5 25

# Readings in Aging and Death:
# Contemporary Perspectives

Harper & Row's
CONTEMPORARY PERSPECTIVES READER SERIES
Phillip Whitten, Series Editor

# Readings in Aging and Death: Contemporary Perspectives

1977-1978 edition

edited by
## Steven H. Zarit

Andrus Gerontology Center
University of Southern California

## Harper & Row, Publishers

New York   Hagerstown   San Francisco   London

Sponsoring Editor: Dale Tharp
Project Editor: Lois Lombardo
Production Supervisor: Stefania J. Taflinska
Printer and Binder: The Murray Printing Company
Cover: "Articulate Man" by Josefina Rubirosa. Courtesy of I.T.T.

**Readings in Aging and Death:
Contemporary Perspectives**

Library of Congress Cataloging in Publication Data
Main entry under title:

Readings in aging and death.

(Harper & Row's contemporary perspectives reader
series)
    1. Aged—Addresses, essays, lectures.   2. Aging—
Addresses, essays, lectures.   3. Death—Addresses,
essays, lectures.   I. Zarit, Steven H.
HQ1061.R36        301.43'5        76–52403
ISBN: 0–06–047056–9

# ACKNOWLEDGMENTS

Prolog. YOU AND DEATH: A QUESTIONNAIRE by Edwin S. Schneidman. Reprinted by permission of PSYCHOLOGY TODAY Magazine. Copyright © 1970 Ziff-Davis Publishing Company

I. AGING—AN OVERVIEW
GERONTOLOGY—GETTING BETTER ALL THE TIME by Steven H. Zarit is reprinted by permission from the author.
SUCCESSFUL AGING AND THE ROLE OF THE LIFE REVIEW by Robert N. Butler. Reprinted by permission from the JOURNAL OF THE AMERICAN GERIATRIC SOCIETY and the author.
JOIE DE VIVRE by Simone de Beauvior is reprinted by permission of G. P. Putnam's Sons from THE COMING OF AGE by Simone deBeauvoir. English translation © 1972 by Andre Deutsch, Weidenfed & Nicoson, and G. P. Putnam's Sons.
Artwork by Evelyn Taylor.
THE ELDERLY IN AMERICA. Courtesy of the Population Reference Bureau, Inc. Washington, D.C. 20036.

II. THE PROCESSES OF AGING
NORMAL AGING—THE INEVITABILITY SYNDROME by Jordan D. Tobin from QUALITY OF LIFE: THE LATER YEARS, L. E. Brown and E. O. Ellis (eds.). Copyright © 1975 The American Medical Association. Published by the Publishing Sciences Group, Inc., Acton, Massachusetts.
A NEW AGE FOR AGING by Bernard L. Strehler is reprinted with permission from NATURAL HISTORY Magazine, February 1973. Copyright © The American Museum of Natural History, 1973.
PHYSIOLOGY OF EXERCISE AND AGING by Herbert A. De Vries, from AGING: SCIENTIFIC PERSPECTIVES AND SOCIAL ISSUES edited by D. Woodruff and J. Birren © 1975 by Litton Educational Publishing, Inc. Reprinted by permission of D. Van Nostrand Company.
TRANSLATIONS IN GERONTOLOGY—FROM LAB TO LIFE by David Schoenfield. Copyright © 1974, by the American Psychological Association from AMERICAN PSYCHOLO-GIST. Reprinted by permission.
AGING AND IQ—THE MYTH OF THE TWILIGHT YEARS by Paul B. Baltes and K. Warner Shaie. Reprinted by permission of PSYCHOLOGY TODAY Magazine. Copyright © 1974 Ziff-Davis Publishing Company.
PERSONALITY AND THE AGING PROCESS by Bernice L. Neugarten is reprinted by permission from THE GERON-TOLOGIST. Photograph by George Gardner.
CHARACTER LASTS: IF YOU'RE ACTIVE AND SAVVY AT 30, YOU'LL BE WARM AND WITTY AT 70 by Margie Casady. Reprinted by permission of PSYCHOLOGY TODAY Magazine. Copyright © 1975 Ziff-Davis Publishing Company.
INSTITUTIONAL POSITION OF THE AGED by Irving Rosow, from SOCIALIZATION TO OLD AGE. Copyright © 1974 by The Regents of the University of California; reprinted by permission of the University of California Press.

III. EXPERIENCING LATER LIFE
AGING IN THE LAND OF THE YOUNG by Sharon Curtin, from NOBODY EVER DIED OF OLD AGE. Copyright © 1972 Little, Brown & Company.
REPORT FROM THE TWILIGHT YEARS by Robert C. Alberts. Copyright © 1974 by The New York Times Company. Reprinted by permission.
Photograph by David Riemer.
LETTERS OF TWO MEN by S. Saul from AGING: AN ALBUM OF PEOPLE GROWING OLD. Copyright © 1974 John Wiley & Sons, Inc.
MIAMI BEACH: REFLECTIONS OF A MORE OR LESS JUNIOR CITIZEN SHOPPING ON WASHINGTON AVENUE by Calvin Trillin. Reprinted by permission. Copyright © 1976 The New Yorker Magazine, Inc.
HAPPINESS IS A KAWASAKI by John D. Dougherty Jr. is reprinted by permission from DYNAMIC MATURITY and the author. Artwork is reprinted by permission from DYNAMIC MATURITY. Copyright © 1976 by the AIM Division, American Association of Retired Persons, 1909 K. Street N.W., Washington, D.C. 20049.
MRS. ELIZABETH HULL—WEDOWEE, ALABAMA by George Mitchell from YESSIR, I'VE BEEN HERE A LONG TIME by George Mitchell. Copyright © 1975 by George Mitchell. Reprinted by permission of the publishers, E. P. Dutton & Co., Inc.
Photograph by George Mitchell.
IN GERONTOLOGY 57 YEARS—AND 85 by Sidney L. Pressey is reprinted by permission from THE GERONTOLOGIST.

IV. SOCIAL PROBLEMS AND SOCIAL POLICIES
OLDER AMERICANS ACT OF 1965 as amended. U.S. Depart-ment of H.E.W., March 1976.
INCOME AND HEALTH CARE OF THE AGING by William Albert and Steven H. Zarit is reprinted by permission from the authors.
THE ABUSE OF THE URBAN AGED by James E. Birren. Re-printed by permission of PSYCHOLOGY TODAY Magazine. Copyright © 1970 Ziff-Davis Publishing Company.
AGE-ISM: ANOTHER FORM OF BIGOTRY by Robert N. Butler is reprinted by permission from THE GERONTOLOGIST.
RETIREMENT AND LEISURE by Morton Puner from TO THE GOOD LONG LIFE: WHAT WE KNOW ABOUT GROWING OLD by Morton Puner. Universe Co. Books, New York, 1974.
COMPULSORY VS. FLEXIBLE RETIREMENT: ISSUES AND FACTS by Erdman Palmore is reprinted by permission from THE GERONTOLOGIST.
FLEXIBLE RETIREMENT—WILL SWEDEN MAKE IT WORK? by Harriet Miller. Reprinted by permission from DYNAMIC MATURITY. Copyright 1976 by the AIM Division, American Association of Retired Persons, 1909 K Street N.W., Washington, D.C. 20049.

# CONTENTS

The young and the old are often the first to suffer when there is widespread social disorganization. When the Ik tribe was forced to change its way of life from hunting to farming, the consequences for the most vulnerable members of society were terrible.

## VII. PSYCHOLOGICAL AND PHYSICAL STRESS    211

is a myth. Even those with brain disorders can be helped, and many supposedly "senile" problems are actually reversible.

For those trying to help an older relative, a Minneapolis program coordinates services that make it possible for them to remain in their own homes, rather than go to a nursing home.

The institutionalization of large numbers of older persons is not an inevitability. Comprehensive mental health programs have allowed people to remain in their home, maximizing their independence and other healthy aspects of personality.

## VIII. DEATH AND DYING — 261

Death is inevitable, but little is known about the process of dying. Though persons can reach a peaceful acceptance of their lives, hospital routines and others' fears of death sometimes impede this process.

Patients, their families, and the hospital staffs may all know that the patient is terminally ill, but they pretend to each other that he/she will get well.

From an early age, children form a concept of death different from adults. Their conceptions are shown in games, nursery rhymes, and play.

Although as inevitable as taxes, death can be postponed for short periods of time to allow a person to celebrate birthdays, holidays, or other special occasions.

The ability to keep persons alive through artificial means has raised important theological and moral issues about the definition of death and the legality of an individual's right to die.

After a death, the bereaved must immediately plan for a funeral. In a state of numbness or confusion, they can be influenced to pay for far more than they actually want.

The dying are sometimes more able than the people around them to face their situation directly, and to explain what has helped them in their final days.

A theorist on death finds in his own dying a test of his theories and an affirmation of his own life.

# PREFACE

Gerontology is the young study of an old problem. Throughout recorded history, humans have been concerned with growing older—sometimes despairing at the relentless passage of time; sometimes searching for a fountain of youth or elixirs to restore declining vigor; and, on occasion, reflecting on the wisdom or calm that the years have brought them. The systematic study of aging, however, is a fairly recent phenomenon, becoming focused with the founding of the Gerontological Society in 1945. Since that time it has grown steadily, both as a discipline and as part of college curricula. One aspect of gerontological research is certainly an understanding of the basic processes of aging, with the age-old goal of discovering those keys that would prolong and improve the quality of life. But more immediately, the study of aging is concerned with integrating the later years into our view of human life.

We have often looked at development as something occurring only in childhood and adolescence, with its goal the attainment of a plateau of maturity and ability we call adulthood. But the possibilities for change and growth throughout the adult years are great, even near the end of life where one may be experiencing a decline in health or in some abilities. Development is the process of our lives, and it does not cease at age 21 or 45 or 65; only its focus changes.

A major purpose of this book is to explore the processes of development in the later years and their impact on people's lives. This search is not without pain or disappointment; however, involvement with older persons will bring students into contact with people who often long for human contact, who can be wise or sad or funny or foolish, but who give us a sense of our past and a view of the present that otherwise would be lost to us. There is a special delight in bridging over age differences with warmth and understanding. In addition to our personal enrichment, a balanced view of aging, emphasizing both the continuing strengths and abilities as well as the difficulties that may confront the old, is of value to the student who may enter a profession that directly serves older persons, or who may work as a volunteer, or for relating to one's parents when they are old. Ultimately, too, we should gain some perspective on our own aging.

In this book there has been an attempt to present aging from a variety of perspectives in articles that are free from excessive professional jargon. They have been chosen as reflective of the major issues in the field of gerontology. Basic concepts of the aging process are presented in the initial two sections. Then the realization of old age in specific social and cultural contexts is depicted: what the aging say themselves, social policies, human relationships, how persons grow old in other cultures, and the problems of aging. The final section (as well as the Prolog and Epilog) deals with an overriding human concern—death and dying.

I am indebted to many people who have assisted in the preparation of this book, including my colleagues at the Leonard Davis School of Gerontology and the Ethel Percy Andrus Gerontology Center who have given me support and encouragement; Penny Manly for her invaluable research assistance; Phillip Whitten, the series editor who developed the concept for this book and who helped me throughout its creation; Leslie Palmer, for her skillful handling of permissions; and Ben and Leora for the time I have been absent from their lives.

S. H. Z.

# You & Death

**D**eath is one of those ubiquitous topics on which every man is his own expert. It is also one of the most taboo topics in our culture.

This questionnaire was designed by Edwin Shneidman of the Center for Advanced Study in the Behavioral Sciences, in consultation with Edwin Parker and G. Ray Funkhouser of Stanford University. It is a modification of a questionnaire Shneidman developed at Harvard with the help of four graduate assistants: Chris Dowell, Ross Goldstein, Dan Goleman and Bruce Smith.

**1** Who died in your first personal involvement with death?

- ⊘ A. Grandparent or great-grandparent.
- ○ B. Parent.
- ○ C. Brother or sister.
- ○ D. Other family member.
- ○ E. Friend or acquaintance.
- ○ F. Stranger.
- ○ G. Public figure.
- ○ H. Animal.

**2** To the best of your memory, at what age were you first aware of death?

- ○ A. Under three.
- ⊘ B. Three to five.
- ○ C. Five to 10.
- ○ D. Ten or older.

**3** When you were a child, how was death talked about in your family?

- ○ A. Openly.
- ○ B. With some sense of discomfort.
- ○ C. Only when necessary and then with an attempt to exclude the children.
- ○ D. As though it were a taboo subject.
- ⊘ E. Never recall any discussion.

**4** Which of the following best describes your childhood conceptions of death?

- ⊘ A. Heaven-and-hell concept.
- ○ B. After-life.
- ○ C. Death as sleep.
- ○ D. Cessation of all physical and mental activity.
- ○ E. Mysterious and unknowable.
- ○ F. Something other than the above.
- ○ G. No conception.
- ○ H. Can't remember.

**5** Which of the following most influenced your present attitudes toward death?

- ○ A. Death of someone close.
- ○ B. Specific reading.
- ○ C. Religious upbringing.
- ⊘ D. Introspection and meditation.
- ○ E. Ritual (e.g., funerals).
- ○ F. TV, radio or motion pictures.
- ○ G. Longevity of my family.
- ○ H. My health or physical condition.
- ○ I. Other (specify):_____

_____

**6** Which of the following books or authors have had the most effect on your attitude toward death?

- ○ A. The Bible.
- ○ B. Camus.
- ○ C. Hesse.
- ○ D. Agee.
- ○ E. Shakespeare.
- ○ F. Mann.
- ⊘ G. No books or authors.
- ○ H. Other (specify):_____

_____

**7** How much of a role has religion played in the development of your attitude toward death?

- ○ A. A very significant role.
- ○ B. A rather significant role.
- ○ C. Somewhat influential, but not a major role.
- ○ D. A relatively minor role.
- ⊘ E. No role at all.

**8** To what extent do you believe in a life after death?

- ○ A. Strongly believe in it.
- ○ B. Tend to believe in it.
- ○ C. Uncertain.
- ⊘ D. Tend to doubt it.
- ○ E. Convinced it does not exist.

**9** Regardless of your belief about life after death, what is your wish about it?

- ○ A. I strongly wish there were a life after death.
- ⊘ B. I am indifferent as to whether there is a life after death.
- ○ C. I definitely prefer that there not be a life after death.

**10** To what extent do you believe in reincarnation?

- ○ A. Strongly believe in it.
- ○ B. Tend to believe in it.
- ○ C. Uncertain.
- ⊘ D. Tend to doubt it.
- ○ E. Convinced it cannot occur.

**11** How often do you think about your own death?

- ○ A. Very frequently (at least once a day).
- ○ B. Frequently.
- ⊘ C. Occasionally.
- ○ D. Rarely (no more than once a year).
- ○ E. Very rarely or never.

**12** If you could choose, when would you die?

- ○ A. In youth.
- ○ B. In the middle prime of life.
- ○ C. Just after the prime of life.
- ⊘ D. In old age.

**13** When do you believe that, in fact, you will die?

- ○ A. In youth.
- ○ B. In the middle prime of life.
- ○ C. Just after the prime of life.
- ⊘ D. In old age.

**14** Has there been a time in your life when you wanted to die?

- ○ A. Yes, mainly because of great physical pain.
- ○ B. Yes, mainly because of great emotional upset.
- ○ C. Yes, mainly to escape an intolerable social or interpersonal situation.
- ○ D. Yes, mainly because of great embarrassment.
- ○ E. Yes, for a reason other than above.
- ⊘ F. No.

**15** What does death mean to you?

- ① A. The end; the final process of life.
- ○ B. The beginning of a life after death; a transition, a new beginning.
- ○ C. A joining of the spirit with a universal cosmic consciousness.
- ○ D. A kind of endless sleep; rest and peace.
- ○ E. Termination of this life but with survival of the spirit.
- ○ F. Don't know.
- ○ G. Other (specify): _____

_____

**16** What aspect of your own death is the most distasteful to you?

- ○ A. I could no longer have any experiences.
- ○ B. I am afraid of what might happen to my body after death.
- ○ C. I am uncertain as to what might happen to me if there is a life after death.
- ○ D. I could no longer provide for my dependents.
- ○ E. It would cause grief to my relatives and friends.
- ○ F. All my plans and projects would come to an end.
- ○ G. The process of dying might be painful.
- ○ H. Other (specify): *NONE*

_____

**17** How do you feel today?

- ○ A. On top of the world.
- ○ B. Wonderful.
- ○ C. Cheerful.
- ⊘ D. On the whole, all right.
- ○ E. About like the average person.
- ○ F. Just fair.
- ○ G. Kind of low.
- ○ H. Down and out.
- ○ I. Wish I were dead.

**18** How do you rate your present *physical* health?

- ○ A. Excellent.
- ① B. Very good.
- ○ C. Moderately good.
- ○ D. Moderately poor.
- ○ E. Extremely bad.

**19** How do you rate your present *mental* health?

- ○ A. Excellent.
- ⊘ B. Very good.
- ○ C. Moderately good.
- ○ D. Moderately poor.
- ○ E. Extremely bad.

**20** Based on your present feelings, what is the probability of your taking your own life in the near future?

- ○ A. Extremely high (I feel very much like killing myself).
- ○ B. Moderately high.
- ○ C. Between high and low.
- ○ D. Moderately low.
- ⊘ E. Extremely low (very improbable that I would kill myself).

**21** In your opinion, at what age are people most afraid of death?

- ○ A. Up to 12 years.
- ○ B. Thirteen to 19 years.
- ○ C. Twenty to 29 years.
- ⊘ D. Thirty to 39 years.
- ○ E. Forty to 49 years.
- ○ F. Fifty to 59 years.
- ○ G. Sixty to 69 years.
- ○ H. Seventy years and over.

**22** What is your belief about the causes of *most* deaths?

- ○ A. Most deaths result directly from the conscious efforts by the persons who die.
- ○ B. Most deaths have strong components of conscious or unconscious participation by the persons who die (in their habits and use, misuse, nonuse or abuse of drugs, alcohol, medicine, etc.).
- ⊘ C. Most deaths just happen; they are caused by events over which individuals have no control.
- ○ D. Other (specify): _____

_____

**23** To what extent do you believe that *psychological* factors can influence (or even cause) death?

- ⊘ A. I firmly believe that they can.
- ○ B. I tend to believe that they can.
- ○ C. I am undecided or don't know.
- ○ D. I doubt that they can.

**24** When you think of your own death (or when circumstances make you realize your own mortality), how do you feel?

- ○ A. Fearful.
- ○ B. Discouraged.
- ○ C. Depressed.
- ○ D. Purposeless.
- ① E. Resolved, in relation to life.
- ○ F. Pleasure, in being alive.
- ○ G. Other (specify): _____

_____

**25** What is your present orientation to your own death?

- ○ A. Death-seeker.
- ○ B. Death-hastener.
- ⊘ C. Death-accepter.
- ○ D. Death-welcomer.
- ○ E. Death-postponer.
- ○ F. Death-fearer.

**26** How often have you been in a situation in which you seriously thought you might die?

- ○ A. Many times.
- ○ B. Several times.
- ○ C. Once or twice.
- ① D. Never.

**27** To what extent are you interested in having your image survive after your own death through your children, books, good works, etc.?

- ⊘ A. Very interested.
- ○ B. Moderately interested.
- ○ C. Somewhat interested.
- ○ D. Not very interested.
- ○ E. Totally uninterested.

**28** For whom or what might you be willing to sacrifice your life?

- ⊘ A. For a loved one.
- ⊘ B. For an idea or a moral principle.
- ⊘ C. In combat or a grave emergency where a life could be saved.
- ○ D. Not for any reason.

**29** If you had a choice, what kind of death would you prefer?

- ○ A. Tragic, violent death.
- ○ B. Sudden but not violent death.
- ⊘ C. Quiet, dignified death.
- ○ D. Death in line of duty.
- ○ E. Death after a great achievement.
- ○ F. Suicide.
- ○ G. Homicidal victim.
- ○ H. There is no "appropriate" kind of death.
- ○ I. Other (specify): _____

_____

**30** Have your attitudes toward death ever been affected by narcotic or hallucinogenic drugs?

- ○ A. Yes.
- ⊘ B. I have taken drugs but my attitudes toward death have never been affected by them.
- ○ C. I have never taken drugs.

**31** If it were possible would you want to know the exact date on which you are going to die?

- ○ A. Yes.
- ⊘ B. No.

**32** If your physician knew that you had a terminal disease and a limited time to live, would you want him to tell you?

- ⊘ A. Yes.
- ○ B. No.
- ○ C. It would depend on the circumstances.

**33** If you were told that you had a terminal disease and a limited time to live, how would you want to spend your time until you died?

○ A. I would make a marked change in my life-style; satisfy hedonistic needs (travel, sex, drugs, other experiences).
○ B. I would become more withdrawn; reading, contemplating or praying.
○ C. I would shift from my own needs to a concern for others (family, friends).
⊘ D. I would attempt to complete projects; tie up loose ends.
⊘ E. I would make little or no change in my life-style.
○ F. I would try to do one very important thing.
○ G. I might consider committing suicide.
○ H. I would do none of these.

**34** How do you feel about having an autopsy done on your body?

○ A. Approve.
⊘ B. Don't care one way or the other.
○ C. Disapprove.
○ D. Strongly disapprove.

**35** To what extent has the possibility of massive human destruction by nuclear war influenced your present attitudes toward death or life?

○ A. Enormously.
○ B. To a fairly large extent.
⊘ C. Moderately.
○ D. Somewhat.
○ E. Very little.
○ F. Not at all.

**36** Which of the following has influenced your present attitudes toward your own death the most?

○ A. Pollution of the environment.
○ B. Domestic violence.
○ C. Television.
○ D. Wars.
○ E. The possibility of nuclear war.
○ F. Poverty.
○ G. Existential philosophy.
○ H. Changes in health conditions and mortality statistics.
⊘ I. Other (specify): *Personal reflection*

**37** How often have you seriously contemplated committing suicide?

○ A. Very often.
○ B. Only once in a while.
⊘ C. Very rarely.
○ D. Never.

**38** Have you ever actually attempted suicide?

○ A. Yes, with an actual very high probability of death.
○ B. Yes, with an actual moderate probability of death.
○ C. Yes, with an actual low probability of death.
⊘ D. No.

**39** Whom have you known who has committed suicide?

○ A. Member of immediate family.
○ B. Other family member.
○ C. Close friend.
○ D. Acquaintance.
⊘ E. No one.
○ F. Other (specify):_____

**40** How do you estimate your lifetime probability of committing suicide?

○ A. I plan to do it some day.
○ B. I hope that I do not, but I am afraid that I might.
○ C. In certain circumstances, I might very well do it.
⊘ D. I doubt that I would do it in any circumstances.
○ E. I am sure that I would never do it.

**41** Suppose that you were to commit suicide, what reason would most motivate you to do it?

○ A. To get even or hurt someone.
○ B. Fear of insanity.
○ C. Physical illness or pain.
○ D. Failure or disgrace.
⊘ E. Loneliness or abandonment.
○ F. Death or loss of a loved one.
○ G. Family strife.
○ H. Atomic war.
○ I. Other (specify):_____

**42** Suppose you were to commit suicide, what method would you be most likely to use?

○ A. Barbiturates or pills.
○ B. Gunshot.
○ C. Hanging.
○ D. Drowning.
○ E. Jumping.
○ F. Cutting or stabbing.
○ G. Carbon monoxide.
○ H. Other (specify): *Don't Know*

**43** Suppose you were ever to commit suicide, would you leave a suicide note?

○ A. Yes. ?
○ B. No.

**44** To what extent do you believe that suicide should be prevented?

○ A. In every case.
○ B. In all but a few cases.
⊘ C. In some cases, yes; in others, no.
○ D. In no case; if a person wants to commit suicide society has no right to stop him.

**45** What efforts do you believe ought to be made to keep a seriously ill person alive?

○ A. All possible effort: transplantations, kidney dialysis, etc.
○ B. Efforts that are reasonable for that person's age, physical condition, mental condition, and pain.
⊘ C. After reasonable care has been given, a person ought to be permitted to die a natural death.
○ D. A senile person should not be kept alive by elaborate artificial means.

**46** If or when you are married would you prefer to outlive your spouse?

○ A. Yes; I would prefer to die second and outlive my spouse.
○ B. No; I would rather die first and have my spouse outlive me.
⊘ C. Undecided or don't know.

**47** What is your primary reason for the answer which you gave for the question above?

○ A. To spare my spouse loneliness.
○ B. To avoid loneliness for myself.
○ C. To spare my spouse grief.
○ D. To avoid grief for myself.
○ E. Because the surviving spouse could cope better with grief or loneliness.
○ F. To live as long as possible.
○ G. None of the above.
⊘ H. Other (specify): *Live it as I come s*

**48** How important do you believe mourning and grief rituals (such as wakes and funerals) are for the survivors?

○ A. Extremely important.
⊘ B. Somewhat important.
○ C. Undecided or don't know.
○ D. Not very important.
○ E. Not important at all.

**49** If it were entirely up to you, how would you like to have your body disposed of after you have died?

○ A. Burial.
○ B. Cremation.
○ C. Donation to medical school or science.
⊘ D. I am indifferent.

**50** Would you be willing to donate your heart for transplantation (after you die)?

○ A. Yes, to anyone.
○ B. Yes, but only to a relative or a friend.
○ C. I have a strong feeling against it.
○ D. No.

**51** What kind of a funeral would you prefer?

○ A. Formal, as large as possible.
○ B. Small, relatives and close friends only.
○ C. Whatever my survivors want.
○ D. None.

**52** How do you feel about "lying in state" in an open casket at your funeral?

○ A. Approve.
○ B. Don't care one way or the other.
○ C. Disapprove.
○ D. Strongly disapprove.

**53** What is your opinion about the costs of funerals in the U.S. today?

○ A. Very much overpriced.
○ B. No one has to pay for what he doesn't want.
○ C. In terms of costs and services rendered, prices are not unreasonable.

**54** In your opinion, what would be a reasonable price for a funeral?

○ A. Under $300.
○ B. From $300 to $600.
○ C. From $600 to $900.
○ D. From $900 to $1,500.
○ E. More than $1,500.

**55** What are your thoughts about leaving a will?

○ A. I have already made one.
○ B. I have not made a will, but intend to do so some day.
○ C. I am uncertain or undecided.
○ D. I probably will not make one.
○ E. I definitely won't leave a will.

**56** To what extent do you believe in life insurance to benefit your survivors?

○ A. Strongly believe in it; have insurance.
○ B. Tend to believe in it; have or plan to get insurance.
○ C. Undecided.
○ D. Tend not to believe in it.
○ E. Definitely do not believe in it; do not have and do not plan to get insurance.

*None of the above*

**57** Assuming that there has been an increase in the amount of concern with death in the U.S. in the last 25 or 50 years, to what *principally* do you attribute this change?

○ A. Wars.
○ B. Domestic violence.
○ C. Pollution of the environment.
○ D. Atomic and nuclear bombs.
○ E. Existential philosophy.
○ F. The drug culture.
○ G. Television.
○ H. No change.
○ I. Other (specify): *Don't Know*

In order to evaluate this survey it is important to know a few things about the background of each person who responds. Please help by answering these questions.

**58** What is your sex?

○ A. Male.
○ B. Female.

**59** What is your age?

○ A. Under 20.
○ B. From 20 to 24.
○ C. From 25 to 29.
○ D. From 30 to 34.
○ E. From 35 to 39.
○ F. From 40 to 49.
○ G. From 50 to 59.
○ H. From 60 to 64.
○ I. Sixty-five or over.

**60** How many brothers and sisters do you have?

○ A. One.
○ B. Two.
○ C. Three.
○ D. Four.
○ E. Five.
○ F. Six or more.
○ G. None; I was an only child.

**61** To what racial group do you belong?

○ A. Caucasian.
○ B. Negro.
○ C. Oriental.
○ D. Other.

**62** What is your marital status?

○ A. Single.
○ B. Married once.
○ C. Remarried.
○ D. Separated.
○ E. Divorced.
○ F. Living with someone.
○ G. Widow.
○ H. Widower.

**63** What is your religious background?

○ A. Protestant.
○ B. Roman Catholic.
○ C. Jewish.
○ D. Other.

**64** How religious do you consider yourself to be?

○ A. Very religious.
○ B. Somewhat religious.
○ C. Slightly religious.
○ D. Not at all religious.
○ E. Antireligious.

**65** What is your political preference?

○ A. Republican.
○ B. Independent.
○ C. Democratic.
○ D. Other.

**66** Would you describe your political views?

○ A. Very liberal.
○ B. Somewhat liberal.
○ C. Moderate.
○ D. Somewhat conservative.
○ E. Very conservative.

**67** What is your level of education?

○ A. Grade school.
○ B. High-school graduate.
○ C. Some college.
○ D. College graduate.
○ E. Some graduate school.
○ F. Master's degree.
○ G. Ph.D., M.D. or other advanced degree.

**68** What is the approximate annual income of your family?

○ A. Less than $5,000.
○ B. From $5,000 to $10,000.
○ C. From $10,000 to $15,000.
○ D. From $15,000 to $25,000.
○ E. From $25,000 to $50,000.
○ F. More than $50,000.

**69** What area of the country would you call your home?

○ A. West.
○ B. Southwest and mountain states.
○ C. Midwest.
○ D. South.
○ E. New England.
○ F. Middle Atlantic
○ G. Other than U.S.

**70** What is the population of the city or community you live in?

O A. Under 10,000.
O B. From 10,000 to 50,000.
O C. From 50,000 to 100,000.
O D. From 100,000 to 500,000.
O E. From 500,000 to 1,000,000.
O F. Over 1,000,000.

**71** What are your present living arrangements?

O A. With my family.
O B. In a dormitory, shared dwelling or apartment with others.
O C. Living alone (in room, apartment or house).

**72** What is your present occupation?

O A. Student.
O B. Elementary or H.S. teacher.
O C. Housewife.
O D. White-collar, clerical or sales.
O E. Technician, craftsman, etc.
O F. College professor or instructor.
O G. Business manager or executive.
O H. Unemployed.
O I. Other.

**73** Do you work professionally as one of the following?

O A. Physician.
O B. Psychologist.
O C. Guidance counselor.
O D. Social worker.
O E. Lawyer.
O F. Engineer or scientist.
O G. Clergyman.
O H. None of the above.

**74** If you have completed one or more of the previous *Psychology Today* questionnaires on
Cities,
Law,
Drugs, or
Sex,
please indicate which ones:

None
_____

**75** What effect has this questionnaire had on you?

O A. It has made me somewhat anxious or upset.
O B. It has made me think about my own death.
O C. It has reminded me how fragile and precious life is.
O D. No effect at all.
O E. Other effects (specify): _____
_____

# Reply Form

# You & Death

**1** A B C D E F G H
**2** A B C D
**3** A B C D E
**4** A B C D E F G H
**5** A B C D E F G H I

_____

**6** A B C D E F G H

_____

**7** A B C D E
**8** A B C D E
**9** A B C
**10** A B C D E
**11** A B C D E
**12** A B C D
**13** A B C D
**14** A B C D E F
**15** A B C D E F G

_____

**16** A B C D E F G H

_____

**17** A B C D E F G H I
**18** A B C D E
**19** A B C D E
**20** A B C D E
**21** A B C D E F G H
**22** A B C D

_____

**23** A B C D
**24** A B C D E F G

_____

**25** A B C D E F
**26** A B C D
**27** A B C D E
**28** A B C D
**29** A B C D E F G H I

_____

**30** A B C
**31** A B
**32** A B C
**33** A B C D E F G H
**34** A B C D
**35** A B C D E F
**36** A B C D E F G H I

_____

**37** A B C D
**38** A B C D
**39** A B C D E F

_____

**40** A B C D E
**41** A B C D E F G H I

_____

**42** A B C D E F G H

_____

**43** A B
**44** A B C D
**45** A B C D
**46** A B C
**47** A B C D E F G H

_____

**48** A B C D E
**49** A B C D
**50** A B C D
**51** A B C D
**52** A B C D
**53** A B C
**54** A B C D E
**55** A B C D E
**56** A B C D E
**57** A B C D E F G H I

_____

**58** A B
**59** A B C D E F G H I
**60** A B C D E F G
**61** A B C D
**62** A B C D E F G H
**63** A B C D
**64** A B C D E
**65** A B C D
**66** A B C D E
**67** A B C D E F G
**68** A B C D E F
**69** A B C D E F G
**70** A B C D E F
**71** A B C
**72** A B C D E F G H I
**73** A B C D E F G H
**74**
**75** A B C D E

_____

# I. Aging—An Overview

# 2

# Gerontology-Getting Better All the Time

## by Steven H. Zarit

Gerontology, the study of aging, is looking into our own futures. But while it is easy to plan for next month, or next year, or even a few years ahead, most of us find it hard to speculate beyond that time span. Try to imagine, for a minute, what you will be like and look like when you are old. It probably is difficult to form a clear impression, even though we probably all have an image of older people in our society.

We tend not to see ourselves as old, or even to think about ourselves aging, in part because of fears about the prospects of growing older. These fears are often focused on losses that can occur—loss of vigor and attractiveness, of one's purpose in life, and a fear of dying. The problems that many older persons have— their loneliness, loss of income, lack of meaningful activities—reinforce our concern.

When we think of those older persons we have encountered, however, we are likely to call forth a variety of impressions: an understanding grandmother; a garrulous old man who was forced to retire from his job; a lonely widow who occasionally stopped by to talk and to bring cookies she baked; the pain and fear felt by older persons in a hospital; the *joie de vivre* of a vigorous old man; the repetitive wandering stories of one person and the vivid accounts of the past by another; the courage of a woman trying to keep her independence despite illness; a sense of despair in a nursing home; the dying person who gropes to find some meaning to her life. Our impressions are mixed: strongly positive for those whose wisdom or wit or caring touched our lives, and feelings of pain for those whose problems consumed them and, to some extent, those around them as well.

Gerontology is the study of these differences in aging: how some persons may age successfully, how others may experience increasing difficulties, how one person may continue learning and growing while another gets stuck, lost in the past. Despite the predominantly negative feelings people have about old age, gerontology is an optimistic discipline. It separates myths of aging from what actually occurs as we grow older, and considers both the potentials and the problems older persons have. The most pervasive myth about aging is that it is a constant downhill course. When viewed from various disciplines, whether physiology, psychology, or from a broader social perspective, the processes of aging are not as deleterious as commonly thought. Decrements which are widely considered to occur with age may be manifested to a lesser extent, may only be found in some individuals, or may not occur at all. Arteriosclerosis, for example, which many people consider an aspect of aging, is actually a metabolic disease which only affects some individuals, and which may be treatable to some extent through diet and exercise (Dovenmuehle, 1970). Similarly, other supposed decrements of aging, including senile brain damage (Butler; Zarit), intellectual decline (Baltes and Schaie); personality deterioration (Neugarten; Casady) and, to some extent, changes in physiological capacities (Tobin; deVries) have been found to occur as the result of illness or disuse, rather than aging per se. Thus, many older persons do not show these changes, while, in others, the possibility exists that decrements can be ameliorated or prevented.

Another myth is that gerontology is concerned only with problems. While many older persons do experience serious difficulties in their lives, there is also a continuing possibility of personal growth. This optimism is reflected in research which emphasizes the extent to which many capacities may be maintained through the lifespan, or diminish only gradually (Baltes and Schaie; Schonfield; Tobin). There may also be gains with aging such as that of aesthetic sense or personal awareness (Alberts). The vivid personal testimony of older persons about their own lives, both past and present, suggests that they have a unique perspective to share on the course of human life.

Another misunderstanding is the feeling that nothing can be done for older persons without a major biological breakthrough to modify aging. While such an advance is no longer just in the realm of science fiction (Strehler), the majority of problems that confront older persons are the result of the social priorities, policies, and practices of society. There is an urgent need to examine our practices concerning income, health care, mandatory retirement of the elderly, and more broadly, to consider how there may be more opportunities for meaningful and fulfilling participation in society in the later years. If health were to be improved in the later years, or if the lifespan was extended another 10 to 20 years, it would make little difference if the aged were consigned to live only in isolated communities of the old, or were not viewed as having anything to contribute to society, or if they had to exist only a bare subsistence income. We must seriously consider how we would prefer living, if we were old today, and then create the economic and social conditions that would facilitate those styles of life.

A major theme in this book is that gerontology is the study of the whole person. People grow older, and that process is reflected in all aspects of functioning. Biological changes are manifested in behavior. Behavior, in turn, affects and is affected by relationships to others and to society in general. And finally, the opportunities for satisfying social relationships and meaningful activities, and for meeting basic needs such as health or nutrition or housing can affect physiological processes. Aging is not the result of a simple process within an individual, but reflects the effects of time on all aspects of one's being.

In this book, aging is viewed from several perspectives. These include basic research findings on the aging process in the sciences and social sciences, social policies and practices that affect older persons, perspectives on aging from other cultures, the types of problems that some elderly people have and programs that can ameliorate them, and the feelings and concerns of older persons themselves. The last section of the book is devoted to an area that is important throughout the lifespan—death. It includes reactions of both young and old, the feelings of the dying and the grief of the survivors. As knowledge of the aging process makes it less fearful, understanding how dying affects us can lead to a sharing of the pain between the ill person and those he or she cares for, so that one's last days can be, in Kubler-Ross' terms, a final stage of growth that gives meaning to the whole of one's life (Kubler-Ross, 1975).

In Part I, "Aging—An Overview," some general concepts are presented. Robert Butler analyzes several of the myths of aging and then presents some suggestions for facilitating successful adaptation in later life. In an excerpt from her book, *The Coming of Age*, the French writer Simone de Beauvoir discusses how our denial and fears of aging affect our lives and those of the aging. Finally, "The Elderly in America," prepared by the *Population Bulletin*, provides a useful demographic profile about those persons who are old, including their education and income, and where and how they live.

## References

Dovenmuehle, R. M. Aging versus illness. In Palmore, E. (Ed.), *Normal aging: reports from the Duke longitudinal study*, 1955–1969. Durham, N.C. Duke University Press, 1970.

Kubler-Ross, E. *Death: The Final Stage of Growth.* Englewood Cliffs, N.J. Prentice-Hall, 1975.

Other references are reprinted in this volume.

# 3

# Successful Aging and the Role of the Life Review*

ROBERT N. BUTLER, MD**

*Washington, DC*

ABSTRACT: The negative view of old age with its outworn stereotypes (particularly "senility") must be changed if the elderly are to have more opportunities for successful aging. It is time for a more balanced attitude. Health in old age involves mental and social as well as physical well-being. There is a distinct difference between the intrinsic features of aging and the reactions of the elderly to their lives. Old age is a period in which unique developmental work can be accomplished. Life review therapy and life-cycle group therapy are effective aids in this direction.

Those who think of old people as boobies, crones, witches, old biddies, old fogies, pains-in-the-neck, out-to-pasture, boring, garrulous, unproductive and worthless, have accepted the stereotypes of aging, including the extreme mistake of believing that substantial numbers of old people are in or belong in institutions. On the contrary, most old people need not be and are not in institutions and, given a fighting chance in a society that has devalued them, can maintain a viable place in society. Indeed, at any one moment, 95 per cent of persons over the age of 65 live in the community. In our social policies and in our therapeutic programs we need to bear in mind a basic standard of health, and not have our thinking dominated by stereotypes of frailty, psychopathology, senility, confusion, decline and institutional living.

However, there is no point in developing illusions concerning healthy, successful old age. Like all periods in life, it has its difficulties. There are problems to be dealt with and needs to be fulfilled. But old age can be an emotionally healthy and satisfying time of life with a minimum of physical and mental impairments. Many older people have adapted well to their old age with little stress and a high level of morale.

The study of "normal" development has sel-

* Presented at the Symposium on Geriatric Medicine co-sponsored by the American Geriatrics Society and the Franklin Square Hospital, Baltimore, MD, March 2, 1974.

** Research Psychiatrist and Gerontologist, Washington School of Psychiatry; Faculty, Howard and George Washington Medical Schools; Consultant, U. S. Senate Special Committee on Aging, National Institute of Mental Health and St. Elizabeth's Hospital, Washington, DC.

*Address:* Robert N. Butler, MD, 3815 Huntington Street, NW, Washington, DC 20015.

dom gone beyond early adult years, and the greatest emphasis has been on childhood. There are relatively few centers for the study of adult human development. These few centers have studied small population samples, usually of white, affluent, middle-class people, composed about equally of men and women. Such work at the University of Chicago, Duke University, the University of California and for a brief period at the National Institute of Mental Health has helped provide us with some understanding of successful mental health in aging.

In our culture few people think of old age as a time of potential health and growth. This is partly realistic, in view of the lot of so many old people who have been cast aside to become lonely, bitter, poor, and emotionally or physically ill. American society has not been generous or supportive of the "unproductive" — in this case old people who have reached what is arbitrarily defined as the retirement period. But in a larger sense the negative view of old age is a problem of Western civilization. The Western concept of the life cycle is decidedly different from that of the Orient since they derive from two opposing views about what "self" means and what life is all about. Oriental philosophy places the individual self, his life span and his death *within* the process of human experience. Life and death are familiar and equally acceptable parts of what self means. In the West, on the other hand, death is considered outside of the self. To be a self or person one must be alive, in control and aware of what is happening. The greater and more self-centered or narcissistic Western emphasis on individuality and control makes death an outrage, a tremendous affront to man, rather than the logical and necessary process of old life making way for new. The opposite cultural views of East and West evolve to support two very different ways of life, each with its own merits. But the Western predilection for "progress," conquest over nature, and personal self-realization has produced difficult problems for the elderly and for those preparing for old age. This is particularly so when the spirit of a nation and of an historical period has emphasized and expanded the notion of measuring human worth in terms of individual productivity and power. Old people are led to see themselves as failing with age, a phrase that refers as much to self worth as it does to physical strength. Religion has been the traditional solace by promising another world wherein the

self again springs to life never to be further threatened by loss of its own integrity. Thus Western man's consummate dream of immortality is fulfilled by religion while integration of the aging experience into his life process remains incomplete. Increasing secularization produces a frightening void which frequently is met by avoiding and denying the thought of one's own decline and death and by forming self-protective prejudices against old people.

In some respects we now deal somewhat more openly with death itself. But aging, that long prelude to death, has become a kind of obscenity, something to avoid.

Medicine and the behavioral sciences have mirrored social attitudes by presenting old age as a grim litany of physical and emotional ills. Decline of the individual has been the key concept, and neglect has been a major treatment technique. Until about 1960 most of the medical, psychologic, psychiatric and social work literature on the aged was based on experience with the sick and the institutionalized even though only 5 per cent of the elderly were confined to institutions. (This 5 per cent, however, is a most significant minority, with major needs. Ultimately, some 20 per cent of older people require institutional care, at least under the current health care system that does not provide comprehensive home care.) The few research studies that have concentrated on the healthy aged give indication of positive potential. Yet the general, almost phobic dislike of the aged remains the norm, with healthy old people being ignored and the chronically ill receiving half-hearted custodial care. Only those elderly who happen to have exotic or "interesting" diseases or emotional problems, or substantial financial resources, ordinarily receive attention for research and treatment by the medical and psychotherapeutic professions.

Health care is approaching a $100 billion annual business, second only to the food industry. The health care industry, however, does not reflect the various human ills in due proportion. Although chronic disease accounts for two-thirds of our nation's health costs, certainly no parallel proportion of our medical school curriculum, medical manpower, intellectual emphasis, research, and health delivery system is devoted to this important group of disorders. With the advent of a national health insurance plan and the ensuing struggle that is now beginning in Congress and in the Administration with respect to the character of that insurance plan, it has to be recognized that not one of the plans under consideration faces realistically the facts of life, of disease and of aging.

## HEALTH IN OLD AGE

What is healthy old age? In thinking about health one must remember that science and medicine have historically been more concerned with treating what goes wrong than with clarifying the complex interwoven elements necessary to produce and support health. Typical of this is the treatment of coronary attacks after the fact rather than establishing a preventive program of diet, exercise, protection against stress, and of smoking. Most of the major diseases of the elderly can be cited as examples of this same phenomenon. The tedious and less dramatic process of prevention requires an understanding of what supports or what interferes with healthy development throughout the course of life. We spend only four cents of every health dollar on prevention.

In 1946 the World Health Organization defined health as "a state of complete physical, mental and social well being and not merely the absence of disease or infirmity." This definition represents an ideal with many possible interpretations. But the three components of health — physical, emotional and social — compose the framework in which one can begin to analyze what is going well in addition to what is going wrong. The attempt must be made to locate the conditions which enable humans to thrive and not merely survive.

One cannot look at health simply as statistical or typical. If one were to do so, the dental caries which affects about 90 per cent of the population might be considered healthy. Moreover, health cannot be regarded simply as a state. It is a *process* of continuing change and growth. What may be apparent health at one moment may already contain the beginnings of illness that will develop fully in still another moment.

Old age is a period when there is unique developmental work to be accomplished. Childhood might be broadly defined as a period of gathering and enlarging strength and experience, whereas the major developmental task in old age is to clarify, deepen and find use for what one has already obtained in a lifetime of learning and adapting. The elderly must teach themselves to conserve their strength and resources when necessary and to adjust in the best sense to those changes and losses that occur as part of the aging experience. The ability of the elderly person to adapt and thrive is contingent upon his physical health, personality, earlier life experiences, and on the societal supports he receives, i.e., adequate finances, shelter, medical care, social roles, and recreation. It is imperative that old people continue to develop and change in a flexible manner if health is to be promoted and maintained. Failure of adaptation at any age under any circumstances can result in a physical or emotional illness. Optimal growth and adaptation may occur all along the course of life when the individual's strengths and potentials are recognized, reinforced and encouraged by the environment in which he lives.

## THE STEREOTYPE OF OLD AGE

To develop a clear depiction of what old age can be like we must contrast the mythologic with a realistic appraisal of old age. Let me present a sketch which I first gave in 1959 to a group of nursing home owners in the State of Maryland (1). This is the stereotype of old age, and it hasn't changed much in the last fifteen years:

"An older person thinks and moves slowly. He does not think as he used to, nor as creatively. He is bound to himself and to his past and can no longer change or grow. He can neither learn well nor swiftly, and even if he could, he would not wish to. Tied to his personal traditions and growing conservatism, he dislikes innovations and is not disposed to new ideas. Not only can he not move forward, he often moves backwards. He enters a second childhood, caught often in increasing egocentricity and demanding more from his environment than he is willing to give to it. Sometimes he becomes more like himself, a caricature of a lifelong personality. He becomes irritable and cantankerous, yet shallow and enfeebled. He lives in his past. He is behind the times. He is aimless and wandering of mind, reminiscing and garrulous. Indeed, he is a study in decline. He is the picture of mental and physical failure. He has lost and cannot replace friends, spouse, jobs, status, power, influence, income. He is often stricken by diseases which in turn restrict his movement, his enjoyment of food, the pleasures of well being. His sexual interest and activity decline. His body shrinks; so, too, does the flow of blood to his brain. His mind does not utilize oxygen and sugar at the same rate as formerly. Feeble, uninteresting, he awaits his death, a burden to society, to his family, and to himself."

There are certain major associated myths.

First, there is the myth of *aging itself*, the idea of chronologic aging, measuring one's age by the number of years one has lived. It is clear that there are great differences in the rates of physiologic, chronologic, psychologic and social aging from person to person and also within each individual.

Second, there is the myth of *unproductivity*. But in the absence of diseases and social adversities, old people tend to remain productive and actively involved in life. There are dazzling examples like the 82-year-old Arturo Rubinstein working his hectic concert schedule, or the 72-year-old Benjamin Dugger discovering the antibiotic aureomycin. Numbers of people become unusually creative for the first time in old age when exceptional and inborn talents may be discovered and expressed. In fact, many old people continue to contribute usefully to their families and community in a variety of ways including active employment.

Third, there is the myth of *disengagement*, related to the previous myth in holding that older people prefer to be disengaged from life and to withdraw into themselves, choosing to live alone or perhaps only with their own peers. Ironically, a few gerontologists hold these views. One study (2) presented the theory that mutual separation between the aged person and society is a natural part of the aging experience. There is no evidence to support this as a generalization. Disengagement is only one of the many patterns of reaction to old age.

Fourth is the myth of *inflexibility*. The ability to change and adapt has little to do with one's age and more to do with one's lifelong character. But even this statement has to be qualified. One is not necessarily destined to one's character in earlier life. The endurance, the strength and the stability in character structure are remarkable and protective. Yet most, if not all, people change and remain open to change throughout the course of life right up to its termination unless they are affected by major destruction of brain tissue or illiteracy or poverty, which are among the common levelers of mankind.

Fifth is the myth of *senility*, the notion that old people are or inevitably become senile (if they live long enough), showing forgetfulness, confusional episodes and reduced attention. This is widely accepted. Senility, in fact, is a layman's term, unfortunately used by doctors to categorize the behavior of the old. Some of what is called senile is the result of brain damage, but anxiety and depression are also frequently lumped in the category of senility even though they are treatable and reversible. Old people, like young people, experience a full range of emotions including anxiety, grief, depression and paranoid states. It is all too easy to blame age and brain damage when accounting for the mental problems and emotional concerns of later life. Benjamin Rush recognized senility as a distinct illness separate from the process of aging (3). Drug tranquilization, much overused in the United States, is a frequently misdiagnosed but potentially reversible cause of so-called senility. Malnutrition or unrecognized physical illnesses such as congestive heart failure and pneumonia may produce "senile behavior" by reducing the supply of blood, oxygen and food to the brain. Alcoholism, often associated with bereavement, is another cause. Late-life alcoholism is a serious and common problem. Irreversible brain damage, however, is no myth. Cerebral arteriosclerosis or hardening of the arteries of the brain and so-called senile brain disease marked by the mysterious dissolution of brain cells, are major and serious disorders that do impair human development in old age.

Sixth is the myth of *serenity*. In contrast to the previous myths which view the elderly in a negative light, this one portrays old age as a kind of adult fairyland. Old age is presented as a time of relative peace and serenity when people can relax and enjoy the fruits of their labors after the storms of life are over. Visions of carefree, cooky-baking grandmothers and rocking-chair grandfathers are cherished by younger generations. In reality, older persons experience more stresses than any other age group, and these stresses often are devastating. The strength of the aged to endure crises is remarkable, and tranquility is an unlikely and inappropriate response under such circumstances. Depression, anxiety, psychosomatic illnesses, paranoid states, garrulousness and irritability are some of the internal reactions to external stresses. Depressive reactions are particularly widespread in late life. *Twenty-five per cent of all suicides in the United States occur in persons over 65.* Grief is a frequent companion of old age, grief either for one's own losses or for the ultimate loss of oneself. Apathy and emptiness are common sequels to the initial shock and sadness that follow the loss of close friends and relatives. Physical disease and social isolation can follow bereavement. Anxiety is another common feature. There is much to be anxious about, with poverty, loneliness and illness heading the list. Anxiety may manifest itself in many forms — rigid patterns of thinking and behavior, helplessness, manipulativeness, restlessness, suspiciousness, and sometimes paranoia.

No less a thinker than Aristotle failed to distinguish between the intrinsic features of aging and the reactions of the elderly to their lives. He considered cowardice, resentment, vindictiveness and what he called "senile avarice" to be intrinsic to late life. Cicero took a warmer and more positive view towards old age. He understood, for example, "if old men are morose, troubled, fretful and hard to please . . . these are faults of character and not of aging." So he explained in his famous essay "De Senectute."

*Ageism.* The stereotyping and myths surrounding old age can be partly explained by lack of knowledge and by insufficient daily and/or professional contact with varieties of older people. But there is another powerful factor, i.e., a deep and profound prejudice against the elderly which is found to some degree in all of us. In thinking about how to describe this I coined the word "ageism" in 1968. "Ageism can be seen as a process of systematic stereotyping of and discrimination against people because they are old just as racism and sexism can accomplish this with skin color and gender. Old people are categorized as senile, rigid in thought and manner, old fashioned in morality and skills. Ageism allows the younger generations to see older people as different from themselves. Thus they subtly cease to identify with their elders as human beings" (4, 5).

## A BALANCED VIEW OF OLD AGE

It is time for a more balanced view of old age. Compare what follows with the earlier stereotype:

"Older people are as diverse as people of other periods in life, and their patterns of aging vary according to the range they show from health to sickness, from maturity to immaturity, activity to apathy, useful constructive participation to disinterest, from the prevailing stereotype of aging to rich forms of creativity.

"Ninety-five per cent of older people live in the community and are not institutionalized or in protective settings. Physical illnesses are frequent and often chronic and limiting. Nonetheless over 80 per cent of older people are ambulatory. This period of life is characterized by complex changes that are multiple, occur rapidly, and with profound effects. Some people are overwhelmed. Others can come to accept or substitute for the loss of loved ones, prestige, social status and adverse physiological changes.

"Old age and brain damage alone do not account for the facade and the modes of adaptation of older people. Diseases, life experience, socio-economic and other forces along with the subjective experience of growing old and approaching death — all interweave to contribute to the picture of old age.

"Older people are apt to be reflective rather than impulsive. Having experienced a great deal and having been burned often, they think before acting. Under suitable conditions the present remains very much alive and exciting to them. But they also turn to the review of their past, searching for purpose, reconciliation of relationships, and resolution of conflicts and regrets. They may become self centered or altruistic, angry or contrite, transcendant or depressed. These old people are optimistic and resourceful and yet at the same time can be painfully aware of the brevity of life and its tragedies. Optimism is tempered by a more balanced view of the joys and sadnesses of life. The old continue to learn and change in response to their experience and of human relationships. Their sexual activity may gain in quality (6). They are not often overwhelmed by new ideas for they recognize how few of them there are. Many are employable, productive and creative. Many wish to leave their mark through sponsoring the young as well as through ideas and institutions.

Over the years I have tried to enumerate certain characteristics which help define tendencies to be observed in older people. They are not inevitable nor are they found to the same degree in each person who manifests them. They do show themselves regularly enough to be considered typical of people who have lived a long time and are viewing the world from the special vantage point of old age.

Old age is the only period of life with no future. Therefore a major task in late life is learning not to think in terms of the future. Children are extremely future oriented and look forward to each birthday as a sign of growing up. The middle-aged, as Schopenhauer said, begin to count the number of years they have left before death rather than the number of years since birth. In old age one's time perspective is shortened even further as the end of life approaches. Some avoid confronting this fact by retreating to the past. Others deny their age and continue to be future oriented. The latter are the people who fail to make wills, leave important relationships unresolved, put off enjoyments, and experience boredom and frustration. A more satisfying resolution is found among those elderly who begin to emphasize the quality of the present and of the time remaining, rather than the quantity. When death becomes imminent, there tends to be a sense of immediacy, of the here and now, of living in the moment.

Only in old age can one experience a personal sense of the entire life cycle. This comes to its fullness with the awareness of death in the forefront. There is the unfolding process of change, the experiencing of a sense of time, the seasoning or sense of life experience with a broadening perspective and the accumulation of factual knowledge of what is to be expected at the different points of the life cycle.

Old age inaugurated the process of the life review, promoted by the realization of approaching dissolution and death. The life review is characterized by a progressive return to consciousness of past experience, in particular the resurgence of unresolved conflicts which can now be surveyed and integrated. The old are not only taking stock of themselves as they review their lives; they are trying to think and feel through what they will do with the time that is left and with whatever material and emotional legacies they may have to give to others. They frequently experience grief. The death of others, often more than their own death, concerns them. Perplexed, frightened at being alone, and increasingly depressed, they at times become wary or cautious to the point of suspicion about the motivations of others. If unresolved conflicts and fears are successfully reintegrated they can give new significance and meaning to an individual's life, in preparing for death and mitigating fears.

## AIDS IN SUCCESSFUL AGING

What can we do to help move society to a more balanced view of older people, and how can we help older people to prevent problems in later life and to favor successful aging? How can we treat already troubled older people to help them successfully age? We cannot review all the relevant factors since they vary so greatly and include preventive measures such as a major attack on the known antecedents of arteriosclerosis which would require a change in dietary habits and physical activity. We certainly must face the enormous problem of alcoholism in the United States. Many people with a lifelong excessive alcoholic intake are now surviving into old age, and many older people are taking up alcohol after experiencing grief and loneliness.

There is need for a major reformation of our culture's sensibility toward old people through use of the media, which can aid in transforming our views of what older people are really like and can provide information about how to help older people enhance their sense of themselves. There is also the political approach. Older people are learning to assert themselves for what they need and win self-respect thereby.

Two forms of psychotherapy can be helpful to older people from both the preventive and therapeutic perspectives: 1) life review therapy, and 2) life-cycle group therapy.

*Life review therapy* includes the taking of an extensive autobiography from the older person and from other family members. Such memoirs can also be preserved by means of tape recordings, of value to children in the family. When the subject is a person of note, the memoirs have considerable historic importance and should be placed in archives for many reasons including furthering our understanding of creativity and improving the image of our elders. The use of the family album, the scrapbook and other memorabilia in the search for genealogies and pilgrimages back to places of emotional import, evoke crucial memories, responses and understanding in aged patients. The summation of one's life work is useful. The consequences of these steps include expiation of guilt, exorcism of problematic childhood identifications, the resolution of intrapsychic conflicts, the reconciliation of family relationships, the transmission of knowledge and values to those who follow, and the renewal of the ideals of citizenship. Such life review therapy can be conducted in a variety of settings ranging from outpatient individual psychotherapy to counseling in senior centers to skilled listening in nursing homes. Even nonprofessionals can function as therapists by becoming trained listeners as older persons recount their lives. Many old people can be helped to conduct their own life reviews. The process need not be expensive.

Reminiscence by the old has all too often been devalued, regarded as a symptom (usually of organic dysfunction), and considered to represent aimless wandering of the mind or living in the past. We recognize the value of reminiscence as seen in the great memoirs composed in old age, which may give fascinating accounts of unusual and gifted people, e.g., Casanova, Benjamin Franklin or Igor Stravinsky. We see the role of the life review in film and fiction. Ingmar Bergman's beautiful 1957 motion picture, "Wild Strawberries," shows an elderly physician whose dreams and visions concerned his past as he changed from remoteness and selfishness to closeness and love. Literature is replete with examples of the life review: Ernest Hemingway's "The Snows of Kilimanjaro," Samuel Beckett's "Krapp's Last Tape" and Leo Tolstoy's "The Death of Ivan Ilych." The National Archives should support a major program to acquire memoirs not only from distinguished contributors to American life but from average citizens who can illuminate the events of history, e.g., the growth of unions. Ethnic groups should help preserve their heritage through life reviews of their elders.

*Life-cycle group therapy.* Since 1970 Myrna I. Lewis, a social worker colleague, and I have conducted four age-integrated psychotherapy groups with about 8 to 10 members each with one contrasting middle-aged group. We have integrated persons ranging from the age of 15 years to over age 80 in each of the four groups, based on the belief that age segregation as practiced in our society leaves very little opportunity for the rich exchange of feeling, experience and support that is possible between the generations. The groups are oriented towards persons experiencing a crisis in their life ranging from near normal to pathologic reactions to adolescence, education, marriage or single life, divorce, parenthood, work and retirement, widowhood, illness and impending death. Thus such groups are concerned not only with intrinsic psychiatric disorders but with preventive and remedial treatment of people as they pass through the usual vicissitudes of the life cycle. Criteria for membership include absence of active psychosis and presence of life crisis, acute, subacute or chronic. Reactions to life crises follow traditional diagnostic categories including depression, anxiety states, hypochondriasis, alcoholism, and drug misuse. Our groups are balanced for age, sex and personality dynamics. We meet once a week for half an hour. Individual membership in a group averages about two years. New group members are asked to participate for a minimum of three months. This life-cycle crisis approach to group therapy is neither strictly encounter nor strictly psychoanalytic. Rather it can be equally concerned with the interaction among group members as determined by

reality and the past histories and problems of each member. The goal is the amelioration of suffering, the overcoming of disability, and the opportunity for new experiences of intimacy and self-fulfillment. Regarding the elderly, some of the phenomena we have observed include pseudosenility (either the type that is psychologically determined by depression and anxiety or the type that is an expression of role-playing), the Peter Pan syndrome or refusal to grow up, leadership preempted by the middle-aged, and neglect or mascoting of the elderly and young. Unique contributions of the elderly include models for growing older, solutions for loss and grief, the creative use of reminiscence, historic empathy, and a sense of the entire life cycle. We believe that both forms of therapy can be very useful in nursing homes, mental hospitals and other institutions. Age integration helps to recapitulate the family, something woefully missing for many older people. The garrulousness of older people reflects a social symptom and an intense desire in the face of death to deal with one's individual life.

These are just two examples of how we can approach older patients, in or out of institutions. Indeed older persons' families, when they exist (one-fourth of older people have no family at all), can themselves participate in therapeutic processes.

## COMMENT

When old people look back on their lives, they regret more often what they did not do rather than what they have done. Medicine should regret its failures to act responsibly in the health care (including mental health care) of the elderly. Physicians, psychotherapists and the public should not assume that nothing can be done for old people. No one should count them out.

## REFERENCES

1. Butler RN: Re-awakening interests, Nursing Home J of ANHA 10: 8, 1961.
2. Cumming E and Henry WE: Growing Old: The Process of Disengagement. New York, Basic Books, 1961.
3. Hader M and Schulman PM: Benjamin Rush: an early gerontological psychiatrist, Gerontologist 5: 156, 1965.
4. Butler RN: Ageism: another form of bigotry, Gerontologist 9: 243, 1969.
5. Butler RN and Lewis MI: Aging and Mental Health. St. Louis, Mo, CV Mosby Co, 1973.
6. Butler RN and Lewis MI: Sex After Sixty. New York, Harper and Row (in press).

# 4

Simone de Beauvoir

# JOIE DE VIVRE

On sexuality and old age

THOSE MORALISTS WHO VINDICATE OLD AGE claim that it sets the individual free from his body. The purification of which the moralists speak consists for them essentially in the extinction of sexual desires: they are happy to think that the elderly man escapes from this slavery and thereby achieves serenity. In his well-known poem, "John Anderson My Jo," Robert Burns described the ideal old couple in whom carnal passion has died quite away. The pair has climbed the hill of life side by side; once they tasted blissful hours; now with trembling steps but still hand in hand they must go together along the road that leads to the end of the journey. This stereotype is deeply imprinted upon the hearts of young and middle-aged people because they met it countless times in the books of their childhood and because their respect for their grandparents persuades them of its truth. The idea of sexual relations or violent scenes between elderly people is deeply shocking.

Yet there also exists an entirely different tradition. The expression, "dirty old man," is a commonplace of popular speech. Through literature and even more through painting, the story of Susanna and the Elders has taken on the value of a myth. The comic theater has endlessly repeated the theme of the ancient lover. As we shall see, this satirical tradition is closer to the truth than the edifying speeches of idealists who are concerned with showing old age as it ought to be.

In childhood, sexuality is polymorphous: it is not centered upon the genital organs. "Only at the end of a complex and hazardous evolution does the sexual drive assume a preeminently genital aspect; at this point it takes on the apparent fixity and finality of an instinct."* From this we may at once draw the conclusion that a person whose genital functions have diminished or become nonexistent is

*J. Laplanche and J.-B. Pontalis, *Vocabulaire de la psychoanalyse.*

not therefore sexless: he is a sexed being—even eunuchs and impotent men remain sexed—and one who must work out his sexuality in spite of a given mutilation.

An inquiry into the sexuality of the aged amounts to asking what happens to a man's relationship with himself, with others, and with the outside world when the preeminence of the genital aspect of the sexual pattern has vanished. Obviously it would be absurd to imagine that there is a simple return to infantile sexuality. Never, on any plane, does the aged person lapse into "a second childhood," since childhood is by definition a forward, upward movement. And then again, infantile sexuality is in search of itself, whereas the aged man retains the memory of what it was in his maturity. Lastly, there is a radical difference between the social factors affecting the two ages.

The enjoyment the individual derives from his sexual activities is rich and manifold to a very high degree. It is understandable that a man or woman should be bitterly unwilling to give it up, whether the chief aim is pleasure, or the transfiguration of the world by desire, or the realization of a certain image of oneself, or all this at the same time. Those moralists who condemn old age to chastity say that one cannot long for pleasures one no longer desires. This is a very short-sighted view of the matter. It is true that normally desire does not arise as desire in itself: it is desire for a particular pleasure or a particular body. But when it no longer rises spontaneously, reflection may very well regret its disappearance. The old person retains his longing for experiences that can never be replaced and is still attached to the erotic world he built up in his youth or maturity. Desire will enable him to renew its fading colors. And again it is by means of desire that he will have an awareness of his own integrity. We wish for eternal youth, and this youth implies the survival of the libido.

Its presence is found only among those who have looked upon their sexuality as something of positive value. Those

20

who, because of complexes rooted in their childhood, took part in sexual activities only with aversion eagerly seize upon the excuse of age to withdraw. I knew an old woman who got her doctor to supply her with certificates so that she could avoid her disagreeable "conjugal duties"; as she grew older, the number of her years provided her with a more convenient alibi. A man, if he is half impotent, or indifferent, or if the sexual act worries him badly, will be relieved when age allows refuge in a continence that will seem normal for that time onward.

People who have had a happy sexual life may have reasons for not wishing to prolong it. One of these is their narcissistic relationship with themselves. Disgust at one's own body takes various forms among men and women; but in either, age may provoke it, and if this happens they will refuse to make their body exist for another. Yet there exists a reciprocal influence between the image of oneself

> **"Never, on any plane, does the aged person lapse into 'a second childhood,' since childhood is by definition a forward, upward movement."**

and one's sexual activity: the beloved individual feels that he is worthy of love and gives himself to it unreservedly; but very often he is loved only if he makes a conscious effort to be attractive, and an unfavorable image of himself stands in the way of his doing this. In this event a vicious circle is created, preventing sexual relations.

Another obstacle is the pressure of public opinion. The elderly person usually conforms to the conventional ideal. He is afraid of scandal or quite simply of ridicule, and inwardly accepts the watchwords of propriety and continence imposed by the community. He is ashamed of his own desires, and he denies having them; he refuses to be a lecherous old man in his own eyes, or a shameless old woman. He fights against his sexual drives to the point of thrusting them back into his unconscious mind.

As we might on the face of it suppose, seeing that there is so great a difference between them in their biological destiny and their social status, the case of men is quite unlike that of women. Biologically men are at the greater disadvantage; socially, it is the women who are worse off, because of their condition as erotic objects. In neither case is their behavior thoroughly understood. A certain number of inquiries into it have been carried out, and these have provided the basis for something in the way of statistics. The replies obtained are always of dubious value, and in this field the notion of an average has little meaning.

## The fear of ridicule

A S FAR AS MEN ARE CONCERNED, the statistics, as it so often happens, merely confirm what everybody knows —sexual intercourse diminishes in frequency with age. This fact is connected with the degeneration of the sexual organs, a degeneration that brings about a weakening of

the libido. But the physiological is not the only factor that comes into play. There are considerable differences between the behavior patterns of individuals, some being impotent at sixty and others very sexually active at over eighty. We must try to see how these differences are to be explained.

The first factor, and one of perfectly obvious importance, is the subjects' marital status. Sexual intercourse is much more frequent among married men than among bachelors or widowers. Married life encourages erotic stimulus; habit and "togetherness" favor its appeasement. The "psychological barriers" are far easier to overcome. The wall of private life protects the elderly husband from public opinion, which in any case looks more favorably upon legitimate love than upon unlawful connections. He feels that his image is less endangered. The word image in this context must be thoroughly understood. Whereas the woman object identifies herself with the total image of her body from childhood on, the little boy sees his penis as an alter ego; it is in his penis that his whole life as a man finds its image, and it is here that he feels himself in peril. The narcissistic trauma that he dreads is the failure of his sexual organ—the impossibility of reaching an erection, of maintaining it, and of satisfying his partner. This fear is less haunting in married life. The subject is more or less free to choose the moment for making love. A failure is easily passed over in silence. His familiarity with his partner makes him dread her opinion less. Since he is less anxious, the married man is less inhibited than another. That is why many aged couples continue sexual activities.

The loss of his wife will often cause a trauma that shuts a man off from all sexual activities, either for a long or short period or forever. Widowers and elderly bachelors obviously have much more difficulty in finding an outlet for their libido than married men. Most have lost their charm: if they try to have an affair, their attempts come to nothing. All that remains is venal love: many men have shrunk from it all their lives, and it would seem to them a kind of giving-in, an acquiescence in the decline of age. Yet some do turn to it: they either go with prostitutes or they have a liaison with a woman they help financially. Their choice, continence or activity, depends on the balance between the urgency of their drive and the strength of their resistance.

Many find an answer in masturbation. A quarter of the subjects questioned by *Sexology* magazine said they had indulged in it either for many years or since the age of sixty: the latter were therefore brought back to it by aging. Statistical cross-checks show that even among married men, many turn to this practice. No doubt many elderly men prefer their fantasies to their wife's age-worn body. Or it may happen that either because deep-rooted complexes or awareness of age turn her against physical love, the companion refuses. Masturbation is then the most convenient outlet.

The subject's sexual activities are also influenced by his social condition. They go on far longer among manual workers, among men with a low standard of living than among those who are well to do. Workers and peasants have more straightforward desires, less dominated by erotic myths, than the middle classes; their wives' bodies wear out early, but they do not stop making love to them. When a working man's wife is old, she seems to him less spoiled than would be the case with a richer husband. Then again he has less idea of himself than the white-collar worker. And he does not take so much notice of public opinion, which has less and less force as one goes down the social scale. Old men and women who live almost entirely outside convention—tramps of both sexes, and inmates of institutions—lie together without any shame, even in front of others.

Finally, the happier and richer sexual life has been, the longer it goes on. If the subject has valued it because of the narcissistic satisfaction it gives him, he will break it off as soon as he can no longer see a flattering reflection of himself in his partner's eyes. If he has intended to assert his virility, his skill, or the power of his charm, or if he has meant to triumph over rivals, then he may sometimes be glad of the excuse of age to relax. But if his sexual activities have been spontaneous and happy, he will be strongly inclined to carry them on as long as his strength lasts.

Yet the elderly man does not take so vehement a pleasure in intercourse as a youth does, and this is because the two stages of ejaculation are reduced to one: he no longer has that piercing sensation of imminence which marks the passage from the first to the second, nor yet the triumphant feeling of a jet, an explosion—this is one of the myths that gives the male sexual act its value. Even when the aged man is still capable of normal sexual activity, he often seeks indirect forms of satisfaction; even more so if he is impotent. He takes pleasure in erotic literature, licentious works of art, dirty stories, the company of young women, and furtive contacts; he indulges in fetishism, sadomasochism, various forms of perversion, and, particularly after the age of eighty, in voyeurism. These deviations are readily comprehensible. The fact is, Freud has established that there is no such thing as a "normal" sexuality: it is always "perverted" insofar as it does not break away from its origins, which required it to look for satisfaction not in any specific activity but in the "increase of pleasure" attached to functions dependent upon other drives. Infantile sexuality is polymorphically perverse. The sexual act is considered "normal" when the partial activities are merely preparatory to the genital act. But the subject has only to attach too much importance to these preliminary pleasures to slip into perversion. Normally, seeing and caressing one's partner plays an important part in sexual intercourse. It is accompanied by fantasy; sadomasochistic elements appear; and often fetishism, clothes, and ornaments evoking the presence of the body. When genital pleasure is weak or nonexistent, all these elements rise to the first place. And frequently the elderly man prizes them very highly because they are manifestations of that erotic world that is still of the greatest value to him. He continues to live in a certain climate, his body still existing in a world filled with other bodies. Here again it is often timidity, shame, or difficulties from the outside that prevent him from indulging in what are called his vices.

WE HAVE A FAIR AMOUNT OF EVIDENCE about elderly men's sexual life. It depends on their past and also upon their attitude toward their old age as a whole and toward their image in particular. Chateaubriand so loathed his aged face that he refused to sit for his portrait. In the first part of *Amour et vieillesse—chants de tristesse*, which he wrote when he was sixty-one, he rejects the amorous advances of a young woman: "If you tell me you love me as a father, you will fill me with horror; if you claim to love me as a lover, I shall not believe you. I shall see a happy rival in every young man. Your deference will make me feel my age, your caresses will give me over to the most furious jealousy. . . . Old age makes a man as ugly as can be wished. If he is unhappy, it is even worse . . ." He was cruelly sensitive to the "insult of the years," and his refusal was dictated by a kind of inverted narcissism.

Old men's loves are not always doomed to failure: far from it. Many of them have a sexual life that goes on very late. The Duc de Bouillon was sixty-six when his son Turenne was born. The famous Duc de Richelieu's father married for the third time in 1702, at the age of seventy. When his son was sixty-two and governor of Guienne, he led a life of debauchery. In his old age he seduced a great many young women. At seventy-eight, bewigged, made-up, and very thin, he was said to look like a tortoise thrusting its head out of its shell; this did not prevent him from having affairs with the actresses of the *Comédie française*. He had an acknowledged mistress, and he spent his evenings with whores; sometimes he used to bring them home —he liked listening to their confidences. He married when he was eighty-four and had recourse to aphrodisiacs: he made his wife pregnant. Furthermore, he deceived her too. He continued his sexual activities right up until his death, at the age of ninety-two.

Tolstoy is a well-known example of sexual vitality. Toward the end of his life he preached total continence both for men and for women. Nevertheless, when he was sixty-nine or seventy he would come back from a very long ride and make love to his wife. All the next day he would walk about the house looking pleased with himself.

Sexuality was of great importance in Victor Hugo's youth and during his middle years. The image of old age that he had always set up for himself allowed him to accept his sexual desires until he was very old: no doubt he thought of Boaz when a young woman offered herself to him. In his view, age was by no means a blemish, but rather an honor; it brought one nearer to God and it was in harmony with everything that is sublime, with beauty and innocence. The aged Hugo certainly suffered from no feeling of inferiority whatsoever. In his opinion he was answerable to no one but himself: at no time in his life did he ever yield to public opinion—if he had desires, he satisfied them.

There are many other examples to show that an elderly man may be importuned by the most urgent sexual desires. H. G. Wells was sixty when he fell in love with Dolores after they had corresponded; he fell passionately in love and found himself possessed of unsuspected sexual powers. "For the first time in my life it was revealed to me that

five, but at fifty-eight he had an odd outburst of eroticism. Bernard Berenson, who died at ninety-four, wrote, "I only really became aware of sex and of women's physical, animal life at the period that might be called my old age."

Many elderly men look for younger partners. Those subjects for whom sex continues to play an important part are gifted with excellent health and lead an active life. Impotence does not exclude desire; desire is most often satisfied through deviations in which the fantasies of middle age are accentuated.

## L'Après-midi d'un faune

WE HAVE ONE MOST REMARKABLE PIECE of evidence concerning an old man's relationship with his body, his image, and his sex: this is Paul Léautaud's *Journal.**
He provides us with a living synthesis of the various points of view that we have considered in this study.

Léautaud always looked at himself with a certain approval. It was from the outside that he learned he was aging, and it made him very angry. In 1923, when he was fifty-three, a railway official referred to him as "a little old gentleman." Furious, Léautaud wrote in his *Journal,* "Little old man! Old gentleman? What the devil—am I as blind as all that? I cannot see that I am either a little or an old gentleman. I see myself as a fifty-year-old, certainly, but an exceedingly well preserved fifty-year-old. I am slim and I move easily. Just let them show me an *old gentleman* in such good shape!" At fifty-nine he looked at himself with a critical eye: "Mentally and physically I am a man of forty. What a pity my face does not match! Above all my lack of teeth! I really am remarkable for my age: slim, supple, quick, active. It is my lack of teeth that spoils everything; I shall never dare to make love to a woman again."

In him we see with remarkable clarity how impossible it is for an old man to realize his age. On his birthday he wrote, "Today I begin my sixty-fourth year. In no way do I feel an old man." The old man is Another, and this Other belongs to a certain category that is objectively defined; in his inner experience Léautaud found no such person. There were moments, however, when his age weighed upon him. On April 12, 1936, he wrote, "I do not feel happy about my health nor about my state of mind; and then there is the sorrow of aging, too. Aging above all!" But at sixty-nine he wrote, "During my seventieth year I am still as lively, active, nimble and alert as a man can be."

I was an astonishing fellow, an extraordinary chap, an outstanding virtuoso. Casanova certainly could never have held a candle to me," he wrote with a smile. The affair turned sour; there were ugly scenes; in the end he could no longer bear Dolores and when he was sixty-six he broke with her. Having done so, he met the girl he called Brylhil; this was the most violent passion of his life—a mutual passion that lasted many years.

Among our contemporaries there are a very great many examples of elderly men married or attached to young women: Charlie Chaplin, Picasso, Casals, Henry Miller. These examples confirm the notion that if it has been rich, sexual life goes on for a long time. But it may also happen that a man who has been indifferent to women for most of his life discovers the delights of sex in his later years. Trotsky had looked upon himself as old since the age of fifty-

"Impotence does not exclude desire: desire is most often satisfied through deviations in which the fantasies of middle age are accentuated."

*Léautaud was a critic and an editor of *Mercure de France,* a literary journal.

Léautaud had every reason to be pleased with himself: he looked after his house and cared for his animals; he did all the shopping on foot, carrying heavy baskets of provisions; wrote his *Journal*; and he did not know what it was to be tired. "It is only my sight that is failing. I am exactly as I was at twenty. My memory is as good as ever and my mind as quick and sharp."

This made him all the more irritable when other people's reactions brought the truth home to him. He was seventy when a young woman lost her balance as an underground train started off with a jerk; she cried out, "I'm so sorry, Grandpa, I nearly fell on you." He wrote angrily, "Damn it all! My age must show clearly in my face. How impossible it is to see oneself as one really is!"

The paradox lies in the fact that he did not really dislike being old. He was one of those exceptional cases I have mentioned, where old age coincides with childhood fantasy: he had always been interested in old people. On March 7, 1942, when he was seventy-two, he wrote, "A kind of vanity comes over you when you reach old age—you take a pride in remaining healthy, slim, supple and alert, with an unaltered complexion, your joints in good order, no illness and no diminution in your physical and mental powers."

But his vanity demanded that his age be invisible to others: he liked to imagine that he had stayed young in spite of the burden of his years.

He only gave way to discouragement at the very end of his life, when his health failed. On February 25, 1945, he wrote, "I am very low indeed. My eye-sight. The horrible marks of age I see on my face. My *Journal* behind-hand. The mediocrity of my life. I have lost my energy and all my illusions. Pleasure, even five minutes of pleasure, is over for me." He was then seventy-five, and his sexual life had come to an end. But except in his very last years one of the reasons for his pride was that he still felt desire and was still capable of satisfying it. We can follow his sexual evolution in his *Journal*.

L EAUTAUD ONLY BECAME FULLY AWARE of women when he was approaching his fiftieth year. At thirty-five he wrote, "I am beginning to regret that my temperament allows me to enjoy women so little." He lacked the "sacred fire." "I always think too much of other things—of myself, for example." He was afraid of impotence and his love-making was over very quickly: "I give women no pleasure since I have finished in five minutes and can never start again. . . . Shamelessness is all I really like in love. . . . There are some things not every woman can be asked to do." He had a lasting affair with a woman called Bl——. He says he loved her very much, but he also says that living with her was hell. When he was about forty, although he was still rather indifferent, since he could give his partner no pleasure, he delighted in looking at pictures of naked women. Yet a few years later he speaks sadly of the "rare love-scenes in my life which I really enjoyed." He reproaches himself for being "timid, awkward, brusque,

oversensitive, always hesitant, never able to take advantage of even the best opportunities" with women. All this changed when at fifty he met "a really passionate woman, wonderfully equipped for pleasure and exactly to my taste in these matters," and he showed himself to be "almost brilliant," although up until then he had thought that he was not very good—as he had only known women who did not suit him. From this time on, sex became an obsession to him; on December 1, 1923, he wrote, "Perhaps Madame [one of the names he gave to his mistress] is right: my perpetual desire to make love may be somewhat pathological. . . . I put it down to a lifetime's moderation—it lasted until I was over forty—and also to my intense feeling for her, which makes me want to make love to her when I see so much as a square inch of her body. . . . I think it is also because I have been deprived of so many things, such as that female nakedness for which I have acquired such a liking. I am quite amazed when I think of what has happened to me in all this. . . . Never have I caressed any other woman as I caress Madame." In the summer they parted, and abstinence lay heavy upon him: he masturbated, thinking of her. "Of course I am delighted to be such an ardent lover at my age, but God knows it can be troublesome."

Madame was a little older than he: all his life he had loved only mature women. A twenty-three-year-old virgin threw herself at his head, and he agreed to have an affair with her; but it did not give him the least pleasure and he broke immediately. Except for this one fling he was faithful to Madame for years. He liked watching himself and her in a mirror during their lovemaking. From 1927—age

---

## "Young people are still very shocked if the old, especially old women, are still sexually active."

---

fifty-seven—on, he was forced to take care not to make love too often; he found consolation in bawdy talk with the Panther (another name he gave to his mistress). He did not get on well with her; "we are attached to each other only by our senses—by vice—and what remains is so utterly tenuous!" But in 1938 he did recall with great satisfaction the "seventeen years of pleasure between two creatures the one as passionate and daring as the other in amorous words and deeds." When he was fifty-nine his affair with the Scourge, as he now called her, was still going on, though she was already sixty-four. He was shocked by couples where the woman was much younger than the man. "I myself at fifty-nine would never dare to make any sort of advance to a woman of thirty."

He was still very much attracted to the Scourge, and he took great pleasure in his "sessions" with her. Yet he did complain, "What a feeble ejaculation when I make love: little better than water!" Later he wrote, "I am certainly better when I do not make love at all. Not that it comes hard—far from it—but it is always a great effort, and I do not get over it as quickly as I did a few years ago. . .

At seventy-two he was still planning idylls that never came to anything, and he had erotic dreams that gave him an erection. "At night I still feel ready for anything." But that same year he observed that his sexual powers were declining. "It is no use giving yourself over to lovemaking when the physical side is dead or nearly so. Even the pleasure of seeing and fondling is soon over, and there is not the least eagerness to begin again. For a real appreciation of all these things, there must be the heat of physical passion." It is clear that Léautaud's greatest pleasure was visual. He retained it longer than any other form of sensual enjoyment, and after the age of forty he prized it very highly indeed. When he lost it he considered that his sexual life was over. It is also clear how a man's image of himself is bound up with sexual activity. He was "in the depths of sorrow" when he could no longer experience these pleasures. Still, his narcissism did survive his sexual decline at least for some time.

## The feminine disadvantage

BIOLOGICALLY WOMEN'S SEXUALITY is less affected by age than men's. Brantôme bears this out in the chapter of his *Vies des dames galantes* that he dedicates to "certain old ladies who take as much pleasure in love as the young ones." Whereas a man of a certain age is no longer capable of erection, a woman "at no matter what age is endowed with as it were a furnace . . . all fire and fuel within." Popular tradition bears witness to this contrast. In one of the songs in the Merry Muses of Caledonia* an old woman laments her elderly husband's impotence. She longs for "the wild embraces of their younger days" that are now no more than a ghostly memory, since he no longer thinks of doing anything in bed except sleeping, while she is eaten up with desire. Today scientific research confirms the validity of this evidence. According to Kinsey, throughout their lives women are sexually more stable than men; when they are sixty their potential for pleasure and desire is the same as it was at thirty. According to Masters and Johnson, the strength of the sexual reaction diminishes with age; yet a woman can still reach orgasm, above all if she is regularly and properly stimulated. Those who do not often have physical relations sometimes find coition painful, either during the act or after, and sometimes suffer from dyspareunia or dysuria; it is not known whether these troubles are physical or psychological in origin. I may add that a woman can take great pleasure in making love even though she may not reach orgasm. The "preliminary pleasures" count even more perhaps for her than they do for a man. She is usually less sensitive to the appearance of her partner and therefore less worried by his growing old. Even though her part in lovemaking is not as passive as people sometimes make out, she has no fear of a particular failure. There is nothing to prevent her from going on with her sexual activities until the end of her life.

What I miss most is female nakedness, licentious attitudes, and playing amorous games."

"Until I was sixty-six or sixty-seven I could make love two or three times a week." Now he complained that his brain was tired for three or four days after making love, but he still went on, and he corresponded with three of his former mistresses.

When he was seventy Léautaud wrote, "I miss women and love terribly." He remembered how he used to make passionate love to the Scourge from the age of forty-seven to sixty-three, and then for two years with CN [another mistress].

"It was only three years ago that I noticed I was slowing down. I can still make love, and indeed I quite often feel sad at being deprived of it; though at the same time I tell myself that it is certainly much better for me to abstain."

---

*Popular Scottish songs collected in the eighteenth century.

Still, all research shows that women have a less active sexual life than men. Kinsey says that at fifty, 97 per cent of men are still sexually active compared with 93 per cent of women. At sixty it is 94 per cent of men and only 80 per cent of women. This comes from the fact that socially men, whatever their age, are subjects, and women are objects, relative beings. When she marries, a woman's future is determined by her husband's; he is usually about four years older than she, and his desire progressively lessens. Or if it does continue to exist, he takes to younger women. An old woman, on the other hand, finds it extremely difficult to have extramarital relations. She is even less attractive to men than old men are to women. And in her case gerontophilia does not exist. A young man may desire a woman old enough to be his mother but not his grandmother. A woman of seventy is no longer regarded by anyone as an erotic object. Venal love is very difficult for her to find. It would be most exceptional for an old woman to have both the means and the opportunity of getting herself a partner; and then again shame and fear of what people might say would generally prevent her from doing so. This frustration is painful to many old women, for they are still tormented by desire. They usually find their relief in masturbation; a gynecologist told me of the case of one woman of seventy who begged him to cure her of this practice—she was indulging in it night and day.

When Andrée Martinerie was conducting an inquiry for *Elle* magazine (March 1969) she gathered some interesting confidences from elderly women. Madame F., a rich middle-class sixty-eight-year-old, a militant Catholic, mother of five and grandmother of ten, told her, "I was already sixty-four. . . . Now just listen: four months after my husband's death I went down into the street just like someone who is going to commit suicide. I had made up my mind to give myself to the very first man who would have me. Nobody wanted me. So I went home again." When she was asked whether she had thought of remarrying, she answered, "That is all I ever do think of. If I dared I would put an advertisement in *Le Chasseur français.* . . . I would rather have a decrepit invalid of a man than no man at all!" Talking of desire, Madame R., sixty years old and living with her sick husband, said, "It is quite true that you don't get over it." She sometimes felt like beating her head against the wall. A woman reader of this inquiry wrote to the magazine, "I must tell you that a woman remains a woman for a very long time in spite of growing older. I know what I am talking about, because I am seventy-one. I was a widow at sixty; my husband died suddenly and it took me at least two years to realize fully what had happened. Then I started to answer advertisements in the matrimonial column. I admit that I did miss having a man—or rather I should say I do miss it: this aimless existence is terrifying, without affection or any outlet for one's own feelings. I even began wondering whether I was quite normal. Your inquiry was a great relief. . . ." This correspondent speaks modestly of "affection," an "outlet for one's own feelings." But the context shows that her frustration had a sexual dimension. The reaction of a young woman who wrote to *Elle* is typical: "In our group

of young people we laughed heartily about the passionate widow (the member of the Action Catholique) who cannot 'get over it.' I wish you would now hold an inquiry on love as it appears to the fourth age of women, in other words those between eighty and a hundred and twenty." Young people are very shocked if the old, especially old women, are still sexually active.

---

## "Whereas a man of a certain age is no longer capable of erection, a woman 'at no matter what age is endowed with as it were a furnace . . . all fire and fuel within.' "

---

A woman, then, continues in her state as erotic object right up to the end. Chastity is not imposed upon her by a physiological destiny but by her position as a relative being. Nevertheless it may happen that women condemn themselves to chastity because of the "psychological barriers" that I have mentioned, which are even more inhibiting for them than for men. A woman is usually more narcissistic in love than a man; her narcissism is directed at her body as a whole. She has a delightful awareness of her body as something desirable, and this awareness comes to her through her partner's caresses and his gaze. If he goes on desiring her she easily puts up with her body's aging. But at the first sign of coldness she feels her ugliness in all its horror; she is disgusted with her image and cannot bear to expose her poor person to others. This lack of assurance strengthens her fear of other people's opinions: she knows how censorious they are toward old women who do not play their proper role of serene and passion-free grandmothers.

Even if her husband wants to make love with her again later, a deeply rooted feeling of shame may make her refuse him. Women make less use of diversion than men. Those who enjoyed a very active and uninhibited sexual life before do sometimes compensate for their enforced abstinence by extreme freedom in conversation and the use of obscene words. They become something very like bawds, or at least they spy upon the sexual life of their young women friends with a most unhealthy curiosity, and do all they can to make them confide their secrets. But generally speaking their language is as repressed as their lovemaking. Elderly women like to appear as restrained in their conversation as they are in their way of life. Their sexuality now shows only in their dress, their jewelry and ornaments, and in the pleasure they take in male society. They like to flirt discreetly with men younger than themselves and they are touched by attentions that show they are still women in men's eyes.

However, it is clear from pathology that in women, too, the sexual drive is repressed but not extinguished. Psychiatrists have observed that in asylums female patients' eroticism often increases with age. Senile dementia brings with it a state of erotic delirium arising from lack of cerebral control. Repressions are also discarded in some other

**"Venal love is very difficult for her to find. It would be most exceptional for an old woman to have both the means and the opportunity of getting herself a partner; and then again shame and fear of what people might say would generally prevent her from doing so."**

forms of psychosis. Dr. Georges Mahé recorded twenty cases of extreme eroticism out of 110 sixty-year-old female patients in an institution; the symptoms included public masturbation, make-believe coition, obscene talk, and exhibitionism. Unfortunately he gives no idea of the meaning of these displays: he puts them into no context and we do not know *who* the patients were who indulged in these practices. Many of the inmates suffer from genital hallucinations such as rape and physical contact. Women of over seventy-one are convinced that they are pregnant. Madame C., seventy and a grandmother, sings barrack-room songs and walks about the hospital half-naked, looking for a man. Eroticism is the most important factor in many delirious states; it also triggers off some cases of melancholia. E. Gehu speaks of an eighty-three-year-old grandmother who was looked after in a convent. She was an exhibitionist, showing both homosexual and heterosexual tendencies. She fell upon the younger nuns who brought her meals; during these crises she was perfectly lucid. Later she became mentally confused. She ended up by regaining her mental health and behaving normally once more. Here again, we should like a more exact, detailed account of her case. All the observations that I have just quoted are most inadequate; but at least they do show that old women are no more "purified of their bodies" than old men.

Neither history nor literature has left us any worthwhile evidence on the sexuality of old women. It is an even more strictly forbidden subject than the sexuality of old men.

There are many cases of the libido disappearing entirely in old people. Ought they to rejoice in it, as the moralists say? Nothing is less certain. It is a mutilation that brings other mutilations with it: sexuality, vitality, and activity are indissolubly linked. When desire is completely dead, emotional response itself may grow loose at its edge. At sixty-three Rétif de La Bretonne wrote, "My heart died at the same time as my senses, and if sometimes a tender impulse stirs me, it is as erroneous as that of a savage or a eunuch: it leaves me with a profound feeling of sorrow." It seemed to Bernard Shaw that when he lost interest in women he lost interest in living. "I am ageing very quickly. I have lost all interest in women, and the interest they have in me is greater than ever and it bores me. The time has probably come for me to die."

Even Schopenhauer admitted, "It could be said that once the sexual urge is over life's true centre is burnt out, leaving a mere shell." Or again, "life is like a play acted at first by live actors and then finished by automata wearing the same costumes." Yet at the same time he says that the sexual instinct produces a "benign dementia." The only choice left to men is that between madness and sclerosis. In fact what he calls "dementia" is the spring of life itself. When it is broken or destroyed a man is no longer truly alive.

THE LINK that exists between sexuality and creativity is striking: it is obvious in Hugo and Picasso and in many others. In order to create there must be some degree of aggression—"a certain readiness," says Flaubert—and this aggressivity has its biological source in the libido. It is also necessary to feel united with the world by an emotional warmth; this disappears at the same time as carnal desire, as Gide understood very clearly when on April 10, 1942, he wrote, "There was a time when I was cruelly tormented, indeed obsessed by desire, and I prayed, 'Oh let the moment come when my subjugated flesh will allow me to give myself entirely to...' But to what? To art? To pure thought? To God? How ignorant I was! How mad! It was the same as believing that the flame would burn brighter in a lamp with no oil left. If it were abstract, my thought would go out; even today it is my carnal self that feeds the flame, and now I pray that I may retain carnal desire until I die."

It would not be truthful to state that sexual indifference necessarily brings inertia and impotence. There are many examples to prove the contrary. Let us merely say there is one dimension of life that disappears when there is no more carnal relationship with the world; those who keep this treasure to an advanced age are privileged indeed.

# 5

# The Elderly In America

By
**Leon Bouvier,**
*Vice President,*
*Population Reference Bureau*

**Elinore Atlee,**
*member of the Gray Panthers,*
*National Council of Senior Citizens,*
*and the American Association of*
*Retired Persons*

**Frank McVeigh,**
*Associate Professor of Sociology,*
*Muhlenberg College*

At the turn of the 19th century, only exceptionally tough or lucky Americans attained the Biblical three score years and ten; as we approach the 21st century, most Americans do. This revolution in length of life has had a profound effect on the population structure of the United States in recent years (see Fig. 1 on the opposite page). It has also changed the lives of the country's elderly citizens.

This *Bulletin* will outline some of those effects, provide statistics and definitions, attempt some forecasts, and relate the experiences of the United States to population trends in the developing countries and their probable consequences.

## Who Are the Elderly?

Physicians, sociologists, and other specialists have yet to reach a consensus on what constitutes aging and who should be included among the elderly.

The Commission on Population Growth and the American Future says: "How we define 'old' and 'young' is always an arbitrary matter, determined in large part by custom. Only at the lower and upper age ranges are the functions which people are able to perform clearly related to biological age. For example, it could be argued that a more appropriate delineation of the working age population would be 21 to 70, rather than 18 to 64 years. This would permit a longer period of schooling and training appropriate to the economy's needs. Also, in a population with higher longevity, health and vitality can be retained until older ages. Sweden, with an older age distribution than ours, places retirement at 70—rather than 65; India, with a much younger age structure, places it at 55."[1]

Biologically, aging begins at birth and continues until death, although not until about the fourth decade of an individual's life does it become obvious—and this, in part, is due to stereotyped ideas about aging. The major physiological changes include a decline in body efficiency and, later, changes in the body structure, an arrest of some growth processes, and a reversal of size.[2]

Aging is, of course, more than a physiological process affected by heredity and modified by environment. It is a social one, as well, and involves changing relationships between the older person and other people, including such subjective factors as whether an individual views himself or herself as elderly or others view the individual so.

In the United States, being "old," or "elderly," is usually considered as having reached the age of 65 years. This view became "officialized" when the Federal social security program was established in 1935. To facilitate the program's implementation, the Social Security Administration had to establish some simple method of assessing eligibility. It selected chronological age to avoid the time-consuming and expensive procedure of evaluating an individual's financial situation and physical and psychological health. The age the Administration initially chose was 65 years.

Recently, however, some official definitions of the elderly have been changing. In 1956 the Social Security Administration selected age 62 for optional eligibility for reduced benefits for retirement of women and in 1961 offered the same participation to men. Then, with the signing into law of the Older Americans Comprehensive Services Amendment of 1973 to the Social Security Act, the optional retirement age was reduced to age 60.

In this *Bulletin,* the elderly will be defined as 65 years of age and over since most of the available data in the United States are for persons in that category, and more people retire at age 65 than any other.

## The Demography of America's Senior Citizens

To better comprehend the social, economic, and political changes in the lives of the elderly citizens of the United States, it is necessary to look in some detail at the demographic factors involved. This review is supplied in the following subsections. As will be seen, many of the important changes are the direct result of numerical increase among the elderly.

Basic data in the following subsections, unless other sources are given, are taken or derived from the U.S. Bureau of the Census Current Population Reports, Series P-23, No. 43, *Some Demographic Aspects of Aging in the United States* (U.S. Government Printing Office, 1973).

### Number

The elderly population of the United States has mounted consistently since 1900 when slightly more than 3 million men and women were aged 65 and over. By 1940, the elderly population had nearly tripled to 9 million, and in 1975 it was more than 22 million (see Table 1). This almost sevenfold gain in 70 years was much greater than that of the total population, which about tripled from 76 million to 215 million over the same period. Several factors have contributed to this rapid expansion.

Perhaps the most important was the high fertility of the late 19th and early 20th centuries. Large birth cohorts around the turn of the century resulted in large numbers of the elderly 65 to 75 years later. It is important to keep this "cohort effect" in mind when in-

## Figure 1. Population in the United States Over and Under 65 Years Old, 1880 Through 1970 and Projected to 2000

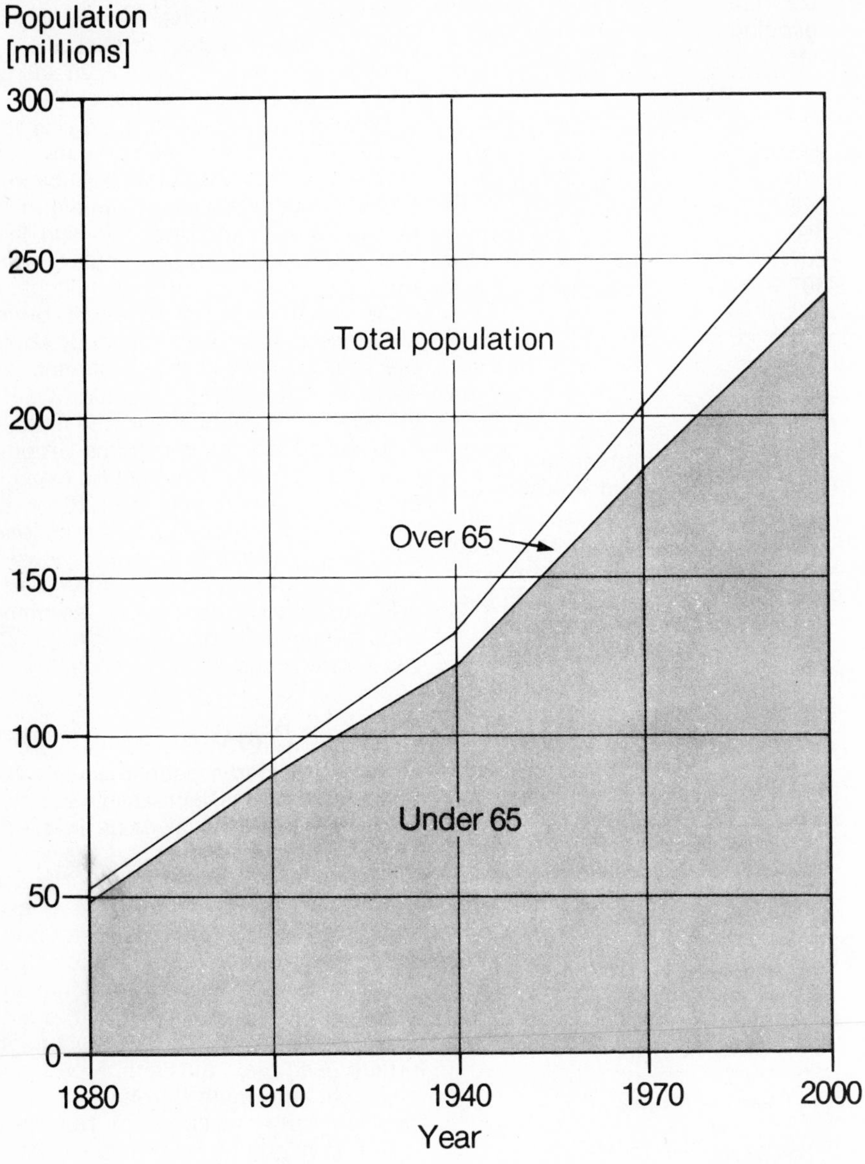

Population
[millions]

Source: The Commission on Population Growth and the American Future, *Demographic and Social Aspects of Population Growth*, (U.S. Government Printing Office, 1972) pp. 52-53.

the Census has projected 24 million elderly by 1980, 27.7 million by 1990, 28.8 million by 2000, 30.9 million by 2010, and 40.2 million elderly by the year 2020.

Note the drop in the growth rate expected beginning around 1990 and lasting about two decades. This would reflect the small cohorts caused by the low birth rate during the depression and up to World War II. But when the post war "babies" begin reaching age 65, shortly after the year 2010, the elderly population will increase dramatically. Later, beyond 2025, the growth rate will probably once again fall sharply because of the rapid decline in births that began in the 1960's and that has since continued almost uninterrupted.

It is important to bear in mind that projections through the year 2020 should be quite accurate as these future elderly are already born. But projections much beyond 2020 could be subject to considerable error because fluctuations in future birth rates are difficult to predict.

### Proportion to the Total Population

The proportion of elderly in the U.S. population has also been changing throughout the century. In 1900 about 4 percent of the nation's 76 million people were 65 years old or over. Forty years later, although their numbers had tripled, they were still only 5.4 percent of the total population. By 1970, however, about one out of 10 Americans (9.9 percent) were elderly.

It is important to realize that changes in the proportion of the elderly (unlike changes in numbers) are affected by variations in the numbers of people in other age categories. Basically, an increase in the proportion of population 65 years and over is more attributable to declining fertility than to lower death rates.

For example, in the first decade of the 20th century, the relatively high fertility of the population and the immigration of young adults combined to limit the proportion of older persons despite the latter's numerical growth. By the 1930's, fertility was much lower, but declines in infant and child mortality kept the proportion of the elderly small. It is only in the past 15 years that lower fertility, low immigration, and the previously explained "cohort effect" have combined and led to large increases in the proportion of the elderly in the U.S. population. Figure 2 illustrates some of these points.

terpreting other demographic data.

Another factor related to the extraordinary increase in the number of the elderly was mortality decline. Progress in medicine and sanitation reduced death rates—especially among infants and youths. This allowed more of the population to survive to age 65. In 1900, for example, only 39 percent of those born that year were expected to survive to their 65th year. Today, 72 percent of the newborn are expected to attain this milestone.

Thirdly, the high level of immigration prior to World War I also had an impact on the large increases in the elderly population in recent years. Generally, the migrants were young adults who swelled the numbers in their respective age cohorts leading to larger numbers of older people decades later.

For the future, the United States can expect a continuing increase in the numbers of older people at least through the year 2020. The Bureau of

**Table 1. Total Population 65 Years and Over, in Thousands, 1900 through 1975, and Decennial Increase, 1900 through 1970**

| Year | Population* | Population increase from the preceding decade | Percent of population increase from the preceding decade |
|---|---|---|---|
| 1900 | 3,099 | | |
| 1910 | 3,986 | 887 | 28.6 |
| 1920 | 4,929 | 943 | 23.7 |
| 1930 | 6,705 | 1,776 | 36.0 |
| 1940 | 9,031 | 2,326 | 34.7 |
| 1950 | 12,397 | 3,366 | 37.3 |
| 1960 | 16,659 | 4,262 | 34.4 |
| 1970 | 20,156 | 3,497 | 21.0 |
| 1975 | 22,300 | – – – | – – – |

*Estimated as of July 1.

Whether the proportion of the elderly will continue to increase depends largely on future fertility rates. If fertility remains at its present low level in the United States with women averaging about two children each, the proportion of the elderly to the total population would increase to about 11 percent in 1990 and then decline slightly as the small birth cohort of the 1930's advances into old age. Should fertility in the near future take an unexpected turn upward to three children per woman on the average, however, the proportion of persons aged 65 and over in 1990 would be only about 9 percent of the total population in the country.

**Figure 2. Age Pyramids, or Percentages in Age Groups, for the United States in 1910, 1940, and 1970**

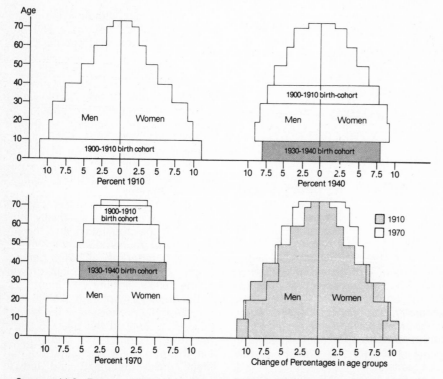

Source: U.S. Bureau of the Census, *General Population Characteristics,* Final Report PC(1)-B1 United States Summary (U.S. Government Printing Office, 1972) p. 1-276.

No matter which fertility projection proves valid, the proportion of the aged will increase between 2010 and 2020 as the baby-boom cohort of the late 1940's and the early 1950's reaches senior citizen status. It can be reasonably expected that the 40 million elderly of the year 2020 will be 13 to 15 percent of U.S. population.

What about projections beyond the year 2020? If the assumptions are made that the present low fertility continues indefinitely, that immigration comes to an immediate halt, and that mortality continues at about today's rate, then the population would presently reach zero growth where births and deaths equal each other. By about the year 2040 when this happened, 16 percent of total U.S. population would be persons 65 years of age and older.

It should be noted that the proportion of the elderly could not be expected to go much higher than 16 or 17 percent of the total population as long as these assumptions are followed. The one-third proportion of the elderly predicted by some writers assumes almost immediate and huge (20- to 30-year) extensions of life expectancy.

## Regional Proportions

While the elderly population in the United States has increased recently, it has not made equal gains in every geographic area or reached the same level in all localities. The Northeast and North Central States have larger proportions of the aged than the South and West (see Table 2 above).

States with a lower share of older residents (less than 8.5 percent) either have populations with relatively high fertility (Georgia, Louisiana, New Mexico, Utah, and South Carolina) or have received large numbers of relatively young in-migrants from other States (Maryland and Nevada).

In contrast, States with relatively large shares of older people (over 12 percent) include Florida, Arkansas, Nebraska, South Dakota, Iowa, and Missouri. Many such States have lost a considerable number of younger people to other areas. When this happens, the elderly are usually left behind, and the age distribution becomes "older." On the other hand, a few States experience an influx of retirees to swell the proportions of the aged.

Florida and Nebraska illustrate contrasting forces that may result in similar proportions of the elderly. In 1970, 14.6 percent of the population of Florida and 12.4 percent of Nebraska were 65 years or over. Between 1960 and 1970, however, the aged population increased by almost 80 percent in

**Table 2. Numbers and Percentages of the Elderly by Region, 1960 and 1970, and Change in Percentage**

| Region | 1960 Number, in thousands | 1960 Percent of total population | 1970 Number, in thousands | 1970 Percent of total population | Change in percentage from 1960 to 1970 |
|---|---|---|---|---|---|
| Northeast | 4,498 | 10.1 | 5,199 | 10.6 | +0.5 |
| New England | 1,122 | 10.7 | 1,270 | 10.7 | - - - |
| Middle Atlantic | 3,377 | 9.9 | 3,930 | 10.6 | +0.7 |
| North Central | 5,078 | 9.8 | 5,727 | 10.1 | +0.3 |
| East North Central | 3,358 | 9.3 | 3,811 | 9.5 | +0.2 |
| West North Central | 1,720 | 11.2 | 1,916 | 11.7 | +0.5 |
| South | 4,582 | 8.3 | 6,043 | 9.6 | +1.3 |
| South Atlantic | 2,099 | 8.1 | 2,937 | 9.6 | +1.5 |
| East South Central | 1,052 | 8.7 | 1,270 | 9.9 | +1.2 |
| West South Central | 1,430 | 8.4 | 1,836 | 9.5 | +1.1 |
| West | 2,401 | 8.6 | 3,096 | 8.9 | +0.3 |
| Mountain | 527 | 7.7 | 695 | 8.4 | +0.7 |
| Pacific | 1,873 | 8.8 | 2,401 | 9.1 | +0.3 |

Florida but by only 12 percent in Nebraska. The high proportion of the elderly in Florida is explained by inmigration of the old; in Nebraska it is caused by the exodus of the young in addition to the longevity of the State's population.

## Life Expectancy

A person born in 1900 could expect to live about 50 years; but a person born today can expect over 71 years. The prime cause of this significant progress has been declining infant and childhood mortality and not any parallel improvement in the life expectancy of the old. As can be seen in Table 3, only moderate gains have occurred in life expectancy for the aged.

For example, a person who achieved age 65 in 1900 could expect to live another 11.9 years while such a person in 1973 could contemplate 15.3—a gain of 3.4 years. And a similar pattern is true of those attaining their 75th year. In 1900 they could look forward, on the average, to 7.1 more years while in 1973 they could plan on an additional 9.5. In both categories, most of the improvement of life expectancy occurred after 1940.

Of course, different categories of the elderly have different expectancies. At all ages, men have shorter life expectancies than women, and, at most ages, blacks have fewer years

ahead than whites. For example, a 65-year-old white woman will probably live 4.1 years longer than a white man, 4.2 years longer than a black man, and 1.1 years longer than a black woman. A 75-year-old black woman could expect to outlive a white man of the same age by 3.2 years, a black man by 2.1 years, and a white woman by 0.9 years.

This difference in the life expectancy

**Table 3. Average Life Expectancy in Years for Persons 65 and Over and 75 and Over by Race and Sex, 1900, 1940, and 1973**

| Age, sex, and race | 1900 | 1940 | 1973 |
|---|---|---|---|
| **All classes:** | | | |
| 65 years | 11.9 | 12.8 | 15.3 |
| 75 years | 7.1 | 7.6 | 9.5 |
| **White males:** | | | |
| 65 years | 11.5 | 12.1 | 13.2 |
| 75 years | 6.8 | 7.2 | 8.1 |
| **White females:** | | | |
| 65 years | 12.2 | 13.6 | 17.3 |
| 75 years | 7.3 | 7.9 | 10.4 |
| **Black males:** | | | |
| 65 years | 10.4 | 12.2 | 13.1 |
| 75 years | 6.6 | 8.2 | 9.2 |
| **Black females:** | | | |
| 65 years | 11.4 | 13.9 | 16.2 |
| 75 years | 7.9 | 9.8 | 11.3 |

of the elderly by sex is increasing. At the turn of the century, the gap was only 0.7 years between white men and women; by the end of the fourth decade it was 1.5 years; and in 1973 it was 4.1 years. The same general progression holds true for blacks.

## Race, Sex, and Age Distributions

Men and women aged 65 and over are far from evenly distributed by race, sex, and age. For example, fewer blacks than whites, proportionally, are elderly; women outnumber men; and the over-65 age group thins unevenly toward advanced old age. Further, some of these patterns have been accentuated recently and may become even more pronounced in the future.

**Race.** While 10.3 percent of all whites in the United States were 65 years or older in 1970, a little less than 7 percent of blacks were elderly. This difference probably results from both a higher infant death rate for blacks in the past, which limited the proportion of those born that survived into old age, and a present relatively high fertility that has increased the percentage of the young.

**Sex.** The majority of older Americans are women, and of these, more than 6 million were widows in 1970. In number, there were almost 3.3 million more older women than men, or—put another way—only 72 men over age 65 for every 100 women age 65 or over. With increasing age, the imbalance becomes even more pronounced, and for the population 75 and over there were only 64 men for every 100 women in 1970.

Elderly men outnumbered older women only in Alaska and Hawaii. This is due chiefly to earlier predominantly male migration to these areas.

A consistent decline in the ratio of elderly men per 100 elderly women has been evident since 1900 (see Table 4) and is expected to continue. Bureau of the Census analysts note that this trend ". . . reflects . . . the progressive effect of higher death rates for males than for females over the entire age range. . . . Furthermore, males have not benefited as much as females by the decline in death rates, resulting in a more rapid reduction in the sex ratio over the age span." The imbalance is less marked, however, for blacks of 65 and over than for whites (80 black men per 100 black women in 1970 as compared to 72 white men per 100 white women).

Largely because of continuing mortality differentials between men and women, the imbalance of the sexes

## Table 4. Men per 100 Women by Age and Race, 1900 to 1990

| Age and race | 1900 | 1930 | 1960 | 1970 | Projection 1990 |
|---|---|---|---|---|---|
| All races: | | | | | |
| Over 65 | 102 | 100.4 | 82.6 | 72.1 | 67.5 |
| Over 75 | 96.3 | 91.8 | 75.1 | 63.7 | 57.8 |
| White: | | | | | |
| Over 65 | 101.9 | 100.1 | 82.1 | 71.6 | 67.7 |
| Over 75 | 97.1 | 92 | 74.3 | 63.2 | 58.4 |
| Black: | | | | | |
| Over 65 | 102.9 | 105.7 | 90.1 | 79.8 | 68.2 |
| Over 75 | 89.6 | 89.6 | 87.6 | 74.7 | 62.6 |

## Table 5. Percent Distribution of the Elderly in Age Groups, 1900 to 1990*

| Age group | 1900 | 1930 | 1960 | 1970 | Projection 1990 |
|---|---|---|---|---|---|
| 65 through 69 years | 42.3 | 41.7 | 37.6 | 33.9 | 34.2 |
| 70 through 74 years | 28.7 | 29.3 | 28.6 | 28 | 26.8 |
| 75 through 79 years | } 29 | } 29 | 18.5 | 18.6 | 19.5 |
| 80 years and over | | | 15.3 | 19.6 | 19.5 |

*Estimated as of July 1.

among the aged is expected to widen in the future. Projections for 1990 indicate that there will be fewer than 68 elderly men for every 100 elderly women.

**Age.** The most obvious trend seen by glancing at Table 5 is that the proportion of the elderly in the 75-and-over age group has increased markedly. In 1900, 29 percent of elderly persons were 75 years of age or over; in 1990, about 39 percent will probably be in that category, of which half will be 80 years or older. In other words, the older population is itself "aging" and is expected to continue to do so in the near future.

This is chiefly due, again, to the large birth cohorts of the late 19th and early 20th centuries, who are now moving into advanced old age, and to the 20th century discoveries in medicine and improvements in health care that have enabled a relatively large proportion of these birth cohorts to survive.

## Table 6. Mortality Rates Among the Elderly per 100,000 Population by Sex and Age for Selected Causes, 1940, 1954, and 1970

| Cause of Death | Persons 65 to 74 years | | | Persons 75 to 84 years | | | Persons 85 years and over | | |
|---|---|---|---|---|---|---|---|---|---|
| | 1940 | 1954 | 1970 | 1940 | 1954 | 1970 | 1940 | 1954 | 1970 |
| All causes | 4,838.3 | 3,785.1 | 3,582.7 | 11,203.9 | 8,603.5 | 8,004.4 | 23,565.1 | 18,157.5 | 16,344.9 |
| Men | 5,462.3 | 4,673.8 | 4,873.8 | 12,126.4 | 9,800.6 | 10,010.2 | 24,639.0 | 18,741.1 | 17,821.5 |
| Women | 4,222.2 | 2,979.1 | 2,579.7 | 10,368.6 | 7,625.9 | 6,667.6 | 22,759.1 | 17,740.0 | 15,518.0 |
| Ratio of men to women | 129.4 | 161.2 | 188.9 | 117.0 | 128.5 | 149.9 | 108.3 | 105.6 | 114.8 |
| Diseases of the heart: | | | | | | | | | |
| Men | 2,129.2 | 2,112.8 | 2,170.3 | 4,962.3 | 4,405.3 | 4,534.8 | 10,343.6 | 8,300.0 | 8,426.2 |
| Women | 1,490.3 | 1,262.0 | 1,082.7 | 4,221.8 | 3,460.2 | 3,120.8 | 9,661.3 | 8,089.9 | 7,591.8 |
| Ratio of men to women | 142.9 | 167.4 | 200.5 | 117.6 | 127.3 | 145.3 | 107.1 | 102.6 | 111.0 |
| Cancer: | | | | | | | | | |
| Men | 737.2 | 839.4 | 1,006.8 | 1,275.2 | 1,371.6 | 1,588.3 | 1,467.0 | 1,688.8 | 1,720.8 |
| Women | 664.9 | 589.4 | 557.9 | 1,047.1 | 972.5 | 891.9 | 1,276.0 | 1,275.3 | 1,096.7 |
| Ratio of men to women | 110.9 | 142.4 | 180.5 | 121.8 | 141.0 | 178.1 | 115.0 | 132.4 | 156.9 |
| Stroke: | | | | | | | | | |
| Men | 593.6 | 550.9 | 449.5 | 1,475.7 | 1,514.9 | 1,361.6 | 2,617.4 | 2,887.2 | 2,895.2 |
| Women | 554.2 | 461.2 | 333.3 | 1,416.9 | 1,414.6 | 1,183.1 | 2,614.5 | 3,179.1 | 3,081.0 |
| Ratio of men to women | 107.1 | 119.4 | 134.9 | 104.1 | 107.1 | 115.1 | 100.1 | 90.0 | 94.0 |
| Influenza and Pneumonia: | | | | | | | | | |
| Men | 253.5 | 92.3 | 129.9 | 719.4 | 258.9 | 376.3 | 2,041.9 | 774.0 | 959.8 |
| Women | 203.2 | 51.4 | 59.3 | 659.4 | 189.2 | 204.4 | 1,945.5 | 669.6 | 733.2 |
| Ratio of men to women | 124.8 | 179.6 | 219.1 | 109.1 | 136.8 | 184.3 | 105.0 | 115.6 | 130.9 |

Source: U.S. Public Health Service, National Center for Health Statistics, *Vital Statistics of the United States 1970,* Vol. II, Pt. A (U.S. Government Printing Office, 1974), pp. 1-26/1-39.

## Causes of Death and Mortality Rates

The leading causes of death among the elderly are "diseases of the heart," cancer, and stroke, in that order. Together, they account for nearly three-fourths of all mortality. "Diseases of the heart" far overshadow other health hazards, and in 1970, 46 percent of all deaths among the aged were so classified. In contrast, cancer and stroke, the next two in rank, each accounted for less than 15 percent. The combined figures for influenza and pneumonia occupy fourth rank, but together they caused less than 5 percent of deaths (see Table 6). Other important causes of mortality for men are accidents and the combined category of bronchitis, emphysema, and asthma. For women, diabetes mellitus and arteriosclerosis are more common.

The mortality rate for each of the four leading causes of death is much higher for elderly men than for elderly women. Furthermore, the difference has increased significantly since 1940. Among persons aged 65 to 74, for example, the 1940 mortality rate for all causes was 29 percent higher for men than for women. By 1970, the difference had widened to about 89 percent.

The two major killers, heart disease and cancer, account for most of the difference. Between 1940 and 1970, the mortality rates for men for these two diseases actually went up. Indeed, the mortality rate for men for cancer increased by 38 percent. During the same time span, the mortality rates for women declined for the same diseases.

This difference explains why the sex ratio (number of men per 100 women) is so low among the elderly and why the life expectancy of elderly women surpasses that of elderly men.

# Some Economic And Social Statistics

While the elderly are no more homogeneous in wealth, education, work, or manner of living than in demographic characteristics, certain patterns are discernible. Some are the outgrowth of past economic conditions or social customs; others suggest probable changes in the social role and economics of the elderly in the future.

## Education

As one might expect, on the average the elderly have completed fewer years

### Table 7. Percent Distribution of Adult Population by Years of School Completed, 1970

| Years of school completed | Persons 25 to 64 years | Persons 65 years and over |
|---|---|---|
| None | 1 | 4.2 |
| Eighth grade or less | 20.6 | 53.2 |
| Some high school | 20.2 | 15.3 |
| High school | 34.8 | 14.8 |
| Some college | 11.5 | 7 |
| College | 11.8 | 5.5 |

Source: U.S. Bureau of the Census, *Educational Attainment,* Subject Report PC(2)-5B (U.S. Government Printing Office, 1973) pp. 1-3.

of formal education than younger adults. For example, in 1970 about 4 percent of those 65 years and over had had no formal schooling, and another 53 percent had completed less than the eighth grade. In contrast, only 1 percent of men and women from 25 to 64 years old had no schooling, and only 21 percent had less than an eighth grade education (see Table 7). The median number of school years completed was 8.7 for the elderly and 12.1 for those 25 to 64 years of age.

These educational characteristics reflect both the values and the available opportunities of the past. By 1990, it is expected that about half the aged population will be high school graduates, and the educational attainments of the future elderly will be even greater as present young adult cohorts enter old age.

## Employment

In 1900, two out of three elderly men worked for a living; now only about one in four does (see Table 8). This turnabout is due chiefly to mass participation by men in voluntary retirement programs and is particularly pronounced among the "younger" elderly in the 65 to 69 age group who are now eligible to collect retirement incomes. (Two other factors may be the decline in self-employment and the stringent retirement rules in some businesses and industries.)

The trend for elderly women, however, has been somewhat different. Between 1940 and 1960, the percentage of elderly women who were employed increased even though the large majority (five-sixths) were economically inactive. Some were utilizing the greater acceptance of women in business and professions; the majority, however, were probably working because their retirement incomes were inadequate and their children and relatives had full financial commitments of their own. The last may have applied especially to elderly black women, who had a higher percentage of employment than their white counterparts.[3]

Since 1960, the trend toward employment by elderly women has softened as more women reaching retirement age are eligible for their own retirement benefits from previously held jobs.

**Unemployment.** Of the elderly men and women who consider themselves an active part of the labor force, roughly 5 percent of the men between

### Table 8. Percent of the Elderly Participating in the Labor Force by Age and Sex, 1940 through 1975

| Sex and age group | 1940 | 1950 | 1960 | 1970 | 1975* |
|---|---|---|---|---|---|
| **Men:** | | | | | |
| 65 through 69 | 59.4 | 59.7 | 44 | 39.3 | 33.3 |
| 70 through 74 | 38.4 | 38.7 | 28.7 | 22.5 } | 14.9 |
| 75 and over | 18.2 | 18.7 | 15.6 | 12.1 } | |
| **Women:** | | | | | |
| 65 through 69 | 9.5 | 13 | 16.5 | 17.2 | 14.6 |
| 70 through 74 | 5.1 | 6.4 | 9.6 | 9.1 } | 5.2 |
| 75 and over | 2.3 | 2.6 | 4.3 | 4.7 } | |

*As of May 1975.

Sources: U.S. Bureau of the Census, *Employment Status and Work Experience,* Subject Report PC(2)-6A (U.S. Government Printing Office, 1973) pp. 31-32.

U.S. Department of Labor, Bureau of Labor Statistics, *Employment and Earnings,* Vol. 21, No. 12 (U.S. Government Printing Office, 1975) pp. 29-30.

the ages of 65 and 75 were out of work in 1970 and between 5 and 7 percent of the women. Nearly 11 percent of women 75 years or over who wanted to work were unable to find jobs.[4]

The attitudes of employers may be an important contributing factor. A Department of Labor study[5] found that physical incapability was the most common reason mentioned by employers for not hiring the elderly despite the fact that 70 percent of those so responding had no factual basis for their attitude.

## Income

Retirement benefits (Social Security and public and private pensions) are the most prevalent and important source of income for the elderly. For elderly couples with a head of household over 65 years old, retirement payments are at least half the income of the majority of couples. For individuals, retirement payments provide nearly two-thirds of total income.[6] Approximately 95 percent of all the elderly in the United States are eligible for Social Security benefits in pensions or aid.

Income derived from wages is second in importance to the elderly, and that from assets in real estate and investments is third. However, only 7 percent of aged couples, and even fewer elderly individuals, obtained all their income from wages, and less than a quarter of elderly couples earned as much as half their incomes.

The fourth-ranking source is public assistance in some form.

While these resources are sufficient

### Table 9. Percent Distribution of Income Among Elderly Couples* and Individuals, 1971

| Income | Couples | Individuals |
|---|---|---|
| $10,000 or more | 17 } | 13 |
| $5,000 to $10,000 | 32 } | |
| $3,000 to $5,000 | 30 | 18 |
| $1,000 to $3,000 | 20 | 59 |
| Less than $1,000 | 01 | 10 |

*Head of household 65 years or older.

Source: U.S. Department of Health, Education and Welfare, Administration of Aging, *New Facts About Older Americans* (Washington, D.C., 1973).

for many elderly couples, a large proportion of elderly individuals is left with incomes inadequate for the usual necessities and comforts of life (see Table 9 and Fig. 3). The contrast is sharp between couples, almost half of whom have joint incomes of $5,000 or more, and individuals, 70 percent of whom live on less than $3,000 a year.

The Social Security Administration confirms that "the proportions at very low income levels are much higher for the nonmarried than the married even when account is taken of differential need."[7] In fact, about half of the nonmarried elderly report incomes below the poverty threshold established for the aged living alone while only 14 percent of married couples are in a similar category. Elderly single men, however, are somewhat better off than older single women—partly because of greater previous earnings.

On January 1, 1974, the Supplemental Security Income program (SSI) replaced the former Federal grants to States for aid to the aged, blind, and disabled. In July of 1974, maximum monthly payments were raised to $146 for individuals without other income and living in their own households and to $219 for couples where both were eligible. This insures annual incomes of at least $1,752 for individuals and $2,628 for couples—a considerable increase for many but still below current poverty levels.

### Figure 3. Median Incomes in 1970 of Elderly Couples and Individuals Compared to Bureau of the Census Poverty Levels and Incomes of Younger Families

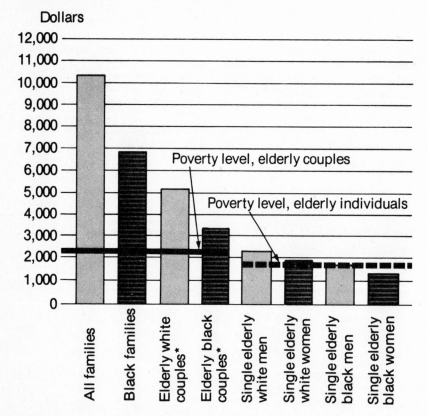

* Head of household 65 years or older; income averaged from 1968 through 1971.

Sources: Office of Management and Budget, *Social Indicators, 1973*, U.S. Government Printing Office (Washington, D.C., 1973) pp. 155, 173, and 175.

U.S. Bureau of the Census, *Current Population Reports*, Series P-23, No. 43, "Some Demographic Aspects of Aging in the United States," U.S. Government Printing Office (Washington, D.C., 1973) p. 29.

## Family Ties and Residence

The majority of the elderly live in a family situation—generally with a wife or husband but sometimes with a child or other relative (see Table 10 on the next page). However, the proportion of men living in families is much higher than that of women; because of their greater longevity, more

## Table 10. Percent of Elderly Men and Women in Various Living Arrangements, 1970

| Living arrangement | Men | Women |
|---|---|---|
| Family | 79 | 59 |
| Head of household | 71 | 10 |
| Wife is head of household | | 33 |
| Other relative is head of household | 8 | 16 |
| Alone or with a nonrelative | 17 | 37 |
| Head of household | 14 | 35 |
| Living with a nonrelative | 3 | 2 |
| Institution | 4 | 4 |

## Table 11. Percent of Elderly Men and Women in Categories of Marital Status, 1970

| Marital status | Men | Women |
|---|---|---|
| Married, spouse present | 68.4 | 33.7 |
| Widowed | 18 | 54.6 |
| Divorced or separated | 5.8 | 4 |
| Never married | 7.8 | 7.7 |

Source: Administration on Aging, *Facts and Figures on Older Americans,* No. 5 (Washington, D.C., Department of Health, Education, and Welfare Pub. [OHD] 74-20005) pp. 4-6.

tion is not good. Adequate homes are not commonly available at prices reasonable to those with limited incomes.

Actually, the elderly are not a very mobile group; 91.2 percent of the elderly in the United States made no residential move at all in 1970-71; and of those who did, most remained within the same county. Only 1.4 percent moved to another State.[9]

Residence patterns of the elderly in both rural and metropolitan areas illustrate their domicile stability. A higher proportion of elderly people than of the general population live in the country—because they've stayed where they lived during their working years. The younger people have moved away to urban centers. Within cities, older people tend to be concentrated in the inner city for the same reason; their children and the young in-migrants have gravitated to the suburbs

while the elderly stayed behind.

Contrary to widespread belief, less than 5 percent of older Americans live in institutions. (Some authorities,[10] however, suggest that since "widows and single people are more likely to be in old age institutions than married persons . . . a continuing decline in the sex ratio might contribute to an increase in demand for institutions.")

### Health and Medical Care and Costs

Although aging does not "cause" any disease, certain ailments—especially chronic ones—are more prevalent among the elderly. For example, in 1972 over 40 percent of noninstitutionalized elderly people had some limitation to normal activity because of a chronic condition compared to only 13 percent of the general popu-

women are widowed and then live alone. In addition, widowed men are apt to remarry because of the availability of single women of their own age group plus the social acceptability of marrying a younger woman. Elderly widowed women, on the other hand, have few potential mates (see Table 11 on the next page).

Most of the elderly also own their own homes and live in them (79 percent of elderly couples and 50 percent of both men and women living alone or with nonrelatives in 1970). Since 85 percent of such homes are free of debt, they are generally economical residences for which the major expenses are property taxes and repairs. They are also a form of inflation-cushioned savings, and the Bureau of the Census reports[8] that the median value of homes owned in 1970 by people between the ages of 65 and 74 was $13,300; that of homes held by men and women 75 and over was $11,000.

For those elderly who wish to move because of convenience, safety, or economy, however, the housing situa-

**Figure 4. Percentages of the Elderly in Nursing Homes in 1969 by Age, Sex, and Race**

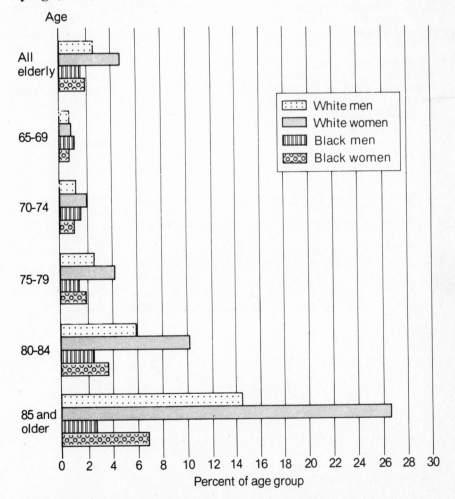

Source: U.S. Office of Management and Budget, *Social Indicators, 1973* (U.S. Government Printing Office, 1973) p. 35.

lation.[11] Heart disease and rheumatism and arthritis were the most common afflictions of the aged, but other frequent problems were auditory and visual impairments, high blood pressure, and mental and nervous disorders.

Acute illnesses (lasting less than 3 months) were less common among the elderly than in the general population; but elderly persons struck by an acute illness were confined to bed or restricted in activity longer than other people. The elderly also averaged two more visits to a physician a year than the general population. Finally, about 2 percent of persons 65 to 74 years old and between 8 and 9 percent of those 75 years and older were in nursing or other institutions.[12] A more detailed distribution by age is shown in Figure 4.

This health pattern imposes a heavy burden of medical and related expenses upon the elderly. They average annual medical bills over three times as great as younger individuals. Private surgical, hospital, and medical insurance pays for some of the outlay, but not everyone has the income to afford adequate insurance coverage, and others may not even be eligible (see Table 12). Medicare and Medicaid take up some of the slack, but the complexity of procedures and rules discourages many of the elderly from obtaining as extensive and frequent treatment as they need.

*Table 12. Percent of the Elderly Privately Insured for Health Care of Specified Types, 1967 Through 1972*

| Care | 1967 | 1968 | 1969 | 1970 | 1971 | 1972 |
|---|---|---|---|---|---|---|
| Hospital | 45.0 | 48.2 | NA | 51.4 | 51.1 | 53.2 |
| Physician: | | | | | | |
| Surgery | 44.1 | 46.7 | NA | 46.7 | 47.0 | 46.3 |
| Hospital visits | 31.1 | 36.6 | NA | 41.1 | 37.7 | 38.5 |
| X-Ray and laboratory | 18.7 | 20.6 | NA | 37.4 | 37.3 | 36.6 |
| Office and home visits | 14.6 | 15.6 | NA | 19.5 | 20.8 | 20.5 |
| Prescribed drugs | 9.7 | 13.1 | NA | 15.9 | 15.9 | 16.6 |
| Nursing: | | | | | | |
| Private | 11.7 | 11.3 | NA | 15.8 | 15.8 | 16.3 |
| Visiting | 13.0 | 14.6 | NA | 18.8 | 19.4 | 21.2 |
| Nursing home | 15.2 | 11.0 | NA | 24.7 | 25.0 | 25.8 |

Source: U.S. Department of Health, Education, and Welfare, Social Security Administration, *Social Security Bulletin,* Vol. 37, No. 2, p. 17.

# Footnotes

1. Commission on Population Growth and the American Future, *Population and the American Future* (U.S. Government Printing Office, 1972) p. 62.
2. Busse, Ewald W., "Changing Concepts: Age Through the Ages" in *Theory and Therapeutics of Aging* (MEDCOM medical update series, 1973) p. 2.
3. U.S. Office of Management and Budget, *Social Indicators, 1973* (U.S. Government Printing Office, 1973) p. 141.
4. U.S. Bureau of the Census, *Employment Status and Work Experience,* Subject Report PC(2)-6A (U.S. Government Printing Office, 1973) p. 2.
5. U.S. Public Health Service, "Biological, Psychological and Sociological Aspects of Aging" in *Working with Older People: A Guide to Practice, Vol. II* (U.S. Government Printing Office, 1972) p. 8.
6. U.S. Social Security Administration, "Relative Importance of Income Sources of the Aged," *Research and Statistics Note 11* (Washington, D.C., Department of Health, Education, and Welfare Pub. [SSA] 73-11701) p. 5.
7. U.S. Social Security Administration, "Income of the Aged Population," *Research and Statistics Note 14* (Washington, D.C., Department of Health, Education, and Welfare Pub. [SSA] 74-11701) p. 2.
8. U.S. Bureau of the Census, *Housing of Senior Citizens,* Subject Report HC(7)-2 (U.S. Government Printing Office, 1973) p. 14.
9. U.S. Bureau of the Census, *Some Demographic Aspects of Aging in the United States,* Current Population Reports, Series P-23, No. 43 (U.S. Government Printing Office, 1973) p. 13.
10. Caplow, Theodore, et al., *The Elderly in Old Age Institutions* (Charlottesville, University of Virginia, 1974) p. 7.
11. Metropolitan Life Insurance Company, "Health of the Elderly," *Statistical Bulletin,* July 1974, pp. 9-11.
12. U.S. Public Health Service, National Center for Health Statistics, unpublished data.

# II. Processes of Aging

What is aging and how does it affect individuals? There is no concise answer to this basic question, but several themes can be identified from basic research in the physiology, psychology, and sociology of aging.

First, estimating what changes occur with aging is methodologically complicated. Cross-sectional studies, which compare old to young, have been found to overestimate the extent of changes with age. Studies of intelligence, for example, have consistently reported that the young score better than the old, but in research which has followed the same persons over time, there appear to be no decrements in functioning with aging, except where speed of response is a factor. This discrepancy can be explained by generational differences: in today's population younger age groups score higher on tests of "intelligence" and other abilities, possibly because of improved education or early-life nutrition. Older persons show decrements in comparison, not because of aging, but due to these generational factors (Baltes and Schaie). Research that follows the same persons longitudinally, however, may underestimate actual changes with age, because of the likelihood of higher drop-out rates and mortality among those individuals who are experiencing declines in functioning (Tobin). In fact, whatever one's age, the period of time preceding one's death may be marked by declines in psychological functioning. There are, then, at least three factors which account for differences between young and old: the aging process, generational differences, and changes occurring because of the nearness of death.

To the extent that age changes can be estimated independently of these two factors, there appear to be considerable individual differences in the process of aging. In comparing young and old, one sees greater variation, or scatter, in the scores of the older group, whether in physiological functioning or in behavior (Tobin; Schonfield). In life styles, values and personality, the aged are a heterogeneous group, as one would expect considering the variety of experiences that can shape development in the adult years. People have different educations, work experiences, family and social relationships; they choose different leisure activities and living patterns. Rather than showing a commonality of characteristics as we grow older, our varied experiences make us increasingly different from one another. There is, in any case, nothing magical about age 65, and a great deal of truth to the cliché that we are as old as we feel.

Another theme is that there is both change and continuity in aging. As noted above, intellectual performance appears to be relatively stable over time. Similarly, major dimensions of personality or of a person's adaptive capacity do not usually undergo change, while, at the same time, the aging may become somewhat more introspective or concerned with their inner life (Neugarten; Casady). One source of change is the special stresses that confront the aging in our society—the generally negative social expectations toward them and the decreasing opportunities they have for taking on meaningful roles in society (Rosow).

Finally, there is the possibility of control of or amelioration in the processes of aging, by controlling the rate at which cells age (Strehler), enhancing physiological functions through exercise (deVries), or through behavioral interventions (Baltes and Schaie).

From basic research in gerontology, then, it appears that the aging process affects people at varying rates, affects various physiological and psychological functions in different ways, and that there are both continuities and changes in the behavior of persons over time. Rather than universally showing decrements, persons show varying rates of changes in some functions and little or no changes in other capacities.

# Normal Aging—
# The Inevitability Syndrome

Jordan D. Tobin*

Aging is a continuum that exists across the entire age spectrum and not something that happens only after one reaches some specific chronological age. It is happening to all of us, all of the time.

We tend to view this ambivalently. We desire the wisdom and experience of age, while retaining the health and vigor of youth. An example of this was a cartoon of "Dennis, the Menace." Five-year-old Dennis is seen speaking to his 3-year-old friend, Joey, and saying, "I wish I was your age knowing what I do now."

Our culture tends to glorify youth, and we try to hold onto it. Aging is something that happens to someone else a variable number of years older than we are. As we pass specific anniversaries, aging is brought home to us.

Personally, when medical students (who, by the way, are getting younger each year) first started calling me "sir," it was a shock. When I first started delivering talks on aging five years ago, comments were usually made about "a young scientist interested in gerontology." People aren't making these comments any more. We are all aging, all of the time.

In describing the physiological changes seen with aging, we must make the distinction between aging of an organism and diseases that affect the organism. This is especially important with the diseases, such as arteriosclerosis, that are more prevalent in the elderly. Thus, we are talking about aging in the absence of disease.

## THE STUDY OF AGING

What is normal aging? It is easy to define normal as what the majority of people do, but this has its pitfalls. To distinguish pathology and disease from normal aging, we have the problem of defining disease. Standards for the definition of a diseased state often are derived from studying young, normal controls. These standards then are applied to the general population. To be considered normal, this places the healthy older person in the situation of performing as well as a young person does.

We recognize that older people, on the average, do not run as fast as younger people. If the time for running a mile, derived from young people, were applied as the standard for older people, one would call a large number of older people abnormal.

### Reserve Capacity

An important concept in the physiology of aging is that of stress, or reserve capacity. There are a number of functions, as we will see later, that are well maintained with increasing age in the basal or unstressed

*Jordan D. Tobin, MD, is associated with the Gerontology Research Center, National Institute of Child Health and Human Development at the Baltimore City Hospitals.

state. Only when the stress of the environment is superimposed on the basal state, do the age changes manifest themselves.

Since this is an aging talk, I would like to illustrate these points by discussing two old men — old in that they are Neanderthal men who would be approximately 80,000 years old.

The fact that Mr. Ugh is younger than, and presumably can run faster than Mr. Mug probably did not influence their usual, basal, day-to-day life. If, however, we superimpose a stress from the environment, a cave lion or a saber-toothed tiger, this age difference becomes important. In an actuarial sense, Mr. Mug's slower speed, which is a normal physiological change, is a risk factor and will limit his chances of survival.

This journey into the past illustrates both the concept of reduced reserve capacity and the potentially harmful effects of a normal physiological change. It also serves to introduce a problem that constantly plagues the gerontologist in the study of aging, that of selective mortality and its effects on cross-sectional studies.

### Selective Mortality

An example of a cross-sectional study is measuring the time it takes Neanderthal men of different ages to run 40 yards. The men could be divided into five-year age groups, and the average time for each age could be plotted against age to describe the age differences in speed.

A longitudinal study of this variable would require retesting the same individuals at a later date to determine how each individual in each age group has changed. If we now include the possible deleterious effect represented by a cave lion or a saber-toothed tiger, we can see the possible conclusions that can be drawn from these two different study designs as demonstrated graphically in Figure 1.

We have plotted variable x, which is the time it takes to run 40 yards, against age. We assume in this example that this time increases

## SELECTIVE MORTALITY

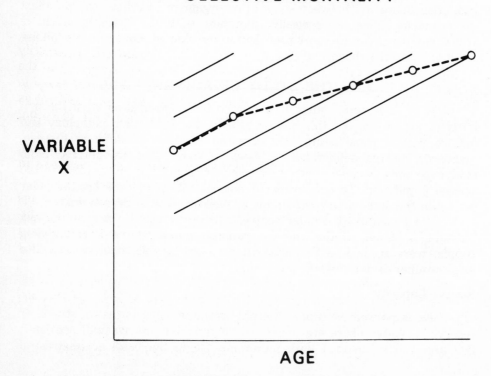

**Fig. 1.** Typical results of cross-sectional study design

linearly with age, as represented by the parallel lines, for five individuals.

Each subject, as he gets older, slows down and takes longer to run the 40 yards. Additionally, we assume that at some particular level this slowing down is lethal for the individual, if he meets up with a faster cave lion.

If we start with the youngest subjects, we see biological variance in that some individuals have higher times than other individuals. The mean is represented by the open circles. If we return five years later, we see that each individual has slowed down but that none has yet reached the lethal level. The mean of the five subjects, when compared with the mean five years previously, accurately represents the change, the slowing down.

If we return again five years later, however, we see that we have only four subjects, since the slowest individual has already reached the lethal level and has been eaten by the lion. The mean of the four remaining individuals is lower than we would have predicted from the previous experience. As we continue retesting the individuals, the progressive loss of subjects leaves us at the end of the study with only the fastest of the original group.

A cross-sectional study, done at one moment in time, would yield the results shown in the open circles connected by the dotted lines and would lead to the conclusion that as one ages, one slows down, but that the rate of change is not as great in later years as it was in the early years.

This conclusion is erroneous and not in accord with the assumption in this experiment that the changes are linearly related to age. This inaccuracy is a result of selective mortality since the only older individuals available to be tested are the survivors, the ones who were the fastest or best performers when they were younger.

With the appropriate combination of patterns of age changes and assumption of lethal levels, it is possible to generate hypothetical curves where cross-sectional results are higher, lower, or of a different pattern than the true longitudinal results of aging. Suffice to say, this is a potential problem in all cross-sectional studies.

### Cohort Differences

A second potential problem in cross-sectional studies is the possibility of cohort differences. Twenty-year-olds in 1974 are not necessarily the same as 20-year-olds were in 1934. They have not been exposed to the same environmental and social stimuli, and this may influence a variable being studied. Thus, 30-year-olds today were not treated to live goldfish as part of their diet, but they may be exposed to more ultraviolet radiation, secondary to the fad of "streaking."

There have been many environmental changes in diet, pollution, education, and so on, that may mask true aging changes of an organism in a cross-sectional study and reflect instead the cohort differences.

Longitudinal studies have the advantage of describing the true age changes of individuals and groups of individuals, and not just the differences between groups of subjects of different ages as in a cross-sectional study. They also have the tremendous disadvantage of taking a long time to conduct, with the investigator aging as fast as the subjects.

To study a man as he ages from 20 to 80 years will require 60 years. A cross-sectional study of a group of 20-year-olds and a group of 80-year-olds could be completed in a fraction of that time.

## RESULTS OF A LONGITUDINAL STUDY OF AGING

The data we are presenting is, for the most part, a cross-sectional look at the ongoing Baltimore longitudinal study conducted by the Gerontology Research Center of NICHD. It is important to take a few moments to describe the study before looking at the results.

Our longitudinal study of aging was started in 1958 by Dr. Nathan W. Shock, the director of the Gerontology Research Center. A retired public health physician, Dr. Peters, felt that gerontologists should be studying healthy, community-dwelling volunteers rather than institutionalized people from the hospitals, nursing homes, and homes for the aged. Therefore, Dr. Peters presented himself to Dr. Shock as a volunteer, recruited his friends, and started the panel that has included over 1,000 men from ages 20 to 103 who have been seen at least once, and over 500 men who have been seen at least four times. At present, there are 650 active participants on the panel.

The study has continued to be largely self-recruited, with participants recruiting their friends and relatives. It is entirely male, though plans for adding women to the panel are in the offing if support is available. The panel is a rather homogeneous group in terms of social characteristics. It is a highly educated group, and most of the participants have college degrees, with a high percentage of them having advanced degrees. Their occupations are largely professional or managerial, and their incomes are relatively high. They are, therefore, not representative of the entire population, but they do represent aging under optimum conditions.

Each participant has volunteered to return to the center every 18 months for the rest of his life. They are admitted to Baltimore City Hospital for 2½ days, where a thorough medical history and physical examination are performed. During their stay, they undergo extensive laboratory, psychological, and physiological testing, including tests of pulmonary, cardiac, renal, neuromuscular, and special sense functions, as well as estimates of body composition, nutrition, and carbohydrate metabolism.

Some of the cross-sectional results of these studies are seen in Figure 2 from the work of Dr. Shock. Here, the performance on each test is expressed for different ages as a percent of the performance of the 30-year-olds, which is taken as 100%.

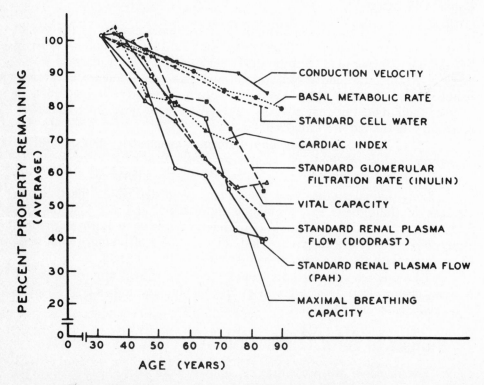

**Fig. 2.** Effect of age on performance on nine physiological tests

There is a general decline in these physiological variances with increasing age. However, different functions and different organ systems seem to decline at different rates. Thus, the conduction velocity, a measure of the speed of transmission of peripheral nervous signals, declines by about 10% over the age span tested. The maximum breathing capacity, a measure of lung function, shows more marked differences between the old and young subjects. The basal metabolic rate, the amount of oxygen used by cells in the basal state, shows a 20% difference, as does the total intracellular water, a measure of the number of cells in the body.

Estimates of heart function (the cardiac index), kidney function (the glomerular filtration rate and measures of renal plasma flow to the kidney), and pulmonary function (the vital capacity as well as the maximum breathing capacity) also show large age differences.

### Intercorrelational Analyses

The description of these age differences on these variables of function between young and old men is important in and of itself. Of potentially greater value is the ability to interrelate the effect of age on these diverse variables to understand better the aging process.

We have a great deal of information on each individual in the study, and we are in a position to ask the question, "Does the entire organism age at the same rate, or do certain systems represent a weak link in the chain of survival?"

Once we have ascertained what the average 60-year-old man's kidney does (its glomerular filtration rate), we can characterize an individual's renal function as average or far below average. If it is far below average, can we expect his pulmonary function, cardiac function, and carbohydrate metabolism also to be below average for his age? If so, this individual, as an entirety, is physiologically older than his peers. Conversely, these other functions may be well preserved, and only his kidney function may be not up to par.

Especially in these intercorrelational analyses, it is important to exclude disease states from true aging. If a subject were to have one kidney removed he would be excluded from the analysis of renal function. He might be suitable for the analysis of pulmonary function, however, and would be included in the studies of the lung. He obviously could not be included in the intercorrelations, since one of the functions would be reduced by a process not attributable to aging.

### Rate of Aging

In addition to describing age differences and intercorrelating the different organs and functions, we are concerned with defining, on a longitudinal basis, the rate of aging of individuals. Do selective mortality or cohort differences play a part in determining these curves? Is the rate of aging linear, or is there some critical level or chronological age at which the rate of aging actually accelerates? What are the actual mechanisms behind the observed age changes? And, of great importance, which changes are detrimental to the survival of the organism, and what, if anything, can be done to optimize survival?

I will go into greater detail on a variable not shown in Figure 2, carbohydrate metabolism. How the body handles ingested glucose, and how it maintains an appropriate blood glucose level after eating or during fasting is an important physiological variable that is profoundly influenced by age. Abnormal carbohydrate metabolism is also the hallmark of the disease diabetes mellitus.

Dr. Reuben Andres, who is head of the metabolism section as well as clinical director of the Gerontology Research Center and the longitudinal study, started studying glucose tolerance in our volunteers in 1963. The following are some of our results.

The subjects included in these studies had no family history of diabetes, were not overweight, were on no medications, had no diseases that influence carbohydrate metabolism, and were eating an adequate diet. There are no age differences in the basal fasting state in the plasma glucose concentration. There is biological variance, with some subjects in each age-range group having higher or lower concentrations, but there is no age trend.

If we now present this system with a stress, not quite as dramatic as a tiger or a cave lion, but that of drinking a load of glucose to stimulate the eating of a meal, we do see marked age effects.

We note that there is no age difference at zero time (fasting). As the glucose is absorbed, all subjects show a similar rise in the plasma glucose concentration. By one hour the 20-year-olds have already started to return toward basal. At two hours the plasma glucose lines up according to age, with the 20-year-olds having the best performance. That is, their glucose concentration has returned closest to the basal. Then come the 30-year-olds, then the 40s, 50s, 60s, 70s, and finally the 80-year-olds, whose performance is the poorest.

This demonstrates that the decline in glucose tolerance is occurring throughout the age range. It is not something that happens only in old age. The 40-year-olds do not perform as well as the 30-year-olds, who do not perform as well as the 20-year-olds.

Eventually, the glucose concentration for all of the subjects will return to the basal level since the fasting values when we started in the morning had no differences. It will, however, take longer to return to basal in the older subjects. Once again we see the factor of time dependence. It takes older subjects longer to meet the objective, be it to run 40 yards, solve psychological tests, or return their blood glucose to basal.

We can look at the individual blood glucose values at two hours for the cortisone-primed glucose tolerance test in Figure 3. Here each dot represents an individual's plasma glucose concentration at two hours on this test and his age. The center line represents the regression of glucose

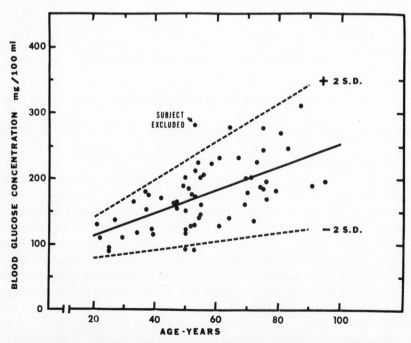

Fig. 3.    Blood glucose concentration 120 minutes after glucose administration among subjects with negative family histories for diabetes (Reproduced with permission from the *Annals of Internal Medicine,* 63:988–1000, Dec 1965.)

versus age, plus and minus two standard deviations. There is a large variance, which increases with age, between better and poorer performers in each group, with the poorer performers being near the top of the graph.

Though on the average, performance decreases with age and the blood sugar is higher, we do have some 60-year-old subjects who perform as well as the average 20-year-old. We do not know whether these individuals were also superior performers when they were 20, and have had a slowing down of their glucose metabolism as they aged, or whether they have maintained the same tolerance all along. Only longitudinal retesting of our present 20- and 30-year-olds and observation of their changes as they age will give us an answer to this question.

If we were to take the worst performers in the young ages, the dots toward the top of the graph of the ones 20 and 30 years old, and defined that as abnormal, we could, by extending that value across the graph, define abnormal for an entire population. If we did that, we would find that almost half of our older population fell above that arbitrary level and would be considered abnormal.

Since an abnormal glucose tolerance test is the hallmark of diabetes, half of the older normal subjects in our group would be called diabetic. As physicians, though, we know that the prevalence of diabetes does increase with age, and we find this high percentage of diabetes not in keeping with the clinical experience.

Some of the individuals in this study are going to develop diabetes at some future time. Are they going to be the worst performers at any given age, the dots at or over the upper line? Or are the people who develop diabetes going to come from the dots above the specific level, regardless of age? Or, as a third possibility, will they come from any point on the graph, meaning that the development of the disease diabetes bears no relation to performance on a glucose tolerance test until one has the disease?

These same questions can be asked, not with the development of a specific disease as an endpoint, but with regard to survival. Is being a poor performer for your age important in determining your life expectancy, or is being above a specific constant level the important criterion in determining life expectancy?

The importance of a high blood glucose value on a glucose tolerance test, with regard to the health of an individual, is a matter of contention, not only among gerontologists, but also among diabetologists. Answers to these questions await the conclusions of prospective studies such as ours.

## DEFINING NORMALITY

Until such answers are forthcoming, we are left with the problem of interpreting the results of our glucose tolerance test, a test profoundly influenced by age, that is used to diagnose a disease. For help in this matter we have turned to the pediatricians, who have similar problems of defining normality at the other end of the age spectrum.

Most of us are familiar with a normal weight chart for growing children that gives age, weight, and a series of percentile lines. Thus, on our chart, a 10-year-old weighing 70 pounds would be at the 15th percentile, an average weight for his age.

If a 7-year-old were to weigh 70 pounds, he would be above the 97th percentile. He would weigh more than 97% of his age-matched peers. He might be considered obese.

We have used this concept of percentile rank to construct a nomogram from our data to characterize each of the subjects in our glucose tolerance test. The nomogram for the oral glucose tolerance test is shown in Figure 4.

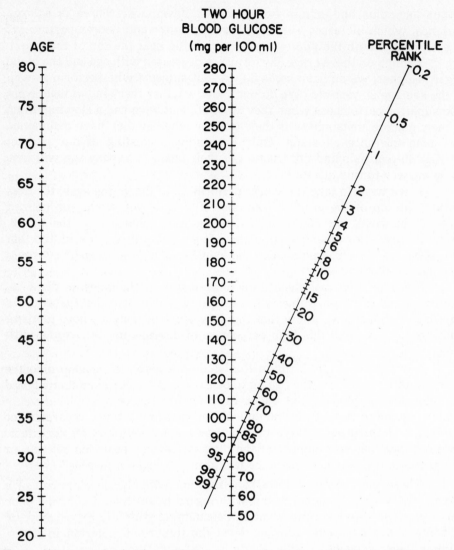

AGE

TWO HOUR
BLOOD GLUCOSE
(mg per 100 ml)

PERCENTILE
RANK

Fig. 4.   Nomogram for judging performance on oral glucose tolerance test (Reproduced with permission from the *Mayo Clinic Proceedings,* 42:674–684, Oct 1967.)

If one knows an individual's age and his two-hour blood glucose value, one can determine his percentile rank. A 20-year-old with a blood glucose value of 140 mg/100 ml at two hours is in the second percentile. Ninety-eight percent of the 20-year-olds would have performed better than he has. If a 60-year-old had the same value of 140, he would be in the 50th percentile. This would be just an average performance for him.

You will notice that nowhere is there a definition of normality or of disease. The nomogram just allows you to compare an individual's performance with his age-matched peers. The actual determination of what rank should be considered abnormal is an arbitrary judgment.

In view of the epidemiological data on the increasing prevalence of clinical diabetes with increasing age, we emphasize that we call the worst 2% of our 20-year-olds diabetic, and increase this one percentile rank for each decade so that 5% of the 50-year-olds and 7% of the 70-year-olds would be called diabetic. This is more in keeping with the clinical realities than the use of nonage-adjusted standards.

At the last meetings of the Gerontology Society, Dr. Jack Rowe presented a comparison of the cross-sectional and longitudinal results on tests of kidney function in our subjects. Standard creatinine clearances, a measure of how well the kidney can clear the blood of waste products, were determined in 548 individuals who had no diseases influencing kidney function. There was a highly significant cross-sectional decline in kidney function with age. Of the 548 subjects, 293 had three or more visits, and their data were used for longitudinal analysis.

There was close correspondence between the cross-sectional age differences and the values that could be predicted by extending the longitudinal age changes. This indicated that, for this variable, selective mortality and cohort differences were not responsible for the cross-sectional age effect.

In the basal state, this decrease in kidney function appears to have no detrimental effects on the older individuals. Given a stress, however, be it excreting drugs, toxins, or excessive nitrogenous wastes, the older kidney, which has lost some of its reserve capacity while it aged, is at a disadvantage when compared to a young kidney. It may do its job, but it will take a little longer.

This chapter refers to normal aging as the inevitability syndrome. Indeed, as we age chronologically, we do slow down physiologically. And if, as in the case of our friend Mr. Mug, there are saber-toothed tigers or cave lions awaiting us, this slowing down can be the limiting factor in our survival.

As gerontologists, our job is to provide a firm scientific basis for the investigation of the aging process. We must define the age changes that occur, differentiate them from disease processes, and determine which of these changes represent significant risk factors. We must determine the rates of change, the patterns of change, and define those factors that lead to optimal aging.

When we have done this, we will be in a position to investigate the mechanism behind the aging process. Then we can better study the effects of intervention, either in earlier years to retard the rate of aging later, or in later years, if possible.

I will close with the words of Satchel Paige. He was asked to what he attributed his ability to pitch baseball professionally at his advanced age. His response was "Don't look back — something might be gaining on you."

48

# 7

# A New Age
# for Aging

*After 30, everyone begins a steady, predictable
decline toward death. Now we are on the brink of an alternative*

## by Bernard L. Strehler

Growing old is a process that few people care to ponder; indeed, most people skirt the issue by spending a surprising amount of time and effort trying to remain youthful. We greet long-lost friends with comments about how well they look (meaning: you haven't aged much). We automatically categorize people according to whether they are younger or older than we are (meaning: I envy your youthful vigor and appearance or you have deteriorated more than I have). Billions of dollars are spent every year on cosmetics (meaning: we want to *look* young). Men dutifully jog around their suburban neighborhoods before leaving for the office (meaning: maybe this will slow down the deterioration of my circulatory system). We adulate youth and respect age (meaning: I would like to be young again; but there must be something good to look forward to—wisdom, perhaps). We advise friends to stop smoking (meaning: you may be shortening your life). The point is that every human being, whether he admits it or not, is at least vaguely apprehensive about the slow deterioration of his structure and functions that eventually ends in death.

Concern about aging and death is an important component of our sub-conscious life and may contribute more than is obvious to the increased mental disease among the middle-aged and elderly. Anxiety about the changed role in life that follows the female menopause or vague fears about potency in aging males are stresses that nearly everyone endures in silence despite the reassuring witticism of gerontologist Alex Comfort: "People give up sex for the same reasons they give up bicycling—it looks silly, arthritis makes it painful, or one has no bicycle!"

With all of the deep and hidden concerns about the processes that cause this sense of impermanence, it seems surprising that society has not invested more in trying to understand, control, arrest, or even reverse the underlying causes of aging. On the face of it, nothing would seem more appealing as a goal for the average person than an extension of the healthful years of life. Certainly most men are more curious about the reasons behind their own ephemeral existence on this globe than about the constitution of the rocks on the moon or whether life is present on Mars. But to date, less has been spent on the entire spectrum of research efforts in biological aging than on a single moon shot.

The reason, of course, is that men have become so accustomed to believing that their individual lives are finite, and that death is the inevitable price we pay for living, that they have refused to consider a biological alternative to individual extinction. After all, if death is inevitable—and unpleasant as well—why waste time, thought, and resources on a hopeless and depressing pursuit? Maybe if we don't think about it, it will go away.

Ironically, the same generation that learned to split and harness the atom, cracked the genetic code, and sent men to the moon may be the very one that will *not* benefit from the eventual amelioration of the aging process—a possibility that could become a practical reality before the end of this century. The control of the atom was the product of the urgencies of war; the understanding of how we are specified in long strings of genetic "beads," which each of our cells contains, was the culmination of a century of effort to understand the modes and mechanics of inheritance and gene expression; the conquest of space was prompted by the preceding successes of our competitors' Sputniks. But until now, the conquest of time itself has not been a social objective, and the President's recent pocket veto of a bill to establish a National Institute for Research on Aging may postpone effective pursuit of this goal for another decade.

Implicit in the drive for federal support of research in this area is the possibility that men will be able to control—and perhaps reverse—part or all of the aging process. But the only way we can accurately predict what the chances are is to understand the nature of the events that lead to human aging. The transformation of life from a young state to an old one encompasses more than the mere passage of time, but the biological processes involved are not generally understood by the public. Perhaps if the basic principles and the rapidly growing body of new data were more openly discussed, there would be greater public support for the needed investment in fundamental research. Only such research, now or in the very near future, may make greatly extended lifetimes available for present generations of humans.

There are two generalizations to keep in mind about the events that occur as we age. The first is that many, although not all, bodily functions decrease gradually as aging takes place. This will not be news to anyone: all schoolboys know they can outrun their grandfathers and that the aged are less active, usually less alert, and more subject to disease than young adults. But this knowledge had not been put on a quantitative basis. During the last thirty years, however, Nathan Shock, the father of American gerontology, and his associates have described the exact rate at which different kinds of bodily functions fail. The essence of these findings is that most functions decrease gradually, at a rate of about 1 percent of the original capacity per year after age thirty. This means that the reserve ability to do all kinds of work will run out at about age 120. It is not surprising, therefore, that about 118 years is the greatest age attained by any human for whom good records of birth and death are available. There are occasional claims that individuals in certain parts of the Caucasus Mountains of the Soviet Union attain ages twenty or more years greater than this, but in the absence of records most such claims can probably be dismissed as folk fables. Once one attains great age, there is a great temptation to exaggerate it.

The second generalization is that the chance of dying does not increase in proportion to the amount of function lost. This was discovered and formulated into a simple mathematical law in about 1832 by an English insurance actuary, Benjamin Gompertz. The Gompertz law states that the chance of dying doubles about every eight years, irrespective of the environment in which one lives. This means that the chance of dying is about 1,000 times greater for a man of 100 than for a man of 25. If we did not age—that is, if we kept the physiology of a 15-year-old indefinitely—the average human life-span would be in excess of 20,000 years. This would mean that the oldest members among us could tell stories about the last Ice Age and give personal accounts of the entire span of recorded human history.

The basic question, of course, is not do we age, but what is the underlying mechanism. This can be summarized as follows: we age primarily because the cells in our bodies that cannot replace themselves either die or lose a small part of their function every year. This law applies to most of the tissues of the body, although some cells and tissues seem immune to the effects of the passage of time. These nonaging tissues include those covering the surfaces of the body (the skin and the lining of the digestive system) and the circulating cells in our blood. The skin forms a new layer of cells every four days or so, the lining of the gut is replenished every day or two, and the red blood cells are replaced on a regular schedule every four months.

Other body cells, such as those of the liver, replace themselves more slowly, although the liver (of experimental animals) can regrow to its original size within a week or so if part of it is removed surgically. Parts of the kidneys and the connective tissues are able to replace themselves more or less on demand.

Key organs and tissues in which cell replacement is either absent or inadequate are the muscles, heart, brain, and certain endocrine and immunity-conferring tissues. The nonreplenishing, or postmitotic, cells involved exhibit two major dif-

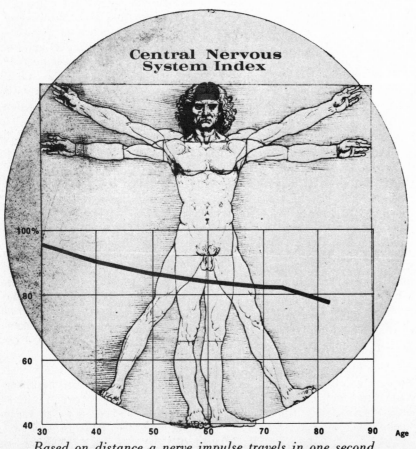

*Based on distance a nerve impulse travels in one second.*

ferences from those in other parts of the body: many of the cells that remain in the tissues of an old animal are either larger or smaller than usual and the resultant irregular appearance of many old tissues is one of disorder; the second, obvious change is the accumulation of yellow-brown colorations known as age pigments. These materials accumulate slowly with age, and in the very old they may occupy nearly the entire cell body. They are believed to be produced by the reaction of oxygen with unsaturated fats in the membranes within cells. This reaction is similar to the one that causes varnish to harden and turn yellow as it dries and ages.

The rate at which it occurs can be reduced, in the test tube at least, by adding substances called antioxidants to the mixture. In this process the antioxidants trap intermediate molecules, called free radicals, and prevent such reactions from becoming self-perpetuating. Vitamin E is one antioxidant that occurs in nature, and BHT, a synthetic compound used to prevent various food products from turning rancid, has similar effects. One group of studies by Denham Harmon of the University of Nebraska indicates that it is possible to extend the lives of experimental animals by adding antioxidants to their diets. Whether the increased longevity is due to the suppression of antioxidative reactions within cells and tissues is not yet certain.

Recent studies also indicate that cells cultured artificially eventually lose their ability to divide or renew themselves. In his careful and imaginative work in this area, Leonard Hayflick of Stanford University has shown that human cells such as embryonic fibroblasts can only undergo about fifty divisions under artificial conditions. Whether such limitations occur in the body itself is not yet clearly settled. It seems likely that skin and gut cells, for example, are able to divide hundreds or thousands of times during the lifetime of a human. Some recent research suggests that all cells manufacture and accumulate materials that tend to prevent their division when the concentration of these substances is large enough. One class of such substances, called chalones, only inhibits the growth of the tissue from which it is extracted.

Lack of materials that inhibit cell division may contribute to the development of cancer—a disease that primarily affects the elderly. One reason that cancer develops could be that the natural inhibitors, perhaps "chalonelike" substances, are either not produced in adequate amounts or no longer have a growth-stopping effect on cells that have become malignant. This is an oversimplification of the origin of cancer, but several lines of evidence indicate that it is at least a part of the picture.

The key to understanding aging is to be found in the mechanisms that control and prevent the division of cells. Much information may fall out of the understanding of cancer, but it seems unlikely that all of the needed facts will result from the pursuit of studies directed toward other goals. What is needed is to focus an adequate research effort specifically on those processes that cause cells to lose vitality with age.

A law of nature states that all systems tend to become more disorganized as time passes unless energy is expended to generate order. Stars burn themselves out; untended gardens go to weed; social institutions become more unmanageable as they age. This also applies to the cells and molecules that make up the individual human being; unless molecules are stored at absolute zero and shielded from all kinds of radiation, they will gradually revert to less ordered arrangements of their atoms.

In one sense, living systems are an exception to this rule, for plants and animals do create order out of chaos. These living organisms are special kinds of machines, which harness the matter and energy about them in order to make more of their kind.

The basic reason that living things are mortal is that this must have favored their evolutionary success. One explanation for this paradox—the death of individuals favoring the perpetuation of the species—was suggested by Peter Medawar, a Nobel laureate in medicine and physiology, who pointed out that some kinds of successful adaptations carry with them side effects that indirectly lead to aging and death. For humans, three such

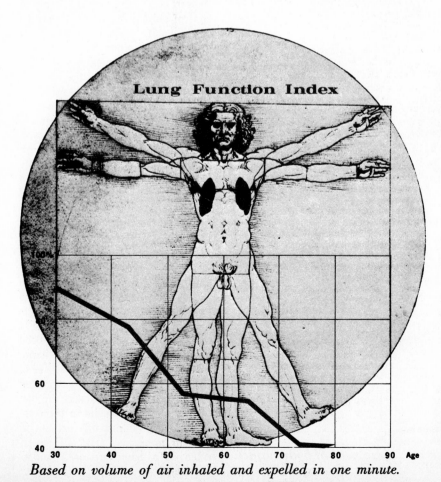

*Based on volume of air inhaled and expelled in one minute.*

adaptations are particularly important: man is best able to function if he has a particular size; man's brain serves as an information storage device, as well as in other ways; our ancestors evolved in competitive environments, which placed a premium on the efficient use of raw materials. What unites these adaptations is that they all involve the "switching off" of certain inherited abilities at specific times in the lifecycle, and it is this process that ultimately causes the system to fail.

The limitation of the human body to a certain optimum size is achieved by the turning off of the genes that would lead to continued growth. The stabilization of memory elements in the brain is achieved, in part, by suppressing the ability of nerve cells in the brain to divide (nerve cell division is a great rarity after birth). Economy in the use of raw materials requires that only those parts that deteriorate rapidly—the skin, gut lining cells, blood cells—are regularly replaced. Tendons, muscles, heart, and brain cells stop replacing themselves as maturity is approached.

The consequence of this switching off of genes is to remove the affected cells from the "living system" category, as defined earlier, with aging and death eventually following. Yet all cells, whether in a functioning or switched-off state, contain the necessary genetic instructions to replenish themselves. When we discover how to unlock the information hidden in the DNA of each nonreplenishing cell, man may indeed possess the knowledge necessary to convert himself into an immortal.

Before the present revolution in biological thinking—the result of understanding how DNA stores the instructions to put the body's parts together—we had exceedingly cumbersome ideas about the regulation of gene expression. It had been thought that each specific event in each kind of cell was controlled by a huge set of genetic instructions. It seemed inconceivable that man could devise nondestructive means for interfering with the enormous complexity of the regulating systems involved.

But it has now been demonstrated that the genetic code is really very simple. It was proved that it is a sequence of just three consecutive "beads," the nucleotide bases in the DNA, which code for a given kind of building block in the working parts of cells. (The building blocks are the body's total of twenty different kinds of amino acids, and the working parts are proteins, which are simply long chains of amino acids arranged in very specific ways according to the instructions provided by the DNA.)

It also has been shown that only two different types of control locations are involved in the regulation of which kinds of genes are expressed. These sites, on the surfaces of the DNA and of the ribosomes, control the copying of the information in specific segments of DNA—a process called transcription—and the decoding of this copied information—a process called translation. In other words, cells can select which of the many products they will make by either controlling the kinds of DNA copied or the kinds of messages decoded.

The importance of these discoveries in terms of the potential control of human aging is enormous. Instead of an imponderable array of control points, the number may be quite small, perhaps only a few dozen. This implies the possibility of producing chemical agents that will selectively change the controls of switched-off cells, thus releasing the latent genetic information needed to produce replacement parts—just as it is possible to produce antibiotics that will destroy infective bacteria without materially harming the body's functions. And far from being an unattainable goal in this generation of humans, selective production of new cells and tissues through pharmacological intervention is on the verge of being tested; at least the basic technology is at hand.

Whether this optimistic view is justified will depend on the results of experiments designed to test a theory of gene regulation proposed about ten years ago. Harvey Itano, now a professor at the University of California at San Diego, suggested that certain genetic diseases are due to the inability of cells to translate some of the code words present in genetic messages. (He was interested in a blood disease, thallas-

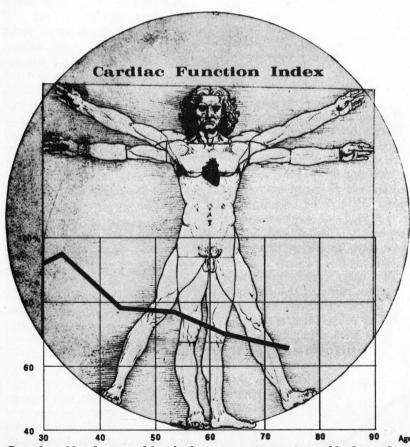

*Based on blood pumped by the heart per square meter of body surface.*

semia, found in the Mediterranean region.) Itano proposed that the mutation responsible for this disease involved the substitution of a poorly translatable genetic code word for a readily translatable one in the defective gene. This idea was independently rediscovered by Gunther Stent, Bruce Ames, and the author, who applied it to aspects of development and aging.

The basic idea behind our thinking and experiments is that as cells mature they may shut off the ability to read, or decode, certain code words. The effect would be that all genetic messages written down in sequences that include nondecodable words could not be used to produce working parts of cells, including replacement parts.

If this idea were correct, one might expect different kinds of cells from the same individual to operate on different genetic languages. A genetic language is definable as a particular combination of code words that includes at least one word for each of the twenty amino acids. Because there are about sixty usable words in the genetic dictionary, it is obvious that a huge number of different kinds of languages are possible. In fact, because there are about three times as many code words as there are amino acids for them to specify, a sequence 100 amino acids in length (about average for a simple protein) can be written down in $3^{100}$ different ways within a given segment of DNA.

Even allowing for some inability to distinguish between certain words, it now appears that at least 10,000 different exclusive sets of code words could be used to specify 10,000 different kinds of cells. This is many times the number of different kinds of cells in the body.

One of the predictions implied in such a theory is that certain steps needed for the translation of a given word will be carried out by certain kinds of cells but not by others. There are now at least fifty studies on various animals and plants that show some deficiencies in the translation machinery from one cell type to another. (Some cancer cells, it now appears, may have reacquired lost translating ability, perhaps as a result of "cancer virus" infection.)

Two findings by Michael Bick and the author are extremely per-

tinent in this regard. The first was that extracts from old soybean cotyledon tissue are unable to fully carry out the step involved just prior to the decoding of genetic information. (This step is the attachment of the proper amino acid to the right decoder molecule.) Young tissues, however, were perfectly capable of doing this.

The second finding was that old tissues contain a substance that specifically seems to block this step. These findings imply that the tissue is programmed to manufacture a "self-poison" (possibly similar to the chalones) late in its lifetime, and that such a "poison" effectively blocks the production of materials needed for an indefinite existence. The lifetime of this very tissue can be extended manyfold by applying a specific plant hormone, kinetin, to the tissue before it ages.

Equally important is an unpublished finding by Gerald Hirsch. He found that cellular material present in extracts of liver cells was unable to produce free soluble proteins if it was given a message from another tissue. These experiments imply that different cells do have different languages.

Roger Johnson and the author have recently made another promising discovery that may be the needed principle that will tie together many of the seemingly different effects of the aging process. Working with dog tissues, we found that nondividing cells lose a particular kind of DNA. This DNA is involved in the manufacture of the machinery needed to produce any kind of protein, the working parts of all cells. This genetic material, known as rDNA, codes for the ribonucleic acid that is part of the ribosomes—the machines through which the genetic messages are threaded as they are translated into working proteins.

It may be highly significant that, in the studies completed so far, this loss of rDNA occurs only in nondividing cells—brain, heart, skeletal muscle. Liver and kidney cells, for example, do not show such losses. The net effect of the gradual loss of some of this genetic material would be to reduce the maximum rate at which protein could be synthesized under stress. Thus, such different afflictions of the elderly as heart

failure (which requires the manufacture of heart muscle proteins if it is to be prevented), inability to detect and reject cancer cells (which requires the rapid manufacture of antibody-like substances to kill off the aberrant cells), and a decrease in the efficiency of the hormonal systems (such as occurs in adult-onset diabetes) may all be ascribable to this fundamental loss of rDNA in nondividing cells. Studies are now under way to test a few of these implications.

It would be too sanguine to state at this time that vital functions could be regenerated simply by reinstating lost abilities to decode one or a few code words. What is needed, of course, is research to find out whether this simple, though versatile, mechanism really dominates the control of development and aging.

Predicting what will happen in, say, the next ten years in the field of understanding and controlling the biological aging process is about like giving a 10-day weather forecast. We know enough about the present situation and the main trends in this area of science to make an educated guess as to what will happen. Barring unforeseen breakthroughs in other areas of biomedicine that might provide important insights into the aging process, the key, limiting factor is whether the needed specific effort will be supported by society. This is an unsettled question right now.

One reason that research on aging has not received the emphasis it deserves has to do with the aging of bureaucracies themselves. New bureaus and institutes are often vital organizations; as they grow older they are concerned more with maintaining the status quo than with imaginative progress.

Within the government (the logical source of funds for basic research), two agencies have a prime interest and obligation toward the health of the elderly: the National Institutes of Health and the Veterans Administration. The National Institutes of Health has been charged with responsibility for support of research on medical problems; the Veterans Administration has responsibility for caring for the veterans of our wars. But both agencies are hampered by inadequate budgets.

Research on aging suffers from a particular disadvantage within the National Institutes of Health because of an absence of experts in decision making and advisory posts sufficiently aware of the details of the process. Instead research proposals are sent to groups of specialists in bacterial genetics, in epidemiology, cell biology, or general biochemistry. The members of each of these review panels or study sections are, almost without exception, leading members of the biomedical research community. But, if the review comments this author has seen are representative, they are quite underinformed about the status of aging research—a field that is alien to their natural interests and, in fact, competitive with the professional objectives (funding) of most panel members.

For a brief time, just before the last election, it looked as though the starvation period for research on aging was about to end, for Congress had passed (by almost unanimous votes in both houses) a bill that would have established a National Institute for Research on Aging. It was jointly sponsored by leading members of both parties and supported by all of the research and service organizations concerned with the needs of the elderly. This bill created the institute that was unanimously called for by the representatives to the 1971 White House Conference on Aging (Research and Demonstration Section), convened by the President in December, 1971.

The euphoria in the aging research community was short-lived, however, for the President killed the bill by pocket veto. The reasons given for the veto were: (1) it would cost $200,000,000 and (2) the work would duplicate work already being carried out within the government. Obviously, there has been some failure in communication, for it is hard to believe that a highly intelligent man would have made this decision if he had been apprised of all of the relevant facts. Perhaps the present governmental shake-up will open the lines of communication and give the President a more balanced view of the needs and opportunities in this field of research when the bill once again is passed and reaches his desk.

What happens in the next ten years thus depends directly on a total imponderable. If the institute is established and adequately and imaginatively funded and administered, it seems likely that by the year 1983 we will understand, in depth, the details of cellular and bodily aging. If no special effort is made to understand this most universal of all human afflictions, the date of understanding and possible control will be pushed back to the beginning of the twenty-first century, a date too late to benefit most of us alive today.

The eventual understanding and control of the aging process will cause a revolution in human affairs. Already a few studies are under way on the social consequences of greatly retarding or abolishing aging and death. A few misconceptions should, however, first be laid to rest. Some of the evidently misinformed opponents of greater, healthy life-spans seem to believe that the world would become populated with decrepit, patched-up, wizened, senile people, perhaps fed through tubes and moving with the aid of electronic prostheses. This ugly picture is totally false, for there is no way to appreciably increase life-span except by improving the body's physical state. Instead, humans that live for 150 years or more will be healthy for a much greater percentage of their total life-span. Men and women of highly advanced age will possess bodies like those of much younger people. In fact, their minds will be even more improved, for the greater years of optimum health will provide more opportunity to assimilate the world's wonders and lead to a greater measure of wisdom—the only intellectual commodity that often improves with age.

Because the healthy middle years of life will be doubled from the present 30 or 40 years, each individual will spend more time as a contributor to society. The average professional of today requires 25 to 30 years to acquire his training—mostly at the expense of the producing members of society. If the post-training years were doubled, every person could give much more back to the pool of resources from which he derived his start.

As the societies of the world evolve, there will be many changes in the kinds of creative activities

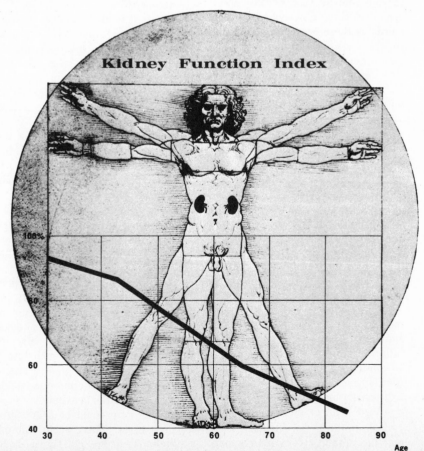

*Based on blood flow through the kidneys.*

open to men and women. People with many decades of optimum health will find it desirable, if not necessary, to move from one kind of occupation to another. One way in which continual retraining in new skills and professions could well take place would be through a regular system of educational leaves-with-pay, much like the sabbatical system that now operates in universities. Every five or seven years, a person could take a year or so to acquire new skills and to refurbish old ones. Plans should be made now for the restructuring of educational institutions so that a continuing re-education will become the rule rather than the exception.

As machines take over the more onerous and repetitive tasks men have performed, opportunities for new careers in the so-called service area will evolve. It is unfortunate that there is not a better word than *service* (from the same root as the word *servant*) to describe the kinds of creative things people can do to make each other's lives enjoyable. Such efforts range from art, music, poetry, and beautiful gardens, to the care of children, entertainment, and creative conversation. As men escape from a subsistence society, in which work must be done to provide for life's necessities, a much more fulfilling kind of work, one directed toward the improved enjoyment of life, will come to dominate.

In time, all of these joyous prophecies will probably come about anyway, provided we have wisdom, foresight, and a little luck. But they will be available to those who read these pages only if the minuscule investment needed to understand and perhaps control human aging is made in this coming decade. What is commonly termed the Protestant ethic encourages some sacrifice now (work, saving, investment, education, research) in order to derive greater benefits in the future. After nearly a decade of disparagement and eclipse, it seems once again to be revealing its wisdom. One can only hope that this resurgence in the appreciation of investment will extend to what is needed to assure a healthier, longer life for all—basic research on the most universal human affliction, aging itself.

# 8

# Physiology of Exercise and Aging

by Herbert A. De Vries

As we grow older there appear to be losses in functional capacity at the cellular level, the tissue level, the organ level, and the system level of organization. However, as pointed out by Shock, the decrements in physiological functions that take place with increasing age become most readily apparent in the responses of the whole organism to stress (Shock, 1961b). As an exercise physiologist my raison d'être lies in the measurement of the human organism's responses to the most physiological of stressors, physical activity, exercise, or the stress of increased energy demands from whatever source. We are most concerned with the various functional capacities of the human individual: how they may be lost through aging or other processes; how they may be improved through such modalities as physical conditioning, improved nutrition, and better relaxation.

Since functional losses are greatest when the whole organism is under stress, we like to think of exercise physiology as the vernier on the scale of general physiology. That is to say, the methods of exercise physiology provide us with a rather sensitive tool for evaluation of physiological decline in aging. Thus, for example, if some of the metabolic capacity is lost at the cellular level, this would not be easily observed or measured under resting conditions, but the measurement of maximal oxygen consumption in the exercise laboratory would display losses in metabolic capacity dramatically. A man of 75, for example, has on the average only about 50 percent of his oxygen consumption value at age 20, while his resting oxygen intake has only declined by 20 to 25 percent over the same period of time (Robinson, 1938). In recent years it has also become apparent to cardiologists that in some cases early ischemic heart disease, which shows no electrocardiogram (EKG) changes at rest, may be successfully diagnosed if the individual's EKG is observed during the stress of a treadmill run or bicycle ergometer ride such as we use daily in the exercise physiology laboratory.

Thus, we are looking at the physiological changes which *accompany* the aging process from the rather

circumscribed vantage point of the exercise physiologist interested not in disease processes but primarily in the gross losses of functional capacity which the aging individual himself experiences as a creeping loss in "vigor." This is not to deny the interest of the exercise physiologist in the entire spectrum of physiological changes, but only to suggest a focus upon those systems which in the "normal" older individual are most likely to be limiting with respect to physical working capacity (PWC) and which are most likely to be amenable to improvement by physical conditioning. Excellent reviews are available for the reader desiring a more comprehensive treatment of physiological age changes than our treatment in this chapter allows. (See, for example, Robinson, 1938; Shock, 1961a).

## Physiological Changes Involved in the Age-Related Loss of Vigor

In evaluating the effects of the aging process on human performance several problems arise. First, it is difficult to separate the effects of aging per se from those of concomitant disease processes (particularly cardiovascular and respiratory problems) which become more prevalent with age. Secondly, the sedentary nature of adult life in the United States makes it very difficult to find "old" populations to compare with "young" populations at equal activity levels. Lastly, very little work has been done involving longitudinal studies of the same population over a period of time. Conclusions drawn from cross-sectional studies in which various age groups of different people are compared must be accepted with reservations because the "weaker biological specimens" are not likely to be represented in as great numbers in the older populations tested as in the younger, due to a higher mortality rate. Thus we must be careful to realize that the age changes described are at best only representative of the average losses and that even these mean values may be derived in some cases from very small samplings.

It must also be realized that just as various individuals within the human species age at different rates, so various physiological functions within the individual seem to have their own rates of decline with increasing age. Indeed, some functions do not seem to degenerate with age (Shock, 1961b). Under resting conditions there to be no changes in blood sugar level, blood pH, or total blood volume, for example. In general, the functions which involve the coordinated activity of more than one organ system, such as aerobic capacity and physical work capacity (PWC), decline most with age. Changes due to the aging process are most readily observed when the organism is stressed. Homeostatic readjustment is considerably slower with increasing age.

## The Cardiovascular System

Assuming appropriate levels of muscle strength and endurance, oxygen transport has been widely accepted as the major factor determining the limits of physical working capacity (PWC) in the young, if the activity lasts more than a minute or two. Oxygen transport as defined by the Fich equation (Oxygen consumption in milliliters/minute = cardiac output in liters/minute $\times$ arteriovenous difference in milliliters/liter blood) depends upon cardiac output and the arteriovenous difference in oxygen. Cardiac output is in turn determined by heart rate and the volume of blood per beat (stroke volume).

Studies of age differences in cardiac output are scarce, but enough work has been done to provide suggestive evidence. With respect to cardiac output at rest, data are available from the work of Brandfornbrener, Landowne, and Shock (1955) on 67 healthy males ranging in age from 19-86. They found a significant age-related decrease of about one percent per year. Their measurements of cardiac output are supported by the ballistocardiographic data of Starr (1964), who estimated a loss in strength of the myocardium (the heart muscle) which was about 0.8 percent per year after the age of 20. This constitutes fairly close agreement from two very different methodological approaches as to the change in function of the heart at rest.

Of the several studies available regarding age changes in cardiac output at submaximal exercise, only two were found in which cardiac output was measured during exercise and in which the subjects and exercise loads were sufficiently similar to allow any meaningful comparison. Becklake et al. (1965) found cardiac output to increase by small amounts with increasing age while Granath, Jonsson, and Strandell (1964) found a small but constant difference in the other direction. Since even in the two studies the methods differed and physical fitness levels were not ruled out among the different age levels, age changes in cardiac output during submaximal exercise must still be considered an open research question.

Most important to our discussion here, however, is the question of what happens to the functional *capacity* of the heart in terms of cardiac output. This means, of course, measurement (or estimation) of *maximal cardiac output*. Only one study was found, but these data from the work of Julius et al. (1967) appear to allow valid age group comparisons and cautious conclusions. They used the indicator-dilution technique to measure cardiac output in 54 subjects in three age groups: I (18–34), II (35–49), and III (50–69). The three groups appear to have been roughly equated in body surface area and physical activity levels. The cardiac outputs at maximum tolerated exercise on a bicycle ergometer were found to be 16.19, 14.96, and 11.98 liters/minute for groups I, II, and III respectively. The age data probably represent a reasonable estimate of the loss in maximum cardiac output with age in a relatively sedentary population. Thus, from the third decade to the sixth and seventh decades we may postulate a loss of some 26 percent. Taking an assumed mean age of 26 for group I and 59 for group III (individual age data were not provided) results in an approximation of the yearly loss at about 0.80 percent per year, a figure roughly similar to the loss rate found for resting cardiac output and myocardial strength.

It has been known that maximum heart rate goes down with age since the classic study by Robinson in 1938. There is also evidence that stroke volume declines with age (Strandell, 1964), so that on these bases we might expect maximum cardiac output to decline at a greater rate than maximum heart rate, which declines almost linearly from 190-195 beats/minute at age 20 to about 160 at age 70 (Robinson, 1938). Assuming a resting rate of 70, this would then result in a lowered capacity for heart-rate response of approximately 0.56 percent per year, over the age range of 20 to 70. Thus the loss of 0.80 percent per year in maximum cardiac output found by Julius et al. (1967) is in the range of what might have been predicted.

## The Respiratory System

It has long been known that maximal ventilation attained during exhausting work shows a gradual decline of about 60 percent from the late teens to the eighth decade (Robinson, 1938). It has also been firmly established that vital capacity (the volume of air that can be expelled by the strongest possible expiration after the deepest possible inspiration) declines with age (Norris et al., 1956; Norris, Shock, and Falzone, 1962; Pemberton and Flanagan, 1956). There appears to be no very good evidence for any change in total lung capacity. Therefore since vital capacity and residual volume (the volume of air remaining in the lungs after the strongest possible expiration) are reciprocally related, residual lung volume increases with age (Norris et al., 1956; Norris, Shock, and Falzone, 1962). Aging therefore increases the ratio of residual volume to total lung capacity, and anatomic dead space also increases with age (Comroe et al., 1962).

The available evidence suggests that lung compliance increases with age (Turner, Mead, and Wohl, 1968), resulting in less elastic recoil to aid in the expiratory process; but even more importantly, thoracic wall compliance decreases in that the elastic stretch and recoil is reduced (Mittman et al., 1965; Rizzato, 1970; Turner, Mead, and Wohl, 1968). Thus the older individual may do as much as 20 percent more elastic work at a given level of ventilation than the young, and most of the additional work will be performed in moving the chest wall (Turner, Mead, and Wohl, 1968).

### Changes in Muscle Function

The many studies which have been reported on muscular strength changes with age have been reviewed by Fisher and Birren (1947), and there seems to be good agreement that for most muscle groups maximal strength is achieved between the ages of 25 and 30. Strength decreases slowly during maturity but seems to decrease at a somewhat faster rate after the fifth decade. However, even at age 60 the total loss does not usually exceed 10-20 percent of the maximum.

With respect to muscular endurance or fatigue rate, Evans (1971) has shown that fatigue rate is significantly greater in the old than the young when holding isometric contractions of 20, 25, 30, 35, 40, and 45 percent of maximal voluntary contraction.

### Physical Working Capacity (PWC)

The best single measure of physical working capacity (PWC) is the maximal oxygen consumption, sometimes referred to as aerobic capacity. Two excellent studies have related this variable to age in men (Robinson, 1938) and women (Astrand, 1960). After a maximum value in early adulthood, there is a gradual decline for both sexes. For men, the maximal values were found at mean age of 17.4 years, and they declined to less than half those values at mean age 75. For women, the maximal values were found in the age group 20-29, and they fell off by 29 percent in the age group 50-65, the oldest tested.

### Body Composition

It is typical (though not desirable) for humans to increase their weight with age. Brozek (1952) has provided interesting data on the composition of the human body as it ages, which clearly show that the weight gain in his sample represented a mean increase of 27 pounds of fat from age 20 to age 55, while the fat-free body weight had actually decreased.

Shock et al. (1963), using estimates of intracellular water as an index of the amount of metabolizing tissue, found losses of active protoplasm (which is protein tissue mass as compared against fat tissue) to average about 0.44 percent per year after age 25. Measurements using total body potassium (Allen, Anderson, and Hangham, 1960) are in relatively good agreement.

Thus we can see that even if we maintained body weight at our young adult value, we would nevertheless be getting fatter since we are losing active protoplasm at approximately 3-5 percent per decade after age 20-25.

## Aging Processes versus Hypokinetic Disease

It is easy to see how the age-related losses in function described above can individually and in concert result in the relatively large losses in PWC which *accompany* the aging process and which are interpreted by the aging individual as a loss in vigor. However, we must be cautious with respect to attributing all of this functional decline to the aging process per se. Indeed, the entire body of knowledge regarding the loss of function with increasing age must be viewed with caution, since in very few cases has the effect of habitual physical activity been controlled or ruled out. Wessel and Van Huss (1969) have shown that physical activity decreases significantly with increasing age. This is not surprising news, but it does provide scientific validation of the need for consideration of this variable in all investigations directed toward aging changes in performance. To support this contention further, Wessel and Van Huss showed that age-related losses in physiological variables important to human performance *were more highly related to the decreased habitual activity level than they were to age itself.*

It would seem that "Hypokinetic Disease," a term coined by Kraus and Raab (1961) to describe the whole spectrum of somatic and mental derangements induced by inactivity, may be of considerable importance as one factor involved in bringing about an age-related decrement in functional capacities.

For example, most of the age-related changes described in previous sections can also be brought about in young, well-conditioned men in as little as three weeks by the simple expedient of enforced bed rest. In one of the outstanding studies in this area, it was found that in three weeks of bed rest, the maximal cardiac output decreased by 26 percent, the maximal ventilatory capacity by 30 percent, oxygen consumption by 30 percent, and even the amount of active tissue declined by 1.5 percent (Saltin et al., 1968). Thus we see that inactivity can produce losses in function entirely similar to those brought about more slowly in the average individual when he grows more sedentary as he grows older (Wessel and Van Huss, 1969). These observations lead us to question how much of the observed losses in function as people grow older are functions of aging and how much may be brought about by the long-term deconditioning of the increasingly sedentary life we usually lead as we grow older. It seems abundantly clear that the physiological changes which accompany the aging process may not be the result of aging alone. Indeed, there is at least one other process which could conceivably account for some of the changes observed. Incipient disease processes, undiagnosible and unrecognized in their early state, could also contribute to the losses in function. For example, the coronary arteries, whose occlusion by fatty deposits ultimately results in a heart attack, may show early changes even in the teenager. Autopsies on 200 battle casualties of the Korean war (mean age 22.1 years) indicated that 77.3 percent of the hearts showed some gross evidence of coronary arteriosclerosis. Some of these casualties were in their teens (Enos et al., 1953).

To summarize, we may hypothesize that the functional losses which have been observed and reported in the medical and physiological literature as age changes must be considered as resulting from at least three composite factors, only one of which is truly an aging phenomenon. Of the other two factors, unrecognized incipient disease processes may or may not be causally related to aging. The third factor, disuse phenomena or "Hypokinetic Disease," is the only one of the three factors which can be easily reversed. The remainder of this chapter is directed toward the physiological and methodological considerations involved in achieving and maintaining physical fitness in middle and old age.

## Trainability of the Older Organism

Only a few years ago, the trainability of older people was still in question. In Germany, it had been concluded that commencement of physical training in a person unaccustomed to sport causes only slight effects of adaptation after the age of 40, while after 60 there is practically no observable effect (Hollman, 1964; Nöcker, 1965). An article from Japan also stated that marked improvement of physical ability by training could not be expected in older people (Katsuki and Masuda, 1969).

On the other hand, Czechoslovakian physiologists had reported better physical performance and functional capacities in a sample of physically active older men than in a comparable sample of sedentary older men (Fischer, Pariskova, and Roth, 1965). Two other investigations had shown significant improvement in physical working capacity and cardiac function by conditioning older people, although the sample size was very small in both—eight in one (Barry et al., 1966) and thirteen in the other (Benestad, 1965). An excellent series of investigations from Stockholm clearly demonstrated the trainability of men in the 34-50 age bracket (Hartley et al., 1969; Kilbom et al., 1969; Saltin et al., 1969). This work demonstrated a 14 percent improvement in aerobic capacity, a 13 percent increase in cardiac output, and some suggestion of decreased numbers of EKG abnormalities. However, it is difficult to consider even the upper end of this age bracket as old, although the investigators did refer to their subjects as "middle-aged and older" men.

We have entered into a series of experiments regarding the trainability and training methodology for older men and women. This work was done at the Laguna Hills retirement community under the sponsorship of the Administration on Aging (H.E.W.).

In the first experiment (deVries, 1970), 112 older Caucasian males aged 52 to 87 (mean = 69.5) volunteered for participation in a vigorous exercise training regimen. They exercised at calisthenics, jogging, and either stretching exercises or aquatics at each workout for approximately one hour, three times per week under supervision. All subjects were pretested and 66 were retested at 6 weeks, 26 at 18 weeks, and 8 at 42 weeks on the following parameters: (a) blood pressure, (b) percentage of body fat, (c) resting neuromuscular activation (relaxation) by electromyogram (EMG), (d) arm muscle strength and girth, (e) maximal oxygen consumption, (f) oxygen pulse at heart rate = 145, (g) pulmonary function, and (h) physical work capacity on the bicycle ergometer. A subgroup of 35 was also tested before and after 6 weeks of training for (a) cardiac output, (b) stroke volume, (c) total peripheral resistance, and (d) work of the heart, at a workload of 75 watts on the bicycle.

The most significant findings were related to oxygen transport capacity. Oxygen pulse and minute ventilation at heart rate 145 improved by 29.4 percent and 35.2 percent respectively. Vital capacity improved by 19.6 percent.

Significant improvement was also found in percentage of body fat, physical work capacity, and both systolic and diastolic blood pressure for the large six-week group (N=66), but with the smaller group which exercised for 42 weeks (N=8) statistical significance was not achieved, although the same trends were observed. Controls did not improve upon any of the above measures. No significant changes were seen in any of the hemodynamic variables tested.

A group of seven men was placed in a modified exercise program because of various cardiovascular problems. This group exercised in the same manner except that they substituted a progressive walking program for the jogging and were restricted to a maximum heart rate of 120 instead of 145 which obtained with the normal group. This group was exercised for six weeks, at which time their improvement showed a similar pattern to that of the harder working normal subjects at six weeks.

Life history of physical activity was evaluated in a subgroup of 53. Neither the mean of high and low years of activity nor the peak level of activity engaged in for a period of six weeks or more correlated positively with physiological improvement found.

It was concluded that the trainability of older men with respect to physical work capacity is probably considerably greater than had been suspected and does not depend upon having trained vigorously in youth.

Since not a single untoward incident occurred during the 18-month tenure of our exercise program, and in view of the improvements in function demonstrated, it was concluded that the exercise regimen as developed was both safe and effective for a normal population of older men in the presence of medical and physiological monitoring.

In a subsequent study, 17 older women (age 52-79) from the same community participated in a vigorous three-month exercise program and again physical fitness was significantly improved, although the women did not show the large improvement in the respiratory system shown by the men (Adams and de Vries, 1973).

On the basis of these studies, we conclude that the older organism is definitely trainable. Indeed the percentage of improvements is entirely similar to that of the young.

## Improvement of Health Factors

Since we had earlier found in our electromyographic investigations that vigorous exercise has a well-defined tranquilizer effect (both immediate and long term) upon young and middle-aged men (deVries, 1968), we decided to evaluate this effect of exercise in our older population. Toward this end, the tranquilizer effect of single doses of exercise and meprobamate (a commonly used tranquilizer pill supplied on prescription as either "Miltown" or "Equanil") were compared with respect to reduction of muscle action potentials in ten elderly, anxious subjects (deVries and Adams, 1972). Thirty-six observations were made of each subject before and after (immediately, 30 minutes and one hour after) each of the five following treatment conditions: (1) meprobamate, 400 mg, (2) placebo, 400 mg lactose, (3) 15 minutes of walking-type exercise at a heart rate of 100, (4) 15 minutes of walking-type exercise at heart rate of 120, and (5) resting control. Conditions 1 and 2 were administered double blind (the investigators did not know which subjects received the drug or placebo). It was found that exercise at a heart rate of 100 lowered electrical activity in the musculature by 20, 23, and 20 percent at the first, second, and third post tests respectively. These changes were significantly different from controls at the one percent confidence level. Neither meprobamate nor placebo treatment was significantly different from control. Exercise at the higher heart rate was only slightly less effective, but the data were more variable and approached but did not achieve significance.

Our data suggest that exercise modality should not be overlooked when a tranquilizer effect is desired, since in single doses, at least, exercise has a significantly greater effect, *without any undesirable side effects,* than does meprobamate, one of the most frequently prescribed tranquilizers. This is especially important for the older individual in that this approach can avoid the further impairment of motor coordination, reaction time, and driving performance, which may occur with any of the tranquilizer drugs. A 15-minute walk at a* moderate rate (sufficient to raise heart rate to 100 beats per minute) is a sufficient stimulus to bring about the desired effect which persists for at least one hour afterward.

Many investigators have found decreases in arterial blood pressure resulting from the physical conditioning process. One of the best-controlled studies is that of Boyer and Kasch (1970) who found highly significant decreases of 12 mm Hg in diastolic and 13 mm Hg in systolic pressures in 23 hypertensive subjects who exercised for six months. The subjects with normal blood pressure showed only small and nonsignificant decreases as expected. It seems likely that this normalization of hypertension may be related to the tranquilizer effect discussed above.

With respect to body composition, Greene (1939), who studied 350 cases of obesity, found that inactivity was associated with the onset of obesity in 67.5 percent of the cases and that a history of increased food intake was present in only 3.2 percent. Pariskova (1964), who analyzed the body composition of 1,460 individuals of all ages, concluded: "One of the most important factors influencing body composition is the intensity of physical activity, and this is true in youth, adulthood, and old age." Many other investigations, too numerous to cite, provide indirect support for the belief that lack of physical activity is the most common cause of obesity. Thus, a clear-cut case can be made for the importance of habitual, lifelong, vigorous physical activity as a preventive measure against obesity.

Furthermore, if we consider the functional capacity of the cardiorespiratory system as an important factor in the health of the older individual, then it is of interest to note that two longitudinal studies have shown that typical loss with age in aerobic capacity can be slowed down (Dehn and Bruce, 1972) or even reversed (Nunneley, Finkelstein, and Luft, 1972) by the physical conditioning process.

It seems then that vigorous physical conditioning of the healthy older organism can bring about significant improvements in: (1) the cardiovascular system, (2) the respiratory system (at least in the male), (3) the musculature, (4) body composition, and in general the result is a more vigorous individual who can also relax better. Other health benefits are likely to include a lower blood pressure and lower percent body fat with the concomitant lessening of "risk factors" for development of coronary heart disease that these factors entail.

# Translations in Gerontology—
# From Lab to Life

## *Utilizing Information*

DAVID SCHONFIELD   *University of Calgary, Alberta, Canada* [1]

When elderly people are asked to participate in investigations on aging, they sometimes object strongly and question the fundamental assumption underlying such research. They suggest that one older person differs so much from another that the quest for generalization is pointless. Although it is easy to attribute such reactions to a negative attitude toward the idea that behavior is in any respect predetermined, the laboratory itself justifies certain reservations. The journey from lab to life must begin with the finding that there are usually greater differences among a group of older people than among the young. In other words, standard deviations tend to increase with age. Figure 1, taken from Heron and Chown (1967), is a typical illustration. Each dot represents one score from a male sample on the Progressive Matrices Intelligence Test, a test of the ability to utilize information. Some people in their 40s, 50s, and 60s do better than the average 20-year-old.

More importantly, there are a few scores among these older groups as good as the best of the younger crowd. It is the lab that provides the caveat for planning and action solely based on average scores. Older people are slower on the average than the young, but it would be wrong to exclude all older workers from jobs that require fast responses—some of the old are just as fast as the young. Sexual drives tend to decrease with age, but a prospective marriage partner with 20 year's seniority may well be one of the many exceptions to that rule. There are, of course, exceptions to rules about the young, too, as can be seen in the 30s and 40s (see Figure 1). However, in general, we can say that there are more older people who behave like the young than young people who behave like the old.

A second pitfall to avoid in the journey from lab to life is due to relativistic and impermanent connotations of the terms *old* and *young*. In Canada a few years ago we considered that we had elected a young prime minister, aged 48, but as a bridegroom of 50, we thought of him as old. In experimental studies, we similarly find that those between 35 and 45 are occasionally labeled as young compared to a group with an average age of 70, but labeled as old compared to a 20-year-old group. The results of such studies are summarized in sentences that begin, "With age, such and such occurs." From the applied point of view, it is of fundamental importance to know whether the difference is between the ages of 20 and 40 or between 40 and 60. The extrapolation type of error is less frequent than the interpolation error, because most studies of human performance employ a group of subjects in their early 20s and another group over 65 years of age, with no one in between. Again the findings are summarized as, "With age, there is deterioration in something or other." The

*Editor's note.* The public demand that psychological research become "relevant" can be met by a demonstration that laboratory findings are indeed relevant to life's problems. In order to apply such findings, a crucial step of translation is required to bridge the gap between the conclusions of experimental investigators and solutions to practical difficulties. The need for bridges is nowhere greater than in gerontology because problems of the aged are so severe. Therefore, the Division of Adult Development and Aging (Division 20) of the American Psychological Association requested three renowned contributors to the literature on performance and aging to make the difficult translation from research findings in the laboratory to the multitude of problems of the aged. This article by David Schonfield and the following two articles by K. Warner Schaie and James E. Birren, respectively, are their responses.

[1] This work was supported by the Canadian National Research Council (APA 89).

Requests for reprints should be sent to David Schonfield, University of Calgary, 2920 24th Avenue, N.W., Calgary, Alberta, Canada T2N 1N4.

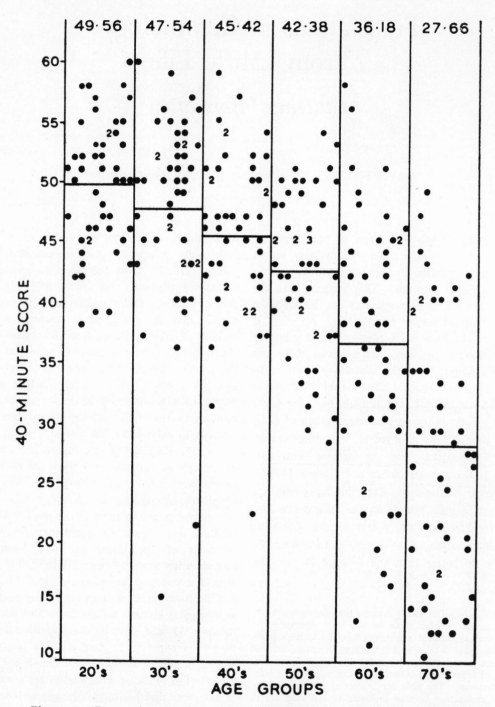

Figure 1.    Progressive matrices (men): Distribution of 40-minute scores with means indicated by horizontal lines. (From *Age and Function* by A. Heron and S. Chown; London: J. & A. Churchill, 1967. Copyright 1967 by J. & A. Churchill. Reprinted by permission.)

suggestion of a gradual and equal decline in each decade between 20 and 70 is unlikely to be correct. When there are only two widely separated, empirically established points on the graph, it is wrong to join them by a straight line and suggest that this represents the age dimension. Figure 2

(Bromley, 1966) provides examples of this kind of interpolation. All of the decline may occur during one or two decades, with a plateau or even improvement during the remaining periods. Personnel officers and policy makers can justify on this basis their refusal to employ people over 45

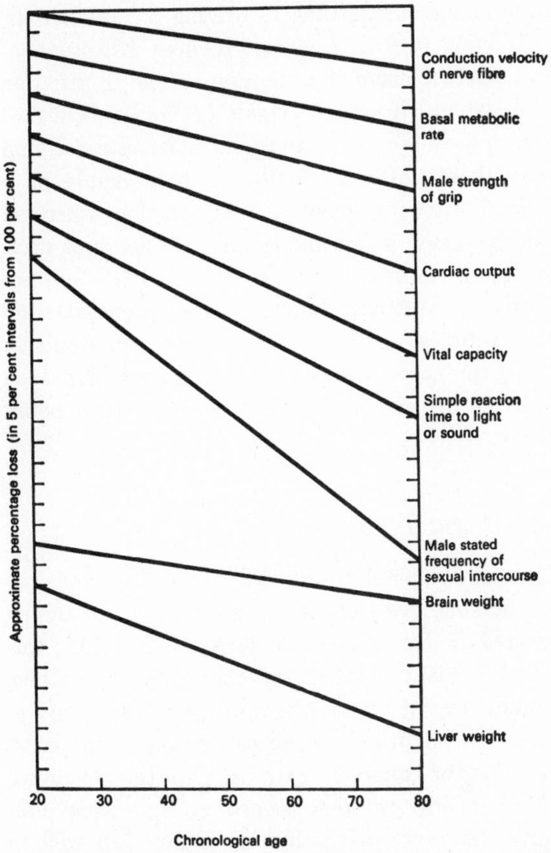
Conduction velocity of nerve fibre
Basal metabolic rate
Male strength of grip
Cardiac output
Vital capacity
Simple reaction time to light or sound
Male stated frequency of sexual intercourse
Brain weight
Liver weight
Approximate percentage loss (in 5 per cent intervals from 100 per cent)
20
30
40
50
60
70
80
Chronological age

Figure 2. Relative age differences for several biological variables expressed as a percentage loss of function from 100% at the age of 20. (From *The Psychology of Human Ageing* by D. B. Bromley; Baltimore, Md.: Penguin Books, 1966. Copyright 1966 by Penguin Books. Reprinted by permission.)

or to press for the early retirement of those in their 50s. In general, we are abysmally ignorant concerning stability and change of behavior during the middle adult years. Be that as it may, the journey from lab to life must begin and end with the same flight number; we should not leave the lab with the 70s and arrive in life with the 40s.

A third methodological issue concerns the absence of age differences in the ability to utilize information. From the applied point of view, any human capacity that shows no difference or minimal change during the adult years should be pinpointed and highlighted. It is on the basis of such *conservation* of ability that older people can compensate for *losses* in ability. The theoretically oriented scientist often ignores findings that show no change with age. He is searching for signs of aging, and the absence of an age change is therefore only of tangential interest. Psychologists should not follow, what might be called, the *biological model* in this regard. We need to emphasize the absence of age differences in order to counteract negative attitudes toward aging. It is just not true that every day in every way we get worse and worse. Situations in which older people have special problems in acquiring information, recalling information, or utilizing information are also of fundamental interest. If such situations can be circumvented, competence can be increased and strain avoided. The most valuable findings of all are those in which the manipulation of one or more variables results in large reductions in age differences. Useful translation from gerontological research to life becomes reasonably straightforward when we can specify situations in which age differences are diminished or disappear.

## *Information Presented in Unusual Ways*

Applied implications of many simple, theoretically based laboratory findings are often easy to envisage. It is not even essential to undertake the physical journey from lab to life—a little imagination suffices for the busy commuters between lab and conferences. Take as an example one of the earliest controlled studies on age effects. Ruch (1934) found that the difference between a middle-aged and an elderly group was much greater when spatial information was provided through a mirror as compared to direct vision. The looking glass difficulty for those over the age of about 55 has been confirmed in settings other than the pursuit rotor task which Ruch employed (Welford, 1958). This difficulty coincides with a general principle about the problem of overcoming longstanding habits. Therefore, we are warranted in alerting those who use mirrors in the "real world." Physiotherapists and speech therapists, for instance, often attempt to provide feedback by means of a mirror when rehabilitating patients following a stroke. During the initial learning period this kind of crutch is likely to be less helpful to the aged than to the young. Ruch's major concern was with the plasticity of nervous tissue, but that theoretical issue becomes superfluous baggage in our journey from the lab. There is at least one danger in this kind of translation of gerontological research. The message that the elderly have difficulty with mirrors and that extra encouragement coupled with patience is required for them can become distorted into a recommendation that mirrors should be avoided in rehabilitation work with older patients. This possible harmful outcome is due to the prevalent carelessness in the use of language which has coincided with our obsessional carefulness about experimental design. An exception to the generalization about the age-associated looking glass difficulties is derived from another conclusion of gerontological research. Well-established skills that continue to be practiced show minor deficits compared to age difficulties in acquiring a new skill (Szafran, 1968). There does not seem to have been any specific investigation on this point with respect to mirrors. Nevertheless, applied psychologists should not be afraid to make the pronouncement that older dentists, for instance, will not experience special difficulties when using mirrors to examine teeth, providing they had their training when they were in their 20s or 30s. On the other hand, starting a second career as a dentist at the age of about 55 is likely to cause problems in utilizing and combining information derived from mirror vision and direct vision.

## Ability to Ignore Irrelevant Information

We turn now from information presented in an unusual way to an age decrement in the ability to ignore irrelevant information. Only one report seems to have been published focusing specifically on the topic, and in that experiment of Rabbitt (1965) the older group's age was over 65. However, an increase in distractibility beginning probably at about 45 is suggested by a number of studies. The evidence on difficulty in identifying concealed figures (Basowitz & Korchin, 1957), in maintaining sets (Talland, 1959), and in maintaining performance on dichotic listening (Schonfield, Trueman, & Kline, 1972) all point toward a problem of excluding from attention material irrelevant to the task at hand. Distraction by irrelevant stimuli is an all-pervasive hazard in the real world, and innumerable examples could be cited in which special consideration should be given to this age-related difficulty. If one does not stick to the main point in conversations with older people information is less likely to be utilized and misunderstandings will ensue. On the other hand, the reputation that the aged themselves have for not sticking to a point can be considered a manifestation of distraction by their own irrelevant memories. When an older person is engaged in the

more dangerous pastime of driving an automobile, distraction by the irrelevant reduces utilization of the vital relevant information. The translation from lab to life should result in the banishing of unnecessary billboards and road signs, especially on busy thoroughfares. Similarly, there should be a general discouragement of conversation when an elderly person is driving during rush hours or driving a new car or driving in a strange city. In other words, if an activity requires greater concentration and if the absence of concentration can result in injury or accident, special procedures are needed to avoid distraction on behalf of the elderly population.

## Speed and Timing

The third example of simple translation from lab to life is derived from the area of speed and timing covered in Birren's article (see pp. 808–815, this issue). Field research in the early Cambridge studies showed that workers in their 50s tended to leave jobs in which performance was paced by a machine or another external source (Welford, 1958). Older workers seemed to have little difficulty, however, in continuing to hold up well in self-paced tasks. The reverse journey from life to lab produced experiments suggesting that acquisition of information was not readily time shared with decisions about responses to be made. Later studies, in particular those of Eisdorfer (1968), led to the conclusion that time limitations can be emotionally upsetting for older people. Ordinary conversation, especially with busy people, often resembles an externally paced task. The questioner impatiently waits for a response while the respondent is attempting both to understand the question and to prepare an adequate answer. By the time an elderly person is ready to talk, the questioner has given up and a new question is posed. Those who are in constant contact with the elderly—family, civil servants, and social workers—should convey an unhurried impression in order to avoid an inquisitional atmosphere with all of its emotional outcome.

## Threshold Level

The raising of thresholds is the source of the fourth translation example. Food remaining near the mouth after eating and the occasional drip of mucus on the nose are sometimes not felt by a younger person. The sensation is at about threshold value for the young and more likely to be below the touch threshold in older people. Alerting the elderly themselves to this kind of reduction of information input could have valuable benefits. Social relationships seem to become more precarious as we age, and they are likely to suffer when appearance is somewhat repulsive. Here, the recommendation is an extra check in the looking glass as opposed to the earlier example of a reduced usefulness of mirror vision.

## Learning and Memory

The next translation example comes from learning and remembering. Theorists wish to pinpoint the locus of the age-associated deficit: Is it short-term memory? Is it acquisition? Is it the transfer from short-term to long-term memory? Is it retrieval? The practical implications, however, of increasing difficulties in reproducing newly acquired information are often straightforward. Surely we can tell physicians that they should provide written instructions for their elderly patients, so that memory can be checked. After verbal instructions, the patient is less likely to remember whether the doctor said, "Do it three times a day," or "four times a day." Did the doctor say, "Swallow the medicine," or "Place it in the anus"?

## Caution

The last example in this series emanates from the tendency toward increased caution with age. Botwinick (1966) has been the major contributor to the literature on this point, but others such as Szafran (1951) in his studies on utilization of vision and Canestrari (1963) on omission errors provide confirming evidence. As we get older we adhere not only to the advice to look before we leap, but we also seem to prefer to look while we are leaping. Industrial gerontologists can use these findings in the counseling they provide about suitable jobs for middle-aged and older workers. Inspection types of occupations, in which carefulness is at a premium, are probably ideal occupations for these age groups.

## Conclusion

These six illustrations—use of mirrors by dentists and others, irrelevant information and driving, self-

pacing in conversation, threshold touch sensation and its social implications, aids to remembering physicians' instructions, inspection-type jobs—suffice to exemplify one approach to translations in gerontology. A specific finding in the lab is recognized as an example of a more general principle, and a jump is made from the finding to a closely analogous situation in the "real world." A prerequisite is considerable knowledge of the discipline so that the practitioner recognizes which specific findings are supported by other investigators. The jump is a nonscientific activity and could perhaps be labeled gerontological common sense. It has been suggested elsewhere (Schonfield, 1972) that all research workers should be encouraged to make this jump by including a section headed "Proposals for the Application of Results" at the end of published articles. The principles will vary according to the breadth of their potential applications. When the breadth is narrow, as in the case of the looking glass example, they might be called "principlettes," and progressively wider applicability would become queen-size principles—for example, the irrelevant information finding—and king-size principles. (The nomenclature is derived from bed size and perhaps because of that it smacks of male chauvinism.)

A king-size principle suggested by the six illustrations is that functioning requires increased attention from about the age of 50. Attention to more than one activity cannot be shared, and concurrent multiple functioning becomes increasingly difficult. Processing of input requires attention because the meaning of signals does not occur so automatically. Processing of output requires attention because "actions do not take care of themselves." (That phrase was used by Sir Frederic Bartlett some 25 years ago in an unpublished lecture.) The fact of time pressure is attended to instead of being ignored, perhaps because paying attention has become a habitual strategy both for relevant and extraneous facets of the task. Even psychological functions, such as remembering, do not "take care of themselves" and remembering to remember demands vigilance. The principle of extra attention has implications for almost all situations in the everyday life of older people.

The use of the term *principle*, rather than *theory*, in these descriptions of translation from lab to life has been deliberate. Following Broadbent (1971), I confess to "distaste for the amount of theory current in psychology" with its "stream of papers giving hypothesis, prediction and verification [p.

5]." Although there is no inherent contrast between theory and practice, the attitude prevails that a theory has greater theoretical value when it has minimal applied value. The pursuit of principles rather than theories and hypotheses may help gerontologists to keep applications at the forefront of our attention. Broadbent (1971) rightly said:

The researcher remote from practical pressures may indeed be free to study major variables in which at this instant society does not seem to be interested, but he should not use this freedom in order to study minor variables, until there are no major ones within reach of our techniques [p. 4].

## REFERENCES

Basowitz, H., & Korchin, S. J. Age differences in the perception of closure. *Journal of Abnormal and Social Psychology,* 1957, **54,** 93–97.

Birren, J. E. Psychophysiology and speed of response. *American Psychologist,* 1974, **29,** 808–815.

Botwinick, J. Cautiousness with advanced age. *Journal of Gerontology,* 1966, **21,** 347–353.

Broadbent, D. E. *Decision and stress.* London: Academic Press, 1971.

Bromley, D. B. *The psychology of human ageing.* Baltimore, Md.: Penguin Books, 1966.

Canestrari, R. E. Paced and self-paced learning in young and elderly adults. *Journal of Gerontology,* 1963, **18,** 165–168.

Eisdorfer, C. Arousal and performance: Experiments in verbal learning and a tentative theory. In G. A. Talland (Ed.), *Human aging and behavior.* New York: Academic Press, 1968.

Heron, A., & Chown, S. *Age and function.* London: J. & A. Churchill, 1967.

Rabbitt, P. M. A. An age decrement in the ability to ignore irrelevant information. *Journal of Gerontology,* 1965, **20,** 233–238.

Ruch, F. L. The differentiative effects of age upon human learning. *Journal of General Psychology,* 1934, **11,** 261–285.

Schonfield, D. Theoretical nuances and practical old questions: The psychology of aging. *Canadian Psychologist,* 1972, **13,** 252–266.

Schonfield, D., Trueman, V., & Kline, D. Recognition tests of dichotic listening and the age variable. *Journal of Gerontology,* 1972, **27,** 487–493.

Szafran, J. Changes with age and with exclusion of vision in performance at an aiming task. *Quarterly Journal of Experimental Psychology,* 1951, **3,** 111–118.

Szafran, J. Psychophysiological studies of aging in pilots. In G. A. Talland (Ed.), *Human aging and behavior.* New York: Academic Press, 1968.

Talland, G. A. Age and the effect of expectancy on the accuracy of perception. *Journal of Gerontology,* 1959, **14,** 202–207.

Welford, A. T. *Ageing and human skill.* London: Oxford University Press, 1958.

# 10

AGING AND IQ

# The Myth of the Twilight Years

Intelligence does not slide downhill from adulthood through old age. By many measures, it increases as time goes by. **by Paul B. Baltes and K. Warner Schaie**

NEWS REPORTERS NEVER TIRE of pointing out that Golda Meir works 20-hour days, yet is in her mid-70s, and a grandmother. *Time*, in a recent story on William O. Douglas, noted that the blue eyes of the 75-year-old Justice "are as keen and alert as ever. So, too, is [his] intellect." This sort of well-intended but patronizing compliment betrays a widespread assumption that intelligence normally declines in advanced adulthood and old age, and that people like Meir and Douglas stand out as exceptions.

In our opinion, general intellectual decline in old age is largely a myth. During the past 10 years, we and our colleagues, (particularly G.V. Labouvie and J.R. Nesselroade) have worked to gain a better understanding of intelligence in the aged. Our findings challenge the stereotyped view, and promote a more optimistic one. We have discovered that the old man's boast, "I'm just as good as I ever was," may be true, after all.

**The Data on Decline.** For a long time, the textbook view coincided with the everyday notion that as far as intelligence is concerned, what goes up must come down. The research that supported this view was cross-sectional in nature. The investigator administered intelligence tests to people of various ages at a given point in time, and compared the performance levels of the different age groups. Numerous studies of this type conducted during the '30s, '40s and '50s led researchers to believe that intelligence increases up to early adulthood, reaches a plateau that lasts for about 10 years, and begins to decline in a regular fashion around the fourth decade of life.

The first doubts arose when the results of longitudinal studies began to be available. In this type of study, the researcher observes a single group of subjects for a period of time, often extending over many years, and examines their performance at different ages. Early longitudinal studies suggested that intelligence during maturity and old age did not decline as soon as people had originally assumed.

As better intelligence tests became available, researchers began to realize that different intellectual measures might show different rates of decline. On measures of vocabulary and other skills reflecting educational experience, individuals seemed to maintain their adult level of functioning into the sixth, and even the seventh decade.

**Resolving the Discrepancy.** In 1956, one of us (Schaie) launched a major project aimed at resolving this disturbing discrepancy between the two kinds of study. Five hundred subjects, ranging in age from 21 to 70, received two intelligence tests, Thurstone and Thurstone's Primary Mental Abilities, and Schaie's Test of Behavioral Rigidity. Seven years later, we retested 301 of the subjects with the same tests.

The tests we used yielded 13 separate measures of cognitive functioning. Using factor-analysis methods, we found that the scores reflected four general, fairly independent dimensions of intelligence: 1) *Crystallized intelligence* encompasses the sorts of skills one acquires through education and acculturation, such as verbal comprehension, numerical skills, and inductive reasoning. To a large degree, it reflects the extent to which one has accumulated the collective intelligence of one's own culture. It is the dimension tapped by most traditional IQ tests [see "Are I.Q. Tests Intelligent?" by Raymond Cattell, PT, March 1968]. 2) *Cognitive flexibility* measures the ability to shift from one way of thinking to another, within the context of familiar intellectual operations, as when one must provide either an antonym or synonym to a word, depending on whether the word appears in capital or lower-case letters. 3) *Visuo-motor flexibility* measures a similar, but independent skill, the one involved in shifting from familiar to unfamiliar patterns in tasks requiring coordination be-

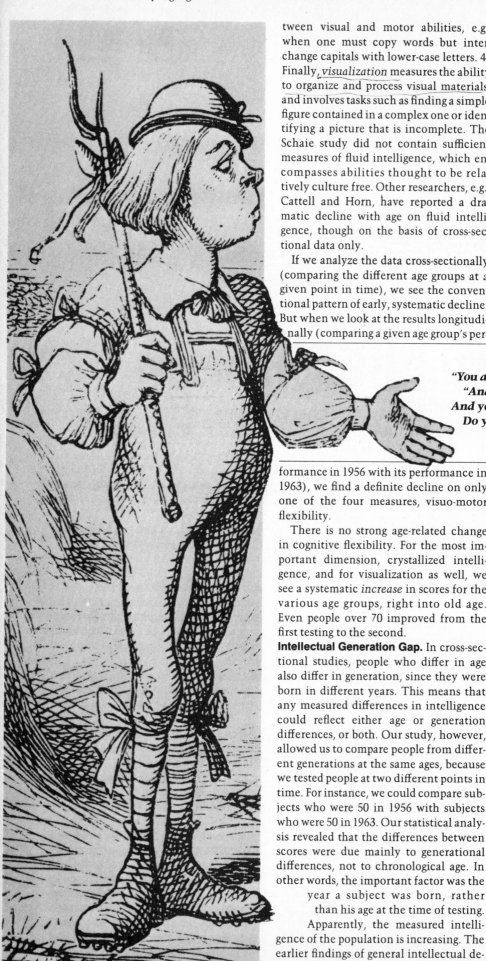

tween visual and motor abilities, e.g., when one must copy words but interchange capitals with lower-case letters. 4) Finally, *visualization* measures the ability to organize and process visual materials, and involves tasks such as finding a simple figure contained in a complex one or identifying a picture that is incomplete. The Schaie study did not contain sufficient measures of fluid intelligence, which encompasses abilities thought to be relatively culture free. Other researchers, e.g., Cattell and Horn, have reported a dramatic decline with age on fluid intelligence, though on the basis of cross-sectional data only.

If we analyze the data cross-sectionally (comparing the different age groups at a given point in time), we see the conventional pattern of early, systematic decline. But when we look at the results longitudinally (comparing a given age group's performance in 1956 with its performance in 1963), we find a definite decline on only one of the four measures, visuo-motor flexibility.

There is no strong age-related change in cognitive flexibility. For the most important dimension, crystallized intelligence, and for visualization as well, we see a systematic *increase* in scores for the various age groups, right into old age. Even people over 70 improved from the first testing to the second.

**Intellectual Generation Gap.** In cross-sectional studies, people who differ in age also differ in generation, since they were born in different years. This means that any measured differences in intelligence could reflect either age or generation differences, or both. Our study, however, allowed us to compare people from different generations at the same ages, because we tested people at two different points in time. For instance, we could compare subjects who were 50 in 1956 with subjects who were 50 in 1963. Our statistical analysis revealed that the differences between scores were due mainly to generational differences, not to chronological age. In other words, the important factor was the year a subject was born, rather than his age at the time of testing.

Apparently, the measured intelligence of the population is increasing. The earlier findings of general intellectual decline over the individual life span were largely an artifact of methodology. On at least some dimensions of intelligence, particularly the crystallized type, people of average health can expect to maintain or even increase their level of performance into old age.

At present, we can only speculate about the reasons for generational differences in intelligence. We believe the answer lies in the substance, method and length of education received by different generations. When we consider the history of our educational institutions, and census data on the educational levels attained by members of specific generations, it seems fair to assume that the older people in our study were exposed to shorter periods of formal education. Furthermore, their education probably relied more heavily on principles of memorization, and less heavily on those of problem-solving.

*"You are old, father William," the young man said,*
*"And your hair has become very white;*
*And yet you incessantly stand on your head.*
*Do you think, at your age, it is right?"*

However, there are other possibilities that must be reckoned with before we can offer a more definite interpretation. Members of different generations may differ in their sophistication in test-taking or their willingness to volunteer responses. They may differ in the extent to which they have been encouraged to achieve intellectually. And tests developed to measure the abilities of one generation may be invalid for another. In any case, the existence of differences between generations makes the search for ''normal'' aging phenomena a Sisyphean task.

**Drop Before Death.** Klaus and Ruth Riegel, psychologists at the University of Michigan, have recently suggested that when intellectual decline does occur, it comes shortly before death [see ''Life, or Death and IQ,'' News Line, May 1973]. In 1956, the Riegels gave intelligence tests to 380 German men and women between the ages of 55 and 75. Five years later they retested 202 of them. Some of the remainder had died, and others refused to be retested. When the Riegels looked back at the 1956 test scores of the subjects who had died, they discovered that on the average, the deceased subjects had scored lower than those who survived. Put another way, the low scores in 1956 predicted impending death.

The Riegels followed up their study in 1966 by inquiring into the fate of the people retested in 1961. Again, some people had died in the interim, and those who had died had lower scores than those who lived. Furthermore, people who had died since 1961 had declined in score from the first test session in 1956 to the second in 1961. These results pointed to a sudden deterioration during the five or fewer years immediately prior to natural death, or what the Riegels called a "terminal drop." Interestingly, the people who had refused to be retested in 1961 were more likely than the others to die before 1966. Perhaps their refusal reflected some kind of awareness of their own decline.

The Riegels' results may offer an alternative explanation for the general decline found by cross-sectional studies: the older groups may contain a higher percentage of people in the terminal drop stage, and their lower scores would not be typical of other older people. If the re-

*"In my youth," father William replied to his son,*
*"I feared it might injure the brain;*
*But now that I'm perfectly sure I have none,*
*Why, I do it again and again."*

**— LEWIS CARROLL**

searcher could foresee the future and remove from his study those subjects nearing death, he might observe little or no change in the intelligence of the remaining group. In fact, the Riegels found that elderly subjects still alive in 1966 did as well, on the average, as persons at the presumed period of peak performance, 30 to 34 years, which of course, is consistent with our own data.

While it is tempting to speculate on the reasons for terminal drop, we feel that the present state of the art is such that interpretation must be tentative at best. Most researchers would probably tend to relate the drop in intellectual functioning to neurophysiological deterioration. However, this position overlooks the possibility that psychological variables contribute both to the drop and to biological death.

**Aged-Biased IQ Tests.** The nature of the tests used to assess intelligence may also contribute to the apparent decline that is sometimes observed. Sidney L. Pressey (who now lives as an octogenarian in a home for the elderly and continues to make occasional but insightful contributions to psychology) first pointed out that the concept of intelligence, as well as the instruments to measure it, are defined in terms of abilities most important during youth and early adulthood. This is not really surprising, since IQ tests came into existence for the purpose of predicting school performance. The format and content of these tests may simply be inappropriate for tapping the potential wisdom of the aged. For example, older people tend to do relatively poorly on tests employing technical language such as the terminology of physics or computer programing. Their performance is better if items are worded in terms of everyday experiences.

Another problem is the distinction between a person's competence and his actual performance. Handicaps that have nothing to do with intrinsic ability may affect the way a person does on a test. For instance, Baltes and Carol A. Furry recently demonstrated that the aged are especially susceptible to the effects of fatigue; pretest fatigue considerably lowered the scores of older subjects, but did not affect the performance of younger ones.

Dwindling reinforcements may also affect the performance of the aged. Elderly individuals, because of their uncertain and shortened life expectancy, may cease to be sensitive to the sorts of long-range rewards that seem to control intellectual behavior in young people (e.g., education, career goals, and development of a reputation). Ogden Lindsley has proposed that the aged may become more dependent on immediate and idiosyncratic rewards.

Even when rewards are potentially effective, they may be unavailable to old people. Most researchers agree that the environment of the elderly is intellectually and socially impoverished. Family settings and institutions for the aged fail to provide conditions conducive to intellectual growth. The educational system discourages participation by the elderly, focusing instead on the young.

Recent work on age stereotypes indicates that some young people hold a negative view of old age. These views may influence them to withdraw reinforcements for competence in the elderly, or even to punish such competence. Aging persons may in time come to accept the stereotypes, view themselves as deficient, and put aside intellectual performance as a personal goal. In the process, the intellectual deficit becomes a self-fulfilling prophecy.

**Compensatory Education for the Aged.** Although educators have made massive attempts to overcome discrimination in early childhood, working through Government-funded compensatory programs, analogous efforts for the aged have barely begun. But, increasing numbers of gerontologists have felt encouraged enough by the reanalysis of intellectual decline to examine, probably for the first time in any vigorous manner, the degree to which intellectual performance can be bolstered. The results are still very sketchy, but they are promising.

Some researchers, working from a biobehavioral perspective, have looked at the effects of physical treatments. For instance, hyperbaric oxygen treatment—the breathing of concentrated oxygen for extended periods to increase oxygen supply to the brain—seems to improve memory for recent events, although the outcome of such research is not at all free of controversy. Treatment of hypertension and conditioning of alpha waves also seem to be promising, and deserve careful study. Other researchers concentrate on studying the psychological aspects of the learning process; they experiment with the pacing of items, the mode of presentation (for instance, auditory versus visual), the amount of practice, the delivery of rewards, training in mnemonics, and so on.

The speed with which a person responds, which is important on many intellectual tests, is usually assumed to be a function of biological well-being. But in a series of pilot studies, Baltes, William Hoyer and Gisela V. Labouvie were able to improve the response speed of elderly subjects rather dramatically, using Green Stamps as a reward for faster performance in canceling letters, marking answer sheets and copying words. After as little as two hours of training, women 65 to 80 years of age increased their speed as much as 20 to 35 percent. The researchers compared the performance of these "trained" subjects with that of untrained controls on 11 different intelligence tests. Although the transfer of the speed training to test performance was not earthshaking, the overall pattern was encouraging.

In the interest of rectifying some of the social injustices that have resulted from the branding of the aged as deficient, social scientists must continue to explore, with vigor and optimism, the research ave-

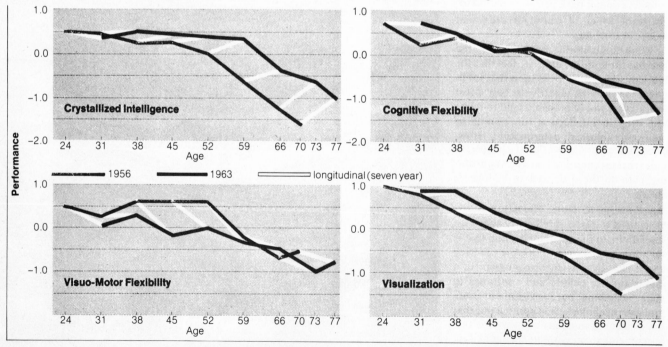

*Reprinted by permission from the* JOURNAL OF GERONTOLOGY, 1972, *Volume 27.*

**AGE & DIMENSIONS OF INTELLIGENCE. The colored lines slope downward, indicating that in both 1956 and 1963, older people scored lower than younger ones on various dimensions of intelligence. However, the white lines, which show how a given age group's performance changed from the first test occasion to the second, reveal that in the older groups crystallized intelligence and visualization go up, not down.**

nues opened during the past few years. This research should be guided by a belief in the potential of gerontological intelligence, and a rejection of the rigid, biological view that assumes an inevitable decline. We should not be surprised to find that the socialization goals and mechanisms of a society are the most powerful influence on what happens to people, not only during childhood and adolescence but also during adulthood and old age.

Social roles and resources can be assigned without regard to age only when the deleterious aspects of aging are eliminated. Toward this end, in 1971 an American Psychological Association task force on aging made some specific recommendations for eliminating the unnecessary causes of decline in intellectual functioning. They included more forceful implementation of adult-education programs; funding of research and innovative programs in voluntary (rather than mandatory) retirement, second-career training, and leisure-time activity; and better utilization of skills that are unaffected by age.

When we consider the vast spectrum of negative conditions, attributes and expectations that most Western societies impose on older people, we must acclaim the impressive robustness of our older population in the face of adversity. At the same time, we hope that society, aided by geropsychology, soon finds ways to make life for the elderly more enjoyable and effective. Acknowledging that intellectual decline is largely a myth is, we hope, a step in the right direction.

# 11

# Personality and the Aging Process

Bernice L. Neugarten, PhD[2]

The lines of inquiry I have chosen to describe today concern changes in personality and behavior with the passage of time, and with the attempt to measure some of the effects of life experience.

## Personality Changes

In one set of studies we asked, What are the changes in personality associated with chronological age in the second half of life? We worked with cross-sectional data gathered in Kansas City on more than 700 relatively healthy men and women aged 40 to 70 from all social-status levels who were living normal lives in the community and data from another group of nearly 300 people aged 50 to 90 whom we interviewed at regular intervals over a 6-year period. We picked successive samples from this large pool of cases, used different conceptual approaches and different variables (this series of studies is reported in Neugarten, 1964).

We found consistent age differences in the covert or intrapsychic areas of personality, in the ways persons see themselves in relation to the environment. For instance, 40-year-olds saw the environment as rewarding boldness and risk-taking, and themselves as possessing energy to take advantage of the opportunities presented in the outer world. By contrast 60-year-olds saw the environment as complex and dangerous, to be dealt with in conforming and accommodating ways. This age difference was described by David Gutmann as a movement from active to passive mastery.

People of different ages deal differently with impulse life. At successive ages, people become more preoccupied with the inner life than with events in the external environment. We described this as increased interiority. There is also less willingness to deal with wide ranges of stimuli or with complicated and challenging situations. Older people seem to move toward

more eccentric, self-preoccupied positions and to attend increasingly to the control and satisfaction of personal needs.

Contrary to these findings regarding intrapsychic processes, age was not significant when we looked at socio-adaptational variables—for example, when we tried to operationalize Erikson's concepts of ego development, or when we tried to measure a whole range of variables related to adaptive, goal-directed, and purposive behavior, processes more readily available to conscious control. Nor were measures of psychological well-being related to age. It would appear that older people, like younger, have different capacities to cope with life stresses and to come to terms with their life situations; and that age itself is not the decisive factor.

A third level of functioning is represented by the nature and extent of the individual's interactions with other persons. Here our studies have shown a long-term decrease with age on several different measures: on social role performance in various life roles, on the amount of each day a person spends in interaction with others, and in the degree of ego investment in present social roles. The general picture regarding social interaction did not show dramatic discontinuities, however, at least through the 60s. For our samples as a whole, a marked drop in role performances did not appear until the late 60s or 70s. While some individuals maintained high levels of activity over the 6-year period in which we followed them, the evidence was nevertheless clear that, over a longer time span, there was shrinkage in social life space, whether it came relatively early or late after middle age.

To sum up these findings, then: in studying the same individuals we found asynchronous trends: in the covert or "inner" life—the eye of the mind—increased interiority and other changes which we interpreted as developmental, occurring as early as the 50s; on the adaptational side, no age-related changes; and in social interaction, decrease occurring not until the late 60s and 70s.

These inconsistent findings—that intrapsychic changes in middle and late life proceed in ways

1. The 1971 Robert W. Kleemeier Award Lecture delivered at the 24th Annual Meeting of the Gerontological Society, Houston, Oct. 28, 1971.
2. Committee on Human Development, University of Chicago, Chicago 60637.

that are not necessarily synchronous with changes in social interaction or in psychological well-being—are compatible with other things we know as students of personality. There are differences between the inner and the outer life; and the inner life is not always translated directly into action. Presumably in older persons, like in younger, there are coping and controlling processes, ego processes, which mediate between different orders of personality; which relate particularly to the ability to organize, to interpret, and to evaluate experience, and to carry out patterns of action in line with one's goals.

## Successful Aging

Stimultaneous to this line of research was another, focused on the question of *successful* aging. Without going into a long recounting of a story that is familiar to many students of gerontology, the disengagement theory, and then a major modification of the theory, emerged from our Chicago group. When first stated in the early 1960s, it set off a controversy in the field that lasted 10 years; a controversy that has now abated, largely, as I like to think, because of some of our own work regarding personality.

The first statement of the theory was based on a recognition of the significance of our findings regarding intrapsychic psychological changes, especially the fact that these changes seemed to precede changes in social behavior. It was observed, as already mentioned, that as people grow old, their social interaction decreases; but looking at the psychological changes, it was postulated that the decrease in social interaction is characterized by mutuality between society and the aging person—the person has decreasing emotional involvement in the activities that characterized him earlier and thus withdraws from those activities. As a second part of

the theory, it was proposed that in old age the individual who has disengeged is the person who has a sense of psychological well-being and will be high in life satisfaction (Cumming & Henry, 1961).

Some of us were uncomfortable with this second part of the theory. As we gathered more data and as we studied the lives of the people in our sample, we did not find the consistent patterns that were predicted from the disengagement theory. Something seemed wrong. Therefore, once all the Kansas City data were in, we devised new and better measures of social interaction and of psychological well-being than the ones originally formulated. Now we found that high life satisfaction was more often present in persons who were socially active and involved than in persons who were inactive and uninvolved. This finding has since been confirmed in our pilot study of men aged 70-75 in six industrialized countries (see Neugarten & Havighurst, 1969).

More important, we found diversity. Some people who were high-high on the two sets of variables; some, high-low; some, low-low; and some, low-high (Havighurst, Neugarten, & Tobin, 1968). Noting that the disengagement theory could not account for this diversity, we asked, how could it be accounted for?

By that time we had worked out, with the aid of sophisticated statistical techniques, a set of empirically derived personality types. Now, in assessing all three kinds of data on each person —extent of his social interaction, degree of life satisfaction, and personality type—we found a high degree of order in the data. Certain personality types, as they age, slough off various role responsibilities with relative comfort and remain highly content with life. Other personalities show a drop in role and in social interaction and show a drop in life satisfaction. Still others have long shown low levels of activity accompanied by high satisfaction and show relatively little change as they age. For instance, in one group of 70- to 79-year-olds, persons who were living in the community and carrying out their usual daily rounds of activities, we empirically derived eight different patterns of aging. We attached the names, Reorganizers, Focused, Disengaged, Holding-on, Constricted, Succorance-seeking, Apathetic, and Disorganized, each name conveying something of the style of aging common to each of the subgroups (Neugarten, Havighurst, & Tobin, 1968).

We have concluded from this line of studies that personality organization or personality type is the pivotal factor in predicting which individuals will age successfully and that adaptation is the key concept.

Furthermore, although we lack systematic longitudinal data to confirm this view, it has appeared from the life-history information available on the people we studied that the patterns reflect long-standing life styles and that consistencies rather than inconsistencies in coping styles predominate as an individual moves from middle age through old age. Within broad limits—given no major biological accidents or major social upheavals—patterns of aging are predictable from knowing the individuals in middle age. (This conviction has led us at Chicago, naturally enough, to expand our perspective on the field of aging to include middle age and then young adulthood: in short, to conceive of a broader time-span, adulthood, as the relevant one for studying aging.)

In demonstrating that there is no single pattern by which people grow old, and in suggesting that persons age in ways that are consistent with their earlier life-histories, it is our view that given a relatively supportive social environment, older persons like younger ones will choose the combinations of activities that offer them the most ego-involvement and that are most consonant with their long-established value patterns and self-concepts. Aging is not a leveler of individual differences except, perhaps, at the very end of life. In adapting to both biological and social changes, the aging person continues to draw upon that which he has been, as well as that which he is.

In giving central importance to personality factors and to the continuities in personality, and in seeing people as active rather than passive, this is not to underestimate the importance of various social, economic, and biological conditions. We know, of course, that if minimum levels of life satisfaction are to be achieved, people need enough money to live on, and decent housing, and health services, and an environment that provides opportunities for social interaction. From this perspective, a major research problem for social scientists interested in successful aging will continue to be that of elucidating the economic, political, and social conditions that are associated with psychological well-being for older people.

At the same time, variations in socio-cultural contexts will not solve the problem of individual variation—that is, why some individuals are more content than others who live in the same social setting. Despite the likelihood that some settings will be found to provide greater freedom and permissiveness for a broad range of life styles, that some will be found to provide greater pressures for social participation, some, greater economic benefits, and so on, we shall still need to look at the ways individual older people adapt to the settings in which they find themselves.

It is the manner in which the individual deals with a variety of contingencies in his life; some of them social, some of them biological, which will continue to be the second important research issue. What does an old person make of his world, and how is the adaptational process influenced by his past life-history and his expectations? In attempting to understand why one individual copes successfully with retirement while another does not, or with illness, we shall have to pursue in much greater depth the ways in which aging individuals relate their pasts with their presents, how they reconcile expectations with reality, and how they interpret and integrate their lives into meaningful wholes.

## Expectations

In the course of our own studies, it has become increasingly evident that each person interprets his present situation in terms of what his expectations have been. Man is a thinking and planning animal, he looks around, compares himself with others, anticipates; then compares reality with his anticipations, and assesses his situation in terms of the congruence between the two. Expectations are therefore an important factor in understanding levels of psychological well-being.

What impressed us, however, was that people's expectations seem always to include a time line or an age referent. For example, our respondents say, "I'm in better health than most people my age," or "things are better (or worse) than I expected them to be." One person who recently suffered a heart attack said, "Well, at my age you have to expect these things."

As psychologists, we have not given enough attention to this area: what are the expectational sets about growing old that people carry with them through adulthood? How are these expectations changing? In our own work we began to see that individuals, whether or not they can easily verbalize it, develop a view of the "normal, expectable life cycle" (a phrase suggested by Dr. Robert Butler). They form expectations based upon consensually-validated sequences of life events: what these events should be, when they should occur, and under what conditions they should occur. They make plans, set goals, and reassess those goals along a time-line shaped by those expectations.

Thus far we have explored only one facet of this question: namely, expectations regarding age-appropriate behavior and the timing of major life events. We began by asking, What is the psychological significance of a given chronological age? How does the person mark off and evaluate the passage of time? It is clear that people do not evaluate lifetime merely by reckoning the number of years since their birth. The statement, "I am 50 years old" has little significance; but, rather, "I am 50 years old and farther ahead than I expected to be," or "farther behind than other men in the same line of work." In such everyday phrases, the individual gives content and meaning to the passage of time, and he refers to an implicit normative system in comparing himself to others.

To understand this normative system we undertook some exploratory studies of age status, age norms, and age expectations, perceiving them as forming a cultural context against which to view the person's evaluation of lifetime. First we studied the extent to which there was consensus regarding age norms. We recognized that in a complex modern society, there are multiple systems of age status that characterize different institutions and that changes in age roles are not synchronous. (For example, in the political institutions of this society, a man is adult at 18 when he can vote; but in the family he is adult when he marries and becomes a parent, usually several years later than 18.) We asked if, nevertheless, there were an age-status system common to the society as a whole.

We interviewed a representative sample of 600 middle-aged and older people and found widespread agreement in response to questions like these:

What would you call the periods of life that people go through after they are grown up? At what age does each period begin for most people? What are the important changes from one period to the next?

We found that middle-aged people perceived adulthood as composed of four different life periods, each with its characteristic pattern of personal and social behavior: young adulthood, maturity, middle age, and old age. Progression from one period to the next was described along one of five dimensions: events in the occupational career; events of the family cycle; changes in health; changes in psychological attributes (e.g., "middle age is when you become mellow"); and/or changes in social responsibilities (e.g., "old age is when you let the other fellow do the worrying").

From these data it was possible to delineate the first gross outline of a system of age expectations that encompasses various areas of adult life. There appeared to be a set of social age definitions that provided a frame of reference by which the experiences of adult life were perceived as orderly and rhythmical. Although perceptions varied by sex and by social class (e.g., old age begins earlier in the perceptions of working-class than in middle-class people) there was nevertheless a striking degree of consensus (Neugarten & Peterson, 1957).

We next asked questions regarding age-appropriate and age-linked behaviors:

What do you think the best age for a man to marry? to hold his top job? for a woman to become a grandmother? What age comes to your mind when you think of a young man? an old man? When a man has the most responsibilities?

There was widespread consensus, also, in responses to items such as these that pertained to work, to family, and to other areas of life. To illustrate, most middle-class men and women agreed that the best age for a man to marry was from 20 to 25; most men should be settled in a career by 24 to 26; they should hold their top jobs by 40; be ready to retire by 60 to 65; and so on. There appears, then, to be a prescriptive time-table for the ordering of major events in the individual's lifeline. Age expectations seemed more clearly focused—that is, consensus was greatest—for the period of young adulthood, as if the normative system bears more heavily upon individuals as they move into adulthood than when they move into middle or old age. There was greater consensus with regard to age-appropriate behavior for women than for men, and again, consistent variation by social class. The higher the social class, the later the ages associated with all major life events.

We moved next to asking, How does this system of age-norms function? How is it demonstrated in the lives of people? We therefore asked respondents about actual occurrences: how old were they when they left their parent's home? married? had their first full-time job? their first child? grandchild? top job? retired? We found that the similarities between occurrences and norms were striking. In short, the actual timing of major life events, especially in young adulthood, tends to adhere to the prescriptive timetable. The normative system seems to function as a system of social control—as prods and brakes upon behavior. In other words, most people do things when they think they "should" do them; and they seem to follow a social clock that becomes internalized so that they can tell an interviewer readily enough if they are late, early, or on time with regard to major life events and with regard to various types of achievement.

We repeated these studies with other groups of respondents: with a group of young married men and women, all around age 25 who lived in a small midwestern city; with a group aged 70 to 80 who lived in a small New England community; with a sample of middle-class blacks who lived in a medium-sized midwestern city. Although some variations appeared, the same general patterns emerged in each set of data, indicating considerable consensus about these types of age norms and age expectations.

We also explored related questions. How do people learn the norms? What are the sanctions in the system, the types of social approval and disapproval that operate to keep people on time? How, in short, does this normative system operate as social control? We have various data showing that age deviancy is always of psychological significance to the individual, but we have not yet obtained good data on how the social mechanisms operate.

Given our conviction that age norms and age expectations constitute a system of social control, we worked out a method for pursuing the question, Do people vary in the degree of constraint they perceive with regard to those norms? We asked such questions as:

Would you approve of a woman who wears a two-piece bathing suit to the beach when she is 18? when she's 35? 55?

What about a woman who decides to have another child at 40?? at 35? at 30?
What about a couple who move across country to live near their married children when they are 40? 55? 75?

We found that middle-aged and old people see greater constraints in the age-norm system than do the young. They seem to have learned that age and age-appropriateness are reasonable criteria by which to evaluate behavior; that to be off-time with regard to major life events brings with it negative consequences. In the young there is a certain denial that age is a valid dimension by which to judge behavior (Neugarten, Moore, & Lowe, 1965).

We have begun to explore the psychological correlates of age-deviancy. For instance, in two studies of Army officers (the US Army is a clearly age-graded set of occupations, where the investigator can create an objective measure of who is on-time and who is off-time) it could be demonstrated that being off-time with regard to career has psychological and social accompaniments. On-time and off-time men differed not only with regard to evaluations of their careers, but also with regard to self-esteem, mobility aspirations, anticipated adjustment to retirement, perception of status in the civilian community, and degree of social integration in the community.

These investigations have been exploratory; some have been carried out as doctoral dissertations (in particular, those by Kenneth Olsen, John Lowe, Margaret Huyck, Helen Warren); not all have been completed; and the studies have not yet been integrated and prepared for publication, a task which lies ahead of us. The studies have been rewarding because we think we have begun to uncover one of the social frameworks that has gone unexplored by social scientists; to point to some of the dimensions by which social-psychological meanings are attributed to age and to time; and to provide a richer context for understanding the changes in behavior and in self-assessments that occur as the individual moves through adulthood. It has not been my purpose here to give a full account of these studies, but rather to use them to illustrate one aspect of expectations that warrants investigation and one way in which expectational frameworks can be studied.

To summarize: I have been interested in change over time in the lives of adults and in the role of personality in predicting patterns of aging. Within broad limits of social and biological conditions, an individual will grow old along a path that is predictable from earlier points in his life, and predictable from knowing something about his personality structure, his coping style, his success in adapting to earlier life events, and his expectations of life. The individual is his own translator and interpreter of experience; he creates his future and recreates his past; he measures his present against the past and against the expectations he has carried forward with him through time. Within that expectational framework he evaluates his situation not only against the present realities—of income, health, social interactions, freedoms and constraints—but also against an internalized social clock, a clock that reflects socially-created age norms and tells him if he is on time. Other aspects of expectational systems need investigation if we are to understand how the personality copes and adapts, and to better understand the enormous complexity of that task we call "successful aging."

## References

Cumming, E., & Henry, W. E. **Growing old.** New York: Basic Books, 1961.

Havighurst, R. J., Neugarten, B. L., & Tobin, S. S. Disengagement and patterns of aging. In B. L. Neugarten (Ed.), **Middle age and aging: A reader in social psychology.** Chicago: University of Chicago Press, 1968.

Moore, J. L., & Birren, J. E. Doctoral training in gerontology: An analysis of dissertations on problems of aging in institutions of higher learning in the United States, 1934-1969. **Journal of Gerontology,** 1971, **26,** 249-257.

Neugarten, B. L. & Associates. **Personality in middle and late life.** New York: Atherton Press, 1964.

Neugarten, B. L., Havighurst, R. J., & Tobin, S.S. Personality and patterns of aging. In B. L. Neugarten (Ed.), **Middle age and aging: A reader in social psychology.** Chicago: University of Chicago Press, 1968.

Neugarten, B. L., & Havighurst, R. J. Disengagement reconsidered in a crossnational context. In R. J. Havighurst, J. M. A. Munnichs, B. L. Neugarten, & H. Thomae (Eds.), **Adjustment to retirement.** Assen, Netherlands: Van Gorcum & Co., 1969.

Neugarten, B. L., & Peterson, W. A. A study of the American age-grade system. **In 4th Congress of the International Association of Gerontology,** Vol. III. Florence: Tito Mattioli, 1957.

Neugarten, B. L., Moore, J. W., & Lowe, J. C. Age norms, age constraints, and adult socialization. **American Journal of Sociology,** 1965, **70,** 710-717. (See also, Neugarten, B. L., & Moore, J. W. The changing age-status system. In B. L. Neugarten (Ed.), **Middle age and aging: A reader in social psychology.** Chicago: University of Chicago Press, 1968.

# 12

Character Lasts

# If You're Active and Savvy at 30, You'll Be Warm and Witty at 70.

Everybody hits rocky years, but a 40-year study of several dozen people shows how healthy personalities adapt from youth to prime to the mellow years. But elderly agony often has roots in youth.

Karen Beckhardt

If you're squared away emotionally and psychologically at age 30, you're likely to stay that way into your 70s. The reverse is also true. Young adults who are depressed, fearful, rigid and sickly are still troubled in life's last years.

Psychologists Henry Maas and Joseph Kuypers brought this finding out of an unusual study by the Institute of Human Development at the University of California in Berkeley. They and their colleagues are now analyzing facts on the personality development of several hundred San Francisco area residents over the past 40 years. By years of interviewing and testing the same people, and their children, the Institute is providing rare insight into the normal development of adults.

Such work fulfills an important goal of psychology. We need to discover the building blocks of a well-integrated personality and to isolate the characteristics and values that are most likely to guide us smoothly through a useful life. In so doing, the Berkeley team often finds that the boy is indeed the father of the man.

**Growth Stages.** Much of the Berkeley evidence now indicates that our personalities appear to be relatively stable throughout life. But another Institute psychologist, Norma Haan, finds that healthy individuals do adjust their personalities and values to reflect changes

throughout the life cycle. Haan compared the personalities of well-adjusted young and middle-aged adults to those of older persons. She learned that both groups had very similar traits, but they tended to rely upon different traits more heavily at specific stages of life.

Young and middle-aged adults attached the most value to intellectual traits and pursuits. They described themselves as interesting, objective persons with high intellectual aspirations. They were verbally fluent, socially poised and interested in a wide variety of subjects and activities.

These adults in their vigorous years valued themselves as dependable, productive, likeable and straightforward. While they also mentioned being warm, giving, and sympathetic, these characteristics came much lower on their self-description lists.

**Mellow Humor.** Haan's older subjects, in their 60s and 70s, emphasized other traits in themselves. They cared less for intellectualism and more for their capacity for intimacy and close interpersonal relations. The older persons were more protective of others and put high value on cheerfulness and gregariousness, and their sense of humor.

Only the older men valued their independence as much as young persons did. But they were more self-satisfied and had more consistent personalities

than the younger adults. They admitted, however, that they were probably less insightful and were more conventional thinkers than their younger counterparts.

Haan was somewhat surprised to find that the older women were more gregarious and responsive to humor than younger men and women. But they were more uncomfortable with uncertainity, less introspective, had lower aspirations and cared less about being powerful.

Haan speculated that the differences between ranking of personality traits among young and old persons reflects a realistic assessment of different life situations. Once older people have left the world of work, they must rely on personal relationships to fill the void. So they develop a desire for warm, empathic connections to spouses, children, grandchildren and friends.

**Trouble Years.** On the other hand, during the mainstream years from 20 to 50, those who are happiest and best adjusted are active participants in life. They are intellectually alert, socially assertive, engaged with environment and other people. They are rewarded by a sense of achievement and a sense of competence.

Haan found that everyone, no matter how well integrated, goes through some rough periods. For men the cobblestones come in early adulthood, when they have to match their occupational skills against others to earn their place in the breadwinner line. Women traveled the bumpiest road as teenagers, struggling to break ties to parents and family and to validate their own female attractiveness.

But for all the struggles and personality differences between ages, two basic personality characteristics were prized by successful persons of all ages. Both young and old stressed the importance of being a dependable, productive person. These two characteristics, reliability and capability, may form the stable core of a well-functioning personality. If so, for all the criticism against it, the Puritan Ethic may be the answer after all.

—Margie Casady

# 13

# Institutional Position of the Aged

## by Irving Rosow

This problem of old age has both practical and theoretical importance: practical because, as a growing social problem, older people affect our society and are in turn affected by it; theoretical insofar as they exemplify numerous issues of social theory, including problems of the life cycle, social roles, and adult socialization.[1]

In the interaction between the aging person and society, deprivation, dependency, and indifference impose strains on both the individual and the social order. Affluence only deepens our vexation with social problems and casts in sharp relief the controversies they evoke over the nature of our institutions, the goals of public policy, and the principles that govern the flow of equity, privilege, and honor in our society.

Older people arouse strains of social conscience. They have done the world's work and met the demands of life, only to fall prey in their later years to growing deprivation and dependence. They have not necessarily failed, so they are not personally responsible for their fate. Diffused in our midst with a quietly insistent presence, they personify uncomfortable issues of social justice. While we could resolve their problems with generosity and commitment, we have not chosen to do so. Thus, the moral dilemma they pose is of our own making and, by the same token, is within our power to dispel.

That the dilemma is one of values is abundantly clear. But this is not the entire picture. Major institutional forces are also at work which systematically undermine the position of older people in American society, depreciate their status, limit their participation, and channel them from the mainstream of social life. This is much less the case in simpler societies, but is increasingly true at an accelerating rate in modern, advanced nations. Thus, the progressive corrosion of the status of the aged is an unintended but direct result of larger social changes.

Analysis has shown that seven major institutional factors govern the status of older people in all societies. In addition to certain patterns of social organization, these concern various resources that old people command and functions they perform. The changes in modern American life have undermined these possible institutional supports and have relegated the aged to a weak position.

We can review these institutional forces briefly as background material for the ensuing analysis. We will simply summarize the broad picture in its most general terms without all the necessary qualifications and available documentation that a detailed treatment would clearly require. Here again, our concern is the forest, not the trees. With this clear caveat, the seven factors are as follows:

## Determinates of Status

### Property Ownership

Property has always been a major resource in providing the aged with security and independence. In simpler societies it also gave them substantial power over the life chances of the young and thereby a claim on their deference. But the power based on property has been weakened in the U.S. by the diffusion of ownership, the growing separation between ownership and management, and the proliferation of opportunities for the young in education and the economy. Thus, the power of the aged has been diluted at the same time that the opportunities of the young have become increasingly independent of them. Although property ownership may assure financial independence, it no longer means control over subordinate younger groups.

### Strategic Knowledge

The tremendous changes—and the *rate* of change —in modern science, technology, and automation steadily depreciate the knowledge, skills, and experience that make old people respected authorities in stable societies. New knowledge and techniques develop so rapidly and are so pervasive, running the gamut from electronic computers to child rearing, that successive generations become "obsolete" at progressively younger ages. The experience of the aged tends to become irrelevant and to count for less and less as radically new specialties and concepts become established. The old even lose their special qualification to instruct the young, who are increasingly trained by formal education and indoctrinated with attitudes and values by middle-age parents, the mass media, and their peers. Thereby the aged have no special claim to cultural

79

authority and are regarded neither as strategic teachers and models nor as respected founts of wisdom by younger groups.

## Productivity

The aged can preserve their social functions longest in low-productivity economies. Primitive technology with limited production tends to preserve the marginal utility of successive increments of labor. Although labor may be cheap, low productivity creates opportunities and functions for old people who are still able to add to the small gross product. But our economy is inordinately productive, and our problem is to maintain demand, not supply. The growth of technology and automation has generally eliminated labor shortages except in certain professions and special labor categories. Old people do not particularly command those new skills which are in short supply. Therefore, with high productivity and no general labor scarcity, their marginal utility in the labor force tends to be low. They have relatively poor employment prospects once they are out of work because their contribution to the economy is not highly valued.

## Mutual Dependence

High productivity has raised living standards and private resources; economic growth and governmental subsidies have also increased opportunities and personal autonomy. These have strengthened individual independence and self-sufficiency, thereby reducing people's reliance on others for help. This weakens mutual obligation and the constraints of reciprocity. As a result, the necessity of personal cooperation has declined, and the solidarity of mutual dependence has been undermined.[2] Self-concern has increased at the expense of group solidarity. Thus, prosperity and autonomy have weakened the informal mutual aid networks that have traditionally been the most important mechanisms for meeting the needs of older people. In a mass society, responsibility for them is becoming increasingly formalized, ritualized, and depersonalized as a public problem.[3]

## Tradition and Religion

In contrast to tradition-bound simpler cultures, we are an innovating society strongly dedicated to "progress." We have only a very limited heritage that present generations carry on and to which the aged are a meaningful link. Our predominant values are materialistic and secular rather than sacred, future- rather than past-oriented, and pragmatic rather than traditional. Hence, older people are not a viable symbol of historical continuity and respected tradition. Certainly they provide no religious ties to the gods, as they do in cultures with ancestor worship, such as the classical Chinese. Thus, social change militates against the traditional orientations that engender respect for the aged.

## Kinship and Family

Our present family structure has fragmented the multi-generation family and the kinship network that typified pre-industrial times. Such organized reciprocal obligations among relatives specifically included old people and respected their needs. But the modern occupational system has put a premium on smaller, mobile families, and these have become the norm. In this context, with increasing residential separation of different generations, obligations are ranked in a hierarchy of priority which leaves older people disadvantaged in comparison with younger generations.[4]

## Community Life

The division of labor and specialized roles underlying modern urban life have weakened those stable local community structures that effectively integrate older people in a broad range of age groups. This loosening of ties has been intensified by residential mobility, changing neighborhoods, and the common impersonality of urban environments. Consequently, local group life tends to be limited, ephemeral, and superficial rather than pervasive, durable, and binding. Hence, people's most significant associates commonly live outside their local neighborhoods.[5] But insofar as people's local dependencies increase as they age and their mobility is reduced, the purely local institutions tend to accommodate them poorly.[6]

In summary, the institutional forces that typically support the position of old people in simpler societies are inimical to them in our own. Paradoxically, our productivity is too high and our mutual dependence too low. We are too wealthy as a nation and too self-sufficient as individuals to need older people, and the significant social functions open to them are shrinking. This both reflects and reinforces other established cultural values, such as our greater concern for the young and our general youth-orientation.

# Consequences for Older People

## Devaluation

The consequences of these institutional patterns are clearly marked. First, the aged are generally devalued.[7] This is reflected in younger groups' negative attitudes, relative indifference to, or even rejection of the elderly. Their basic devaluation and its concomitants are absolutely basic factors in their prospective socilization to old age. We shall presently consider this.

## Stereotyping

Second, they are commonly viewed in stereotypes, as are other devalued minority groups. Thus, they are seen more as representatives of an age group than as individuals, and various negative characteristics are attributed to them.[8] Significantly, these images of the old are not confined to younger people alone, but are also widely shared by the aged themselves.[9] Old persons depreciate other aged persons, and in the same terms. Furthermore, these images of older people do not vary according to others' direct contact or experience with them, but tend to be fairly stable, regardless of exposure.[10] Hence, the stereotyped conceptions are not easily subject to change through direct association.

## Exclusion

Third, the aged are excluded from equal opportunities for social participation and rewards enjoyed by younger members of their social class, ethnic, or racial group.[11] To this extent, they become relatively disadvantaged in the later years and lose significant bases of their earlier social integration.

## Role Loss

Fourth, not the least of such attrition is their role losses.[12] This constitutes a conspicuous alienation from major family and work roles: through widowhood and retirement, through the damage to symbolic life styles from lower income after retirement, and through the general decline in health, which can impair sheer independence. Except for a minority who are disengaged, the loss of roles is mainly involuntary and unwelcome, even when illness forces retirement.[13] Role losses inevitably affect previous group memberships, lower prestige, and reduce one's status sets and the social integration that they provide the individual. We will return to this presently.

## Role Ambiguity

Fifth, role loss entails a sharp reduction of responsibility and a limitation of function, the net result of which is role ambiguity. There is comparatively little prescribed activity that attends old age. The role tends to be open, flexible, and unstructured.[14] It may be defined with a maximum of personal preference and individual choice. This seeming boon, however, calls heavily on people's initiative and inner resources in the absence of definite role expectations by others.[15] Such negative demands are not always easily met and may generate as much strain as do conflicting role pressures.[16] Indeed, role loss and ambiguity are generally quite demoralizing; they deprive people of their social identity and frequently affect their psychological stability.[17] The apparent freedom is often a burden because earlier in life, roles typically structured expectations, requirements, and activities for them.[18] Most workaday routines do not result from intention, but merely from occupying a particular social position and from several decisions at crucial points in the life cycle. The unstructured situations of later life are inherently depressing and anxiety-generating. Older people must fill the vacuum of social expectations with personal definitions, and they must develop private standards in the absence of established norms for them. Many of the elderly respond to their devaluation and ambiguous role by clinging to youthful norms as a means of dealing with the new uncertainties.

## Youthful Self-Images

Finally, older people also cling to youthful self-images. Or, as Bernard Baruch expressed it, "To me old age is always fifteen years older than I am." One of the most consistent findings of surveys of old people is their refusal to acknowledge that they are old.[19] Most of them claim that they consider themselves as middle-aged or young.[20] And the older they are, the later they think that "old age" begins.[21] This indicates a deep and widening split between older people's self-images and the conceptions that others have of them. Indeed, the discrepancy between these perspectives and old people's self-images inevitably creates a strain. Nonetheless, it reflects how much the aged accept the larger views and values of their society.

In summary, the position of the elderly has several consequences: they are devalued, viewed in invidious stereotypes, excluded from social opportunities; and they lose roles, confront severe role ambiguity in later life, and struggle to preserve self-esteem through youthful self-images.

1. The analysis in this section is based upon an earlier publication, Irving Rosow, "Old Age: One Moral Dilemma of an Affluent Society," *Gerontologist,* 2 (1962) 182–91.

2. For an analysis of how proliferating opportunities may weaken primary group ties, see Irving Rosow, "Affluence, Reciprocity and Solidary Bonds," paper prepared for the Biennial Meeting of the International Society for the Study of Behavioral Development: Ann Arbor, August, 1973.

3. Indeed, the steady shift of responsibility for aged parents from their children to the state has been stimulated by the courts in rulings that establish the prior claims of adult children's self-advancement over the needs of their parents. See Alvin Schorr, *Filial Responsibility in the Modern American Family* (Washington: Social Security Administration, 1960).

4. Cf. Talcott Parsons, "Revised Analytical Approach to the Theory of Social Stratification," in Reinhard Bendix and Seymour Lipset (eds.), *Class, Status and Power* (Glencoe: Free Press, 1953) 92–128; "The Social Structure of the Family," in Ruth Anshen (ed.), *The Family: Its Function and Destiny* (New York: Harpers, 1949) 173–201. On the other hand, Eugene Litwak argues that the modern extended family retains significant cohesion, viability and mutual aid, even in the face of major geographic and social mobility ("Geographic Mobility and Extended Family Cohesion," *American Sociological Review,* 25 [1960] 385–94). Aside from important weaknesses which may be criticized in the sample at Litwak's disposal, he focuses on family solidarity in meeting sundry crises, such as major illness or financial aid in securing a child's college education. While this may be true, this is drastically different from the cohesion which develops from continued proximity. Sustained

daily interaction results in viable group living and integration of older people in family groups, as opposed to the intermittent help to overcome emergencies. Indeed, Peter Townsend finds that in the face of intergenerational occupational and social mobility, the meaningful emotional ties between generations in a family become strained, ritualized and atrophied in contrast to the sustained solidarity when mobility does not disrupt family structure and interaction (*Family Life of Old People* [London: Routledge and Kegan Paul, 1957]). And social contact and interaction are indispensable to morale (Bernard Kutner, *et al. Five Hundred Over Sixty* [New York: Russell Sage, 1956]; Sheldon Tobin and Bernice Neugarten, "Life Satisfaction and Social Interaction in the Aging," *Journal of Gerontology*, 16 [1961] 344–46). Townsend's evidence sharply contradicts Litwak's case. The entire problem is quite subtle and difficult to resolve without careful research that can cut through ritualistic behavior to establish its significance for the participants. Recent work, however, has clearly called into question the extreme formulations of Parsons on the extent of nuclear family isolation within larger kinship networks. See the Duke University symposium on this problem: Ethel Shanas and Gordon Streib (eds.), *Social Structure and the Family: Generational Relations* (Englewood Cliffs, N.J.: Prentice-Hall, 1965).

5. Joel Smith, William Form and Gregory Stone, "Local Intimacy in a Middle-Sized City," *American Journal of Sociology*, 60 (1954) 276–84.

6. Wendell Bell and Marion Boat, "Urban Neighborhoods and Informal Social Relations," *American Journal of Sociology*, 62 (1957) 391–98; Irving Rosow, "Retirement Housing and Social Integration," *Gerontologist*, 1 (1961) 85–91, also in Clark Tibbitts and Wilma Donahue (eds.), *Social and Psychological Aspects of Aging* (New York: Columbia University Press, 1962) 327–40; Joel Smith, William Form and Gregory Stone, *op cit.*

7. Milton Barron, "Minority Group Characteristics of the Aged in American Society," *Journal of Gerontology*, 8 (1953) 447–82; Raphael Ginzberg, "The Negative Attitude toward the Elderly," *Geriatics*, 7 (1952) 297–302; Peggy Golde and Nathan Kogan, "A Sentence Completion procedure for Assessing Attitudes toward Old People," *Journal of Gerontology*, 14 (1959) 355–63; Bertram Hutchinson, *Old People in a Modern Australian Community* (Carlton, Australia: Melbourne University Press, 1954); Maurice Linden, "Effects of Social Attitudes on the Mental Health of the Aging," *Geriatrics*, 12 (1957) 109–14; Joost Meerloo, "Some Psychological Problems of the Aged Patient," *New York State Journal of Medicine*, 58 (1959) 3810–14.

8. Joseph Drake, "Some Factors Influencing Students' Attitudes toward Older People," *Social Forces*, 35 (1957) 266–71; Raphael Ginzberg, *op. cit.*; Joost Meerloo, *op. cit.*; Jacob Tuckman and Irving Lorge, " 'When Aging Begins' and Stereotypes about Aging," *Journal of Gerontology*, 8 (1953) 489–92.

9. Milton Barron, *op. cit.*; Robert Havighurst and Ruth Albrecht, *Older People* (New York: Longmans & Green, 1953); Nathan Kogan, "Attitudes toward Old People in an Older Sample," *Journal of Abnormal and Social Psychology*, 62 (1961) 616–22; Nathan Kogan and Michael Wallach, "Age Changes in Values and Attitudes," *Journal of Gerontology*, 16 (1961) 272–80; Bernice Neugarten and David Garron, "The Attitudes of Middle-Aged Persons Toward Growing Older," *Geriatrics*, 14 (1959) 21–24; Jacob Tuckman and Irving Lorge, "Attitudes toward Older Workers," *Journal of Applied Psychology*, 36 (1952) 149–53 and "Old People's Appraisal of Adjustment over the Life Span," *Journal of Personality*, 22 (1953–54) 417–22; Jacob Tuckman, Irving Lorge and G. A. Spooner, "The Effect of Family Environment on Attitudes toward Old People and the Older Worker," *Journal of Social Psychology*, 38 (1953) 207–18; Irving Zola, "Feelings About Age Among Older People," *Journal of Gerontology*, 17 (1962) 65–68.

10. Joseph Drake, *op. cit.*

11. Wilma Donahue, Harold Orbach and Otto Pollak, "Retirement: The Emerging Social Pattern," in Clark Tibbitts (ed.), *Handbook of Social Gerontology* (Chicago: University of Chicago Press, 1960) 330–406; Margaret Gordon, "Aging and Income Security," in Clark Tibbitts (ed.) *op. cit.*, 208–60, "The Older Worker and Hiring Practices," *Monthly Labor Review*, 82 (1959) 1198–1205, and "Work and Patterns of Retirement," in Robert Kleemeier (ed.), *Aging and Leisure* (New York: Oxford University Press, 1961), 15–53; William Harlan, "Meaning of Economic Security to Older Persons," *Transactions of the Illinois State Academy of Science*, 44 (1951) 182–86; Irving Rosow, "Old Age: One Moral Dilemma of an Affluent Society"; Harold Sheppard, "Unemployment Experiences of Older Workers," *Geriatrics*, 15 (1960) 430–33.

12. Bernard Phillips, "A Role Theory Approach to Adjustment in Old Age," *American Sociological Review*, 22 (1957) 212–17; K. W. Schaie, "The Effect of Age on a Scale of Social Responsibility," *Journal of Social Psychology*, 50 (1959) 221–24.

13. Benjamin S. Prasad, "The Retirement Postulate of the Disengagement Theory," *Gerontologist*, 4 (1964) 20–23; Herbert Rusalem, "Deterrents to Vocational Disengagement Among Older Disabled Workers," *Gerontologist*, 3 (1963) 64–68.

14. Robert Havighurst, "Flexibility and the Social Roles of the Retired," *American Journal of Sociology*, 59 (1954) 309–11; Robert Havighurst and Ruth Albrecht, *op. cit.*; Aaron Lipman, "Role Conceptions and Morale of Couples in Retirement," *Journal of Gerontology*, 16 (1961) 267–71; Harold Orbach and David Shaw, "Social Participation and the Role of the Aging," *Geriatrics*, 12 (1957) 241–46; William Smith, Joseph Britten and Jean Britten, *Relations within Three-Generation Families*, Research Publication 155 (University Park, Pennsylvania: Pennsylvania State University, College of Home Economics, 1958); Richard Williams "Changing Status, Roles and Relationships," in Clark Tibbetts (ed.), *Handbook of Social Gerontology* (Chicago: University of Chicago Press, 1960) 261–97.

15. Woodrow Hunter and Helen Maurice, *Older People Tell Their Story* (Ann Arbor: University of Michigan, Division of Gerontology, 1953); Bertram Hutchinson, *op. cit.*

16. Leonard Cottrell, "Adjustment of the Individual to his Age and Sex Roles," *American Sociological Review*, 7 (1942) 617–20; Arnold Rose, *Theory and Method in the Social Sciences* (Minneapolis: University of Minnesota Press, 1954).

17. Alfred Heilbrun and Charles Lair, "Decreased Role Consistency in the Aged: Implications for Behavioral Pathology," *Journal of Gerontology*, 19 (1964) 325–29; Louis Leveen and David Priver, "Significance of Role Playing in the Aged Person," *Geriatrics*, 18 (1963) 57–63.

18. Leonard Goodstein, "Personal Adjustment Factors and Retirement," *Geriatrics*, 17 (1962) 41–45.

19. Milton Barron, "The Dynamics of Occupational Roles and Health in Old Age," in John Anderson (ed.), *Psychological Aspects of Aging* (Washington: American Psychological Association, 1956) 236–39; Zena Blau, "Changes in Status and Age Identification," *American Sociological Review*, 21 (1956) 198–203; Bernard Kutner, *et al., op. cit.*; Evelyn Mason, "Some Correlates of Self-Judgments of the Aged," *Journal of Gerontology*, 9 (1954) 324–37, and "Some Factors in Self-Judgments," *Journal of Clinical Psychology*, 10 (1954) 336–40; Bernice Neugarten and David Garron, *op. cit.*; S. Payne, "The Cleveland Survey of Retired Men," *Personnel Psychology*, 6 (1953) 81–110; Jacob Tuckman and Martha Lavell, "Self-Classification as Old or Not Old," *Geriatrics*, 12 (1957) 661–71; Jacob Tuckman and Irving Lorge, "Classification of the Self as Young, Middle-Aged or Old," *Geriatrics*, 9 (1954) 534–36; Jacob Tuckman, Irving Lorge and F. Zeman, "The Self-Image in Aging," *Journal of Genetic Psychology*, 99 (1961) 317–21; Irving Zola, *op. cit.*

20. Such youthful self-images are reflected in choices that people make in identifying themselves as young, middle-aged or old. These responses indicate preferences on an implicit value

scale where they accept society's youth orientation and the valuation of youthfulness. This may well be similar to the dilemmas of choice of identity and reference groups exhibited by other marginal groups. For example, light skinned Blacks often had the option of living as Blacks or of "passing" as white. It is an old story that in various self-assignments, whether on social class position or power in small groups, people tend to upgrade themselves in relation to assignments that others make of them. That is, they describe themselves as closer to the preferred social norm than others describe them.

And in their youthful self-images, older people also accept and reflect the dominant social norms about age.

21. Raymond Kuhlen and Everett Luther, "A Study of the Cultural Definition of Prime of Life, Middle Age, and of Attitudes toward the Old," *Journal of Gerontology*, 4 (1949) 324; Woodrow Morris, "Age Attitudes and Health," *Adding Life to Years*, 8 (March, 1961) 3–6; Jacob Tuckman and Irving Lorge, " 'When Aging Begins' and Stereotypes about Aging," *op cit.*, and "When Does Old Age Begin and a Worker Become Old?" *Journal of Gerontology*, 8 (1953) 483–88.

# III. Experiencing Later Life

Older persons, themselves, describe aging best. It is in their reports, or from the observations of those who have shared their lives for a period of time, that we may discover what it is like to be old and about the unique perspective that the aging have of the past and of the human lifespan.

Historical events that the young learn about in books or from the media—the Depression of the 1930s, the World Wars, the Prohibition Era—were experienced first-hand by the old. Today's aged have seen remarkable changes in technology and in society, and those of us who speculate about the quality of life in the present can find new insights from persons who grew up in a less-complicated past. Many older persons have also participated in another unique event—immigrations, whether from Europe or Asia to this country, or within this country from farm to city, or South to North; and these older persons are now our only personal link to the culture of our ancestors. Having seen the human comedy unfold across a lifetime, the aging may be able to share a rare wisdom with us.

Perhaps the first impression from the articles that follow is that these unique possibilities are rarely utilized. As the title to the selection by Curtin suggests, this is the "Land of the Young," where youth alone is valued and there is not time to listen to or care for the old. What does emerge in those who have been left alone or have been segregated among their own age peers, is their courage and sometimes feistiness in trying to maintain their dignity (Curtin, Trillin).

A second impression is the variety of their lives. As described in the previous section, the increasing individual differences which occur with aging are manifested in the thoughts, feelings, and life-styles of individuals. In these readings we meet two old hoboes (Curtin), a woman who lived and grew old in the rural South (Mitchell), a solidly middle-class couple who have made a comfortable retirement for themselves (Alberts), those who eke out a life from meager incomes amidst their age peers in Miami Beach (Trillin), a man who finds he is not too old to enjoy a motorcycle (Dougherty), and one of the founders of the study of aging in this country reflecting on his own career and life (Pressey).

Finally, there is the richness of the vision that they convey—whether reflecting on the sadness of a loss shared by brothers-in-law (Saul), or on the pleasures of art or music, or in looking over a lifetime of experiences. There is much to be gained by bringing the experience of the aging back into our consciousness, not as an occasional oddity, but as an integral part of human life.

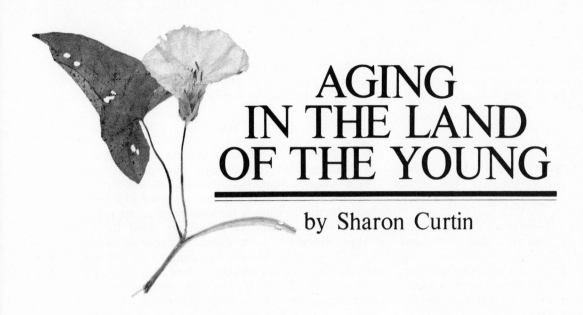

# 14

# AGING IN THE LAND OF THE YOUNG

## by Sharon Curtin

What burden are years if you have lived no more than thirty? The author has searched for answers from friends and strangers twice and three times her age, and writes of what it is like to learn the feeling of no longer growing, in a culture that worships youth.

1.

Old men, old women, almost 20 million of them. They constitute 10 percent of the total population, and the percentage is steadily growing. Some of them, like conspirators, walk all bent over, as if hiding some precious secret, filled with self-protection. The body seems to gather itself around those vital parts, folding shoulders, arms, pelvis like a fading rose. Watch and you see how fragile old people come to think they are.

Aging paints every action gray, lies heavy on every movement, imprisons every thought. It governs each decision with a ruthless and single-minded perversity. To age is to learn the feeling of no longer growing, of struggling to do old tasks, to remember familiar actions. The cells of the brain are destroyed with thousands of unfelt tiny strokes, little pockets of clotted blood wiping out memories and abilities without warning. The body seems slowly to give up, randomly stopping, sometimes starting again as if to torture and tease with the memory of lost strength. Hands become clumsy, frail transparencies, held together with knotted blue veins.

Sometimes it seems as if the distance between your feet and the floor were constantly changing, as if you were walking on shifting and not quite solid ground. One foot down, slowly, carefully, force the other foot forward. Sometimes you are a shuffler, not daring to lift your feet from the uncertain earth but forced to slide hesitantly forward in little whispering movements. Sometimes you are able to "step out," but this effort—in fact the pure exhilaration of easy movement—soon exhausts you.

The world becomes narrower as friends and family die or move away. To climb stairs, to ride in a car, to walk to the corner, to talk on the telephone; each action seems to take away from the energy needed to stay alive. Everything is limited by the strength you hoard greedily. Your needs decrease, you require less food, less sleep, and finally less human contact; yet this little bit becomes more and more difficult. You fear that one day you will be reduced to the simple acts of breathing and taking nourishment. This is the ultimate stage you dread, the period of helplessness and hopelessness, when independence will be over.

There is nothing to prepare you for the experience of growing old. Living is a process, an irreversible progression toward old age and eventual death. You see men of eighty still vital and straight as oaks; you see men of fifty reduced to gray shadows in the human landscape. The cellular clock differs for each one of us, and is profoundly affected by our own life experiences, our heredity, and perhaps most important, by the concepts of aging encountered in society and in oneself.

The aged live with enforced leisure, on fixed incomes, subject to many chronic illnesses, and most of their money goes to keep a roof over their heads. They also live in a culture that worships youth.

A kind of cultural attitude makes me bigoted against old people; it makes me think young is best; it makes me treat old people like outcasts.

Hate that gray? Wash it away!

Wrinkle cream.

Monkey glands.

Face-lifting.

Look like a bride again.

Don't trust anyone over thirty.

I fear growing old.

Feel Young Again!

I am afraid to grow old—we're all afraid. In fact, the fear of growing old is so great that every aged person is an insult and a threat to the society. They remind us of our own death, that our body won't always remain smooth and responsive, but will someday betray us by aging, wrinkling, faltering, failing. The ideal way to age would be to grow slowly invisible, gradually disappearing, without causing worry or discomfort to the young. In some ways that does happen. Sitting in a small park across from a nursing home one day, I noticed that the young mothers and their children gathered on one side, and the old people from the home on the other. Whenever a youngster would run over to the "wrong" side, chasing a ball or just trying to cover all the available space, the old people would lean forward and smile. But before any communication could be established, the mother would come over, murmuring embarrassed apologies, and take her child back to the "young" side.

Now, it seemed to me that the children didn't feel any particular fear and the old people didn't seem to be threatened by the children. The division of space was drawn by the mothers. And the mothers never looked at the old people who lined the other side of the park like so many pigeons perched on the benches. These well-dressed young matrons had a way of sliding their eyes over, around, through the old people; they never looked at them directly. The old people may as well have been invisible; they had no reality for the youngsters, who were not permitted to speak to them, and they offended the aesthetic eye of the mothers.

My early experiences were somewhat different; since I grew up in a small town, my childhood had more of a nineteenth-century flavor. I knew a lot of old people, and considered some of them friends. There was no culturally defined way for me to "relate" to old people, except the rules of courtesy which applied to all adults. My grandparents were an integral and important part of the family and of the community. I sometimes have a dreadful fear that mine will be the last generation to know old people as friends, to have a sense of what growing old means, to respect and understand man's mortality and his courage in the face of death. Mine may be the last generation to have a sense of living history, of stories passed from generation to generation, of identity established by family history.

2.

In a hill town in eastern Kentucky, I met an old woman called Granny Sukie. She was more than a hundred years old, according to her family, and now spent most of her time wrapped in a quilt sitting by the fireplace in the winter and on the porch in the summer. Granny Sukie was cared for by "Aunt" Mary, no blood relation but considered kin by marriage. Aunt Mary was pushing seventy when I first met her, and she told me she had been caring for "the old lady" for thirty years. Their relationship had begun quite naturally: Granny Sukie needed someone to care for her, and Aunt Mary needed somewhere to live.

Granny Sukie was blind now, had been for many years. But she knew her way around in the way only a woman who has cleaned and scrubbed every inch of space can know a house; and she knew every tree and shrub in the small yard the same way. She had planted them, had nurtured them, had watched them grow. Even though she could not see anymore, things in the area of her home remained so familiar that her step never faltered.

She told me one day, "The last years of a woman's life should be spent in trying to settle what's inside. Early on a woman is so filled with things outside—her looks and her husband, her children and her home—that she never has a chance to be just private. I've had more private time, now, than I need; but I value these years all the same. I miss readin' and I wonder sometimes if the hills have changed any. I've buried two husbands and three children . . . right up till now, my life's been good. But I wonder if Aunt Mary is gonna last long enough? Seems to me her arm feels thinner, and she isn't moving so quick. If Mary goes, I haven't much kin left . . . and if she gets sick, well, can I take care of her?"

Her face was so full of wrinkles and folds that sometimes I thought it would look the same upside down as right side up. Being blind had made her face appear eyeless, as if a sculptor's thumb had been drawn from temple to temple, leaving only a continuous deep crevice. She was tiny, so tiny I wondered if she would just shrink away. Compared to her body, her hands seemed outsized. They were still the hands of a homemaker; large, with red knuckles, the skin tightly drawn from washing clothes by hand with lye soap. Sometimes her hands would reach out as if looking for a job to do, a baby to bounce or a coat to mend. Those hands weren't used to being still. But now she spent her time dozing in her chair, wrapped in her quilt (she could tell stories about each of the *age, āj* n *fr. L.* aetas, *fr.* aevum, *lifetime 1. The part of an existence extending from the beginning to any given time. (Webster)*

pieces in the quilt. It was very old, so old that even Aunt Mary didn't know whether or not the stories were true), and living in a "private place" in her mind.

Granny Sukie and Aunt Mary lived on a stipend from the state welfare office called "Old Age Assistance." At the time, for the two of them, they received about $180 a month. The house was owned "outright," but they paid for taxes and insurance. The utility bill was negligible, since they cooked but one big meal a day on the old wood stove, and they went to bed with the sun and rose with the dawn, thus using very little electricity. They managed, with the small vegetable garden and a few pretty sad looking chickens, to eat fairly well. Neighbors frequently brought over fresh bread, or a pie, as was the custom in that part of the country. In fact, someone came by the house nearly every day, just to check on the old women and see that they were all right. They still had some family. They were as rich in resources as they were in years.

Some bright young man at the bank noticed one day that the signatures on the welfare checks were identical and he called the welfare office. That office, failing to find anything out from the old ladies, had asked that a member of the family look into the matter.

Aunt Mary was, quite properly, furious that someone would suspect that she was trying to cheat Granny Sukie. She straddled a worn spot in the linoleum, looking for all the world like an ancient sea turtle, her head darting from side to side and her eyes shining, and her low-built, almost legless body never moving an inch. Damn right, she signed both the checks. Did those fools in that office think the old lady could read and write, her with no sight for thirty-more years? She always knew those ladies-aide women or social women or whatever you called them wouldn't give something for nothing. What did they want? The house? Granny's jewelry? Were they going to send her, send Aunt Mary, to jail so's they could come and drag Granny away and take it all? You never got something for nothing, she knew it, always knew it, shouldn't have started accepting the money in the first place. Well, she'd pay back every last cent. She'd never done nothing dishonest . . .

Aunt Mary against the society of social officialdom was something to see. She had done nothing wrong and that was that. "They" had offered *them* the money; a busy woman with a leather case like a man's came out one day, years ago, and filled out some papers. The money came to the letter box every month, and once in a while some snoopy lady would come and ask questions, refusing tea or any refreshment like she was too good . . . Social officials were simply routed. First of all, Aunt Mary had no idea of their existence. She wouldn't talk to them. And sec-

ond, to stop the checks now would mean someone had been making an error every month for years. So the old sea turtle beat the great black birds. In the little house in the gentle hills, things go on much as they have for years. Agelessly aging.

3.

I decided to spend some time in the hotel because of the sign painted on the building: Pensioners Welcome. The sign meant just this: the owners would accept pensioners as lodgers, not provide any special service or anything. They would tolerate old men and women. The hotel itself was located in an unlovely section of a singularly unlovely city, full of small hotels, greasy spoons, liquor stores that advertise specials on muscatel and Tokay wines, and over all was a feeling of decay.

If the owner had had any sense and any insurance coverage, he would have been out looking for a good arsonist. The building seemed structurally sound—at least, it didn't lean—but the minute you walked inside the door, you could smell it, feel it: the place couldn't be saved. There are some buildings where too much has happened, where the walls can't support any more life. They are full, finished.

My own mood as I walked down the street was like that of the hotel. I felt finished, depressed, abandoned. I had begun research on the problems of old people, had spent three weeks working in a nursing home and a month as a visiting nurse, and was very full of other people's misery. My marriage had not long before been declared a disaster, and I was just beginning to come out of numbness into the real despair. I had been able to sit for hours, for days, without moving, just staring straight ahead. Now I was trying hard to "pull myself together" and "straighten UP." I felt like the old people I was trying to understand: sick and lonely and wondering if it was worth the trouble to take another breath.

The carpet in the lobby had once had an elaborate pattern, maybe even colorful, like that found in old movie theaters. Time and dirt had erased everything but shadows. Here and there a certain brightness in the pattern suggested the past presence of some piece of furniture, but now there was only the clerk's desk in one corner and some uncomfortable chairs. A few old men sat around, successfully blending in with the walls and furniture.

I walked in carrying my own burden of loneliness. It seemed like an appropriate place for me, at the time, even if I wasn't a pensioner. I needed a totally new and undemanding environment. I wanted to be someplace where nothing reminded me of normal happy things; someplace where a deep, ragged sigh would not sound unusual. The lobby was still, so quiet it seemed to be waiting for an earthquake or a

thunderstorm. It was an empty quietness, somehow, not the quiet of content or the stillness that follows good conversation, but just the absence of sound.

The desk clerk was a hostile cretin. He did not talk but interrogated. Was I from welfare? From the state? The city? What agency did I represent? Whom was I investigating? Anything I wanted to know, I could ask him. No sense bothering the old fools. Was I a cop? Maybe some kind of fed? Well, what did I want?

"A room. With bath, if you have it."

The clerk was not accustomed to listening, unless it was through a keyhole. Direct human communication seemed impossible. His face was webbed; in fact, the wrinkles were so dense that it seemed all expression was caught in a net.

"We don't handle day trade, lady. This here is a resident hotel. But maybe we can make a deal . . ."

Behind me I could feel ears straining to hear every word. I began to realize that the desk clerk knew of only two kinds of young women who could come to that hotel: social workers and hookers. Either way, he was out to make a buck, as long as he was protected. I knew I was blushing, and embarrassment made me angry. He had rooms available; I had seen the sign in the window. He was also the kind of person you couldn't let get by with anything. He was a small-time, small-brained creep; but he would be capable of sneaking up to my room with a passkey, or peeking through the keyhole, or making a grab as I walked by.

Anger was a dangerous emotion, because I was so hurt and confused over the direction my life was taking that I could not control rage. I would have cheerfully murdered that man, and something in my face must have frightened him. I repeated my request, quietly, not daring to look into his face because of my own anger, and he quickly closed a deal. A room, shared bath, two weeks in advance, $40. He overcharged me.

As I closed the door of the room behind me, I almost regretted my persistence. I didn't mind being considered a dirty young lady so much as I minded living like one. I knew country poor, but not city poverty. The room was about 8 by 10 feet, just large enough for a bed, a bureau (the top covered by the scars of lonely drinking bouts, hundreds of circles left by wet glasses, and the edge marked by forgotten cigarettes) and a straight-backed chair. The room wasn't noticeably clean, but someone had been very generous with a scented spray. No obvious signs of insect occupation. It was a tiny, smelly, ugly room.

I was also worried about my motives for being there. I wasn't particularly interested in social reform, and I wasn't a reporter. I liked old people, and was interested in the problems of aging, but I didn't intend to make it my life's work. I had thought about writing a book, about organizing old people as a revolutionary political force, because it seemed to me they were natural revolutionaries. They had time, and nothing to lose. But most of this was speculation, idle thought. Why was I here in this pensioners' hotel, populated by forty or so old, poor, independent people?

Why was I there? Partly, the atmosphere of the place suited me. Like the old people there, I guess I felt more abandoned than independent. Oh, I could manage. But it wasn't as if I had a choice, really. The place was right for me and for the old people who lived there. It was a kind of junkyard for rejected human beings.

When I had come upstairs the lobby had been buzzing. The conflict and hatred between myself and the clerk had been quite obvious. I hoped this would make the old men feel they could trust me, but I had no idea how to approach them. I felt stiff, awkward; I didn't know the rules observed by people who lived this way. I didn't want to hurt or embarrass anyone, and I couldn't afford to be hurt or embarrassed myself. I couldn't offer to pay someone to let me follow them around. (Excuse me, sir. I am doing research on dirty old men. Could I step into your shoes for a week? For a price? No? Why not? Because, even here at the bottom, you have a right to privacy and a right to choose your own company. Right, sir.) I felt they might be more friendly outside, maybe in one of the local diners.

I met Harry and Al over a salt shaker on the corner. They were both in their seventies, old enough and tough enough so that they remain difficult to describe. They looked alike, stringy in body and sour of face, with eyes that were never still. After a while I noticed that Harry did most of the talking, because Al seemed to have a slight drool, perhaps the result of a stroke. They had both been drifters since the Depression. Though ancient, they retained the moves of much younger men; like good athletes, they had learned to care for their bodies, to conserve their energies, to keep moving. I was impressed with their strength from the very beginning. They had nothing, hadn't ever been much, loved no one, and regretted nothing. They accepted things in a way that was difficult for me to understand.

Harry and Al didn't exactly seek my company, but they agreed to spend some time with me after I convinced them that I sincerely believed they had something to teach me, that I wasn't trying to cheat them, and that I wasn't any "do-gooder" either. They were pretty contemptuous of the human race in general, not having generous natures themselves, but were especially suspicious of "guv'ment do-gooders." I think

*The latter part of life; an advanced period of life;
also, seniority; state of being old. ("Nor wrong mine
age with this indignity." Shakespeare)*

their final analysis of me was that I was a fairly harmless crank.

That first afternoon we spent in a nearby park. They had one bench they always sat on, close to the street so they wouldn't lose the comforting smell of the city. Both men hated the country; they distrusted anything that looked too close to the earth. I would lie on the grass and they were both convinced I would die of worms or some other dread disease. They never saw any contradiction between this and the fact that they continually itched and scratched from various bug bites.

We agreed to meet in the morning outside their room in the hotel. I glanced in when Harry opened the door; the room was so small that they had to turn sideways and scuttle to move between the beds; they had no bureau, and clothing was simply tossed in piles around the room. Everything seemed both dusty and water-stained, like a very old and slightly leaky tomb. They wore the same clothing every day. It never seemed to get any dirtier or cleaner; maybe they each had several outfits in the same stage of filth and disrepair.

A day with Harry and Al always started with coffee and a doughnut at a diner twelve blocks away, to which one walked. Twelve blocks, in the morning, before coffee. All three of us would silently move down the cement wrapped in our own misery. I felt sorry for myself. Harry tried to move in a way to minimize the pain in a bad knee. Al would blink, blink, mutter, and wipe his mouth every fifth step. The reason we went twelve blocks was that in that diner one could buy day-old pastries: 15 cents fresh, 7 cents day old; coffee 10 cents, refill for a nickel. That was breakfast. No talking. Everyone in the diner was in the same state of early-morning sorrow, that moment of gathering strength to face a day over which one has no control. You have to be ready for anything, surprised by nothing.

Neither man was on any kind of public assistance. Al insisted he had tried to get aid and had been turned down. Harry didn't say much, but my guess is that he had some reason for failing to apply; maybe a family abandoned somewhere or jail time not yet served. Their days were spent scurrying around the city, like chiggers under the skin of civilization. They lived by panhandling and petty thievery (mostly shoplifting), occasionally taking a job "on the docks" or washing cars or with a moving company that hired day labor for a buck an hour, a quarter kicked back. In my honor they free-lanced a few days. They showed me how to work a street: at the stoplights, each would rush a car, preferring two women or an older couple in it, wipe the windshield, and ask for money. Refusal meant they had a right to hurl unspeakable obscenities in the "customer's" face. Working the street usually meant more money than

just straight panhandling, but sometimes you would be hassled by the cops. And you didn't do it when high school kids were on their way home. (Both men were terrified of teen-age males. It was an almost mystical terror, like primitive devil fear. They would rather be hassled by cops than by teen-age boys.)

I tried panhandling. I was terrible at it. Harry said I asked as if I expected to be refused, and didn't deserve any help. He was a master. He could make himself look older, yet still proud. He would shuffle up, plant himself in front of the "mark" as if by accident, and say, "I's old, cold, hungry. Can't work, bad knee. Could you give me a little change to get to the Veterans Hospital?" It always worked. I think Harry usually chose to ask older affluent men, men who were facing their own retirement and old age. They would give him money just to get him out of the way. Al would hit on women. With his drool and slightly lopsided appearance, he frightened money out of them.

Actually, I think they preferred to work rather than panhandle. But some days, physical labor was impossible for them. So they would beg. Or steal. One of the reasons Harry and Al finally accepted me was that I was a better shoplifter than they were. They were obviously out to steal. I could go into one of the big supermarkets, pass for a shabby student or maybe a sloppy housewife, and come out with enough food for lunch every day. I also tried to get them some new clothes—shirts, sweaters, underwear—but they promptly sold everything I gave them.

We lived in a pretty tight little world, the three of us. I began to find myself neglecting to bathe at night, and leaving my hair in braids instead of washing it. Since we did the same thing everyday, I wore the same clothes. Just like Harry and Al.

People would really stare at the three of us. At first I was self-conscious, but I learned to stop *feeling* their eyes. I didn't need anything from them, and they didn't need anything from me. Just like Harry and Al.

We shared a boundless contempt for the hotel clerk. Harry called him the "Gutless Wonder," because he would steal from anyone, even the dying. Harry told me about the man who had been in my room, lived there a long time, slowly dying.

"There lay old Eddie, dying inch by inch, and swearing he didn't want to go to the city hospital. He knew they'd do some dreadful experiments or something, and he wanted to die in peace. So we would bring him food and medicine. But the Gutless Wonder couldn't wait to figure what was in it for him. You know how he charges 10 percent of value to cash checks? Well, pretty soon, he was taking 50 percent of Eddie's check, plus room rent, plus something for not calling the hospital. And when Eddie died, old Gutless stole his clothes. Would have taken his teeth, too, but they stopped him. Man oughtn't be buried without his teeth, even if he is buried by the city."

Gutless did steal everything he could. Besides charging me four times the normal rent for my room, he had another small business on the side. Some of the winos in the area would give the hotel as their home address to the welfare office, and their checks would come there. But they preferred to stay on the street or in the cheaper flophouses which were unacceptable to the welfare department. Gutless would report that they lived in the comparative opulence of the "Pensioners Welcome" hotel, accept the mail, split the checks with the winos, and everyone was happy. The drunks could afford to drink, welfare could feel it was performing a social service by keeping drunks off the streets, and Gutless had more money. What he did with it was beyond me; he lived in two rooms off the lobby, dressed like the other old men, and was too unimaginative to have any expensive vices.

Since I was able to steal lunch, Harry and Al spent hours in the park with me, just taking it easy, talking about their lives, other people in the hotel, the world in general. They didn't believe in God or Man or the Devil, yet were capable of mouthing the most awful sanctimonious and patriotic clichés. I began to think they never had an original thought or noble moment. Everything about them—their faces, their bodies, their minds, their souls—was stunted and soiled. They lacked the ability even to *experience* their lives as real. Harry and Al were professional survivors. They saw only what was directly in front of them, they asked no questions, felt no anger, demanded no love; they just made do, just kept body and soul together. They reminded me of a couple of antique cockroaches, those marvelous insects that no amount of civilization can kill. Cockroaches survive everything; and so had Harry and Al. But at what a price. They had paid by giving up almost all human softness or warmth. I would sit on the park bench and wonder if that was the only way to survive, if you have to stop feeling, stop loving, stop caring, in order to live. It was frightening, but the longer I stayed around the hotel, the more convinced I became that nobody cared.

At the same time, I was aware that Harry and Al liked me. When I was more depressed than usual, they would try to cheer me up. They would tell horrible corny jokes, and even talk to me in the morning. Their efforts were awkward, but they tried to be my friend. And friendship was their one decent instinct. They had total loyalty and friendship for one another. It wasn't love that kept them together, but something stronger. Need. They had met on the road about twenty years previously, and discovered that as a team they were able to survive with less trouble. Two men could cover more ground panhandling; two heads knew twice as many diners where you got bread and butter with soup, not just crackers; two men could work both sides of the street. And if there were two of them, they were less vulnerable to attack when tired or weak or asleep.

Their friendship for each other was really the only thing these two had; life had knocked everything else out. I began to be afraid I would disrupt their lives in some awful way, that I was disturbing some precarious equilibrium, some carefully nurtured blindness and insensitivity which enabled them to survive. The other old men in the hotel began to tease them, asking which one I preferred.

One night in the local Mom's Café I tried to talk about all this with the boys. Those "Mom's Café" signs mean that for 99 cents you get a complete meal—soup or salad, meat loaf, potatoes, gravy, dessert, coffee. The soup is watered-down canned soup, just like Mom's in the Depression. And the meat loaf is mostly bread crumbs. But the good places serve things hot and give you extra coffee free. So Mom's was a treat.

The problem was my inability to accept the responsibility of their friendship. I couldn't guarantee loyalty or support. I was just passing through.

Harry and Al stared dumbly into their coffee as I tried to explain my problem. They sensed my fear, maybe even before I did. The more I tried to talk, the sorrier I sounded. Before long I was ready to cry, ready to say I would take them home and take care of them forever and they wouldn't have to live like this anymore. I don't think I really meant it—I wasn't ready to give that much yet—I just felt so damn guilty about being young enough to leave that hotel and that neighborhood and live another way.

When Harry began to talk, his voice was so low I could barely hear. He and Al knew I was worried about them, knew I thought they should be different, better than they were. But they had learned to live one way and that was that. They liked it. Couldn't ask for more, couldn't settle for less. It was their way. But not mine. Besides, they didn't need me, didn't need my sentimentality. They had one another.

Their greatest fear was being so disabled or so sick they wouldn't be able to get on their feet again. Little things they could handle between them: the days Harry's knee wouldn't work, Al would do the running. But they didn't want to end up as "vegetables."

So like Huck and Tom they had cut their thumbs and sworn that if one became so ill that complete recovery was a remote possibility, the other would smother him with a pillow.

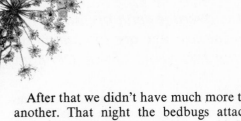

After that we didn't have much more to say to one another. That night the bedbugs attacked in full force and I packed my carpetbag and left old Gutless Wonder with two days' rent paid in advance.

4.

We walked slowly through the pretend garden, just a narrow walk surrounded by tiny evergreen bushes and casually placed rock. The old woman clutched my arm and begged to be taken back to her room. She was too weak to walk, too tired, she didn't want to be outside. I was younger, stronger, pulling her along, ignoring her plea. She needed to exercise, needed to be out of that place; if she just stayed in bed she would soon die. Walk, I told her, walk. You must get your strength back. Come on, I said, tugging not so gently now and hearing my voice impatient, you simply must move around.

She had been my friend. We had met months before at a lecture when, bored and feeling guilty, both of us had tried to leave the hall without being noticed and collided in the doorway. I had smiled because she looked so startled, like a child caught with forbidden sweets. "It's like leaving church in the middle of a sermon," I said. "You feel you've offended God." We laughed and left the building together.

There was seventy years' difference in our ages. We shared a mild cynicism, met frequently for lunch, and tore apart the reputation and motives of public figures. She considered herself a conservative, I was a radical. Nothing ever changes, she would say, you must save the things that are good and familiar, otherwise people become confused and destroy everything. Nobody has ever tried to change *enough,* I would retort; everything must change if the world is to be a fit place to live.

And so we would talk. She was ninety-six years old. Her passion was bridge. She liked order, quiet, things properly arranged. For thirty years she had taught mathematics to uninterested high school students; she had never found a pupil, she said one day, who could understand the beauty of numbers, of problems neatly solved, how beautiful the arrangement of a difficult problem on a page. That was the only time I ever heard her express an unfulfilled hope. She had been one of the first women to graduate from Stanford University and still wore her hair cut in a boyish bob, a style once considered a threat to home and family and country. Deep-set, lively blue eyes peered at the world with stubborn distrust. I think she had been beautiful, the bones of her face cleaned of superfluous flesh, her aquiline nose stretching out and the nostrils flaring with each breath. She was rather like mathematics; a cipher, a code, a human being pared down to the essential

parts. Nothing sloppy or sentimental about Miss Larson. She was ninety-six years old, a maiden lady without family and with few friends.

After she was forced to retire from teaching she moved into a private residence club and lived there for thirty years. Her life was orderly—I was the first new variable, she said, in twenty years. She desired nothing, lacked nothing, did what she pleased in the order she pleased. She thought my life utter chaos, my politics anarchy, my appearance slovenly, my habits unhealthy. I thought her rigid, frozen, unemotional, detached; I once told her I thought I injected a bit of healthy dirt into her life. I was very fond of her and had no idea why she tolerated me.

She became ill during a bridge tournament. That morning, Miss Larson had wakened early, excited and looking forward to a long day of playing her favorite game with first-rate opponents. She was conscious of mild nausea and a sharp pain in her side. But she was old and accustomed to functioning with occasional discomfort. Just excitement, she told herself as she carefully dressed. The pain in her side was enough to make her move carefully and slowly. I am ninety-six years old, she thought, and I still get a catch in my side when I am excited. I remember my first day of teaching, it was the same thing. I couldn't eat, felt so weak, and those high school boys all looked so huge and menacing. Well, I soon showed them who ruled the classroom. And today, well, today I feel I am going to play fine bridge.

She did play fine bridge that day, and when the final cards were played, she asked that someone call her doctor. She felt too faint to stand and the pain had become a grasping, digging presence, making breathing difficult. An ambulance was called, and she went directly from six hours of tournament bridge to the hospital operating room. Miss Larson had gallstones.

The operation was a complete success, no physical difficulties were experienced, she simply entered what she later referred to as her "psychedelic stage." Three days after surgery, the night nurses were surprised to hear a loud, argumentative voice coming from her room. When they entered, they found her standing by her bed shaking her fist at a corner of the room and demanding that her pupils pay attention to the algebra lesson. She was confused when confronted by the nurses and began to cry. Throughout that night and early morning, the staff found it necessary to keep someone in the room.

The next morning, the doctor ordered private-duty nurses twenty-four hours a day for Miss Larson, and she became the first patient I had cared for in four years. She found this very amusing, during her lucid moments, because we had often argued about my reasons for disliking nursing.

"I see things," she announced to me that first

*The period equal to the average span of human life:*
*generation ("Actions of the last age are like almanacs*
*of the last year." John Denham)*

morning. "I think someone gave me some drug. At night, when the hospital is sound asleep, I wake and the room is filled with colors, with dimly remembered faces, with funny music. Sometimes I will find myself talking quite lucidly to someone who just isn't there, someone who died a long time ago. I feel one moment like I am five years old, and my father is holding me on his lap; or I am on a train and have cinders in my eyes. Last night I taught my first class all over again—and, oh, I didn't want to do it then or now. I argued with my father about going to graduate school. 'I must,' I told him. 'I can be a really great mathematician.' But as I was talking to him, his face became a rainbow and slid off down the wall and he disappeared. The nurses came in . . . if they've given me some drug, for experiments, they should tell me. It isn't fair, I shouldn't have to relive all that again. If every night for the rest of my life is going to be this way; if all my dreams are going to be distortions of the past, with time and color and everything all running together, I would just as soon die now. I can't do it all again, I can't be that strong all over again, not now. Not after all these years."

During the day she was fine, if tired and dozing most of the time. But when darkness came she entered a shadowy world, a world seen only by her. In hospitals they call it "sundowning" and it is a common thing with old people when they are removed from a familiar environment and placed in the hospital. The darkness, the lack of familiar things around them, the strange sounds from the corridors cause a sort of sensory confusion which brings on hallucinations. Usually the simple act of turning on a nightlight will chase away the shadows, and the old people will sleep. But in Miss Larson's case, a light was not enough. For ten days her nights were filled with horrors, and her days spent in exhausted, fitful dozing. She seemed well on her way to becoming a senile old lady.

But gradually the lucid moments became more frequent, and she began to beg to be taken home. The hospital was a malignant presence to her, a place filled with ghosts and sudden, unexplained noises in the night. She was coherent but unreasonable in her demands. She could not walk, could barely stand without help. She continued to be suspicious of all nurses, but she had always been suspicious. She was extremely demanding, even more so after she discovered the private-duty nurses received $40 a shift. She expected to receive her money's worth. The night nurse quit after Miss Larson caught her dozing in a chair and threw a pitcher of water in that general direction.

The next morning her doctor announced that, owing to her slow recovery and the general overcrowding in the hospital, she must consider moving to a convalescent hospital. Since she lived alone, she must be physically able to care for herself before discharge. Meals and maid service were available in the residence club, but no personal care. Now Miss Larson became really upset. She had friends who had simply disappeared in such places; she believed people went there when there was no chance for recovery. "Death houses for the old," I heard her mutter. "I'll go to the street first." But it wasn't as if she really had a choice. The hospital needed her bed for acutely ill patients, and other facilities were available for long-term care.

The doctor informed the nursing staff and the hospital social worker that Miss Larson was to be transferred to an "extended-care facility." He recommended several places in the vicinity, and the social worker came to talk to her.

"Social Worker." A strange title and an even stranger woman. Her job at this particular hospital consisted in finding places to send people who were no longer in need of intensive nursing care, who could not be helped by all the technology gathered in a modern hospital, who were, in short, no longer medically interesting or likely to improve drastically. The job was more like that of a travel agent, and Miss Larson was convinced that this woman was selling only one-way tickets.

"You're very lucky, Emily, my, you don't look ninety-six years old, we've found a perfectly lovely place just down the block from here, a new place run by perfectly lovely competent people recommended by your doctor. Everything will be taken care of before you leave here; I just need a few answers to some simple questions and you can be moved immediately, and doctor says you are to have nurse with you for a few days until you get used to the change. . . . Now, Emily, if you will just tell me your social security number . . . Is she listening to me?"

"I think she turned off her hearing aid when you called her by her first name. She regards that as impertinent; she doesn't want to go to this place, and I don't blame her for being uncooperative," I answered. "If you need any information, it should be on her admission forms here. I think Miss Larson understands that she is being moved on orders from her doctor, and there isn't much we can do. But she doesn't feel any need to be polite."

"Doctor says . . ." The woman was only doing her job. I didn't want to be rude, but she showed no understanding of the crushing blow Miss Larson had received. For years, she had managed to avoid a nursing home, and now, through the benevolence of Medicare, she was eligible for, and forced to accept, institutionalization. There was no way the social worker could sugarcoat the pill, no family she could smile at and be helpful to, no gratitude from the withdrawn old lady in the bed.

First impressions of Montcliffe Convalescent Hospital were favorable. It was small, just thirty-six patients, and fairly new. The design and decoration of the building was modern California motel; long and low, with large expanses of glass covered by serviceable beige drapes. Every floor was carpeted, and walls were newly painted beige. Large and fantastically colored sprays of plastic flowers dominated every flat surface and each room had sliding glass doors opening onto a narrow walk surrounding the building. The place was unimaginative, impersonal, tasteless, but not really objectionable. It was simply ugly.

Miss Larson and I were directed to a four-bed room; no, they didn't have space available in a two-bed room; yes, they knew it was requested and as soon as space was available . . . please just fill out these forms.

The woman in charge of the Montcliffe Convalescent Hospital was a registered nurse. She was required by law, a fixture like fire doors or ramps; new to her job, frightened of old people, she had a tendency to avoid looking you in the eye. She bustled, chirped, patted, pulled, and quickly disappeared. All of the actual patient care was done by the "aides" or "attendants." They are not trained to do their jobs, and they learn by watching other attendants. Their skill and interest depend a good deal on whom they work with the first days. Some are good, some terrible. All are underpaid. It's a job for the unskilled, for women with children to support and no hope in their future; for women whose legs are already swollen and tired from thankless day labor in a million other jobs like this one; they must work, and it's a job.

Three of the beds in the room were occupied, two by silent unmoving figures, looking as if a child had placed pillows under the sheets to fool his parents, and the bed nearest Miss Larson's (I already thought of it as "her" spot as she sat in the wheelchair, head down, hearing aid off, hands moving restlessly in her lap) was completely filled by an extremely obese—grayly fat, no pink skin, just mounds of bulging, unfeeling flesh—woman, who moved her lips constantly, pulling them in and out like a baby waiting to be fed.

It was nearly four o'clock, time for me to be leaving. I wanted out of that place very badly. It was all so clean, so neat, but underneath it felt just like the "Old Folk's Home" I had known. The smell, the ambience were alike, but the surface was different. We have certainly improved care of the aged in all those highly visible ways like clean linen, modern buildings, professional staff, even fire regulations. The package has been sanitized, wrapped in plastic, and labeled fit for public funding. But it feels the same as it did before modernization set in.

I didn't want to leave Miss Larson. However, I smiled a very professional nursy smile, efficiently tucked her into bed without letting myself feel compassion, and thought that the doctor *must* know best; after all, he is the doctor. I refused to meet Miss Larson's miserable, half-uttered pleas that I not leave her alone. I went home, and by morning had convinced myself that the place wasn't so bad, that I was simply against institutions without really giving any particular place a chance to be different, and resolved that I would do my best to make Miss Larson's stay comfortable, easy, and as short as possible.

That first morning began with a lecture by the charge nurse. I must help Miss Larson adjust to being in Montcliffe . . . As the charge nurse talked, I could see the aides pushing patients in wheelchairs out of their rooms and into the hall. Under thin cotton bath blankets, the old people were naked. Some were confused, pulling the cloth off their wrinkled flesh, mouths and hands constantly working, sometimes uttering small wordless cries. Others sat miserably hunched in their chairs and held the thin blankets tightly around bent shoulders. Someone had pulled Miss Larson out of bed, and she was sitting in the line, looking around wildly, her neck rigid with indignation. "No, no, I have a nurse. No, no . . ." I could hear her protest. "No, no, I can bathe myself, just let me alone, I can do it." Some of the other patients were looking at her, without interest and without pity. We all have to do it, they seemed to be saying. Don't fight it. No distinctions. What makes you think you're so different? Men, women, confused, coherent, all the same. To the showers!

Two aides, one on each side, would pick up the old carcass, place it in a molded plastic shower chair, deftly remove the blanket, push the person under the shower and rather haphazardly soap her down. A few minutes for rinsing, a quick rubdown with an already damp towel, back under the blanket and ready for the next. The aides were quick, efficient, not at all brutal; they kept up a running conversation between themselves about food prices, the new shoes they had bought, California divorce laws. They might have been two sisters doing dishes. Lift, scrub, rinse, dry, put away. Lift, scrub, rinse, dry, put away. And did you hear the one about . . .

I gave Miss Larson a bath in her room that morning, over the strenuous objections of the charge nurse, who felt I was encouraging separation and dependence. I felt guilty, and my hands were unnecessarily rough as I turned and bathed Miss Larson. It was as if I blamed her for placing me in a position where I had to be miserable, observe misery. How could she do it to me?

The resentment I felt so strongly that first morning

*Act one's age or be one's age: to behave in a reasonable manner.*

seems endemic in places where the aged live. The custodians, whether medically trained or administrative, always seem to have some anger, some residual hatred or fear of their charges. Sometimes I felt it was fear of one's own aging process, or just anger at having to do a very difficult job. Sometimes I saw it as a sort of natural turning away from another's misery, the way one will ignore the open trousers of an old man on the subway. But even if it was a sense of delicacy, of not wanting to intrude on the last years these old people had on earth, it soon progressed to another level. Because the attendants had physically to care for, handle the aging bodies of these old people, they began to treat them as if they were infants, unhearing, uncaring, unable to speak or communicate in any way. The patients were uniformly called honey or dearie or sweetie—or sometimes naughty girl if they soiled their beds—just as one tends to call children by pet names. The attendants expected gratitude or at least silent acquiescence from the old people and their families. The bodies were kept clean, fed, powdered, combed, and clothed, but they were like infants, without modesty or sex or privacy.

At times the patients were even treated as inanimate objects rather than as human beings, adult or infant. This attitude was most frequent in older staff members, and it is understandably defensive. "Ahhh, she's *just* an old lady," they would say. "She's *just* an old lady." And that seemed to justify all manner of things, including the way blind patients were fed or not fed, according to whim; or how soon an old man was cleaned and his linen changed after he soiled his bed. And Montcliffe Convalescent Hospital is a *good* hospital.

Besides the nursing-care program (baths twice a week, enemas when required, tranquilizers and sleeping pills as directed, part of each day spent out of bed, and so forth), Montcliffe also boasted a part-time recreation therapist. She hadn't been trained for her job, but she had the right disposition and character for it. Nothing depressed her, and she seemed oblivious to the depression around her. Surrounded by "her girls," who were all nodding and fidgeting in wheelchairs and who had not uttered a sound, she would chirp, "Oh, this is such fun, isn't it, girls? We must do this [watch television, play bingo, clap hands, whatever] more often!"

The programs took place in what Miss Larson and I began calling "the parking lot." This was a large room, beige brightened by a touch of orange, designated the recreation room by Miss Smiles. Most of the day it was filled with old people, who had either been pushed in in wheelchairs and left to doze in long lines against the wall, or had tottered in, pulled by the hand of an impatient aide, and were seated in low, plastic chairs, expressly designed for the discomfort of old bones. Miss Larson refused to patronize the "parking lot"; she said the sight of that many old bodies lined up waiting for the undertaker depressed her. No conversation between patients ever took place in the parking lot. The only people who spoke were those whose job it was to entertain. When no program was scheduled, a large color television set was turned on. The patients were not to touch the set, and it was frequently out of focus.

Miss Larson entered Montcliffe the last week in October. The air was cool and fresh and in the sun it was quite warm, so we spent a good part of our day outside. I was becoming increasingly impatient with her; her condition was deteriorating in spite of my efforts. No matter what I did she simply refused to get better. I blamed her for imposing her weakness on me; but whenever she became too demanding, I would just walk away and have a cigarette in the dining room. Shortly after her admission, I arrived one morning at 7 A.M. to find the night nurse indignant and angry. Miss Larson had climbed over the side rails during the night, and had been found in the bathroom. "She didn't ring or call out," said the nurse, "her room is right opposite the desk, and I would have heard her. Why, she might have been hurt, and she is so confused. I want the doctor to order more sedation. We can't have her carrying on and disturbing all the other patients. Finally, we had to put her in restraints and I repeated her sleeping pill. But she kept yelling all the same."

I walked in the room and Miss Larson was indeed in restraints; the look on her face was so angry, it seemed to me someone had tied her up in order to prevent murder. "Get me out of these!" she ordered. "How dare they try and stop me from getting out of bed. I always have to relieve myself at night; and they never answer my bell. Usually they come and hide the cord so I can't even find it. So I crawl over the edge; I've been doing it ever since I came to this place. Now, you get me out of these, and tell that doctor I want to see him!"

Miss Larson was not confused; but in a place where all the patients are so sedated that they scarcely move a muscle during the night, she was counted a nuisance. I didn't want them to increase her sedation; barbiturates frequently make old people confused and disoriented. Even if she was a pain in the neck, I liked her better awake and making some sense. The problem was she had no rights. She was old, sick, feeble. Therefore she must shut up, lie still, take what little was offered, and be grateful. And if she did that, she would be a "good girl." There she was, ninety-six years old and didn't even know she was dependent on society. She thought her thirty years of teaching, her careful hoarding of the

*Age, vb.: to grow older: become old: show the
effects of or undergo change with the passage of time
("His mind did not* age." *R.W. Firth)*

little she inherited from her family, and the benevolence of the Social Security Act, with amendments,
would guarantee humane treatment in her old age.
"You get what you pay for," she told me, "and I
want a nurse here, at least during the day, until I'm
strong enough to manage on my own. I don't want to
depend on those"—with a scornful jerk of her head—
"people for anything. I'll pay for your services, but
I'm asking as a friend. Don't leave me alone with
them. They just want to keep everyone in the parking
lot until it's over."

I didn't want to leave her alone, and certainly understood her fears. The place was driving me crazy. I
would catch myself sitting and staring at the wall
with a vacant smile, my hands folded in my lap, just
like one of the old people in the parking lot. I found
myself ignoring the calls for the help that came from
rooms other than Miss Larson's because the aides
had become so hostile to my "interference." The
charge nurse gave me daily lectures on my letting
Miss Larson become too dependent, how bad it was
for her to get everything she wanted, how demanding
she was to the other nurses, poor things.

She was my friend and I wanted her well, healthy,
back at the bridge table. But I couldn't stay with her
forever. I became impatient, even angry, sometimes
rough. I could feel a great distance between us—I was
young, she was old—that had never existed on the
outside. The hostility of them, the others, those
people who worked in the hospital, was beginning to
permeate the relationship we had. I began really to
dislike Miss Larson. And we had been friends.

Miss Larson understood the stakes long before I
did. It was a battle for her soul, a fight for her mind,
with her weakened physical condition the trump
card. Either she could give up, and wheel into the
parking lot, or she could keep fighting and have everybody hate her, receive extra sedation to keep her
mouth shut, be placed on mind-fogging tranquilizers
to stop her demands.

In late October Miss Larson and I reached an
uneasy agreement; I would stay a few more days,
then come back only for a few hours in the morning
to help her bathe and dress. I explained to her that I
was interested in seeing other places where old
people lived and had accepted a temporary job as a
visiting nurse in order to do some quiet investigation.
She glanced at me sharply, snorted unbelievingly,
and turned off her hearing aid. I left the room.

It was Halloween. As I hurried down the hall to
the dining room, I could hear Miss Smiles tittering
away, pretending joy, fulfilling Montcliffe's promise
for a balanced and interesting program of activities
geared to the interest and rehabilitation of the old
people in their care. The afternoon's activity was to
be a party. "I ought to make the old lady go," I
thought. "A Halloween party would really set her

off!" The cook had prepared cupcakes decorated
with tiny candy pumpkins, and apple cider in juice
glasses. Miss Smiles, in her untidy blue smock, had
been racing around all morning, trailing black and
orange streamers. Every patient, with the exception
of an old man who said he was dying that day, was
wheeled or pushed into the parking lot to attend the
party.

Halloween. Hallowed Eve, the day before All
Saints Day, the day that unfulfilled souls walk the
earth and demand satisfaction. The door to the parking lot was filled with flickering light; they must have
candles, I thought. I stopped outside the door and
glanced in.

Smiles had outdone herself. Thirty-four old men
and women sat lined up in the semidarkness, unmoving and quiet. One would give a phlegmy cough, another would clear her throat; hands picked at blankets or grasped the arms of the chairs tightly to
prevent the tremors. The room was decorated as for a
first-grader's dreams of Halloween; all orange and
black and skeletons dangling from the ceiling. Plastic
pumpkins held flickering candles. No games were
being played, no one spoke or moved, except Miss
Smiles, who was fluttering about, "Oh, what fun,
what fun! Are you excited, darling? Isn't this just
lovely? We really must have parties more often!"

I watched her move about, stopping before each
one of the old people and moving her hands about
their faces as if to evoke a spell, a running stream of
words following her around the room. I had thought
her an incredibly stupid woman, unimaginative and
insensitive, but from the doorway, on this day, in her
dark dress, she looked somehow sinister and evil.
Suddenly she stopped her fluttery movements and
stepped back, brushing her hands together briskly as
if she had completed a hard and dusty task. "There!"
she said. "Finished. Isn't it wonderful?" And she
turned toward me, and flicked on the light.

Then I could see what she had been doing. The
faces of the old people were covered with masks, with
crudely drawn skulls, garish pumpkins, little elves,
evil witches. The old gray heads halved by elastic
turned toward the door slowly as if all the masks
were attached to one string and Miss Smiles had
pulled them in my direction. There they were, drool-
ing, twitching; some able to think coherently, some
senile; women, men; private and charity cases; all
distinctions gone, they joined the living dead.
Witches, goblins, ghosts, skeletons, twisted bodies
topped by a child's nightmare of faces.

I backed out of the room, fleeing from some vision
of my own future, locked in a world like this, forced
to attend meaningless functions, eat tasteless food,
live friendless, penniless, sour, and old. Was that the
future? "No," I thought. "No, I don't want to get
old."

# 15

It's possible to be
as happy in old age as at 40

# Report from
# the twilight years

## By Robert C. Alberts

The young man was good, but as sometimes happens with reporters, he told me more than he needed to about why he was doing the story. While he didn't say it in so many words, I gathered that his editor's assignment went something like this: "I want you to do a piece on an old party. He retired in 1969, at the age of 62, and has taken up a new career as a writer. He collects things. He's surprisingly active for someone almost 68 years old." (The editor, I learned later, is 44.)

"Make it a personal sort of piece on the experiences of aging by a man who seems to be functioning fairly well. Get him to express his feelings about advancing age, its problems, its pleasures. Make him open up a bit about his personal affairs, not in a gossipy way but so as to illuminate such an important part of life for the reader. He apparently is making good use of his retirement. What does he know about other upper-

*Robert C. Alberts, in the years since his retirement, has had one book published and is currently writing a biography of the artist, Benjamin West.*

middle-income people who have retired? What does he know about the matter of women vs. men in adjusting to age and retirement?

"Most of the material I read about older people is sheer calamity: What inflation is doing to them, and do they want to suffer to a miserable end or be put away by euthanasia? Reasonably intelligent, articulate people go off into that September twilight and they don't often report back to us on how it is out there. Maybe this character can tell us something favorable about old age and make us believe it."

The young man took a slow look around the living room and uttered a few pleasantries. He indicated that he had read some of the things I'd written. "You took early retirement after 28 years with an advertising agency," he began. "Would you tell me what was in your mind when you did it?"

"The usual things. To put an end to commuting, deadlines, pressures, corporate competitiveness. I had been doing some writing of my own in the nineteen-sixties and I figured with the company pension and income from books and articles, and by working at home, I could make a go of it. I wanted to experience some of the pleasures of semiretirement before I hit 65. I thought I might

accept gracefully what Cicero called 'our common burden of old age . . . which all men wish to attain and yet reproach when attained.' Marcus Tullius Cicero, the Roman statesman, orator and writer."

I paused to give him time to write it down. Instead, he asked, "Did he say that in 'De Senectute'?"

"Yes."

"Around 45 B. C., I believe. Have the pleasures of retirement lived up to your expectations?"

"Yes and no. The thing that struck me was how very quickly you get used to what a few months earlier would have been pure joy. We're both early risers, my wife and I, but we like to have breakfast in bed and read the morning paper and look at the news. Within a month or two, I was taking it as something quite normal, as though I had been doing it all my life. The human spirit isn't geared to steady, unalloyed pleasure. Things soon level off. Nature is sort of unfair that way. You suffer anguish when you have to go to work every morning, but you don't experience an equivalent sense of joy when you don't have to go to work every morning."

The young man looked disappointed.

"There is one retirement pleasure, however, that has continued to be a joy forever. It happens on

Sunday evenings at our place in the mountains east of here. The visitors gather up their children and picnic baskets and leave around, say, 7 o'clock. For 25 years, we've packed the station wagon, put the damned shutters up and started back to the city ourselves, bucking the Sunday night traffic, a 90-minute drive. Nowadays, we just relax. We take two walks around the pond, read the Sunday Times, look at "Masterpiece Theater" and purr. We go back Monday afternoon. Maybe Tuesday. Or Wednesday. If there's a heat wave in the city, why go back at all? When you have

a place in the mountains, your pleasure rises right along with the thermometer in the city. It embarrasses me to tell you this, but not very much."

"You seem to be able to fill up your time and keep busy."

"The observation, if you'll permit me to say so, doesn't have much meaning. It's not applicable. In the first place, I haven't really retired: I have to earn enough by writing to keep us in the style to which, et cetera. And nobody who has bought an old farmhouse ever has to worry about filling up his time. Wherever the eye alights, there is work to be done.

"It's good advice, but it doesn't work with me. The genes of my Germanic and

"John Kenneth Galbraith writes about that in 'The Liberal Hour.' He holds that the biggest mistake you can make is to begin fixing up the place. It has probably been around a lot longer than you have, and if the roof doesn't leak, just take it as it is and enjoy. If you feel you have to do something, he recommends that you buy a pint of paint and a cheap brush and paint something. If you still can't resist the impulse to improve after that, equip yourself with a brush hook.

Huguenot ancestors go to work and I start to remodel and repair. We've fixed up a big 1820 log house. There's always the rationalization that your efforts will be repaid some day when you have to sell the place.

"The fact is, within a few months of retirement, people who are self-starters are wrestling with the same three big problems they've always had: never enough money, never enough room, never enough time.

"Money. You have to have or be able to get a decent amount of it or your retirement and old age can be a disaster. Leonard Merrick said

in 'Cynthia' that poverty is no disgrace but there are few disgraces that cause such keen humiliations.

"Time. We couldn't take the trip to the Newberry Library last spring with the Bibliophiles because we were too busy. We couldn't go to Sandwich this fall to the meeting of the Early American Industries Association, the 'Old Tools Fools,' for the same reason. So many things to do and so little time to do them. We've been buying old hand tools and implements at farm auctions since 1950. I thought I might be able to make a proper accession list, clean them up, burnish and put a coat of carnauba wax on the iron pieces, and display them properly. I thought I might do a monograph on Karl Hofer, the German Expressionist painter we knew and admired when I was with the Army of Occupation. I wanted to become really fluent in my German and master the uvular r. There are a dozen ladderback chairs hanging in the barn I should weave splint seats for. I don't know to what purpose, except that they're there. About 4,000 books that should be catalogued, and one-third of them I haven't read, including Proust and Plutarch and Melville. I have a habit of memorizing poetry. I used to do it when I had a hilly 15-minute walk twice a day between the parking lot and the office. My belief is that the only way to get really inside a great poem is to memorize it. I've memorized 56 of Shakespeare's sonnets and I thought I might take on the other 98. Well, there hasn't been time for any of that."

"What do you miss most in your retirement?"

"I miss the companionship and conversation of the lunches I used to have with the people I worked with. I ate lunch far too often with my colleagues instead of with clients. David Ogilvy, the advertising man, called that 'career suicide.' Now a group of us, we have a sort of unofficial luncheon every Tuesday at the Athletic Association. My wife calls it my Golden Age Club. Some of us were discussing the problems of retirement the other day, and one of the men gave us a pluperfect put-down. He said, 'What I miss most is the company plane.'

"Another thing I miss is a secretary. I miss the Xerox machine down the hall. I long for the day when they make a home copier I can afford, one that will take book pages and reproduce them at good speed on regular paper. I miss the scruffy boys who, three times a day, used to pick up the letters in my out box. I never appreciated the mail boys enough and I apologize to them now. Outgoing mail is, to put it delicately, a pain in the backside I have to travel at least a mile to mail a letter to be sure it will be picked up the same day I mail it, and if I drive there's always some thoughtful person who has parked his car on the yellow line by the drive-in mailbox, and there's nowhere else to park. Every sixth trip, on an average, I forget to take the letters with me, and every fourth trip I find the letters in my pocket when I get back home.

"I've wondered if such forgetfulness is an evidence of approaching senility. I'm working at my desk and I go upstairs to get a book. Since I'm upstairs I might as well go to the bathroom. Having accomplished this, I go back down to my desk and find I have forgotten the book. I storm upstairs again in a rage, cursing my stupidity. This is what psychologists recognize as responding to the emotions aroused in yourself by a situation rather than by the situation itself, which is trivial. This is probably my worst quality and I hate myself for it, but I can't seem to do anything about it.

"I'm comforted by the fact that other people who aren't 67-going-on-68 are also forgetful. My wife read an amusing passage to me the other day out of Sir Walter Scott's "Journal." He was always misplacing his galleys or page proofs. This time, he got a letter, wrote an answer and began to search for the piece of paper that had the person's address on it. He found the address the next day, but in the meantime he had mislaid the letter. Over the next week, he often had the two pieces of paper in his hands, but never at the same time. Scott wondered if his brain was softening. I feel that in my case it is not really absentmindedness but rather intense concentration focused on one thing at a time. My wife says I'm quite right.

"I confess this to make a point. You carry with you into retirement and old age the temperament, the personality, the attitudes you've always had. You aren't going to change them, and the chances are that your strong and weak qualities, for better or worse, will be intensified. If you were a nagger at 45, or a chronic complainer, or a melancholic, you're likely to be worse at 65. If you've had a pleasant disposition, you'll have it in your old age, unless you run into special problems. I could wish that more of us who are old would work harder at being pleasant. Old age tends to become querulous, irritable, at the very time when we are least attractive physically and most need to have a pleasant disposition. Elsie de Wolfe, Lady Mendl, long ago had a recipe for social success that is especially good advice for the old: 'Be handsome if you can, be witty if you must, but be agreeable if it kills you.'

"People have the sentimental notion that the old are fortified by the pleasant memories they've stored up in a lifetime. Happy recollections of happy occasions. I'm afraid we're just as likely to brood on our store of painful memories, on thoughts of past failures, past angers and remorse. Memory can be two-faced—a blessing and a curse. It depends on the temperament. I dwell much more on my failures than on any successes I've had. When I can't sleep, I begin to think of the stupid things I've done, of the narrow escapes I've had from injury, ruin or disgrace, of the people I was once unkind to, or rude to, or offended in some way, many of them long dead. It's not a serious hang-up, but I wish I could push a 'Clear Memory' button like the one on my pocket calculator. I'm too old to improve my conduct by reflecting on the errors I've made. A person is a fool to remember anything he doesn't need to remember or doesn't want to remember. H. L. Mencken claimed he had a special drawer in his desk into which he ceremoniously dropped the thoughts he wanted to forget. They disappeared forever when he closed the drawer—or so he said. I've tried it and it doesn't work."

The young man had stopped taking notes. "It would help me in my work," he said, "if you could think of some of the pleasures of growing old. Some cheerful advantages?"

"There's an amusing story about that in the book Garson Kanin did, 'Remembering Mr. Maugham.' W. Somerset Maugham, English playwright and novelist."

The young man caught it and smiled. "Died in 1965," he said, "at the age of 91."

"Well, this happened as part of his 80th-birthday celebration. As Kanin tells it, Maugham was being honored by the Garrick Club. Only three other men had been so honored: Dickens, Thackeray and Trollope. Maugham got a standing ovation when he was introduced. He expressed appropriate greetings and thanks, paused and began: 'There are many virtues in growing old.' A very long pause followed. Maugham seemed to be struggling, perhaps because of his stammer, head down. The audience grew nervous, then apprehensive. Finally, at the last drawn-out moment, he looked up and said, 'I am just trying to think what they are.'

"One of the unexpected compensations for me is that somehow the past, instead of receding, draws closer as you grow older. The 18th century, for example, seems a lot nearer to me now than it did 50 years ago, when I was 17. The young have no depth perception in time. Ten years back or 10 years forward is an eternity.

"When I was 17, I kept a diary, filling it with ecstasy, anguish and profound ideas no one had ever thought before, and when I was 21 I used to read and reread it, mooning over the past and my departing youth. I am always a little startled when I think that Adams and Jefferson died only 81 years before I was born—only one long lifetime away. And when I remember that my father's father was wounded at the Battle of the Wilderness. Thus the past becomes more real, more believable, and therefore more interesting."

I heard my wife come back from her daily swim and go into the kitchen.

"Another compensation is that as you grow old your tastes broaden. Your enthusiasms may diminish, but your tolerance expands. You are receptive to authors, music, schools of art that you scorned when you were young and might scorn if you were young today. It is no longer necessary to assert yourself by scorning anything or anybody. You can accept and admire baroque and Greek revival, late Victorian and Bauhaus. You have to have years behind you to enjoy both the Parthenon and the Albert Memorial. Mary McCarthy commented on this pleasant development in a lecture I heard this year. She observed that you not only can absorb such new material, but that you can do so without losing your liking for any of the old — 'except perhaps the poetry of Swinburne.'

"You have lost some of your youthful capacity for rapture when you come to a great work of art—not many goose pimples or shivers up the spine—but you gain almost as much in the understanding you bring to it. You come equipped with an accumulation of knowledge, perhaps of wisdom, and a cluster associations, and a set of honed perceptions. You have the exhilarating experience of focusing upon the work the experience of decades of reading, listening, looking.

"Young people sometimes sense this. They may realize —I think dimly—that you've had a lifetime of stored-up experience far beyond anything they have known. But young people can be arrogant about this even when they don't consciously mean to be. A young couple who spent a weekend with us in the country were astonished when I put on some jazz records— first that they were jazz, second that they were Muggsy Spanier's 'Relaxin' at the Touro,' Bessie Smith's 'Empty Bed Blues,' Wingy Manone's 'Jumpy Nerves.' I almost think they suspected me of having bought them the day before to make an impression, or to be hep, or with it, or whatever the phrase is now. They thought they had discovered that music. I've been listening to those records since 1939, when a friend taught me to take this music seriously, almost 20 years before my young friends were born."

"What changes have you seen in your lifetime in the way old people manage in our society?"

"I'm sure you know what the changes are. The whole

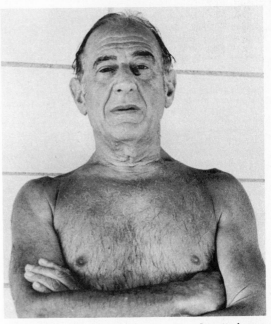

Abe Olanoff, 71, of Swampscott, Massachusetts is one of the top Masters swimmers in the United States in his age division. Mr. Olanoff, swims at least one mile each day, bicycles the two miles between his home and the pool.

structure has changed. Parents seldom live with their grown children now, and from what I remember of some of those households, it's a mercy. The youngest daughter doesn't sacrifice her life and stay heme to nurse mamma and papa, with small thanks from her brothers and sisters Most old people have some income from Social Security now — maybe not enough to live on, but enough to give them some resources and self-respect. And there's television. Whatever its faults, it's a well-recognized godsend for people who are more or less housebound. No other period has ever had anything remotely like that.

"It occurs to me that no other period has seen the aging process as we are seeing it, close up in hundreds of people we have come to know. One evening, you see a 1933 movie, perhaps with James Cagney or Joan Blondell. A few nights later, you see them again, as they are today, 40 years later. Instant old age. Actors, public figures have been made immortal by the movies and television. The young Ronald Colman, with all his good looks and charm, still talks and smiles and breathes."

"What does your wife think of your retirement?"

"That's a good question and I hoped you wouldn't ask it. Let's begin by saying that it can be rough on almost any wife. She has had the house to herself all day for some years, and now she has the 24-hour companionship of her mate. You know the little jokes women make: 'Twice as much husband on half as much money' and 'I promised to love, honor and obey, but not for lunch.'"

My wife Zita appeared as if on cue, pushing the tea cart. I made the introduction. She poured the smoky tea that young S. H. G. Twining gave me when I did a piece on his 18th-century Twining ancestor. I said, "You really should ask my wife about that." The young man reworded the question.

"Older women do talk a great deal among themselves about retired husbands," she said. "Some of them are happy to have the constant company, in real Darby and Joan fashion. Most aren't. Of the women I swim with, one likes the house at a 68-degree temperature, her husband wants it at 72. Another wants the radio on while she works around the house—it doesn't much matter what it's giving out, it's contact with the rest of the world. Her husband objects.

"My friend Sally's husband is mad about opera. When he retired he spent hours each day stretched out on the sofa listening to his records. The 'Anvil Chorus' at full sound. Sally retreated to the attic with her sewing and stuffed rugs under the door, but it didn't help. We got frequent reports on that in the locker room. She began to have headaches that obviously were caused by the tension of that situation. Yet they were very fond of each other. One day her husband said he had been offered a position and an office as consultant with a trade association in the city, and did she think he ought to take it. She managed to wait 60 seconds, thinking hard about it, and then suggested that perhaps he should take it. Now they're both as happy as can be.

"I like to look at the afternoon soap operas with one eye while I'm ironing or putting up peaches or whatever. I ask myself, with columnist Erma Bombeck, 'Why do I bother with this junk?' but I do. The Head of the House here — he's known as The Mister among our friends in the mountains — he hates them, and he insists that the sound penetrates even to the other end of a large house. I feel the same way about his Pirate football games."

"Baseball," I said. "I tried an outside office but it was no good. I work late at night. I like to work sitting up on a bed. Wherever I was, home or office, the papers I needed were at the other place. And we're in the country five months of the year. I may try it again, though. One of the real problems of working at home is that it is assumed you are always 'available' to run errands, do household chores and entertain visiting relatives."

"Every normal woman," my wife said, "spends a lot of time on the telephone chattering with Jane or Midge or Peggy. It's one of the ways she survives monotony and maintains her identity. I gather that many men, for some reason, simply can't bear this and are interfering about it. Some husbands prowl around the kitchen, not to help but to see what's going on. 'Why did you buy this brand of tomatoes when the other brand was two cents cheaper?' The wife knows very well why she bought that particular brand."

"They aren't interested in the two cents," I said. "It would be some other reason. Retirement is terribly hard on

some men. There's generally a horrendous loss in income, and there's a drop in status, especially if they were important people in their jobs. More than that, they've had a structure to their lives, going off to an office or shop five days a week. I think people want that, no matter how much they bitch about it. Call it a rhythm. The heart beats to a rhythm. But when they retire, the rhythm is disrupted, the structure is dismantled."

"It's not the same with women," my wife said. "A woman's life is structured to her household, even when she works at an outside job. It's with her from birth to death, part of her inheritance, part of being a woman, part of her feminine mystique. Her retired husband may be an intrusion into her daily routine, but the routine, the rhythm is not basically changed."

The young man indicated appreciative interest. My wife exchanged glances with me and continued.

"The greatest blessing of age for me is the freedom it brings from the pressures of convention. You're just not deeply concerned any longer with the things that seemed so important when you were younger. You don't have to prove yourself, or save face, or try to impress anyone, or go anywhere unless you really want to. I feel so sorry for young people, because I remember my own youth and the part convention played in it. The fear of a Saturday night without a date. Your life was ruined if you didn't have someone to take you to the junior prom. A harsh word was enough to shrivel your soul. Young people today think they are unconventional, and perhaps by old standards they are, but they have imposed on themselves a rigid set of new conventions, many of them false, some of them worse than ours. One is that you are to be loved for your inner self alone, not for outward charm, or physical beauty, or nice clothes, or grace and kindness. Therefore you must dress all alike in ugly clothes and look as drab as you can and confront the world with an impassive cold stare. You wish you could pass on some of your experience to the young, but of course you can't."

"A really beautiful girl of 18," I said, "it doesn't matter what she wears."

"Remember, my dear, that to a really beautiful girl of 18,

any man over 40 is as old as Rip Van Winkle. Most of the women I know agree that one of life's finest pleasures is the enjoyment you take in your small grandchildren. It's a kind of calm pleasure, detached but deep, a week of love and fun at the seashore with no responsibility beyond tomorrow. These are the women who have been fortunate in their children and grandchildren. They are always fully aware that they're among the lucky ones, and they have a positive sense of gratitude for it. Some of the women are silent. They have stories to tell or to conceal that simply make your heart ache.

"One of the things you discover about yourself as you grow old is that you're more conscious of other old people. You study them in the stores and on the bus, and you find yourself making judgments on how they're getting along. I think this comes out of a stronger sense of common humanity, because you know that regardless of background you're all in the same situation. When you see someone neat and trim, shoes shined, appropriate clothes, the men with a clean neckline and the hair trimmed out of their ears, you honor them for it. They're still in there as people.

"I would add that growing old is especially hard on women. They've had a pride in their bodies, and they diet and work hard to continue to look nice. But the face begins to sag under the accumulated weight of years, and eventually there almost always comes a stomach, a . . . well, a potbelly. Even if the waist doesn't thicken, it comes, and, large or small, it's a terrific shock. It's apparently a sex-linked characteristic. You can exercise like mad to get rid of it, but it doesn't go away. It just turns to muscle."

"The time comes," I said, "even if you're in good health, when you are aware of failing physical powers. My eye man tells me that old people burn up a larger percentage of their energy in the physical effort of using, focusing their eyes. This happens just when they have less energy available. It's one reason, he says, why old people snooze so much. I snooze several times a day myself, but I call it 'resting my eyes.' At the farm, I never wrestle the shutter into place on the front door without wondering how soon the day will come when I will no longer have the strength to do it. I have been running a mile three times a week on an indoor track. I used to do the mile in 4 minutes, 35 seconds, which wasn't such bad time in 1928. It annoys me that I can't get down to 8 minutes, 30 seconds without pushing harder than I should. Any month now, one of the girl runners is going to do the half-mile faster than I ran it in my senior year at college. Probably little Mary Decker, who is 17, wears pigtails and weighs 85 pounds. When that happens, I may put my head in the oven. Or I may just send her some flowers."

"Do you find that older people have a calmer, more reasoned outlook on the world's ills?"

"I don't know. I would doubt it. I suppose we should have. We've fought four wars, suffered a nine-year Depression, seen three Presidents wrenched from office by natural death, assassination and shame, and endured the riots of the nineteen-sixties. We shared the deepest gloom and fear I think the country has ever felt, in June of 1940, when Hitler overran Europe. Anyone who has experienced all that should be able to stand up to anything—to take

---

**'A man in retirement can be rough on any wife. It's twice as much husband for half as much money.'**

---

the long view, the calm, measured overview of events.

"My own feelings have been influenced by something Ernest Hemingway wrote. Nothing that can happen to the human race, he said, could be any worse than what it has already suffered. I also carry around in my intellectual baggage an idea I developed for an article in 1969. It occurred to me then that not one of the impending disasters we had all worried about in the nineteen-fifties was of any real concern to us in 1969. I listed them. Fear of massive technological unemployment caused by automation. The shortage of engineers. Concern whether we could educate the tidal wave of young people. The belief that Russia was a dedicated, efficient leader of a united, monolithic and possibly irresistible international movement. The fear that Russia was outstripping us in the rate of economic growth, basic scientific re-

search, training of engineers, development of missiles and space exploration. Those problems either never existed or had silently vanished by 1969, with hardly one cheer or nod from us to mark their departure. We were worried about a whole new set of problems in 1969, almost none of which we had foreseen in the nineteen-fifties.

"In other words, the big problems we are worrying about today were not on the front burner 15 years ago. Perhaps the impending disasters we're wrestling with today will be just as remote by the end of the nineteen-eighties. I guarantee that the problems we'll have then will be grave, but maybe they'll be new, different, and not at all what we now expect. You are welcome to any optimism you can squeeze out of that.

"For those of us who are pushing 70, of course, the optimism is moderate. If we

think about it at all, we must know that we are getting closer to what Turgenev called 'the insufferable insult of extinction.' We cheerfully assume that it will be long delayed. We pray that it will not be the Big C, that we will be among friends and that it will not involve prolonged suffering for ourselves or too much trouble for others. Somebody said—one of the penalties of a lifetime of reading is that you sometimes can't remember whom to credit—someone, maybe a Scandinavian, described us all as walking out on ice that grows progressively thinner One by one, later or sooner, each of us reaches a place where we break through and go under."

"Is there any word of advice you would offer to those who are taking that walk?"

"Yes," I said. "If you can figure out any way to avoid it, by all means do so. And please let me know what it is."

"In the meantime," my wife said, "bring money."

"Bring a variety of consuming interests," I said.

"Bring good health," she said.

"If a person can manage those," I said, "he should be at least as happy in his old age as he was when he was 40." ∎

# 16

# Letters of Two Men

*By Themselves*

by S. Saul

February 10
Santa Monica, California

Dear Avrom,

I am writing to you on this, the first anniversary of Judith's death . . . my dear sister and your beloved wife. Though we live a continent apart, we are close to each other through our love for her. I can never forget how you took care of her during her illness—pushing her wheelchair to the hospital and back. I have kept her letters and yours—I have read them over and over . . . to remember how fortunate she was to have you as a husband . . . you, who did everything possible to make her life easier during the last long months of her illness. Your relationship as husband and wife are beautifully described in your letters—and I, far away from you both, am grateful for the way you shared it all with me.

We are two old men—without our wives. Your letters to me are always a source of pleasure . . . and a reminder of our long standing friendship . . . for this, as for other things . . . I shall never forget my sister.

Sincerely,

Sam

February 20
New York City

My dear brother Sam,

Your letter touched a vulnerable spot in my heart . . . that is, our Judith. In our society (which I see as quite swampy politically, economically and morally), it is often frowned upon to express one's sentiments. I ask, why should that be? Is not a person entitled to express his thoughts and feelings? Is not every day of one's life a holiday . . . a day of joy, or sometimes grief . . . but yet a holiday? I believe that no person has the right to insult another. . . . to make him feel bad. But how does society dare to oppress an individual's feelings . . . shame from expressing his happiness or suffering?

Judith is very much alive in my memory. A picture of our little family hangs over my desk . . . both of us, much younger . . . and little Sarah. Now Sarah has grown children . . . how the years fly! Judith's name is often spoken, not only in my house, but in Sarah's house, and in the homes of our mutual friends. It is no accident that we speak of her . . . for her lifetime she earned the love of so many through the way she lived her own life, through her relationships with people, her kind deeds, her sweet and friendly face, her beautiful eyes . . . her susceptible heart.

You know, dear Sam, I am not a hypocrite. I am a plain honest man who likes to speak as he thinks. I do not write you these things because you are her brother . . . but because they are true. She and I were a real team. This was so, not because we both came from the same small town in Russia . . . not because our parents prayed in the same small synagogue; not because your father, who was the town miller, bought hardware from my father's store back there in the Ukraine; but because we just seemed to fit together. I remember, the first week after we were married, you wrote her a letter asking how it felt to live far away from her family, with a stranger like me! Her answer to you warmed my heart . . . I felt so much a man when I read it, for she wrote, "Even though I've lived with him only one week, I feel as if I've known him all my life!"

Those were her feelings toward me, and mine toward her . . . even though this was my second marriage, and I already had my little child. She helped me bring up my daughter . . . for this alone, I should adore her. She fitted in with my own family . . . and she tactfully and beautifully helped me remain friends with Sarah's mother's family.

You speak of my pushing the wheelchair. Who else should have done that? She was my wife, my comrade, my flesh and blood. She was so sick, then, it tore the heart out of me. And, to top it off, I had to perform a daily injection into her thigh . . . not with a thin needle but with one as thick as the tooth of a fork because the liquid itself was so thick it couldn't pass through a small lumen. Her thigh was so perforated from these daily injections, it looked like a sieve. I used to curse myself whenever I did it, but she had to have it every day, or else she would die. One might almost think this was a punishment from heaven (why upon me?) to inflict needles into the body of my best friend, my beloved wife.

Even as I write to you, my hands shiver with the memory.

People like her are a rarity. How she respected you and your father. How she worried over her younger brothers. And to the youngest, Jacob, she was like a mother! When your sister Ninotchka fell ill, she traveled, sick herself, to Chicago, hoping to persuade her to change her ways. And, finally, when Nina had to be brought to New York from Chicago, how Judith embraced me when I said I would go fetch her! When your father was ill, Judith cared for him . . . she was the only one who could make him comfortable . . . and would sit up in a chair all night watching him.

Was there, then, a limit to her gallantry? I am a poor writer, and cannot describe the treasures of this human soul. You knew her as a sister, a young kid, a schoolgirl, and a young lady. I knew her as a grown up person, a woman, wife and mother. As a housewife . . . member of her community. As a friend to others.

When she became ill, she never complained. To all her visitors, at home or in the hospital, she would say, "How are you? Tell me about yourself."

I would have pushed that wheelchair from here to California. Now she is gone. I have no guilt before anyone to speak of her. She was the brightest element in one important epoch of my life. A beautiful memory, which I cherish along with others.

Thank you for your note, dear Sam. Let us write often.

Avrom

# 17

by Calvin Trillin

# U.S. JOURNAL: MIAMI BEACH

## REFLECTIONS OF A MORE OR LESS JUNIOR CITIZEN SHOPPING ON WASHINGTON AVENUE

WASHINGTON AVENUE, the main shopping street of South Beach, is sometimes called Yenta Alley. In Yiddish, a yenta is a shrew or a battle-axe. As shoppers, yentas make the new brand of suspicious and aggressive consumers—those truth-in-packaging advocates and coöp-food-purchasing organizers and unit-measurement freaks—seem like a gaggle of impulse buyers. Washington Avenue is a tough place to run a fruit stand. It is also a tough place to shop. The clerks are as contentious as the customers.

"Is this papaya ripe?" I heard a woman ask a clerk at a Washington Avenue fruit stand one day.

The clerk looked at the papaya. "Yeah, it's ripe," he said.

"To me, it doesn't look ripe," the woman said.

"You don't believe me, why ask me?" the clerk said. "Decide for yourself."

"This is not a ripe papaya," the woman said, putting it back in the bin and reaching for another.

At the Big Chips fruit stand on Washington Avenue, I once happened to be standing next to a woman who was asked repeatedly by the clerk to refrain from squeezing the strawberries with such gusto—a request that a Washington Avenue shopper is likely to treat the way a customs inspector might treat the request of a bearded and long-haired young traveller not to break the seal on a clear-plastic envelope full of unidentified white power. On

Washington Avenue, fruit is not casually tossed into a market basket; it is inspected. A Washington Avenue shopper goes over a tomato the way the bomb squad goes over a metal fragment found at the scene of the blast. The woman I heard being warned about bruising the strawberries told the clerk that, her eyesight have deteriorated over the years, an educated sense of touch was the only means at her disposal for guarding against imperfections in strawberries. She continued her inspection, sighing occasionally to indicate how she felt about the quality of the berries circumstances had forced her to examine. When she had finally finished, and the clerk was pouring the strawberries into a paper sack, one strawberry apparently missed the sack and fell back into the bin.

"You dropped one," the woman said. "One of them fell out!"

"Oh, that you can see," the clerk said. "Before, you had such bad eyes you had to feel every strawberry. But one strawberry falling you can see from five feet away."

"Brute!" she said. "You ought to be ashamed of yourself."

"I'm not the one handled all the strawberries."

"You should be ashamed. Oh, you should be so ashamed—treating an elderly person like that," she said.

"Now she can see," the clerk mumbled. He picked a strawberry out of the bin and put it in the sack.

South Beach, the southernmost dozen or fifteen blocks of Miami Beach, is

dominated by elderly European-born Jews who have retired from the cities of the Northeast; its style of shopping is partly the result of so many shoppers' being people who have severe restrictions on their budgets and virtually no restrictions on their time. It may be that shopping under such circumstances could bring out yenta-like behavior in Maharishi Mahesh Yogi. It has occurred to me, though, that some normally easygoing residents of South Beach may assume a combative posture as they enter Big Chips or the Thrifty Supermarket the way heavyweight prizefighters suddenly start bragging and growling at each other at the weigh-in. Could it be, I have sometimes wondered, that the smiling, warm-looking woman sitting on the bench over there, showing off pictures of her grandchildren, is suddenly transformed into one of the Eumenides by entering Lundy's Supermarket? Like boxing, after all, shopping on Washington Avenue is carried on as a self-contained activity bound by set rules. Everybody knows what days the Thrifty has specials. Everybody knows that Lundy's will not give refunds or exchanges on "any jar or canned goods that have been unnecessarily refrigerated." Some of the shouting that goes on during shopping hours on Washington Avenue must be caused by the impatience and irritability associated with old age; some of it is undoubtedly caused by the anxiety associate with living on a fixed income during a period of terrifying inflation.

But I think clerks on Washington Avenue sometimes absorb punishing remarks for the same reason that heavyweights sometimes absorb punishing uppercuts—because somebody good at the game has seen an opening.

Thenever my father was in the Miami area, he used to drive to South Beach to hear women argue with the butcher, the way other people drove down to watch the dogs race. As a tourist, my father was unvaryingly contrary. The marked spots that places like Disney World now provide to indicate where amateur photographers should point their cameras would have puzzled him; when he first took his movie camera to Florida he used it to take films of stout bathers approaching the ocean on a slightly chilly day. It says right in the tour book left in Miami Beach hotel rooms that the Bal Harbour shopping center—a collection of stores in northern Miami Beach that includes branches of Neiman-Marcus and Mark Cross and a number of other well-known retailers— is a "must-visit sight for every visitor to South Florida," but my father preferred the stores on Washington Ave, particularly the butcher shops. He had a non-scholarly but lively interest in the development of the Yiddish curse that came out of the Eastern European ghettos—"May you have an itch in a place impossible to scratch" and "May streetcars grow on the back of your throat" and that sort of thing—and he thought kosher butcher counters in South Beach were good places for hearing particularly imaginative curses, perhaps because the shoppers were inspired by the added irritant of kosher meat's being even more expensive than non-kosher meat. He loitered around butcher counters on Washington Avenue the way American folklorists used to hang around remote Tennessee mountain towns. While he was there, of course, he bought the specials. His favorite curse was one that seemed to indicate an attempt to adapt the form to modern American life: one woman said to a Washington Avenue butcher, "May you have an injury that is not covered by workmen's compensation."

WHEN a checker at the Thrifty Supermarket has trouble reading the price on a box or a can, she holds it up and shouts over to the next checker in Spanish. On Washington Avenue, both the clerks and the people who sweep out the stores are likely to be Cubans. South Beach has not only Cuban workers but Cuban residents. By some estimates, thirty per cent of the population of South Beach is Spanish-speaking. The newest supermarket on Washington Avenue specializes in Cuban food instead of schmalz herring and stuffed kishke. One of the kosher butcher shops on Washington Avenue now has a small sign saying "*Se Habla Español*." A visitor to South Beach could get the impression that every young person he sees is Cuban and every old person is Jewish, but, as it happens, some of those little old Jewish men playing pinochle in, say, the pavilion of Friendship Corner #2, one of the centers run by the Miami Beach Park and Recreation Department, are actually little old Italian men playing knock rummy.

Still, retired Jews are an overwhelming majority, and South Beach is culturally Jewish. (It is not a religiously Jewish as all the kosher signs and advertisements for cantorial concerts would lead a stroller on Washington Avenue to believe. In a article for the Sunday magazine of the Miami *Herald* several years ago, a reporter named Mel Ziegler took the trouble to do some mathematics with population figures and synagogue seats and service attendance, and concluded that the elderly Yiddish-speaking residents of South Beach did not necessarily clutch at religion in their final years.) In America, an ethnic culture is partly something that provides additional hobbies for the retired. An elderly Italian has not just shuffle board but bocce. An elderly Jew has not just television but the Yiddish music hall. And arguing. The ethnic culture of Anybody who ahs survived one of the immigrant neighborhoods of New York or Boston or Philadelphia is likely to include contentiousness. According to Chaim Rose, who presides over Friendship Corner #2 and has worked with the elderly in Miami Beach for more than twenty years, South Beach residents are contentious not just with clerks but with card partners and landlords and thypeople in the next apartment and with old political opponents who still can't seem to grasp what the only true course for a revolutionary was in Lithuania in 1912.

The Jewishness of South Beach is also partly a matter of packaging—the sort of packaging that makes pancake-mix pancakes served in a Pennsylvania hotel "Pennsylvania Dutch pancakes" instead of just pancakes. Along Washington Avenue, the packaging is designed for an audience that is elderly and Jewish. A movie theatre that features a stage show between showings of the film ("You've all heard of Mario Lanza, and this next singer . . ." "I know you all know who Liza Minnelli is; well, this young lady I'm about to introduce . . .") does not call its stage show local-talent night but Five Acts of Vaudeville. The Famous, a well-known restaurant on Washington Avenue that is popular with the people who stay in the more expensive lodgings uptown, advertises "Jewish-American Cuisine—from Boiled Beef to Lobster Tails."

ONE day, at a Washington Avenue fruit stand, I came across a tiny woman who was having difficulty picking the best ten oranges out of a bin that held perhaps two hundred of them. The oranges were ten for thirty-nine cents. She had already chosen six. The problem she was encountering in selecting her final four was that the bin was so wide it kept at least a third of the oranges beyond her reach. A clerk was only a few feet away—picking cucumbers from a box and tossing them into a bin next to the oranges. She explained her problem to him. He just looked at her for a moment, and then went back to tossing cucumbers.

"Will you help?" she asked him.

"No," he said.

Not being one of the combatants, I felt free to move down a few dozen oranges for her. "Thank you very much," she said. "Taller people can reach. It's not fair."

"You're right," I said.

Under the circumstances, a finely developed sense of justice seemed reason enough for her request, although that is not the motivation normally mentioned in explaining why South Beach shoppers are inclined to examine all two hundred oranges in order to find the best ten for thirty-nine. There are those who say that the elderly of South Beach buy only a few items at a time at the Thrifty because they can afford only necessities or specials, and there are those who explain the same phenomenon by saying that people with nothing much to do prefer to make a daily ritual of shopping rather than fill a shopping cart to overflowing in the manner of a suburban housewife trying to get the supermarket chore off her back for a few days.

There are undoubtedly people living in South Beach who are desperately poor and people who are desperately lonely. There are also people who are quite comfortable. A lot of South Beach looks more or less the same— whitewashed two- and three-floor apartment buildings with efficiencies and "pullmanettes," small hotels built in the days when toniness was simulated with English names (The Shelley, The Chesterfield, The Essex, The Kent, The Carlton) instead of with the French names that were in vogue after the war, when the larger hotels (The Sans Souci, The Versailles, The Deauville, The Fontainebleau) were built farther uptown. But someone like Chaim Rose can usually make a good guess at a resident's former occupation and retirement income by looking at his address in South Beach. When some of the residents of South Beach first came from Europe to New York, someone familiar with the lower East Side could have used their addresses to make a good guess at the villages they came from; sixty or seventy years in America has at least sorted them out economically instead of geographically. But they all go to the Thrifty for the specials.

All of them, of course, have lived for sixty or seventy years in a country that treats shopping as a skill and a hobby as well as a necessity. The selling technique of, say, an automobile dealer is based on treating the customer as a fellow-expert—familiar with the jargon and the motor-magazine ratings and even the markup. The Bal Harbour shopping center really is considered a "must-visit sight" for a lot of tourists in South Florida. For a retired person—a retired Jew in Miami Beach or a retired Lutheran in Arizona—shopping can become the skill and hobby and necessity that dominates all others. Women who were mildly proud of being able to feed a large family in a thrifty way monitor the butcher's movements with a concentration they could never manage with two children pulling at their skirts. Men who formerly used their business sense to run a store apply it instead to comparing the McIntosh-apple prices at Big Chips with the McIntosh-apple prices at the Thrifty.

FOR a big special at the Thrifty or the Food Fair, it is said, people come to South Beach from the expensive condominiums in northern Miami Beach or even Hollywood—the huge high rises that crowd up against the shoreline like some hopelessly lost monsters looking for a way back to Manhattan. There are now several such condominiums in South Beach—on the bay side, facing Miami—and just about everybody having anything to do with the Chamber of Commerce or the tourist industry in Miami Beach would like to see more. They would also like to see fewer old people—particularly old people of limited means. A concentration of elderly people is bad for the image of a tourist town—especially a tourist town that seems to have a steadily rising median age even in the neighborhoods of expensive hotels and condominiums.

The occupation of South Beach by the elderly is not merely a problem of image but a problem of real estate. As a tourist center built on the concept of "last year's hotel" being replaced by "this year's hotel" (or, more recently, this year's condominium; a new hotel hasn't been built in years), Miami Beach has more or less used itself up. The only way new development can take place is to begin all over again— at South Beach, where development started, and where, ironically, the retired waiters living in pullmanettes can walk to a broad sand beach instead of the pathetic strip that has been left for the seventy-five-dollar-a-day luxury hotels farther north. For several years, there has been talk in Miami Beach about how to redevelop South Beach. A building moratorium has been in effect while options are being considered, and last year the city council went as far as to officially declare the section below Sixth Street a "blighted area"—a designation necessary to qualify for certain state funds. For a while, it was said that any sensible plan for redevelopment of South Beach—a plan that would presumably include expensive hotels and marinas and new condominiums—would result in the relocation of the elderly people who live there now. But apparently everyone concerned decided that relocation would be too damaging politically. As soon as the subject was mentioned, the elderly people of South Beach began shouting at city-council meetings and telling reporters the council was planning a "final solution" to the problem of the elderly—a reference to the Holocaust that, as an example of unrestrained arguing, compares with claiming impending blindness as a reason for squeezing strawberries. The level of contentiousness in South Beach means that councilmen, like clerks, have to treat the residents not as passive and perhaps pathetic old folks but as combatants. Any battles that the elderly of South Beach lose will not be lost quietly. The residents would obviously react to someone's offering them relocation the same way they would react to someone's offering them an overpriced brisket.

—CALVIN TRILLIN

# Happiness is a Kawasaki

### by John C. Dougherty Jr.

**I'm beating the high cost
of gas and having
the time of my life doing it.**

The day I sneaked through the rear door of my Kawasaki dealer's, I felt as if I were entering an X-rated theater. After all, I was 60, looked 60, and had never been on a motorcycle in my life.

But when I saw my first Kawasaki, it was love at first sight. As soon as I straddled the black, banana-shaped seat, I was hooked. I bought the cycle—a shiny orange and black beauty with matching helmet, face shield, aluminum ramp, and tie-down straps to secure the bike to the back of my truck.

The all-too-quick briefing I received was not the fault of the dealer. I may have led him to believe that I knew how to ride. It's also possible I may have intimated that the bike was a gift for my grandsons. OK, so I lied a little.

I called my insurance agent to inform him of what I had done, while Bud, the dealer, loaded my bike onto the truck. My agent was speechless, and I think I hung up before he could have the call traced

**"My grandsons contributed
to my education . . ."**

to alert the men with the white suits and butterfly nets.

A year earlier, I wouldn't even have known what a Kawasaki was if anyone had asked me. I would have guessed it was something you

ordered in a Japanese restaurant—with that "saki" on the end, probably a Japanese cocktail.

But with the increasingly high cost of gas, the idea of owning a motorcycle began to intrigue me. My son, who started his education on a Vespa and graduated to a Triumph, filled me in on the facts of life about gas consumption and motorcycles. My grandsons, too, contributed to my education. They scoffed at my ignorance and proceeded to give me a crash course on dirt bikes, street bikes, and anything else I might want to know—and didn't want to know—about cycles. They volunteered the information in good faith, with a dash of tolerance, but it was all so confusing to me that they might as well have been speaking Japanese.

The main obstacle I had to overcome was my impression that motorcycles were bought by the younger generation to dismantle in the center of driveways, in a conspiracy to keep the head of the

house from using the garage. But I soon learned that cycles really were made to be kept in one piece; they really did run for thousands and thousands of miles trouble-free, with far less maintenance than a car; and you actually could go miles on a gallon of gas.

So there I was, the day after buying my cycle. Armed with the operations and instructions manual, I had parked on a deserted road out in the country among the Florida scrub palmettos and sand spurs.

My audience consisted of several bored Brahma steers and some ominous-looking turkey buzzards lining a split-rail fence. At least the birds weren't circling.

The moment of truth had arrived. I consulted my checklist, calling out each step, and touched every item like a copilot on a 747. Switch on —bike in neutral—choke full—little gismo pointing down, indicating full gas flow. Then one pump and my bike started to purr like a young cougar.

Elated, I "varroomed and varroomed" a couple of times just for the hell of it. I lifted the clutch pedal a notch, lurched forward and staggered erratically down the road.

**"It might as well have been Japanese."**

Two hours later, proud, sweaty and feeling 20 years younger, I pushed my little jewel up the ramp of my truck, tied it down and triumphantly headed for home.

That was 3,000 miles ago. Confident, cautious miles to my business, the post office, the bank. No parking worries and no more gas problems. Although I check the

tank every day, I strongly suspect a Japanese leprechaun is inside, busily manufacturing gasoline. Maintenance? One spark plug (I changed it myself), a spray can of chain lube, and an occasional pat on the handlebars.

I love riding my bike during the week, but on Sundays I am truly a free spirit. Up at sunrise, I cross the bridge spanning Sarasota Bay, zoom along Gulf of Mexico Drive, stopping whenever I want at all the unspoiled, scenic spots inaccessible to the 4-wheeled monsters. Relaxed now, and confident, I've even learned to wave jauntily to my fellow cyclists. And I can honestly say, a man of 60 *can* find happiness on a Kawasaki. But I still don't do "wheelies"—at least, not yet.

# 19

# Mrs. ELIZABETH HULL

## WEDOWEE, ALABAMA

### by George Mitchell

My mother died when I was nine months old. My grandmothers on both sides and some aunts taken me and raised me. I came up without the love of a mother, but they were so good it always seemed like they was Mama. Yeah, they was mighty good to me. One of the ones that took care of me, an aunt, she was married and she had a baby that was nursing and he had one breast and me one. A lot of strangers just thought we was twins, but we was just cousins.

The earliest memories I can remember about when I was a child was making snuff. I was just a little kid. They would raise their tobacco, and they'd parch it and fix it and put it in a big old rag, and I'd get out yonder to the flat rock they had in the yard to set your washpan on, and I'd get out there with a hammer and beat it up fine. They would all cough themselves to death when they were beating it, but I wouldn't. After I beat it, they'd fill up their vessels full and give me that real fine stuff in the bottom of the rag, and that's what made me a 'bacco worm. I used to dip, smoke and chew. I had it all. But I had to leave it all off, all but my snuff. I still dip my snuff.

I've had to stop doing a lot of things I used to do, but I'm not going to give up until I just have to give up and stay in the bed. I'm going to go just as long as the Good Lord gives me strength. Let me go! Don't tie me down here and just make me stay in one place! I want to get out and see the flowers and the birds and the bees and be out in the open air.

Some of the happiest times I used to have was when I'd be by my lone self, and I'd get my Bible and my songbook, and I'd be just as happy in my home—nobody but me—as I ever was in a church or anywhere else. But now I can't see to read, and so I can't read to pass off the time. The time seems mighty long, too. My son and daughter-in-law live here with me, and I'll get them to give me something or nuther that I can ravel and tear up and fix and make a mess out of to pass off the time, I get so lonesome. I can get outdoors to walk about a little, but I can't hold out long. Go across the road to the garden and back, then I'm just tired down. Have to get a chair, sit down and rest. Yeah, Lordy.

Lots of times I sit here and I think back when I was just a child, and I can see the old homestead, the old places, the wells and all the things that was there when I was a kid coming up. I have my imagination now; I can see a lot of them places where I was when I was just a child. Yessir. Down ten miles below Goodwater—that's where I was mostly raised in my child days—and I study about that old place down there now.

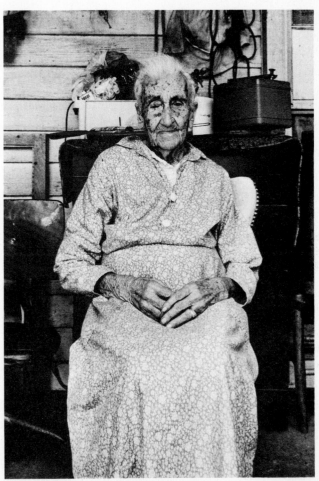

Mrs. Hull is 109 years old.

There was a row of cedar trees in the front yard, a bench under them. I can see them cedar trees and that bench there now. And the well stood around this away, and it was a big oak tree stood there. Now I can't see them, but I imagine I can see them just like I could when I was there.

Yessir, I've been here a long time. I won't be here that much longer now. No, it can't be that long. But I want to stay here just as long as the Good Lord will let me. Whenever he sees fit to call my number, I want to be ready to go. That's just the way I am. Of course, I'm glad to be here where I can see my friends and my children and talk with them and enjoy being with them. But we've all got to go someday, and the thing we've got to do is try to be prepared and ready. For it's a'coming sometime or nuther; it may be in the day, it may be in the night, we may be on the road; we don't know. But we do know it's coming to one and all, sometime.

The Lord's got his work for us to do and when we complete what he aims for us to do, then He's going to call us home. Whenever we complete what He aimed for us to do, then we're going up yonder—where there won't be no more sad farewells, no more sorrow, no heartaches and pain—all be peace and love.

My husband's been dead a good long time now. I've got it down in my Bible, I think it was in '45. But I see him every once in a while. Last time I seed him, he come back, he was right out there in the yard. Had on his coat and his hat, and looked like he was trimming his fingernails or trying to get something out of his finger; I seed him just as plain. And I went to him, and I was asking him how he was getting along, and he said, "Very well. How are you?" I said, " 'Bout like common." Then he was gone again. He come back where I can see an imitation of him. He's coming at me some of these days, and I'm going to go with him when he comes after me. Folks may say that's crazy talk, but it ain't; it's a warning or something or nuther to me that he keeps coming back. And he's gonna come one day and I'm gonna go with him.

Yessir, Lord, I sure do miss him. Yeah, I miss him. Oh me. We always miss them when we lose them—we'll always miss them. But sometimes look like we can feel their presence near us. They ain't forgotten us; we all gonna be together again some day or nuther.

# 20

Dear Dr. Kaplan:

You have asked for "an autogerontological page or two." Will this look back-and-around so serve?

Sidney L. Pressey
Professor emeritus, Psychology
Ohio State University

# In Gerontology 57 Years—and 85

Sidney L. Pressey[1]

In 1917, while a psychological intern at the Boston Psychopathic Hospital, I published a paper reporting measurement of mental deterioration in elderly psychotics. Now I am working on a report regarding problems and potentials of institutional living as seen by an 85-year-old resident—me! So I might claim 57 years in the field and ask if that might be a record!

But there was a gap. After obtaining my doctorate in psychology at Harvard, I plunged into 15 years of exhilerating but exhausting work ranging wide over educational and developmental problems in school and college and resulting in some 75 papers by myself, my wife, and our students, also 4 books, 26 widely used tests, and 6 "teaching machines" of various types. Then chronic problems of health became insistent. A torturing divorce was followed by a healing second marriage. I realize that, at 45, the most exhilerating of all periods of life—the prime—was over, and I was beginning change-decline into age. And with the collaboration of two of my students I wrote what I considered the most distinctive of my books, **Life: A Psychological Survey** (1939), believed to be the first volume systematically to cover human development from birth to death with consideration of socioeconomic as well as biological factors. And having stressed major applications of that perspective to problems of time-saving for students involved in World War II, I was made director of research regarding educational acceleration and published some 24 papers and a monograph then on that topic and several papers since.

In the meantime, circumstances made me again interested in age. My 88-year-old father came to live with us. Though physically slowing down, he continued intact in intellect and personality until his death at 93. Indeed there seemed gains with age—more tolerant judgments, humor, kindliness. Sundry of my older friends showed similar mellowing. Looking back to the middle and younger adult years of those I had long known, I thought I often glimpsed sources of such outcomes. But the gerontologists of 30 years ago seemed mostly stressing the losses in age and neglecting the middle years. So I initiated and was elected first president of the Division on Maturity and Age of the American Psychological Association (1948).

And I sought more material about superior old people. Thus I asked advanced students in summer sessions in

an Ohio, a California, and a Canadian university to prepare case studies of the finest old person they had known well and the oldster most a problem. Usefulness even into the 90s was richly reported. And to make intensive study of cases in the Columbus metropolitan area, funds were obtained from the National Institutes of Health to study outstanding old people there, and something as to the factors making them so (1957). Meanwhile, to make practical contact with such issues, I became active in sundry local, state, and national welfare organizations as well as those concerned with the aged, attended their meetings and reported our work, extended such trips to include visits to programs for the old across the country, fostered very practical "action research."

Thus a local clergyman studied the older people in his church and developed programs for them; several such programs were fostered and appraised. A retired YWCA worker investigated ways in which such organizations might serve older women—and became the first director of the city recreation program for the elderly. A wealthy alumnus gave the university funds to investigate retirement—research reported in some 15 papers in professional journals. It was early evident that those who could (as independent professional and business people) usually preferred "tapering"—lessening their work load as they aged—and might then continue some work into their 80s. Thus an aging physician might continue to see his older patients but turn over most of his practice to a younger partner. But big organizations could have some such flexibility. A famous eastern university had 66 as retirement age; but outstanding men were invited to continue longer—a few part-time to 80. A big department store kept some salespeople on part-time till that age, also found older occasional workers more reliable than youngsters they had been hiring (1954, 1958, 1962). And all this was reported at professional and business meetings and dealt with in courses in adult education (1957).

Though I thought "teaching machines" might have special values for older learners, such as letting each progress at his own rate and guiding him to correct answers, unfortunately I did not so experiment. An effort to build a test battery which would in content and tasks be as appropriate to older adults as the Binet to children showed such adults scoring much higher than men in their 20s (1957). Though very promising, the project was not completed. A deceptively simple little person-

1. 1870 Riverside Drive, Apt. 28, Columbus, Ohio 43212.

ality inventory asked that those items thought wrong be marked in a list of 125 such as "smoking" and "immodesty," worried about as "money," liked as "flirting" and "church." This little folder was in 1923 thus marked by some 1700 youngsters from the 8th grade through college, repeated at decade intervals for 50 years, and in 1953 given also to a wide sampling of adults, some elderly. From childhood through college and from 1923 to the near present there was a marked liberalizing in attitudes. Older adults seemed not so much to become conservative as to remain with the attitudes of their young adulthood. But a few oldsters showed delightful mellowed tolerance. Surely more (and better!) such simple checks on attitude-aging are to be desired (1955).

Papers on older psychologists and professional retirement (1955) led to a foundation grant to open opportunities for retired faculty. My friend and former student, Ray Kuhlen, and I collaborated on a book reviewing development and change through the life-span (1957). And in 1959 at age 70 I retired with an invitation to UCLA and later to the University of Arizona; in both places I insisted on only half-time work to conserve energies and also to give me time to study programs for the elderly and their folkways in these two areas—and our own aging.

Since retirement, I have published 32 papers of which 11 concerned teaching machines and programmed learning and 9 educational acceleration—two major controversial topics with which I have long been closely identified. Twelve concern age.

And even more than my earlier publications on that topic, they had two characteristics: I viewed the aged as one of them, and I tried to be of help. Thus I found how indeed wrenching retirement from a position long held can be—and how then enlivening an offer of a post-retiremet position. We saw and felt how lonely oldsters can be, in crowds of their kind in a strange place—and then how helpful were programs bringing them into friendly acquaintance. Returning from the Southwest after 4 years, we found our lovely big home now a burden; a pleasant apartment involved no resources for emergencies of health; all these needs were met in a retirement village to which we finally went. And in evaluation of these various types of living we kept detailed records, hopefully of help to other oldsters (1966). A recent paper tells of my wife's final illness and how the resources of the Village, and the kindnesses of neighbors there, all helped (1973). So, as others had need, I have tried to do. . . . Residency in this retirement community has also given me opportunity to accede to the request of a committee of educators to prepare an autobiography, which puts my gerontological work in the perspective of my total career (1971).

Finally—at 85, my wife recently gone, friends about me ailing and dying, I think of death. Medical science may distressingly, even horribly, prolong that process through long misery, pain, perhaps years of degrading senility. Surely the old **should** have the right to die with dignity, when they truly wish. Euthanasia surely **should** be a topic of major gerontological concern.

**Selected References**

*Life: A psychological survey.* New York: Harpers, 1939.
*The new Division on Maturity and Age: Its history and potential service.* **American Psychologist**, 1948, **3**, 107-109.
*Employment potentialities in age, and means for their possible increase.* Report of New York State Joint Legislative Committee on Aging, 1954, 92-94.
*1923-1953 and 20-60 age changes in moral codes, anxieties, and interests, as shown by the "X-O Tests."* **Journal of Psychology**, 1955, **39**, 485-502.
*Certain findings and proposals regarding professional retirement.* **Bulletin American Association of University Professors**, 1955, **41**, 503-509.
*Tests "indigenous" to the adult and older years.* **Journal of Counseling Psychology**, 1957, **4**, 144-148.
*Potentials of age: An exploratory field study.* **Genetic Psychology Monographs**, 1957, **56**, 159-205.
*Psychological development through the life span.* New York: Harpers, 1957.
*Jobs at 80.* **Geriatrics**, 1958, **13**, 678-681.
*Most important and most neglected topic: Potentials.* **Gerontologist**, 1963, **3**, 69-70.
*Two insiders' searching for best life in old age.* **Gerontologist**, 1966, **6**, 14-17.
*Genius at 80; and other oldsters.* **Gerontologist**, 1967, **7**, 183-187.
*Sidney Leavitt Pressey: An autobiography.* In **Leaders in American education**, 70th yearbook of the National Society for the Study of Education. Chicago: Univ. of Chicago Press, 1971, 231-265.
*Old age counseling: crises, services, potentials.* **Journal of Counseling Psychology**, 1973, **20**, 356-360.

# IV. Social Problems and Social Policies

Older persons, as a group, are among the most disadvantaged in society. Whether one considers income, health care, housing, or opportunities for satisfying activities and interactions, substantial minorities of aging individuals face problems in these areas.

Current policies and practices toward the aged are contradictory. Overtly, society endorses the principle that older persons deserve the conditions necessary for leading a decent life. But perhaps because of strong age biases, or "age-ism" (Butler), programs for the aged fail to meet their objectives. The Older Americans Act of 1965, which has subsequently been reaffirmed in principle by Congress in a series of amendments, sets out noble objectives of social policy toward this country's elderly. The readings that follow it in this section need to be considered with a view toward how well the principles of the Older Americans Act have been translated into practice.

The first two objectives of that Act concern income and health care. A report published in 1976 by the Social Security Administration indicated that the average health care bill for a person 65 or older was $1360 in fiscal 1975, almost six and one-half times the average health care expense of persons under age 19 and three times that of people aged 19 to 64. Health care for the aged rose 18 percent in fiscal 1975, compared with an 11.4 percent increase in 1974, the report stated. Medicare, which promised to meet the needs of the elderly, has failed in some basic ways, including providing preventive care and reducing costs. The impact of medical expenses that are not covered by Medicare and the cost of other basic life necessities on the limited incomes of many older persons is dramatic, and the student is invited to complete a sample budget to estimate these costs (Albert and Zarit). Another facet of their declining incomes is that many aging persons have little choice in housing or lifestyle (Birren), while attempts to provide safe housing alternatives have been met by a surprising degree of opposition (Butler).

The principle area where the aged face legal restrictions is mandatory retirement. While this practice is currently being challenged in New York State and other places, over half of those who currently retire do so because of compulsory regulations (Palmore). Many persons look forward to having more leisure upon retiring, but the transition from work can be difficult even when a person has adequate income (Puner).

There are some social benefits to mandatory retirement, such as increasing the opportunities for work and advancement of younger persons. These gains are important, especially in a time of high unemployment. But they must be weighed against the waste of skills and human potential that ensues when persons are prevented from working beyond an arbitrary age (Palmore). Often overlooked in the arguments over mandatory retirement is the possibility of continuing one's work on a part-time basis into the later years. Miller describes an exciting experiment in that direction which currently is taking place in Sweden, and its impact on the lives of Swedish elderly.

# 21

# OLDER AMERICANS ACT OF 1965, AS AMENDED

### (42 U.S. Code, § 3001, Et. Seq.)

*Public Law 89–73 (July 14, 1965), as amended by*

*Public Law 90–42 (July 1, 1967),[1]*

*Public Law 91–69 (September 17, 1969),[2]*

*Public Law 92–258 (March 22, 1972),[3]*

*Public Law 93–29 (May 3, 1973),[4]*

*Public Law 93–351 (July 12, 1974),[5] and*

*Public Law 94–135 (November 28, 1975)[6]*

## An Act

To provide assistance in the development of new or improved programs to help older persons through grants to the States for community planning and services and for training, through research, development, or training project grants, and to establish within the Department of Health, Education, and Welfare an operating agency to be designated as the "Administration on Aging".

*Be it enacted by the Senate and House of Representatives of the United States of America in Congress assembled,* That this Act may be cited as the "Older Americans Act of 1965".

———

[1] *Hereinafter referred to as the "1967 Amendments".*

[2] *Hereinafter referred to as the "1969 Amendments".*

[3] *Hereinafter referred to as the "1972 Amendments".*

[4] *Hereinafter referred to as the "1973 Amendments".*

[5] *Hereinafter referred to as the "1974 Amendments".*

[6] *Hereinafter referred to as the "1975 Amendments".*

# TITLE I—DECLARATION OF OBJECTIVES:
## DEFINITIONS

### DECLARATION OF OBJECTIVES FOR OLDER AMERICANS

SEC. 101. The Congress hereby finds and declares that, in keeping with the traditional American concept of the inherent dignity of the individual in our democratic society, the older people of our Nation are entitled to, and it is the joint and several duty and responsibility of the governments of the United States and of the several States and their political subdivisions to assist our older people to secure equal opportunity to the full and free enjoyment of the following objectives:

(1) An adequate income in retirement in accordance with the American standard of living.

(2) The best possible physical and mental health which science can make available and without regard to economic status.

(3) Suitable housing, independently selected, designed and located with reference to special needs and available at costs which older citizens can afford.

(4) Full restorative services for those who require institutional care.

(5) Opportunity for employment with no discriminatory personnel practices because of age.

(6) Retirement in health, honor, dignity—after years of contribution to the economy.

(7) Pursuit of meaningful activity within the widest range of civic, cultural, and recreational opportunites.

(8) Efficient community services, including access to low-cost transportation, which provide social assistance in a coordinated manner and which are readily available when needed.

(9) Immediate benefit from proven research knowledge which can sustain and improve health and happiness.

(10) Freedom, independence, and the free exercise of individual initiative in planning and managing their own lives.[8]

### DEFINITIONS

SEC. 102. For the purposes of this Act—

(1) The term "Secretary" means the Secretary of Health, Education, and Welfare.

(2) The term "Commissioner" means, unless the context otherwise requires, the Commissioner of the Administration on Aging.

---

[8] *In addition to the Declaration of Objectives of the Older Americans Act, embodied in sec. 101, the 1973 Amendments stated their objectives, as follows:*

"SEC. 101. The Congress finds that millions of older citizens in this Nation are suffering unnecessary harm from the lack of adequate services. It is therefore the purpose of this Act, in support of the objectives of the Older Americans Act of 1965, to—

*(1) make available comprehensive programs which include a full range of health, education, and social services to our older citizens who need them,*

*(2) give full and special consideration to older citizens with special needs in planning such programs, and, pending the availability of such programs for all older citizens, give priority to the elderly with the greatest economic and social need,*

*(3) provide comprehensive programs which will assure the coordinated delivery of a full range of essential services to our older citizens, and, where applicable, also furnish meaningful employment opportunities for many individuals, including older persons, young persons, and volunteers from the community, and*

*(4) insure that the planning and operation of such programs will be undertaken as a partnership of older citizens, community agencies, and State and local governments, with appropriate assistance from the Federal Government."*

# TITLE II—ADMINISTRATION ON AGING

### ESTABLISHMENT OF ADMINISTRATION ON AGING [1]

SEC. 201. (a) There is established in the Office of the Secretary an Administration on Aging (hereinafter in this Act referred to as the "Administration") which shall be headed by a Commissioner on Aging (hereinafter in this Act referred to as the "Commissioner"). Except for title VI and as otherwise specifically provided by the Older Americans Comprehensive Services Amendments of 1973, the Administration shall be the principal agency for carrying out this Act. In the performance of his functions, the Commissioner shall be directly responsible to the Office of the Secretary. The Secretary shall not approve any delegation of the functions of the Commissioner to any other officer not directly responsible to the Commissioner.

(b) The Commissioner shall be appointed by the President by and with the advice and consent of the Senate.

### FUNCTIONS OF ADMINISTRATION

SEC. 202. (a) It shall be the duty and function of the Administration to—

---

[1] *The 1973 Amendments, sec. 201(a), completely revised sec. 201, by (a) requiring that the Administration on Aging be in the Office of the Secretary, (b) requiring that AoA, with exceptions, be the principal agency for carrying out this Act, (c) requiring that the Commissioner, in the performance of his functions, be directly responsible to the Office of the Secretary, and (d) prohibiting approval by the Secretary of any delegation of the Commissioner's functions to "any other officer not directly responsible to the Commissioner", unless the Secretary took certain actions. However, the 1974 Amendments, sec 2, changed this to an absolute prohibition against such delegation.*

(1) serve as a clearinghouse for information related to problems of the aged and aging;

(2) assist the Secretary in all matters pertaining to problems of the aged and aging;

(3) administer the grants provided by this Act;

(4) [2] develop plans, conduct and arrange for research in the field of aging, and assist in the establishment of and carry out programs designed to meet the needs of older persons for social services, including nutrition, hospitalization, preretirement training, continuing education, low-cost transportation and housing, and health services;

(5) provide technical assistance and consultation to States and political subdivisions thereof with respect to programs for the aged and aging;

(6) prepare, publish, and disseminate educational materials dealing with the welfare of older persons;

(7) gather statistics in the field of aging which other Federal agencies are not collecting;

(8) stimulate more effective use of existing resources and available services for the aged and aging;

(9) [3] develop basic policies and set priorities with respect to the development and operation of programs and activities conducted under authority of this Act;

(10) provide for the coordination of Federal programs and activities related to such purposes;

(11) coordinate, and assist in, the planning and development by public (including Federal, State, and local agencies) and nonprofit private organizations of programs for older persons, with a view to the establishment of a nationwide network of comprehensive, coordinated services and opportunities for such persons;

(12) convene conferences of such authorities and officials of public (including Federal, State, and local agencies) and nonprofit private organizations concerned with the development and operation of programs for older persons as the Commissioner deems necessary or proper for the development and implementation of policies related to the purposes of this Act;

(13) develop and operate programs providing services and opportunities as authorized by this Act which are not otherwise provided by existing programs for older persons;

(14) carry on a continuing evaluation of the programs and activities related to the purposes of this Act, with particular attention to the impact of medicare and medicaid, the Age Discrimination Act of 1967, and the programs of the National Housing Act relating to housing for the elderly and the setting of standards for the licensing of nursing homes, intermediate care homes, and other facilities providing care for older people;

---

[2] *The 1973 Amendments, sec. 201(b)(1), revised paragraph (4). It previously read: "(4) develop plans, conduct and arrange for research and demonstration programs in the field of aging;".*

[3] *The 1973 Amendments, sec. 201(b)(2), added paragraphs (9) through (16).*

(15) provide information and assistance to private nonprofit organizations for the establishment and operation by them of programs and activities related to the purposes of this Act; and

(16) develop, in coordination with other agencies, a national plan for meeting the needs for trained personnel in the field of aging, and for training persons for carrying out programs related to the purposes of this Act, and conduct and provide for the conducting of such training.

(b) [4] In executing his duties and functions under this Act and carrying out the programs and activities provided for by this Act, the Commissioner, in consultation with the Director of Action, shall take all possible steps to encourage and permit voluntary groups active in social services, including youth organizations active at the high school or college levels, to participate and be involved individually or through representative groups in such programs or activities to the maximum extent feasible, through the performance of advisory or consultative functions, and in other appropriate ways.

# 22

# Income and Health Care of the Aging

by William C. Albert and Steven H. Zarit

The eradication of poverty has long been a part of the American dream and yet income maintenance is an alien idea to many Americans. This contradiction has the greatest effect on the aged, who represent the most economically depressed group in society. Older persons are increasingly barred from continuing employment past 65. Over half of those who retire are forced to do so because of compulsory regulations (Palmore, 1972), while the various other sources of income available to them often fail to reach an adequate level. To fully appreciate this situation it is necessary to consider from a historical perspective the development of income supplements, and then to look at total income available to the aged. At that point, estimates of the expenses of basic necessities for older persons, including health care, can be made as a way of assessing the adequacy of current income levels.

We have developed a complex system of piecemeal categorical income programs which individually and in combination offer some assistance, but often inadequately meet human needs: Unemployment Insurance to aid the unemployed; Workman's Compensation to assist those injured on the job; Old Age Survivors Disability and Health Insurance (popularly referred to as Social Security) to provide aid to the aged, to the survivors of deceased workers and to the disabled, and to assure medical services under Medicare. We provide Public Assistance to families with dependent children and the Supplemental Security Income program in the federalized Old Age Assistance, Aid to the Blind, and Aid to the Disabled programs. Whatever one's philosophical leanings we have in fact had what essentially constitutes a guaranteed annual income, however meager, for many years.

## History of Income Supplements and Old Age Insurance

Much of the unwieldy complexity in these programs exists because the entire concept of income maintenance goes against the grain of our cultural and social history. We continue to be bound to roots of the English Poor Law of 1607 which arrived with the colonists from England. The Poor Law remained the basis for public welfare and practice until the depression of the 1930s. "Up to that time, such principles of the Poor Law as local responsibility for care of the needy, the obligation of relatives to take care of their own, and settlement laws designed to discourage the indigent traveler survived the changing conditions of life" (Vasey, 1958; 25). Such policies were reflective of the attitude of rugged individualism—the idea that anyone with enough determination, thrift, and hard work could be a success. As applied to old age pensions, this attitude included even ex-Presidents. Ulysses S. Grant was found living in poverty at the end of his life.

Some early attempts to provide specific assistance to the elderly failed. In 1907 William B. Wilson introduced in Congress the first bill to provide old age pensions to all elderly people. In 1911 Victor S. Berger made another attempt, but the issue of public relief remained dormant for another two decades. Then the crushing effects of the Depression forced recognition of our interdependence as a society, and the realization that at times even the industrious and able-bodied are at the mercy of a fluctuating economy. Even those who bought the American dream and had worked hard and saved for some future rainy day learned that the unexpected storms of life could render them destitute.

By Executive order, on June 29, 1934, Franklin D. Roosevelt appointed the Committee on Economic Security to develop income maintenance programs. This committee was composed of the Secretary of Labor as chairman, the Secretaries of the Treasury and Agriculture, the Attorney General, and the Federal Energy Relief Administration. In the same executive order, Roosevelt created an Advisory Council to the Commission on Economic Security. This council was composed of 23 experts on social insurance from the fields of industry, labor, and social work.

Edwin E. Witte of the University of Wisconsin was chosen as the Executive Director to implement the executive order, and a Technical Board was also created to help develop the program. The reports of the staff members comprised more than a dozen large volumes. The Advisory Council submitted its report on December 18, 1934 and the Committee on Economic Security its report on January 15, 1935.

Supporting data for an old age pension program showed that many of our aged were without economic resources. In Connecticut, for example, it was found in 1932 that 49% of the aged had incomes of less than $300.00 per year, and that more than 33% had no income of any kind. Other studies in New York and Massachusetts revealed that from 23 to 65% of the aged had less than $300.00 annually and less than $5000 in property. A traditional approach to the problem of indigent aged, almhouses, was considered and rejected as a solution since shocking deficiencies were found in this type of care. Such houses suffered from having too many diverse groups of disabled all thrown together with too little financial resources to provide adequate care. The Committee on Economic Security formulated a plan which provided two programs for the aged. One, an "insurance" program, would provide payments as a matter of right to wage-earners who would contribute to the system. The other was an old age assistance program which would cover only those in need and would be financed from general tax revenues. After hearings in both houses of Congress, the Social Security Bill was introduced. It passed by a margin of 371 to 33 in the House and 76 to 7 in the Senate.

In 1935 the basic Social Security payroll tax rate was 1% from both employer and employee on the first $3,000 of income. By 1977, employers and employees were each contributing 5.85% on the first $16,500 of earned income. The Social Security tax is perhaps the most regressive federal tax in existence. Those earning $16,500 or less are taxed on their entire income. It allows no exemptions and does not apply to income from interest, dividends, rent, or capital gains. Only income from wages is taxed.

## Current Social Security Benefits

Social Security currently does not adequately meet the needs of some participants and many others have never been included in the program. This situation reflects the contradictory attitudes of Congress toward income benefits. Social Security was not intended to guarantee an adequate income to the elderly but to supplement savings, investment returns, and private pensions, thus representing a compromise between our individualistic ethic and the needs of many elderly who have simply never been able to amass such supplements. The minimum Social Security benefit, as of May 1976, was $101.00 per month. The maximum Social Security benefit for an individual is presently $364.00 per month. A wife drawing on her husband's account will increase benefits by approximately 50%. For example, if an elderly single male entitled to $200.00 per month were to marry a woman over 65, they would receive about $300.00 per month. This example is probably not far from the average individual payment. The U.S. Department of Health, Education, and Welfare reported an average monthly payment of $161.97 in December of 1972 (*Social Security Programs in the U.S.*: 37). Wives who have worked, however, cannot draw on the full benefits of their own Social Security and many single older persons who consider marrying would suffer a loss of some of the income they currently receive individually. The amounts of Social Security payments are summarized in Table 1.

Table 1    A Perspective on Income

| | | White | Black | |
|---|---|---|---|---|
| Median family income by age and race of family head: | total | $9,910 | $6,035 | |
| 4 year average 1968–1971 | 65 & over | $5,143 | $3,309 | |
| | | **White** | **Black & others** | **All Persons** |
| Persons below the low-income by age and race: 1973 | total | 8.4% | 29.6% | 11.1% |
| | 65 & over | 14.4% | 35.5% | 16.3% |
| | | **Minimum (May 1976)** | **Maximum (May 1976)** | **Average (Dec. 1972)** |
| Monthly Social Security Payments | | $101.00 | $365.00 | $161.97 |
| | | **Single** | **Couple** | |
| Federal Supplemental Security Income Payment (May 1976) | | $157.70 | $236.60 | |

Sources: *Social Indicators*, 1973, and the Social Security Administration. Income figures on other minority groups were not available.

Since Social Security did not establish a minimum income, but was designed to provide supplements to those who worked, Public Assistance programs were created in the Social Security Act to aid the indigent. Categorical programs included Old Age Assistance, Aid to the Disabled, Aid to the Blind, and Aid to Families with Dependent Children. In 1974, the Supplemental Income program federalized the adult categories of public assistance: Old Age Assistance, Aid to the Blind, and Aid to the Disabled. Social Security Insurance removed persons in those categories from federal-state welfare programs and established a national minimum income for them at $140.00 per month (raised to $157.70 in 1975 and to $167.95 in July 1976). Persons with no income would receive the total amount, while those with any sources of money under the minimum would receive supplements up to that base level. In addition, some states augment the S.S.I. program. In California, the combined programs augmented by California's contribution can provide up to a maximum of $279.00 monthly to an elderly individual.

When computing expenses for an elderly individual whose income is provided in part by S.S.I., it is important to note that the S.S.I. recipient is not eligible to participate in the Food Stamps program and may be deprived of other benefits of state welfare systems, as in New York, where rent subsidies were taken away when older persons were administratively transferred from the Old Age Assistance Program to S.S.I. Levels of income that S.S.I. will raise an individual to are shown in Table 1.

## Other Income Sources: Employment and Pensions

The basic effect of Social Security is to provide some minimum levels of support, which then may be supplemented from other sources to allow for a more comfortable income. One way to augment Social Security is through working, but there are two obstacles. First, there are few full or part-time jobs that will take an employee over 65. In fact, only 1 in 4 men and less than 1 in 10 women over 65 participate in the labor force (*The Elderly in America*, 1975). Second, persons who are on Social Security and earn from employment more than $2760 a year will have their payments reduced by one dollar for every two earned above that amount. Thus a person receiving $200 per month Social Security could, by earning the maximum amount allowed in wages, have a combined income of $5160 annually. This reduction in Social Security payments does not apply to pensions or interest from savings, bonds, or other sources.

Probably the major source of income that people intend for supplementing Social Security during retirement is private pensions to which they have contributed through their employers; however, participating in a pension fund has not guaranteed that the worker will qualify for any benefits upon retirement. Until new federal legislation regulating pension funds was approved by Congress in 1974, complicated rules governed the vesting process, that is, how a person became eligible for a pension. In many instances, one needed 30 years or more of continuous service for the

same company, or same union, or even, in some cases, the same union local, in order to be vested (Nader and Blackwell, 1973). A person who changed jobs before becoming vested would not carry over any benefits paid into the pension fund at his or her previous employment. Those workers who were laid off for periods of time during their working years sometimes did not qualify because the vesting procedure stipulated that continuous service was required. In some cases, persons who were disabled, or who were laid off or retired before a certain age, and who had accumulated the required years of continuous service, did not receive benefits because their pension stipulated that they had to work to a certain age to become eligible for payments. When companies went out of business or were purchased by other companies, pension funds sometimes were terminated with no distribution of money to participants, even to those individuals who already were receiving pensions. There were, additionally, specific episodes of abuse where workers were laid off or retired within a few months before they became vested, even after 20 or more years of employment ("Major Provisions of the Pension Bill," 1974).

Given these complicated restrictions that often governed vesting, Nader and Blackwell (1973) conclude that a large proportion of persons who have contributed to pension funds have never received any benefits. They write:

> In fact, nobody even knows exactly how many people who expect pensions end up getting them. One out of two is probably the most optimistic guess. But many people believe that figure is too high. Senator Javits estimates that pension benefits go to as few as one of twelve—certainly not much more than one of ten—covered employees.[1] The Western Conference of Teamsters says that only one of six employees who enroll in the union's pension plan collects a benefit.[2] A study of pension plans in ten low-wage industries covering 60,000 workers found that only one of ten employees could expect to receive a pension.[3]

Many of the inequities in the pension system will potentially be corrected under the 1974 federal legislation. That law sets up procedures for vesting, for determining eligibility of workers to receive a pension, for financing pension funds so that the promised levels of payments will be guaranteed, and for covering the possibility that the firm might go out of business. With respect to vesting, for example, the legislation sets up three options for private pension funds:

1. Gradual Vesting: Each participant is vested in at least 25 percent of his/her accrued benefits from the

1. *Preliminary Report of the Private Welfare and Pension Plan Study,* 1971, The Committee on Labor and Public Welfare, Subcommittee on Labor, U.S. Senate, 92nd Cong., Ist Sess. (Washington, U.S. Government Printing Office, 1971).
2. James H. Schulz, *Pension Aspects of the Economics of Aging: Present and Future Rules of Private Pensions,* prepared for the Special Committee on Aging, U.S. Senate (Washington, U.S. Government Printing Office, 1970), pp. 38–39.
3. *Private Welfare and Pension Plan Legislation,* Hearings, General Subcommittee on Education and Labor, U.S. House of Representatives, 92nd Cong. 1st and 2d Sess. (Washington, U.S. Government Printing Office, 1970), p. 262.

**Table 2    Estimated Minimum Monthly Benefit for an Older Person living Alone**

*Estimated Monthly Cost*

1. Food            Weekly——————    ————————

2. Housing
   (rental)                         ————————

3. Utilities
   phone                            ————————
   gas                              ————————
   electric                         ————————

4. Clothing        Yearly ——————    ————————

5. Miscellaneous                    ————————

6. Medical                          ————————

TOTAL MONTHLY EXPENSE               ————————

## Budget Items

1. *Food:* One area where many older individuals attempt to save money is on food. But proper nutrition is as important during the later years as at other times of life. Inadequate eating habits can complicate existing medical problems, or lead directly to new problems, including acute organic brain syndromes (Butler and Lewis, 1973).

The U.S. Department of Agriculture has prepared a "Food Guide for Older Folks," which details the necessary nutritional requirements for older persons, and includes a sample menu for one week.[1] Based on their recommended diet, an older person's daily intake should include:

a. Dairy: 2 cups or more of milk or its equivalent every day.
b. Vegetables and Fruits: 4 or more daily servings, including 1 source of Vitamin C and one serving containing Vitamin A every other day. A serving portion is ½ cup, or the usual serving portion, such as 1 medium apple, banana, orange or potato, one half grapefruit, or cantelope.
c. Meat: 2 or more servings of meat, poultry, or fish every day. A serving is defined as 2 to 3 ounces of lean, boneless cooked meat, poultry, or fish. The Food Guide also gives alternative sources of protein with the following equivalent to 2 ounces of meat: 2 eggs, 1 cup of cooked beans, dry peas, or lentils; and 4 tablespoons of peanut butter.
d. Cereals and Breads: Four or more servings a day. A serving consists of 1 slice of bread; 1 ounce of ready-to-eat cereal; and ½ to ¾ cup of cooked cereal, cornmeal, grits, macaroni, noodles, rice, or spaghetti.

1. This pamphlet is available by writing: Superintendent of Documents, U.S. Government Printing Office, Washington, D.C. 20402. Cost is 30 cents.

The cost of a weekly food budget that contains these minimum food requirements can be estimated by developing a menu for one week based on the nutritional guide and pricing the cost of the meals in a supermarket. This figure can then be multiplied by 4 and entered into a monthly budget.

2. *Rent:* The minimum that an older person living alone has to pay for housing can be estimated by pricing what an average two or three room apartment costs per month in the reader's community. Those who own their own homes are often faced with the problem of tax and maintenance costs that are rising, in many instances faster than their incomes. Students may wish to estimate the cost of taxes and maintenance in a house, as an alternative to rent.

3. *Utilities:* What is the average cost for phone, gas, electric in your community?

4. *Clothing:* What would be an estimate of the minimum amount of new clothing necessary in a one-year period, and what would that clothing cost? This figure can then be divided by 12 and entered into the monthly budget.

5. *Miscellaneous:* What other items are necessary at minimal levels for a monthly budget? These items can include: use of public transportation; any entertainment; meals taken in a restaurant; gifts; or other items that seem appropriate.

6. *Medical Expenses:* While many persons may expect that Medicare pays the great bulk of medical expenses for persons over 65, this is not the case. In fact, medical expenses and getting adequate medical care remain a major problem for older persons. Because of the importance and complexity of these issues, medical expenses and medical care will be discussed in detail.

employer's contributions after 5 years of service, with increments in vesting over the next 10 years, leading to full vesting after not more than 15 years.

2. Rule of 45: a worker receives 50 percent vesting when the sum of his/her age and years of service equal 45, with vesting increasing by 10 percent for each additional year.

3. 10-Year Vesting: employees become fully vested after 10 years of service.

This legislation also requires that all funds offer survivors benefits of at least 50 percent of the pension ("Major Provisions of the Pensions Bill," 1974).

These regulations of vesting and financing of private pensions will undoubtedly increase the numbers of retired persons who receive supplementary income to Social Security. As the law is not retroactive, however, it does not apply to those who are already retired; nor will all provisions of the law be in effect before 1981, so that workers retiring before that time may in some cases not be included under these procedures ("Major Provisions of the Pensions Bill," 1974). Further, this law does not allow for transfer of payments from one fund into another, if an employee has not worked long enough to become vested. It should also be noted that many workers, particularly those receiving lower wages, are not currently covered by private pension plans and can expect to receive only Social Security upon retirement. The effects of pension reform, then, will be to guarantee levels of payment to those workers who are covered by private pensions. It will not affect those currently retired, some of those who will retire before 1981, and those workers not covered by private pension plans.

### Living on an Older Person's Income

The result of these contradictory policies toward income of the elderly has been that large numbers of persons are forced to exist on inadequate levels of income. As shown in Table 1, median income of families in which the head of the household is over 65 is $5,143 for whites and $3,309 for blacks, which is approximately 50% of the median income of all families (*Social Indicators*, 1973). Similarly, the proportion of older persons falling below federal levels of subsistence income as of 1973 is larger than for the total population. S.S.I. supplements have come into effect since the figures on median income and of poverty level were calculated so that there has been some relative inmprovement among those who have received the least amounts.

The impact of the restricted incomes that many older persons have can be demonstrated by completing the budget shown in Table 2, and comparing that with the range of income that older persons receive in Table 1: median family income, minimum and average Social Security payments, and S.S.I. payments. The budget is comprised of estimates of costs in the communities in which readers live for food, housing, utilities, clothing, medical expenses, and miscellaneous expenses for a one-month period. By following the instructions described below, minimum amounts necessary for subsistence can be calculated for an older person living alone. Students may also wish to construct budgets for older couples, or budgets that include leisure activities or incidental expenses.

### The Cost and Provision of Health Care

Medicare is a national health insurance program financed by the federal government through the Social Security tax and from the general fund. It was passed by Congress in 1965 as part of the amendments to the Social Security law, Title XVIII, in order to protect the elderly from rising medical costs. But this program has not freed older persons from health bills. Out-of-pocket expenses for medical care for the elderly were $178.00 in 1966. In 1974 those out-of-pocket expenses had reached $415.00. In 1967, Medicare's first full year, the plan covered 46% of the medical bills of the elderly; today it pays for only 38% (Main, 1976). There is separate coverage under Medicare for in-patient (Part A) and out-patient (Part B) services, but enrollment in Part B is not automatic. To receive Part B an individual must pay a monthly premium of $7.20. There are also deductibles on both out-patient and in-patient care that the subscriber must pay before receiving benefits (see Table 3).

A major reason for high out-of-pocket expenses is the types of service which are not covered by the program (see Table 3). These include treatments of such common problems of the elderly as sight, hearing, dental, feet, and any out-of-hospital prescriptions, for whatever reason. Certain areas, such as psychiatric care, transfusions, and physical rehabilitation are minimally covered. In-patient care is extensively insured but there are more minimal benefits for preventative and out-patient services, which might deter certain deteriorative processes (Kerschner and Hirschfield, 1975). This lack of ameliorative care is most apparent with respect to nursing homes. Medicare will cover expenses in nursing homes for 100 days and then, if the person cannot pay for additional care, he or she will be covered by Medicaid. In 1971, $3.5 billion of public money was spent on nursing homes (Mendelson, 1973), a figure which may have already doubled. Despite this tremendous outlay, the types of services that could prevent institutionalization—home health services, homemakers, day care, and other forms of community supportive assistance—are generally not covered. Even such services as physical rehabilitation, which is effective in restoring to community life persons who have had strokes, back or head injuries, or fractures may be disallowed. Those administering Medicare can decide, with a "Catch-22" reasoning, that the prospective rehabilitation candidate is either "too well" or "too sick," although without retraining that person would otherwise have to go to a nursing home (Tager, personal communication). At the present time in California, for example, virtually no individuals with hip fractures are eligible for rehabilitation.

Medicaid is not specifically for elderly people. Nevertheless one out of every three Medicaid dollars is spent for skilled nursing home care (U.S. Department of Health, Education and Welfare, 1971). Older people

**Table 3    Coverage Available from Medicare and Medicaid**[1]

| Item | Medicare | Medicaid |
|---|---|---|
| Administration | Administered solely by federal gov't. | Administered by states, localities, and federal gov't. |
| Age Coverage | Only for people 65 and over and the disabled | For medically indigent persons of any age as determined by states. |
| Eligibility | Persons 65 and over and disabled Social Security recipients automatically enrolled for limited hospital and nursing home insurance as part of Social Security. People not receiving Social Security may also be eligible. | Persons must apply and meet state requirements. |
| Benefits | Benefits same throughout country. | Benefits may vary from state to state. |
| Types of benefits | Part "A" coverage For each spell of illness provides up to 90 days hospital care ($40 deductible) and up to 100 days of nursing home care after hospitalization. Visiting nurse service, home health aides, physical therapy, prosthetic devices, and limited care by a podiatrist | In most states, more expanded hospital and nursing home care and services of visiting home nurses and home aids for those eligible. |
|  | Part "B" Coverage Care by a physician in the office, home, or hospital (pays 80% of expenses after $50 deductible) out-patient clinic services, prosthetic devices in home, and limited ambulance service if patient signs up for $4 voluntary payments to S.S. | More expanded care by physician, including preventive check-ups. |
| Drugs and other Health Services | Drugs for home use and services of health professionals other than physicians not covered (except for limited podiatry service). | Some states cover drugs, dentistry, podiatry, optometry, prosthetic devices, eyeglasses, hearing aids, ambulance service, and oxygen. |
| Payment | Patient can pay directly and be reimbursed by federal government. | Most cases do not pay physician directly. Doctor bills state or agency responsible. |
| Fee Schedule | Pays usual and customary fees. | Some states have fixed fees, otherwise pay regular fees. |
| Finances | Social Security deductions. | Tax monies, federal-state-city. |

1. From Alexander and Podair, 1968, pp. 11–12.

can be eligible for Medicaid if they fall within prescribed income limits. Initially, Medicaid was designed to account for inadequacies of Medicare. It has often been confused with Medicare, yet both programs have distinctive features as indicated in Table 3.

Medicare and Medicaid were conceptually designed to assure the elderly and the medically indigent access to medical services. When catastrophic situations arise, Americans discover that these programs encourage hospitalization, fail to provide many needed services, and often result in a depletion of resources before one can qualify for Medicaid. And yet, Medicare is far from adequate and it is doubtful that major reform will be initiated in the near future.

## Income: Is It Enough?

In returning to the older person's budget, students can make their own estimate of the adequacy of incomes of older persons. Clearly, however, there are gaps and deficiencies in the various assistance programs that leave many older persons without income to meet essential needs.

Overall, the attempts since the 1930s to provide adequate income level and health care for older persons have had mixed results. At this point, a majority of older persons are able to meet basic needs and to live comfortably, but for a sizable group, the prospects of old age are for a continuing struggle to meet ends on a minimum level. There is agreement, in principal, and as evidenced by our social legislation, that persons who have worked all their lives are entitled to a guaranteed pension and health care, especially as their employment prospects have become more limited. But this commitment has not eradicated the poverty that some persons must endure in their old age.

## References

Alexander, S. R. and Podair, S., *Medicaid: the people's health plan*, Public Affairs Pamphlet, 1968.

Butler, R. N. and Lewis, M. I. *Aging and mental health.* St. Louis: Mosby, 1973.

Kerschner, P. A. and Hirschfield, I. S. "Public policy and aging: analytic approaches." In D. S. Woodruff and J. E. Birren (Eds.) *Aging: scientific perspectives and social issues*, New York: D. Van Nostrand, 1975.

Main, Jeremy "What ails medicine," *Money, 3,* 5, May 1976.

"Major provisions of the pension bill signed by Ford." *The New York Times*, September 3, 1974, p. 24.

Mendelson, M. A. *Tender loving greed: how the incredibly lucrative nursing home industry is exploiting America's old*, New York: Knopf, 1974.

Nader, R. and Blackwell, K. *You and your pension.* New York: Grossman Publishers, 1973.

Palmore, E. "Compulsory versus flexible retirement: issues and facts." *Gerontologist*, 1972, *12*, 343–348.

*Report of the Committee on Economic Security.* Washington, D.C.: U.S. Government Printing Office, 1935.

*Social indicators: 1973.* Office of Management and Budget, Washington, D.C.: U.S. Dept. of Commerce, 1973,

Tager, R. M. Personal communication.

"The elderly in America." *Population Bulletin, 30,* No. 3, 1975, 1–36.

U.S. Department of Health, Education and Welfare, *Social Security programs in the United States*, Washington, D.C.: DHEW Publication No. (SSA) 73-11915, 1973.

Vasey, Wayne. *Government and Social Welfare*, New York: Holt, Rinehart and Winston, 1958.

# 23

# The Abuse of the Urban Aged

"When the bulldozers come, they have to go, along with everyone else. But there's almost no place for the aged to go."

by James E. Birren

THE AGED POOR have been unable to join the flight of younger and affluent families to suburbia to avoid the noise, smog, dirt, social tension and poor housing of the central city. Instead, millions of them remain in unattractive, inadequate and necessarily inexpensive housing, trying to cope with the inadequacies of the contemporary city, getting less and less a fair share of its goods and services. Urban development thus far has failed to relieve them and in fact often has worsened matters for them. Most of the time the urban aged are simply displaced by urban redevelopment, which is accompanied by new shopping areas, apartment buildings, restaurants and hotels that are too expensive for them.

The wretchedness of this huge, silent minority is an incredibly challenging problem. Part of the difficulty stems from the fact that builders, if not planners, ignore the critical reality that cities are primarily social organizations—that they are only secondarily collections of concrete, steel and wooden structures. The principle that structure follows function has been obscured; much of the agony in the cities suggests that builders and planners mistakenly believed that function would be determined by structure.

True, business and industry have learned to survey sites and buildings to determine economic feasibility; they do it well, but precious few have worked up equal skill at surveying the social functions of proposed physical facilities. And even fewer can properly weigh the extent to which the facilities meet social functions. Persons who can best judge safety and material design have control of construction. Yet the first function of urban buildings and land is social.

Building designs as well as city plans should be submitted to panels of behavioral and social scientists competent to analyze the social system into which they are supposed to fit. There are now too few such specialists, which suggests that the universities should be training them so that future planners will have access to this competence. The concept of *life space* should be used in any discussion of cities because it implies the functional

relations of people to their environment. Ideally a city should provide a life space that offers many options and opportunities to express individual differences in needs and desires. Because they are poor, more than half of the over-65 citizens have very little to say about where they will live, or about much of anything else in their life space.

We know that an aged person tends to live with relatives because he is poor —that if he had an adequate income, he would live near his children or other kin but would be independent of them. In fact, the number of aged persons living with relatives has been declining.

We know that most elderly persons have lived a long time in their communities. The 1963 Social Security Survey of the Aged indicated that 80 per cent of couples over 62 have lived 10 or more years in their communities. On average they had lived in their communities 32 years and in their homes 16 years. Two thirds of the married had median equity of $10,000 in nonfarm homes and median assets of $11,180 (including homes). Among couples with at least one partner over 65, 41 per cent were classified as poor or they got less than $2,500 a year. If all the assets of individuals are prorated as annual income over expected life, the median income for married couples over 65 would be $3,795. Thus, even if the over-65 couple spent one-third of their annual income (plus assets) for housing, it would be only $1,265 a year, or about $105 a month.

Though the aged often appear to dislike their housing, they do not move as frequently as the young. About one fifth of the national population changes residence each year. Yet, a survey in Los Angeles showed that while about 90 per cent of individuals over 50 were dissatisfied with their living arrangements, only 13 per cent actually moved during a one-year period. Thus we know that there is more dissatisfaction and less mobility among the aged than the young. Moreover, at least half of the aged couples would appear to be locked into living arrangements simply because they are too poor to move.

We also know that a massive effort to

**"... they are subject to the same passions and colors and vices and politics and biases that divide the rest of mankind."**

make matters better probably would misfire if it followed a simple-minded notion of the poor as a single, self-contained group. It is questionable whether the aged regard themselves or behave as a minority group, or that they cross ethnic, religious and occupational lines to associate with each other. Thus the future urban environment for the aged must accommodate wide differences in interests, education, energy level, health, religion and customs.

Any approach to the place of the aged in the city should be organized around the concept of life space—that part of the city the individual occupies physically, socially and psychologically. Good or pleasant housing is big in the individual's life space but it is not the biggest aspect of urban life. Obviously it is simpler to analyze housing needs than to go into the infinitely more complex relations of housing to other aspects of urban environment.

Optimum life space for the aged would offer support in the context of familiar objects and persons. It would also let the individual choose patterns of both privacy and involvement—he should have both private sanctuary and easy contact with others. It should be socializing and it should put him in a stream of useful and emotionally supportive information.

Even good housing may cease to be supportive of adequate life space when an individual ages. He may still live where he settled as a young adult but may be suffering a lonely symbolism of his early life. If, in fact, you count the number of his daily contacts and an estimate is made of the intimacy of these contacts, you may find that he is poorly related to the community where he has lived for a long time but has been an increasingly marginal resident.

Young adults, because they are agile, can adapt more easily to the increasingly scattered nature of urban functions. The mere reduced agility of the aged individual markedly reduces the life space available to him in the cities. It is easier for him if he moves into an older neighborhood with clustered small shops and narrow streets. Paradoxically, it is in the most deteriorated areas of cities that aged persons may live independent lives, piecing together for themselves the combinations of needed services. That's why

such care should be taken in the redevelopment of these areas. The replacement of deteriorated areas with high-rise housing may put shopping areas out of reach at the same time that it drives rents too high for the aged poor. It is often almost impossible to get to new shopping centers on foot.

The specialized nature of modern cities scatters social functions widely: shopping centers replace corner stores, far-away cemeteries take the place of churchyards, neighborhood doctors and dentists move to medical centers. All betoken the impersonal atmosphere of the modern city. Services are perhaps more efficient—and more generally available—but you have to be mobile to use them.

Coping and associating with unfamiliar customs produces emotional and mental tension in the aged. Left to their own tendencies they will seek out companionship with their mirror images, members of the same ethnic, religious, occupational and social-class groupings. This is why religious groups have provided so much of the specialized housing for the very aged. They provide physical care while they reduce the older person's feeling of alienation in an impersonal urban society. The proliferation of clubs for the aged is evidence that the needs of the elderly are not commonly being met by place of residence alone. The nonworking retired resident in an apartment building largely occupied by middle-aged adults can be a remarkably isolated person. Since friendships often grow out of work relationships, the retired person has lost a prime source of new friendships in urban life. With the shrinking life space that follows advancing age, objects that are near at hand provide more and more of a person's psychological support. That is why the immediate environment assumes such importance for the aged. Mobile young adults rarely perceive this.

Not surprisingly, the aged, like the young, most enjoy the company of their contemporaries. Even the new friends of the aged are likely to be elderly. Such friends are important in the enjoyment of life's activities and they also provide a shock-absorbing quality in crisis situations. The candid, mutual soul-searching that is permitted by a confidante appears to be an important factor in maintaining mental health in crises. Quite possibly, if we were to look at the mental health of the aged in as much detail as we have that of the young, we would find a considerably higher proportion of psychopathology than we now recognize. Certainly more people could lead more productive, contented lives in the city if we had ways of detecting individuals who require special help—and if we had special facilities to offer the needed services.

A wide range of living facilities is necessary to handle the transition from independent living with a large family unit to the more dependent, less mobile life of the aged. Yet the progression of change from complete independence to restricted dependence proceeds at individual rates. A fortunate few may never be confined to a home, a room, or a bed at life's end, but many will, and in cramped quarters. Some of the aged will outlive their peers, siblings and in some cases their children, and if they become infirm there will be no one to provide the protection and help they require.

Then there is death, the universal, which can never be far from the thoughts of the aged. Its circumstances, and the need for contact with the familiar, are dominant concerns of the older person. Almost nothing about today's urban environment can help the aged meet death with dignity. There is a large population of widows in our society, resulting from earlier deaths in men and the male tendency to marry younger women. Our urban way of life thus must offer a good life for millions of widows.

As areas of cities deteriorate and become economically unproductive, there is a desire to clean it all up and when the bulldozers come, the aged have to go, along with everyone else. But there's almost no place for the aged to go—because they have so little mobility and money. And they can't return to the redeveloped site. Even if public housing has been put up, it is usually impossible for the displaced aged to qualify for it.

It is easier to design and construct housing units than to create a community social design that replaces familiar people, objects and places. It is unsurprising, then, that the aged are reluctant to stay and reluctant to go. When they move, no matter how, it's a sorry swap: they give up familiar, supporting things; they get a clean, new apartment. Also, the ordinary frustrations of moving and the tax on energy are formidable, and for many of the elderly, they are just too much. Rehousing plans should deal with these psychological and social factors.

Older persons become discouraged by a succession of obstacles that would not inhibit the young: high bus steps, the need to cross wide, busy streets to catch a bus, fast-changing traffic lights, high curbs and inadequate building labels. The aged may do without banks, doctors, repair services, dentists, shops, lawyers and parks because of the energy it takes to get to them.

The range of options in living arrangements available to older adults should be even greater than those available to the young-adult population. Access to goods, services and recreation must be fashioned with the aged in mind. For example, every major cultural event in a metropolitan area should provide for the aged—information, access, ticketing and seating.

The aged frequently have television sets and can watch scheduled programs when others are otherwise occupied. Television could provide valuable information services and educational programs for the elderly.

Whole cities for the aged have been proposed, it being argued that the elderly find the good life with their contemporaries. This is not necessarily so; it could be wrong. Most of the aged prefer to live independently, near persons their own age and within easy reach of one or more of their children or other relatives. The aged should be able to share the use of buildings, parks, beaches, cultural centers and churches with members of other age groups since they tend to use them at different times. Congregate living arrangements for the aged should be distributed in communities so that they can share facilities and services with the whole community . . . with all age groups.

Although there are more than 19 million of the aged in our midst, planning for them is inadequate and often comes only as an afterthought. The reason for this is that the aged do not have a clear relationship with industry and that they are not particularly good consumers. Another reason is that the aged are not a homogeneous group—they are subject to the same passions and colors and vices and politics and biases that divide the rest of mankind. The urban environment must be planned to accommodate their wide range of individual differences.

The best planning would encourage congregate living arrangements of older persons—small apartment buildings preferably—adjacent to areas where they can share community facilities with other age groups. The aged are best housed in a community where they can walk to the shops and offices that meet their daily needs. Generally speaking the older the individual, the greater the number of services that must be near at hand.

Architects and city planners should involve behavioral and social scientists in developing the goals and patterns of living arrangements for the aged. Only through exchange of information can we even begin to describe the social system in which the older person functions and thus design a flexible supporting system with options. Moreover, we must follow up with evaluations so that we can learn from mistakes. This means even wider interdisciplinary involvement—architects, planners, behavioral and social scientists, engineers and biological scientists. Clearly more such people must be trained to meet the planning and construction needs of the future. Otherwise what we euphemistically call urban redevelopment will continue its cruel disruption of the lives of the elderly.

# 24

# Age-Ism
# Another Form of Bigotry

by Robert N. Butler

Malcolm X, the Kerner Commission Report, and a variety of other persons, events, and materials have made the concept of racism familiar. Social class discrimination also needs no introduction. However, we may soon have to consider very seriously a form of bigotry we now tend to overlook: age discrimination or age-ism, prejudice by one age group toward other age groups. If such bias exists, might it not be especially evident in America; a society that has traditionally valued pragmatism, action, power, and the vigor of youth over contemplation, reflection, experience, and the wisdom of age?

In the affluent community of Chevy Chase, recent events have revealed a complex interweaving of class, color, and age discrimination that may highlight the impact of these forces in our national life.

On January 30, 1969, the National Capital Housing Authority, the public housing agency of the District of Columbia, held hearings on its proposal to purchase Regency House, a high-rise apartment building in Chevy Chase, for the elderly poor. If finally approved, Regency House would be the first public housing project west of Rock Creek Park, the traditional boundary between black and white in Washington, D.C.

The middle-class and middle-aged white citizenry of Chevy Chase appeared at both the hearings and at the Chevy Chase Citizens' Association meeting at a local public school on February 17. They vigorously protested on a variety of grounds the National Capital Housing Authority proposal. Some of these aroused citizens demonstrated that they could practice the politics of protest and confrontation in a manner as impassioned as that of the young and alienated.

Chevy Chase residents were irritated and angered by a proposal to provide what they considered luxury housing (there is a swimming pool on the roof of Regency House) for older people who were not accustomed to "luxury."

Among statements heard at the meetings and quoted in the local newspapers were: "You would open the door for people who don't know how to live." "Slums are made by the people who live in them." "It (public housing) has to come sometime but not this time or in this place." "I am not against old folks, believe me." "Who wants all those old people around." Zoning, tax losses, costs, and property values were also mentioned, but it was clear that more than concern over the pocketbook was operating.

Class, color, and age have always been parts of the structure of American communities. Since the passage of the Public Housing Act of 1937, we have tended to increase the divisions within America by separating the poor and segregating the non-white. Today, despite Social Security, the elderly poor are common, and they are frequently black. There has also been a trend in recent years toward segregation of the middle-class elderly in "retirement communities" and "housing for the elderly."

Neighborhood reaction against the use of Regency House for the elderly poor carries implications beyond Chevy Chase. The classic or scapegoat explanation for prejudice turns upon the unconscious effort to justify one's own weaknesses by finding them in others—in other races, religious, or nationalities. Personal insecurity, once generalized, becomes the basis of prejudice and hostility.

Age-ism describes the subjective experience implied in the popular notion of the generation gap. Prejudice of the middle-aged against the old in this instance, and against the young in others, is a serious national problem. Age-ism reflects a deep seated uneasiness on the part of the young and middle-aged—a personal revulsion to and distaste for growing old, disease, disability; and fear of powerlessness, "uselessness," and death.

Cultural attitudes in our society reinforce these feelings. We have chosen mandatory retirement from the work force and thus removed the elderly from the mainstream of life. Age-ism is manifested in the taunting remarks about "old fogeys," in the special vulner-

1. Washington School of Psychiatry and George Washington University Medical School, 3815 Huntington St., NW, Washington, D.C., 20015.

132

ability of the elderly to muggings and robberies, in age discrimination in employment independent of individual competence, and in the probable inequities in the allocation of research funds. Although persons 65 years of age and over account for 25% of all public mental hospital admissions, only 3% of the research budget of the National Institute of Mental Health is spent in relevant research. Less than 1% of the budget of the entire National Institutes of Health is devoted to the study of aging phenomena.

The issue goes deeper. It is the middle-aged, after all, upon whom the "burdens imposed" by both ends of the life cycle, the young and the old, necessarily fall. From their purses come hard-won earnings to educate the young and to care for the elderly (in our time collectively, although inadequately, through Medicare and Social Security). Middle life has been labeled the period of "gravity" because of its manifold responsibilities. It is not surprising that some members of the middle group "cop out" of marriages, of jobs, even of society while others rigidly and tenaciously hold on to what they have struggled so hard to achieve. Many middle-aged people, of course, respond flexibly and creatively to both young and old.

Age-ism is also seen in other groups. The young may not trust anyone over 30; but those over 30 may not trust anyone younger. The Walker Commission report has described how young people were beaten-up in the "police riot" in Chicago during the Democratic Convention. These attacks have been viewed as class-determined (lower-class police punishing middle-class children) and the age factor has been minimized. Yet future historians may find in the political year 1968 the elements of a counter-revolution by the middle-aged against both the young and old.

Many different objections were raised to the National Capital Housing Authority proposal for housing the elderly poor in Chevy Chase. Color and class were surely most significant, yet racism alone cannot account for the "middle-aged riot"—for screeching, shouting, booing, and stomping of feet that occurred at the hearings and the citizens' meeting. A local official noted that the same arguments against public housing had been heard from middle-class Negro families in the Northeast, a predominantly black section of Washington.

The proposed purchase of the nine-story 172-unit apartment building gave rise to an extraordinary amount of misinformation. In the first place, Regency House is not particularly luxurious. The National Capital Housing Authority now houses about 1600 elderly individuals or couples, and over the last two years, has spent $8.3 million to buy three high-rise apartment houses that had been privately constructed and rented. These buildings, all less than 5 years old, contain more than 600 apartments and are well equipped with air conditioning, off-street parking, garbage disposals, and swimming pools. A swimming pool, so offensive to the affluent Northwest Washingtonians who objected to the Regency House proposal, could be beneficial for the health and recreation of older people.

Second, contrary to the apparent fears that only elderly Negroes on welfare could occupy Regency House, NCHA housing is for low-income elderly and not just for welfare or black elderly. The maximum annual income that an elderly person may have to live in NCHA housing is $3,300 for an individual and $4,300 for a couple. Retired school teachers, railroad employees and others, both black and white, would seek to live in Regency House and indeed these groups make up 10% of the 1,200 persons who have been on NCHA housing waiting lists for an average of 2 years. Tenants at Regency House would have to pay $50 per month for an efficiency and $55 per month for a one-bedroom apartment. Preference is given to veterans and to those evicted by urban renewal.

Some opponents of the Regency House proposal expressed fear that families with children would eventually move in, although the apartment house contains only efficiencies and one-bedroom apartments.

Others considered that "these people" were undeserving and should have been more provident. Yet the stereotype of the undeserving poor seems curiously outmoded. Many of "these people" were at the height of their earning power and productive years during the Depression when income and the possibility of saving were minimal. With inflation spiraling at a rate of 4 to 6%, it has been difficult for people of all ages living on fixed incomes to save, irrespective of prudence. Despite a 13% across-the-board increase in Social Security benefits in January, 1967, more people have fallen below the poverty line because of inflation than have risen above it. Fortunately, consideration is now being given to include escalator clauses in Social Security to provide for cost of living increases.

Other opponents of the Regency House proposal misunderstood the financial basis of the plan. They feared that monies for the purchase of this building would come out of their own pockets through local taxes. The costs actually do come out of their pockets in part, but through the federal Internal Revenue receipts that provide for partial subsidies for public housing throughout the country.

Still another point in the opposition was that "these people" would have a higher cost of living in Chevy Chase than elsewhere. Actually there has been some evidence that living costs are higher in Washington's ghetto areas.

Among the positive features of the area is the location of Regency House close to conveniences useful to older people: drug stores, reasonably priced restaurants, cafeterias, and supermarkets. A community center, a library, and public transportation are also nearby.

Prior to the selection of Regency House, the National Capital Housing Authority had to study carefully the 200 apartment buildings it has been offered to determine soundness of construction, proper location, and appropriate price. Under an executive order from President Johnson, National Capital Housing Authority is required to space public housing throughout the city of Washington. If National Capital Housing Authority had not selected Regency House, it would have chosen some other apartment building in a comparable area of Northwest Washington.

Commissioner Walter E. Washington approved the

purchase on March 6 and the Department of Housing and Urban Development gave its approval. There was talk among the middle-aged opponents of legal action against the decision. One stated ground was that public monies should not be used to enforce social policies.

H. G. Wells once said that history is a race between education and catastrophe. The NCHA might have mitigated the storm of controversy and, more important, facilitated the reception of the elderly poor into Chevy Chase through an educational campaign with the assistance of the press (both the *Washington Post* and the *Star* have supported the NCHA), and various interested groups and individuals within and without the community. Many groups testified in favor of Regency House, including the Northwest Washington Fair Housing Association. City-wide organizations, such as the League of Women Voters and the D.C. Democratic Central Committee have supported the proposal. However, there was a large measure of good will within the community that was not mobilized.

The experience of other housing for the elderly sponsored by NCHA could have been reported and potential residents themselves asked to participate in neighborhood meetings. Chevy Chase residents, imprisoned in such myths as "deterioration," could have been invited to visit other NCHA housing.

Such a program would have been political education in the very best sense. Perhaps the same number of Chevy Chase residents would have objected; but their protests would have been drowned out by a better informed, articulate majority. Moreover, both the youth and the middle-aged of the area would have learned something about themselves, including the implacable course of their own aging.

To explore the bigotry in age-ism is not to minimize the other more salient features of racial and class discrimination observed in Chevy Chase. But aging is the great sleeper in American life. By the year 2000, according to current population projections, there will be approximately 33 million retired people each with an average of 25 years of retirement time. Should there be major breakthroughs in finding deterrants to aging along with the present steady pace of medical progress, there would be still greater numbers of old and retired people. How are they (that is, we) to be supported: What are they (we) to do? The Beatles sing:

> "Will you still need me,
> Will you still feed me,
> When I'm sixty-four.
> You'll be older, too..."

Chevy Chase residents, like Americans in general, are unaware of or unwilling to acknowledge the poverty of the elderly. George Santayana said that, but for the excellence of the typical single life in a society, no nation deserves to be remembered more than the sands of the sea. If it may be said that the quality of a culture can be measured by its regard for its least powerful members, for example, its care for the elderly and its protection and education of its children, the readings for ours are disappointingly low.

Social Security and Medicare, which most Americans consider landmarks in social legislation, are little more than sops to the conscience. The average income of the person over 65 in America is $1,800 per year. Nearly 7 million of our 19 million elderly are below the poverty line. The average monthly Social Security check of a retired male worker in America today is $86.04. Since Medicare pays an average of only 35% of medical bills, it has thus far failed to provide adequate financial support for the health care of the elderly. Medicare, Social Security, and public housing are examples of tokenism. They are not fundamentally meeting human needs for health care, income, and housing.

In the District of Columbia there are 73,000 people of age 65 and above. The immediate area of Regency House has a heavy concentration of older people (and four old age homes) but in Washington, as in other cities, the elderly tend to be locked in older, slum-ridden areas. Many elderly, for example, live in Washington's Model Cities area, which includes the Shaw section. Much of the public housing in the District has been built in the Anacostia area across the river.

Ironically, one could question the wisdom of concentrating old people in specific housing. Sweden, for example, has been giving up high-rise enclaves for its older citizens. Rather than a housing program for older citizens, it might be more desirable socially to provide rent supplements or, ultimately, appropriate income maintenance so that the elderly could live anywhere throughout the city. Of course, some older people do want to live together and coordinated services—medical, social, and recreational—can be placed in housing for the elderly. For those with increasing limitation, congregate living with available services is mandatory. Thus it is probably wisest for a society to provide a range of alternatives. One of the greatest losses of old age is that of choice.

One thing is certain: further concentration of public housing in limited sections of any city—concentrating the poor or the rich or the black or the old or the young—only contribute to the divisiveness of our society particularly the separation into two societies in the Kerner Report.

I do not want my children to grow up in an isolated neighborhood, knowing neither the realities of old age nor the meaning of racial heterogeneity. Age, race and social class discrimination are clearly inimical to the developing human community and to the extent that our community of Chevy Chase is "closed," *it* is inherently disadvantaged.

Age-ism might parallel (it might be wishful thinking to say replace) racism as the great issue of the next 20 to 30 years and age bigotry is seen within minority groups themselves.

Seventeen per cent of our electorate is over 65 already, but at present it is not voting as a group. Consequently politicians are not zealously seeking the votes of older citizens. Yet this may well change; perhaps one day we will be hearing of Senior Power. We don't all grow white or black, but we all grow old.

# 25

# Retirement and Leisure

by Morton Puner

In the year 1973 it was finally recorded that, on the occasion of his retirement dinner after 32 years of devoted service, a man got up and said: "I'll be brief. The working conditions here are terrible. I haven't liked a day of it. I'm glad I'm out of it." And sat down. The news story does not go into reactions of boss, colleagues, friends, or family. Nor does it tell of the new retiree's feelings the morning after. But clearly before making his brief speech, he had faced a moment of truth—and decided, for once, not to play the game.

Work ethic and guilt feelings aside, the truth is that most people do not like their daily toil. Abraham Lincoln once said, "My father taught me to work, but not to love it. I never did like to work and I don't deny it. I'd rather read, tell stories, crack jokes, talk, laugh—anything but work." It is different for some professionals and creative workers or for those who are specially driven. But for the great majority, work is hardly the soul-satisfying experience that the "joy-in-work" philosophers have assumed. Juanita M. Kreps of Duke University, a pioneer in the study of the economics of aging, says that "work is often tiring, boring, and quite unpleasant. It is no accident that the pressure for shorter working hours (albeit, with no reduction in pay) has come from industrial and commercial workers, who are much less satisfied with their working conditions than the professional."

To those who remember the Great Depression—and the desperation of men seeking any kind of job—the result of a study of attitudes today must seem astonishing. Nearly 400 white male blue-collar workers were asked: "If you could retire with as much money as you need for a good pension, and not have to work anymore, would you do it right away, or would you wait a while?"

The level of the job bears upon the answer. Two-thirds of all men over 55 in low-level tasks (with little variety, responsibility, or autonomy) said, "Yes. I want to retire right away." So, too, did fully half of all the men *under 40* in low-level tasks. Of men in higher-level tasks, half of those over 55 and a third of those under 40 also said they preferred immediate retirement.

In practice, a growing number of persons do indeed pick early retirement—age 60 or even 55—and tighten their belts, accept lower pensions and Social Security benefits (even in face of rising prices and taxes) in order to get out from under their work a few years earlier. It is not just physical surroundings or tedium or rigors of the job they wish to escape. "Health" is often given as the reason for retiring; emotional, as well as physical, health is at stake. For there are also the matters of not being one's own man or woman, of subservience in countless ways, of being pigeonholed and frustrated and angry and insecure.

Why then is there so often the fear of being retired—and of having all that long-cherished leisure time to fill up? The businessman or executive considers the prospects gloomily and says, in some desperation: "Golf is not enough. I'll take up painting or pottery—or something." A working man worries about having enough to live on, about spending all his days around the house, and says, "Maybe I can find a part-time job, here or somewhere else." Even those who calculate they can get by on their pensions often try at the last moment to cling to their jobs—although they may have spent the previous twenty years cursing boss, rat-race, or the stupidity of the job itself. Trade unions talk of lowering retirement ages—and also of bargaining for "flexible retirement" so that a worker can stay on a few more years, according to his ability. Wives of retirees have their doubts about it, too. They've been heard to define retirement as "twice as much husband on half as much income." That they don't really mean this as a joke is borne out by a Duke University finding that 55% of the wives of retired men (and 67% of the wives of early retirees) are sorry about the whole thing. Still, the loss of occupation is felt much more acutely by men than by women. The women continue to have care of home and family to busy themselves with. "To many working class men, retirement is a social disaster," notes Peter Townsend.

There are at least three good reasons why those who retire often seem to be victims as well as beneficiaries of the pension system. One is the matter of reduced income; a second is the tradition of the work ethic and the loss of role in society; and a third is lack of preparation for retirement and simply not knowing how to use leisure time. Sociologist A. J. Jaffe, taking the extreme view, is not at all sure the problem can be solved for many of the old. "Retirement in our society is a contradiction of the work ethic," he says, and training a man to enjoy retirement after a lifetime spent in the throes of work (and in the belief that work is moral and right) "seems to be difficult, if not impossible."

Even if the contradiction can be overcome, Dr. Jaffe is not sure the results may be desirable. "For men to enjoy their retirement, they will need years of practice to overcome the work ethic," he says. "And with the diminution of our work ethic we may ask: What will happen to our economy? There is reason to believe that societies that value leisure greatly have trouble achieving large economic growth."

Society must be served; industry must be served; fortunately there are spokesmen for the individual man and woman, too. As we seek to reconcile many interests, the subjects of retirement and the use of postretirement time have become the most hotly and lengthily discussed of all aspects of aging. The conflict of interests is seen most clearly in the debate on "compulsory" versus "flexible" retirement, a debate which has escalated as more and more workers are affected by retirement policies (and as national costs of maintaining incomes and health care go up, too). The charge has been raised in the United States and Great Britain that compulsory retirement is a clear case of discrimination against an age group and should be banned, along with other forms of age, sex, and race discrimination in employment. Leonard Davis, honorary president of the American Association of Retired Persons, says unequivocally that the United States must abolish mandatory retirement if it is to meet its responsibilities to its older population. Still, it takes an enlightened big-scale industrial employer to see it that way; if any employer thinks of his workers as cogs in a machine, he may also think that it is easier and more profitable to treat them as cogs, disposing of them and replacing them in uniform fashion as they wear out.*

The issue is being resolved to some degree: More and more companies are adopting forms of flexible retirement, with valued or key employees staying on beyond normal retirement age, negotiating and renegotiating the length of their service from time to time, depending on their health and function.

All the while, the counter-trend toward earlier retirement continues. In 1970, the United Auto Workers union first adopted the slogan, "30 and out," calling for full retirement benefits at any age after thirty years of service. The UAW settled for improved benefits at age 58 in 1971, and at age 56 in 1972. "30 and out" has caught on with blue-collar and professional workers

alike, but agreeing on what is adequate income—and getting it—will be a critical issue in labor-management negotiations for a long time to come. This is, indeed, the paradox of the moment: There are greater social and economic pressures to have the elderly retire earlier from the labor market. But, in the United States most of all, millions of the old must continue to work if they are to avoid ending their lives in poverty. More than a quarter of all Americans over 65 still work full or part time because they must. Leonard Davis says that "as things now stand, the overwhelming majority of older Americans must retire on less—often much less—than half of their preretirement income." Among others, he and William E. Oriol, staff director of the U.S. Senate Committee on Aging, call inadequate retirement income "the number one problem of older Americans."

The problem, alas, does not end there. A statement of the United Steelworkers gives an idea of the scope of other union concern. Apart from income, there are still "vital needs" to be met: "Appropriate housing and enjoyable use of leisure time are not available to large numbers of retirees and pensioners. Too often, drabness and loss of pride and dignity are the lot of many who were unprepared for retirement or who live in a community that has failed to provide services and living conditions suitable for retirees . . ."

Leisure, as retirement's blessing, seems to be a mixed one—even when the financial problem is held at bay. An international gerontological conference was held in 1972 devoted solely to leisure as a contemporary problem; one of its reports stressed that many old people spend several hours a day doing "absolutely nothing." (The term was not further defined.) Sociologist Jaffe warns that societies that value leisure greatly may have trouble with their economic growth. Joseph J. Spengler of Duke University has an apocalyptic view: "Ultimately, no issue is of greater long-run concern than the question of *how* man uses his increasing income and discretionary time. Poets have told us that every empire expires in the soft lap of luxury. Gibbon describes how, in a few years, indolence and luxurious living reduced the Vandals, once fierce conquerors of the Romans, to cowardice, ignominy, and self-pity. Manifestations of dissipative processes are already evident in the West . . ."

It may take a long, long time for the "dissipative processes" to take effect. Retirement and the new leisure have already produced their own burgeoning industries —sometimes frantic ones—which allow no one involved any rest or chance to become decadent. Dozens of books and hundreds of articles are published each year explaining "how to make the most of your retirement" and exploring "the creative use of the new freedom." There are a host of organizations concerned with the rights and opportunities of retirees and preretirees. Probably the largest is the American Association of Retired Persons—"pioneering the new world of retirement"—which has about 6 million members, two magazines, *Dynamic Maturity* (for preretirees 50 to 65 years old) and *Modern Maturity* (for all persons 55 and over), and—with its sister organization, the National Retired Teachers Association—a score of "better retirement" booklets and other publications, along with

---

* There is considerably more to the issue and a better case may be made for mandatory retirement than suggested here. A fair listing of both sides is presented in "Compulsory versus Flexible Retirement Issues and Facts," by Erdman Palmore in the next article in this book.

the rest of its genuinely creative and valuable program. Other voluntary and professional groups of many types are also devoted to the practical aspects—helping retirees to find new jobs or careers, make money, get all available government benefits, meet their budgetary, housing, health, nutritional, social, and recreational needs. The business of keeping old people active and well in retirement extends into dozens of fields; a well-directed letter or phone call from an anxious retiree may start him on the road to receiving more guidance and advice than he can keep up with.*

On the road—but it still may take him years to adjust successfully to his new station in life. The act of retirement, its immediate prospects, continue to be a fearsome thing. Gerontologists consider that retirement —along with the death of a mate—are the two most shattering, traumatic events of later life. The day his retirement starts, a man is apt suddenly to feel very old. (It is an actuarial cliché that the first year of retirement has among the highest of all mortality rates.) It is, of course, not just the end of his usual job and the prospect of living on a reduced income that so affect him. The state of being retired is a new and difficult category in societies just beginning to be defined; past societies had aged people, but no retired ones. With retirement comes loss of status, association, and role— that and the fear of uncertainty of change. At a retiree's farewell dinner, those around him may feel a sense of relief; some deadwood is being removed, their chances for advancement enhanced. He, in turn, may feel that he cannot be replaced and things will never be the same after he leaves—or, at least, he hopes so. Unlike the case that opens this chapter, both parties usually lie a lot about their real feelings, all in a spirit of bonhomie and farewell. But the feelings are there, the damage done. After the shows of goodwill and appreciation— and the presentations of watch, luggage, or loving cup— the retiree is unalterably alone, no longer a member of any team, on his own as he slips into the uncharted and final phase of his life.

## Notes

Juanita M. Kreps is professor of economics and dean of the Women's College at Duke University. Her remarks appear in *Lifetime Allocation of Work and Income: Essays in the Economics of Aging* (Durham, N.C.: Duke University Press, 1971), which is also the source of the quotation about Abraham Lincoln's aversion to work.

The study of blue-collar workers is reported in *Where Have All the Robots Gone?*, by Harold L. Sheppard and N. Q. Herrick (New York: Free Press-Macmillan, 1972).

The Peter Townsend quotation is from *The Family Life of Old People*

Professor A. J. Jaffe is associated with the Bureau of Applied Social Research, Columbia University. His article, "The Middle Years: Neither Too Young nor Too Old," appears in *Industrial Gerontology* (Washington, D.C.: National Institute of Industrial Gerontology, National Council on Aging, 1971).

Leonard Davis's remarks appear in "Tomorrow's Role for Retirees," *Modern Maturity*, August-September 1972.

The United Steelworkers statement is quoted in *The Aging Worker and the Union: Employment and Retirement of Middle-Aged and Older Workers*, by Ewan Clague, Balraj Palli, and Leo Kramer (New York: Praeger, 1971).

William E. Oriel's remark appears in "Congress, Politics, and the Elderly," in *The Future of Aging and the Aged*, edited by George L. Maddox (Atlanta, Ga.: Southern Newspaper Publishers Association Foundation, 1971).

Joseph J. Spengler is James B. Duke professor of economics, Duke University. This quotation comes from his introduction to *Lifetime Allocation of Work and Income, op. cit.*

* There is good reason for this emphasis on postretirement activities and problems in the United States. In most countries, retirement is accepted as a time of rest after a lifetime of work. In the United States, it is seen as something else, according to *Old People in Three Industrial Societies*. Comparing postretirement practices in the United States, Britain, and Denmark, the study says that "the data suggest that activity is so highly valued by older Americans that the pastimes of retirement take on the aspects of work."

# 26

Compulsory retirement is increasing so that about half of wage and salary workers who retire at age 65 do so because of compulsory retirement. Compulsory retirement is discrimination against an age category and prevents many older workers from continuing employment. Flexible retirement would better utilize the skills and experience of older persons and increase the income of the aged. It may also increase life satisfaction and longevity. The facts do not support most arguments for compulsory retirement.

# Compulsory Versus Flexible Retirement: Issues and Facts

Erdman Palmore. PhD[1]

The local, state, and national conferences involved in the 1971 White House Conference on Aging have increased concern with one of the most controversial issues in gerontology: that of compulsory retirement at a fixed age versus flexible retirement based on ability. Debate on this perennial issue also seems to increase as compulsory retirement policies affect more and more workers who are still able to work and as the national costs of maintaining incomes and health care for the retired steadily escalate. Some argue that compulsory retirement is a clear case of discrimination against an age category and should be banned along with other forms of age, sex, and race discrimination in employment (Gould, 1968).

Various arguments and theories supporting one side of the other have appeared in scattered reports and articles (Busse & Kreps, 1964; Havighurst, 1969; Hyden, 1966, Kreps, 1961; Koyl, 1970; Lambert, 1964; Mathiasen, 1953; Palmore, 1969a). This article attempts to summarize these arguments and present the relevant facts as a basis for future private and public policy.

We will first present the facts on the extent of compulsory retirement, then discuss the theories and facts supporting flexible retirement, and third, discuss those supporting compulsory retirement. Finally, we will present three proposals for encouraging flexible retirement policies.

### Extent of Compulsory Retirement

The practice of compulsory retirement apparently became widespread only in this century and grew along with the swift industrialization and growth of large corporations in the early 1900s (Mathiasen, 1953). A series of national surveys conducted by the Social Security Administration and others show that compulsory retirement policies affect a large and growing proportion of older workers. A comparison of the reasons for retirement given in the 1951 and the 1963 Social Security surveys of the aged indicate that the proportions of male beneficiaries who retired because of compulsory retirement provisions doubled during those 12 years (11% in 1951 and 21% in 1963 for wage and salary workers retired within the preceeding 5 years [Palmore 1967]). In their 1969 Survey of Newly Entitled Beneficiaries, the Social Security Administration found that 52% of the nonwork-

I. Duke University Medical Center, Durham 27710. Research on this paper was supported in part by Grant HD-00668, NICHD, USPHS.

ing beneficiaries, who had been wage or salary workers and who became entitled at age 65, had retired because of compulsory retirement (Reno, 1971) (those who retired before they reached 65, about 2/3 of the new beneficiaries, usually gave poor health or job discontinued as the main reason, rather than compulsory retirement). A national survey of retirement policies found that 73% of companies with pension plans (which includes most large companies) had compulsory retirement at a fixed age for some or all workers (Slavick & McConnell, 1963). The majority of these had compulsory retirement at age 65. The 1966 SSA survey of retirement systems in state and local governments found that 79% had compulsory or automatic retirement at a fixed age (Waldman, 1968). This is an increase from the less than one-half of the systems in 1944.

Thus, it appears that compulsory retirement policies may affect about half of the male wage and salary workers retiring at age 65 and will affect more in the future if recent trends continue.

### The Case for Flexible Retirement

1. Compulsory retirement is by definition discrimination against an age category, contrary to the principle of equal employment opportunity. Federal law now prohibits discrimination in employment based on race, sex, or age for persons under 65. It is ironic that the present law against age discrimination in employment is limited to persons under 65, because persons over 65 are the ones who are most likely to be discriminated against by such policies as compulsory retirement. It seems possible that restricting this law to persons under 65 could be considered unconstitutional in the sense that it does not provide equal protection of the law to all persons.

Supporters of compulsory retirement might argue that such discrimination is as legal and justifiable as child labor laws and policies which restrict the employment of children. However, there seems to be a valid difference in that child labor restrictions are designed primarily for the protection of children while compulsory retirement policies are usually justified on grounds other than those of protecting older persons.

2. Age, as the sole criteria for compulsory retirement, is not an accurate indicator of ability because of the wide variation in the abilities of aged persons. Twenty years ago the National Conference on Retirement of Older Workers concluded that

Both science and experience indicate that the aging process and its effects show such wide variance among

individuals as to destroy the logic of age as the sole factor in determining whether a persons should retire or continue to work (Mathiasen, 1953).

Recently the Gerontological Society's Committee on Research and Development Goals in Social Gerontology echoed this conclusion by stating

age limitations for employment are both socially and economically wasteful, since chronological age is rarely a reliable index of potential performance (Havighurst, 1969).

All the available evidence agrees that despite the declining abilities of some aged, most workers could continue to work effectively beyond age 65 (Riley & Foner, 1968).

3. Flexible retirement would better utilize the skills, experience, and productive potentials of older persons and thus increase our national output. If the millions of persons now forced to retire were allowed to be gainfully employed, the national output of goods and services could increase by billions of dollars. In a previous review (Palmore, 1969a) we concluded,

Many gerontologists have pointed out that because of the aged's extensive experience and practice, many have developed high levels of skills, emotional stability, wise judgment, and altruism. They agree that these abilities can and should be channeled into constructive roles.

4. Flexible retirement policies would increase the income of the aged and reduce the transfer payments necessary for income maintenance. Since the average income of retired persons is about one-half that of aged persons who continue to work (Bixby, 1970), it follows that flexible retirement policies might double the average incomes of those who were forced to retire but are willing and able to work. Similarly, over twice as large a proportion of retired aged persons have incomes below the poverty level as do aged persons who continue to work. Thus the millions of aged persons with poverty incomes

might be substantially reduced by flexible retirement, which would increase their employment opportunities. This in turn would substantially reduce the amount of old age assistance and other welfare payments currently given to the aged with inadequate incomes. Similarly, Social Security payments could be reduced substantially because of the provision which reduces retirement benefits for earnings of over $1,680 per year. Considering the fact that over 20 billion dollars a year are paid by Social Security to retired workers and their dependents, it is easy to see that several billion dollars could be saved from income maintenance programs if only a minority of the aged could avoid forced retirement.

5. Flexible retirement, in providing more employment, would improve life satisfaction and longevity of the aged. Most evidence indicates that retirement does tend to decrease life satisfaction. A recent review concluded:

> Overall satisfaction with life is greater among older persons who are still working than among those who have retired. This pattern seems to arise in part (but only in part) because the kinds of people who remain in the labor force are very different from those who retire (tending to be healthier, better adjusted, more advantaged on the whole). Yet quite apart from such factors as health or socioeconomic status, the pattern of lower satisfaction among the retired persists. (Riley & Foner, 1968).

Streib (1956) found that even for persons with similar levels of health and socioeconomic status, morale still tends to be comparatively higher among the employed. Thompson (1960) found that decreases in satisfaction over 2-year period were somewhat greater among older persons who retired than among those who continued to work; and decreases in satisfaction were substantially greater among reluctant retirees. The Duke Longitudinal Study (Palmore, 1968) found that reductions in economic activities including retirement were closely associated with reduction in life satisfaction. Dr. Thomas Green (1970), of Syracuse University's Educational Policy Research Center, has concluded,

> Surely there is nothing more damaging to the human spirit than the knowledge—or belief—that one's capacities are unused, unwanted . . .

There is less evidence supporting the idea that retirement has negative effects on health and longevity. Most of the association of poor health and greater mortality with retirement is probably due to the fact that people in poor health and with shortened life expectancies are the ones who tend to retire (Martin, Doran, 1966; Riley,

1968). However, we found that work satisfaction was one of the strongest predictors of longevity in our longitudinal study of normal aged (Palmore, 1969b). It may be that lack of work satisfaction, which can occur among the employed as well as among the retired, is the factor which reduces longevity.

6. Flexible retirement reduces the resentment and animosity caused by compulsory retirement. Apparently, many workers bitterly resent being thrown on the trash dump while they are still capable of working. Flexible retirement policies, by allowing such workers to continue work, eliminates this problem.

## The Case for Compulsory Retirement

1. Compulsory retirement is simple and easy to administer. Flexible retirement would require complicated tests which would be difficult to administer fairly and difficult to explain and justify to the worker. This may be the main reason for the popularity of compulsory retirement among administrators. Proponents of flexible retirement agree that it would be somewhat more difficult to administer, but many with experience in the administraton of flexible retirement plans assert that the complications have been exaggerated and that adequate tests of retirement based on ability are "not the monsters they were made out to be" (Mathiasen, 1953). Various groups have been working on improving techniques for measuring functional ability as a basis for retirement practices (Koyl, 1970).

In fact, most organizations have implicit or explicit standards, more or less based on ability and merit, which they use to decide who should be hired, fired, transferred, or promoted among workers under 65. Flexible retirement policies can use these same standards, or somewhat more exacting standards, to decide who should be retained and who retired among workers over 65.

2. Compulsory retirement prevents caprice and discrimination against individual workers. Proponents of flexible retirement also grant this point, but point out that prevention of individual discrimination is bought at the price of wholesale discrimination against an entire age category. They argue that the net number of workers willing and able to work who are forced to retire would be much less under policies of flexible retirement.

3. Compulsory retirement provides predictability. Both employer and employee know well in advance that the employee must retire on a fixed date. Thus, both can plan ahead better.

On the other hand, some predictability can be built into flexible retirement by requiring workers and management to give a certain amount of advance notice to the other party of any intended retirement.

4. Compulsory retirement forces management to provide retirement benefits at a determined age. Most compulsory retirement plans are accompanied by retirement pension systems (Slavick & McConnell, 1963). On the other hand pension systems are often combined with flexible retirement policies with no great difficulty (Mathiasen, 1953).

5. Compulsory retirement reduces unemployment by reducing the number of workers competing for limited jobs. This is especially important in declining or automating industries or plants with an over supply of workers. On the other hand, it could be pointed out that compulsory retirement tends to increase unemployment among older workers by forcing them to leave one job at which they are experienced and seek another job in a new area in which they may be disadvantaged. Using compulsory retirement to reduce unemployment is analogous to firing all women or all blacks in order to reduce the number of workers competing for jobs. A better solution to the unemployment problem is for the government to stimulate the economy or to create additional jobs by being the "employer of the last resort." In a previous analysis we concluded,

> The idea that society can provide only a limited number of jobs and that therefore it cannot provide enough jobs for aged workers is no longer accepted by most modern economists. Society could create a useful role for every adult if it were willing to devote the necessary attention and resources to this end. Certainly there would be major economic and political problems involved. But there is an unlimited amount of goods and services needed and desired in our American society (Palmore, 1969a).

If a smaller work force is really desired, this could be accomplished by shorter work weeks, longer vacations, delayed entry into the labor market by more education, etc. (Kreps, 1969).

6. Compulsory retirement prevents seniority and tenure provisions from blocking the hiring and promotion of younger workers. This is certainly true when seniority and tenure provisions are used to retain workers who have become less efficient and productive. A solution to this problem under flexible retirement would be to eliminate seniority and tenure provisions at a fixed age and require the older workers to compete periodically for their jobs on the basis of ability rather than seniority.

7. Compulsory retirement forces retirement in only a few cases because most workers 65 and over want to retire or are incapable of work. This claim is probably not true as shown by the surveys cited earlier.

It is true that 69% of men over 65 not at work say they are not well enough to work and another 16% say they are not interested in work, but many of these responses may be rationalizations for inability to find suitable employment (Palmore 1967; Sheppard, 1969). The only way to accurately determine how many older workers are forced to retire, but willing and able to work, is to eliminate compulsory retirement and count how many take advantage of the opportunity to continue working.

8. Compulsory retirement saves face for the older worker no longer capable of performing adequately. The older worker does not have to be told and does not have to admit that he is no longer capable of working but can blame his retirement on the compulsory retirement policy. Such a face-saving device undoubtedly has important value for many workers, but the number of such workers should be balanced against the perhaps equal number of capable workers forced to retire by compulsory retirement and the resulting frustration, loss of status, reduction of income and of national productivity.

9. Most workers 65 years old have impaired health or only a few years of health left. The facts do not support this argument. Life expectancy for a 65-year-old person is now about 15 years, and the majority of aged do not appear to have disabling impairments. Only 37% of persons 65 and over report any limitation in their major activity (National Center for Health Statistics, 1971).

Seventy percent of the Social Security male beneficiaries retiring at age 65 because of compulsory retirement report no work limitation (Reno, 1971). Furthermore, despite compulsory retirement and other discrimination against the aged, about one-third of men over 65 continue to do some work (Bogan, 1969). Thus, it appears probable that the majority of workers age 65 can expect a substantial number of years in which they will be capable of productive employment.

10. Most older workers are inferior and cannot perform most jobs as well as younger workers. This appears to be another of the stereotypes about the aged which has little or no basis

in fact. A recent review of the evidence concluded,

> Studies under actual working conditions show older workers performing as well as younger workers, if not better, on most, but not all, measures. Thus, those men and women who remain in the labor force during their latter years are not making generally inferior contributions, despite their frequently poor performance under laboratory conditions (Riley & Foner, 1968).

11. Compulsory retirement does little harm because most workers who are forced to retire could get other jobs if they wanted to. Again the evidence is contrary to this theory. When workers 65 and over lose their jobs, they have much more difficulty in getting another one than younger men. The proportions of older workers in the long-term unemployed categories are about twice as high compared to workers age 20-35 (Riley & Foner, 1968). Educational differences do not explain these differences in long-term unemployment (Sheppard, 1969). More than one-half of all private employees in states without age-discrimination legislation in 1965 admitted age limits in hiring practices and many more probably informally discriminate against older workers (Wirtz, 1965).

12. Most workers forced to retire have adequate retirement income. Again the facts appear to be to the contrary. We do not know exactly what percentage of those forced to retire are in poverty, but 30% of all retired couples and 64% of the retired non-married persons have incomes below the official poverty level (Bixby, 1970). And it is precisely those forced to retire early who have incomes substantially lower than those who retire early voluntarily (Reno, 1971).

## Proposals for Increasing Flexible Retirement

As may be obvious from the preceeding review, I favor flexible retirement policies primarily because I conclude compulsory retirement is unfair to the capable older worker, psychologically and socially damaging, and economically wasteful. The remaining question then is how to bring about more flexible retirement policies.

The most extreme proposal would be to outlaw all compulsory retirement by removing the age limitation in the present law against age discrimination in employment. The main objections to such a proposal is that at present it would be politically difficult if not impossible to pass such a law and that even if it could be passed it would be extremely difficult to enforce effectively. A counter-argument would be that the difficulty of enforcement should not prevent passage of a just law. We have many excellent laws which are difficult to enforce, such as laws against murder, robbery, and racial discrimination. Another serious objection is that while compulsory retirement may usually be unjust, in some situations it may be less unjust than a system with no retirement criteria or with completely arbitrary decisions as to who must retire.

A more moderate proposal would be to provide tax incentive for flexible retirement policies. A reduction in the amount of Social Security tax paid by the employer with flexible retirement policies could be economically justified by the savings in Social Security benefits that would result from continued employment of workers not forced to retire.

The most modest proposal would be to encourage some kind of compromise between complete compulsory retirement and flexible retirement based on ability alone. Brown (1950) of Princeton University proposed such a compromise plan over 20 years ago. Under this plan a definite age would be set at which all employees recognize that the promise of continued employment ends. At this time all seniority rights and further accumulation of pension credit ends. Then retired employees can be recalled to work as temporary employees, subject to the needs of management.

In this way, selected individuals can be recalled for specific needs on the basis of changing demands for personnel and the physical, mental, and personality adjustment of the particular worker to advancing age.

Such plans are in fact already operating smoothly in many businesses and institutions.

In conclusion, I hope that this article may clarify the issues and facts involved and may become a basis for reducing the millions of cases of compulsory retirement and the resulting social and economic waste of our older citizens' talents and skills.

## References

Bixby, L. Income of people aged 65 and older. **Social Security Bulletin**, 1970, **33**, 4, 3-34.

Bogan, R. Work experience of the population. **Monthly Labor Review**, 1969, **92**, 44-50.

Brown, J. The role of industry in relation to the older worker. In **The aged and society.** New York: Industrial Relations Research Assn., 1950.

Busse, E., & Kreps, J. Criteria for retirement: a re-examination. **Gerontologist**, 1964, **4**, Pt. I, 117-119.

Gould, D. Let's ban retirement. **New Statesman**, 1968, **75**, 411.

Green, T. Panel examines new technology. **New York Times**, Jan. 30, 1970.

Havighurst, R. J. (Ed.). Research and development goals in social gerontology. **Gerontologist**, 1969, **9**, Part II.

Hyden, S. **Flexible retirement age.** Paris: Organization for Economic Cooperation & Development, 1966.

Koyl, L. A technique for measuring functional criteria in placement and retirement practices. In H. Sheppard (Ed.), **Towards an industrial gerontology.** Cambridge, Mass: Schenkman, 1970.

Kreps, J. Case study of variables in retirement policy. **Monthly Labor Review**, 1961, **84**, 587-91.

Kreps, J. Economics of retirement. In E. Busse & E. Pfeiffer (Eds.), **Behavior and adaptation in late life.** Boston: Little, Brown, & Co., 1969.

Lambert, E. Reflections on a policy for retirement. **International Labor Review**, 1964, **90**, 365-75.

Martin, J., & Doran, A. Evidence concerning the relationship between health and retirement. **Sociological Review**, 1966, **14**, 329-343.

Mathiasen, G. (Ed.). **Criteria for retirement.** New York: G. P. Putnam's Sons, 1953.

National Center for Health Statistics. Current estimates from the Health Interview Survey—1969. **Vital & Health Statistics**, Ser. 10. No. 63, 1971.

Palmore, E. Retirement patterns. In L. Epstein & J. Murray, **The aged population of the United States.** Washington: Government Printing Office, 1967.

Palmore, E. The effects of aging on activities and attitudes. **Gerontologist**, 1968, **8**, 259-263.

Palmore, E. Sociological aspects of aging. In E. Busse & E. Pfeiffer (Eds.), **Behavior and adaptation in late life.** Durham: Duke University Press, 1969. (a)

Palmore, E. Predicting longevity. **Gerontologist**, 1969, **9**, 247-250. (b)

Reno, V. Why men stop working at or before age 65: Findings from the Survey of New Beneficiaries. **Social Security Bulletin**, 1971, **34**, 6, 3-17.

M. Riley & A. Foner, **Aging and Society**, Vol. II. New York: Russell Sage Foundation, 1968.

Sheppard, H. Aging and manpower development. In M. Riley & A. Foner, **Aging and Society**, Vol. II. New York: Russell Sage Foundation, 1969.

Slavick, F., & McConnell, J. Flexible versus compulsory retirement policies. **Monthly Labor Review**, 1963, **86**, 279-81.

Streib, G. Morale of the retired. **Social Problems**, 1956, **3**, 270-276.

Thompson, W., Streib, G., & Kosa, J. The effect of retirement on personal adjustment. **Journal of Gerontology**, 1960, **15**, 165-169.

Waldman, S. **Retirement systems for employees of state and local governments**, 1968. Washington: Government Printing Office, 1968.

Wirtz, W. **The older American worker.** Washington: Government Printing Office, 1965.

---

### The Project

I called him as soon as I got home. I rambled on about the old lady I had just seen. I told him that some organization called me about a woman who needed a companion and I agreed to visit her. It was a new project and I love new projects. I described the way she lay on the couch, I holding her hand, staring at her teeth on the table, telling her that she'd pull through. I rubbed alchohol under her nose. A little of it dribbled into her cake and I watched it fuse with the melted ice cream. Her skin was like the lizard's that my brother gave me for my birthday. The house didn't smell, but all the blinds were closed and there was no light in the room. She had millions of books scattered around the room—mostly romance stories. She'd been sick for two years with heart trouble. I stared at her chest making sure that her heart kept beating. She propped her legs on two pillows. Her skin bubbled under her garters. I wondered why she even bothered to get dressed. She told me about her son, talking very slowly.

I left after an hour when the doctor finally arrived despite her pleas for me to stay for the night. I told her that I hoped she'd feel better and that I'd call. She said "Goodbye Princess." I waved, half stunned, because that's what my father calls me.

Sharon Grollman

Submitted by the author with the thought that the viewpoint of an adolescent (18 years old) concerning geriatrics might be of value.

# 27

# Flexible retirement— will Sweden make it work?

**by Harriet Miller**
Executive Director

On July 1, Sweden will begin a national experiment that could change the way governments and industries think about retirement.

The idea is to ease the transition from full-time employment to complete retirement by allowing people between the ages of 60 and 70 to get part of their pension payments while they work part-time. Thus, for a time, they could combine the freedom of retirement with the familiar routine of their job.

A worker will be able to vary the ratio between retirement time and job time to fit his or her personal circumstances—with corresponding adjustments in job income and pension payments. Workers can also come out of retirement to work full-time whenever they choose.

As long as a worker is employed for at least 17 hours a week, he or she will be eligible not only for pension payments but also for the wide range of fringe benefits available to all Swedish workers. Since income earned from part-time jobs will be taxed for pension purposes, workers participating in this program will still be able to collect a full pension upon complete retirement after age 65.

In essence, Sweden is offering its older workers a smorgasbord of retirement options from which they may choose those most suitable to their individual situations. At the same time, employees would be encouraged to stay in the work force longer—if only on a part-time basis —thus increasing the nation's productive capacity.

The benefits are not purely economic.

"We've found that some people just die after one or two years of retirement," said an official of the National Social Insurance Board, the Swedish equivalent of our Social Security Administration. "They've worked 40 or 50 years. They need time to calm down and adjust to retirement. People should be able to stay on at work as much as they want and retire slowly . . . so they don't face the shock at 65."

This is, of course, completely contrary to the prevalent—and erroneous—assumption that everyone reacts to the approach of retirement in the same way. In actuality, some may welcome retirement as an escape from jobs they've hated and felt trapped in for years. Others may regard it as a threat, and dread being deprived of the feeling of accomplishment they derive from doing work they enjoy.

Over the years, there has been much talk about how the retirement process should be more flexible in its response to individual needs. The Swedish experiment, however, represents the first nationwide effort to test these theories.

But any program offering so many potential benefits must also have a catch, and this one is no exception.

"Newspaper surveys have indicated that industries vary greatly in their ability to create part-time slots," notes Richard J. Litell in a background article released by the Swedish Institute. "Many large firms, while sympathetic to the idea . . . do not know how they can create the required part-time openings."

And, he adds, "It has been pointed out that a worker can hardly expect to keep his old job if he switches to part-time employment and will most likely have to accept less-qualified, and, therefore, less satisfying work."

But Litell also reports that "one industrial leader has suggested that it is not inconceivable for two persons to share an 8-hour shift, although he admits that finding a lighter job for an older person will be difficult."

It is significant that this experiment was conceived during a period when the Swedish economy was at a record high and unemployment was virtually nonexistent. Now, as the testing is about to get under way, Sweden is finally beginning to feel the effects of the current recession, and unemployment is being seen in that country for the first time in many years.

Despite these factors — which could cause problems—the Swedish experiment is worth watching by our nation's policy planners. If it works there, perhaps it should be tried here. If it fails, perhaps we can learn from Sweden's experience. □

# V. Love, Families, Relationships

The vitality and excitement of life depends on sharing one's experiences with intimates, whether family, lovers, or friends. Deep caring relationships are important in the lives of many older persons but there is also a risk of losing these supporting persons at the point in life when they are needed most. As one grows older, those we are close to may die or move away, and it is difficult to replace these valued relationships. We can readily imagine how distressed and lonely we would be if those we love were suddenly taken away from us, but that is the condition that many aging people face.

An important aspect of relationships is sexual intimacy and the closeness and sense of well-being that successful sexual relationships bring. Far from being sexless, the aging retain both the capacity for sexual expression and the ability to respond to treatment if specific sexual problems develop. They are limited not by age but by the lack of available partners, by myths about losing one's sexuality, and by the ridicule that they may be exposed to by showing an interest in sex (Sviland, Wax). Menopause, for example, long viewed as a detriment to sexual functioning and to the emotional state of older women, appears to have only minimal effects (Boston Women's Health Book Collective). Similarly, men do experience some changes in sexual responses as they age, but there is no reason to equate old age with an absence of sex. For those individuals fortunate enough to break out of the straitjacket of sexual prohibitions and misinformation, satisfying, complete sexual relationships can have a dramatic impact on their lives.

For many aged persons, the major source of social relationships and of help for specific problems comes from their families. Rather than disintegrating in modern society, as has often been predicted, the family continues to serve these functions, although we need to know more about how well these needs are met (Black).

A significant dimension for a woman is that, if she marries, she is likely to become widowed at some point during her lifetime. Women live longer than men by an average of about 7 years and have tended during this century to marry men who are older than they. For either a man or woman, loss of a spouse following a long relationship is a devastating experience. The widow, in particular, is likely to find major changes occurring as the result of the death of her spouse, including a loss of status and income, loneliness, and a lack of understanding from friends, who may even exclude her from many activities because she is no longer part of a "couple" (Caine, and "Don't Cry in Front of Your Friends"). One exciting alternative for the aging widow lies in the development of mutual, self-help groups of widows, to provide comfort and social opportunities, and generally to assist in actualizing the potentials of older women (Silverman).

# V. Love, Families, Relationships

# 28

Trapped by fixed
incomes and lonely rooms, the
country's 22 million old
people are beginning to rebel.
Increasingly, elderly
couples are pooling retirement
benefits and living together
without marriage

# SEX AND THE SINGLE GRANDPARENT

## By Judith Wax

"Lonely widow, 72, wishes to correspond with older man, preferably liberal." Near the first anniversary of her husband's death—she'd been married for 43 years—Lila Hascomb (all names have been changed) put her ad in the *New Republic* personal column. Less modest, she might have added: "Still good-looking, laughs easily, could model dentures on TV." When her husband expired before his *New Republic* subscription did, Mrs. Hascomb found the magazine too weighty a companion for lonely Sioux City nights, she confesses. "But I thought the kind of man who might *see* my ad there could prove interesting. And he did!" Other women have found Max Kornblum—a small, aged Philip Roth with a Myron Cohen delivery—

interesting, too, in the span of his 86 years. They included his late wife, to whom he was married for 35 years, and two short-term brides (both divorced). Time has trifled with Kornblum's hearing and prostate, but not his young ideas. Mrs. Hascomb's ad led to a three-month exchange of soul-baring letters. ("He quoted the Bible to tell me he didn't have marriage in mind; I answered with a nursery rhyme that goes, 'Nobody *asked* you sir, she said.'") Chicagoan Kornblum made a reconnaissance flight to Sioux City to meet his pen pal and says, "Our decision to live together was thereby cemented." A week later—nearly two months ago—they sublet a Chicago apartment.

"This is a trial period." Fond of rhetorical flourish, Kornblum speaks carefully. "The *goal* is to find an oasis of happiness." So, like the burgeoning new breed of well-seasoned citizens, courtly Mr. Kornblum and stately Mrs. Hascomb are shacking up in their twilight years.

Are we witnessing—in such out-of-wedlock, out-of-the-closet combines as Hascomb/Kornblum (a conservatively estimated 18,000 couples over 65, according to the U.S. Census Bureau)—the arrival of the last stragglers in the sexual revolution? Does "the best is yet to be" bode geriatric swinging? Will Whistler's Mother turn Weinstein's Mistress? The answers, it seems, are less frequently Hugh Hefner's department than Health,

Education and Welfare's. Half the income of those over 65 comes from pensions, mostly Social Security, and if a widow who has been dependent on her late husband's benefits remarries, she either forfeits 50 percent of that income or all of it if she applies for new payments as a married woman. Pooled individual benefits, however, are higher than those allowed to a couple; since a quarter of the nation's elderly lives below federal poverty guidelines (and many more survive only marginally), such luxuries as marriage certificates are being sacrificed to the economic realities of shelter, food and

*Judith Wax is a free-lance writer living in Chicago.*

health care. Loss of any income, however small, can threaten love *and* existence.

There are more than 22 million Americans past 65—10 percent of the population today, and a projected 25 percent by the middle of the next century. There will be more of those Mr. Kornblum calls "*senior* senior citizens," too, though he decries the life-extending efforts of gerontologists. "They want to increase the longevity of old people," he snorts angrily, "but to what *purpose* if someone lives to an exalted age—like me—and has no place to live."

When Kornblum's sublease expires in a few months, he faces the housing crisis that threatens many post-65ers and his modest budget. The 1971 White House Conference on Aging concluded that 120,000 new housing units for the elderly would be needed each succeeding year; in the last eight, only 45,000 units were constructed. Last June, the General Accounting Office reported that the Department of Housing and Urban Development had illegally impounded $214.5 million in housing funds for the elderly.

Despite such problems, says Kornblum, "My ultimate interest in the pursuit of happiness includes a companionship that is definitely to the interest of both male and female; we have a desire to live a better life than either one of us could accomplish living alone. *Everyone* yearns for wholesome and sincere companionship!"

Companionship is the word older unmarrieds use most often to describe the core of their coupling. It means everything from dependable dinner/movie/walk-around-the-block company, to fondling and hugging, to nightly "we-try-all-positions" rapturous unions. For many, what is most missed of a dead spouse is reliable "thereness"—even, it would seem, abrasive omnipresence. Touching and embracing can have warm associations with courtships long past. And, like early New Englanders, oldsters who find sustenance in variations of "just holding each other" are not far from young campus couples who describe the same sort of comforting, but noncoital bedsharing for months before actual intercourse.

Kornblum/Hascomb line up with the fondler/holders. Is there satisfaction in that? "Well, there *has* to be," says 86-year-old Kornblum, "because that's all there *is*. I'm in good physical condition, so I can really give out with the love and affection; it exists in there by the *tons*, just waiting for an outlet. Now any person

who isn't ready for that naturally will not get the full benefit of living with me. But I'd have to invent something if I wanted to call it sex."

"It's better than nothing," Mrs. Hascomb philosophizes, "though my husband and I could occasionally manage everything, if you know what I mean, into our seventies. But I was so lonely after he died, and Max *is* attentive and affectionate."

"I'm not defending myself on the sex business," says Kornblum, pulling up one errant white sock. "Twenty-five years ago, I encountered prostate surgery, which can slow a male up. If I didn't have *that* difficulty, I'd be a ten-day wonder. . . because I could *impregnate,* even at this age. And I *can* say, without fear of contradiction," he intones sonorously, "that there are *zillions* of women who would *give their right arms* for a guy like me!"

"Oh, bullshit," trills the beloved.

## "Loneliness is the worst disease there is; you can't catch anything more horrible"

Other lovers, other stories. Arthur and Jean—he's 70, she's 65—have separate rooms in a Cleveland retirement hotel. Jean, carefully made up and trim in light blue slacks, has chronic respiratory problems that require occasional public-aid financed hospitalizations ("I tell the old gossips around here she's gone for an abortion," snorts Arthur). Widow's benefits and public aid supplement the rental for her tiny room, shared bath and hotel services and meals. "I couldn't have paid for her medication, let alone her last hospital bill," Arthur says, "and if we married—which I'd love—she'd lose too much of her benefits. My pension, including Social Security, amounts to $400 a month, so I'd be asking her to live in abject poverty. What a crazy law!"

"I hate having to sneak out of his room at dawn," says Jean, "but I don't want to appear with him in the morning and be an embarrassment to the hotel, though I don't care what anybody thinks. It *would* be nice if we could live together all the time—my grandchildren think so, too—but I'm grateful for the happiness we have, even without a piece of legal paper we can't afford."

Jean and Arthur both describe depression and hopelessness before finding each other six months ago. "I made up my mind everything was over when I came here," she says, "and then I met Arthur and found out life is wonderful and I can be happy." Arthur takes her hand and explains, "Loneliness is the worst disease there is; you can't catch anything more horrible. And Jean cured me of it."

When Jean was 30, her serious post-childbirth illness so alarmed her husband that, fearful of making her pregnant again, he developed an impotence that lasted until his death 25 years later. Unable to help him, Jean says, she was faithful for 12 years, until a kiss on the way to a party with a casual friend led—within minutes—to a motel and a series of affairs with younger, single men ("I'd never do anything to harm a marriage") which she's sure had her husband's unspoken approval. "But it was all just sex, never love. There's a big difference, and—till Arthur—I had reconciled myself to never finding anyone again who really cared for me."

"I hadn't felt any sexual desire for several years before I met Jean," he says, slipping a cushion behind her. "She created it; not by suggestiveness or actions, but because I felt important and loved. We'll be playing Scrabble and it just comes over me. . . I have to put my arms around her and kiss her. She's a *rotten* Scrabble player! You don't desire sex as often at my age as a younger person does; you conserve it until you can get fulfillment. But to be perfectly frank, I have no idea how often we—"

"You have a heck of a time going a week without it, dear," she says indulgently to his very pleased laughter.

Jean privately confides, in warm grandmotherly tones, "Arthur didn't know anything about half the things I've taught him. He was used to regular old-fashioned intercourse and—I guess his wife wouldn't have liked it—he'd never experienced oral sex or fondling in the 45 years they were married. But he got the idea fast. Well, that's all part of loving, and now he knows there's nothing dirty or obscene; if you love somebody, you love *all* of them. He tells me I'm the most beautiful woman who ever was. . . that my *body* is beautiful. I've looked in the mirror and I know that's ridiculous, but he's made me *feel* lovely, and I have the same kinds of orgasms I did when I was young."

"Sex can be a continuing activity for septuagenarians, octogenarians and

even nonagenarians," says psychiatrist Dr. Eric Pfeiffer of the Center for the Study of Aging and Human Development at Duke University. Taboos related to sexual expression among the elderly stem not only from a cultural bias that equates young flesh with desirability (firm breasts merit firm erections) but, says Dr. Pfeiffer, old people remind us of our parents who from childhood we resist thinking about as sexual beings. Masters and Johnson report that "having permission" is a crucial factor in sexual functioning; desire dies when people think it *ought* to. If we get the idea it is no longer "nice" to have such needs, the body will conform to the psyche. Decreased demand for ejaculation need not, say M & J, interfere with erection *or* pleasure for the male well into his eighties; an elderly woman may be slower to lubricate—the female equivalent of erection—and lose some vaginal sensation (often treated with replacement hormones). Such physiological changes may slow, but need not and *should* not—the experts assure—end sexual function that helps healthy, aging men and women *stay* healthy.

Research, however, has shown that most older women need a *sanctioned*

sexual partner. (Mrs. Hascomb fears her Sioux City friends may get wind of her "arrangement"; others report terror of gossip.) The ratio of over-65 females to males is nearly four to one; those mature women who *do* find partners but cannot afford to lose current pension income by marrying often insist—true or not—that the relationship precludes sex. The attitudes of a pre-liberation lifetime seldom permit such acknowledgment.

Widowed Mynna Sackman, for instance, admits to 67 and a four-year passion for lifelong bachelor Lester Rabin, 64. "I love *him,* darling; he is everything a woman could want! He is my whole life! I mean this with all my heart and every word I'm telling you is the truth, the same as if the good Lord would be talking to you!" But she denies, at least till second blush, sexual union. . . while Lester proclaims daily beddings down. "She doesn't think it's nice to say, because it isn't legal," he explains. "I'd marry her in a minute—she's the first girl who ever appealed to me that way—if we could afford it without her husband's Social Security."

The "first girl who ever appealed that way" to conservatively suited, albeit

sneakered, Lester Rabin festoons her eternal yellow curls with five velvet hairbows of assorted hues and sizes. The stockings end beneath her knees, the miniskirt well above that and Mynna herself at about four feet ten. One gold tooth, dead centered, like Oliver Dragon's, is the upper gum's only tenant; a nervous hand has wrought aqua eyeshadow and skittery Swansonesque brows. "I just never came across anyone I ever wanted until I saw *her*—her whole makeup, the way she keeps herself! And she can really cook, oh gosh, she can really cook out of this world! She made a potato salad, and I'm not a potato salad person but this. . . *this!* Amazing! And her pot roast cannot be told by experts from filet mignon!"

Because of Mynna's near deafness, and unwillingness to wear a hearing aid amid the velvet bows, she and Lester carry on contrapuntal and frequently contradictory conversations with others. "You find in all cities men and women who live together without that piece of paper," says Mynna. "*I* would not do that!" "Well, we *rent* two rooms," Lester says of their arrangements in a low-rent retirement hotel, "but we *live* in one." "I try to please him the best I can," she touches hand to breast, implores the heavens, and the Sophie Tucker tremulo convulses voice and body. "But let's talk plain; you're a married woman. THIS MAN CAN RAISE AN ERECTION JUST BY LOOKING AT ME! But for me, darling, sex is a closed book; I am not an oversexed woman." Lester is unperturbed. "We do it every night," he says. "She loves it." "I'll admit," says the unhearing Mynna, "we've *tried* it. Sex is sex; they even have it on TV. And Lester is very genteel."

"The trouble is she's jealous, terribly jealous," Rabin confides. "I can't even go to the grocery store; she thinks I'm making phone calls, dates."

"He's an oversexed man," Mynna erupts, "and I don't trust him because he can have any woman in this building. *He's* jealous, too; if he ever saw me in another man's arms, he'd murder! But I am honest; I am sincere; I am true. I was a virtuous girl, before God and man, when I got married at 17. Nobody told me a thing about sex. If *I* were explaining it to a young girl, I'd go very deep and use deep words. I would say, 'Don't go in the dark. . . have dinner! Have a soda! There are sex organs in a man,' I would say, 'and sex organs in a woman and the man gets aroused and wants to put his sex RIGHT IN YOUR PRIVATE! Then you can have a child and be an unmarried mother! Can he support you? Can he give you a home?' " She pauses for breath, her solitary golden tooth catching the light and Lester's admiring glance. "As for me, I've given this man four years of my honest, decent life and I'm never going to leave him. Marriage, schmarriage, darling; they'll have to kill me first!"

Lester Rabin may reveal secrets of the boudoir, but in another retirement hotel—this one elegantly resortish for those who don't feel pension's pinch— 78-year-old, still-dashing Dr. Barkham gallantly protects *his* lady's reputation. Mrs. Mitchell is a fresh-faced 72, with the assurance of a woman who has always known herself to be attractive to men ("I have a large bust"). Unlike so many other older unmarrieds, financial concerns don't bar matrimony. "If I had her money," jokes Barkham, "I'd marry her. But she's independent, liberated." "I don't want to marry," she says placidly, patting the curly white hair with jeweled fingers. "I admit she's got young ideas; she's well-balanced, a college graduate. . . there are dentists in her family. But who would have sex with an old man

like me?" he asks waggishly. "Say, she *does* have pretty legs; don't you think so?" He quickly points out that exposure to "thousands" of women patients in the course of his long medical practice has made him invulnerable to feminine charms. And he adds, for him and Mrs. Mitchell (whom he calls "this young lady") desire is only remembrance of tingles past. But his neighbors complain that Mrs. Mitchell wakes them nightly by mistaking their door for the doctor's, and—says the hotel management— Barkham ordered a larger bed when "this young lady" took a nocturnal slide off his single-bliss mattress. Whatever the exertions of the night, though, Dr. Barkham— his claims of geriatric immunity aside—is no daytime slouch. "Maybe we could all go out together sometime," he tells a 35-years-younger new acquaintance. "Do you—perhaps—tango, my dear?"

Dr. Barkham and Mrs. Mitchell

## "He has a nice body and I don't know if I should say this, but we take baths together"

hunger for each other, perhaps, but not— unlike so many of their contemporaries— for their daily three squares. Food market managers across the country suspect that increased dog food consumption is reflected in Grandpa's dish, not Fido's. Whatever the merits of geriatric pairing, Ken-L Ration is hardly more palatable à deux. The Ford Administration has so far failed in its attempts to raise the cost of food stamps, a move that would be discriminatory as well as catastrophic, since it hits hardest at the fixed-income old. Community feeding programs, conceived as a method for bringing the isolated elderly together for the nourishment of companionship as well as food, have been funded but—for the most part—are unimplemented, and the Administration was sued recently to force the spending of such authorized money.

Living modestly, however, hasn't subdued Celia Sampson. The only thing she bothers to hide (under a picture of Jesus) is a gag calendar featuring fat male nudes. . . . "I keep it there in case the nun visits." Celia is a snappy 74: a dimpled smiler in gilt-framed glasses with a body

more main chance than last chance. Her lover, Jim Henning, is 60.

"Did I know him a long time before I slept with him?" she asks wide-eyed. "Oh, y-e-s-s! At *least* two weeks. God bless America!" she explodes with laughter and does a little buck-and-wing. "He said, 'Let's have sex,' and I said, 'Okay, let's go.' He told me I was the fastest undresser he ever met.

"Sex isn't as powerful a need as when you're young, but the whole feeling is there; it's as nice as it ever was. He puts his arms around you, kisses you and it comes to you—satisfaction and orgasm— just like it always did. . . don't let anybody tell you different. Maybe it only happens once every two weeks, but as you get older, it's such a release from the tensions. I'm an old dog who's even tried a few new tricks. Like oral sex, for instance; I figured it was time to find out what that's like. We weren't too crazy about it though.

"He has a nice body and I don't know if I should say this," she hesitates; then the smile takes over, "but we take baths together and he washes *my* body and I wash his. I know I'm getting old and my skin could use an ironing, but we love each other—so sex is beautiful."

Celia's neighbors cut her off when the affair started, she reports. "They called me a prostitute and some of my friends stopped talking to me. Jim said, 'You're not doing anything wrong; hold your head up high!' And I told my children, accept him or not; he's the big thing in my life. And everybody *does* accept now. Why should we sleep alone and lonely? Anyway, I've got to watch him good; he might get someone else!" she laughs and pounds the table. "I like this arrangement and I'm not missing one thing in life!"

Fanny Weiss is 82 and doesn't think *she's* missing anything *without* sex, either, since she and pencil-mustached Morris A. Gotkin announced their engagement six months ago. ("I gave her a ring and party like she never saw in her life.")

"How did I fall in love with him?" the big woman in thick glasses asks incredulously. "*He* fell in love with me!" She is evasive about a wedding date—and there is some gossip in their hotel that a live Mrs. Gotkin is stashed away elsewhere despite Morris A.'s assurances that the wife to whom he awarded "the best 30 years of her life" has been dead several years.

"Let's be realistic," says Gotkin,

dwarfed by baggy azure pants and his fleshy fiancée. "Sex appeal is never out of the question, but at our age I've done all I could." He has also, says the hotel management, asked to be changed from his room on the second floor to one near hers on the eighth. "I can't take the commuting," he complains, one ear perpetually hand-cupped in aid of failed audio.

"Sex is finished; you get arthritis," shrugs Fanny. "Though some are always after what they can get," she adds ominously. "But you can do kissing."

"I gave her a birthday party, very elaborate. That's a Longine I gave her that she's wearing, and I gave her a Bulova with diamonds all on the band. She's got a lot of other jewelry coming, when she makes up her mind about the wedding. It's not her money, you understand; she's got $100,000 AND I DON'T WANT ANY OF IT!"

"He *counted* it," she laughs uproariously. "Listen, about the sex, a man can't after a certain age, so who can tell if a woman *could?*"

(Says her fragile neighbor, an 80-year-old widow in failed support hose and lace-up shoes, "*I'm* not marrying again till I see if he can get it up!") Late-show love isn't limited to second-time-arounders. Sally O'Hare, 78 and described as the Mary Poppins of her retirement home, calls smooth-faced Tom Houlihan, a dauntless widower pressing 90, her "first romance."

"I don't take any credit for being a virgin at 78," she says. "I was never tempted beyond my strength. I *am* disillusioned with the Catholic faith, because they taught me in school that if a boy puts a hand on you, something terrible will happen. Tom here has had surgery that makes physical relations impossible, but how can I miss what I never experienced? He's a strong man, though, even if he's a little weak in the legs," she says with a proprietary pat on his left knee. "And there's gratification in hugging and kissing. . .for *me*, anyway."

"Works both ways," says taciturn Tom.

"When I first came here, I didn't know a soul and I wanted to die," she says, still smiling. "My niece told me,

'This is it, Aunt Sally; you better learn to like it.' Then Tom came; I was shy, a late bloomer. He brings me the morning paper and a sweet roll every day. He's not much for giving compliments, but he makes me feel like a *woman*. . . for the first time in my life!"

Love's maiden voyage can be bumpy, though, according to May ("You're talking to a single girl") Miller. A decade younger than her 80-year-old suitor, Harvey Robinson, she describes agonizing seizures of "first-time-in-my-life" jealousy. "I don't blame her," he says proudly. "The woman just won't let me alone."

In most retirement residences, women far outnumber male eligibles and jaunty widowers are looking for anything but monogamous restraints. One hale septuagenarian said to service an unending lineup of elderly lovelies is dubbed "The Stud of Sunset House" by the dietician. "Somebody told him eggs are good for potency, so he brings *extra* ones for us to cook for him every morning," she says. "Well, he'd never swing like that on Cream of Wheat!" Another senior satyr haunts a nearby eye clinic to offer the comfort of his room across the street, "till your vision clears from the drops, dear."

"Once in a while we'll find an old couple playing with each other in the ballroom," says the affable manager of a posh suburban retirement hotel, "and we say, 'Wouldn't you be more comfortable upstairs?' We don't care what they do in the privacy of their own rooms—although a maid almost lost her teeth when she walked in on a great-grandmotherly type of 80 with *two* old bucks in her bed!"

Sometimes when mind and memory suffer loose connections, feeling can still send a message through. When Becky and Barney, both in their eighties, arrived at the retirement hotel their children found for them—modest rental, food and linen service, small clean rooms and planned activities—both were lost and apathetic. They have been blissfully inseparable since their mutual discovery three years ago, and it is so unusual to see either solo that when panda-like Barney lumbered into the dining room alone one day, the concerned social director immediately asked his tiny consort's where-

abouts. "I follow Barney," a small voice wavered behind him, "and I always *will*, till I die!" ("They go up at night together," says the social director. "They neck in the theater, they help one another on the potty.")

"I didn't think about getting married, yet," says Becky, blinking guileless, faded blue eyes. "I'm waiting." The wispy grey hair is haphazardly spiked with combs to produce sparse Dorothy Lamour pompadours.

Becky and Barney can always be found in his room—according to switchboard reports—and "we kiss once in a while"; but both recoil at hints of shared beds. Becky explains, "God wouldn't want you should sleep with a fella you're not engaged." "*After,*" says Barney, "why not?"

There will, it seems, be no "after." "Barney's children think their father has deteriorated because of Becky, that she's led him down the primrose path," said one hotel staffer. "They need more care, now, than they can get here, but they'd probably die without each other." At the insistence of Barney's children, however, the couple has been dispatched to separate nursing homes. "Let's face it," says the pretty young social director, "Barney's kids just don't like the girl he goes with."

W.H. Auden wrote: "Man must either fall in love/with Someone or Something/or else fall ill."

Becky didn't get her chance to follow Barney "till I die" and if—far from her "pel" now at another nursing home—she lapses into her occasional old habit of wearing two dresses at the same time, no beaming old man thinks it makes her look twice as devastating. But Dr. Barkham whistles "It Takes Two to Tango" during his pre-date shave, Celia Sampson and Jim Henning get dreamily bombed (then take a double bubble bath) to celebrate her 75th birthday. As another poet *might* have said, "Do Not Go Gentle Into That Good Night. . .Take a Roommate."

When the circus is nearly over, one last swing—two on the trapeze—is a thrilling, death-defying act. There is, after all, no retirement age for the feeling heart.

# 29

# Helping Elderly Couples Become Sexually Liberated: Psycho-Social Issues

Mary Ann P. Sviland
Sepulveda Veterans Administration Hospital
Los Angeles, California

This article describes a therapy program for helping elderly couples become sexually liberated and some critical age-related sexual problems of which the counselor must be aware in working with the elderly. To provide an adequate context for the objectives and methods of the treatment, it is necessary to first describe some psycho-social issues of sexuality which influence sexuality in the elderly. These issues include: negative social attitudes towards elderly sexuality, knowledge of sexual behavior in the elderly, and cultural-physiological factors interacting to restrict elderly sexuality.

## Negative Social Attitudes

Sexual discrimination against the elderly still exist in this era of expanding sexual understanding and corresponding liberalization of attitudes. Until recently, society has found amusing or insignificant the sexual needs of elderly persons. Jokes involving old people and sex bring inevitable laughter. The insignificance of elderly sexuality is reflected in sexual research. Only three out of 1700 pages in the two Kinsey reports are devoted to the older age group (Claman, 1966). The Masters and Johnson (1966) study of sexual response included only 31 male and female subjects beyond age 60 in a total population of 694 subjects. Part of this inadequate study-subject population is an artifact of difficulty in eliciting active cooperation in elderly subjects. Apparently societal strictures make the elderly defensive regarding disclosure of their sexual life. But old people are terribly confused and vitally interested in information about the norms of sexuality in the elderly population (Feigenbaum et al, 1967).

The general social belief that sexuality is the domain of the young has resigned many senior citizens to premature impotence, frustration, self-depreciation or loneliness. The cultural myth that impotence is a natural phenomenon of aging is so entrenched that even informed aging physicians are capable of becoming unexplainably panicked at one or two erectile failures. More pathetic is the elderly patient seen in counseling practice who is laden with guilt and shame at his or her continuing sexuality and masturbation because of partner unavailability. Since the feelings and behaviors of the elderly are related to societal expectations, many elderly people feel guilty about healthy feelings because they are unacceptable to themselves, the physician or other people they live with (Newman and Nichols, 1966). Counselors too may need to examine their own social biases regarding aged sexuality and increase their understanding of elderly sexual function to foster a supporting climate for the resolution of healthy sexual function in their elderly patients.

Counseling elderly patients in improved sexual function and adjustment is not an end in itself but a means of fulfilling a deeper core — the timeless need of all humans for intimacy and love. Sexuality is one avenue of facilitating trust, affection, and caring. As Dean (1966) observed:

> We know that old people do not cease to be human just because they are old; they have many of the desires of the young, and their need for companionship is even greater. Nor does the desire for romance, intrigue or even sex necessarily disappear with advancing years.

Thwarted sexuality may be a greater contribution to depression in the elderly than previously assumed. The lack of an intimate and empathetic relationship may account for much of the clinical depression currently diagnosed as involutional. Loneliness and feelings of not being attractive or wanted or needed create depression irrespective of age. The positive value of companionship to general physical health is seen in the higher illness and morbidity rates of older single persons.

Primary opposition to sexuality in the aged arises from adult children who view their aged parents' normal urges for intimacy and romance as a threat to social disgrace and/or signs of second childhood (Dean, 1966). The negative attitude of the children towards their parents holds much more strongly for the mother than the father which then generalizes to all elderly females. Claman (1966) describes the identification of parent ideals with old people which blocks acceptance of their sexuality thus:

> Our aversion to serious discussion about sex in

older people may be based on the fact that we identify old people with our parents, and are therefore made uncomfortable when we think of our parents in this connection. Sam Levinson, the school-teacher-homespun philosopher of television fame, once said: "When I first found out how babies were born, I couldn't believe it! To think that my mother and father would do such a thing! . . ." Then, after reflection, he added: "My father — maybe, but my mother — never!"

Mateless parents who express loneliness are told to take up a hobby and are pressed into household service thereby adding to their social isolation instead of being encouraged to reenter the mainstream of life through another marriage. The horror towards parental sexual acting out is readily observed in the strict nursing home sexual prohibitions designed to appease the bill-paying adult children. Cognizant of the positive value of sexuality in the aged, Kassel (1974) advocated the free acceptance of sexuality in homes for the aged as humanistic.

### Research Findings on Physical and Circumstantial Effects on Elderly Sexuality

Contrary to popular mythology, the greater sexual interest, activity and capacity in earlier life, the greater the interest, activity and capacity in later years (Claman, 1966), which supports the concept of continuity of life style. Early termination of sexual activity occurs where sex is not important in life (Pfieffer and Davis, 1972). While prior activity and interest affects later male activity, elderly female sexuality is only related to past sex enjoyment (Pfieffer and Davis, 1972).

Male sexual function shows a steady decline after peak responsiveness attained around age 18 while female sexuality reaches peak responsiveness in the last thirties and early forties and maintains this level into the 60's (Kaplan, 1974). After the fifties, frequency of orgasm and length of refractory period has changed significantly in the male; while in sharp contrast to men, elderly women remain capable of enjoying multiple orgasms (Kaplan, 1974). Between 50 and 60 years the wife may want sex more than the husband is able to give (Kinsey et al, 1948, 1953).

Partner availability and good health are crucial variables to sexual continuence. Any acute or chronic illness lowers male sexual responsiveness and if his wife is ill the aging male is restricted in sexual opportunity (Masters and Johnson, 1966). Seven out of ten healthy married couples over 60 years were sexually active, some into their late eighties (Swartz, 1966). In contrast only 7% of the single, divorced, and widowed over 60 years were found sexually active (Newman and Nichols, 1966).

Surveys undertaken at the Kinsey Institute (Kinsey et al, 1948) and at Duke University (Newman and Nichols, 1960) have disclosed that 70% of married males aged 70 remained sexually active with a mean frequency of .9 per week with some males maintaining a frequency of three times per week. By age 75, 50% of married males are still sexually active (Claman, 1966).

Regarding female sexual incidence, 70% of married females and 12% of postmarried females aged 60 engaged in coitus. The incidence of masturbation was higher for postmarital females with 25% of single females aged 70 still masturbating (Christenson and Gagnon, 1965). Sexual abstinence in the elderly woman is not primarily biological but influenced by social and psychological factors since they do not seek partner replacements unless they are unusually attractive and secure with exceptional personal assets (Kaplan, 1964).

Worry over sexual failure can create secondary impotence. Culture induced unconscious sex anxiety may cause premature sex abandonment; therefore the supernormal frequencies found in some elderly males may more accurately reflect innate capacity and could become the average expectation in a more guiltless, biologically natural culture (Stokes, 1951). Abnormal sex behavior in the elderly can not be described when normal sex behavior is still unknown due to lack of published research (Hirt, 1966). We are realizing that the decline of sexual activity in the elderly is less a factor of physiology than an artifact of social prohibitions and lack of willing partner availability.

### Interaction of Restricting Cultural and Physiological Factors

If it is true that sexuality in the elderly is primarily spouse related and that companionship increases life expectancy and self-worth, then elderly patients who miss intimacy and sexual expression should be directed in counseling to finding a mate. Counseling should also be directed to increasing their sexual satisfaction. Given that sex and companionship are important for the elderly, the interacting physical and cultural limitations to their sex adjustment must next be examined.

Although the culture imposes some restrictions on the elderly male, his sexuality is primarily limited by physical factors. In contrast the elderly female, where physical capabilities and responsiveness has not depreciated, is primarily limited from sexual expression by cultural factors. Understanding of this distinction is necessary for a more rational approach to sexuality in the aged.

The elderly male experiences reduced sexual stamina which adversely affects his sex life. Biological changes included: decreased orgasm frequency, longer refractory periods following orgasm, loss of awareness of pending orgasm and greater need for direct stimulation for arousal (Kaplan, 1974). Sexual adjustment and satisfaction in the elderly male may require shifts in the sexual pattern. The female may need to take a more active role in sexual situations and both partners may need to learn new behaviors to increase compatibility and minimize the functional effects of aging on male sexuality.

Since aging does not substantially affect sexual capacity of elderly females, compared to elderly males, cultural factors such as the double standard impede sexual actualization in elderly females. Women are faced with approximately eleven yeras of matelessness since they tend to marry males four years older and the life expectancy for males is seven years shorter. Elderly females glut the marketplace which makes it easier for widowed males to remarry. Females outnumber males 138.5 to 100 at age 65 and 156.2 to 100 at age 75. (Pfieffer and Davis, 1972).

To avert the problem of protracted widowhood,

solutions from prolonging the vigor and life of the male to polygamy have been proposed (Pfieffer and Davis, 1972; Kassell, 1966). Dean (1972) proposed a more parsimonious solution:

It is an irony of fate and an anatomico-physiological paradox that a male-oriented society has propagated the custom of a man's marrying a woman younger than himself. Many a woman, after reaching the menopause and being freed of the fear of pregnancy, is more desirous of sex than ever before, but it is precisely at such a propitious time that her husband, who is five or ten years older, may begin to show impotence. Many think there would be much less sexual frustration in later years — and perhaps fewer widows — if the chronological trend were reversed so that women marry younger men to begin with.

If not initial marriage, at least dating in older life should allow elderly females access to younger males without social censure based on mother-son incest taboos. There is no need to view sexual contact with an older person as physically repugnant stemming from our cult of youth as beauty. Much of the physical signs of aging, the paunch and the wrinkles, are due to poor body caretaking, not the aging process. Many elderly people who lived prudently are remarkably attractive without the physical signs we attribute to old age. People, both male and female, should be allowed to pick their life partners on the sole basis of compatibility. This would make acceptable the relationship of the younger male with an older female. Age discrepent relationships do not necessarily indicate psychopathology for either party. Since the younger male would benefit from the experience of the older female, the positive sexual and psychological benefits afforded each party would make this combination as rewarding as a liaison with a partner of one's same age. In dealing with the expanding geriatric population and their sexual needs, society will have to take a more liberalized view regarding alternate life styles. People should be allowed to choose their mates on the basis of psychological compatibility, not preconceived standards of propriety or normalcy.

### Sexual Therapy to Help Elderly Couples Become Sexually Liberated

Many therapists and sexual therapy programs are now directing themselves to enhancing sexuality (Kaplan, 1974). Therapy modalities which range from weekend sexual workshops directed to body awareness and non-demand mutual pleasuring to the more traditional techniques are helping elderly people obtain a more fulfilling sexual adjustment. Their needs are no less important sexually and no less desirable socially than the needs of younger people.

I have been involved in a therapy program to help elderly couples become sexually liberated (Sviland, 1974). This included couples over the age of sixty with a basically sound marital relationship and no sexual dysfunction who wanted to decrease their sexual inhibitions and expand their repetoire of sexual behaviors to conform to recently liberated mores. Raised in a more prohibitive era they wanted to erase still prevalent internal taboos towards such activities as oral-genital sex or sex for pleasure.

The primary therapy goal is increased sexual satisfaction. A universal subgoal is permission to accept one's sexuality without guilt or shame. The therapist then hooks the superego and becomes a stronger authority figure granting permission for sexual curiosity and exploration. The therapist must remain flexible throughout the therapy shifting from exercises to psychotherapy with insight as needed. Assignments are always in "the here and now" of what the couple currently feels comfortable to work on. Exercises proceed slowly with patient control to prevent anxiety or negative emotional response. The basic attitude gotten across is that sex can be playful and enjoyable and another way of expressing affection. One does what one wants when one feels like it. Sex is not a ritual.

### Procedure

Voluntary treatment occurred in a hospital setting with referral from medical services. The flood of applicants attests to the needs of elderly couples in the community at large for this type of counseling.

Outpatient treatment consisted of weekly one hour sessions with homework assignments. Treatment combined educational materials, sexual exercises, assertion training and traditional psychotherapy techniques according to the needs and goals of each couple. Since the whole issue of sexuality is highly personal with different value systems, the therapist never advocated specific behaviors but helped the couple achieve self-stated goals.

First sessions focused on exploration of: 1) current sex life; 2) subjective feelings about current sex life; 3) marital dynamics; 4) degree of attitude change mutually desired; and 5) definition of goals and approximate number of sessions required.

In the conduct of therapy with the aged it is very important to recognize that the sexual values, attitudes and especially capabilities may differ markedly among the elderly. Therefore the rate of progress of introducing various information and techniques requires astute pacing to fit the characteristics of the clients.

Educational materials may be introduced at this point for the purpose of: 1) desensitization to previously taboo behaviors; 2) technique learning; 3) increasing eroticism; and 4) increasing sexual fantasy. Couples may be sent into the field to view X-rated movies, self-selected, and to puruse sexual handbooks such as Comfort's *Joy of Sex* (1972) and Otto and Otto's *Total Sex* (1973). Couples generally experience a sense of naughty intrigue with these assignments. Their responses to these materials are then explored and used to establish sexual exercise goals. Increasing the fantasy system and general level of eroticism facilitates later homework sex assignments. The wife may especially need help with integration of increased, explicit sex fantasies and her self-ideal. In other words, to understand that a woman can enjoy and think about sex and still be a lady.

At this stage, increased physical attractiveness and flirtation techniques may be included where the relationship is dull because the couple take each other for granted and do not satisfy each other's romantic needs. Each spouse defines explicit attire and mannerisms which would increase erotic attraction. The husband is told, 'If your wife was a young secretary, how would you have to look and what would you have to say to get her to take you seriously as a potential lover?" The wife is told, "If you were widowed and wanted to trap this man in a field of rough competition, how would you have to dress and act and talk to turn him into an ardent suitor?" Simultaneous homework exercises to replicate the playfulness, intrigue and joy of dating may include candlelight dinners, unexpected love notes, flirtatious telephone conversations, etc.

Couples write in detail their ideal sexual fantasy before body contact exercises are introduced. The couple exchanges their fantasies and behavior to supplement each party's fantasy. Frequently the wife's fantasy indicates a need for more romanticness with behaviors to enhance nurturance and tenderness rather than specific sex act concerns.

Next sessions involve selected sexual exercises. Sensate focus exercises involving hand, foot and head caresses may be initially employed. Opening communication is vital so partners can frankly convey without shame or anxiety what their sexual needs are, which may not agree with what the textbooks state is normative. To this end the non-threatening pleasuring exercises developed by Masters and Johnson and Hartman and Fithian are very useful. Specific sex techniques are approached in a graduated series of steps to prevent anxiety or negative emotional response.

This treatment was remarkably successful in changing behavior and attitudes within weeks. Following goal attainment of increased sexual happiness, therapy is extended with minor variations on the exercises to insure a stable system of consistent positive response to recently acquired behaviors with absence of ensuing marital or intrapsychic conflict.

In general, where elderly couples have a good relationship and no sexual problems but want to become sexually liberated, they are given permission to experiment with as wide a range of sexual behaviors as desired. Later they discard or incorporate these behaviors into their sexual patterns according to their own values of meaningfulness. It is a mistake for one partner to engage in any specific act to please the other if unconscious aversion is not extinguished. In one case where the wife was highly motivated to sexually liberalize, she expressed conscious enjoyment of recently learned fellatio, yet loss of voice occurred four days following a dream of gagging to death on a penis. When this was interpreted and she was given permission to permanently discontinue fellatio, her voice rapidly returned. Since the couple now enjoy a wide range of other learned pleasuring behaviors, discarding fellatio was no significant loss to the husband.

*Summary*

For maximum long-lasting therapeutic benefit, sexual therapy should focus beyond specific training of sexual behaviors to treating the total interpersonal relationship. With the elderly couple, therapy must extend to working through depression at the confrontation of age-related physical limitations to integration of acceptance of current sexual capacity. Sexual therapy directed to helping elderly couples becomes sexually liberated not only has positive social value but has enabled elderly couples to open communication, increase intimacy and self-esteem and enjoy without guilt sexual pleasures society accords as acceptable to its youth. Society should provide more such services to elderly couples and publicize their availability.

# References

Berne, E. *Games people play.* New York: Grove Press, 1964.

Christenson, C.V. & Gagnon, J.H. Sexual behavior in a group of older women. *Journal of Gerontology*, 1965, 20, 351-356.

Claman, A.D. Introduction to panel discussion: Sexual difficulties after 50. *Canadian Medical Association Journal*, 1966, *94*, 207.

Comfort, A. *Joy of sex.* New York: Crown, 1972.

Dean, S.R. Sin and senior citizens. *Journal of the American Geriatric Society*, 1966, 14, 935-938.

Dean, S.R. Sexual behavior in middle life. *American Journal of Psychiatry*, 1972, *128*, 1267.

Feigenbaum, E.M., Lowenthal, M.F. & Trier, M.L. Aged care confused and hungry for sex information. *Geriatric Focus*, 1967, *5*, 2.

Hirt, N.B. The psychiatrist's view. Panel discussion: Sexual difficulties after 50. *Canadian Medical Association Journal*, 1966, *94*, 213-214.

Kaplan, H.S. *The new sexual therapy.* New York: Brunner Mazel, 1974.

Kassell, V. Polygamy after 60. *Geriatrics*, 1966, *21*, 214-218.

Kassell, V. You never outgrow your need for sex. Presented at 53rd Annual Meeting New England Hospital Assembly, Boston, March 27, 1974.

Kinsey, A.C., Pomeroy, W.B. & Martin, C.I. *Sexual behavior in the human male.* Philadelphia: W.B. Saunders, 1948.

Kinsey, A.C., Pomeroy, W.B., Martin, C.I., & Gebhard, P.H. *Sexual behavior in the human female.* Philadelphia: W.B. Sanders, 1953.

Masters, G. & Johnson, V.E. *Human sexual inadequacy.* Boston: Little, Brown and Company, 1970.

Newman, G. & Nichols, C.R. Sexual activities and attitudes in older persons. *Journal of the American Medical Association*, 1960, *173*, 33-35.

Otto, H.A. & Otto, R. *Total sex.* New York: New American Library, 1973.

Pfeiffer, E. & Davis, G.C. Determinants of sexual behavior in middle and old age. *Journal of the American Geriatrics Society*, 1972, *20*, 151-158.

Stokes, W.R. Sexual functioning in the aging male. *Geriatrics*, 1951, *6*, 304-308.

Sviland, M.A.P. Helping elderly couples become sexually liberated. Presented at Western Psychological Association Convention at San Francisco. April 28, 1974.

Swartz, D. The urologist's view. Panel discussion: Sexual difficulties after 50. *Canadian Medical Association Journal*, 1966, *94*, 213-214.

# 30

# MENOPAUSE

*My first sign of menopause was the night sweat. Even though I knew why I was having the sweats, it was a little frightening to wake up in the middle of the night with my sheets all drenched. It was hard not to feel that something was very wrong with me. And I lost a lot of sleep changing sheets and wondering how long the sweats would go on. Sometimes I felt chilled after sweating and had trouble going back to sleep. It was a good thing I could absorb myself in a book at times like that.*

*I also had hot flashes several times a week for almost six months. I didn't get as embarrassed as some of my friends who also had hot flashes, but I found the "heat wave" sensation most uncomfortable.*

*I felt generally good around the time of menopause. My children were supportive and patient, particularly when I was irritable from lack of sleep. My husband, unfortunately, was quite insensitive and frequently accused me of "inventing" my "afflictions." Without the help of friends and children who did try to understand what I was going through, it might have been harder for me to be around him.*

Even though menopause has been a neutral or positive experience for many women, the physical and emotional changes associated with it are often misunderstood and mystifying. Since lack of knowledge may easily lead to anxiety, it's not surprising that some women have felt that the worst part about menopause was that they did not know what to expect or had no resources to refer to.

*I received no emotional support during menopause. It was my fault really. I was too ignorant of the facts, both physical and otherwise, to get the support I could have used.**

*I feel that far more education should be done (or did I just happen to miss it?) as to menopause, its onset, what to expect, and more specific help and understanding and explanation of all its aspects. I used to ask my doctor*

*Many of the quotes and insights found in this chapter are taken from responses to a menopause questionnaire sent out by the Boston Women's Health Book Collective in 1974. See p. 233.

*when I would know I was in menopause, and he would smile benignly and not answer; I would ask if I shouldn't be taking pills, and he'd say he'd tell me when.*

This chapter will try to help women reduce the anxiety which results from a lack of knowledge. We will provide factual information about the menopausal experience—its causes, symptoms, and possible alternatives for treatment if this should be necessary. By better understanding menopause and by seeking medical help when appropriate, we women will be better equipped to deal with this phase in our lives. This chapter also seeks to encourage women to research and study menopause, a subject which has been inexcusably neglected by the male-dominated medical profession.

Even when physical symptoms are minimal or under control, menopause is often a more negative experience than it needs to be because of our society's attitude toward us during that time. The popular stereotype of the menopausal woman has been primarily negative: she is exhausted, irritable, unsexy, hard to live with, irrationally depressed, unwillingly suffering a "change" that marks the end of her active (re)productive life.

*I usually think of geriatric types: little old white-haired women in wheelchairs in nursing homes. It's such an ugly word and image. Dried-up womb—bloodless insides. I'll never forget a man's description of an elegant hotel in the Virgin Islands as "menopause manor"! It made me glad at that time that I was still menstruating and didn't qualify for his derogatory observation. Now, ten years (and Women's Liberation) later, I can see the folly of his remarks and his machismo. But the word by itself still gives me a chill. It seems so final—as if an important bodily function had ceased, and with it all the fun of youth—which, of course, isn't true.*

Our ideas of menopause have often been shaped by ads like the one in a current medical magazine that pictures a harassed, middle-aged man standing by a drab and tired-looking woman. The drug advertised is "for the menopausal symptoms that bother him most." This ad, like many others, presents menopause as an affliction which makes us a burden to our family and friends.

Our youth-oriented culture tends to present menopause as a descent into "uncool" middle and old age. In a society which equates our sexuality with our ability to have children, menopause is wrongly thought to mean the end of our sexuality—the end of our sexual pleasure, or even the total end of our sex lives.

We women are now changing these views. As we value ourselves as more than baby machines; as we increasingly view middle age as a welcome time offering new freedom to pursue activities that interest us; and as we make selective use of hormones, vitamins and drugs to minimize the more severe menopausal discomforts, we can make menopause a more positive experience.

---

*I am constantly amazed and delighted to discover new things about my body, something menstruation did not allow me to do. I have new responses, desires, sensations, freed and apart from the distraction of menses [periods].*

---

*I felt physically in better shape—in my prime—unencumbered by the cycle of pain, swelling, discomfort, nuisance, etc.*

---

*I was immensely relieved that my periods were ceasing. I hated them and resented their prolongation for so many years after childbearing had ceased. It was a damn nuisance.*

---

*I felt better and freer since menopause. I threw that diaphragm away. I love being free of possible pregnancy and birth control. It makes my sex life better.*

---

If we feel good about ourselves and what we are doing at this time in our lives, we will cope better with whatever menopause problems we may have. It is important to be able to talk openly with those who are close to us and to ask for the support we need.

## WHAT IS MENOPAUSE?

The menopause is the time when menstruation permanently ceases. Up until menopause a woman's ovaries have periodically released estrogen during the monthly menstrual cycle. But as a woman approaches menopause her ovaries stop producing a monthly ovum (egg) and stop secreting the cyclic supply of estrogen. (Well past the menopause a much smaller amount of estrogen continues to be produced by the ovaries and the adrenals.) At the same time there is a decline in the production of the hormone progesterone, which each month has been building up the lining of the uterus in preparation for the fertilized egg (see Chapter 2). These hormonal changes mean that we will no longer be able to conceive and bear children, and that we might experience some uncomfortable physical symptoms as our bodies adjust to the often rapidly diminishing supply of estrogen.

The gradual decrease in the cyclic release of estrogen and progesterone usually begins some years before the end of menstruation. Most women are aware that menopause is coming closer when the menstrual periods become scantier, shorter and farther apart. Sometimes whole months are skipped.

---

*My menses were very regular all my life, every twenty-seven days. Then the intervals between menses gradually lengthened during menopause.*

---

In some women the cycles become shorter and the flow more prolonged and profuse.

---

*My periods ceased abruptly and I was grateful, but for the final two or three years preceding menopause they were excessively lengthy and torrential.*

---

It is not possible to predict the exact age at which a woman will begin menopause, though it usually happens between forty-eight and fifty-two; there is some indication that the age may vary with national or geographic origin. It is not true that the younger a woman starts menstruation the earlier she will go through menopause.

An early menopause can occur when a woman's ovaries are removed (oophorectomy) or as a result of ovarian disease. A hysterectomy, the removal of the uterus, will *not* bring on menopausal symptoms (unless, of course, both ovaries are removed in addition to the

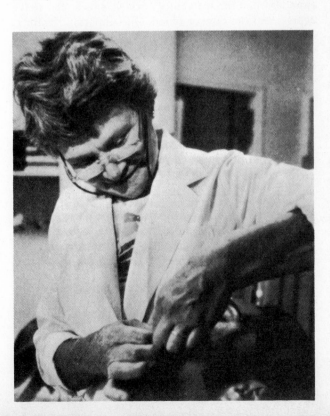

uterus). The removal of one ovary does not bring on menopause, since the remaining ovary continues to produce sufficient estrogen. When the ovaries are removed in a younger woman who still has her uterus, estrogen is usually administered afterward to maintain menstrual periods.

---

*In my case I was glad to have the hysterectomy—no more worry about profuse bleeding, no more heavy feeling, no more muss and fuss. Since I cannot take hormones, I expected much more of a jolt. I was somewhat nervous and excited—but not much. Compared to other things that can happen in life, I think the "problem" of menopause is much overrated.*

---

## Symptoms of Menopause

The two predominant symptoms characteristic of the menopausal period are "hot flashes" (also called flushes, flushing, sweats) and a decrease of moisture and elasticity in the vagina ("vaginal atrophy" is the medical term). A hot flash is a sudden sensation of heat in the upper body, sometimes accompanied by a patchy redness of skin. It usually lasts from several seconds to a minute and may involve some sweating. When it is over, a woman often feels chilly. These hot flashes may average four or five a day, most often occur at night, and may disturb sleep.

Women who have experienced them describe the hot flash as "an all-over hot feeling with profuse perspiration." "They happen unpredictably and momentarily, as if I had a fleeting fever with perhaps a slight dampness on my forehead." "It is a feeling of heat and sweat flooding one's head without warning."

Hot flashes are not fully understood. They may result from "vasomotor instability," which affects the nerve centers and the flow of blood. One important factor is that the pituitary gland increases its production of the ovary-stimulating hormone FSH (follicle stimulating hormone) in response to the decreased production of estrogen and progesterone. The large amount of FSH in the blood causes an upset in the intricate glandular balance of the body. Symptoms such as the hot flash may occur as a result of the body's attempt to achieve a new hormonal balance. Another, slightly different explanation suggests that hot flashes result from estrogen deprivation or withdrawal in an individual whose vascular system (blood vessels) has long been supported by the presence of circulating estrogen. When a woman's body has adjusted to the new levels of estrogen, hot flashes diminish and cease.

The other predominant symptom of the menopausal transition, vaginal dryness and inelasticity, results from the greatly reduced secretions of the vaginal walls. When this occurs, it is most often during the latter part of menopause (and more severe cases usually don't de-

velop until five or ten years after menstruation has ended).

---

*The physical discomfort due to the dryness of the vagina was very sexually inhibiting. We were both concerned about the problem with intercourse. I am now using a cream to counteract the dryness. But for a long while ignorance plus poor gynecological care were responsible for a lot of discomfort.*

---

Often vaginal dryness can cause irritation and an increased susceptibility to vaginal infections. During intercourse, a substitute for the missing lubrication may be necessary to prevent uncomfortable friction. A water-soluble lubricant such as K-Y Jelly works well. A woman who experiences painful intercourse should seek medical help, since problems other than vaginal dryness and inelasticity may be the cause (see p. 58 in Chapter 3).

So far, medical research has not proven that symptoms other than these two are clearly linked with menopause. However, a small percentage of women have reported other troubling symptoms during menopause. Like the hot flash, some of these secondary symptoms possibly result from "vasomotor instability." Palpitations, anxiety, dizziness and swollen ankles may be related in some as yet undefined way to the body's readjustment to a different level of estrogen. Other symptoms, such as sleeplessness, less energy, headaches and fatigue, may be indirect results of the annoying hot flashes.

There is not yet enough clear information about the effects of reduced estrogen levels on our mental health. But it is understandable that a night's sleep disrupted by hot flashes might result the following day in tiredness, irritability and a nervous edge. If hot flashes occur during the day, a woman may feel chagrined, anxious, or tense.

---

*I once saw another woman having a hot flash. Her face reddened, she started to cry, and went to bed.*

---

*Hot flashes may be uncomfortable, but if you know what they are you can live with them.*

---

It may be embarrassing to have such an obvious and uncontrollable menopausal symptom, especially since the connotations of menopause in Western culture have been negative. As we women demystify menopause we may see that these negative connotations have been more harmful than the physical symptoms themselves.

Although it is not certain that any symptoms other than hot flashes and vaginal atrophy are related to estrogen deficiency, some doctors treat a whole group of symptoms, ranging from depression, dizziness and headaches to bloatedness, diarrhea and so on as part of the "menopausal syndrome." Since medical viewpoints differ, it is important for us to understand the present controversies as to what are and are not menopausal symptoms and how those symptoms should be treated. We do not need to accept automatically whatever our particular doctor may suggest. We should be especially wary of doctors who put every woman on medication and, equally, of those who tell us that our symptoms are "only in the mind." There are cases when severe symptoms *may* require treatment, and we have a right to medical help that will provide such treatment.

# TREATMENT OF MENOPAUSE

About one out of every five women will have no (or just a few) menopausal symptoms. Although most women do experience some bothersome symptoms, many of these will not actually require treatment. We should seek help whenever symptoms significantly interfere with our normal activities, particularly because continuous and unrelieved physical distress may result in depression.

---

*At the time when I felt the hot flash and sweating I also experienced a feeling of tension; it is hard for me to tell which triggered which. At the moment I felt tension, worry about some problem came to mind.*

---

Physicians treat menopausal discomforts in a variety of ways. Some prescribe treatment only on the basis of a woman's symptoms; others prefer to consult laboratory tests first (for example, to check the level of estrogen in a woman's body) and recommend treatment on the basis of these tests.* Neither we women nor our physicians can be guided by imperfect laboratory tests alone to determine estrogen deficiency and the beginning of menopause. We must also consider our medical history, our appearance and all the symptoms we may be experiencing. On the basis of examinations and tests, a number of physicians suggest tranquilizers, sleeping pills, or aspirin to relieve various symptoms. Other physicians prescribe estrogen replacement therapy (ERT) in the form of injections, or pills containing some form of estrogen, sometimes along with progesterone. Discussion of this follows.

*There are certain laboratory findings which are characteristic of the menopause, such as a higher level of FSH (follicle stimulating hormone) in the blood and urine. This indirectly indicates that there is an estrogen deficiency—a *normal* deficiency for menopause. Some evidence of the extent of estrogen deficiency in a woman's body can also be detected with vaginal smears, but these are not always reliable. More research into ways of establishing the precise degree of estrogen deficiency is needed.

## Estrogen Replacement Therapy (ERT)

Some doctors recommend ERT for almost all menopausal women who go to them, while others warn against its indiscriminate use and reserve ERT only for the more severe cases of hot flashes and vaginal atrophy.* The kind of treatment a physician prescribes will usually depend upon his/her own view of menopause; some doctors will define menopause as a diseased state (e.g., as an "estrogen deficiency disease"), while others will view it as a fundamentally normal, if troublesome, phase in a woman's life. Those doctors who view menopause as a deficiency disease strongly argue the usefulness of widespread estrogen therapy. Others recommend a much more cautious use of ERT (see below).

We want to stress that ERT involves serious risks.† Only a woman whose normal functioning is seriously hindered by menopausal discomforts should consider it, and then only after learning about the latest research on estrogen. Since it is not always easy to determine which ailments are menopausal and which are simply related to aging or other life crises, we appreciate how difficult a decision it may be to take ERT. But these are complexities which we women must consider while seeking help from the medical establishment.

Estrogen is neither a fountain of youth, nor does it keep us from growing old. It does not change any of the real life crises we may be going through, but it may help some of us to adjust more easily to a possibly difficult period of our lives.

---

*As a modern liberated woman, the major myth I had to overcome was the one which maintained that menopause was only a problem for neurotic women. I was taught that if a woman was physically active, busy, enjoying life, career-oriented and fulfilled, she would not experience any special discomfort during menopause, as these symptoms are all neurotic and psychosomatic. I am healthy, very busy and active, and was amazed to discover that certain physical menopausal symptoms did indeed occur. Night sweats, joint pains, dreadful nervous instability, terrible feelings of anxiety, impending disaster— This all prompted me to talk to my gynecologist, who prescribed estrogen replacement.*

---

There are at least three groups of women who should not take estrogen at all: women who have a history of cancer, recurrent cysts, or blood clots. Since estrogen has a tendency to cause the retention of salt and water, it is not usually prescribed for patients with kidney or liver

*For discussion of the controversy surrounding ERT, see the cover article in *Medical World News* for June 28, 1974.

†For example, ERT is now being related to endometrial cancer. See D. Smith, *New England Journal of Medicine* (Dec. 4, 1975).

disease, certain kinds of heart disease, or endometrial hyperplasia (see below). Women who have endometriosis or fibroids (see Chapter 6) usually should not take estrogen. However, exceptions are sometimes made in cases of extreme menopausal symptoms. When doctors make such exceptions in recommending ERT, they should fully explain the risk factors.

There is not yet *one* preferred method for administering ERT: the type, amount, frequency and duration of the dosage will vary, depending on the doctor and the individual woman.*

Most cases of vaginal dryness and hot flashes—both of which can result from lowered levels of estrogen in the body—are relieved by ERT. For many cases of vaginal dryness it is sufficient to use an estrogen cream (applied to the vagina), thus avoiding the possible dangers of orally ingested estrogen, which affects the whole body.

Although ERT is often successfully used to treat other symptoms thought to be related to estrogen deficiency—such as insomnia, irritability, nervousness, depression, nausea and constipation—there is not yet any medical data to support this practice. It is not clear why or how ERT is effective in such cases or if in fact it is ERT and not something else that is really relieving the symptoms. It does appear, however, that ERT *can* and *does* help many menopausal women by relieving symptoms and imparting a greater sense of well-being.

---

*When the doctor gave me estrogen my period started up again. He reduced the dosage and is presently trying to regulate it. The estrogen did relieve the hot flashes and dry vagina.*

---

How long should hormone therapy continue? Some believe that whenever possible the dosage of estrogen should gradually be cut down. This reasoning is based on the fact that so much about estrogen remains unknown and the possibility that the dangers of estrogen therapy may outweigh the benefits (see below). Some women *do* get habituated to a high estrogen level, so that when medication is stopped, hot flashes and other previous symptoms may come back. Some physicians are less concerned with possible dangers and believe that hormone therapy once begun should continue through-

*The usual dosage is .625 to 1.25 mg. of a conjugated estrogen given daily, orally, in 21- to 25-day cycles. The cyclic use of estrogen is especially important in order to avoid possible harmful effects of prolonged and uninterrupted ERT. In cases where conjugated estrogen is not well-tolerated, natural crystalline estrogen is administered. Ethinyl estradiol (.02 to .05 mg.) and diethylstilbestrol (.25 to .50 mg.) have also been prescribed by some doctors, though for many women both produce more negative side effects than conjugated estrogens. Sometimes progesterone is given along with estrogen toward the end of the cycle. For a discussion of the classifications of different kinds of estrogen, see *A Clinical Guide to the Menopause* (1968), Ayerst Laboratories, Information Publishing Co., 3 West 57th St., New York, N.Y.

out a woman's life. Occasionally they will even increase the dosage when an attack of serious infection, surgery, severe emotional stress, flu, or even a prolonged heat wave results in a relapse of severe menopausal symptoms.

### Side Effects and Risks of ERT

Besides the difficulties involved in gradually reducing dosage, ERT has some risks and side effects. As with the pill, taking estrogen increases the risk of blood clots and hypertension. The risk of blood clots increases with age. (See p. 190 in Chapter 10 for important details.)

Usually the goal with ERT is to prescribe as small an amount of estrogen as possible, to control the menopausal symptoms without precipitating side effects (such as weight gain and swelling, breast tenderness, nausea and increased cervical secretions) or stimulating the lining of the uterus to proliferate and produce "breakthrough" or "withdrawal" bleeding (see p. 192, in Chapter 10). This bleeding, which occurs in as many as 30 percent of women taking ERT, may happen either during the few days of every cycle when *no* estrogen is being taken (withdrawal bleeding), or irregularly, at any point in the cycle. Such proliferation, caused by too much estrogenic stimulation, may lead to endometrial hyperplasia, a condition in which the uterine lining becomes thick and produces an abnormally large number of cells.

---

*I was satisfied with the estrogen treatment at the time, for it did relieve my symptoms; but I learned (after my hysterectomy) that I had developed hyperplasia of the uterus and should not have been given estrogen replacement because of a higher possibility of developing uterine cancer in my case.*

---

In a small number of women who have this condition, uterine cancer may eventually develop, so it is wise to treat breakthrough bleeding to avoid that possibility. Some doctors recommend a lower dosage of estrogen to prevent such bleeding. If it is not possible to find a dosage small enough to prevent breakthrough bleeding and still high enough to relieve menopausal symptoms, some doctors then recommend a combined estrogen-progesterone therapy in order to produce *regular* bleeding. The progesterone—usually a synthetic progestin—produces a more complete shedding, or "sloughing off," of the uterine lining and usually reverses any hyperplasia that may exist. Some doctors think that such combination therapy should even be used preventively (before any bleeding occurs), while others claim that the benefits of progesterone have not yet been proven, especially its role in preventing uterine cancer. In particular, some pathologists believe that there are small immature areas of the uterine lining which do not respond to the progestational hormones and are not sloughed off periodically.

Thus, these isolated areas would be constantly subjected to estrogen stimulation and its possible harmful effects.

In a woman taking ERT, any abnormal bleeding is probably breakthrough or withdrawal bleeding. However, there is a small chance that endometrial cysts, polyps, or uterine cancer could be the cause. To distinguish ERT-related bleeding from other kinds, most doctors recommend combined estrogen-progesterone therapy (see above). Such therapy will stop ERT-related bleeding, while it usually won't affect other kinds of abnormal bleeding. (To determine the cause of non-ERT-related bleeding, an endometrial biopsy, a D & C, or a suction procedure similar to menstrual extraction—see p. 223— is usually performed in order to examine the endometrial tissue for abnormal cells.) Some doctors think that combined estrogen-progesterone therapy may, in rare cases, stop even bleeding caused by uterine cancer. To rule out this possibility, they always recommend an endometrial biopsy or a D & C in addition to the combined estrogen-progesterone therapy.

Estrogen replacement therapy has other side effects besides breakthrough and withdrawal bleeding. Some women on estrogen experience gastrointestinal disturbances, fluid retention and weight gain. Some have experienced breast and pelvic discomfort due to tissue engorgement. Headache, vaginal discharge and changes in skin pigmentation have also been noted. The kinds of side effects vary with the different oral forms of estrogen; natural conjugated estrogens are the most easily tolerated.

### Estrogen Replacement Therapy and Other Diseases: Cancer, Osteoporosis, Heart Disease

Estrogen hormones have a profound and widespread effect on the entire metabolism of the body in addition to their effect on the reproductive system. Perhaps the most consistent worry has been the influence of estrogen on *cancer*. *There are no conclusive data as yet*, but there are suggestions that an excess of estrogen over a long period of time may be related to the development of breast cancer and, as we have said, cancer of the lining of the uterus in some women. Estrogen therapy has only been in use since 1940, so we do not as yet have sufficient data concerning long-term effects. However, it does seem safe to say that it appears to stimulate such processes as cystic mastitis, possibly culminating in a true malignancy.

Estrogen's effect on *osteoporosis* is controversial. Osteoporosis is a condition which affects the human skeleton. Gradually, small amounts of bone mass are reabsorbed by the body. The bony mass which remains becomes fragile and susceptible to fracture. There is no evidence as yet that ERT can prevent osteoporosis. ERT apparently keeps osteoporosis from progressing for a limited time (3 to 9 months), but after this time osteoporosis usually resumes, sometimes at an even more

rapid rate. The high dosages required to stop osteoporosis in these latter cases may induce bleeding and may increase the risk of heart disease (see next paragraph). Since osteoporosis also occurs in the male, a great many people believe it is simply part of the aging process rather than estrogen-deficiency-related, and that adequate calcium and protein intake along with exercise are the best treatment* (this seems to have preventive value too). It is important to remember that osteoporosis is not just an inevitable aspect of aging, but can also be a consequence of poor calcium and protein intake and insufficient exercise.

Studies have not yet shown any definite benefits of ERT with respect to *heart disease*. There is even a strong statistical indication that heart disease may not be related to the menopause, ovarian function, or estrogen. One study indicates that ERT may contribute to an increase in triglyceride levels in the blood. These higher levels are apparently related to an increased risk of heart disease.

Much more research is needed in the area of ERT, particularly its effect on osteoporosis, heart disease, cancer and mental depression. Because of present uncertainties, many women are very cautious about ERT, choosing it only when symptoms are severe and when no contraindications are present. In most women, postmenopausal production of estrogen (primarily by the adrenals) is sufficient, and no therapy is indicated. For some women, an alternative is found in carefully planned tranquilizer therapy and the strong psychological support of family, friends and medical personnel. Studies of such substances as anti-hypertensive agents are now in progress to find satisfactory alternatives to

*Medical World News* (June 28, 1974), p. 41.

ERT, especially for women who are unable to take estrogen. As it stands now, the positive value of ERT must be balanced against the possibility of negative side effects.

## MENOPAUSE FROM THE WOMAN'S POINT OF VIEW

Those of us looking ahead to menopause or just beginning to experience it can find little material that explores what most women go through during menopause. Most research has been done on "clinical samples"— that is, on the minority of women who have chosen or been forced to seek medical care because of the severity of their symptoms. Consequently we know very little about what menopause is like for all the women who never seek medical help.

At least one woman, the sociologist Bernice Neugarten, has done research on the menopausal experience of the average woman. One of her studies* involved 100 women aged forty-three to fifty-three, from working-class and middle-class backgrounds, all in good health, all married and living with husbands, all mothers of at least one child, and none having had a hysterectomy. These women were asked about their expectations regarding menopause; whether they considered themselves pre-menopausal, menopausal, or post-menopausal (and what the basis of their assessment was); and what changes in their lives they attributed to the menopause.

Interestingly enough, the women in Neugarten's study did not view menopause either more positively or more negatively as a result of their being "pre-menopausal," "menopausal," or "post-menopausal." Also, women with more severe menopausal symptoms did *not* tend to view menopause more negatively than women with less severe symptoms. Only 4 out of the 100 women thought of menopause as a major source of worry. "Losing your husband," "just getting older" and "fear of cancer" were much more frequent concerns.

When asked how menopause affects sexuality, 65 percent of these women maintained that there was no effect. Of the remaining women, "half thought sexual activity becomes less important and half thought sexual relations become more enjoyable because menstruation and fear of pregnancy were removed."†

Those women who reported more negative experiences in the areas of menstruation, first sexual experience, pregnancy and childbirth also reported more severe menopausal symptoms. There could be a variety of explanations for this correlation. Conceivably, the physical cause or causes of previous reproductive or sexual difficulties could also be the cause of menopausal problems. Or maybe negative attitudes that our culture teaches us about our bodies and about our reproductive processes continue throughout our lives to have a negative effect on all our sexual and reproductive experiences.

### Our Menopause Questionnaire

Our Collective, unable to find much information about menopause as most women experience it, in 1974 sent out almost 2,000 menopause questionnaires to women all over the United States. Since we wanted to know if certain symptoms did in fact occur more frequently around the time of menopause, we asked women aged twenty-five and up (*not* just older women) to fill out the questionnaire. We asked about personal background, symptoms, medical treatment and, when relevant, the menopausal experience itself.

In this chapter we can present only a small fraction of the information that has been gathered from these questionnaires. We are hoping to prepare a longer publication that will more thoroughly describe and analyze all the responses we have received. Please remember that this study is in no sense a "scientific" one. The women answering the questionnaire do not represent a cross section of women. However, these responses give us a better idea of what research needs to be done and also give us the privilege of hearing the voices of many women talking about this experience which society presents so negatively. In general, our questionnaires corroborate the findings of Bernice Neugarten.

#### The Sample

Following is a brief description of the 484 women who answered the questionnaire:

| Age Range | % of Total Sample |
|-----------|-------------------|
| 25–40     | 37%               |
| 41–50     | 26                |
| 51–60     | 26                |
| over 60   | 11                |

About two-thirds of the women were married, about one-fifth divorced or widowed, and about one-tenth single. Four-fifths of the married women had been married more than 21 years.

Most of the women who responded were living in large cities or suburbs. Three-fourths had children; of these, about one-half had one or two children, and half had more than two children. Almost all were, or had been at some point in their lives, involved with full-time housework and/or child-rearing. Of the menopausal and post-menopausal women, about two-thirds worked outside the home during their menopause. Including volunteer work, this figure rose to about three-fourths. Post-menopausal women worked outside the home slightly more often than menopausal women.

One-fifth of the women had had a hysterectomy. (See

---

*Neugarten, *et al.*, "Women's Attitudes toward the Menopause" (see bibliography).

†*Ibid.*, p. 82.

Chapter 6 for information about hysterectomies.) Half of these operations included the removal of both ovaries. Two-thirds of the women had sought a second medical opinion before deciding to have the surgery. Slightly less than two-thirds had primarily positive things to say about having had the operation.

### Our Survey: Attitudes Toward Menopause

We were especially interested in finding out more about the different attitudes women have toward menopause, so the first thing we asked on the questionnaire was, "What comes to mind when you first see the word 'menopause'?"

About half the women gave positive or neutral associations, while half referred to negative aspects. In general, younger women were more fearful and felt more negative about menopause. Older women, especially post-menopausal women, were more matter-of-fact about this particular stage in life. This suggests to us that younger women tend to have a distorted view of the menopausal experience, anticipating it as much worse than it usually turns out to be. Is this because of all the myths about menopause that surround us? Is it because younger women especially fear our society's attitude toward aging women and look upon menopause as a key symbol of the aging process? If younger women have such fear, why don't older women answering the questionnaire express as much fear or even extreme frustration with living in a society that treats the aging with so little respect? Possibly the older women in our sample represent a unique group of fairly active women (two-thirds of them had jobs outside the home during and/or after menopause) who have managed to feel basically good about themselves despite society's generally negative attitude toward them. Another possibility is that since most (two-thirds) of these older women felt that they received emotional support from family and/or friends during menopause they were more likely to have positive attitudes toward menopause. There are probably a number of likely explanations, and we would like to encourage more groups to explore these kinds of questions.

### Our Survey: "Symptoms" Experienced by Younger and Older Women Alike

One question asked all women (age twenty-five and up) to check off any of 23 various "symptoms" (excluding hot flashes and vaginal dryness) they might have experienced during different decades of their lives. (All of these were symptoms often associated with menopause.) The question had very interesting results. Women twenty-five to forty years old checked more symptoms much more frequently than women in any other age group. And women over sixty checked by far the fewest symptoms. It is not clear what this difference might reflect: Do older women have difficulty remembering and thus recall fewer symptoms than they have actually ex-

perienced? Or do older women tend to see themselves as less "laden" with symptoms? Or do they define a "symptom" differently (that is, would they check off only very severe symptoms)? The checklist results suggested that menopausal women *weren't* more likely than other women to report having symptoms (other than hot flashes and vaginal dryness).

### Our Survey: The Experiences of Menopause

Another part of the questionnaire asked older women who were going through or who had gone through menopause to describe their actual experiences at that time.

About two-thirds of the menopausal and post-menopausal women reported hot flashes. Although very few women mentioned vaginal discomfort or painful intercourse, many of them may not have known that this symptom can be related to menopause. The incidence of vaginal dryness therefore may well have been higher than reported.

There were a variety of symptoms experienced during menopause, some more extreme than others. For most women menopause was reported to have lasted about 2 years or less, but for others it seemed to last as many as 4, 5, or 6 years. This is partly due to the 15 percent of the post-menopausal women who resumed their periods after they had not been menstruating for a whole year. It would be interesting to know why this happens to so many women.

Following are some of the emotional and psychological changes women reported having around the time of menopause: "Relief" . . . "Tearfulness" . . . "Unexplainable periods of nervousness and irritation" . . . "Rage at aging" . . . "Disorientation, crying, sense of being 'over the hill,' sense of failure" . . . "Delight that childbearing years were coming to a close" . . . "Happy to anticipate relaxed intercourse without need of contraceptive devices—disappointed because of vaginitis."

Here are some individual feelings and reactions to the various changes that women experienced around the time of menopause: "I merely feel regret at the evidence of aging" . . . "There hasn't been that much change" . . . "I like not needing contraceptives" . . . "I feel much better now. I had feared menopause because I was told that I would go crazy" . . . "The lack of sex desire really bothers me" . . . "I believe that the hot flashes I experi-

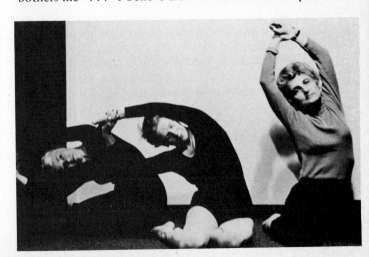

enced were milder than most. I was always so busy with my work I didn't have time to think about them" . . . "The changes were not drastic. I have just accepted them. They will stop one of these days" . . . "Most of the problems at this time were due to other causes: aging, role-stereotyping, other people's attitudes toward me" . . .

In general, about two-thirds of the menopausal and post-menopausal women felt neutral or positive about the changes they experienced. One-third felt clearly negative. When asked specifically about the loss of childbearing ability, 90 percent felt either positive or neutral. Although our culture has attached great importance to a woman's ability to reproduce, most women in our sample were not upset by the end of menstruation. Possibly this reflects the fact that, for these women, childbearing ability was only part of their self-image: after menopause they were able to value (and had the opportunity to develop) their talents and capacities beyond childbearing. Perhaps for most of these women it was a simple matter to accept this biological change as an inevitable and natural part of aging.

### Our Survey: Sexuality and Menopause

The women also expressed a variety of feelings about their sexuality and sexual desire. About half of the menopausal and post-menopausal women reported no changes in their sexual desires, while the rest indicated about equally often either an increase or decrease in sexual desire. When asked if they felt differently about themselves sexually, two-thirds of these women said no. (Note how similar this is to Neugarten's finding.)

The responses to our questionnaire clearly indicate that many of us need much more accurate information about menopause. We hope that more women will do research in this area, both to improve the medical treatment of menopause and to increase our own knowledge of what menopause really is. On the brighter side, our questionnaire definitely suggests that most women feel positive or neutral about menopause, are untroubled by the loss of fertility, and go through the two years or so with minimal discomfort.

## CONCLUSION

The most unpleasant aspects of menopause for many women are not necessarily the specific physical problems. Menopause comes at a time in a woman's life when her relationships may be changing. It is a time when her parents may be starting to get feeble or to fall ill. They may be needing her in new ways, putting new demands on her physical and emotional strength. It may take new inner resources to deal with this problem. If she is married, her husband may be seeking her help with his own life changes. If this is the case, this could be a time when a couple could find new and more profound ways of offering mutual support. If a woman has children, her children are becoming more independent

or have families of their own. This can be a difficult transition, but the delightful bonus of grandchildren is a great joy to many women. (Some communities have adoptive grandparent programs. Investigate, or start one!)

If a woman has spent a large part of her life to date raising a family, she now has some important decisions to make about what to do with her new freedom and the next thirty years of her life. She may find that her options are terribly limited, since the labor market does not value her abilities and potentials. She may want to talk with other women about these problems, and there are groups getting together to discuss just these issues.* The women involved in them recognize that the needs of older people are not separate from the needs of society as a whole. We are all going to grow older, and we must all work to eliminate age discrimination.

We as women must work to change society's negative attitude toward aging. We know that we can be as valuable to others and to ourselves after menopause as before—in fact more so as we grow in wisdom and experience. It may be hard to grow older in a society that worships youth, but we must challenge the stereotypes which minimize our abilities; we must challenge social and economic forces in our culture which falsely glorify youthfulness. Let us reaffirm our potential for personal growth and meaningful contribution to society at every stage in the continuum of life.

*For information, write to: (1) The Gray Panthers, 3700 Chestnut St., Philadelphia, Pa. 19104; (2) Tish Sommers, Coordinator, Now Task Force on Older Women, 434 66th St., Oakland, Calif. 94609; (3) *Prime Time, an Independent Feminist Journal*, 168 W. 86th St., New York, N.Y. 10024.

# The Older Person and the Family

by Dean Black

Discussing the family is a challenge for anyone because the topic is so very broad. There is so much to say that one hardly knows where to begin. A second problem in talking to others about families is that almost everyone lives in families. It may surprise you when I say that our living in families could be a problem. When I give talks, however, it often is. It's so easy for people to say either, "I already knew that. Why can't you tell me something new?" Or else, "You don't know what you are talking about. I have lived in a family all my life, and it never happened that way."

The family is important. I am sure that all of you know that. I know it, not only from my academic study of family sociology, but from many aspects of my own experience. For example, whenever I tell someone that I am a gerontologist, I get either one of two reactions. Some people react as did a man I met recently in a Sunday School class. He asked then, as do so many, "What in the world is Gerontology?" When I told him, he got one of those looks on his face that said something like, "I wish you never told me." I understand why he said that when I asked him what he did for a living. He was a mortician. The other common reaction to my work is one that lets me know people are concerned about their families and about their old people. So often, when I tell people that I study aging, they step closer and, almost in a confidential tone, say to me, "I am so happy that I have had a chance to meet you. Can you tell me what I should do about mother?"

There is an interesting thing that lets us know family ties are important to older people. That is the very common existence of what we call "fictive kin." Fictive kin are people you pretend are related to you, even though they are not. Perhaps we can all remember as children that we had various "aunts" and "uncles" who were adult friends of our parents. Such fictive kin are actually quite common. In a class I once had, I asked my students how many of them had an older

person whom they called by a family title, even though there was no actual blood relationship. Over one half of the students raised their hands. When I questioned them further, I discovered that for many of those young people, those relationships were as meaningful as the relationships they shared with actual blood kin. This willingness of people to create family relationships where none previously existed has been used by the government to develop an effective program for helping both older people and young children. This is the Foster Grandparents Program. This program helps elderly men and women overcome many of the problems that seem to accompanying aging: loneliness, a feeling of uselessness, and so on. The older person becomes involved as a foster grandparent with a child who needs the warmth and benefits of a close personal relationship. Since the program was started in about 1966, it has experienced dynamic growth. It has demonstrated very convincingly the importance to both young and old of a family type relationship, whether it be artificially established or the product of a blood relationship.

I would like to emphasize that the family is not a single, readily recognizable, entity. The family is many things. A well known family sociologist, Marvin Sussman, wrote an article in 1971 in which he identified something like twenty different family forms. New family forms are continually evolving in this time of rapid social change. For a practitioner working with older people, the "family" is usually not difficult to define. The family consists of the people who brought the older person to the facility; it includes those who come to visit. The family members are also often defined as those who are financially responsible for the older person's care. Of course, what I have described here is really a very limited segment of the older person's entire family. Service providers probably deal most often, for example, with a daughter rather than a son. Women seem to maintain parent-child ties more than men do. And the issues dealt with are apt to be somewhat limited as well. For example, the children must be helped to handle their guilt. They feel guilty and insecure because

* Assistant Professor of Sociology, University of Southern California.

165

they have to bring the older person into the facility. They need help to work that through. There are other things. Some family members don't know how to visit properly. It may be that Mom used to be the sounding board for all of the family problems. So, when the children come to visit they bare their souls and their griefs to Mom. After they feel better, they leave. Mom may feel better too, if she has gained a sense of usefulness from the experience. But it can also be a depressing, damaging experience for her. So families sometimes must be taught to be good visitors. Another problem often arises if the older person is released from a convalescent facility. We often speak of the problems the older person has in adapting to his release. Since the older person is most often released into the family, that family has to be prepared to take the older person back.

Each of us has had a limited experience with families, and so we also have a somewhat limited perspective. Yet I think we can better serve older people and their families by recognizing that there are a great variety of family forms, and that the particular nature of your challenge with the older person and the family is a product of the nature of the entire family of the older person you serve.

Many older people live alone. Of those who live alone, a small percentage have no family still living. Most of those with no living family are probably found among the eight percent of those sixty-five and over who have never married. The others have simply outlived the other members of their family. It is apparent that this group of older people includes many widows. There are over eleven million widowed persons in the United States today, and three-fourths of those are over the age of sixty-five. Every year, 251,000 men and 592,000 women are widowed. Widowhood is a severe crisis. In fact, a group of researchers who were studying the impact of many events involving a change in a person's life discovered that death of a spouse was rated as the most severe crisis event that could be encountered in life. Nevertheless, most widowed persons are not left totally alone and do have other living relatives, although they may not share the same household with them. Of those sixty-five and over, seventy-five to eighty percent have living children. Statistics show that even more of them have living siblings. One study reported that eighty-two percent of their respondents had living siblings. A slightly greater percentage of them reported living children. This can be partially explained by the greater family size of a few generations ago, but it is an amazing thing nevertheless.

More common than the single aged individual is the aging couple. Sixty-eight percent of men and thirty-four percent of women over sixty-five are married. Two thirds of those who are married live independently of other family members; that is, although they may have other living relatives—siblings and children, for example—they do not share their household with them. The figures I just cited reflect the much higher number of widowed women than men. There are, of course, two reasons for this. First, women tend to outlast men, and so the chances of a woman losing her husband are greater than are his chances of losing her. The second

factor is the phenomenon of remarriage. In the fairly recent past, remarriage was less an acceptable option for the older person who is widowed than it is today. People tended to feel that the sexual aspects of marriage were no longer of interest to the elderly, an idea that has since been discredited by researchers from Kinsey to Masters and Johnson. Often, an older person who wanted to marry again would find that society looked at that idea with disapproval. His friends, his children, and the larger community might discourage his remarriage as being somehow foolish and improper. Although the general public has still not fully accepted the idea that marriage in the later years is appropriate, social barriers against remarriage are breaking down, particularly for men. If the trend continues, there may yet be a time when remarriage is not only an accepted but an expected event for both men and women following the death of a spouse.

There are older persons who live in what might be called a multi-generation or complex family household. Thirty-six percent of elderly people live with their children; ten percent live with their siblings; and, amazingly, as many as five percent of elderly people over sixty-five live with aging parents.

Many children undoubtedly expect to have their parents live with them when they become unable to take care of themselves. They probably feel as well that this would be expected and desired by their parents. However, research has shown that only about eight percent of elderly people feel that it is desirable to live with their children. In one study, seventy-seven percent of the elderly people interviewed, said they would choose to live somewhere other than with their children when they are no longer able to care for themselves. I once mentioned this fact to a friend of mine, and she said, "but they only say that because they feel they will be a burden. I have that problem with my mother. She insists that she doesn't want to come to live with us, but I know that it is only because she feels it would be hard on us."

What my friend means by this was that the figures I cited were misleading. She feels that older people may say that they don't want to live with their children, but underneath they really do. I think I would tend to disagree with her. Parents often genuinely do not want to live with children though the children do not believe that their reasons are acceptable. An older person who feels he is being a burden will be miserable whether he is actually being a burden or not. And children who persist in saying things like, "But mother, I told you time and again that I don't mind taking care of you," can often do little to relieve the older person's anxieties. Under conditions like that, it is not unreasonable that they should want to live with someone they feel would not be overburdened by their presence.

I have been concerned so far with different family forms. There are single older people living alone, some with no living family, some never married, some widowed, some with living children, some with living siblings, and so on. There are aging couples, some with their spouse of half a century, some newlyweds, and even some who may merely be continuing a lifelong pattern of one marriage after another. Then there are multi-generational families, helpful in so many ways, and yet a potential source of anxiety to young and old alike.

There are still other important differences between families. Those are the result of ethnic and cultural differences. For example, I recently heard a very interesting talk by a psychologist who grew to her adult years on the Chinese mainland; her name is Dr. Yung-Hua Liu, and she is now with the Student Counseling Center at U.C.L.A. She pointed out to us that the attitude of the young towards the old in China is very different than it is here in our country. She stated that one important reason for this is the philosophical heritage that all Chinese children of her era learned by word of mouth from their parents. That philosophy speaks very directly of the value of old age. For example, she cited one of the sayings of Confucius which went something like this:

At 15, I applied myself to the study of wisdom,
At 30, I grew stronger in it,
At 40, I no longer had doubt,
At 50, there was nothing on earth that could shake me,
At 70, I could follow the dictate of my heart without disobeying moral law.

Can you see what this teaches them about their old people? Another important influence on the Chinese attitude towards aging is their vocabulary. In English, our word, "old," often has a negative connotation. But in Chinese, the word for "old" has a neutral value, and even tends toward a positive kind of feeling. I believe Dr. Liu said the word was "lao." She told us that the word is rarely used by itself, but is rather used in combination with other words to form new words with very different meanings. For example, when combined with another word, it means honesty. And she went on to list other words that could be formed with the Chinese word for old. All of them were words that almost invariably referred to things of honor and value. Beyond these philosophical and linguistic factors which make old age a positive thing can be added the practice of ancestor worship. Ancestor worship brings reverence for old age and things old directly into the family context. Ancestor worship anchors family roots deep in historical time, living and dead, within the Chinese family. I believe that this example serves to illustrate the fact that the cultural heritage can greatly influence the nature of an older person's experience within a family, and the feelings of family members toward the older person.

There are indeed many family forms, and the family can mean many different things to different people. But in spite of the variations, there are some general features of families that are important to the understanding of the role of the family in later life. The first feature has to do with the sort of personal relationships that exist in families. The second feature has to do with the way the family can organize itself as a helpgiving unit. Family relationships are personal; they are face-to-face; they are intimate relationships. They are relationships in which the people are important, and not the positions they hold. In order to understand this more clearly, let me contrast the personal, intimate family relationship with the sort of relationship which exists in a bureaucratic institution. For example, when you go into a bank, you expect a teller to help you. Suppose that in the middle of the transaction, someone taps your teller on the shoulder and tells him that he had a telephone call, then steps into the teller's window and says to you, "Hello, I am Mr. Wilson. The other teller had to answer a telephone call." This probably would not bother you. If it did, your main concern would be this: does Mr. Wilson know how to be a teller? If he does, there is no reason to worry; the important thing is that he know how to carry out the position of being a teller. In contrast, suppose a child goes home one afternoon after school, walks into the house, and meets a strange lady who says, "Hello there. Your mother has been transferred to another family, and I am here to take her place. Don't worry; I know all about being a mother. I can cook, wash clothers, and do everything a mother must do." Will the child accept that? Would you accept it? Of course not! Because in a family the people are important, not what they do. And this is why families are undoubtedly the source of our most meaningful, personal relationships. And the same intimacy is the reason why in the family comes some of the most destructive inter-personal violence. We have all seen examples of the strength of the family bond. I recall seeing a well known poster that showed a small child carrying another little boy. The caption read something like, "He ain't heavy, Mister, he is my Brother." Once on the television show, "Leave it to Beaver," Beaver saw a boy and a girl fighting. In the best tradition of chivalry, little Beaver stepped in to break it up. Suddenly he found himself being attacked by both children. You see, they were brother and sister, and, even though they fought, the bond between them was strong enough to make them unite against anything that threatened either one of them.

These were examples using children, but what they illustrate persists throughout life. The evidence shows that the family is still a very important source of meaningful social interaction for the elderly. Research studies have found things like this: sixty-two percent of people aged sixty-five and over have a son or a daughter within walking distance; eight-four percent live within one hour of at least one of their children; and only seven percent live further away than two hours. Family members are generally quite available to an older person as a source of interaction.

But you might ask whether or not they take advantage of their availability. One study found that sixty-five percent of the older people had seen at least one of their children during the previous twenty-four hours; and over eighty percent had seen at least one child in the preceding week. It is apparent that the family is indeed a key source of social interaction during the later years. That is not to say that interaction is always positive; in fact, one study showed that older women who live near a married child who had young children, tended to have low morale. I guess grandmother can be asked to be a babysitter once too often. Another study showed that one of the main reasons why people in the lower classes moved from one city to another was to get away from the close contact of their kin. Whether the interaction is positive or negative, or as is more likely the case, whether it has both positive and negative aspects, the family is an important and meaningful source of social support during the later years.

The second general feature has to do with the family as a help-giving unit. Again, a contrast with a bureaucracy will help to illustrate this. Bureaucratic organizations have a fixed, inflexible schedule of activities for handling certain pre-defined problems. Since they have handled about every problem that could come up, they have also devised set ways of doing things. If someone comes along with an unusual problem, the response is likely to be, "I am sorry; we don't handle that sort of thing." But, families are not like that. They are flexible; they are diffuse in their activities and have no specific single purposes. As a result, the family is very often able to handle emergencies that demand speed of action and flexibility in a much better way than can the service bureaucracies.

After the major flood that hit Denver in the early sixties, some people did a study to find out what were the victims' major sources of help. They wondered: do people rely on the service agencies provided for them by the local, state and national governments? Or, do they rather seek the help of friends, neighbors, and kin? They found that family and kin were by far the most important source of aid. People tended to go to the more formalized service agencies only as a last resort. The reason, again, is that the family is a flexible kind of organization that can quickly mobilize itself around a particular problem. This flexibility is, of course, supported by the kind of intimate feeling for one another I spoke of earlier. This sort of thing has been found in study after study. I don't feel it is necessary to burden you here with the details of research. It is enough, I believe, to simply point out that there is overwhelming evidence for a two-way pattern of help and support flowing between the older and the younger generations in American families. The aid may be in the form of money or services, it may be a response to an immediate and potentially destructive crisis, or it may be an integral part of the pattern of daily life. But, whatever the form, there is little doubt that the family is the most important source of aid for the majority of older people today. There is one more thing regarding the family as a source of help that often tends to be ignored. That is the fact that some old people have a great capacity to tyrannize their families. I read of one instance of an eighty-two year old father of five, named Mr. Jones. He had been a successful businessman, and, as a result, was well-off financially and accustomed to having his orders obeyed. His wife died a few years before, and since he was in a wheel chair, he needed someone to take care of him. He demanded that his forty-five year old bachelor son give up his job and move in to become his caretaker. This seemed to be a reasonable solution to everyone, because Buddy did not like his job anyway. So, Buddy became his dad's nurse, with an allowance of $50.00 a week, a new car, and free board and room. But the problem is that now, after several years, the arrangement still goes on. Dad is completely satisfied and refuses to even consider any other arrangement. But what will happen to Buddy when his father finally dies? Will he have a chance to get a job again? Mr. Jones may have felt that the arrangement was ideal, but the cost to Buddy could be very great indeed.

Patriarchal tyranny was the theme of the movie, "I Never Sang for my Father." In that movie, the middle-aged son of an elderly father wanted to get married again following a period of widowerhood. But the father clung to his son. It was as though his life depended upon whether or not he could prevent his son from marrying once again and moving into a home of his own. The movie traced the course of this struggle, which eventually erupted into a final, bitter and angry separation.

I have now traced two important meanings of the family to an older person. The family is a source of intimate social relationships. It is also the most important source of help in time of need. But there is another, perhaps more subtle, meaning of the family that is well illustrated in a screen play that was written by Dick Eribes that is called, "I Remember the Future as Though It Were Yesterday." It tells of an elderly father who was moving from the large home where he had raised his family and seen his wife pass away, into some kind of retirement housing, where he couldn't take along many of the things that seemed to collect in houses where children grow up. So he had a garage sale, and one of his sons, who was by now a middle-aged man, was helping him to get things set up for the sale. They placed everything out on tables in the front yard, and soon the people began to come. The father and the son played two different roles in the drama that began to unfold. The son was the bargainer. He would talk to the people and try to get the prices up. He took very seriously the idea that he could best serve his father by helping him raise money that was so important now during his retirement years. The father didn't look at all like a salesman. In fact, he walked around like a customer picking up the various articles, looking them over as though he were considering which one to buy. A little boy came along and began to look at a bicycle that had once belonged to the old man's son. The old man watched him for awhile and then bent down beside the boy and said, "You know, my boy used that bike when he was your age." The little boy said, "Gosh, it sure is a nice bike." The father said, "How would you like to have that bike?" The little boy said, "Oh, I wish I could, but I haven't got enough money." And, then the father stood up and said to the boy, "You don't have to pay for it; I want you to have it. Go on, take it. Get on it and let me see how you can ride it." And off the boy rode.

The son was angry. "Dad," he said, "I could have gotten $20.00 for that bike." You see, he didn't understand what the father was doing. The old man had created for himself a bit of a future out of the past. He had taken something out of his past and given it a future in that little boy. "I Remember the Future as Though It Were Yesterday."

People seek immortality in a variety of ways. Some believe in an after-life; some hope for monuments and physical evidences of their life. But for many, their future exists only as a part of them carried on by those who bear their name.

I'd like to close by drawing your attention to something that Irving Goffman talks about in his book called, *Asylums*. When Goffman talks about "Asylums," he is referring to the whole variety of institutions where people go to be protected from intrusions of the world outside, and so that the world outside might be protected from them. In many ways, institutions for the aged can be considered as such total institutions. Goffman speaks of the "stripping" process that people are often required to undergo as they enter an institution. They are stripped of many things. Sometimes, it is the clothing they wear; often it will be what Goffman calls "The Identity Kit," a comb, a mirror, make-up; or, it may be things like clocks or books. But, whatever it is, it is virtually certain that an older person must lose some things as he comes into an institution. There simply is not enough space for everything he once had. But, there are some things that cannot be taken away from an older person, and I believe that the most important of these is this: Every older person that you encounter is a person with a history in a family. For most older people, that family is still the most important aspect of their social world.

# 32

# "Don't Cry in Front of Your Friends"

**Widows, as individuals, have enough problems. But looking at them as a group, one sociologist sees them also as among the country's most oppressed minorities. Consider a minority as any group that receives unequal treatment because of its lifestyle or cultural patterns — regardless of size or ethnic character. By these standards, Dr. Helena Znaniecki Lopata, who chairs the sociology department at Chicago's Loyola University, is certainly right.**

Ballroom dance studios convince them to "put a little fun in their lives" and bilk them out of $10,000 in lessons. They arrive at formal dinner parties full of anticipation, only to find their name tags crowded together on the same table. They tune out loneliness with civic-minded busy work and resign themselves to a life on the sidelines of society.

They are, in the opinion of one Chicago sociologist, our most oppressed and most ignored minority: the nine million widows of America.

In terms of social status, widows are losers on all counts. They face discrimination as women, as old people, as poverty cases and often as racial or ethnic minorities. And while they are battling social pressures, they must switch emotional gears from a secure past to an uncertain and lonely future.

For Helena Lopata, professor of sociology at Chicago's Loyola University, widowhood has become a complete field of investigation—and since social scientists, like society, have given a back seat to the subject, there is much to explore. With numerous studies and a book, *Widowhood in an American City,* to her credit—Lopata is about to launch a four-year cross-cultural study financed by the Social Security Administration. She will investigate the social, economic and emotional support, or lack of it, available to Chicago widows while other research teams are working in Zagreb, Yugoslavia and Warsaw, Poland. "We don't know what other things we can do for widows," Lopata says, "but when we see what other societies do, we'll know better."

How are widows stigmatized as second class citizens? For urban women especially, a husband's death means a plunge in social status—an interesting commentary on women's position in our society, which still bases their worth on their relationships with men. The loss of a male escort curtails their activities and transforms them into an awkward fifth wheel at two-by-two social functions.

Women friends suspect widows of husband-snatching, while the husbands themselves have been known to proposition them on the sly. Widows often escape the whole sticky situation by limiting their socializing to each other.

Lopata sees widows in their new living arrangements as the victims of a double bind. Older women in particular have been acculturated to live in the homes of male providers, whether fathers or husbands, and have gotten the message that they could not and should not fend for themselves.

But rather than be unwanted guests in their children's homes, most widows prefer to live alone and suffer the loneliness and inconveniences involved. Lopata estimates that 49 percent of Chicago widows aged 50 or over are solitary dwellers. She points out that it is difficult for older widows to view their new independence

Illustration by Deanna Glad

formerly social and economic equals. "Downward mobility in a society idealizing upward mobility is psychologically difficult," states Lopata.

Added to these disadvantages is the fact that 1.6 million of the country's elderly women are members of ethnic or racial minority groups. As housewives, they have had less contact with American society than their husbands and children, who work and go to school, and, as widows, they are all the more alienated from the dominant culture. Lopata believes that this foreignness also cuts them off from their own ethnic community, which is Americanizing itself faster than elderly stay-at-homes can tolerate.

As a native of Poland, Lopata is particularly aware of the plight of Polish widows in Chicago. Her father, a prominent Polish sociologist, emigrated to this country when she was a child. Although Lopata has never experienced widowhood herself—her husband is a management consultant in Chicago—she became conscious of its unresolved problems while researching *Occupation Housewife*, a book on the limited opportunities and expectations of American women, published last year.

Lopata is convinced that there are almost as many internal obstacles to a widow's readjustment as there are external roadblocks. "Grief makes people more passive," she says.

For widows, this passivity translates into a kind of giving up. Some women are so immobilized by loneliness and a longing for the past that they resist new friendships and retreat from old ones. Others feel the weight of new responsibilities that husbands formerly handled—mowing the lawn, servicing the car and even adjusting the color television.

The loneliness is intensified by society's squeamishness about displays of open grief. Many widows complain that even good friends suddenly pull away, rationalizing that the bereaved must work out their sorrow alone. "I'm still grieving," remarked one widow. "My husband has been dead a little over one year, but no individual has helped me at all." Said another, "Don't cry in front of your friends; you just embarrass them and they can't help you."

But most widowed women pull out of their inertia and search for activities to give their lives some meaning. For many, new concerns are as pedestrian as joining the local bridge club or making cookies for an orphanage. But they supply an essential mainstay: the knowledge that, as one woman put it, "the space you're occupying counts for something."

with pride, since most Americans still swallow the myth that ideal lifestyle for older women is that of doting matriarch in a three-generation household.

In yet another area—supporting themselves—widows are victims of sex inequalities. After a lifetime of taking clerical jobs for pin money and raising children to the exclusion of a career, widows are pathetically ill equipped to be self-sufficient economically. In one study of some 300 urban widows, Lopata found that 26 percent had never worked, that 40 percent did not work during marriage and that almost half were forced to seek jobs after their husbands' deaths. Most of the older widows had not improved their job status since they married. After some 20 years of little or no job activity, they were something less than valuable commodities on an already glutted job market.

Their work situation is all the harder because of another deeply-rooted American prejudice—our dislike of old age. In a society which finds youthful innocence more attractive than mature experience, widows have a rough time convincing themselves or potential employers that life begins at 56—the average age of widowed Americans.

Then there's the question of poverty. Most of the older people living alone are women, and many of them live on $1,350 a year or less. In polling groups of widows in rural Missouri and metropolitan Chicago, Lopata found that 88 percent of the former and 60 percent of the latter squeeze by on less than $3,000 a year. A lack of funds can curtail a widow's already narrow range of activities, making luxuries out of emotional necessities like visits to far away relatives and friends, or membership fees in organizations.

The poverty that follows the loss of a bread-winner can send a widow into a demoralizing economic tailspin, often forcing her to move into a poorer neighborhood and live on a tighter budget than friends who were

# 33

# Crazy Lady

## by Lynn Caine

When that protective fog of numbness had finally dissipated, life became truly terrifying. I was full of grief, choked with unshed tears, overwhelmed by the responsibility of bringing up two children alone, panicked about my financial situation, almost immobilized by the stomach-wrenching, head-splitting pain of realizing that I was alone. My psychic pain was such that putting a load of dirty clothes in the washing machine, taking out the vacuum cleaner, making up a grocery list, all the utterly routine household chores, loomed like Herculean labors.

I was alone. Alone. Without Martin. Forever. And I didn't know what to do. I was beset with problems, some real, most imagined. I did not know how or where to start to put my life in order. If only I had known that the wisest course of action was inaction. Doing nothing at all. At least until I had regained the ability to cope with the essentials of everyday life.

If that hypothetical wise person had existed who would have told me about grief's seasons, he would have also stressed that the widow has no conception of what she is doing for many, many months after her husband's death.

Helen Hayes, the actress, confessed, "For two years [after her husband's death] I was just as crazy as you can be and still be at large. I didn't have any really normal minutes during those two years. It wasn't just grief. It was total confusion. I was nutty," Miss Hayes said, "and that's the truth. How did I come out of it? I don't know, because I didn't know when I was in it that I was in it."

I didn't know I was in it either; all I know was that I hurt. But looking back, I was certainly a crazy lady. Oh, I thought I was eminently sane, that I was making wise decisions. But I was acting like an idiot.

And I was idiotically inconsistent. I swung from outlandish attempts to solve my problems (and money loomed the largest; I equated it with security and stability) to maudlin, childish endeavors to set the clock back and try to pick up the threads of my life from the years before I knew Martin. Few of my actions had much to do with reality. They were freakish, inconsistent. Crazy.

That's really what it was. Craziness.

I was not prepared for craziness. But it was inevitable. Folk wisdom knows all about the crazy season. Friends and acquaintances tell the widow, "Sit tight. Do nothing. Make no changes. Coast for a few months. Wait . . . wait . . . wait." But the widow, while she hears the words, does not get the message. She believes that her actions are discreet, deliberate, careful, responsible.

I certainly did. I believed that every step I made was carefully thought out, wisely calculated. But the record shows otherwise.

One bizarre caper of mine was to write a rich politician.

"You are fat and rich; I am poor and thin," I wrote. "My husband died leaving me with no life insurance and two small children to support on a publishing salary. Would you please send me $500,000.

"I met you at a literary cocktail party in Washington last year and you drove me to the airport.

"I look forward to hearing from you."

Crazy! It was one of those things that one might have fantasies about, but never, never do. I did it. And I expected him to reply. Every night I'd riffle through the mail. I knew what the check would look like. It would be bright yellow and the amount would be typewritten. $500,000.

Finally it came. An envelope in the mail. A typewritten letter on the politician's official letterhead.

"Sorry, I cannot comply with your request," he wrote.

I was crushed. Heartbroken. What had I expected? I'm afraid I had expected a check for half a million dollars.

This was just the tip of the iceberg. My craziness went deep. I was a lost child and yearned for someone to take care of me, to love me. Anyone.

Before I met Martin, I had had a love affair that ended disastrously. Very unpleasant and messy. Yet, less than two months after Martin died, I telephoned that man. For some reason, I thought he would still be waiting for me. As I dialed the number, that same old number of eighteen years ago, I had a fantasy that he would send me yellow roses and promise to cherish me forever.

When he answered I said, "You told me I could

always call you if I were in trouble." I started crying. "I'm in very bad trouble," I sobbed. "Martin is dead and I have two children."

He didn't know who I was!

"It's Lynn," I told him. "You said you'd never be able to forget my eyes." I stammered through half a dozen reminiscences, determined that he must remember me. It was terribly embarrassing. When I finally had the sense to hang up, I sat huddled in the chair by the telephone for the rest of the evening.

Most of my craziness involved money and security. I was terrified because Martin had left no insurance and the money had stopped. This was realistic enough. A widow with two children has to be concerned with money. What was unrealistic was that I never stopped to consider the fact that I was still earning a decent salary and that I was now getting Social Security payments for the children. We were certainly not going to starve. But somehow, after Martin died I was possessed with the idea that I was penniless.

Today it is a shock to realize my financial incompetence at the time. It ranged from the trivial to the staggering. When Martin was alive, I used his credit card to telephone home every night when I was out of town on business. One evening after he died, I started dialing home from Boston. And I panicked. "Martin's dead!" It hit me hard, as if for the first time. "I can't use his credit card any more. And I don't have enough change to make the call." There I was in a public telephone booth at the airport, shaking and crying. It did not dawn on me that I could reverse the charges—although I had made collect calls all my life. And it took months before I realized I could apply for my own credit card.

There were other aberrations, less grotesque. I knew Martin was dead, but somehow it took a long time for the reality to seep in, become part of me. I would go to the supermarket and think, "Oh, they have endive today. I'd better get some. Martin likes it so much." I would pick out an avocado for him, a fruit! I've never really liked. Then I would realize, "My God! He is dead!" and put the avocado back as if it were burning me.

When something funny happened, I'd say to myself "Oh, wait until I tell Martin about this tonight! He'll never believe it." There were times in my office when I would stretch out my hand to the telephone to call him, to chat. Reality always intervened before I dialed that disconnected number.

I have learned that most widows do similar things. One woman told me it took weeks for her to stop setting the table for two every night. And another said that she had renewed her late husband's subscription to a motor car magazine for three years running although she hadn't the slightest interest in automobiles herself and never took the magazines out of their wrappers. She simply stacked them beside her easy chair month after month until it dawned on her that this was crazy.

One day when I was on the Fifth Avenue bus I spotted a man who looked like Martin. I pulled the cord and plunged after him. I knew it wasn't Martin, but I tried desperately to catch up with him. I couldn't. I lost sight of him and it made me very depressed, as if Martin had rejected me.

And I had dreams. I would dream that I heard the door open while I was in the kitchen getting the ice for our evening drink. It was Martin, home from work. I would be so happy to hear him come in. But I always woke up before I saw him.

I had a sense of Martin, of some quality of Martin that had filtered into me. A very real feeling that part of me was Martin.

I thought this was some very special psychic phenomenon until I discovered that it was not peculiar to me at all, but part of the phenomenon of grief. Dr. Parkes reported that one widow who participated in a study of bereavement insisted, "My husband is in me, right through and through. I can feel him in me doing everything."

My identification was not this strong. But I very often felt like some character in a Victorian novel, the young widow, for instance, whose husband has died and left her alone to run the family estate. She lies in bed at night mulling over some problem that she must cope with the next day. "What would the squire tell me to do?" she wonders. And in her sleep, the answer is given. When she wakes in the morning, her thoughts are clear, she knows how to proceed. For many months, I would routinely think to myself, "What would Martin tell me to do?" when faced with some problem. I usually came up with a satisfactory answer. I still do it, but much less often. I have learned that the best answers come from myself. I no longer have to rely on the dreary mystique of "Martin knows best."

There is nothing shameful about the widow's temporary insanity. It is remarkable, in fact, that so many widows are able to live through this distressingly crazy time and come out as strong or stronger than they were before.

A psychiatrist, Dr. Thomas Holmes, has isolated forty-three events or crises that the average person may expect to experience and given them stress ratings, which he calls "life change units." The death of a spouse, by far the most stressful, is rated at one hundred life change units. Change in one's financial status, something experienced by most widows, has a rating of thirty-eight. And if the change involves the widow having to go to work, there are an additional twenty-six life change units to add on.

I had not known about stress ratings before I was widowed. If I had, it might have helped me proceed with a bit more caution. As it was I accumulated more life change units in the course of a year than I could handle. According to Dr. Holmes's rating, this is how mine added up:

| | |
|---|---|
| Death of spouse | 100 |
| Change in financial state | 38 |
| Mortage over $10,000 | 31 |
| Change in living conditions | 25 |
| Revision of personal habits | 24 |
| Change in residence | 20 |
| Change in social activities | 18 |
| Change in sleeping habits | 16 |
| Change in eating habits | 15 |
| Christmas | 12 |

A psyche-shattering total of 299 life change units. Dr. Holmes's research showed that an accumulation of 200 or more life change units in a year is usually more than a person can cope with. He advises people with 200 or more units to "lie low" for a little while and suggests that it is a good idea to talk things over with a physician or a qualified counselor.*

*Here are stress ratings for other life crises that widows may encounter:

| | |
|---|---|
| Death of close family member (other than spouse) | 63 |
| Personal injury or illness | 53 |
| Change to different line of work | 36 |
| Foreclosure of mortgage or loan | 30 |
| Son or daughter leaving home | 29 |
| Trouble with in-laws | 29 |
| Change in work hours or conditions | 20 |
| Vacation | 13 |

If anyone had intimated that I was not supremely sane and suggested that I could use some counseling, I would have been insulted. Unbelieving. I would have retorted, "If ever I have been practical in my life, if ever I have measured my words and actions, this has been the time." I was convinced that everything I was doing made sense. The truth was that most of it was nonsense. It took me a long time to undo some of the ridiculous—and expensive—mistakes I made. And the emotional fallout verged on the disastrous. I did eventually reach the point where I sought counseling. But if I had understood earlier the unbearable degree of stress I was subjecting myself to . . . Well, what then? I like to think that it might have stopped me from acting so precipitously, thus reducing the number of life change units I accumulated. And I like to think I would have gotten the psychological help I needed earlier.

# 34

# Widowhood and Preventive Intervention*

PHYLLIS R. SILVERMAN**

*This paper discusses the needs of the new widow to make a transition from the role of wife to that of widowhood. It points to the lack of a transition ritual in American culture which helps the bereaved individual know how to make the needed changes in his life. A mode of intervention, developed in the Widow-to-Widow program is described in which another widow is the primary caregiver. Using their own experience as widows they offer the newly bereaved individual an opportunity to get some help in coping with their grief and then point the way to making the transition. The widow aide is helpful in at least three ways. She provides support, is a role model, and is a bridge person.*

Widowhood can be viewed as that social category which every married person will enter when one of the couple dies first. Most people put aside any thought that this change of status will happen to them. Most contemporary traditions and patterns of behavior support people in their reluctance to face death and its consequences for family life. In fact few people understand what it means to be widowed.[1] While it is common to rehearse for marriage during courtship no similar rituals prepare the individual for the inevitable termination of this marriage when one of the partners will die. Any verbal discussion of what widowhood involves rarely occurs even when the spouse is seriously ill and death is anticipated. On the other hand

*silent* consideration of what is involved may be taking place in an older population as people observe their friends who are becoming widowed.

Berardo (1968) pointed out that the examination of widowhood is a neglected aspect of study in the family life cycle. He noted that the widowed are a growing population and that they have a high risk of developing social and emotional difficulties. (Berardo, 1968)

In 1968 there were approximately 11,000,000 widowed individuals in the United States, while in 1960 there were only 9,000,000. For all age groups: men were becoming widowers at the rate of 5.9/1000 or 251,000 a year while women were becoming widows at the rate of 13.9/1000 or 592,000 per year. The widowed are increasingly a female population. Widowhood is not solely a problem of the elderly as one-fourth of those widowed are under 65. However, many people grow to old age as widows and widowers. For example, of those who die of old age, on the average women have been widows for 18.5 years and men have been widowers for 13.5 years. (Carter and Glick 1970)

Berardo (1968) raised questions about what life is like for these men and women who no longer have a husband or wife with whom to share their life. Other researchers have approached the question of widowhood from other view-

* The work reported in this paper was financed by a special grant from the National Institute of Mental Health No. MH09214. The author would like to thank Mrs. Adele Cooperband, Mrs. Dorothy MacKenzie, Mrs. Mary Pettipas, Mrs. Elizabeth Wilson, and Mrs. Carrie Wynn, who as widow aides did the basic intervention reported here.

** Phyllis R. Silverman, Ph.D., is Lecturer in Social Welfare, Department of Psychiatry, Harvard Medical School and Director of Widow-to-Widow program, Laboratory of Community Psychiatry, Harvard Medical School.

[1] The very word "widow" has very negative connotations. Many widows feel as if it implies they are damaged, a second class citizen. The same associations are not true for the word "widower."

points. For example, the sociologists, Marris (1958) and Lopata (1969, 1970), have looked at the content of the widow's social life; Maddison (1970) and Parkes (1964, 1967, 1970) as psychiatrists have been concerned with the mental health implications of widowhood; and the insurance companies (LIAMA, 1970) have examined the adequacy of their programs for meeting the needs of the surviving widow. This growing interest is beginning to influence caregiving practices. (Gerber, 1969) The Widow-to-Widow program is one effort to develop appropriate modes of helping the widowed. (Silverman, 1969)

### The Widow-to-Widow Program

This paper will discuss several aspects of what it means to be widowed based on the experiences of the Widow-to-Widow program. The program developed in response to the finding that most caregivers who might normally be available to the widowed were fearful of a bereaved individual, attempting to shut off his or her mourning prematurely and then withdraw while there was still great need. (Silverman, 1966) Most people hope that the widow's grief will be short lived and time bound. They find it difficult to tolerate the prolonged anguish of acute grief. The recital of a few platitudes by the clergy or the offering of a prescription by the physician may give these caregivers a sense of doing something but in fact the widow reported that this helped very little.

Most widowed people did not seek out mental health professionals since they were not seen as appropriate to their need. They did not see themselves, and correctly so, as having psychiatric problems. Instead, as Silverman (1966) reported, they found another widowed person to be most helpful. The Widow-to-Widow program was an experiment to test the feasibility of another widow becoming a caregiver to the newly widowed. It was hypothesized that she would be able to use her own experience to help others, that her special empathy would enable her to understand the sup-

port needed, that she could accept the new widow's distress over an extended period of time, and that she would be accepted if she offered her assistance to the new widow. (Silverman, 1967)

In this program the new widow did not solicit help. In part this was because a newly bereaved person is usually too disorganized and too unsure of his or her needs to reach out and ask for assistance. Since the widowed are at a high risk of developing psychiatric problems (Volkart and Michael, 1957), the question was asked: could intervention such as the Widow-to-Widow program prevent such disabilities from occuring? A public health model of prevention was followed, i.e., attempting to reach every member of the target population even those who might be "immune" and not need any assistance. Therefore, the Widow-to-Widow program tried to reach all the widowed women under the age of 60 in a given community. For another widow this contact was easier since she seemed to have a legitimate interest in helping and could act in the context of a neighbor or friend who had similar personal experience. (Silverman, 1971) The goal of such intervention is not simple, since it is difficult to say what is being prevented. What is poor mental health? The findings of the Widow-to-Widow program indicate that widows and widowers often develop emotional disturbance when they cannot give up their role of wife or husband, i.e., when they try to continue to live as they had when their spouse was alive. A good part of the intervention seems to involve helping them make this transition from wife to widow.

Widowhood does not just happen when a spouse dies. A woman may legally become a widow at this point; however, the legal fact does not always coincide with her social and emotional acceptance of the role. Goffman (1961) wrote of a moral career in a role. This is a useful concept here. In his terms the widow becomes a member of a social category after undergoing a dramatic status transition. There is a regular "sequence of change that this career entails in the person's self, and in his framework of imagery for judging himself and others." (Goffman, 1961, 127-128) A "change over time, as is basic and common to the members of this social category takes place and the individual becomes socialized to the role." (Goffman, 1961)

To assume the role of widow, one needs to know how to play this part. In some cultures the role is clearly defined. (Mathison, 1970) The widow is expected to be in mourning the remainder of her natural life. Mourning, and the public behavior which is viewed as an expression of it, is the dominant force in her life. It may not be pleasant but at least she knows who she is and what is expected of her and she never has to give up what attachment she has to her deceased husband. In sharp contrast in the United States a person's mourning is supposed to be of short duration and to end before the new widow or widower understands what the new role means or how it will affect his life. This pressure to not express one's bereavement can in fact only intensify the grief. (Gorer, 1967) It seems safe to say that the period after the death of a spouse is an "anomic" situation; an individual at the threshold of a career as a widow or widower does not know what to do, what it means, and what to expect of himself and for himself.

The remainder of this paper is devoted to examining this dilemma created by widowhood and describes one way of helping to cope with it. The experience on which this paper is based is primarily with widows under 60. From other experience[2] it would seem that the critical transition involving a role change is no different for widowers (with necessary modifications specific to the role of husband) or for people over 60.

### Giving Up the Role of Wife

Initially the new widow is numb.[3] Very often at the time of the funeral she appears calm and able to cope with her various social responsibilities and all the many chores connected with the funeral and the ongoing care of her family. At this time it is normal and appropriate for her to act as if she is still her husband's wife. She plans the funeral according to his wishes or as she thinks he would have wanted it. In her initial reactions, in how she expresses her feelings, and in what she tells the children she behaves in ways that are true to his style and their life together. She does not think of herself as a widow.[4]

It is safe to say the real anguish and distress of grief has not yet begun. As the numbness lifts, something changes and the widow falls apart. The pain seems to emanate from the growing awareness of the finality of the loss, as the widow is forced to confront the terrible fact: her husband is gone permanently. It can take up to two years to accept this fact. Mourning, however, is not something that ends and then the widow is able to return to her life as before.

Evidence from the Widow-to-Widow program indicated that one does not recover from grief. It is not a disease from which one is cured. It is a necessary process which if avoided creates its own problems.[5] A woman's sense of self is changed, and the very nature of her

---

[2] Since September 4, 1970, one aide has been working in a neighborhood center reaching out to an elderly population of new widows. A telephone "Hot Line" was also started at that time, staffed by volunteers who are widowed and serving both widows and widowers. Data from both these programs substantiates the hypothesis that this problem is universal for all newly widowed people regardless of their age.

[3] Mourning has been characterized as a process. Bowlby (1961) described three stages: impact, recoil, and recovery or adjustment. These phases have been helpful in understanding and describing the widows' behavior during the first year of bereavement.

[4] Personal communication: Ruth Abrams, M.S.W., first noticed this continuing interaction between the widow and her deceased spouse when analyzing data from Bereavement Project of the Laboratory of Community Psychiatry, Harvard Medical School.

[5] Lindemann (1944) and Parkes (1967) describe some of the negative consequences for people who cannot or do not grieve, noting that this can lead to serious mental illness.

outer world is different. She has to recognize that it can never be the same.[6] There is no *restitution ad integrum*.[7] It is more accurate to talk of making an accommodation or an adjustment or of making the past history, and therefore a prologue to the future.

Before reaching this accommodation several widows served by the Widow-to-Widow program, talked of experiencing a low point, where in fact they felt they could as easily die as live.[8] One of these women described her experience:

"I looked around and I saw people worse off than me; they had no money or no family. One woman I know really died after her husband went. The way I was going that could happen to me; I wasn't sure that I wanted that to happen. Then I began to take stock. I was doing things I had never done before, going to meetings (of a widow group), driving

---

Parkes (1970) noted that the individual who still pines for her husband, feels his presence in the house, and cannot accept the fact that he is gone one year after his death is most likely to have a poor outcome from the mental health point of view.

[6] Lindemann (1944) wrote "the bereaved is surprised to find how large a part of his customary activity was done in some meaningful relationship to the deceased and has lost its significance. Especially the habit of social interaction—meeting friends, making conversation, sharing enterprises seems to have been lost."

[7] Von Witzleben (1958), found a reference in the work of Freud that is not often quoted: ". . . there was no restitution ad integrum after a serious affective loss. The structure of one's inner world. . . will never be the same. Not only is the identity of self changed but also that of the outer world is different." . . . Freud wrote to a friend who lost his son. "We know that the most poignant grief is blunted after such a loss; but we remain inconsolable and never can we find a substitute. Whoever takes his place, even if he were to fill it completely will always remain totally different, and actually that is as it should be. It is the only way to preserve a love that in reality one does not wish to relinquish."

[8] Faye Snider, M.S.W., in an unpublished manuscript talked about the "wrenching away" process. Ruth Abrams looked for ways in which the widow "gave up the ghost." Most widows it would seem only begin to consider finding ways of making the past history during the second year after their husband died. For others it took longer.

---

people there, people who are counting on me. I was needed. I was the one who was always so helpless and here I was helping someone else. I never thought I could change like that — and I knew then that I had to go on living."

What helped her make the choice was her ability to see another role for herself, other than wife. Widowhood involved a different way of life, but nonetheless it could be meaningful as well.

The direction the change took in part was related to how much the role of wife permeated the lives of these women; did they have a total commitment to this role or did it occupy only a part of their life?

The woman who works has a good part of her identity invested in her role as a secretary, a physician, a salesgirl, and so forth. Her marital status can be irrelevant to this situation. Even if she still maintains her image of herself as wife, this does not create a conflict for her at work and she still can function well there. This may be why many women return to work as soon as possible. However, the fact that a woman can still identify herself with an intact role may postpone a confrontation with her new reality at home. Some of these women, to their surprise, found that six months or a year later they began to feel lonely and to mourn in a way they had not done before:

"I have worked for many years. When my children got older I wanted to get out and meet new people and be busy all the time. When my husband died, work became more important. At work I was fine. I had supper at my various children's homes and then with friends. One evening I came home early and I got panicky. I started to cry and I couldn't understand what was happening to me."

When she could no longer keep running this woman began to mourn.

A woman whose entire sense of self was invested in being a wife and mother, will begin her career as a widow with less delay:

"The funeral was over and suddenly I was all alone; no one to shop for, no one to talk to. The loneliness was so awful I thought I would go out of my mind."

Her life is suddenly barren and she has no meaningful role available to her.

These women have to find a way of accepting an altered reality in which they have no one to share their daily lives. They have lost the opportunity for an intimate social and emotional relationship that for most people comes only in marriage. (Lopata, 1969) Unlike the working woman who has at least one viable role available to her, these women have to develop new roles for themselves sometimes from whole cloth. (Lopata, 1970)

Even socially a new widow may do well until she tries to socialize with other couples. She is the fifth wheel and it is unclear to whom she relates. What is expected of another woman's husband in seeing that she is comfortable, in paying her check, and the like?

"I met my friends for lunch. They came to visit during the day as before. Then someone suggested going with the men to the theatre. It was awful I felt so alone. My husband's name came up, because he would have enjoyed this play. They got embarrassed. Imagine I had to comfort them. When we left there was some discussion about taking me home. I had wanted to drive myself, even though I had never gone out alone at night. Then they got into this kind of nonsense. I'll never agree to do that again, and I'm not sure they want me anymore either."

There are other roles available to the new widow. In some instances the woman's role as mother, sister, or daughter was more important than that of wife. When her husband dies these roles do not change and her life can continue as before. In an older population a woman is seldom the first to be widowed in her group and her widowed friends provide her with a ready reference group. This may not be acceptable to her since she may not be able "to accept herself as one of them yet."

In summary, the drama of the status transition the individual undergoes to become a widow can be described as starting when the new widow realizes that this word applies to her. At this point she knows there is no returning from the grave, and the loneliness, the pining, the pain really burst out. She has passed what can be called an initiation stage, but she is not necessarily able to act on

her recognition of this reality.[9] Grief can be seen as an inner struggle not to assume the widow role, to deny at some level the reality of the loss, to recapture and to live in the past. When this fails for her then a woman can recover, and her career as a widow begins, and it is with this definition of herself that she must live until she either remarries or dies. It is here that an educational process must begin for she is finding her way in a social category always known to mankind, but yet ignored in the present day so that she is essentially a pioneer since neither religious nor social tradition can really guide her.

## Helping

What help can be provided to help these women through the transition from the role of wife to that of widowed? Not every widow needs assistance from someone like a widow-aide to adjust to her new situation. Many women have had a lifetime of successful experience adapting to new situations. Some have had a life outside of their marriage in which their identity did not depend on their role as wife, some could accept their loneliness and had no need to change their style of life. Others accepted a new dependency and went to live with their grown children. Whatever their range of options these women did tolerably well. Many of them were pleased to see the aide and enjoyed the additional moral support the encounter provided, others refused her offer of help.[10] In these instances, however, one might say these women had a natural immunity and they did not need any additional intervention to help them

---

[9] Several women reported that it took a year to change their food buying habits. This is one aspect of role specific behavior that they have to learn.

[10] On occasion an adult child called to insist that the aide not bother his mother. He or she would take care of her. In a follow-up study we are trying to reach some of these people to evaluate the success of this plan. In two instances the widow herself overruled the children and called the aide back. She could not accept this dependency on her children.

through their mourning and to accept their widowhood.

In this paper the focus is on those women who wanted the additional assistance offered to make the transition.[11] For them the most important fact was that the intervener was another widow. It was not necessary to justify or to clarify how they felt. There was an immediate exchange of common feelings, and the offer of help was accepted because of this. (Silverman, 1970)

The help[12] in fact varied according to what point the individual had reached in her career as a widow. Initially she needed to feel she was not all alone. One widow, who had no living relatives, talked about her fear and loneliness as she sat alone in her apartment, afraid to go out because the neighborhood was run down. She said:

"If I died no one would have known the difference. When Mrs. C. called it was as if a bit of heaven had come into my living room."

Another widow talked about the perspective she had gotten from talking to the aide:

"I thought I was doing fine. In fact I was numb. The aide warned me that things could get worse before they got better. It made a big difference to understand what was happening when I began to feel so miserable. It seemed as if nothing would be right again, I wanted to know how she managed. Looking at her now I couldn't believe she ever felt like I did."

The aide was comfortable talking about her own grief and her difficulties in accommodating to it. She was very aware of the many ways in which a woman could avoid acknowledging that her husband was dead, such as saying: "I can't work, he didn't want me to." She could recognize that this was a way of avoiding the reality of the change in her life

[11] The older women who seemed to do well initially often refused help but as their sense of loss and loneliness increased they sought out the aide.

[12] Guilt was rarely an issue in helping these women cope with their loss. They were remorseful, they had regrets but they were not guilty. This seemed to be the issue in the exceptional situation, if then, of extreme psychopathology when it might be appropriate to consider psychiatric care.

and she knew when it was time to say: "He is dead — there is no coming back and you are going to have to accept it. It's your life now — what's right for you."

She was able to listen, to be empathic, and to understand the turmoil of grief. She was not upset by tears, nor distressed by the length of time it could take for a widow to find a new direction but she could get annoyed and push a little when she knew it was time to take hold and try something new.

The most important help was in learning what it meant to be widowed. The aide becomes a model of what can be:

"When I first saw Mrs. M. I knew that there was hope for me. Here she was the same age as me, and she was able to think about helping others. . . ."

She was a bridge person back into the real world. One widow remembered the aide told her: "There is a great big world out there, why don't you go out and explore it." To help in doing this she introduced the widow to other women who had similar interests. One woman had given up on a trip to Europe that she had planned with her husband after he died. She subsequently planned to go on that trip with a group of widows and widowers whom she met in a new group that developed in the community. This woman had put off the aide initially. One year later she was on her way to the cemetery to visit her husband's grave on what would have been his seventieth birthday when her daughter saw a note from the aide the mother had put aside inviting her to a cookout. The daughter encouraged her to go and this was a turning point in helping her find a new direction.

One of the older women complained about the social isolation she was experiencing. She was worried because she found herself feeling too much self pity, and since she had nothing else to do was day dreaming a lot about the past. She talked about what the aide did for her:

"She told me about these groups, and introduced me to another widow my age who lived two blocks away. She was so close and yet we never knew each other. We go to meetings together and all of a sudden there are lots of people in my life and many new things to do."

Another important way of helping was in teaching the widow how to do things differently:

"She told me it was time to go out and get a job — that I wasn't too old. Then she helped me figure out what I could do. She even drove me down once for the interview."

Education for these women is not an academic process. They need concrete direction to find their way out of the house and get involved in new activities. For the younger women this may mean learning to drive and getting a job. For the older women it is finding ways into car pools, learning what resources are available and where their talents and energies can be used. The aide encourages, prods, insists, and sometimes even takes the widow by the hand and goes through the motions with her. As one woman said:

"The aide was there every step of the way. She gave me moral support and after every driving lesson I called to tell her how I did."

Another woman with one unmarried son at home remembered the aide always asking:

"She wanted to know why I was always cleaning house. She reminded me most times my son didn't even come home for supper. I finally realized she was right. I began to wonder what else I could do? I wondered about volunteering and she had all sorts of ideas about what was available."

When the widow had some positive definition of herself in a new role then it may be possible to say that her career as a widow has begun or perhaps ended. In the words of one widow:

"I guess I see myself as single. I enjoy the theatre, and traveling. I like to meet people."

Another widow remarked:

"It is important to feel needed. If I can help someone else then I feel good and life makes sense to me."

This woman has become a volunteer in the Widowed Service Line. About this experience she has said:

"I have lived a long time, and I learned a lot from it. However, I never realized how important it was to have someone to listen to you who understood what you were feeling. I listen and I get all my experience together. We always come up with some solution. It's a whole new thing for me."

The aide, then, is a teacher, a bridge person, (Silverman, 1970) and is instrumental in helping the widow repeople her life to find new roles for herself.

## Discussion

What has been proposed here is a method of intervention in a normal life crisis. The method of intervention to a large extent bears many similarities to a self-help program since the primary caregiver is a widow and she is serving other widows. In addition, the widows served can move into the role of caregiver. This is one of the new roles available to them as they move to redefine their lives without a spouse. The caregiver in turn then is helped. This is another aspect of self-help efforts that the person helping is being helped by this activity.

One of the points made is that the widow caregiver is the most effective intervener. Her own experience makes her most able to provide appropriate service to the newly bereaved individual and to help her move in the direction of finding a new role. One reason for this is that there are few other caregivers who are sufficiently able to involve themselves with a bereaved person and who understand how to really be helpful. Help comes not only from understanding but also in being able to give specific directions and have real alternatives available to offer the widowed individual.

Lopata (1970) points to the lack of facilities for helping people who are socially disengaged to find new ways of reengaging in society. She also notes that if people need additional assistance with this they are often viewed as deviant or defective. In this context people experiencing acute grief and the dilemmas of role transition are referred to psychotherapy for what she calls "adjustment treatment." As noted earlier in the paper, the engagement prior to marriage can be seen as a period of transition to help an individual disengage from the role of child or single person and to engage themselves in the role of husband or wife. This is the institutionalized *rite de passage*. Something similar is needed at the end of the family cycle to help the individual move from their role as husband or wife to widow or widower.

The Widow-to-Widow program provides a systematic effort at reengaging the bereaved individual in a new but acceptable role. A widow caregiver bears no stigma of illness, or disability. To take help from such a person does not reflect negatively on the individual's own competence. As a teacher, as a role model, as a bridge person she helps make order out of the chaos of grief and provides the widow direction in the role transition. This is the essence of prevention.

REFERENCES:

Berardo, Felix M. Widowhood Status in the United States: Perspective on a Neglected Aspect of the Family Life-Cycle. *The Family Coordinator,* 1968, 17, 191-203.

Bowlby, John. Processes of Mourning. *The International Journal of Psychoanalysis,* 1961, 13, 317-340.

Carter, Hugh and Paul C. Glick. *Marriage and Divorce: A Social and Economic Study.* Cambridge: Harvard University Press, 1970.

Gerber, Irwin. Bereavement and Acceptance of Professional Service. *Community Mental Health Journal,* 1969, 5, 487-496.

Goffman, Erving. The Moral Career of a Mental Patient. *Asylums.* New York: Doubleday and Co., 1961.

Gorer, Geoffrey. *Death, Grief, and Mourning.* Garden City: Doubleday Co., and Anchor Book, 1967.

Life Insurance Agency Management Association. *The Onset of Widowhood,* 1970, 1.

Lindemann, Erich. Symptomatology and Management of Acute Grief. *American Journal of Psychiatry,* 1944, 51, 141-148.

Lopata, Helena Z. Loneliness: Forms and Components, *Social Problems,* 1969, 17, 248-261.

Lopata, Helen Z. The Social Involvement of American Widows, *American Behavioral Scientist,* 1970, 14, 41-57.

Maddison, David. The Relevance of Conjugal Bereavement for Preventive Psychiatry, *British Journal of Medical Psychology,* 1968, 41, 223.

Maddison, David and W. L. Walker. Factors Affecting the Outcome of Conjugal Bereavement, *British Journal of Psychiatry,* 1967, 113, 1057-1067.

Marris, Peter. *Widows and Their Families.* London: Routledge and Kegan Paul, 1958.

Mathison, Jean A. Cross-Cultural View of Widowhood. *Omega,* 1970. 1, 201-218.

Parkes, C. Murray. Recent Bereavement as a Cause of Mental Illness. *British Journal of Psychiatry,* 1964, 110, 198-204.

Parkes C. Murray. Nature of Grief, *International Journal of Psychiatry.* 1967,3, 5-8.

Parkes, C. Murray. The First Year of Bereavement, *Psychiatry.* 1970, 33, 444.

Silverman, Phyllis R. Services for the Widowed During the Period of Bereavement. *Social Work Practice.* New York: Columbia University Press, 1966.

Silverman, Phyllis R. Services to the Widowed: First Steps in a Program of Preventive Intervention. *Community Mental Health Journal,* 1967, 3, 37-44.

Silverman, Phyllis R. The Widow-to-Widow Program. *Mental Hygiene,* 1969. 53, 333-337.

Silverman, Phyllis R. The Widow as Caregiver. *Mental Hygiene,* 1970, 54, 540-547.

Silverman, Phyllis R. Factors Involved in Accepting an Offer of Help. *Archives of The Foundation of Thanatology,* 1971, in Press.

Volkart, E. H. and S. T. Michael. Bereavement and Mental Health. In A. H. Leighton, J. H. Clauser, and R. N. Wilson (Eds.) *Explorations in Social Psychiatry.* New York: Basic Books, 1957, 281-307.

Von Witzleben, Henry D. On Loneliness. *Psychiatry,* 1958, 21, 37-43.

# VI.  Culture and Aging

Many of our concepts of what it means to be old are based on the experience of aging in this society. But the status of aging persons, the respect they are given, and the roles they play, vary considerably, depending on culture and social organization. There is a tendency, in looking to other societies, to idealize those pre-literate or pre-industrial groups who have maintained their aged as an integral part of the social fabric. In many places, however, life is, as once described by the English philosopher Thomas Hobbes, "nasty, ugly, brutish, and short." Often where there is extreme poverty or when other stresses are placed on the social order, the old and the young suffer (Turnbull).

In many nonindustrial societies however, the aged occupy an important place in society. We can find instances where there is a harmony of interests between the old and young, and where we can see some of the special contributions that only the aged can make in providing a continuity of our traditions, values and history (Coles). We can discover in different lifestyles and social practices ways to improve the opportunities for self-expression for older persons in our society (Palmore and "Retirement to the Porch").

The most striking example of older persons living well is in those societies in which many people live to advanced ages. In Abkhasia in the southern Soviet Union (Benet), a sizable proportion of the population claims to live to 90 or 100 years, apparently with good physical and mental health. The ages of persons in Abkhasia and other long-lived societies, such as the Hunza in Pakistan, or in parts of the Andes region in Ecuador, have not been thoroughly documented, and some researchers seriously question the claims of longevity, pointing out that in cultures where age is valued, there is a tendency to exaggerate (Medvedev, 1974). If the ages are accurate, those factors which contribute to a lengthened lifespan are not yet to be discovered. Some variables that may be significant in the case of the Abkhasians are diet, climate, physical exercise, sexual practices, and heredity. One clear thread among those cultures with long-lived peoples, however, is the respect and value accorded to the aging, with older persons encouraged to participate in the social life and work of the community to the extent that they wish and are able. While this factor may not facilitate long life, it is a good prescription for successful aging in any society.

### References

Medvedev, A. Z. "Caucasus and Altay Longevity: A Biological or Social Problem?" *Gerontologist*, 1974, *14*, 381–387.

# 35

# The Mountain People

By Colin M. Turnbull

**Can human beings survive without love? Is society merely a survival mechanism? The Ik may hold the answers—for us.**

## PREFACE

In what follows, there will be much to shock, and the reader will be tempted to say, "how primitive, how savage, how disgusting," and, above all, "how inhuman." The first judgments are typical of the kind of ethno- and egocentricism from which we can never quite escape. But "how inhuman" is of a different order and supposes that there are certain values inherent in humanity itself, from which the people described here seem to depart in a most drastic manner. In living the experience, however, and perhaps in reading it, one finds that it is oneself one is looking at and questioning; it is a voyage in quest of the basic human and a discovery of his potential for inhumanity, a potential that lies within us all.

Just before World War II the Ik tribe had been encouraged to settle in northern Uganda, in the mountainous northeast corner bordering on Kenya to the east and Sudan to the north. Until then they had roamed in nomadic bands, as hunters and gatherers, through a vast region in all three countries. The Kidepo Valley below Mount

Morungole was their major hunting territory. After they were confined to a part of their former area, Kidepo was made a national park and they were forbidden to hunt or gather there.

The concept of family in a nomadic society is a broad one; what really counts most in everyday life is community of residence, and those who live close to each other are likely to see each other as effectively related, whether there is any kinship bond or not. Full brothers, on the other hand, who live in different parts of the camp may have little concern for each other.

It is not possible, then, to think of the family as a simple, basic unit. A child is brought up to regard any adult living in the same camp as a parent, any age-mate as a brother or sister. The Ik had this essentially social attitude toward kinship, and it readily lent itself to the rapid and disastrous changes that took place following the restriction of their movement and hunting activities. The family simply ceased to exist.

It is a mistake to think of small-scale societies as "primitive" or "simple." Hunters and gatherers, most of all, appear simple and straightforward in terms of their social organization, yet that is far from true. If we can learn about the nature of society from a study of small-scale societies, we can also learn about human relationships. The smaller the society, the less emphasis there is on the formal system and the more there is on interpersonal and intergroup relations. Security is seen in terms of these relationships, and so is survival. The result, which appears so deceptively simple, is that hunters frequently display those characteristics that we find so admirable in man: kindness, generosity, consideration, affection, honesty, hospitality, compassion, charity. For them, in their tiny, close-knit society, these are necessities for survival. In our society anyone possessing even half these qualities would find it hard to survive, yet we think these virtues are inherent in man. I took it for granted that the Ik would possess these same qualities. But they were as unfriendly, uncharitable, inhospitable and generally mean as any people can be. For those positive qualities we value so highly are no longer functional for them; even more than in our own society they spell ruin and disaster. It seems that, far from being basic human qualities, they are luxuries we can afford in times of plenty or are mere mechanisms for survival and security. Given the situation in which the Ik found themselves, man has no time for such luxuries, and a much more basic man appears, using more basic survival tactics.

*Turnbull had to wait in Kaabong, a remote administration outpost, for permission from the Uganda government to continue to Pirre, the Ik water hole and police post. While there he began to learn the Ik language and became used to their constant demands for food and tobacco. An official in Kaabong gave him, as a "gift," 20 Ik workers to build a house and a road up to it. When they arrived at Pirre, however, wages for the workers were negotiated by wily Atum, "the senior of all the Ik on Morungole."*

The police seemed as glad to see me as I was to see them. They hungrily asked for news of Kaabong, as though it were the hub of the universe. They had a borehole and pump for water, to which they said I was welcome, since the water holes used by the Ik were not fit for drinking or even for washing. The police were not able to tell me much about the Ik, because every time they went to visit an Ik village, there was nobody there. Only in times of real hunger did they see much of the Ik, and then only enough to know that they were hungry.

The next morning I rose early, but even though it was barely daylight, by the time I had washed and dressed, the Ik were already outside. They were sitting silently, staring at the Land Rover. As impassive as they seemed, there was an air of expectancy, and I was reminded that these were, after all, hunters, and the likelihood was that I was their morning's prey. So I left the Land

Rover curtains closed and as silently as possible prepared a frugal breakfast.

Atum was waiting for me. He said that he had told all the Ik that Iciebam [friend of the Ik] had arrived to live with them and that I had given the workers a "holiday" so they could greet me. They were waiting in the villages. They were very hungry, he added, and many were dying. That was probably one of the few true statements he ever made, and I never even considered believing it.

There were seven villages in all. Village Number One was built on a steep slope, and even the houses tilted at a crazy angle. Atum rapped on the outer stockade with his cane and shouted a greeting, but there was no response. This was Giriko's village, he said, and he was one of my workers.

"But I thought you told them to go back to their villages," I said.

"Yes, but you gave them a holiday, so they are probably in their fields," answered Atum, looking me straight in the eye.

At Village Number Two there was indisputably someone inside, for I could hear loud singing. The singing stopped, a pair of hands gripped the stockade and a craggy head rose into view, giving me an undeniably welcoming smile. This was Lokeléa. When I asked him what he had been singing about, he answered, "Because I'm hungry."

Village Number Three, the smallest of all, was empty. Village Number Four had only 8 huts, as against the 12 or so in Lokeléa's village and the 18 in Giriko's. The outer stockade was broken in one section, and we walked right in. We ducked through a low opening and entered a compound in which a woman was making pottery. She kept on at her work but gave us a cheery welcome and laughed her head off when I tried to speak in Icietot. She willingly showed me details of her work and did not seem unduly surprised at my interest. She said that everyone else had left for the fields except old Nangoli, who, on hearing her name mentioned, appeared at a hole in the stockade shutting off the next compound. Nangoli mumbled toothlessly at Losiké, who told Atum to pour her some water.

As we climbed up to his own village, Number Five, Atum said that Losiké never gave anything away. Later I remembered that gift of water to Nangoli. At the time I did not stop to think that in this country a gift of water could be a gift of life.

Atum's village had nearly 50 houses, each within its compound within the stout outer stockade. Atum did not invite me in.

A hundred yards away stood Village Number Six. Kauar, one of the workers, was sitting on a rocky slab just outside the village. He had a smile like Losiké's, open and warm, and he said he had been waiting for me all morning. He offered us water and showed me his own small compound and

that of his mother.

Coming up from Village Number Seven, at quite a respectable speed, was a blind man. This was Logwara, emaciated but alive and remarkably active. He had heard us and had come to greet me, he said, but he added the inevitable demand for tobacco in the same breath. We sat down in the open sunlight. For a brief moment I felt at peace.

After a short time Atum said we should start back and called over his shoulder to his village. A muffled sound came from within, and he said, "That's my wife, she is very sick —and hungry." I offered to go and see her, but he shook his head. Back at the Land Rover I gave Atum some food and some aspirin, not knowing what else to give him to help his wife.

I was awakened well before dawn by the lowing of cattle. I made an extra pot of tea and let Atum distribute it, and then we divided the workers into two teams. Kauar was to head the team building the house, and Lokelatom, Losiké's husband, was to take charge of the road workers.

While the Ik were working, their heads kept turning as though they were expecting something to happen. Every now and again one would stand up and peer into the distance and then take off into the bush for an hour or so. On one such occasion, after the person had been gone two hours, the others started drifting off. By then I knew them better; I looked for a wisp of smoke and followed it to where the road team was cooking a goat. Smoke was a giveaway, though, so they economized on cooking and ate most food nearly raw. It is a curious hangover from what must once have been a moral code that Ik will offer food if surprised in the act of eating, though they now go to enormous pains not to be so surprised.

I was always up before dawn, but by the time I got up to the villages they were always deserted. One morning I followed the little *oror* [gulley] up from *oror a pirre'i* [Ravine of Pirre] while it was still quite dark, and I met Lomeja on his way down. He took me on my first illicit hunt in Kidepo. He told me that if he got anything he would share it with me and with anyone else who managed to join us but that he certainly would not take anything back to his family. "Each one of them is out seeing what he can get for himself, and do you think they will bring any back for me?"

Lomeja was one of the very few Ik who seemed glad to volunteer information. Unlike many of the others, he did not get up and leave as I approached. Apart from him, I spent most of my time, those days, with Losiké, the potter. She told me that Nangoli, the old lady in the adjoining compound, and her husband, Amuarkuar, were rather peculiar. They helped each other get food and water, and they brought it back to their compound to eat together.

I still do not know how much real hunger there was at that time, for most of the younger people seemed fairly well fed, and the few skinny old people seemed healthy and active. But my laboriously extracted genealogies showed that there were quite a number of old people still alive and allegedly in these villages, though they were never to be seen. Then Atum's wife died.

Atum told me nothing about it but kept up his demands for food and medicine. After a while the beady-eyed Lomongin told me that Atum was selling the medicine I was giving him for his wife. I was not unduly surprised and merely remarked that that was too bad for his wife. "Oh no," said Lomongin, "she has been dead for weeks."

It must have been then that I began to notice other things that I suppose I had chosen to ignore before. Only a very few of the Ik helped me with the language. Others would understand when it suited them and would pretend they did not understand when they did not want to listen. I began to be forced into a similar isolationist attitude myself, and although I cannot say I enjoyed it, it did make life much easier. I even began to enjoy, in a peculiar way, the company of the silent Ik. And the more I accepted it, the less often people got up and left as I approached. On one occasion I sat on the *di* [sitting place] by Atum's rain tree for three days with a group of Ik, and for three days not one word was exchanged.

The work teams were more lively, but only while working. Kauar always played and joked with the children when they came back from foraging. He used to volunteer to make the two-day walk into Kaabong and the even more tiring two-day climb back to get mail for me or to buy a few things for others. He always asked if he had made the trip more quickly than the last time.

Then one day Kauar went to Kaabong and did not come back. He was found on the last peak of the trail, cold and dead. Those who found him took the things he had been carrying and pushed his body into the bush. I still see his open, laughing face, see him giving precious tidbits to the children, comforting some child who was crying, and watching me read the letters he carried so lovingly for me. And I still think of him probably running up that viciously steep mountainside so he could break his time record and falling dead in his pathetic prime because he was starving.

Once I settled down into my new home, I was able to work more effectively. Having recovered at least some of my anthropological detachment, when I heard the telltale rustling of someone at my stockade, I merely threw a stone. If when out walking

I stumbled during a difficult descent and the Ik shrieked with laughter, I no longer even noticed it.

Anyone falling down was good for a laugh, but I never saw anyone actually trip anyone else. The adults were content to let things happen and then enjoy them; it was probably conservation of energy. The children, however, sought their pleasures with vigor. The best game of all, at this time, was teasing poor little Adupa. She was not so little—in fact she should have been an adult, for she was nearly 13 years old—but Adupa was a little mad. Or you might say she was the only sane one, depending on your point of view. Adupa did not jump on other people's play houses, and she lavished enormous care on hers and would curl up inside it. That made it all the more jump-on-able. The other children beat her viciously.

Children are not allowed to sleep in the house after they are "put out," which is at about three years old, four at the latest. From then on they sleep in the open courtyard, taking what shelter they can against the stockade. They may ask for permission to sit in the doorway of their parents' house but may not lie down or sleep there. "The same thing applies to old people," said Atum, "if they can't build a house of their own and, of course, *if* their children let them stay in their compounds."

I saw a few old people, most of whom had taken over abandoned huts. For the first time I realized that there really was starvation and saw why I had never known it before: it was confined to the aged. Down in Giriko's village the old ritual priest, Lolim, confidentially told me that he was sheltering an old man who had been refused shelter by his son. But Lolim did not have enough food for himself, let alone his guest; could I . . . I liked old Lolim, so, not believing that Lolim had a visitor at all, I brought him a double ration that evening. There was a rustling in the back of the hut, and Lolim helped ancient Lomeraniang to the entrance. They shook with delight at the sight of the food.

When the two old men had finished eating, I left; I found a hungry-looking and disapproving little crowd clustered outside. They muttered to each other about wasting food. From then on I brought food daily, but in a very short time Lomeraniang was dead, and his son refused to come down from the village above to bury him. Lolim scratched a hole and covered the body with a pile of stones he carried himself, one by one.

Hunger was indeed more severe than I knew, and, after the old people, the children were the next to go. It was all quite impersonal— even to me, in most cases, since I had been immunized by the Ik themselves against sorrow on their behalf. But Adupa was an exception. Her madness was such that she did not know just how vicious humans could be. Even worse, she thought that parents were for loving, for giving as well as receiving. Her parents were not given to fantasies. When she came for shelter, they drove her out; and when she came because she was hungry, they laughed that Icien laugh, as if she had made them happy.

Adupa's reactions became slower and slower. When she managed to find food—fruit peels, skins, bits of bone, half-eaten berries—she held it in her hand and looked at it with wonder and delight. Her playmates caught on quickly; they put tidbits in her way and watched her simple drawn little face wrinkle in a smile. Then as she raised her hand to her mouth, they set on her with cries of excitement, fun and laughter, beating her savagely over the head. But that is not how she died. I took to feeding her, which is probably the cruelest thing I could have done, a gross selfishness on my part to try to salve my own rapidly disappearing conscience. I had to protect her, physically, as I fed her. But the others would beat her anyway, and Adupa cried, not because of the pain in her body but because of the pain she felt at the great, vast, empty wasteland where love should have been.

It was *that* that killed her. She demanded that her parents love her. Finally they took her in, and Adupa was happy and stopped crying. She stopped crying forever because her parents went away and closed the door tight behind them, so tight that weak little Adupa could never have moved it.

The Ik seem to tell us that the family is not such a fundamental unit as we usually suppose, that it is not essential to social life. In the crisis of survival facing the Ik, the family was one of the first institutions to go, and the Ik as a society have survived.

The other quality of life that we hold to be necessary for survival—love —the Ik dismiss as idiotic and highly dangerous. But we need to see more of the Ik before their absolute lovelessness becomes truly apparent.

In this curious society there is one common value to which all Ik hold tenaciously. It is *ngag,* "food." That is the one standard by which they measure right and wrong, goodness and badness. The very word for "good" is defined in terms of food. "Goodness" is "the possession of food," or the *"individual* possession of food." If you try to discover their concept of a "good man," you get the truly Icien answer: one who has a full stomach.

We should not be surprised, then, when the mother throws her child out at three years old. At that age a series of *rites de passage* begins. In this environment a child has no chance of survival on his own until

he is about 13, so children form age bands. The junior band consists of children between three and seven, the senior of eight-to twelve-year-olds. Within the band each child seeks another close to him in age for defense against the older children. These friendships are temporary, however, and inevitably there comes a time when each turns on the one that up to then had been the closest to him; that is the *rite de passage,* the destruction of that fragile bond called friendship. When this has happened three or four times, the child is ready for the world.

The weakest are soon thinned out, and the strongest survive to achieve leadership of the band. Such a leader is eventually driven out, turned against by his fellow band members. Then the process starts all over again; he joins the senior age band as its most junior member.

The final *rite de passage* is into adulthood, at the age of 12 or 13. By then the candidate has learned the wisdom of acting on his own, for his own good, while acknowledging that on occasion it is profitable to associate temporarily with others.

One year in four the Ik can count on a complete drought. About this time it began to be apparent that there were going to be two consecutive years of drought and famine. Men as well as women took to gathering what wild fruits and berries they could find,

digging up roots, cutting grass that was going to seed, threshing and eating the seed.

Old Nangoli went to the other side of Kidepo, where food and water were more plentiful. But she had to leave her husband, Amuarkuar, behind. One day he appeared at my *odok* and asked for water. I gave him some and was going to get him food when Atum came storming over and argued with me about wasting water. In the midst of the dispute Amuarkuar quietly left. He wandered over to a rocky outcrop and lay down there to rest. Nearby was a small bundle of grass that evidently he had cut and had been dragging painfully to the ruins of his village to make a rough shelter. The grass was his supreme effort to keep a home going until Nangoli returned. When I went over to him, he looked up and smiled and said that my water tasted good. He lay back and went to sleep with a smile on his face. That is how Amuarkuar died, happily.

There are measures that can be taken for survival involving the classical institutions of gift and sacrifice. These are weapons, sharp and aggressive. The object is to build up a series of obligations so that in times of crisis you have a number of debts you can recall; with luck one of them may be repaid. To this end, in the circumstances of Ik life, considerable sacrifice would be justified, so you have the odd phenomenon of these otherwise singularly self-interested people going out of their way to "help" each other. Their help may very well be resented in the extreme, but is done in such a way that it cannot be refused, for it has already been given. Someone may hoe another's field in his absence or rebuild his stockade or join in the building of a house.

The danger in this system was that the debtor might not be around when collection was called for and, by the same token, neither might the creditor. The future was too uncertain for this to be anything but one additional survival measure, though some developed it to a fine technique.

There seemed to be increasingly little among the Ik that could by any stretch of the imagination be called social life, let alone social organization. The family does not hold itself together; economic interest is centered on as many stomachs as there are people; and cooperation is merely a device for furthering an interest that is consciously selfish. We often do the same thing in our so-called "altruistic" practices, but we tell ourselves it is for the good of others. The Ik have dispensed with the myth of altruism. Though they have no centralized leadership or means of physical coercion, they do hold together with remarkable tenacity.

In our world, where the family has also lost much of its value as a social unit and where religious belief no longer binds us into communities, we maintain order only through coercive power that is ready to

uphold a rigid law and through an equally rigid penal system. The Ik, however, have learned to do without coercion, either spiritual or physical. It seems that they have come to a recognition of what they accept as man's basic selfishness, of his natural determination to survive as an individual before all else. This they consider to be man's basic right, and they allow others to pursue that right without recrimination.

In large-scale societies such as our own, where members are individual beings rather than social beings, we rely on law for order. The absence of both a common law and a common belief would surely result in lack of any community of behavior; yet Ik society is not anarchical. One might well expect religion, then, to play a powerful role in Icien life, providing a source of unity.

The Ik, as may be expected, do not run true to form. When I arrived, there were still three ritual priests alive. From them and from the few other old people, I learned something of the Ik's belief and practice as they had been before their world was so terribly changed. There had been a powerful unity of belief in Didigwari—a sky god—and a body of ritual practice reinforcing secular behavior that was truly social.

Didigwari himself is too remote to be of much practical significance to the Ik. He created them and abandoned them and retreated into his domain somewhere in the sky. He never came down to earth, but the *abang* [ancestors] have all known life on earth; it is only against them that one can sin and only to them that one can turn for help, through the ritual priest.

While Morungole has no legends attached to it by the Ik, it nonetheless figures in their ideology and is in some ways regarded by them as sacred. I had noticed this by the almost reverential way in which they looked at it—none of the shrewd cunning and cold appraisal with which they regard the rest of the world. When they talked about it, there was a different quality to their voices. They seemed incapable of talking about Morungole in any other way, which is probably why they talked about it so very seldom. Even that weasel Lomongin became gentle the only time he talked about it to me. He said, "If Atum and I were there, we would not argue. It is a good place." I asked if he meant that it was full of food. He said yes. "Then why do Ik never go there?" "They do go there." "But if hunting is good there, why not live there?" "We don't hunt there, we just go there." "Why?" "I told you, it is a good place." If I did not understand him, that was my fault; for once he was doing his best to communicate something to me. With others it was the same. All agreed that it was "a good place." One added, "That is the Place of God."

Lolim, the oldest and greatest of the ritual priests, was also the last. He was not much in demand any longer, but he was still held in awe, which means kept at a distance. Whenever he approached a *di*, people cleared a space for him, as far away from themselves as possible. The Ik rarely called on his services, for they had little to pay him with, and he had equally little to offer them The main things they did try to get out of him were certain forms of medicine, both herbal and magical.

Lolim said that he had inherited his power from his father. His father had taught him well but could not give him the power to hear the *abang*—that had to come from the *abang* themselves. He had wanted his oldest son to inherit and had taught him everything he could. But his son, Longoli, was bad, and the *abang* refused to talk to him. They talked instead to his oldest daughter, bald Nangoli. But there soon came the time when all the Ik needed was food in their stomachs, and Lolim could not supply that. The time came when Lolim was too weak to go out and collect the medicines he needed. His children all refused to go except Nangoli, and then she was jailed for gathering in Kidepo Park.

Lolim became ill and had to be protected while eating the food I gave him. Then the children began openly ridiculing him and teasing him, dancing in front of him and kneeling down so that he would trip over them. His grandson used to creep up behind him and with a pair of hard sticks drum a lively tattoo on the old man's bald head.

I fed him whenever I could, but often he did not want more than a bite. Once I found him rolled up in his protective ball, crying. He had had nothing to eat for four days and no water for two. He had asked his children, who all told him not to come near them.

The next day I saw him leaving Atum's village, where his son Longoli lived. Longoli swore that he had been giving his father food and was looking after him. Lolim was not shuffling away; it was almost a run, the run of a drunken man, staggering from side to side. I called to him, but he made no reply, just a kind of long, continuous and horrible moan. He had been to Longoli to beg him to let him into his compound because he knew he was going to die in a few hours, Longoli calmly told me afterward. Obviously Longoli could not do a thing like that: a man of Lolim's importance would have called for an enormous funeral feast. So he refused. Lolim begged Longoli then to open up Nangoli's *asak* for him so that he could die in *her* compound. But Longoli drove him out, and he died alone.

Atum pulled some stones over the body where it had fallen into a kind of hollow. I saw that the body must have lain parallel with the *oror*. Atum answered without waiting for the question: "He was lying looking up at Mount Meraniang."

Insofar as ritual survived at all, it could hardly be said to be religious, for it did little or nothing to bind Icien society together. But the question still remained: Did this lack of social behavior and communal ritual or religious expression mean that there was no community of belief?

Belief may manifest itself, at either the individual or the communal level, in what we call morality, when we behave according to certain principles supported by our belief even when it seems against our personal interest. When we call ourselves moral, however, we tend to ignore that ultimately our morality benefits us even as individuals, insofar as we are social individuals and live in a society. In the absence of belief, law takes over and morality has little role. If there was such a thing as an Icien morality, I had not yet perceived it, though traces of a moral past remained. But it still remained a possibility, as did the existence of an unspoken, unmanifest belief that might yet reveal itself and provide a basis for the reintegration of society. I was somewhat encouraged in this hope by the unexpected flight of old Nangoli, widow of Amuarkuar.

When Nangoli returned and found her husband dead, she did an odd thing: she grieved. She tore down what was left of their home, uprooted the stockade, tore up whatever was growing in her little field. Then she fled with a few belongings.

Some weeks later I heard that she and her children had gone over to the Sudan and built a village there. This migration was so unusual that I decided to see whether this runaway village was different.

Lojieri led the way, and Atum came along. One long day's trek got us there. Lojieri pulled part of the brush fence aside, and we went in and wandered around. He and Atum looked inside all the huts, and Lojieri helped himself to tobacco from one and water from another. Surprises were coming thick and fast. That households should be left open and untended with such wealth inside . . . That there should have been such wealth, for as well as tobacco and jars of water there were baskets of food, and meat was drying on racks. There were half a dozen or so compounds, but they were separated from each other only by a short line of sticks and brush. It was a village, and these were homes, the first and last I was to see.

The dusk had already fallen, and Nangoli came in with her children and grandchildren. They had heard us and came in with warm welcomes. There was no hunger here, and in a very short time each kitchen hearth had a pot of food cooking. Then we sat around the central fire and talked until late, and it was another universe.

There was no talk of "how much better it is here than there"; talk revolved around what had happened on the hunt that day. Loron was lying on the ground in front of the fire as his mother made gentle fun of him. His wife, Kinimei, whom I had never seen even speak to him at Pirre, put a bowl of fresh-cooked berries and fruit in front of him. It was all like a nightmare rather than a fantasy, for it made the reality of Pirre seem all the more frightening.

The unpleasantness of returning was somewhat alleviated by Atum's suffering on the way up the stony trail. Several times he slipped, which made Lojieri and me laugh. It was a pleasure to move rapidly ahead and leave Atum gasping behind so that we could be sitting up on the *di* when he finally appeared and could laugh at his discomfort.

The days of drought wore on into weeks and months and, like everyone else, I became rather bored with sickness and death. I survived rather as did the young adults, by diligent attention to my own needs while ignoring those of others.

More and more it was only the young who could go far from the village as hunger became starvation. Famine relief had been initiated down at Kasilé, and those fit enough to make the trip set off. When they came back, the contrast between them and the others was that between life and death. Villages were villages of the dead and dying, and there was little difference between the two. People crawled rather than walked. After a few feet some would lie down to rest, but they could not be sure of ever being able to sit up again, so they mostly stayed upright until they reached their destination. They were going nowhere, these semianimate bags of skin and bone; they just wanted to be with others, and they stopped whenever they met. Perhaps it was the most important demonstration of sociality I ever saw among the Ik. Once they met, they neither spoke nor did anything together.

Early one morning, before dawn, the village moved. In the midst of a hive of activity were the aged and crippled, soon to be abandoned, in danger of being trampled but seemingly unaware of it. Lolim's widow, Lo'ono, whom I had never seen before, also had been abandoned and had tried to make her way down the mountainside. But she was totally blind and had tripped and rolled to the bottom of the *oror a pirre'i;* there she lay on her back, her legs and arms thrashing feebly, while a little crowd laughed.

At this time a colleague was with me. He kept the others away while I ran to get medicine and food and water, for Lo'ono was obviously near dead from hunger and thirst as well as from the fall. We treated her and fed her and asked her to come back with us. But she asked us to point her in the direction of her son's new village. I said I did not think she would get much of a welcome

there, and she replied that she knew it but wanted to be near him when she died. So we gave her more food, put her stick in her hand and pointed her the right way. She suddenly cried. She was crying, she said, because we had reminded her that there had been a time when people had helped each other, when people had been kind and good. Still crying, she set off.

The Ik up to this point had been tolerant of my activities, but all this was too much. They said that what we were doing was wrong. Food and medicine were for the living, not the dead. I thought of Lo'ono. And I thought of other old people who had joined in the merriment when they had been teased or had a precious morsel of food taken from their mouths. They knew that it was silly of them to expect to go on living, and, having watched others, they knew that the spectacle really was quite funny. So they joined in the laughter. Perhaps if we had left Lo'ono, she would have died laughing. But we prolonged her misery for no more than a few brief days. Even worse, we reminded her of when things had been different, of days when children had cared for parents and parents for children. She was already dead, and we made her unhappy as well. At the time I was sure we were right, doing the only "human" thing. In a way we *were*—we were making life more comfortable for ourselves. But now I wonder if the Ik way was not right, if I too should not have laughed as Lo'ono flapped about, then left her to die.

Ngorok was a man at 12. Lomer, his older brother, at 15 was showing signs of strain; when he was carrying a load, his face took on a curious expression of pain that was no physical pain. Giriko, at 25 was 40, Atum at 40 was 65, and the very oldest, perhaps a bare 50, were centenarians. And I, at 40, was younger than any of them, for I still enjoyed life, which they had learned was not "adult" when they were 3. But they retained their will to survive and so offered grudging respect to those who had survived for long.

Even in the teasing of the old there was a glimmer of hope. It denoted a certain intimacy that did not exist between adjacent generations. This is quite common in small-scale societies. The very old and the very young look at each other as representing the future and the past. To the child, the aged represent a world that existed before their own birth and the unknown world to come.

And now that all the old are dead, what is left? Every Ik who is old today was thrown out at three and has survived, and in consequence has thrown his own children out and knows that they will not help him in his old age any more than he helped his parents. The system has turned one full cycle and is now self-perpetuating; it has eradicated what we know as "humanity" and has turned the world into a chilly void where man does not seem to care even for himself, but survives. Yet into this hideous world Nangoli and her family quietly returned because they could not bear to be alone.

For the moment abandoning the very old and the very young, the Ik as a whole must be searched for one last lingering trace of humanity. They appear to have disposed of virtually all the qualities that we normally think of as differentiating us from other primates, yet they survive without seeming to be greatly different from ourselves in terms of behavior. Their behavior is more extreme, for we do not start throwing our children out until kindergarten. We have shifted responsibility from family to state, the Ik have shifted it to the individual.

It has been claimed that human beings are capable of love and, indeed, are dependent upon it for survival and sanity. The Ik offer us an opportunity for testing this cherished notion that love is essential to survival. If it is, the Ik should have it.

Love in human relationships implies mutuality, a willingness to sacrifice the self that springs from a consciousness of identity. This seems to bring us back to the Ik, for it implies that love is self-oriented, that even the supreme sacrifice of one's life is no more than selfishness, for the victim feels amply rewarded by the pleasure he feels in making the sacrifice. The Ik, however, do not value emotion above survival, and they are without love.

But I kept looking, for it was the one thing that could fill the void their survival tactics had created; and if love was not there in some form, it meant that for humanity love is not a necessity at all, but a luxury or an illusion. And if it was not among the Ik, it meant that mankind can lose it.

The only possibility for any discovery of love lay in the realm of interpersonal relationships. But they were, each one, simply alone, and seemingly content to be alone. It was this acceptance of individual isolation that made love almost impossible. Contact, when made, was usually for a specific practical purpose having to do with food and the filling of a stomach, a single stomach. Such contacts did not have anything like the permanence or duration required to develop a situation in which love was possible.

The isolation that made love impossible, however, was not completely proof against loneliness. I no longer noticed normal behavior, such as the way people ate, running as they gobbled, so as to have it all for themselves. But I did notice that when someone was making twine or straightening a spear shaft, the focus of attention for the spectators was not the person but the action. If they were caught watching by the one being watched and their eyes met, the reaction was a sharp retreat on both sides.

When the rains failed for the second year

running, I knew that the Ik as a society were almost certainly finished and that the monster they had created in its place, that passionless, feelingless association of individuals, would spread like a fungus, contaminating all it touched. When I left, I too had been contaminated. I was not upset when I said good-bye to old Loiangorok. I told him I had left a sack of *posho* [ground corn meal] with the police for him, and I said I would send money for more when that ran out. He dragged himself slowly toward the *di* every day, and he always clutched a knife. When he got there, or as far as he could, he squatted down and whittled at some wood, thus proving that he was still alive and able to do things. The *posho* was enough to last him for months, but I felt no emotion when I estimated that he would last one month, even with the *posho* in the hands of the police. I underestimated his son, who within two days had persuaded the police that it would save a lot of bother if he looked after the *posho*. I heard later that Loiangorok died of starvation within two weeks.

So, I departed with a kind of forced gaiety, feeling that I should be glad to be gone but having forgotten how to be glad. I certainly was not thinking of returning within a year, but I did. The following spring I heard that rain had come at last and that the fields of the Ik had never looked so prosperous, nor the country so green and fertile. A few months away had refreshed me, and I wondered if my conclusions had not been excessively pessimistic. So, early that summer, I set off to be present for the first harvests in three years.

I was not surprised too much when two days after my arrival and installation at the police post I found Logwara, the blind man, lying on the roadside bleeding, while a hundred yards up other Ik were squabbling over the body of a hyena. Logwara had tried to get there ahead of the others to grab the meat and had been trampled on.

First I looked at the villages. The lush outer covering concealed an inner decay. All the villages were like this to some extent, except for Lokeléa's. There the tomatoes and pumpkins were carefully pruned and cleaned, so that the fruits were larger and healthier. In what had been my own compound the shade trees had been cut down for firewood, and the lovely hanging nests of the weaver birds were gone.

The fields were even more desolate. Every field without exception had yielded in abundance, and it was a new sensation to have vision cut off by thick crops. But every crop was rotting from sheer neglect.

The Ik said that they had no need to bother guarding the fields. There was so much food they could never eat it all, so why not let the birds and baboons take some? The Ik had full bellies; they were good. The *di* at Atum's village was much the same as

usual, people sitting or lying about. People were still stealing from each other's fields, and nobody thought of saving for the future.

It was obvious that nothing had really changed due to the sudden glut of food except that interpersonal relationships had deteriorated still further and that Icien individualism had heightened beyond what I thought even Ik to be capable of.

The Ik had faced a conscious choice between being humans and being parasites and had chosen the latter. When they saw their fields come alive, they were confronted with a problem. If they reaped the harvest, they would have to store grain for eating and planting, and every Ik knew that trying to store anything was a waste of time. Further, if they made their fields look too promising, the government would stop famine relief. So the Ik let their fields rot and continued to draw famine relief.

The Ik were not starving any longer; the old and infirm had all died the previous year, and the younger survivors were doing quite well. But the famine relief was administered in a way that was little short of criminal. As before, only the young and well were able to get down from Pirre to collect the relief; they were given relief for those who could not come and told to take it back. But they never did—they ate it themselves.

The facts are there, though those that can be read here form but a fraction of what one person was able to gather in under two years. There can be no mistaking the direction in which those facts point, and that is the most important thing of all, for it may affect the rest of mankind as it has affected the Ik. The Ik have "progressed," one might say, since the change that has come to them came with the advent of civilization to Africa. They have made of a world that was alive a world that is dead—a cold, dispassionate world that is without ugliness because it is without beauty, without hate because it is without love, and without any realization of truth even, because it simply is. And the symptoms of change in our own society indicate that we are heading in the same direction.

Those values we cherish so highly may indeed be basic to human society but not to humanity, and that means that the Ik show that society itself is not indispensable for man's survival and that man is capable of associating for purposes of survival without being social. The Ik have replaced human society with a mere survival system that does not take human emotion into account. As yet the system is imperfect, for although survival is assured, it is at a minimal level and there is still competition between individuals. With our intellectual sophistication and advanced technology we should be able to perfect the system and eliminate competition, guaranteeing survival for a given number of years for all, reducing the demands made upon us by a social system, abolishing desire and consequently that ever-present and vital gap between desire and achievement, treating us, in a word, as individuals with one basic individual right—the right to survive.

Such interaction as there is within this system is one of mutual exploitation. That is how it already is with the Ik. In our own world the mainstays of a society based on a truly social sense of mutuality are breaking down, indicating that perhaps society as we know it has outworn its usefulness and that by clinging to an outworn system we are bringing about our own destruction. Family, economy, government and religion, the basic categories of social activity and behavior, no longer create any sense of social unity involving a shared and mutual responsibility among all members of our society. At best they enable the individual to survive as an individual. It is the world of the individual, as is the world of the Ik.

The sorry state of society in the civilized world today is in large measure due to the fact that social change has not kept up with technological change. This mad, senseless, unthinking commitment to technological change that we call progress may be sufficient to exterminate the human race in a very short time even without the assistance of nuclear warfare. But since we have already become individualized and desocialized, we say that extermination will not come in our time, which shows about as much sense of family devotion as one might expect from the Ik.

Even supposing that we can avert nuclear holocaust or the almost universal famine that may be expected if population keeps expanding and pollution remains unchecked, what will be the cost if not the same already paid by the Ik? They too were driven by the need to survive, and they succeeded at the cost of their humanity. We are already beginning to pay the same price, but we not only still have the choice (though we may not have the will or courage to make it), we also have the intellectual and technological ability to avert an Icien end. Any change as radical as will be necessary is not likely to bring material benefits to the present generation, but only then will there be a future.

The Ik teach us that our much vaunted human values are not inherent in humanity at all but are associated only with a particular form of survival called society and that all, even society itself, are luxuries that can be dispensed with. That does not make them any less wonderful, and if man has any greatness, it is surely in his ability to maintain these values, even shortening an already pitifully short life rather than sacrifice his humanity. But that too involves choice, and the Ik teach us that man can lose the will to make it. That is the point at which there is an end to truth, to goodness and to beauty, an end to the struggle for their achievement, which gives life to the individual and strength and meaning to society. The Ik have relinquished all luxury in the name of individual survival, and they live on as a people without life, without passion, beyond humanity. We pursue those trivial, idiotic technological encumbrances, and all the time we are losing our potential for social rather than individual survival, for hating as well as loving, losing perhaps our last chance to enjoy life with all the passion that is our nature.

# 36

# Two Languages, One Soul

by Robert Coles

The Spanish-speaking people of the Southwest continue to be considered one of this nation's "problems," and for understandable reasons. In large measure they are poor, and their lot has by no means improved universally in recent years, for all the steps taken in the 1960s to make life easier for our so-called minorities. In the Rio Grande Valley of Texas even the vote cannot be taken for granted by many Mexican Americans, as they are called there. In the barrios of Los Angeles the "brown berets"—one more term—struggle on behalf of people plagued by joblessness and a host of discriminatory practices. "Chicano power!" one hears—yet another phrase; and looking at the power others have, it is not easy to disagree with the exhortation. In New Mexico there are distinct differences; unlike Texas or California, the state has long been responsive to its Spanish-speaking people. In fact, along with the Indians, they made up its "first families," and to this day, despite Anglo political and economic dominance, Spanish surnames are to be found everywhere: among holders of high political office, in the business world and the professions, and among storekeepers, small landowners, and blue-collar workers. Such a state of affairs has to be contrasted with conditions in Texas, where thousands of "Mexicanos" (as "gringos" sometimes call them with barely concealed disdain) are either migrant farmworkers or go jobless, or in California, where César Chávez continues his not altogether successful struggle, and where "Latinos" (one hears that word used, too) share with blacks all the misery of the urban ghetto, most especially the sense that there is no one very important to call upon for help.

Still, even in New Mexico there is no reason to rejoice at the position the state's Spanish-speaking people occupy—especially when one compares it with the social and economic condition of Anglos. In many towns and villages those who speak Spanish are desperately poor; they lack work, or, if they do have jobs, they are menial ones, the only kind available. In the schools their children are often enough treated badly; reprimanded for using Spanish words, told that they are not suited

for school, and made to feel that they will soon enough be living the same circumscribed lives their parents have known. Many who want better for the poor and struggle on their behalf—whether for the Anglo poor, black poor, Spanish-speaking poor—know how particularly destructive that kind of educational experience can be for young children, whose whole sense of "expectation" (What do I dare see ahead for myself, aim at, hope for?) is so crucially determined by the atmosphere in the elementary school.

Efforts to improve the condition of the Spanish-speaking poor of New Mexico have been predominantly educational. No one in the state has difficulty in voting, and the economy is unfortunately not advanced enough for those on the bottom to have any great success in demanding a larger share of the available wealth. Businesses are very much being courted, not with quite the desperation one sees in Alabama or Mississippi, but with a certain grim determination. And labor unions are not the power they are in Michigan or Pennsylvania. But the schools have traditionally been the hope for the future all over this country; and they lend themselves more easily to change than a newly arrived factory or a firmly entrenched political hierarchy. So, one hears about "culturally disadvantaged" children and "culturally deprived" children; and among those both more knowledgeable and less given to condescension, "bilingual" education. Such terms are meant to convey the difficulties Spanish-speaking people have as outsiders of sorts. "America is Anglo," one hears Indian and Chicano children say in various parts of the Southwest, and that is that.

At least those children are granted a degree of hope by those of us who spend our time making judgments about the fate or destiny of one or another racial or ethnic group: they are young; changes are taking place; their lives will be less shame-ridden, more fulfilled. There are "job opportunity" programs. There are also various "enrichment" programs in the schools. Spanish is now increasingly allowed in those schools—to be spoken, even to be used by teachers. In the words of one Chicana social worker I have talked with: "We are determined to move ahead, even if there is great resistance from the power structure. No longer will Chicanos in New Mexico grow up feeling like second-class citizens. No longer will they feel misunderstood or scorned. In the old days they received the worst kind of schooling. They were made to feel stupid and awkward. They were made to feel they have nothing worthwhile to say or contribute. The Anglo teachers, the Anglo-run school system looked down on Chicanos. We were given no credit for our own values, for our culture and traditions. And the contempt showed on the people; they felt ashamed, inferior. They never learned to speak English the way the teachers did. They never learned to express themselves in school and they dropped out soon, usually well before high school was over. We hope to change that. We can't do anything about what has already happened. The old people are the way they are—it is too late for them to change. But it will be difficult for the young. They will have pride in themselves, and they will not only think well of themselves, but speak well. They won't have memories of Anglo teachers laughing at their Spanish, or punishing them for using it. They will speak Spanish with joy."

As she said, "the old people are the way they are." But exactly how is their "way" to be characterized? That is to say, how badly have they been scarred by the awful conditions described so forcefully by this particular political activist, among others? No doubt she is right—down to the last detail of her remarks; in recent years I have seen enough first-hand to more than confirm the basis for her sense of outrage. Still, I have to think of the people I have come to know in New Mexico—the old, thoroughly poor, certainly rather uneducated people, who have lived the hard, tough, sometimes terribly sad lives that the Chicana just quoted describes, and yet don't quite feel as she does about themselves. Nor do they speak as if they have been systematically brutalized, robbed of all their "self-esteem," as social scientists put it. In their seventies or eighties, with long memories of hardships faced and perhaps only partially (if at all) surmounted, "deprived" of education, made to feel hopelessly inarticulate, and obviously out of "the American mainstream," they are nevertheless men and women who seem to have held on stubbornly to a most peculiar notion: that they are eminently valuable and important human beings, utterly worth the respect, even admiration, not to mention the love, of their children and grandchildren.

Moreover, they are men and women who, for all the education they lack, all the wrongheaded or just plain mean teachers they once ran up against, all the cultural bias and social discrimination they may have sensed or experienced outright, still manage not only to feel fairly assured about themselves as human beings, put here by the Lord for His own purposes, but also to say rather a lot about what is on their mind—and in such a way that they make themselves unmistakably clear. In fact, I have found myself at times overwhelmed by the power of their speech, the force that their language possesses, the dramatic expressions they call upon, the strong and subtle imagery available to them, the sense of irony and ambiguity they repeatedly

and almost as a matter of course demonstrate. Perhaps my surprise and admiration indicate my own previous blind spots, my own ignorance and even prejudice. If so, I have been more than brought up short again and again.

Here are the words of an elderly woman who has had virtually no schooling and speaks a mixture of Spanish (which I have translated) and terse but forceful English. She lives in a small, isolated mountain community well to the north of Santa Fe and enjoys talking with her visitor: "Sometimes I have a moment to think. I look back and wonder where all the time has gone to —so many years; I cannot say I like to be reminded how many. My sister is three years older, eighty this May. She is glad to talk of her age. I don't like to mention mine. Maybe I have not her faith in God. She makes her way every day to church. I go only on Sundays. Enough is enough; besides, I don't like the priest. He points his finger too much. He likes to accuse us— each week it is a different sin he charges us with. My mother used to read me Christ's words when I was a girl—from the old Spanish Bible her grandmother gave to her on her deathbed. I learned that Christ was a kind man; He tried to think well of people, even the lowest of the low, even those at the very bottom who are in a swamp and don't know how to get out, let alone find for themselves some high, dry land.

"But this priest of ours gives no one the benefit of the doubt. I have no right to find fault with him; I know that. Who am I to do so? I am simply an old lady, and I had better watch out: the Lord no doubt punishes those who disagree with His priests. But our old priest who died last year was so much finer, so much better to hear on a warm Sunday morning. Every once in a while he would even lead us outside to the courtyard and talk with us there, give us a second sermon. I felt so much better for listening to him. He was not in love with the sound of his own voice, as this new priest is. He did not stop and listen to the echo of his words. He did not brush away dust from his coat, or worry if the wind went through his hair. He was not always looking for a paper towel to wipe his shoes. My husband says he will buy this priest a dozen handkerchiefs and tell him they are to be used for his shoes only. Here when we get rain we are grateful, and it is not too high a price to pay, a little mud to walk through. Better mud that sticks than dust that blows away.

Well, I should not go on so long about a vain man. We all like to catch ourselves in the mirror and find ourselves good to look at. Here I am, speaking ill of him, yet I won't let my family celebrate my birthdays any more; and when I look at myself in the mirror a feeling of sadness comes over me. I pull at my skin and try to erase the lines, but no luck. I think back: all those years when my husband and I were young, and never worried about our health, our strength, our appearance. I don't say we always do now; but there are times when we look like ghosts of ourselves. I will see my husband noticing how weak and tired I have become, how hunched over. I pretend not to see, but once the eyes have caught something, one cannot shake the picture off. And I look at him, too; he will straighten up when he feels my glance strike him, and I quickly move away. Too late, though; he has been told by me, without a word spoken, that he is old, and I am old, and that is our fate, to live through these last years.

"But it is not only pity we feel for ourselves. A few drops of rain and I feel grateful; the air is so fresh afterwards. I love to sit in the sun. We have the sun so often here, a regular visitor, a friend one can expect to see often and trust. I like to make tea for my husband and me. At midday we take our tea outside and sit on our bench, our backs against the wall of the house. Neither of us wants pillows; I tell my daughters and sons that they are soft—those beach chairs of theirs. Imagine beach chairs here in New Mexico, so far from any ocean! The bench feels strong to us, not uncomfortable. The tea warms us inside, the sun on the outside. I joke with my husband; I say we are part of the house: the adobe gets baked, and so do we. For the most part we say nothing, though. It is enough to sit and be part of God's world. We hear the birds talking to each other, and are grateful they come as close to us as they do; all the more reason to keep our tongues still and hold ourselves in one place. We listen to cars going by and wonder who is rushing off. A car to us is a mystery. The young understand a car. They cannot imagine themselves not driving. They have not the interest we had in horses. Who is to compare one lifetime with another, but a horse is alive and one loves a horse and is loved by a horse. Cars come and go so fast. One year they command all eyes. The next year they are a cause for shame. The third year they must be thrown away without the slightest regret. I may exaggerate, but not much!

"My moods are like the church bell on Sunday: way up, then down, then up again—and often just as fast. I make noises, too; my husband says he can hear me smiling and hear me turning sour. When I am sour I am really sour—sweet milk turned bad. Nothing pleases me. I am more selfish than my sister. She bends with the wind. I push my heels into the ground and won't budge. I know enough to frown at myself, but not enough to change. There was a time when I tried hard. I would talk to myself as if I was the priest. I would promise myself that tomorrow I would be different. I suppose only men and women can fool themselves that way; an animal knows better. Animals are themselves. We are always trying to be better—and often we end up even worse than we were to start with.

"But now, during the last moments of life, I think I have learned a little wisdom. I can go for days without an upset. I think I dislike our priest because he reminds me of myself. I have his long forefinger, and I can clench my fist like him and pound the table and pour vinegar on people with my remarks. It is no good to be like that. A man is lucky; it is in his nature to fight or preach. A woman should be peaceful. My mother used to say all begins the day we are born: some are born on a clear, warm day; some when it is cloudy and stormy. So, it is a consolation to find myself easy to live with these days. And I have found an answer to the few moods I still get. When I have come back from giving the horses each a cube or two of sugar, I give myself the same. I am an old horse who needs something sweet to give her more faith in life!

"The other day I thought I was going to say good-bye to this world. I was hanging up some clothes to dry. I love to do that, then stand back and watch and listen to the wind go through the socks or the pants or the dress, and see the sun warm them and make them smell fresh. I had dropped a few clothespins, and was picking them up, when suddenly I could not catch my breath, and a sharp pain seized me over my chest. I tried hard to stand up, but I couldn't. I wanted to scream but I knew there was no one nearby to hear. My husband had gone to the store. I sat down on the ground and waited. It was strong, the pain; and there was no one to tell about it. I felt as if someone had lassoed me and was pulling the rope tighter and tighter. Well here you are, an old cow, being taken in by the good Lord; that is what I thought.

"I looked at myself, sitting on the ground. For a second I was my old self again—worrying about how I must have appeared there, worrying about my dress, how dirty it would get to be. This is no place for an old lady, I thought—only for one of my little grandchildren, who love to play out here, build their castles of dirt, wetted down with water I give to them. Then more pain; I thought I had about a minute of life left. I said my prayers. I said goodbye to the house. I pictured my husband in my mind: fifty-seven years of marriage. Such a good man! I said to myself that I might not see him ever again; surely God would take him into Heaven, but as for me, I have no right to expect that outcome. Then I looked up to the sky and waited.

"My eye caught sight of a cloud. It was darker than the rest. It was alone. It was coming my way. The hand of God, I was sure of it! So that is how one dies. All my life, in the spare moments a person has, I wondered how I would go. Now I knew. Now I was ready. I thought I would soon be taken up to the cloud and across the sky I would go, and that would be that. But the cloud kept moving, and soon it was no longer above me, but beyond me; and I was still on my own land, so dear to me, so familiar after all these years. I can't be dead, I thought to myself, if I am here and the cloud is way over there, and getting further each second. Maybe the next cloud—but by then I had decided God had other things to do. Perhaps my name had come up, but He had decided to call others before me, and get around to me later. Who can ever know His reasons? Then I spotted my neighbor walking down the road, and I said to myself that I would shout for him. I did, and he heard. But you know, by the time he came I had sprung myself free. Yes, that is right, the pain was all gone.

"He helped me up, and he was ready to go find my husband and bring him back. No, I told him, no; I was all right, and I did not want to risk frightening my husband. He is excitable. He might get some kind of attack himself. I went inside and put myself down on our bed and waited. For an hour—it was that long, I am sure—my eyes stared at the ceiling, held on to it for dear life. I thought of what my life had been like: a simple life, not a very important one, maybe an unnecessary one. I am sure there are better people, men and women all over the world, who have done more for their neighbors and yet not lived as long as I have. I felt ashamed for a few minutes: all the complaints I'd made to myself and to my family, when the truth has been that my fate has been to live a long and healthy life, to have a good and loyal husband, and to bring two sons and three daughters into this world. I thought of the five children we had lost, three before they had a chance to take a breath. I wondered where in the universe they were. In the evening sometimes, when I go to close loose doors that otherwise complain loudly all night, I am likely to look at the stars and feel my long-gone infants near at hand. They are far off, I know; but in my mind they have become those stars—very small, but shining there bravely, no matter how cold it is so far up. If the stars have courage, we ought to have courage; that is what I was thinking, as I so often have in the past—and just then he was there, my husband, calling my name and soon looking into my eyes with his.

"I'm all right, I told him. He didn't know what had happened; our neighbor had sealed his lips, as I told him to do. But my husband knows me, so he knew I looked unusually tired; and he couldn't be easily tricked by me. The more I told him I'd just worked too hard, that is all, the more he knew I was holding something back. Finally, I pulled my ace card. I pretended to be upset by his questions and by all the attention he was giving me. I accused him: why do you make me want to cry, why do you wish me ill, with those terrible thoughts of yours? I am not ill! If you cannot let me rest without thinking I am, then God have mercy on you for having such an imagination! God have mercy! With the second plea to our Lord, he was beaten and silent. He left me alone. I was about to beg him to come back, beg his forgiveness. But I did not want him to bear the burden of knowing; he would not rest easy by day or night. This way he can say to himself: she has always been cranky, and she will always be cranky, so thank God her black moods come only now and then—a spell followed by the bright sun again.

"I will say what I think happened: I came near going, then there was a change of heart up there in Heaven, so I have a few more days, or weeks, or months, or years—who knows? As for a doctor, I have never seen one, so why start now? Here we are so far away from a hospital. We have no money. Anglos don't like us, anyway: we are the poor ones, the lost ones. My son tells me the Anglos look down on us—old people without education and up in the hills, trying to scrape what we can from the land, and helped only by our animals. No matter; our son is proud of us. He is proud to stay here with us. He says that if he went to the city he would beg for work and be told no, no, no: eventually he might be permitted to sweep someone's floor. Better to hold on to one's land. Better to fight it out with the weather and the animals.

"Again I say it: doctors are for others. My mother and my aunt delivered my children. I once went to see a nurse; she worked for the school and she told me about my children—the diseases they get. Thank you, I said. Imagine: she thought I knew nothing about bringing up children, or about the obstacles God puts in their way to test them and make them stronger for having gone through a fever, a rash, some pain. No, I will see no nurse and no doctor. They are as far from here as the stars. Oh, that is wrong; they are much farther. The stars I know and recognize and even call by name.

They are my names, of course; I don't know what others call the stars. Is it wrong to do that? Perhaps I should ask the priest. Perhaps the stars are God's to name, not ours to treat like pets—by addressing them familiarly. But it is too late; my sins have been recorded, and I will soon enough pay for each and every one of them."

True, I have pulled together remarks made over a stretch of months. And again, I have translated her Spanish into plain, understandable English, or at least I hope I have done so. I have even "cleaned up" her English to an extent; that is, I have eliminated some of the repetitive words or phrases she uses—as we all do when we talk informally to visitors in our homes. On the other hand, I have made every effort to keep faithful to the spirit, and mostly to the letter, of her remarks. I have found that her Spanish is as bare, unaffected, and strong as her English. I have found that in both languages she struggles not only to convey meaning, but to enliven her words with her heart's burden or satisfactions. I have found that she struggles not only with her mind but with her body, her whole being, to express herself. Nor is she unique, some peculiar or specially gifted person whose manner of expression is thoroughly idosyncratic. She certainly can be saddled with negatives, however compelling her way of speaking. She is uneducated. She is superstitious. She has never attended any bilingual classes. She is poor. Maybe some doctor would find her at times forgetful, a little "senile." She and others like her are rural people; they belong to a social and economic "system" that we all know is "out of date," because the future of America is to be found in cities like Albuquerque and their suburbs. Or so we are told.

Nor is she saintly. She can be morose, and at times quite cranky and reticent. Once she asked me, "What is the point of trying to talk to those who are deaf?" She had in mind some Anglo county officials who refused to give food stamps to a needy cousin of hers. She had in mind an Anglo teacher or two, and yes, a Spanish-speaking teacher or two; they had said rude things to her grandchildren and to their parents, her children. So, she becomes bitter and tense, and after a while she explodes. She admits it is not in her nature to hold in her beliefs, her feelings. She must have her say. And when she does her hands move, her body sways a bit, and sometimes, when she is especially worked up, there is a lurch forward from the chair, so that suddenly she is standing—giving a sermon, almost like the priests she has listened to all these years. A hand goes out, then is withdrawn. The head goes up, then is lowered. A step is taken forward, then back she goes—and soon she is seated again, ready to sew and continue the conversation on a less intense level. When she searches for a word, be it in Spanish or English, she drops her needle and thread, drops a fork or spoon, drops anything she may have in her hands. She needs those old, arthritic fingers of hers. They flex and unflex; it is as if before her is a sandpile of words, and she must push and probe her way through it until she has found what she is looking for. Then the fingers can stop, the hands can relax and go back to other business, or simply be allowed a rest on her lap.

The more time I spend with this woman and her husband and their friends and neighbors and relatives, the more confused I become by much of what I read about them and their so-called cultural disadvantage. I have no inclination to turn such people into utterly flawless human beings, to create yet another highly romanticized group that can be used as a bludgeon against the rest of the country. They can be mean and narrow at times; the woman I have been quoting says things about hippies, and even, at times, about Anglos, that I disagree with or find exaggerated, unfair, distorted. As for her own disposition, she is clearly aware of her personal limitations. Still, she and her kind are at best pitied by many who have described their "plight." If there are grounds for pity (poverty, substantial unemployment, a degree of prejudice even in New Mexico, never mind Texas or California), there are also grounds for respect and admiration—maybe even envy. Some of us who have gone through all those schools and colleges and graduate schools, who have plenty of work and who live comfortable upper-middle-class lives, might want to stop and think about how *we* talk.

Occasionally I come home from a day spent with Chicano families or Indian families and pick up a psychiatric journal, or for that matter, the daily newspaper. Or I happen to go to a professional meeting and hear papers presented, or, afterwards, people talking in lobbies or corridors or restaurants—all those words, all those ideas, spoken by men and women who have no doubt about their importance, the value of their achievements, and certainly not about their ability to "communicate." No one is proposing that jargon-spewing scholars of one sort or another overcome their "cultural disadvantage." Few are examining closely the rhetoric of various business and professional people, or that of their elected leaders—the phony, deceiving, dull, dreary, ponderous, smug, deadly words and phrases such people use and use and use. Relatively few are looking at the way such people are taught in elementary school and high school and beyond. Who is to be pitied, the old lady who can't recognize a possible coronary seizure and instead sees the hand of God approaching her, or some of us who jabber with our clichés and don't have the slightest idea how to use a metaphor or an image in our speech?

True, we have no "illusions"; we are educated, and pain in the chest is for us pain in the chest. Nor do we get carried away with ourselves; we are as sober as can be—so sober the whole world trembles at what we as the owners of this nation can do and have done amid our sobriety, our controlled speech and controlled actions. No hysteria for us. No gesticulations. No demonstration of exuberance, passion, heartiness, excitability. We are cool, calculating; we keep under wraps whatever spirit we have left, if any. And no doubt about it, the grandchildren mentioned so often by this particular old lady are not going to be like her: they are learning in school all sorts of valuable information—but also how to curb their imaginations, restrain their lively interest in harnessing language to the mind's rush of ideas, the heart's movements.

Their grandmother, soon to die, she knows, has said it far more precisely than I can—if with unintended irony: "My grandchildren will not struggle as I do to make myself clear. They are being fed words, Anglo words, by their teachers. They are learning the Spanish language; I only speak it, I don't know how to pick it apart! My oldest granddaughter showed me a book; it was about the Spanish language. I told her she does not need it; she can speak Spanish quite well. No, she said, she has to learn more, and the same with English. Who am I to disagree? Children have so much to learn. The better they can speak, the better it is for them. My grandchildren will speak better Spanish than I; and they will be good at English, too. There is change; there is progress. I am grateful. When I wonder whether there is any hope for my people, I look at my children's children and I say to myself: yes, there is hope. My husband says he hears the little ones chattering away: back and forth they go, from Spanish to English and then to Spanish again. I tell him that we haven't done so bad ourselves; we can make ourselves understood in both languages. But he says—and he is right—that it is not the struggle for them that it has been for us. There is enough struggle for any of us in this world; so, the less the better.

"I only worry that the more people have, the less grateful they feel to God. I know, because a while back, when we had an even harder time than now, we prayed to Him more often. Now our stomachs are full, our children give us money—not a lot, because they don't have much themselves, but some; and the result is that we ignore Him, or we only thank Him on Sundays, when we are in church. I have always felt that He listens more to our daily prayers at home, rather than those we offer in church, when it is a mere habit being practiced. But I am speaking out of turn; I have no right to speak for Him! He knows which prayers mean the most to Him. I have no right to feel sorry for my grandchildren, either. There are moments when I wish they put more of themselves into their fine English and their fine Spanish, but misery likes company, I guess. My husband and I reach out, cry out, for our words, and we are so surprised at the little ones: what we can never take for granted, they have in such large supply. No wonder they have other things to think about than how to get their message across to people! No Anglo is going to make them feel speechless. I can't say I've felt speechless with Anglos, either; but I am sure that they have looked down on me, or not understood my English. As for my Spanish, it has served me well. The Anglos don't understand it, and a Spanish gentleman, one of great learning, would no doubt feel sorry for me, the way I use his language. But I repeat, it has served me well, the way I talk; that is as much as I can say, no more.

"Well, I do have another thought to offer. My daughter told me the other day that all our lives we have been split: we are Spanish, but we are Americans; we have our Spanish language, but in this country the Anglos are kings, and everyone has to speak their English or pay the penalties. I could not disagree. I took my daughter to me and told her she was right to listen to those teachers. I only worry that she and her children will take the message too seriously—will feel ashamed of their own parents, their own people's history. After all, even if there has been trouble, there has been God's grace: He has helped us; He has healed us; He has enabled us to try to be worthwhile and decent people. We have two languages, I know. We are in the middle; we don't know where to go, who to turn to. Or is it that we turn in one direction, then another? But God has given each of us a soul, and it is the soul that really counts. I do not have a Spanish soul, or a soul that is part Anglo. The soul is the place where each of us, no matter what language we speak, no matter our color, meets the Creator. We live the best we know how to live, and our actions are words to God, and He makes His judgment. Through our soul we speak to Him and He to us. Oh, I am not very clear today! This is the end of my life, the month of December for me; and I fear my talk shows it! I only want to say that even though there are two languages to speak, there is only one soul. But maybe the time has come for me to stop speaking in any language. The soul finally tires of the body; it is a prison, and the soul wants to leave. Words struggle to leave us, but once spoken they are dead. The soul leaves and lives forever. I believe it does. I hope it does."

She makes that last distinction between faith and hope rather innocently. Not for her a dramatic division: I want something to be, but I'm not sure my wish will be realized; and so there is my religious conviction as opposed to my intuitive sense that one cannot be certain by any means. As for those words she mentions, they do indeed struggle for expression. She knows all the pain of the translator. She knows she has one range of expression given her by the Spanish language and another that is set by the English she uses. She moves back and forth, calls upon words and phrases and expressions and proverbs and sayings she has gathered together over the decades and made into her own particular way of both thinking and speaking. Who can (who wants to?) titrate the mixture, resort to percentages or long analytic statements about which idiom makes for what degree of her "pattern" of speech? In each home I visit, the language differs; it all depends on so much—a particular person's manner of getting on with people, a person's responsiveness to sounds (in contrast, say, to visual images), a person's experiences as a worker, a host of accidents and incidents and encounters that may have caused one person to be more talkative, more expansive, more sensitive to the requirements of "bilingual" life than others turn out to be. (A kind Anglo boss, for instance, who took pains once to offer some help with pronunciation, or with the mysteries of a given phrase of construction; or a priest who is especially devoted to the life of a parishioner, including his or her interest in self-expression; or a teacher who was encouraging rather than intimidating.) Beyond all those "variables" there is the daily rhythm of a given kind of living—close to the land, in touch with nature, very much part of a community's collective experience. We who have become locked up

in city apartments or small suburban lots may find the language of an old "illiterate" grandmother—from a settlement in north central New Mexico too small even to qualify as a village—unusually vivid or figurative. The fact is that such a woman has her heritage, her surroundings, her everyday experience, even as we have ours—hence the difference in language. But the power is ours, and also the numbers—we are the vast majority. Moreover, historically America is a "melting pot"; there is, there has been all along, the expectation that those who come here, or for that matter (the gall!) were here before anyone else, respond to the nation's "manifest destiny"—and such a destiny has its cultural as well as its brute military or political components. Meanwhile that woman and thousands like her, old and tired, proud and energetic, do what we all try to do: look at the world, listen to its sounds, figure out its outlines, its structure, its significance. Then comes that attempt at coherence which is language—and with it the connections that words provide: one person to another, the two of them to a neighborhood, and beyond.

There is no point holding up anyone's struggle with language as a standard by which others must measure themselves. I have probably not emphasized strongly enough the silences I have heard, the almost desperate search for words which quite frequently turns out to be unsuccessful. I am myself a writer, hence wordy. And my work makes me utterly dependent on the words of others—or at least when I write up that work I have to come forth with those words. The point is not to deny her wish—at least for her grandchildren, if not herself—to speak better, more fluent, English, maybe even a "higher" form of Spanish, too. The point is simply to emphasize the particularity and complexity of her life; and, not least, its integrity.

Against considerable odds she and her husband have carved out a "moment" for themselves on this earth. They happen to be alert, vigorous, stubborn people. They don't let things go; their ears prick up, their eyes dart, they love to smell food as well as taste it, and they enjoy touching people, objects, animals. They possess adequate if not superior intelligence. That being the case, for all their cultural and educational "deficits," for all the "handicaps" they have had to face, for all the difficulties of a "bilingual" life, they nevertheless prove themselves altogether adequate to the demands of their day-to-day existence. They make themselves known. They affirm themselves. They speak out of their minds and hearts. They reveal once again that a lean and willing soul can find its own carefully chosen if hesitantly uttered words, even as others, grown fat and sassy spiritually, can pour forth statements and remarks but worry little about what they sound like. After all, there is so much to lay claim upon through words, there are so many people to keep up with and impress and win over or argue down—rather than, as is the case with the woman I have quoted, simply reach and arouse and stir.

# 37

# Retirement to the Porch

Oftentimes, when people get on in years, they are relegated to the back room. But in Laurel Creek, West Virginia, they are usually accorded an honored place on the front porch. In that small, rural Appalachian settlement, according to sociologist-anthropologists John Lozier and Ronald Althouse of West Virginia University, there is a definite cultural phenomenon they call "retirement to the porch."

The front porch, which used to be an important place for socialization regardless of age, is now "useless for most Americans. New houses are built with a vestigial stoop in front, and outdoor leisure life focuses on the backyard or patio. The wide front porches of older houses often stand empty, if they have not been enclosed to provide more 'useful' interior space," Lozier and Althouse point out.

**Observing.** Well, the front porch is still a tradition for Laurel Creek senior citizens. (Lozier and Althouse have limited their reportage to the male inhabitants.) Typically, a man will begin to spend time on the porch when he is no longer competing for regular work. From his vantage point, he observes activity on the road and swaps tales with those who stop, often hitching a ride into town with them. In those first years, he arranges for occasional paid or volunteer work through social interactions initiated on his porch. "As long as he is active and able," say the investigators, "it is important that he continue to be available to help others and to provide for himself, associating with others in a way that is established from patterns of reciprocity in earlier years."

When his health begins to fail or when others relieve him of some of his obligations, he begins full retirement to the porch. He then can draw on the social credit he has stockpiled over the years, say Lozier and Althouse. It thus becomes acceptable to ask passersby he knows to pick up his groceries or to spend a few more minutes visiting. If his presence on the porch has become usual, a sudden absence causes community concern. After a reappearance on the porch following a health crisis, "there is an increased urgency about providing him with appropriate social interaction."

When he is close to death and spending most of his time indoors, whenever possible, those who care for him will bring him out on the porch. Such an appearance will be broadcast throughout the community, and "for a couple of hours, perhaps, he will receive his final public attention."

Not all old people receive such solicitous attention. Those who have recently moved into the neighborhood ("cash-ins," Lozier and Althouse call them) have weak social networks and don't spend much time out in front; in fact, they often live in trailers or in other porchless dwellings. Then there are the "no-counts," people who have never earned much social standing and who can't start now simply by parking a rocking chair out front. Others have always stuck to themselves and have never been involved with the community at large. For a successful retirement to the porch, a person needs to have a good amount of social standing.

Laurel Creek provides much more than the rudimentary services to many of its old people. All elderly people deserve at least that much, say the investigators. "What is required for successful old age is the continuing existence of community or neighborhood systems which can recognize and store credit for the performance of an individual over a whole lifetime and which can enforce the obligation of juniors to provide reciprocity. Without such a system, the help that is provided to an elder robs him of his dignity, for there is no recognition that this is his due, and not a form of charity," conclude Lozier and Althouse.

**"In Laurel Creek, West Virginia, the elderly are often accorded an honored place on the front porch."**

*For the retired in rural West Virginia, porches are for seeing and being seen.*

# 38

Japan has maintained a high level of respect and integration for their aged. Japanese practices suggest many ways that the USA could improve the status and integration of its aged: Senior Citizens Day, special celebration of the 65th birthday, precedence for older persons, exercise and sports for the aged, free health examinations and medical care, more employment opportunities for the aged, more senior centers, and political action by the aged.

# What Can the USA Learn from Japan About Aging?[1]

Erdman Palmore, PhD[2]

## Status and Integration

Aging in Japan is almost a mirror image of aging in the United States. Despite high levels of industrialization and urbanization, the Japanese have maintained a high level of respect for their elders and a high level of integration of their elders in the family, work force, and community. While there is considerable prejudice and discrimination against the aged in America (Palmore, 1969, 1973), old age is recognized by most Japanese as a source of prestige and honor. The most common word for the aged in Japanese, *Otoshiyori*, literally means "the honorable elders." Respect for the elders is shown in the honorific language used in speaking to or about the elders; rules of etiquette which give precedence to the elders in seating arrangements, serving order, bathing order, and going through doors; bowing to the elders; the national holiday called Respect for Elders Day; giving seats on crowded public vehicles to the elders, and the authority of the elders over many family and household matters.

The high level of their integration into Japanese society is demonstrated by the following facts. Over 75% of all Japanese aged 65 or more live with their children (Office of the Prime Minister, 1973) in contrast to 25% in the United States (Epstein & Murray, 1967). The majority of Japanese men over 65 continue to be in the labor force (Japan Census Bureau, 1965), compared to 29% of men in the United States over 65 (Palmore, 1964). Most of the Japanese elders who are not actually employed continue to be useful in housekeeping, child-care, shopping, and gardening, often freeing their daughters or daughters-in-law for employment outside the home. The vast majority of Japanese elders also remain active in their communities through Senior Citizens Clubs, religious organizations, and informal neighborhood groups. And, most surprising of all, there appears to have been little decline in these high levels of integration during the past 20 or 30 years (Palmore, 1975).

This high status and integration of the elders has roots in the "vertical" structure of the society and in the religious principles of filial piety. Japan has often been called a "vertical society" because most relationships tend to be hierarchical rather than horizontal or equalitarian (Nakane, 1970). Age grading is one of the most important dimensions determining who is above or below. The principles of filial piety go back to both Confucian precepts and to ancestor worship, "the real religion of Japan" (Hearn, 1955). The principles of filial piety specify that respect and duty toward parents is one of the most important virtues of all.

Thus, the most general thing we can learn about aging from the Japanese is that high status and integration can be maintained in a modern industrialized society.

## Suggestions for the United States and the West

Obviously, many of the practices and attitudes of Japanese toward their elders are not likely to be imported as such. However, many of these practices do suggest ways in which the situation of older Americans in the United States as well as the Western world could be improved.

1. Much of the material for this article is adapted from my forthcoming book, **The Honorable Elders: A Cross-cultural Analysis.** This study was supported in part by Grant # HD 00668, NICHD, and by the Duke Bio-medical Sciences Support Grant 5-S05-RR07070-07. The Tokyo Institute of Gerontology provided office facilities and translators. Mikio Mori of the Dept. of Health and Welfare provided materials and assisted in various ways.

2. Professor of Medical Sociology and Scientific Associate, Duke Center for the Study of Aging and Human Development, Durham 27710.

(1) Respect for the Elders Day is a popular national holiday and apparently succeeds in encouraging respect for the elders and a greater awareness of their problems, as well as actions to reduce these problems. Labor Day and Veterans Day in the United States are similar national holidays which recognize the contributions of labor and veterans as well as encouraging more recognition of their problems. Mother's Day and Father's Day in the United States are not official government holidays but are widely observed in a variety of ways to recognize the contributions of mothers and fathers. Thus, there seems to be ample precedent for establishing an Older Americans Day in the United States which would be similar in function to Japan's Respect for Elders Day. One difficulty is that while laborers, veterans, mothers, and fathers are generally proud, or at least not ashamed, of their status, many older Americans are ashamed of their status and try to deny their old age. Presumably, if an Older Americans Day could be established, it would help reduce this shame about old age.

(2) The Japanese also use the 61st birthday as an occasion to honor the elders and to express affection for them. In the United States, Americans sometimes use the 21st birthday as an occasion to recognize the new adult. Other rites of passage for the young are christening, confirmation or bar mitzvah, graduation, and marriage ceremonies. There are few such ceremonies for older persons. Sometimes a golden wedding anniversary (after 50 years of marriage) becomes an occasion for recognizing and showing affection for older couples. Sometimes retirement parties are held to recognize an employee's contribution. It might also be useful for the Americans to observe the 65th birthday with special celebrations in order to encourage more respect and affection for our elders.

(3) In an egalitarian society, it is unlikely the West would adopt forms of deference toward older people such as bowing and honorific language. Nevertheless, we do have a weak tradition of "age before beauty" when going through doors and when serving people. This saying, unfortunately, implies that the aged are not beautiful. However, it may be that strengthening and extending the tradition of precedence for older persons would help restore more respect for elders and more self-respect among older persons themselves.

(4) The United States also has a weak tradition of giving seats to elders on crowded public transportation. This could be reinforced, as the Japanese have done, by regulations which give priority to older persons for a certain number of seats in each bus or train. In addition to recognizing special privileges for elders, this would facilitate the ease of travel of older persons, more of whom must rely exclusively on public transportation.

(5) All older Japanese are eligible for a minimum income payment from the government. While this amounts to little more than pocket money at present, the principle of a minimum income guaranteed by the government for older persons is a good one. As of January, 1974, the United States started a program guaranteeing a minimum income to persons over 65 of $140 per month ($120 for a couple). Thus, the principle of minimum incomes for the aged has only recently been adopted and the next step would be to raise the level of this minimum from its present poverty level to a more adequate income.

(6) Several cities in Japan have established programs in which elders living alone are visited or called on a daily basis in order to see if they are all right or need anything. Such a program in the United States, which is sporadically conducted in stead of being universal, would not only reduce the fears of older persons living alone that they might have some kind of accident or even die before anyone could be reached, but it would also reduce their isolation. There is evidence that isolation can lead to mental and even physical deterioration among the aged (Lowenthal, Berkman, Brisette, Buehler, Pierce, Robinson, & Trier, 1967; Roth & Kay, 1962).

(7) It is a widespread practice for Japanese of all ages to begin their day with some kind of group exercise. This is carried over into homes for the aged in which the day typically begins with a combination of group exercise and folk dance in rhythm to music. Such morning exercise is widely recognized as an excellent way to preserve physical and mental functioning. When it is done on a group basis, there is the added satisfaction of social support and interaction. Instituting such programs of exercise for older people in the West should improve their physical and mental health (Palmore, 1970; Palmore & Luikart, 1972).

(8) The Japanese government encourages and subsidizes sports day for the elders. Generally, this takes the form of various track and field events which are not too strenuous for healthy older persons. If the USA government encouraged and subsidized such sports days for older

Americans, this too should improve the physical and mental health of those who participate.

(9) Another program to improve the health of Japanese elders is the free annual health examination, which is followed by more detailed examinations and treatments for those who need it. The present Medicare program in the United States does not cover such routine examinations. It would seem that with only a modest cost to the program, it could be extended to cover an annual examination in order to detect and prevent the development of many serious diseases.

(10) Starting in 1973, the Japanese government began providing completely free medical care to most Japanese over age 70. Some cities provide free medical care to their residents between the ages of 65 and 70. The present Medicare program in the United States covers only 40% of the medical care cost of older Americans (although other public programs cover another 24%) (Cooper & Piro, 1974). Completely free medical care would remove the high financial barriers that remain between many older people in the USA and adequate medical care. This would not only improve the health of people in the USA and thus improve their life satisfaction directly, but it would also prevent the depletion of financial resources which so often results from the expenses of serious illness.

(11) Perhaps the most important single idea the United States could benefit by is the provision of more employment opportunities for older persons. Japanese older persons are not only permitted, but are *expected* to continue working or doing housework of some kind as long as they are able. There are many ways one could expand job opportunities for older USA people to approach those in Japan. The 1971 White House Conference on Aging recommended the USA earmark a minimum amount of federal manpower funds to improve employment opportunities for older workers; that the USA vigorously enforce and extend the present legislation against discrimination in employment; that the government become the "employer of last resort" for those older workers unable to find other jobs; and that the government establish a computerized national "job bank" and work-related centers to locate and bring together older persons and potential employers on both a full-time and part-time basis (White House Conference on Aging, 1973). During the 3 years following this conference, *none* of these recommendations have been carried out. The Japanese believe that voluntary employment of older

persons contributes to their physical and mental health, to their satisfaction, to their financial independence, and to the nation's productivity. There is considerable evidence in Japan and in the USA that they are correct in this belief (Palmore, 1972).

(12) Another idea with potentially great benefit is more integration of older persons in the families of their children and grandchildren. It appears unlikely that USA citizens will greatly increase the proportions of older persons living with their children. But it may be feasible and desirable for more older Americans to live near enough to their children and grandchildren to contribute more fully to their household activities. On the one side, this would decrease the isolation and inactivity of many older persons, and on the other side it would reduce the mother's and father's burdens of child care, housekeeping, and household maintenance.

(13) The Japanese have a nation-wide system of government-supported Elders Clubs, to which about half the elders belong. These clubs function not only to provide community service, group study, and recreation, but also provide mutual support and self-pride among the elders. The USA has some Senior Citizens Clubs and some get modest government support. But, compared to Japan, these clubs are few and weak. The National Institute of Senior Aging estimates that less than 5% of Americans over 65 belong to any such club. If the USA follows Japan's example and establishes more, and more active, Senior Citizens Clubs, the benefits of greatly expanded community service as well as providing opportunities for group study and recreation, mutual support and self-pride to the majority of our older citizens would be reaped.

(14) A related program in Japan is the building of welfare centers for the aged, where various educational, recreational, and consultation services are provided with little or no charge. The centers are subsized by the government and now exist in most large communities. Again, while the USA has a few such centers, they are rare compared to the Japanese. The 1971 White House Conference on Aging recommended:

In every community and neighborhood, as appropriate, there should be a multi-purpose senior center to provide basic social services, as well as link all older persons to appropriate sources of help, including home-delivered services. The basic services, in clearly identifiable sites, i.e., senior centers, action centers, department of social services, etc., financed as an on-going government program, could be the foundation for such additional services as various levels of government and the voluntary sector, including organizations of the aged, would desire and sponsor.

So far, this recommendation has not been officially implemented.

(15) Perhaps most important in terms of getting these and other recommendations implemented is organized political action and demonstrations by the aged. In Japan, the elders are a recognized political force. This is true not only because they themselves constitute a sizeable proportion of the voters, but because they exert a strong influence over the votes of their family and younger friends. Furthermore, because of the high level of organization and self-pride among the elders, they are able to mount massive demonstrations and other forms of political pressure to get the government to meet their needs better. There are signs in the USA that more of the aged are beginning to realize the necessity for developing more political "clout." They are joining and working through such organizations as the American Association of Retired Persons and the National Council on the Aging in ever-increasing numbers. But massive demonstrations and effective political pressure is still rare. Older people in the USA could learn from their Japanese counterparts more effective ways of organizing and applying political pressure to improve their situation.

(16) Finally, the most complex and yet fundamental way in which one could learn from the Japanese relates to respect for elders and self-respect among the elders. Respect for Japanese elders is rooted in the basic social structure of their "vertical society" and in their religion of ancestor worship and filial piety. But the very idea of a vertical society and of ancestor worship would seem alien, if not completely repugnant to most USA citizens. Yet it appears that respect for the aged is the key element which can maintain the status and integration of the aged in modern industrial societies. Therefore, in order to improve the status and integration of older Americans, it is necessary to improve respect for the aged somehow. Instead of the vertical society, perhaps one could use egalitarian ideology that all persons are entitled to respect because they are humans, regardless of race, sex, or age. Instead of ancestor worship, perhaps one could use the Judaic-Christian commandment, "Honor thy father and mother," to increase respect for the aged. Perhaps the beliefs that "experience is the best teacher" and that knowledge can come from books but only years of experience can provide wisdom can be revived. Whatever the method or ideological

base, it seems probable that respect for older Americans must be substantially increased before their status and integration will be substantially increased.

The commentary above is not intended to propose a culture which assumes the aged are superior simply because they are old (as was true in old Japan). Nor is this intended to be an argument for a gerontocracy in which the aged have most of the power and rewards of the society (as in ancient Japan). It is intended, instead, to suggest that stereotypes and prejudices in the USA and other Western countries should be overcome to provide the elderly equal respect with all other humans; and, therefore, in the USA discrimination against the aged in employment, in our families, and in our communities should be stopped so that they can regain an equal share of power and rewards.

Those who agree with these ideals may be able to learn something from the land of "The Honorable Elders."

### References

Cooper, B., & Piro, P. Age differences in medical care spending, fiscal year, 1973. **Social Security Bulletin,** 1974, **37,** 3-14.

Epstein, L., & Murray, J. **The aged population of the United States.** USGPO, Washington, 1967.

Hearn, L. **Japan: An interpretation.** Charles E. Tuttle, Rutland, VT, 1955.

Japan Census Bureau. **1965 population census.** Japan Census Bureau, Tokyo, 1965.

Lowenthal, M. F., Berkman, P. L., Brisette, G. G., Buehler, J. A., Pierce, R. C., Robinson, B. C., & Trier, M. L. **Aging and mental disorder in San Francisco.** Jossey-Bass, San Francisco, 1967.

Nakane, C. **Japanese society.** Univ. of California Press, Berkeley, 1972.

Office of the Prime Minister. **Public opinion survey about problems of old age.** Office of the Prime Minister, Tokyo, 1973.

Palmore, E. Work experience and earnings of the aged in 1962. **Social Security Bulletin,** 1964, **27,** 3-15.

Palmore, E. Sociological aspects of aging. In E. W. Busse & E. Pfeiffer (Eds.), **Behavior and adaptation in late life.** Little Brown, Boston, 1969.

Palmore, E. Ageism compared to racism and sexism. **Journal of Gerontology,** 1973, **28,** 363-369.

Palmore, E. Health practices and illness among the aged. **Gerontologist,** 1970, **10,** 313-316.

Palmore, E. Compulsory versus flexible retirement. **Gerontologist,** 1972, **12,** 343-348.

Palmore, E. **The honorable elders.** Duke Univ. Press, Durham, NC, 1975.

Palmore, E., & Luikart, C. Health and social factors related to life satisfaction. **Journal of Health & Social Behavior,** 1972, **13,** 68-80.

Roth, M., & Kay, D. Social, medical and personality factors associated with vulnerability to psychiatric breakdown in old age. **Gerontologica Clinica,** 1962, 147-160.

White House Conference on Aging. **Toward a national policy on aging,** Vol. II. USGPO, Washington, 1973.

# 39

# Why They Live to Be 100, Or Even Older, in Abkhasia

## by Sula Benet

SULA BENET is a professor of anthropology at Hunter College, New York City. Her book, "Abkhasia: The Long Living People of the Caucasus," was published in 1972.

Not long ago, in the village of Tamish in the Soviet Republic of Abkhasia, I raised by glass of wine to toast a man who looked no more than 70. "May you live as long as Moses (120 years)," I said. He was not pleased. He was 119.

For centuries, the Abkhasians and other Caucasian peasants have been mentioned in the chronicles of travelers amazed at their longevity and good health. Even now, on occasion, newspaper reports in the United States and elsewhere (never quite concealing bemusement and skepticism) will tell of an Abkhasian who claims to be 120, sometimes 130. When I returned from Abkhasia to New York displaying photographs and statistics, insisting that the tales are true and preoccupied with the question of why, my American friends invariably responded with the mocking question that contained its own answer: "Yogurt?" As a matter of fact, no, not yogurt; but the Abkhasians do drink a lot of buttermilk.

Abkhasia is a hard land—the Abkhasians, expressing more pride than resentment, say it was one of God's afterthoughts—but it is a beautiful one; if the Abkhasians are right about its mythical origin, God had a good second thought. It is subtropical on its coast along the Black Sea, alpine if one travels straight back from the sea, through the populated lowlands and valleys, to the main range of the Caucasus Mountains.

THE Abkhasians have been there for at least 1,000 years. For centuries they were herdsmen in the infertile land, but now the valleys and foothills are planted with tea and tobacco, and they draw their living largely from agriculture. There are 100,000 Abkhasians, not quite a fifth of the total population of the autonomous Abkhasian Republic, which is, administratively, part of Georgia, Joseph Stalin's birthplace; the rest are Russians, Greeks and Georgians. However, most of the people in government are Abkhasian, and both the official language and the style of life throughout the region are Abkhasian. The single city, Sukhumi, is the seat of government and a port of call for ships carrying foreign tourists. They are often visible in the streets of the city, whose population includes relatively few Abkhasians. Even those who live and work there tend to consider the villages of their families their own real homes. It is in the villages—575 of them between the mountains and the sea, ranging in population from a few hundred to a few thousand—that most Abkhasians live and work on collective farms.

I FIRST went there in the summer of 1970 at the invitation of the Academy of Sciences of the USSR. The Abkhasians were fascinating; I returned last summer and will go again next year. It was while interviewing people who had participated in the early efforts at collectivization that I became aware of the unusually large number of people, ranging in age from 80 to 119, who are still very much a part of the collective life they helped organize.

After spending months with them, I still find it impossible to judge the age of older Abkhasians. Their general appearance does not provide a clue: You know they are old because of their gray hair and the lines on their faces, but are they 70 or 107? I would have guessed "70" for all of the old people that I encountered in Abkhasia, and most of the time I would have been wrong.

It is as if the physical and psychological changes which to us signify the aging process had, in the Abkhasians, simply stopped at a certain point. Most work regularly. They are still blessed with good eyesight, and most have their own teeth. Their posture is unusually erect, even into advanced age; many take walks of more than two miles a day and swim in the mountain streams. They look healthy, and they are a handsome people. Men show a fondness for enormous mustaches, and are slim but not frail. There is an old saying that when a man lies on his side, his waist should be so small that a dog can pass beneath it. The women are dark-haired and also slender, with fair complexions and shy smiles.

THERE are no current figures for the total number of aged in Abkhasia, though in the village of Dzhgerda, which I visited last summer, there were 71 men and 110 women between 81 and 90 and 19 people over 91—15 per cent of the village population of 1,200. And it is worth noting that this extraordinary percentage is not the result of a migration by the young: Abkhasians, young and old, understandably prefer to stay where they are, and rarely travel, let alone migrate. In 1954, the last year for which overall figures are available, 2.58 per cent of the Abkhasians were over 90. The roughly comparable figures for the entire Soviet Union and the United States were 0.1 per cent and 0.4 per cent, respectively.

Since 1932, the longevity of the Abkhasians has been systematically studied on several occasions by Soviet and Abkhasian investigators, and I was given full access to their findings by the Ethnographic Institute in Sukhumi. These studies have shown that, in general, signs of arteriosclerosis, when they occurred at all, were found only in extreme old age. One researcher who examined a group of Abkhasians over 90 found that close to 40 per cent of the men and 30 percent of the women had vision good enough to read or thread a needle without glasses, and that over 40 per cent had reasonably good hearing. There were no reported cases of either mental illness or cancer in a nine-year study of 123 people over 100.

In that study, begun in 1960 by Dr. G. N. Sichinava of the Institute of Gerontology in Sukhumi, the aged showed extraordinary psychological and neurological stability. Most of them had clear recollection of the distant past, but partially bad recollection for more recent events. Some reversed this pattern, but quite a large number retained a good memory of both the recent and distant past. All correctly oriented themselves in time and place. All showed clear and logical thinking, and most correctly estimated their physical and mental capacities. They showed a lively interest in their families' affairs, in their collective and in social events. All were agile, neat and clean.

Abkhasians are hospitalized only rarely, except for stomach disorders and childbirth. According to doctors who have inspected their work, they are expert at setting broken arms and legs themselves—their centuries of horsemanship have given them both the need and the practice.

The Abkhasian view of the aging process is clear from their vocabulary. They do not have a phrase for "old people"; those over 100 are called "long living people." Death, in the Abkhasian view, is not the logical end of life but something irrational. The aged seem to lose strength gradually, wither in size and finally die; when that happens, Abkhasians show their grief fully, even violently.

FOR the rest of the world, disbelief is the response not to Abkhasians' deaths but to how long they have lived. There really should no longer be any question about their longevity. All of the Soviet medical investigators took great care to cross-check the information they received in interviews. Some of the men studied had served in the army, and military records invariably supported their own accounts. Extensive documentation is lacking only because the Abkhasians had no functioning written language until after the Russian Revolution.

But why do they live so long? The absence of a written history, and the relatively recent period in which medical and anthropological studies have taken place, preclude a clear answer. Genetic selectivity is an obvious possibility. Constant hand-to-hand combat during many centuries of Abkhasian existence may have eliminated those with poor eyesight, obesity and other physical shortcomings, producing healthier Abkhasians in each succeeding generation. But documentation for such an evolutionary process is lacking.

When I asked the Abkhasians themselves about their longevity, they told me they live as long as they do because of their practices in sex, work and diet.

THE Abkhasians, because they expect to live long and healthy lives, feel it is necessary self-discipline to conserve their energies, including their sexual energy, instead of grasping what sweetness is available to them at the moment. They say it is the norm that regular sexual relations do not begin before the age of 30 for men, the traditional age of marriage; it was once even considered unmanly for a new husband to exercise his sexual rights on his wedding night. (If they are asked what is done to provide substitute graitifications of normal sexual needs before marriage, Abkhasians smile and say, "Nothing," but it is not unreasonable to speculate that they, like everyone else, find substitutes for the satisfaction of healthy, heterosexual sex. Today, some young people marry in their mid-20's instead of waiting for the "proper" age of 30, to the consternation of their elders.)

Postponement of satisfaction may be smiled at, but so is the expectation of prolonged, future enjoyment, perhaps with more reason. One medical team investigating the sex life of the Abkhasians concluded that many men retain their sexual potency long after the age of 70, and 13.6 per cent of the women continue to menustrate after the age of 55.

Tarba Sit, 102, confided to me that he had waited until he was 60 to marry because while he was in the army "I had a good time right and left." At present, he said with some sadness, "I have a desire for my wife but no strength." One of his relatives had nine children, the youngest born when he was 100. Doctors obtained sperm from him when he was 119, in 1963, and he still retained his libido and potency. The only occasions on which medical investigators found discrepancies in the claimed ages of Abkhasians was when men insisted they were younger than they actually were. One said he was 95, but his daughter had a birth certificate proving she was 81, and other information indicated he was really 108. When he was confronted with the conflict he became angry and refused to discuss it, since he was about to get married. Makhti Tarkil, 104, with whom I spoke in the village of Duripsh, said the explanation was obvious in view of the impending marriage: "A man is a man until he is 100, you know what I mean. After that, well, he's getting old."

ABKHASIAN culture provides a dependent and secondary role for women; when they are young, their appearance is stressed, and when they are married, their service in the household is their major role. (As with other aspects of Abkhasian life, the period since the revolution has brought changes, and some women now work in the professions; but in the main, the traditions are still in force.) In the upbringing of a young woman, great care is taken to make her as beautiful as possible according to Abkhasian standards. In order to narrow her waist and keep her breasts small, she wears a leather corset around her chest and waist; the corset is permanently removed on her wedding night. Her complexion should be fair, her eyebrows thin; because a high forehead is also desirable, the hair over the brow is shaved and further growth is prevented through the application of bleaches and herbs. She should also be a good dancer.

Virginity is an absolute requirement for marriage. If a woman proves to have been previously deflowered, the groom has a perfect right to take her back to her family and have his marriage gifts returned. He always exercises that right, returning the bride and announcing to the family. "Take your dead one." And to him, as well as all other eligible men, she is dead: in Abkhasian society, she has been so dishonored by his rejection that it would be next to impossible to find a man to marry her. (Later on, however, she may be married off to an elderly widower or some other less desirable male from a distant village. When she is discovered, she is expected to name the guilty party. She usually picks the name of a man who has recently died, in order to prevent her family from taking revenge and beginning a blood feud.)

For both married and unmarried Abkhasians, extreme modesty is required at all times. There is an overwhelming feeling of uneasiness and shame over any public manifestation of sex, or even affection. A man may not touch his wife, sit down next to her or even talk to her in the presence of strangers. A woman's armpits are considered an erogenous zone and are never exposed, except to her husband.

A woman is a stranger, although a fully accepted one, in her husband's household. Her presence always carries the threat that her husband's loyalty to his family may be eroded by his passion for her. In the Abkhasian tradition, a woman may never change her dress nor bathe in the presence of her mother-in-law, and when an Abkhasian couple are alone in a room, they keep their voices low so that the husband's mother will not overhear them.

Despite the elaborate rules—perhaps, in part, because they are universally accepted—sex in Abkhasia is considered a good and pleasurable thing when it is strictly private. And, as difficult as it may be for the American mind to grasp, it is guiltless. It is not repressed or sublimated into work, art or religious-mystical passion. It is not an evil to be driven from one's thoughts. It is a pleasure to be regulated for the sake of one's health—like a good wine.

AN Abkhasian is never "retired," a status unknown in Abkhasian thinking. From the beginning of life until its end, he does what he is capable of doing because both he and those around him consider work vital to life. He makes the demands on himself that he can meet, and as

## There'll Always Be an Abkhasia

The Abkhasian culture has survived intact despite centuries of warlike raids by, and against, neighboring herdsmen, and domination by the Greeks, Turks and Russians; in Abkhasian history, the rule of the Turks was especially cruel. Many Abkhasians were sold as slaves, but it is a certainty that that depredation left Abkhasian vigor intact. In the 5th century, under Justinian, orthodox Christianity was imposed on the Abkhasians, and in the 15th and 16th centuries, the Sunni sect of Islam. Traces of those religions remain, and some Abkhasians will identify themselves as Christians or Moslems. But they always have been pagans, and their underlying beliefs are pagan, connected to the family structure. They make animal sacrifices at family shrines. Asked to reconcile paganism with the mid-20th century, Abkhasians smile and say, "Oh, we don't believe in it. It's just a tradition."

The years since the Russian Revolution have brought still another wave of change; as usual, the Abkhasians have not been swamped. The economy and political structure have changed greatly: what were once isolated, semi-pastoral homesteads producing at a subsistence level are now collectives, prospering by comparison to pre-revolutionary days. It is the Soviet policy to retain and enhance the national cultures within the U.S.S.R. but after the revolution the shift to collectives produced violent reactions among the peasants in many parts of the Soviet Union. Not in Abkhasia. The village elders opted for collectivism, and the Abkhasians followed. The transition was relatively smooth, and the Abkhasian culture remains intact.

Even the trappings of modernism have been absorbed. Radios are ubiquitous, television sets present but less frequent, and even less frequently watched. Tractors and helicopters please the Abkhasians but an expert horseman and an excellent horse are still prized over a pilot and his plane.—S.B.

those demands diminish with age, his status in the community nevertheless increases.

In his nine-year study of aged Abkhasians, Dr. Sichinava made a detailed examination of their work habits. One group included 82 men, most of whom had been working as peasants from the age of 11, and 45 women who, from the time of adolescence, had worked in the home and helped care for farm animals. Sichinava found that the work load had decreased considerably between the ages of 80 and 90 for 48 men, and between 90 and 100 for the rest. Among the women, 27 started doing less work between 80 and 90, and the others slowed down after 90. The few men who had been shepherds stopped following the herds up to the mountain meadows in spring, and instead began tending farm animals, after the age of 90. The farmers began to work less land; many stopped plowing and lifting heavy loads, but continued weeding (despite the bending involved) and doing other tasks. Most of the women stopped helping in the fields and some began to do less housework. Instead of serving the entire family—an Abkha-

The Abkasian Republic, between the Caucasus Mountains and the Black Sea, has been dominated by Turks, Greeks and Russians in its 1,000-year history.

sian family, extended through marriage, may include 50 or more people—they served only themselves and their children. But they also fed the chickens and knitted.

Dr. Sichinava also observed 21 men and 7 women over 100 years old and found that, on the average, they worked a four-hour day on the collective farm—the men weeding and helping with the corn crop, the women stringing tobacco leaves. Under the collective system, members of the community are free to work in their own gardens, but they get paid in what are, in effect, piecework rates for the work they do for the collective. Dr. Sichinava's group of villagers over 100, when they worked for the collective, maintained an hourly output that was not quite a fifth that of the norm for younger workers. But in maintaining their own pace, they worked more evenly and without waste motion, stopping on occasion to rest. By contrast, the younger men worked rapidly, but competitively and tensely. Competitiveness in work is not indigenous to Abkhasian culture but it is encouraged by the Soviet Government for the sake of increased production; pictures of the best workers are posted in the offices of the village collectives. It is too soon to predict whether this seemingly fundamental change in work habits will affect Abkhasian longevity.

The persistent Abkhasians have their own workers'

heroes: Kelkiliana Khesa, a woman of 109 in the village of Otapi, was paid for 49 workdays (a collective's workday is eight hours) during one summer; Bozba Pash, a man of 94 on the same collective, worked 155 days one year, Minosyan Grigorii of Aragich, often held up as an example to the young, worked 230 days in a year at the age of 90. (Most Americans, with a two-week vacation and several holidays, work between 240 and 250 days, some of them less than eight hours, in a year.)

Both the Soviet medical profession and the Abkhasians agree that their work habits have a great deal to do with their longevity. The doctors say that the way Abkhasians work helps the vital organs function optimally. The Abkhasians say, "Without rest, a man cannot work; without work, the rest does not give you any benefit."

That attitude, though it is not susceptible to medical measurements, may be as important as the work itself. It is part of a consistent life pattern: When they are children, they do what they are capable of doing, progressing from the easiest to the most strenuous tasks, and when they age, the curve descends, but it is unbroken. The aged are never seen sitting in chairs for long periods, passive, like vegetables. They do what they can, and while some consider the piecework system of the collectives a form of exploitation, it does permit them to function at their own pace.

OVEREATING is considered dangerous in Abkhasia, and fat people are regarded as ill. When the aged see a younger Abkhasian who is even a little overweight, they inquire about his health. "An Abkhasian cannot get fat," they say. "Can you imagine the ridiculous figure one would cut on horseback?" But to the dismay of the elders, the young eat much more than their fathers and grandfathers do; light, muscular and agile horsemen are no longer needed as a first line of defense.

The Abkhasian diet, like the rest of life, is stable: investigators have found that people 100 years and older eat the same foods throughout their lives. They show few idosyncratic preferences, and they do not significantly change their diet when their economic status improves. Their caloric intake is 23 per cent lower than that of the industrial workers in Abkhasia, though they consume twice as much vitamin C; the industrial workers have a much higher rate of coronary insufficiency and a higher level of cholesterol in the blood.

The Abkhasians eat without haste and with decorum. When guests are present, each person in turn is toasted with praise of his real or imaginary virtues. Such meals may last several hours, but nobody minds, since they prefer their food served lukewarm in any case. The food is cut into small pieces, served on platters, and eaten with the fingers. No matter what the occasion, Abkhasians take only small bites of food and chew those very slowly—a habit that stimulates the flow of ptyalin and maltase, insuring proper digestion of the carbohydrates which form the bulk of the diet. And, traditionally, there are no leftovers in Abkhasia; even the poor dispose of uneaten food by giving it to the animals, and no one would think of serving warmed-over food to a guest—even if it had been cooked only two hours earlier. Though some young people, perhaps influenced by Western ideas, consider the practice wasteful, most Abkhasians shun day-old food as unhealthful.

The Abkhasians eat relatively little meat—perhaps once or twice a week—and prefer chicken, beef, young goat and, in the winter, pork. They do not like fish and, despite its availability, rarely eat it. The meat is always freshly slaughtered and either broiled or boiled to the absolute minimum—until the blood stops running freely or, in the case of chicken, until the meat turns white. It is, not surprisingly, tough in the mouth of a non-Abkhasian, but they have no trouble with it.

At all three meals, the Abkhasians eat *abista*, a corn meal mash cooked in water without salt, which takes the place of bread. *Abista* is eaten warm with pieces of homemade goat cheese tucked into it They eat cheese daily, and also consume about two glasses of buttermilk a day. When eggs are eaten, which is not very often, they are boiled or fried with pieces of cheese.

The other staples in the Abkhasian diet—staple in Abkhasia means daily or almost so—include fresh fruits, especially grapes; fresh vegetables, including green onions, tomatoes, cucumbers and cabbage; a wide variety of pickled vegetables, and baby lima beans,

## Doctoring Themselves

The Abkhasians practice an elaborate folk medicine, using more than 200 indigenous plants to cure a wide variety of ills. They apply plantain leaves to heal severe wounds, take ranunculuses for measles, use poligonaceae as anticoagulant and asafetida (also known as Devil's Dung) as an antispasmodic. When all else fails, a doctor is called and the aged Abkhasian is taken to the hospital—but always with the expectation, including his own, that he will recover. They never express the fatalistic view, "Well, what do you expect at that age?" Sickness is simply not considered normal and natural.—S.B.

cooked slowly for hours, mashed and served flavored with a sauce of onions, peppers, garlic, pomegranate juice and pepper. That hot sauce, or a variant of it, is set on the table in a separate dish for anyone who wants it. Large quantities of garlic are also always at hand.

Although they are the main suppliers of tobacco for the Soviet Union few Abkhasians smoke. (I did meet one, a woman over 100, who smoked constantly.) They drink neither coffee nor tea. But they do consume a locally produced, dry, red wine of low alcoholic content. Everyone drinks it, almost always in small quantities, at lunch and supper, and the Abkhasians call it "life giving." Absent from their diet is sugar, though honey, a local product is used. Toothaches are rare.

Soviet medical authorities who have examined the Abkhasians and their diet feel it may well add years to their lives; the buttermilk and pickled vegetables, and probably the wine, help destroy certain bacteria and, indirectly, prevent the development of arteriosclerosis, the doctors think. In 1970, a team of Soviet doctors and Dr. Samuel Rosen of New York, a prominent ear surgeon, compared the hearing of Muscovites and Abkhasians, and concluded that the Abkhasians' diet—very little saturated fat, a great deal of fruit and vegetables—also accounted for their markedly better hearing. The hot sauce is the only item most doctors would probably say "no" to, and apparently some Abkhasians feel the same way.

ALTHOUGH the Abkhasians themselves attribute their longevity to their work, sex and dietary habits, there is another, broader aspect of their culture that impresses an outsider in their midst: the high degree of integration in their lives, the sense of group identity that gives each individual an unshaken feeling of personal security and continuity, and permits the Abkhasians as a people to adapt themselves—yet preserve themselves—to the changing conditions imposed by the larger society in which they live. That sense of continuity in both their personal and national lives is what anthropologists would call their spatial and temporal integration.

Their spatial integration is in their kinship structure. It is, literally, the Abkhasians' all-encompassing design for living: It regulates relationships between families, determines where they live, defines the position of women and marriage rules. Through centuries of nonexistent or ineffectual centralized authority, kinship was life's frame or reference, and it still is.

KINSHIP in Abkhasia is an elaborate, complex set of relationships based on patrilineage. At its center is the family, extended through marriage by the sons; it also includes all those families which can be traced to a single progenitor; and, finally, to all persons with the same surname, whether the progenitor can be traced or not. As a result, an Abkhasian may be "kin" to several thousand people, many of whom he does not know. I first discovered the pervasiveness of kinship rules when my friend Omar, an Abkhasian who had accompanied me from Sukhumi to the village of Duripsh, introduced me to a number of people he called his brothers and sisters. When I had met more than 20 "siblings" I asked, "How many brothers and sisters do you have?"

"In this village, 30," he said. "Abkhasian reckoning is different from Russian. These people all carry my father's name."

I took his explanation less seriously than I should have. Later, when I expressed admiration for a recording of Abkhasian epic poetry I had heard in the home of one of Omar's "brothers," Omar, without a word, gave the record to me as a gift.

"Omar, it isn't yours," I said.

"Oh yes it is. This is the home of my brother," he said. When I appealed to the "brother," he said, "Of course he can give it to you. He is my brother."

The consanguineal and affinal relationships that make up the foundation of the kinship structure are supplemented by a variety of ritual relationships that involve lifetime obligations—and serve to broaden the human environment from which Abkhasians derive their extraordinary sense of security. Although there are no alternative life styles towards which the rebellious may flee, the Abkhasians are ready to absorb others into their own culture. During my visit, for instance, a Christian man was asked to be the godfather of a Moslem child; both prospective godfather and child were Abkhasians. When I expressed surprise, I was told, "It doesn't matter. We want to enlarge our circle of relatives."

The temporal integration of Abkhasian life is expressed in its general continuity, in the absence of limiting, defining conditions of existence like "unemployed," "adolescent," "alienated." Abkhasians are a life-loving, optimistic people, and unlike so many very old "dependent" people in the United States—who feel they are a burden to themselves and their families—they enjoy the prospect of continued life. One 99-year-old Abkhasian, Akhba Suleiman of the village of Achandara, told his doctor, "It isn't time to die yet. I am needed by my children and grandchildren, and it isn't bad in this world—except that I can't turn the earth over and it has become difficult to climb trees."

The old are always active. "It is better to move without purpose than to sit still," they say. Before breakfast, they walk through the homestead's courtyard and orchard, taking care of small tasks that come to their attention. They look for fences and equipment in need of repair and check on the family's animals. At breakfast, their early morning survey completed, they report what has to be done.

Until evening, the old spend their time alternating work and rest. A man may pick up wind-fallen apples, then sit down on a bench, telling stories or making toys for his grandchildren or great-grandchildren. Another chore which is largely attended to by the old is weeding the courtyard, a large green belonging to the homestead, which serves as a center of activity for the kin group. Keeping it in shape requires considerable labor, yet I never saw a courtyard that was not tidy and well-trimmed.

DURING the summer, many old men spend two or three months high in the mountains, living in shepherds' huts, helping to herd or hunting for themselves and the shepherds (with their arrested aging process, many are excellent marksmen despite their age). They obviously are not fearful of losing their authority during their absence; their time in the mountains is useful and pleasurable.

The extraordinary attitude of the Abkhasians—to feel needed at 99 or 110—is not an artificial, self-protective one; it is the natural expression, in old age, of a consistent outlook that begins in childhood. The stoic upbringing of an Abkhasian child, in which parents and senior relatives participate, instills respect, obedience and endurance. At an early age, children participate in household tasks; when they are not at school, they work in the fields or at home.

There are no separate "facts of life" for children and adults: The values given children are the ones adults live by, and there is no hypocritical disparity (as in so many other societies) between adult words and deeds. Since what they are taught is considered important, and the work they are given is considered necessary, children are neither restless nor rebellious. As they mature, there are easy transitions from one status in life to another: a bride, for instance, will stay for a time with her husband's relatives, gradually becoming part of a new clan, before moving into his home.

From the beginning, there is no gap between expectation and experience. Abkhasians expect a long and useful life and look forward to old age with good reason: in a culture which so highly values continuity in its traditions, the old are indispensable in their transmission. The elders preside at important ceremonial occasions, they mediate disputes and their knowledge of farming is sought. They feel needed because, in their own minds and everyone else's, they are. They are the opposite of burdens; they are highly valued resources.

The Abkhasians themselves are obviously right in citing their diet and their work habits as contributing factors in their longevity; in my opinion, their postponed, and later prolonged, sex life probably has nothing to do with it. Their climate is exemplary, the air (especially to a New Yorker) refreshing, but it is not significantly different from many other areas of the world, where life spans are shorter. And while some kind of genetic selectivity may well have been at work, there simply is not enough information to evaluate the genetic factor in Abkhasian longevity.

MY own view is that Abkhasians live as long as they do primarily because of the extraordinary cultural factors that structure their existence: the uniformity and certainty of both individual and group behavior, the unbroken continuum of life's activities—the same games, the same work, the same food, the same self-imposed and socially perceived needs. And the increasing prestige that comes with increasing age.

There is no better way to comprehend the importance of these cultural factors than to consider for a moment some of the prevalent characteristics of American society. Children are sometimes given chores to keep them occupied, but they and their parents know there is no *need* for the work they do; even as adults, only a small percentage of Americans have the privilege of feeling that their work is essential and important. The old, when they do not simply vegetate, out of view and out of mind, keep themselves "busy" with bingo and shuffleboard. Americans are mobile, sometimes frantically so, searching for signs of permanence that will indicate their lives are meaningful.

Can Americans learn something from the Abkhasian view of "long living" people? I think so.

# VII. Psychological and Physical Stress

The problems in functioning that may develop in the later years often have a great impact on the individual, but are usually exacerbated by society's responses. People generally take the attitude toward the aged that nothing can be done about their problems, that they are just old, and what can you expect. Some physicians refer to their older patients as crocks, whereas mental health professionals usually have excluded elderly persons from treatment, even from community mental health centers that are mandated to serve everyone (Kahn, "The Mental Health System and the Future Aged"). This reluctance to treat the old is based on our negative cultural attitude toward aging, and sets up a self-fulfilling prophecy: Because nothing is done for and nothing is expected of the aged, they often do not improve when they otherwise might. This situation is illustrated by the "excess disabilities" that are manifested in institutionalized persons—that is, these individuals give the impression of having greater impairment than is actually present (Kahn, "Excess Disabilities"). As the following articles demonstrate, however, older persons—even those with dramatically debilitating illnesses—can respond and benefit from caring treatment.

A central developmental theme in the later years is that of grief and restitution (Butler). Older persons are vulnerable to losses; for example, the death of a spouse or of friends, declines in health, income, and status. Losses often lead to a sense of despondency and isolation. These feelings can be overcome by working to re-include the older person into the world through listening, giving support, touching, and caring (Burnside; Moustakas; Geba). One exciting direction is the formation of self-help groups that seek to counter stereotypes about aging and to provide alternative lifestyles for the old (Elwell; Kellogg and Jaffe). Even those older persons who are considered senile may either be improperly labeled or have the potential for improvement in functioning, despite the presence of brain disease (Zarit).

Unfortunately, the trend in providing assistance for the elderly has been in the opposite direction—to exclude them from the larger community. Nursing homes have become, more and more, the final home for older persons. While some nursing homes do provide excellent care, others are degrading, humiliating places to live and die (Townsend). Many persons who currently reside in nursing homes may not actually need that level of care (Gottesman and Boureston); but there usually are few supports or services available to maintain an older person in the community or with his or her family. Families are often faced with a terrible choice: keep the person in the home at great emotional or financial sacrifice, or place him or her in a nursing home (Margolius). Greater provision of community services, however, would diminish this dilemma, by offering to the family those services they need to maintain the person in their home and by allowing that individual to live in a familiar, comfortable setting. Community care has been effective in reducing the need for long-term care in other countries and may be the best way to maximize the independence and dignity of even severely impaired individuals (Kahn, "The Mental Health System and the Future Aged"). Successful treatment of many of the problems of aging does not require a major scientific breakthrough, but the application of practices that recognize the worth and potential of older persons.

# 40

## TOWARD A PSYCHIATRY OF THE LIFE-CYCLE: IMPLICATIONS OF SOCIOPSYCHOLOGIC STUDIES OF THE AGING PROCESS FOR THE PSYCHOTHERAPEUTIC SITUATION

ROBERT N. BUTLER, M.D.*

OLD people and children have become increasingly socially visible since the seventeenth century. Augmented survivorship, joined with certain socio-cultural conditions, has "unfolded" the life-cycle, making its stages or phases prominent. Rousseau, Victor Hugo, the Swedish sociologist Ellen Key, and the French historian Philippe Ariès are among those who have emphasized the social and historical evolution of the child in the last two centuries (Ariès, 1962). In this century, old people have grown conspicuous in number and social significance.

The social and psychologic sciences and the professions have not succeeded in keeping pace with these changes. Sociology remains primarily class-conscious (Gordon, 1949). Psychology has demonstrated great interest in child development in this century, but the majority of these studies do not go beyond early adulthood. The life-cycle as a whole, in all its phases, has not been a central preoccupation of the psychologic and social sciences. The mass media seem somewhat more conscious of the significance of age-grading in human affairs, of stages of life, and of inter-generational conflicts (Poppy, 1967; Demography, 1966; Twenty-five and Under, 1967). Medicine, includ-ing psychiatry, has been most fascinated by the younger, attractive, well-paying patients with acute and/or esoteric diseases.

I have no identification with "geriatric psychiatry" per se nor with a "young people's" psychiatry. I am interested in how people live their lives, how they change in the course of time, and how they die. I am particularly inter-ested in the interior subjective experience of the life-cycle, of aging, of changes in the body image and the self-concept ("the changing self"), and of approach-ing death (Butler, 1960; 1963b; 1963c). I would like to see the development of a comprehensive body of knowledge concerning the life-cycle as a whole, its stages, its modes, and the complex interplay of individual life-cycles with socioeconomic, cultural, and historic conditions. I am interested in life-cycle-ology or life-cycle psychiatry.

The paper might have been entitled: "How the concepts of the life-cycle and of historic psychology should be considered in psychotherapy and in social organization." I wish to consider the influences of stage-characteristics, of certain features of middle and later life, upon psychotherapy with old people and upon potential social changes.

Evidence from many sources supports the conclusion that the immediate personal, social, and medical situation significantly influences the adaptation of the aged. Variations in personality and life history help account for the

* Research Psychiatrist and Gerontologist, The Washington School of Psychiatry; Faculty, Washington Psychoanalytic Institute and George Washington University Medical School; Consultant, St. Elizabeths Hospital, Washington, D. C.

lack of uniform effects of personal, social, and medical variables, for example, the impact of widowhood, retirement, and increasing blindness. I assume that characteristics pertinent to stages in the life-cycle also contribute to adaptation. I assume that the degree of realization of these life-cycle stage-characteristics may be influenced by psychotherapy and by the sociocultural situation.

There are many aspects of psychiatric work with the elderly. I have dealt with some of these elsewhere, ranging from technique to countertransference to organic brain disorders in both inpatients and outpatients (Butler, 1960; 1963b; Butler, Dastur, and Perlin, 1965). Here I will concentrate upon psychotherapy with patients having predominantly psychologic problems and functional disorders of old age. I will use my psychotherapeutic work primarily as a source of data about later life rather than as a basis for discussing psychotherapeutic technique or results.

My work with old people, begun in 1955, has ranged from the healthy experimental subject (Birren *et al.*, 1963; Butler, 1963a) to the private office patient to the patient in the more extreme situations of private and state hospitals and nursing homes (Butler, 1960; Butler *et al.*, 1965). In the preparation of this paper I have reviewed my records from the comprehensive and intensive study of 17 hospitalized patients at Chestnut Lodge, 71 patients from private office practice, and 47 community-resident, healthy, aged volunteer research subjects. These samples have been characterized elsewhere (Butler, 1960; 1966; Birren *et al.*, 1963).

GRIEF AND RESTITUTION

Of the many matters that could be discussed respecting psychotherapeutic experience with the aged, I shall begin with the proposition that a fundamental issue of psychotherapy with old people is the problem of death and loss. It is death that sets in motion all the basic questions that must be faced by both the therapist and the old person. What kind of life have I led? What am I to do now, in the face of death? I am referring to psychologic events and not to a moral drama, although for some persons, the latter defines the experience of old age, that is, the resolution of the problem of guilt.

All sociopsychologic studies pertain in some way to the central problem of the relations between the interior psychologic experience of approaching death and the social and cultural conditions that further shape and influence it. However, many sociopsychologic studies tend to approach this essential problem cautiously, dealing with limited or partial aspects of the problem, such as interaction and/or isolation, or morale and life satisfaction (Cumming and Henry, 1961; Neugarten, 1966; Neugarten, Havighurst, and Tobin, 1961; Kutner *et al.*, 1956; Lowenthal, 1965). However, the factor of death has been directly studied by some (Glaser and Strauss, 1965).

In research work with older people and in practice, one sees the problem of death manifest in many different ways. One observes the defensive and adaptive maneuvers that older people undertake, including counterphobic behavior and denial (Birren *et al.*, 1963). Counterphobic behavior may be revealed in the almost obscene efforts of some older people to be young, wearing inappropriate dress and make-up and undertaking a variety of activities unsuitable to their age. One sees old people who cannot bear to look at themselves in a mirror and whose drawings show signs of dissolution despite intact cognitive and psychologic functions (Butler, 1963c).

One finds older people preoccupied by recollections of the aging and death of their own parents and their own fears of possible replication of their parents' experience. On the other hand, some older people make unusual efforts to appear dignified and gracious in the face of illness and death. Through analysis one learns that insomnia may be a fight to stay awake rather than a fight to go to sleep, and thus reflects the fear of death. Fears of death may reach paranoid proportions marked by the belief that medicines are poison, and to the point of misinterpreting aging changes and disease states as the results of external agents (Butler, 1966). Thus, intimations of mortality may be revealed in projection. Fears of death are exploited by business charlatans who play upon the magic wishfulness of old people by quackery and fraud. Hypochondriasis not uncommonly (but not exclusively) expresses concern with death.

It is quite correct that many old people show no direct signs of fear of death. However, one must not conclude, therefore, that the problem of death does not exist for them. One may study the person at a particular stage of his adaptation to the reality of death. In our National Institute of Mental Health sample (Birren *et al.*, 1963), for example, overt fear was present in 30 per cent and denial in 15 per cent. A realistic adjustment to, or the resolution of, the problem of death had occurred in 55 per cent of this healthy sample. Medical diseases, disadvantageous social circumstances, and so forth, may compound the problem. However, if one can imagine the most idealized socioeconomic conditions, the most culturally-enriching circumstances, there would remain the essential question of man's resolution of the issues of his past life when confronted with death.

Case history:

*Chief complaint:* "I can't catch my breath." This is the case of an otherwise fortunate man who was always in a hurry and had eventually to stop to catch his breath.

A sixty-eight-year-old, highly intelligent and intellectual sociologist developed a severe cough upon his return from an extended and exciting journey abroad. An X-ray shadow increased the medical suspicion of a malignancy. Without prior discussion and preparation the patient was inadvertently but directly told this by a secretary arranging his admission for surgery. The operation revealed a lung abscess and the patient responded well physically both to the operative procedure and in the recovery period, with one exception: he could not catch his breath. His internist suggested an extended vacation and later tranquilizers, and gave reassurance. After some months the doctor strongly recommended psychotherapy as he realized the patient was becoming increasingly agitated and depressed without adequate medical explanation. The patient was extremely tense and restless. He appeared somewhat slovenly. His pants hung loose from his suspenders and his fly was partly open. In short, he gave an impression of organic mental disorder but he spoke clearly and well. Despite his obvious gloom, he managed some humor and clarity in giving his present and past history.

His situation was socially and personally favorable. He had a good relationship with a devoted wife. He had many good friends and professional colleagues. He was well regarded professionally. He was under no pressure to retire, and consultancies were open to him. He had a wide range of interests in addition to his professional field. His relationships with his brothers and sisters were good. With the exception of the chief complaint, his physical status was excellent. He believed his physician that there was no major organic disease, that is, he was not suffering from a fear that he was being misled. But despite all of this he was tense and depressed. Recurrent dreams included one in which "a paper was due" and another in which he was "behind in an exam." He had never taken out any life insurance. He had made no conscious admission to himself that he might age. He had made nothing of birthdays. He did not have a very clear concept of the natural evolution of the life-cycle. He did not have a sense of stages and development of middle and later life. He had an enormous capacity for work and had kept busy all his life as though unaware of the passage of time. He had never been bored. He had great capacity for self-discipline and was not given to marked expression of either grief or anger but only to a narrow spectrum of affects, including fearfulness and pleasure. He was a kind of Peter Pan and he and his wife eventually concluded in the course of his psychotherapeutic work that he, and in some measure she, had imagined themselves to remain in their twenties instead of in their late sixties. As he reviewed his life and the realities of aging and death, he became freer in his expression of more negative affects. His depression and tension improved and he had remained well in a follow-up of some six months. He was no longer short of breath.

The problem of death, then, is a central theme of late life, a primary characteristic of this stage of the life-cycle. The problem of death, of course, is divisible into partial deaths or losses or separations or irreversible changes or crises, depending upon how one wishes to describe them. Psychotherapeutic work with older people involves the management of these small deaths, these intimations of mortality. Put succinctly, the psychotherapy of old age is the psychotherapy of grief and of accommodation, restitution, and resolution. "Coming to terms with," "bearing witness," reconciliation, atonement, construction and reconstruction, integration, transcendence, creativity, realistic insight with modifications and substitutions, the introduction of meaning and of meaningful, useful, and contributory efforts: these are among the terms that are pertinent to therapy with older people.

However, one obviously cannot operate in the vacuum of an idealized socioeconomic and medical situation. One must be the physician first of all, treating the patient from the comprehensive viewpoint (Butler, 1963c). When the modifiable, the treatable, has been dealt with, then one is the psychotherapist of grief.

But also of ambiguity. Our society, and the persons immediately around the older person, tend to create situations of ambiguity in order to overcome their own anxiety and because of their wish to help the older person. Thus, in addition to the problem of grief, there is often the problem of ambiguity, of uncertainty, of transition, for example, not knowing whether and not having been told whether a disease exists or not, not being certain one's driver's license will be renewed. Ambiguity may be transmuted into a major stereotypic expectation. Families and society may expect dignified and gracious aging requiring the suppression and delay of grief. In summary, then, there are three concerns: How to live in the present with one's losses, how to account for one's past life, and how to meet death.

One major premise exists in this work and that is the assumption of human elasticity. To put it differently, one must consider the reality of forces toward inner change, toward intrapsychic alterations, making possible accommodation, restitution, and resolution. In this sense, the goal of psychotherapy is to define and seek possibilities. Psychotherapy, conditioned by our culture and conducted by therapists in turn conditioned by our culture, often occurs in an atmosphere of futility. Yet the possibilities for intrapsychic change may be greater in old age than at any other period in life (in the absence of severe organic brain disease). One motive for change is the proximity of death. The patient and the therapist must collaborate in assessing together assets as well as deficits.

Elsewhere I have presented summary tables of the changing internal and external conditions that affect the subjective experience, the behavior, and the adaptation of old people, based on studies at the National Institute of Mental Health, at Chestnut Lodge, and in private practice (Butler, 1966). A person may attain old age and die without any losses—personal losses, such as widowhood, as well as social and economic losses—but this is extremely unlikely. Kramer (1965), for instance, has indicated the importance of widowhood to the development of psychopathology and to psychiatric hospital admission in old age. There is a meshing of the social and the personal—it is conflictual retirement or conflictual widowhood that is important. Mysterious but still obscure aging-changes, in addition to physical disease, add their losses.

Personality profoundly shapes the experience of old age. Despite many writings to the contrary, however, the generalization that personality characteristics are accentuated or exaggerated with age is a poor one. In fact, certain personality features mellow or entirely disappear. Others prove insulating and protective, although they might formerly have been impairing, such as a schizoid disposition (Birren *et al.*, 1963).

I began by referring to the changing historic conception of the life-cycle.

History is pertinent in two respects: first, with respect to the variation over time in the status and roles of old people; and, second, with respect to the way in which his own era influences the older person. Barbara Tuchman's *The Proud Tower* and Frederick Lewis Allen's *The Big Change* give one a sense of the impact of historic experience upon older people. Our work as psychotherapists, our understanding of the patient, is much enhanced by our effort to empathize with the historic era through which the older person has passed. Presently-living old people have experienced more profound and a greater number of social and technologic changes than probably any other generation.

History shows itself also in the language of old people. Certain euphemisms such as "delicate condition" or "limbs," are heard; "machines" may be used in place of cars and "marketing" may occur instead of shopping, and so forth. But we are concerned not only with such historic and cultural variations in language but with idiosyncratic psychodynamic translations in language that are relevant to age. For instance, an older person's seemingly unfounded fear of going blind may be translated as a subjective concern that he has been blind to significant experiences and feelings throughout his life.

We need a historic psychology or paleo-psychiatry pertinent to our considerations of the psychologic development of man over his life-cycle. The nineteenth century virtues of conscientiousness and ambitiousness have become represented in the twentieth century under the term compulsiveness, as a pejorative. Fletcherism, ptomaine poisoning, Lactobacillus bulgar, focal infections, laxatives, are some of the special features of the medical-cultural heritage to be found in the language of the elderly.

Historic and other variables may blend. For instance, relocation through urban renewal may adversely affect a particular individual, who may have a personal reaction to being removed from the familiar immediate structure. And it is not uncommon today to see a person in his sixties grieving over the death of his parents (whose long survival was the result of medical advances, a historical variable).

Table I suggests several features salient to survival, that is, anti-obsolescence. Heredity is beyond individual human control, but other variables are subject

TABLE I. Features Salient to Survival: Anti-Obsolescence

| Features | Positive Pole | Negative Pole |
|---|---|---|
| 1. Biologic Survival (Heredity; Disease; Accident) | Health | Illness |
| 2. Energy (Psycho-physical) | Activity Level* | Quiescence |
| 3. Life-enhancing Attitude (Berenson) | Vitality* (Liveliness) | Inertia (Early Senility) |
| 4. Affirmation (Adaptiveness) | Resourcefulness (Modifiability) (Complexity) | Resignation |
| 5. Centrality (Center of Forces) | Power (Usefulness) | Powerlessness (Uselessness) |
| 6. Interpersonal Responsiveness | Self-Revelation (Candor) | Reticence |
| 7. Intimacy (Mutuality) | Affiliation (Bonds) | Loneliness (Isolation) |
| 8. Changeableness (Wish to change identity) (Forces of Contra-Identity) | Sense of Possibility (Incompleteness) | Closure (Completeness) |
| 9. Renewal Function | Self-Education (Autodidacticism) | Obsolescence |

* Activity and Vitality are not synonymous; quiescent vitality and inert activity are not uncommon.

to varying degrees of individual and social influence—for example, chronic cigarette smoking, accidents, and disease, not to mention suicide and war. There is an old adage—we do not die; we kill ourselves.

The features numbered 4-9 are of a psychosocial character and derive from the National Institute of Mental Health study (Butler, 1967) and from observations in the course of psychotherapy. In the table, the positive pole represents a possible goal of psychotherapy.

Much is made of the wish to maintain a sense of identity. Little attention has been paid to the wish to change identity, to preserve and exercise the sense of possibility and incompleteness against a sense of closure and completeness. This emphasis is not in contradiction to Erikson's concept of a maintenance of the sense of identity as critical to health. This concept implies process and not status.

There has been some disagreement in the literature concerning education as a significant force in maintaining the mental health of older people. Goldfarb and his associates (Pollack, Kahn, and Goldfarb, 1958), for example, found education to be important. On the other hand, in our NIMH sample, where the range of health and education was narrow, education did not carry any significant weight (Birren *et al.*, 1963). I suggest that the important variable may be not formal education per se as measured by the number of years or even by the quality of education, but rather the extent to which the individual becomes capable of a continuing self-education process.

## PSYCHOLOGIC ISSUES IN LATER LIFE

Table II delineates some features observed to be salient in late life and to the resolution of the problem of death or the contraction of futurity. These features are believed to contribute to the behavior of old people along with the immediate situation of losses described above and the past history of the

TABLE II. FEATURES SALIENT TO LATE LIFE AND THE RESOLUTION OF THE PROBLEM OF DEATH (THE CONTRACTION OF FUTURITY)

| Features and Issues | Positive Pole | Negative Pole |
| --- | --- | --- |
| Legacy (Forwardness) | Continuity (Historicity) (Relation to "benign indifference to the universe") Succession; Organ Legacy | Discontinuity (Absence of Sense of Life-Cycle and Posterity) |
| Elder Function (Direct Transmission) | Counseling (Teaching; Sponsoring) | Withholding (Nothing to Offer) |
| Autobiographic Process | "Life Review" | Denial |
| Serenity | Sense of Value of Time | Time Panic Boredom |
| Attachment to Objects (Memorial; Orientation) | Familiarity | Unfamiliarity Wish for Permanence Collecting; Hoarding |
| Presentness (Immediacy) | Surprise (Sense of Wonder; Expectation) | Disillusionment (Cynicism) |
| Perspective | Acknowledgement (Innocence) (Authenticity) | Imposture (Pretense) |
| Identity* | Generativity | Self-Absorption (Stagnation) |
| Identity* | Integrity | Despair (Hopelessness) |

* These dimensions are based on Eriksonian concepts of identity.

individual. It is likely that these features interrelate with each other. Their relative importance varies from individual to individual, and they are not automatically fulfilled qualities; rather they reflect potentialities. It is undecided whether these features are to be regarded primarily as psychobiologic or as acquired psychosocial characteristics.

Mark Twain, bitter and despairing in his old age, said that the future does not worry about us, so why should we worry about the future? However, it would appear that the older person who does show concern about the future tends toward greater psychologic health. Here again, the positive pole represents a possible goal of psychotherapy. Legacy, for example, is not only a theoretic notion but also may be illustrated practically. A businessman finds it difficult to "let go" and retire, despite increasingly incapacitating physical and perhaps mental changes. He must be helped to acknowledge these changes and to collaborate in setting up appropriate succession within his firm. The alternative would be continued denial of his waning capacities and a willful, angry insistence upon his ability to run the firm himself—even if it means "running it into the ground." A sense of continuity following the successful development of a mechanism of succession is infinitely more free of anxiety and despair than is the feeling of discontinuity.

In passing, one may make an important clinical point. At times one will see an older person who suddenly has received a prescription from a doctor or a spouse to quit a job or to retire before methods of succession have been established or before new plans have been laid out by or for the individual. In such circumstances, it may be much wiser to introduce partial and gradual retirement or to take a leave of absence rather than to undertake a sudden and complete change.

Those older people who exercise what I have called the "elder function" also appear to experience less despair and anxiety. These persons participate directly in counseling, teaching, sponsoring, consulting—carrying out functions that only older people with their accumulated experience and knowledge can carry out. One also can make a point concerning technique. When the patient feels that the doctor is learning from him, there is considerable therapeutic benefit, providing this is not a contrived strategy.

The "autobiographic process" manifests itself in many ways throughout the life-cycle, at times reflecting predominantly self-analytic or introspective qualities, at other times suggesting a need for self-documentation. The daily journal or diary is distinctly different from the retrospective memoir. I have proposed elsewhere that with old age comes the inauguration of a process I have called the life review (Butler, 1963b), which is "prompted by the realization of approaching dissolution and death" and "characterized by the progressive return to consciousness of past experiences, and, particularly the resurgence of unresolved conflicts," which can be "surveyed and reintegrated," and if successfully reintegrated, can give "new significance and meaning to one's life" and "prepare one for death, mitigating one's fears." I have found this naturally occurring process to be useful and central in my psychotherapeutic work, and harness it to that end. Etigson and Tobin (1966) have pursued the life review concept and found that "in spite of remarkable thematic consistency in reminiscences, changes were found which were related to current life stress." They are further studying how the "qualities of the life review . . . covary with adaptation." Gorney, of the Committee on Human Development, University of Chicago, has found an increased and intense introspection in later life that appears to wane again after the early seventies (Personal Communication). The life review process may not be apparent unless one becomes involved in an intensive, inquiring, psychoanalytically-oriented relationship. Defensive and selective denial may be prevalent. One underlying question is that of King Lear: "Who is it that can tell me who I am?"

Man lives by the calendar, the more so as he ages. Old people tend to come early for their psychotherapeutic sessions and to be concerned about time and schedules. This may or may not have any bearing on the pre-existence of obsessional-compulsive behavior. At times one may see frank "time panics." Some older people report boredom or the experience of time being heavy upon their hands. These subjective states do not relate exclusively to clinical depression, but do express a connection with the use of one's time in the proximity of death. In the course of therapy it is striking when the individual begins to show both tranquility and an increasing sense of the value of time.

The attachment to objects that is seen with age has a memorial function and contributes to the maintenance of orientation. Such familiarity is not to be confused, however, with an undue and pathologic collecting mania or need to hoard. The latter symptom may be present at any point in the life-cycle although it is somewhat more frequent in old age and is connected with fears of ruin and of loss that, again psychodynamically, often relate to the fear of death. The presence of objects with which one is familiar is orienting, comforting, and pleasurable. Pets can be most important to old people.

An immediacy or sense of presentness is very important. Goethe, at eighty, said that he was still capable of being surprised. A sense of wonder and expectation counters the possibility of disillusionment and cynicism. Apparently related is the sense of perspective, of appropriate acknowledgement rather than pretense or imposture. This is an important clinical point. It can be unfortunate if the psychotherapist tends to invoke inappropriately the *deus ex machina* of "irrational guilt." It is to the benefit of the patient if he can acknowledge any specific acts hurtful to others whether by commission or omission. It can, of course, be easy for the patient to fall into global self-condemnation that may dilute the specific issue(s). This defense should be openly handled.

Erikson (1963) was among the first of the psychoanalysts to make an effort to delineate the life-cycle as a whole. With respect to the middle-aged, Erikson has emphasized generativity and integrity.

Middle age is the fulcrum or working center of the younger and older generations. Table III, like my other tables, is offered tentatively, as an effort to hypothesize issues of heightened significance in the latter half of the life-cycle. These formulations derive from reviewing the material of 40 office patients aged forty to sixty years.

While in old age the autobiographic process appears to manifest itself as the life review, in middle age it has the quality of stocktaking, in which a greater opportunity to consider possibilities, alternatives, and the organization of commitments occurs. The other possibilities are closure and fatalism on the one hand, or an over-expansiveness on the other.

Fidelity appears as a critical element in mid-life. Fidelity refers to the testing of personal, professional, and other commitments. In adolescence one is concerned about the hypocrisy of others; in middle age with one's own; and in old age with neither or both. The problem of hypocrisy on the one hand and of self-deception on the other are the negative alternatives to the test. To my mind, this problem of fidelity underlies and includes the narrower question of marital fidelity. The latter is frequent in middle age and its nature is insightfully described in Tolstoy's *Anna Karenina*. Indeed, Konstantine Levin, a principal character, struggled with social fidelity. Levin's situation occupies a large part of this book and is as important as Anna's affair.

Naturalness in the handling of the relation of growing and dying is another critical issue in middle life. The man may begin to envy his son's increasing sexuality; the middle-aged woman, or man, may make obscene or phrenetic

## TABLE III. FEATURES SALIENT TO MIDDLE LIFE

| Issues | Positive Pole | Negative Pole |
|---|---|---|
| Stock-Taking | Possibility; Alternatives Organization of Commitments | Closure; Fatalism |
| Fidelity | Commitment to Self, Others, Career | Hypocrisy Self-Deception |
| Growth-Death (To Grow is to Die) (Juvenescence and Rejuvenation Phantasies) | Naturality | Obscene or Phrenetic Efforts (e.g. to be youthful) Hostility and Envy toward Youth and Progeny; Longing |
| Credulity | Ego-Beliefs Profound Realistic Convictions | "The True Believer" Right (Past) or Left (Future) Radicalism (e.g. Eric Hoffer) |
| Simplification { of Persons Conservation { Time Settling-In { Place | Centrality { of Specification { Relationships, Rootedness { Places and { Ideas | Diffusion Confusion |
| Communication Complexity (Cues) | Abbreviation: "Matters Understood" Continuity: "Picking up where left Off" | Repetitiveness Boredom Impatience |
| "Prime of Life" | Maturity-Process Productivity | "Winner-Loser" |

efforts to be youthful. Hostility toward and envy of youth may come to a head. Some people with the "Peter Pan problem" detest aging because it means symbolically the murder of the parent, that is, for oneself to grow, the parent must die. Phantasies of rejuvenation and juvenescence may be more frequent than is recognized.

The evolution of deep convictions or ego beliefs rather than stereotyped and fanatic beliefs is another central problem in middle life. Eric Hoffer's class of "true believers," either to the right or to the left, is indicative of the negative alternatives. Other features concern the reduction of communication complexity, a point emphasized by Bernice L. Neugarten, and the further simplification of living. Finally, middle age is often viewed as the "prime of life." In its best sense, it is a period of maturity and productivity but it is also the period in which preoccupations with being a "winner" or "loser" can have a harsh and phrenetic edge.

One "stage" of life is "mobile." Contemporary idiom refers to the "teeny-bopper" who is "in," "with it." A "teeny-bopper" can be eleven or twelve, that is, a pubescent "going on twenty," or can be a middle-aged forty-year-old, "going on twenty." This point is made to remind us of the still far from decisive delineation of the issues and features of the life-cycle. How many of these "stages" are "mobile" because they are in part the consequences of social, cultural, and historical conditions remains a relevant question.

### DISCUSSION

Before making a final summary statement, I will touch upon the range and limits of psychotherapy with older people, and suggest some sociopsychologic research that would be of great value to the psychotherapist.

No intensive psychotherapeutic units for aged patients existed when we established one at Chestnut Lodge in 1958 (Butler, 1960). Here, intensive psychotherapy was employed that was defined as individual, insight-oriented psychotherapy involving up to four or five sessions a week with patients in residence in a psychotherapeutically-oriented milieu. Also, my private office practice derives principally from a psychoanalytically-oriented position.

However, over the years, I have dealt with a wide range of older patients and have employed an equally wide range of approaches. The range of problems met and the development of various strategies and techniques in psychotherapy and in the general management of psychiatric problems of later life will be the subject of another paper.

However, psychotherapy and the psychiatric treatment of the aged is a "drop in the bucket," considering the major problems that confront people in old age. Psychiatry cannot possibly cope with the accumulated problems of an entire individual life time, despite the typically American belief in total cure, nor can psychiatry begin to play a significant role in overcoming the enormous social problems that older people face. Indeed, we must be careful that a Gresham's law does not evolve in community psychiatry wherein bad psychiatry drives out good psychiatry. We need all kinds of first aid efforts and measures in our work with older people in the community, but these are slight, indeed, and await more fundamental social, cultural, and economic changes. Poverty among the aged remains an enormous problem, for a prime example. Society requires remodeling, balancing the requirements of each stage of the life-cycle and extending beyond purely economic considerations. For instance, age discrimination in employment is tied to the problem of economic productivity. Our social system is economically rather than comprehensively and humanistically oriented. A humanistic social reorganization would be likely to include programs of continuing education throughout the life-cycle. A portfolio of possibilities should exist to meet the many exigencies of the stages of the life-cycle.

It is interesting to speculate upon the kinds of sociopsychologic research that would aid the psychotherapist in his work. Certainly, the social processes involved in succession, which we discussed earlier, would be very helpful. For instance, one wishes for further understanding of the most appropriate timing for the increasing delegation of authority and the final giving up of control to a successor. Consideration of mechanisms other than those of consultancies and appointments as chairmen of the board would be useful.

The problem of relocation, transplantation, or geographic mobility is an important one (Aleksandrowicz, 1961; Lieberman, 1961). It would be interesting to compare the effects of various living arrangements of the elderly according to their association with death ("the last stop," *etc.*). Other studies, pertaining to integration within the life-cycle, are indicated (Rosow, 1961). The memorial function, orientation, is important to problems of housing and moving.

A major problem is the social usefulness of older people. Social psychologists could contribute immeasurably by studying voluntary agencies and determining how to identify factors conducive to and impeding the appropriate utilization of the various skills and "stage" characteristics of older people; this is the matter of the logistic matching of skills with social needs. Studies of the usefulness and the problems of older people in Vista and the Peace Corps would be pertinent. It is surprising how often one will see someone with a Ph.D., with intact intellectual functioning, licking stamps for a charitable agency. Recent interest in the Swedish legal development of the Ombudsman leads one to pause and wonder if certain qualified older citizens might not make excellent Ombudsmen (Gellhorn, 1966). The older person has the accumulated experience and the leisure and he is comparatively free from worldly competition.

Critics of studies of the outcome of psychotherapy repeatedly refer to the need for information concerning the natural course of disorders for purposes of control. We need, in fact, data on the natural courses of lives. Studies of lives, the examination of the differential durability of the emotions, the characteristics and processes of change (Group for the Advancement of Psychiatry, 1966) and irreversibility, are all necessary. Major stereotypes still exist regarding the early fixity and stability of character, the resistance to change, and the time required to change; these are interrelated but all pertain directly to the understanding of the life-cycle as a whole and of late life in particular.

## FINAL NOTE

Solon, the Greek lawgiver, said that no man could consider his life happy until it was over. And Nietzche stated, "that which does not kill me makes me stronger." This is a sensitive aspect of the psychotherapeutic situation and most certainly of the situation of old age. An increasing awareness on the part of both the patient and the therapist of aspects of survival and of adaptation to it are important. Obviously, the therapist, too, must be prepared to survive the painful losses of his older patients.

The therapist must not in any way be destructive to the processes of illusion and denial needed by his patients. One must discuss the fact of death, the facts of loss, the problems of grief, but always in the context of possibilities, restitution, and resolution. The same principle applies in work with older people as applies in work with patients of all ages: one must work compassionately and carefully to get behind the defenses rather than to attack them overtly As Dr. Relding said, in Ibsen's *The Wild Duck*, "Rob the average man of his life-illusion, and you rob him of his happiness at the same stroke."

In this paper, I have drawn upon my psychotherapeutic and research studies of middle-aged and older persons to suggest certain features as characteristic of the stages of later life. The subjective experience, behavior, and adaptation of people at any age depend upon the degree of fulfillment of the stage-characteristics as well as upon the immediate situation and past history (including personality structure). With old age come increasing losses and the reality of death. Psychotherapeutic and social efforts must both emphasize the possibilities of the present and deal with grief. Because of the wide variation in personalities, individualization must be considered in any planned alterations of social institutions just as it is in psychotherapy. Life-stage features, on the other hand, being universal, offer the psychotherapist and society broad guidelines for useful intervention on behalf of the elderly. How would the social and personal situation of the elderly differ if such needs as those for continuity, familiarity, and usefulness were more effectively met in our culture?

## References

ALEKSANDROWICZ, D. R. 1961. Fire and its aftermath on a geriatric ward. Bull. Menn. Clin., **25**:23-32.

ARIÈS, P. 1962. Centuries of Childhood. A Social History of Family Life. Trans. by R. Baldick. New York: Alfred A. Knopf.

BIRREN, J. E., BUTLER, R. N., GREENHOUSE, S. W., SOKOLOFF, L., and YARROW, M. 1963. Human Aging: A Biological and Behavioral Study. Public Health Service Publication Number 986. Washington, D. C.: Government Printing Office.

BUTLER, R. N. 1967. Aspects of survival and adaptation in human aging. Amer. J. Psychiat., **123**:1233-1243.

BUTLER, R. N. 1963a. The facade of chronological age: An interpretative summary. Amer. J. Psychiat., **119**:721-728.

BUTLER, R. N. 1960. Intensive psychotherapy for the hospitalized aged. Geriatrics, **15**:644-653.

BUTLER, R. N. 1963b. The life review: An interpretation of reminiscence in the aged. Psychiatry, 26:65-76.

BUTLER, R. N. 1963c. Psychiatric evaluation of the aged. Geriatrics, 18:220-232.

BUTLER, R. N. 1967. Research and clinical observations on the psychological reactions to physical changes with age. Mayo Clin. Proc. 42:596-619.

BUTLER, R. N., DASTUR, D. K., and PERLIN, S. 1965. Relationships of senile manifestations and chronic brain syndromes to cerebral circulation and metabolism. J. Psychiat. Res., 3:229-238.

CUMMING, E. and HENRY, W. E. 1961. Growing Old: The Process of Disengagement. New York: Basic Books.

DEMOGRAPHY. The Command Generation. 1966. Time, 88:50-54 (July 29).

ERIKSON, E. H. 1963. Childhood and Society. New York: W. W. Norton, 2nd ed.

ETIGSON, E. C. and TOBIN, S. S. 1966. Effects of stress on reminiscence in the aged. Paper presented at the American Psychological Association meeting, New York, New York, September.

GELLHORN, W. 1966: Ombudsmen and Others; Citizens' Protectors in 9 Countries. Cambridge: Harvard University Press.

GLASER, B. G. and STRAUSS, A. L. 1965. Awareness of Dying. Chicago: Aldine Publishing Co.

GORDON, M. M. 1949. Social class in American sociology. Amer. J. Sociol. 55:262-268.

GROUP FOR THE ADVANCEMENT OF PSYCHIATRY. 1966. Psychiatric Research and the Assessment of Change. Report Number 63. New York: Group for the Advancement of Psychiatry.

KRAMER, M. 1965. Trends in the usage of psychiatric facilities by the aged and their implications for community mental health programs and related research. Mimeographed.

KUTNER, B. D., FANSHEL, A. M., and LANGNER, T. S. 1956. Five Hundred Over Sixty. New York: Russell Sage Foundation.

LIEBERMAN, M. A. 1961. The relationship of mortality rates to entrance to a home for the aged. Geriatrics, 16:515-519.

LOWENTHAL, M. F. 1965. Antecedents of isolation and mental illness in old age. Arch. Gen. Psychiat., 12:245-254.

NEUGARTEN, B. L. 1966. Adult personality: Toward a psychology of the life cycle. Paper presented at the American Psychological Association meeting, New York, New York, September.

NEUGARTEN, B. L., HAVIGHURST, R. J., and TOBIN, S. S. 1961. The measurement of life satisfaction. J. Gerontol., 16:134-143.

POLLACK, M., KAHN, R. C., and GOLDFARB, A. I. 1958. Factors related to individual differences in perception in institutionalized aged subjects. J. Gerontol 13:192-197.

POPPY, J. 1967. The generation gap. Look, 31:26-32 (February 21).

ROSOW, I. 1961. Retirement housing and social integration. The Gerontologist, 1:85-91.

TWENTY-FIVE AND UNDER. The inheritor. 1967. Time, 89:18-23 (January 6).

# 41

# Organic Brain Syndromes

**by Steven H. Zarit**

Perhaps the most common assumption about older persons is that they have become, or are in the process of becoming "senile," and that, therefore, little can be done for them. Behavior problems that occur are often viewed as "senile" manifestations, with other causes and the possibility for treatment overlooked. Despite this stereotype, development of senility or "chronic brain disease," does not seem to be an intrinsic part of the aging process and it is not a condition affecting all older persons. The type of brain damage that leads to senility and senile behavior, such as extreme forgetfulness and inability to perform simple cognitive tasks, actually is found only among approximately 5% of the population of persons over 65. (Busse, 1973) The incidence of brain changes seems to increase with age, but many persons do live to 100 years or more without experiencing the dramatic decline associated with senile brain disease.

There are two processes of change that may occur in the brain as one grows older. (Kay, 1972) The first might be termed *expected* or *normal age changes*, and involves a continuous loss of functioning brain neurons over the adult years. Unlike other body cells, neurons do not reproduce after the early formative years. When a cell is damaged or dies, it is not replaced. In addition, there are other irreversible changes in the structure of brain tissue that occur over time. (Vogel, 1969) These changes, of themselves, do not lead to the massive cognitive deficits that characterize senile behavior. In fact, other than leading to a slowing in reaction time, the relation of these changes to behavior is uncertain and may vary from person to person. For most, the impact of this decline may be minimal, except, perhaps, under particularly stressful circumstances (Zarit and Kahn, 1975).

When persons do experience the dramatic behavior changes found with senility, more extensive brain damage is almost always present (Malamud, 1965; Blessed, et al. 1968; Kay, 1972). This damage may result in some instances from a specific disease process, such as arteriosclerosis, heart disease or a cerebrovascular accident. In other cases, extensive deterioration including deaths of large numbers of brain cells, occurs in an individual, with the cause of this decline unknown at this time. While this type of damage may represent a speeding up of the normal aging process, some research has pointed to a process that is qualitatively different from normal aging that may have a viral or genetic origin (Busse, 1973).

Two older persons, then, might be quite different in the degree of brain dysfunction that is present, with one individual having only minimal decline while another manifests these extensive, senile changes. Most older persons do not show this second type of change to any great extent. In other words, senility is not a common state in old age, and may not even be an inevitable outcome of aging.

### Organic Brain Syndromes

While most older persons are not and will never become senile, organic brain syndromes are a significant problem for a minority. An important distinction must be made between *acute, or,* what Butler and Lewis (1973) term "reversible," *brain syndrome*, and *chronic brain syndrome*, which corresponds to what is commonly referred to as senility.

There is considerable misunderstanding of the nature of behavior changes that occur with organic brain syndromes. In practice, acute and chronic syndromes are sometimes confused with one another, or "senility" is diagnosed when none is present. Older persons often are labeled as having chronic brain syndrome because of some action such as momentary forgetfulness or apparently inappropriate or disorganized behavior. Common incidents, such as losing one's way in a complicated building, forgetting where one put something, or even repeating the same stories or questions, can occur at any age and do not necessarily indicate chronic brain syndrome. There are, however, significant types of cognitive deficits that occur with organic brain syndromes, which, if assessed, give a valid indicator of whether brain dysfunction is present. These cognitive changes are usually manifested in responses to simple orientation and information questions, such as in the Mental Status Questionnaire. This type of structured assessment is important for two reasons: to rule out the presence of an organic brain syndrome in those cases

## Mental Status Questionnaire[1]

1. Where are you now? (What place is this? What is it called?)
2. Where is it located? (What is the address?)
3. What is the date today? Day?
4. What month is it?
5. What year is it?
6. How old are you?
7. When were you born? Month?
8. Year of birth?
9. Who is the president of the United States?
10. Who was the president before him?

What is your main trouble? (Why did you come here?)

Have you ever been in another (place with same name)?

Have you ever seen me before?

What do I do? (What is my job called).

Where were you last night?

1. Modified from Kahn, R. L. et al. Brief objective measures for the determination of mental status in the aged. *American Journal of Psychiatry*, 117: 326–28, 1960.

where it is mistakenly thought to occur, and to evaluate instances in which there is an acute condition which may be reversible, if properly treated.

The specific behavior changes that are seen with an acute brain syndrome involve answering questions, such as those in the Mental Status Questionnaire, in a different symbolic context than they are asked. The question "Where are you?" or "What is my job called?" are factual—that is, they have right or wrong answers. The person with an acute brain syndrome does not try to give the correct answer and instead responds metaphorically (Weinstein and Kahn, 1955; Weinstein, et al., 1964). A person who is in a hospital may say he is in a hotel, retirement home, or repair shop. If shown sheets or towels that have the hospital name printed on them, he may maintain that the linen must have gotten there by mistake. Often, these responses deny one's current problems or difficulties. Other responses of this nature include placing the location of the hospital in a different part of town, stating one was in another hospital with the same name, fabricating a journey (as when a person states he had been somewhere other than where he actually was on the previous night), or identifying the interviewer as a person having a function not connected to hospitals or mental health. Other behavioral changes that may occur with an acute brain syndrome include paranoid delusions and inappropriate sexual behavior.

The type of metaphorical language that characterizes an acute brain syndrome may also be present when there is extensive chronic brain damage. The distinction between these two conditions can be made on the basis of history: whether the behavior changes have been of sudden onset or the result of a long, insidious process. This type of metaphorical language is usually not seen in persons with functional psychoses.

An acute brain syndrome can be brought on by incidents that lead to permanent damage, including brain tumors, cerebrovascular accidents (strokes), or severe head injuries. Many transient conditions, however, may provoke this problem, for example, toxic reactions to medications, malnutrition and somatic infections (Butler and Lewis, 1973). Sometimes even stressful events, for example relocation into an unfamiliar setting such as a hospital or nursing home, may cause an acute brain syndrome, as indicated in the case of Mrs. C. When the causal agent is removed or treated, the person usually returns to his or her previous level of functioning. Often, the behavioral changes are dramatic, with a disorganized, delusional patient becoming a functioning, capable person. Unfortunately, persons with an acute brain syndrome are sometime inappropriately diagnosed as senile or schizophrenic. Their real problem, then, may go untreated.

With chronic brain syndrome, there is difficulty in performing cognitive tasks, especially those involving memory and new learning. The difficulties are usually so pronounced that simple information, such as that elicited by the Mental Status Questionnaire, can differentiate between intact and impaired brain function. In contrast to an acute brain syndrome, persons with chronic brain syndrome do try to answer these questions in the same conceptual framework, but cannot provide the information. They may not know the hospital name, or will give the wrong name, or the wrong date, or say that they do not know. The criterion for diagnosing chronic brain disease is making three or more errors on the Mental Status Questionnaire (Kahn, et al., 1961). While anyone might, on a given day, not know the date or miss one of the other items, it almost never happens that a person with intact brain function will miss three questions. The scores on this type of test have been found to correlate highly with direct measurements of the degree of cerebral atrophy such as in postmortem examination or computerized temography, an x-ray procedure to assess brain damage (Blessed, et al., 1968; Nathan and Gonzalez, 1975; Kazniak, et al., 1975).

Unlike acute brain disease, chronic brain syndrome is not reversible. There have been attempts to modify the behavior of persons with this problem, but they have not succeeded. One approach, Reality Orientation, involves frequently telling patients the answers to the items on the Mental Status Questionnaire, such as what the date is. This procedure ignores the fact that the reason for cognitive difficulties is an underlying substrata of brain damage, which does not change whether the person knows the correct answer or not. In fact, little improvement on test scores has been demonstrated in controlled studies in which this procedure has been used. A second approach has been the use of hyperbaric oxygen treatment. This procedure involves inhaling a mixture of air with a higher-than-normal concentration of oxygen. Underlying this approach is the hypothesis that increased concentration of oxygen in the brain will improve the efficiency of brain functioning. While potentially promising, this technique has been shown to be ineffective in improving mental impairment in persons with chronic brain syndrome (Goldfarb, et al., 1972; Thompson, et al., 1976).

While no successful treatment exists once chronic brain syndrome occurs, a preventive approach for

## Acute Brain Syndrome

Mrs. C was a 77-year-old woman who had been an active, hard-driving person all her life. Despite limited formal education, she had managed to achieve a position of status through community and cultural activities, which she had maintained up to the present. Approximately four months prior to being evaluated psychologically, she broke her leg in a fall and was hospitalized for rehabilitation. She made good progress but fell again, this time fracturing her hip. She was now facing the prospect of a few additional months in the hospital, largely confined to bed. She lived with her son, who wanted to take her home, but was uncertain he could manage while she was still disabled.

Though up to this point she had been a model patient, a pyschological consultation was called because she mentioned to a nurse she felt like jumping out the window. She was initially interviewed on a Friday afternoon. When interviewed she correctly identified the hospital but stated she had been in another hospital with the same name that was a few blocks away. (No such hospital existed.) She further incorrectly identified the year and her age and reported a confabulated journey, that she had been in another place the previous evening. She also made many errors on a battery of other memory tests, and was positive on the Face-Hand test. The latter is a neuropsychological assessment of perception of stimuli that are applied simultaneously to the cheek and hand, and which reliably indicates the presence of brain dysfunction if persistent errors are made (Kahn, et al., 1961).

Mrs. C was interviewed again the following Monday. Before the interview, however, a treatment plan had been worked out with her son, so that she would be able to go home at the end of the week and receive continued therapy on an outpatient basis. She had been informed of this decision. When retested on Monday afternoon, she gave no evidence of symbolic or other errors on the Mental Status Questionnaire, made no errors on the Face-Hand test, and performed significantly better on other memory procedures. Her improvement after this episode was unimpeded.

This example illustrates the reversible nature of an acute brain syndrome. While often precipitated by illness or medications, in this case the only apparent cause was the stress of facing a potentially long-term hospitalization. Mrs. C's functioning returned to normal when the stress was alleviated.

arteriosclerosis, hypertension, and related difficulties might reduce the incidence of brain damage among the old. The presence of chronic brain syndrome, however, does not mean that there is nothing more that can be done for an individual. While the extent of brain damage usually correlates with overall functioning (Kahn, et al., 1961), there are some individual differences in adapting. Some persons who manifested few behavioral deficits have been found in postmortem examinations to have suffered extensive brain damage (Blessed et al., 1968). Personality factors may account for these differences. In one study, for example, persons who denied their illness showed greater difficulties in functioning than nondeniers who had incurred the same degree of brain damage (Zarit and Kahn, 1974). Persons with chronic brain syndrome who are depressed or who manifest other disturbances can make positive, though limited, gains in response to a caring relationship, and in some instances to psychotherapy (Butler, 1960).

### References

Blessed, G., Tomlinson, B. E., and Roth, Martin., The association between quantitative measures of dementia and of senile change in the cerebral gray matter of elderly subjects. BRITISH JOURNAL OF PSYCHIATRY, 1968, *114*, 797–811.

Busse, E. W. Mental disorders in later life—organic brain syndromes. In E. W. Busse and E. Pfeiffer (eds.), MENTAL ILLNESS IN LATER LIFE. Washington, D.C. American Psychiatric Association, 1973.

Butler, R. N., Intensive psychotherapy for the hospitalized age. GERIATRICS, 1960, *15*, 644–53.

Butler, R. N. and Lewis M. I. AGING AND MENTAL HEALTH, St. Louis: Mosby, 1973.

Goldfarb, A. E., Hochstadt, N. J., Jacobson, J. H., II., Weinstein, E. A., Hyperbaric oxygen treatment of organic mental syndrome in aged persons. JOURNAL OF GERONTOLOGY, 1972, *27*, 212–17.

Kaszniak, A. W., Garron, D. C., and Fox, J. H. Mental status questionnaire scores, short-term memory and cerebral atrophy as measured by computerized temography. Paper presented at the Gerontological Society, Louisville, Ky., 1975.

Kay, D. W. K. Epidemiological aspects of organic brain disease in the aged. In C. M. Gaitz, (ed.), AGING AND THE BRAIN. N. Y., Plenum Press, 1972.

Malamud, N., A comparative study of the neuropathological findings in senile psychoses and in "normal" senility. JOURNAL OF AMERICAN GERIATRICS SOCIETY, 1965, *13*, 113–117.

Nathan, R. J. and Gonzalez, C. Correlations between computerized transaxial tomography (C.T.T.) and the extent of dementia. Paper presented at the meeting of the American Gerontological Society, Louisville, Kentucky. 1975.

Thompson, L., Davis, G. C., Obrist, W. D., and Heyman, A. Effects of hyperbaric oxygen on behavioral and physiological measures in elderly demented patients. JOURNAL OF GERONTOLOGY, 1976.

Vogel, F. S. The brain and time. In E. W. Busse and E. Pfeiffer (eds.), BEHAVIOR AND ADAPTATION IN LATE LIFE. Boston, Little, Brown, 1969.

Weinstein, E. A., Cole, M., Mitchell, M. S., and Lyerly, O. G., Anosognosia and aphasia. ARCHIVES OF NEUROLOGY, 1964, *10*, 576–586.

Zarit, S. H. and Kahn, R. L. Aging and adaptation to illness. JOURNAL OF GERONTOLOGY, 1975, *30*, 67–72.

# 42

# Excess Disabilities in the Aged

**by Robert L. Kahn**

Recently there has been a good deal of discussion about aspects of behavior related to brain damage. We have found that one of the most common prevailing patterns of pathology in the institutionalized aged was what we called withdrawal. These people just sat without responding to questions, without showing much of an interest in what was going on about them, and if they did respond, at most might say, "I don't know." Our observations were based on a random sample survey of institutionalized aged in New York City, and repeated with followup studies for the past five years (Goldfarb, 1962; Kahn, et al., 1961).

The withdrawal behavior I have described is like certain patterns of behavior seen in adults with brain damage; it is commonly described as kinetic mutism, and in adults with brain damage, the literature attributes it to lesions in particular parts of the brain.

However, research has shown, first, that it never occurs as an isolated behavior pattern; it always occurs in context with other kinds of withdrawal or avoidance. Second, it is very much related to the personality of the individual. Third, it is much related to the context of the situation.

Let us take as an example a patient who will not respond to a doctor who goes up to query him about his illness. A nurse then goes up and speaks to the patient and the patient responds. In this case you cannot say that the behavior follows automatically from the brain damage. With aged people, we know that there certainly is brain damage, but the problem is that we expect this kind of behavior as a natural part of the aging process. We think, this is what happens with the aged brain.

One way of clarifying the differences between normal aging and brain damage is to study disorientation. There was much talk yesterday about disorientation, but what is it? How frequent is disorientation in the aged? In our sample, we found that only 9 per cent of the patients actually misnamed the place—gave it another name—which is the kind of error that you find commonly in your adults with brain damage who are called disoriented.

But what happened in the aged patients? Thirty-seven per cent said they *did not know* where they were. They did not know the name of the place. I call this behavior unorientation. I think it is a markedly different phenomenon from disorientation, though the two are almost always lumped together. I think the difference has tremendous consequences, because unorientation, we believe from our studies, is deeply related to the character of the milieu and the degree of interaction that the person has with his environment. For example, we did a control study comparing an open state hospital with a closed state hospital, randomly testing patients admitted during the same period. We found that while 30 per cent of the ambulatory patients in the closed state hospital showed the kind of withdrawal phenomenon represented by unorientation, none of the ambulatory patients in the open hospital showed this type of behavior.

Our research has also led us to define a concept that we call "excess disability." We have tried to define this concept operationally in terms of some of our measures. For example, we gave the patients a test of motor tasks to perform, such as, "Lift both your legs. Comb your hair. Tie your shirt. Get out of bed." And then we rated them in terms of a series of everyday functional tasks done not in a test situation, but for daily maintenance: Did they feed themselves? Were they ambulatory?

In some patients, we found a discrepancy between their motor performance on request and what they were able to do when integrating such performances into meaningful units of living. Where we found this discrepancy, we called it excess disability, where the functional disability was greater than that warranted by actual physical and physiological impairment of the individual.

We found excess disability in about 40 per cent of all institutionalized aging. To cite one brief anecdotal example of how this works in practice, at one place we found a patient who propelled herself around by sitting on the floor and just pushing herself with her hands.

Everybody smiled and was pleasant to her, she was affable right back, and they carefully stepped around her. We examined her and found that while six months before she had had some condition which required temporary bed rest, now there was no longer any physical reason to keep her from walking. She had been behaving this way for about five months because this is the way the institution expected older people to act. They were surprised when we initiated the most rudimentary kind of rehabilitation procedure: we got her a walker, and in a couple of days we had her walking around.

This reflects what goes on in institutions, and perhaps more subtly in old people outside institutions, where by stereotyped expectations of "appropriate" roles for the aged, we induce disability greater than that warranted by their actual condition.

Another issue we tackled was the problem: What kind of facility should aged people go to when there is need for an institution? When we started our survey, we were charged with trying to find out what mistakes were made—how many patients were inappropriately sent to a state hospital when they should have gone to a home for the aged or a nursing home, but we were trying to develop criteria for determining what kind of institution would be appropriate for various types of aged persons.

We began by assuming that each institution serves a different kind of need—the state hospital serves the patients with psychiatric needs, the nursing home those with physical needs, and the home for the aged those with social needs. However, our survey found that the populations in all three institutions were much alike and could not be significantly differentiated in terms of intrinsic factors. There were, of course, relevant extrinsic factors, like ethnic background or race, that were crucial.

Finally, the last study I would like to mention bears on a topic discussed yesterday, the one of psychogenic versus organic problems in the aged. On the basis of our research and in support of the points made yesterday, the dichotomy seems false. The psychogenic and organic interact. Given a substrate of brain damage, the kinds of behavior we see, though they look organic, may be more related to psychological factors; some apparently psychogenic conditions can be related to organic factors.

When our patients were given a functional diagnosis by psychiatrists (e.g., paranoia, depression) and we compared these with an objective rating scale of intellectual functioning, we found that the people who made one or two errors were the ones most likely to be rated as having a functional disorder. Those people with no errors or a large number of errors were less likely to be so diagnosed. Thus, with minimal brain damage, there are behavioral changes—either adaptive or a direct consequence of the brain damage—that have the character of functional disorders.

We also used an operational index of depression. We asked all patients: If you had one wish, what would you wish for? We found 10 per cent who wished they were dead. Using this as an operational index of depression, we found again that it occurred relatively infrequently in people who showed no mental impairment, most often in those who had minimal impairment, and then decreased until it vanished in those with maximum impairment.

# 43

# Loss: A Constant Theme in Group Work With the Aged

IRENE MORTENSON BURNSIDE, R.N., M.S.
*Lecturer, School of Nursing*
*University of California*
*San Francisco, California*

*I am not resigned to the shutting away of loving*
   *hearts in the hard ground.*
*So it is, and so it will be, for so it has been, time out*
   *of mind:*
*Into the darkness they go, the wise and the lovely.*
   *Crowned*
*With lilies and with laurel they go; but I am not*
   *resigned.*

—Edna St. Vincent Millay

THE AGED PERSON knows much about "the shutting away of loving hearts in the hard ground." For 18 months I worked weekly with a group of aged patients in a nursing home, and the one pervasive theme in our discussions was loss. There were many variations, but loss was central. An analysis of my meeting summaries confirms the impression.

By far the most painful loss and the most difficult for those in our group to accept was the loss of a loved spouse. Some of the group members had been married from 30 to 50 years, and they often shared poignant memories of their loved ones. I sometimes wondered if these memories did not sustain them in their present unhappy situation. At times their memories seemed to bear a close similarity to Victor Frankl's memories of his wife while he was interned in a concentration camp:

"My mind still clung to the image of my wife . . . I knew only one thing—which I had learned very well by now: Love goes far beyond the physical person of the beloved. It finds its deepest meaning in his spiritual being, his inner self. Whether or not he is actually present, whether or not he is alive at all, ceases somehow to be of importance."[1]

One 80-year-old man told me he had lost his wife six months before, and he talked about his former drinking habits: "I had been drinking pretty heavily for a long time. One night I came home and found my wife sitting and crying about the excessive drinking I had been doing. That did it. I stopped drinking for 17 years. I can still see her . . . ." I replied, "It must be rough for you now without her." He said softly, almost to himself, "I have not gotten over it yet and don't know if I ever will." I, like

---

[1] Victor Frankl, *Man's Search for Meaning*, Washington Square Press, New York City, 1969, p. 60.

other workers, have noticed that men seem to find it more difficult to cope with the loss of a spouse than women do.

If during a group meeting one person mentioned his loss, another usually picked up the theme. At times they seemed to be talking to no one in particular, and we would all sit quietly and listen. Often there was repetition, something common in the communications of aged persons; perhaps it is necessary for them to retell some of the events of their lives, particularly the happier ones.

SOME OF THE MEETINGS were somber to the point of sadness. Only one man in the group had never married and he was quiet during these discussions. All the others had lost their spouses, and this alone gave the group commonality. The participants had not been selected because of their widowhood, but bereavement is one of the realities we must face in group work with the aged.

Kaplan writes that losing relatives and friends makes an older person feel insecure and without protection.[2] Hyams writes that the use of group therapy with the aged "may improve motivation by encouraging interpersonal relationships and by providing instances of other similarly disabled patients making progress toward independence."[3] The group also helps a grieving person by offering support and solace from associates who "have been there too."

I vividly recall a woman who came to the group only once. Her husband had died recently, and she was in a very slowed-down state due to her depression. At the meeting she sat next to a blind man in the group, and when I introduced them, they shook hands. He did not release her hand but sat quietly holding it. She stared intently into his face for some moments. Only recently admitted to the convalescent hospital, she was obviously having difficulty with adjusting to dependency on others and, indeed, with all her interpersonal relationships. She had been left to do the work of grief pretty much on her own. I sometimes think we have to give patients permission to care for someone, or at least to create an environment in which they can care.

Lidz writes, "When both partners continue into old age, sooner or later the invalidism or death of one brings the need for another major adjustment. It often forms a critical juncture, for the couple have managed through their interdependence upon one

another; and their familiarity and devotion have eased the way. The old person must not only assimilate the loss of a partner who has become an integral part of his life, but he must often also adjust to becoming dependent on others."[4]

Death of friends through the years is another significant loss. As Vischer writes, "The smaller a group of contemporaries becomes, the greater is the sense of isolation of those who still survive. Congeniality is a prerequisite for the emergence and maintenance of close relations between people of the same age."[5] Being in a small group that meets weekly is one way for aged patients in institutions to develop friendships and close relationships.

The disabilities of most of the group members were multiple. One man was blind, another had glaucoma, and only two could see well enough to read a newspaper. During one meeting, a member told us she had been to an eye doctor who had said she was losing her sight and there was not much to be done. She was a wheel-chair patient, and had been unable to walk or stand for three years, yet she had anticipated living to 90 as her mother and grandmother had done. But that day she said sadly, "I don't want to live to be 90 if I am not going to be able to see."

Loss of eyesight was especially difficult for the patients to accept. They would say, "I have fog before my eyes" or "I drop things and cannot see to pick them up." The blind man did not want to leave his room for fear of not finding his way. Nurses are needed when such losses occur. A nurse is a day-to-day worker who can help aged persons both in their struggle with their changing body image as they pass through physical crises and with the crisis of a personal loss when they need support in their lonely work of grief.

OUR GROUP DISCUSSED all the physical losses except one—the loss of sexual activity. I attribute this both to the solid Protestant ethic of the members and also to the fact that I did not fully explore the matter with the group. Celibacy is imposed upon them, after all, when they are institutionalized. My observations agree with Vischer's, who says, "Older people tell one another little or nothing about their sexual experiences."[6]

The loss of money and economic security was another topic of discussion, sometimes quite a lively

2 Jerome Kaplan, "The Day Center and Day Care Center," *Geriatrics*, Vol. 12, April 1957, pp. 247-251.

3 D. E. Hyams, "Psychological Factors in Rehabilitation of the Elderly," *Gerontologica Clinica*, Vol. 11, March 1969, pp. 129-136.

4 Theodore Lidz, *The Person*, Basic Books, New York City, 1968, p. 479.

5 A. L. Vischer, *On Growing Old*, translated by Gerald Onn, Houghton Mifflin, Boston, 1967, p. 28.

6 *Ibid.*, p. 43.

one. It was pointed out to me that the patients who had worked and earned Social Security got no more spending money than "the guy who spent his days drinking cheap wine." Everyone received $15 a month out of their pensions or Social Security. If they were destitute, Medi-Cal (our state's form of medicaid) paid them $15 a month for personal expenses. Often relatives handled the money and in some instances made the small purchases. A constant problem was that money was stolen, apparently because there was no way a patient could lock up his possessions. Said one man, "They'd steal the eyes out of a snake here." It did seem a pity patients did not have small lockers in which to keep their spending money and cherished personal possessions.

Group discussions also centered on loss of clothing. For instance, personal clothing would sometimes be taken from the owner's closet and put on an incontinent patient. One man hung his clothes at the head of his bed so that the staff would wake him if they reached over his head to get them. It seemed to be a challenge for the patients to outwit the staff and other patients to retain their own belongings. As Goffman wrote, "The personal possessions of an individual are an important part of the materials out of which he builds a self, but as an inmate the ease with which he can be managed by staff is likely to increase with the degree to which he is dispossessed."[7]

ONE DAY a man who had missed only one meeting in a year refused to attend. He was very angry, and at first I thought it was because we had changed the usual meeting place. But as I talked with him before the meeting, I became aware that his anger was displaced. Only a few moments before, a woman patient had scurried into his room, grabbed his bathrobe, and run out. The man had glaucoma and could not see well, but he shuffled along and managed to catch her. With the help of his cane, he retrieved his bathrobe, which he was now wearing over his white shirt and pants. He wrapped it around him with a gesture that said, "No one else will get my robe, to be sure!" I persuaded him to come into the group, where he talked with us about his anger. It was not easy for him to do so, because in extreme anger he usually withdrew. In response, other patients related how many shirts they had lost, what the laundry did to their clothing, and similar grievances.

In institutions where there are many confused and disoriented persons, it is easy to shrug off their complaints, saying, "He doesn't know what he is talking about." But it is my experience that even some of the most confused patients often do know. With all the other losses he is experiencing in old age, the aged hospitalized patient should not be stripped of anything that is an integral part of his self.

LOSS OF DIGNITY was another familiar and consistent theme in the group. The members felt they were often treated like children, or "pushed around like cattle," as one patient described it. They felt that in general people were not willing to listen to them. Often staff addressed them in too-familiar terms, such as "grannie" or "auntie," or called them by their first names. They had grown up in an era when one respected one's elders, and familiarity was difficult for many of them to tolerate. Vischer points out that "Old men and women often find themselves placed in a situation in which they are required to recognize and even to admire the leadership of those whom they had once known as immature young people."[8]

The loss of dignity was closely related to the loss of privacy. The 90-year-old man repeatedly told us of his embarrassment when he entered the nursing home. He was undressed and bathed even when he told them he had been bathing himself for 85 years and was still quite able to care for himself. "The elderly patient may react to his changed environment by feeling a loss of identity and dignity, and disorientation may ensue," says Hyams. "His confidence must be won, and the team can do this by their attitudes and actions."[9] It would seem that if we treat aged people like children, we can expect them to behave like children. It also seems that if we treat them with respect and concern, their behavior in turn will be more desirable.

In his discussion of geriatric nursing, Davis points out that unfamiliar surroundings or the permanent or momentary loss of contact with friends, spouse, or relatives makes an elderly patient generally apprehensive.[10] There are a number of ways in which patients lose touch with their former world. Many have been placed in hospitals quite far from their relatives and friends and their former communities. The way of life is different, too, and patients miss former routines—one of our men missed having a beer and a sandwich at a certain lunch counter. They also miss the particular foods and drinks they

7 Erving Goffman, *Asylums*, Doubleday, New York City, 1961, p. 78.

8 Vischer, *op. cit.*, p. 28.
9 Hyams, *op. cit.*
10 Robert W. Davis, "Psychologic Aspects of Geriatric Nursing," *American Journal of Nursing*, Vol. 68, April 1968, pp. 802-804.

used to know; one group member missed raw cucumbers, and another hot biscuits. They have to give up wine and beer when they enter the hospital unless the doctor specifically orders them, but even then such beverages are served like medicine—not in the leisurely, social way to which the patients were accustomed.

In most institutions, smoking rules are strict, curtailing the pleasure for some. The favorite pipe of one man had been stolen; although he used a cheap corncob pipe as a substitute, he still missed his old favorite. As Hyams says, "A disabled person lives at the center of a small world, for his environment has effectively shrunk on account of his disability."[11] That statement is also applicable to elderly people admitted to nursing homes. Their world has become considerably smaller—for some, so small that their bed comprises their entire territory.

Another loss is independence. Some elderly people give it up rather gladly, and indeed have been driven to somatic complaints to get attention and concern. But others fight fiercely for autonomy and do not easily give it up, even when they should do so for the sake of their health. Davis writes, "Every older person feels, more intensely than at any time since adolescence, the conflict between the need for dependency and the urge to remain independent. When self-esteem is lost, there is a tendency to submerge oneself in the person or being of another. A crucial issue in nursing care is the patient's continuing struggle to maintain his independence."[12]

Many in our group had been forced to become dependent because of declining health, but in spite of their physical disabilities, some of them retained a marvelous sense of autonomy. One day I went to the blind man's room to bring him to the meeting, and watched him lower his side-rail and maneuver himself into his wheel chair with no help from me. He took the risks necessary to maintain that degree of independence. One day he told the group how he had misjudged the distance in the bathroom and had fallen. He could not of course see the call bell to signal for help, so he had to wait until someone came. This man's independence and courage often served to encourage other group members, especially those who were beginning to lose their own vision.

Vischer noted another loss: "The withdrawal of work and consequently the withdrawal of the opportunity to give service, the discovery that there is no work for them and that they are not meant to work, is an experience which aging people find hard to bear."[13] The opportunities to feel useful are certainly sharply decreased for institutionalized patients; group members often said they wished they could do something for me to repay me for being the group leader.

Perhaps one of the bitterest losses is the decrease of mental acuity. Patients are often aware of their memory losses and their inability to think as fast as before, and many became quite embarrassed. Sometimes in meetings a member could not think of the answer to a question I asked. He would apologize, and we would pass it over without much comment. I tried to keep the group members mentally alert by encouraging them to discuss world affairs as well as their own problems and concerns, and by helping them recall what had happened during previous meetings.

Even the loss of me as a leader threatened these elderly patients. They would be angry, sullen, or silent, and noticeably withdrawn, when I returned after an illness or a vacation. It seemed to be their way of punishing me for being away. During my absences, they lost the intimacy of the group meetings, because no one else was willing to take over until I returned. They lost my sharing of my own world and the outside world, and they feared the possible disintegration of the group. However, after about a year, the members would be euphoric when I came back after an absence, and would begin chattering immediately. Eventually they quite openly said they did not like me to be away and waited for my return. In the interim they saved things to share with me and the group.

In some ways, I undertook certain "family duties" for them, because I saw some things as necessary input to help expand the small dot their world had become. I did not handle their money, but I did read letters for them when they asked me. I brought in sweets or beer in hot weather, or a cake when one of us had a birthday. In such ways I think I became a pseudo-family-member for them.

My group never shied away from talking about the greatest loss of all, their own death. They started discussing it in the second meeting. In the 45th meeting, they talked about suicide and why they would not attempt it. And sometimes they would laugh at death. The blind man said, "I really can't die; I have such a bad conscience that I am afraid to." The group loved that remark and burst out laughing. I was reminded of a line I had written long ago, in a poetic mood: "Because I know you are the wind blowing out stars, I shall laugh."

11 Hyams, *op. cit.*
12 Davis, *op. cit.*
13 Vischer, *op. cit.*, p. 29.

The ultimate loss—the loss of their own life—was the most difficult for me to listen to and share. It took me a long time to become comfortable in the group when the members discussed this particular variation on the theme of loss. Somehow I found the subject easier to handle when talking individually with a patient. But if I, as their leader and their friend, could not listen while group members spoke of their death, then who could? For as Davis says, "Fear of death is reduced by making the patient feel he is not alone."[14] That was the function of the group and the responsibility of its leader.

Nurses, whose primary duty is to give or supervise bedside care, can do much with individuals and with groups to help assuage the pain of the losses that aged people experience. They can support and console patients during the work of grief in order to prevent further depression. They can immediately intervene when a patient meets a new crisis in his health—a broken hip, failing sight, exacerbations of previous illnesses, or final commitment to a wheel chair. They can help patients accept changes in their body image, and can assist coherent and alert patients to keep the cherished personal possessions that constitute their "self system."

Nurses can help by bringing creativity and zest to their responsibilities. They can help patients retain a measure of independence and autonomy in self-care even when it would be "easier to do it for them." It is a fine judgment as to when to let a patient become dependent and when to encourage him to maintain his independence. Nurses can insist that everyone who comes in contact with elderly patients treat them with dignity and respect regardless of their age, illness, race, or disability. Nurses should be the role models for less educated workers who give nursing care to the aged. They can collaborate with other disciplines and share ideas about different ways of providing care.

Group work with the aged is indeed useful; it allows patients to discuss and share their losses. But where can we find people to lead such groups? We shall have to call on our creativity to find new people to work with the aged and new methods to help them. Vischer, himself an old man, writes, "We often hear old people complain that, although they receive sympathy, there is no longer anybody there to share their experiences and their pleasures."[15] The challenge exists for nurses to help the aged and to alleviate the pain of their many inevitable losses.  •

14 Davis, *op. cit.*

15 Vischer, *op. cit.*, p. 25.

# 44

# COMMUNAL LONELINESS

CLARK E. MOUSTAKAS

*Merrill-Palmer Institute, Detroit*

He stood in the doorway of my office, a terribly stooped old man. Pain and misery, heavy wrinkles, lined his face. He stared beyond me, fiery, piercing eyes fixed to the floor, a face filled with indescribable loneliness and defeat. "Won't you come in and sit down?" I asked gently. He entered the room, but he did not sit. He began to pace, back and forth, back and forth. Increasingly, I felt the turbulence inside him which electrified my office, with a kind of frozen tension. The tension mounted, becoming almost unbearable. Heavy beads of perspiration fell from his face and forehead. Tears filled his eyes. He started to speak several times but the words would not come. He stroked his hair roughly and pulled at his clothing. The pacing continued.

I felt his suffering keenly, deep inside me, spreading throughout my whole body. I remarked, "So utterly painful and lonely." "Lonely," he cried. "Lonely!" "Lonely!" he shouted, "I've been alone all my life." He spoke in rasping tones, his nerves drawn taught. "I've never been an honest person. I've never done anything I really wanted to do, nothing I truly believed in. I don't know what I believe in anymore. I don't know what I feel. I don't know what to do with myself. I wish I could die—how I have yearned, how I have longed for death to come, to end this misery. If I had the courage, I would kill myself. These headaches. Have you ever known such lasting pain? I don't know how much more I can stand. I haven't slept for months. I wake up in the middle of the night. Everything is dark, black, ugly, empty. Right now my head is throbbing. I take pills. I try to rest. I avoid becoming upset. Nothing helps. My head is splitting. I don't think I can take this pain much longer. I wake with a start. My heart fills with terror. My wife and children are asleep, with me in the house—but I am entirely alone. I am not a father. I am not a husband. I'm no one. Look! See these tears? I could weep forever. Forever. I sometimes feel I cry for the whole world—a world that's sour and lost."

All this the old man uttered—sobbing, choking, sighing, gasping for breath. The sounds were thick. His tongue was fastened to his gums. Only with the greatest effort did he talk. It was almost unendurable. The lancinating physical pain and mental anguish mounted unrelentlessly. There was not even a moment of suspension so we could breathe normally and recapture our resources. His distress was cumulative, increasingly exhaustive.

In his completely weakened state, unknown urges, unknown capacities, a surprising strength enabled him to continue. From the beginning he had never been a real person. It was too late now, he felt. Nothing in life was real. For seventy-four years he had lived by other people's descriptions of him, others' perceptions of him. He had come to believe that this was his real self. He had become timid and shy, when he might have discovered and developed social interests. He was silent when he might have something to say. He played cards every Tuesday and attended club meetings every Thursday when he might have enjoyed being alone, or conversing with his wife, or developing an avocation or hobby. He listened to the radio and watched television every evening when he might have discovered values in music and books. He did not know his real interests and talents, his real aspirations and goals He never gave himself time to discover himself.

He asked in agony, "Do you know what it means not to feel anything, to be completely without feeling? Do you understand what it is to know only pain and loneliness? My family doesn't understand me. They think I have these headaches because my business is failing. They think I roam the house at night, moving from bed to couch to chair to floor, because I'm worrying about my business. They think I'm worrying about new possibilities and plans. So they soften me and treat me gingerly. Husband and father must have a quite house, so the house is quite. He must not be upset, so he is avoided. He must not be expected to be friendly and sociable because he is passive and shy. He must be indirectly talked into doing what they want, in the right way, at the right moment. It takes careful planning. He must have sympathy, even if it's false, to be able to face the tough, competitive world outside. They cannot and will not recognize that this man they handle with kid gloves, whom they fear upsetting, whom they decide has to be coddled and manipulated into buying new clothes, a new car, a new home, all the other possessions a family feels it must have, this man does not really exist and never did. But who is he? He doesn't know and he doesn't know how to find out. Can't you see? I do not really exist. I am nothing. Do you know what it is not to know how you feel, not to know your own thoughts, not to know what you believe, not to know what you want, not to be sure of anything but endless pain and suffering? And everyone else takes you for granted, on already formed opinions and actions, the same words, the same ways. How do I start to live again? I'm dying and I can't stop breathing. I can't stop living."

These were the themes of our talks together—self-denial, estrangement, rejection, excruciating pain, spreading loneliness. We met eight times. In each visit, his suffering and sense of isolation increased, reaching unbelievable heights. Often, I thought: "Surely this is it. He has reached the breaking point." He seemed at the very end of his power and resources. But he kept coming until I wondered whether I had not reached the breaking point. The only thing that kept me going was the certainty that without me there would be no one —no one at all. I could not give up, abandon him, even when I questioned my own strength to continue to live through our conversations and the lonely terror not expressible in words. I suffered deeply in these hours with him. Each time he came I felt on the verge of sinking into total despair. Often when he wept, there were tears in my eyes too, and when his head ached painfully, I felt the pain all the way through me. And when he paced and pulled at himself, I felt a terrible restlessness and agitation. And when he was utterly alone and lonely, I was alone and lonely too. My full, complete presence was not enough to alleviate his suffering, his self-lacerating expressions. I felt an awful loneliness and desolation as I was not able to help him find a beginning, locate a direction, a new pathway of relatedness to himself and others. It hurt me deeply to see him grow increasingly, unbelievably tortured and not be able to help him find a meaning or even some beginning belief in the possibility of a good life. He was dying before me and something within me was dying too. I could not reach him. I do not know what effort of will power, what inner strivings of the heart, what forces kept me going in the face of this unendurable, mounting desolation, despair, and loneliness. I felt defeated and weakened, yet each time he came I met him squarely, honestly, directly. Each time my capacity for bearing with him seemed to be reaching a terminal point, new threads inside revived me. Somehow fresh strength flowed into me, mysteriously encouraging me and enabling me to continue. I listened to him and believed in him. I was convinced he had the power within himself to find a new meaning to life. I continued to live with him in the crucial hours of psychic dying. My entire office filled with his aching. I could feel it everywhere in the room—in the floor, the walls, the furniture,—the papers and books on my desk. It settled irrevocably and held stationery. For some time after he left, I did not move. I remained heavy as the feeling he left when he departed.

Then on the ninth appointment he did not come. What could this defection mean? How had I failed? Had he sensed my own growing struggle, my own exhaustion, my own loneliness? I searched within my self and within our relations but I could find no satisfactory answer.

Two weeks passed before he called. He spoke in a calm voice, in a totally different way from any previous words. "It's all so fresh and raw," he said, "and so new and startling that I'm constantly uncertain, but I feel I am coming into a totally new existence. I sometimes doubt th t what I am feeling will last, but the feelings have persisted now almost two weeks and I'm beginning to recognize them as my own. I do not know what is happening or how, but by some strange miracle or inner working, I am beginning to breathe again and to live again. I do not want to see you just now because I must have further confirmation, but I will call you soon."

Six weeks later the old man came for the last time. I could barely recognize him. He looked youthful. His face was alive. His smile was radiant and so thrilling I felt tingling sensations everywhere inside me. He spoke warmly, confidently, "I came only to see your face light up, to be warmed by the gleam in your eyes. I know how much you suffered. I have seen your tortured face even after leaving you. I'll just sit here with you quietly a few minutes." So we sat in silence, each revelling in the birth, each warmed by a bond that emerged from deep and spreading roots in the hours of anguish and loneliness. We were no longer alone or lonely. We had found a new strength and sustenance in each other.

The fundamental communion in which we suffered enabled him to get to the very depths of his experience. Perhaps in arriving at the foundation of his grief and loneliness, immediate death or immediate life were the only choices within reach. He chose to live. From his rock bottom loneliness emerged a new life and a real self was restored.

MS. received, VII 18, 6).

**Clark E. Moustakas**　Staff member of the Merrill-Palmer Institute. Child-centered play therapy and adult counseling. Author of "Children in play therapy" 1953; "Psychotherapy with children. The living relationship" 1959; Editor of "The self" 1956.

# 45

# Creating a Human Bond

## by Bruno Gelba

I work with people. A lot of information filters through me during the day. People tell me about their lives—their problems, their aspirations. They tell me about their childhood, their marriage, their joys, their disappointments and their fear of death. It is a never ending list.

George A., one of my students, tells me that he is 64 years old and a widower. He used to work for the city as a bus driver. It seems easy for him to talk to me in complete honesty about himself. I pay close attention to him, to the tone of his voice, his posture, his facial expressions, the movement of his hands, his eyes, yes, particularly his eyes, because they are truly the mirror of a person's soul. "I can't see how you can be interested in all this stuff I'm telling you," he says to me. "You must get tired of hearing the same old things over and over again." While we talk something else is taking place. Without our being aware of what is really happening, we are coming closer to each other. We have formed a bond, an area of mutual understanding, a human bond. It is created through feelings of trust, sincerity, respect and empathy. I can't really explain how it all comes about. I only know when it is there and when it isn't. The human bond is a spontaneous event. It evolves directly from person-to-person contact.

George is aware of what has happened. He tells me he has experienced an inner certainty about me. "I have a feeling that you hear me. I sense that I am also beginning to understand myself better." Yes, we hear each other all right. We have established a good relationship. Older people, more than any other age group, need such a confidant, someone to share their memories and feelings with.

They also need—and we have seen this over and over again—to be touched. Touching plays an im-

portant part in the work we are doing. The teacher uses many opportunities to establish this direct physical contact with the student. The most neutral and least threating area to touch or to be touched is, of course, the hands. Let me illustrate this point with a story one of my assistants told me recently. This assistant is an older woman in her late seventies, extremely active in our association and a living example of what we believe in.

The following is her story:

"The other day when we visited the retirement home on Center Avenue an old lady was sitting almost completely hidden in a corner. While most of the other women in the room were chatting with each other and asking me all kinds of questions about our program, she remained extremely withdrawn. After I had talked to all the other people, I walked over to her and asked how things were going. She responded with an empty and forlorn look. Then it came to my attention that her fingernails and cuticles were in very bad condition and that a lot of rough skin on her fingers was starting to break open. So I reached for my handbag and took out my manicure set. I took her left hand and began to cut her fingernails and snip off some of the hard skin particles around her fingertips. As I did this, I asked her a few questions directly related to what I was doing like, "Does this hurt you? Do you want me to do the other hand too?" And this is when she said her first words, "Yes, please." This is how our conversation started. She began to tell me how thankful she was to me for doing this for her. After I had finished I took some cream out of my handbag and began masssaging her hands. This is when I really experienced the first emotional reaction in her. Her face became a bit flushed. She began to sit up a little bit straighter, and I recognized the strange mixture of upcoming tears and a certain delight in her eyes. She said that I really had been the first person in a long time to touch her in this way, by massaging her hands. She had forgotten how good it felt and how much she needed to be touched by another person.

Touching plays a very important role in creating a trusting and caring relationship. From our experience we can say that older people as a rule have a tremendous need to be touched because they are sorely neglected in this respect. It always amazes us after working a couple of weeks in a convalescent home to see how hugging can become a part of everyday living. Through this direct body contact the human bond is vitally strengthened and a new degree of intimacy and trust is established.

# 46
# The SAGE Spirit

**by C. C. ELWELL II**

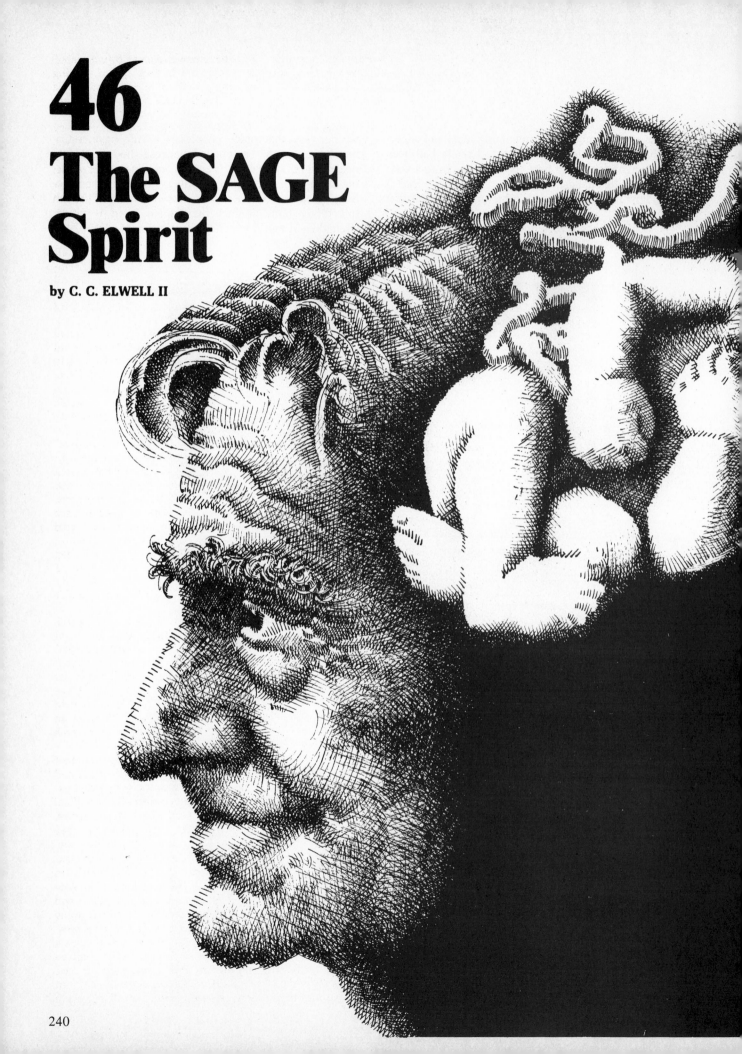

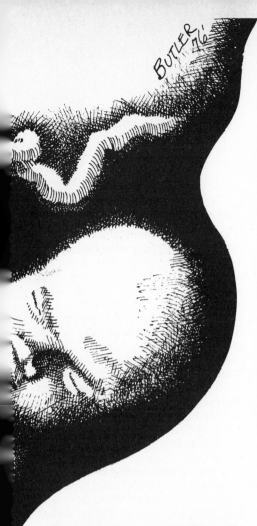

BUTLER '76

O ld people too often accept the clichés of advancing age—the debilitating aches and pains and the sinking energies. But a remarkable group in Berkeley, California, seems to have found a way to fight back. The techniques are simple and they work, but it takes a lot of caring.

**C. C. Elwell II lives in Claremont, California, and is a frequent contributor to HUMAN BEHAVIOR.**

I came to Berkeley, California, because I had heard about some aging people who were finding joy and fulfillment in their declining years. And I had heard about the people who were helping them, free of charge and without hope of personal gain. The program that they were offering was called SAGE—Senior Actualization and Growth Exploration.

There are around 150 elderly participants in SAGE, I had been told. In charge of them are seven group leaders, or teachers, or guides—they really would prefer no title at all. The groups of 10 to 20 persons meet once or twice a week. They do various exercises in deep breathing for relaxation; they do some yoga and some Western exercises such as gentle pushaways from a wall. Sometimes these old folks growl like

Illustration by Chris Butler

lions or let out a war whoop. Very often they laugh. Usually, they end their sessions stretched out full-length on the floor, lost to the occasional voice or the distant hum of traffic in the outside world. During these quiet times, no one pries into the inner world they are experiencing. Some are Christians, some are Yogi, many don't call themselves anything. But just about all are feeling some connection with a force much bigger than the forces of this world, and through this connection they are less afraid—less afraid of living and less afraid of dying.

The meeting this day is at 828 Arlington Avenue, and getting there entails a drive through those winding, narrow old streets in the Berkeley foothills, a walk through a cool cave of dense trees and, finally, to a large, brown, Charles Adams-like house. A thick wooden door is opened by Gay Luce—china-blue eyes searching out of an oval face, at once hopeful and vulnerable. She's the founder of SAGE, an award-winning science writer-turned-teacher. Within the next several minutes of amenities, she does something that threatens my professional balance: she reaches up and gently removes a twig that has lodged itself in my graying hair. Still, I like it. And Gay Luce and I are just folks.

Inside, the large carpeted living room is beginning to fill with elderly people. They are starting their exercises, trying out one called "the back scratcher," lying out on the floor rocking back and forth like babies in their cribs. "It's starting to feel much better," says a man they call Mac. "Must have been some tensions in my spine I didn't know about."

"The crux of our entire program is deep muscle relaxation—first of body, then emotions and finally of the mind," says Gay Luce. "The one thing we do with all participants, no matter how weak or incapacitated, is to work on proper slow, deep breathing. We begin by placing an object or a hand on the stomach and asking them to move it up and down as they breathe. This promotes breathing in the diaphragm, the way babies breathe and the way we are supposed to breathe. This kind of breathing relaxes the body, the emotions and the mind. It also opens the self to repressed emotions. Beyond proper breathing, all exercises are geared to the capacity of the members."

There are some pushaways from the wall and some talk about somebody's arthritis flaring up (Gay Luce is very attentive, sympathetic and suggests an exercise to remedy it); there is a film on the importance of deep breathing for re-

laxation; there is a "meditation walk," everybody with eyes closed, taking seemingly forever to walk across the room, experiencing whatever they are experiencing.

SAGE participants come from every social, economic and educational level. Among members is an itinerant hobo who never made it past the third grade; another is a former Berkeley intellectual; there are several elderly women prominent in Bay Area social circles. Some participants are still physically active; others are confined to wheelchairs; and still others are deaf and half blind. The one problem all have in common is that of aging in America; all other differences seem to fade as they share their hopes and fears, joys and sorrows.

"I came here afraid of dying and even more afraid of being a burden in my old age," says Herb. "Now, I'm not nearly so afraid." When you think of Herb, think square and solid. Here is a man who looks many years younger than his 77—thick leathery face, large meaty hands—the kind of guy you could depend on in a crisis. "As for the changes," he says, "I came here with arthritis in my hands, terrible backaches and a stiff neck. I still have some trouble with the arthritis, but the backache is gone, and I can now twist my head and see the traffic behind me on the road. I used to smoke two packs a day, and now I don't smoke. You can't smoke and deep breathe at the same time, you know. I still drink a quart of wine a day. My wife says I'm an alcoholic. I don't know . . . "

Next, Frances. She is very beautiful. At 68, it's incredible—she brings out the romantic in me. Softly rounded face, dark hair and deep marble eyes. As if this weren't enough, she lowers her voice in conspiracy and asks, "Have you got a cigarette? I'm the only one in the group who smokes." We light up together. Two sinners saving each other from guilt.

"I had this tension thing," Frances tells me. "Bad pain in my shoulder and arm, almost constant. I had tried physical therapists, osteopaths, medical doctors. I even tried acupuncture. Nothing helped. I came here, and they told me deep breathing would help. How could just breathing deeply, relaxing completely on the outgoing breath before I took the next breath . . . how could that do anything? But I did it, and slowly I realized the pain was going away. And it's completely gone now. As for the spiritual part, I came here a very skeptical person. I didn't believe anything my five senses didn't tell me was so. Now, I don't understand it, but there is some force, something much

241

greater than scientists can understand. I used to think death just meant oblivion. Now, I'm beginning to wonder."

Such testimony is not unique. Other reports include that of an elderly woman who came to SAGE with severe leg pains. "For 30 years doctors have told me there is nothing they could do. By practicing these exercises and breathing properly, my leg has completely realigned itself, and the pain is gone." Another woman reported on a common aging complaint—fatigue: "As we grow old we face a real energy crunch. Here we're learning to tap new power sources through our spiritual growth. I'm finding energy I haven't had in years."

While many come to SAGE for relief of physical ailments, just as many find themselves confronting various emotional blocks. Eleanor, 73, talks about working through the long-repressed grief of losing six people including her brother within a short period of time. "One day I was doing the deep breathing at a SAGE session," says Eleanor, "when these emotions came up and I had to leave the room. I wept bitterly for two hours, and I wept away a score of sorrows. And, finally, I started to laugh, thinking of the people who have loved me all my life and still love me. Now I find that any time I want to use the breathing method, I can wipe out my sorrows and trapped emotions."

And yet there seems to be no obvious formula in SAGE to account for any of this. Says Gay Luce: "It's hard to describe a typical SAGE session because we don't have a set recipe. Each session evolves differently if we remain open to the needs of the group. For example, when a 75-year-old woman has just lost her husband, the group responds to her grief. Or when an introverted shut-off member expresses joy for the first time, there is a feeling of elation for all of us. No two sessions are ever the same. The leaders never pose as professionals. Those of us who have Ph.D.s may as well throw them in the wastebasket. Everything here is on a first-name, person-to-person basis. Our whole premise is that the 70-year-old can grow just as much as the 7-year-old, given the same love and encouragement."

As unstructured as SAGE is, the results are impressive, and word of the program is drawing inquiries from all over the country. A recent week-long SAGE training workshop drew 120 professionals in the field of aging to the Mills College campus in Oakland, California, and other training sessions are being planned around the nation. Letters and phone calls have come in from groups in Southern California, Pennsylvania, Florida and New York. The National Institute of Mental Health—which has declared the isolation and depression of the elderly to be a top priority in mental health—is currently studying SAGE to see if it might contain the seeds of a national model. Surely, nowhere more than in youth-worshipping America is the need so great as tens of thousands of Americans each year pass the magical 65 mark, only to sink into the abyss of feeling useless and unwanted.

SAGE teacher Susan Garfield, 37, a former documentary filmmaker, has thought a lot about this phenomenon. "The big problem in the United States is this severe segregation of older people," she says. "There is this general cultural message that if you pass a certain age—and it's rapidly dropping—a person is useless. Those old people who can't see beyond the values of our society incorporate these feelings into themselves, and they feel worthless and isolated, depressed and unhappy. In our program, we try to offer an opportunity for older people to experience life in a different way. Their whole notion of what it means to be alive changes. The importance of each day is not 'Did I achieve such and such today?' or 'Did I do this job well for my boss?' The important thing is 'How did I feel today?' 'What was my inner experience?' In other words, our purpose is not to make older people be like 30-year-olds but to realize that this period of their lives can be one of the most significant and rewarding of times.

"Other countries are far advanced in this," Garfield continues. "In India, for instance, the middle years are for raising the family and being a householder. The last third of life is meant for spiritual development. Throughout China, the elderly are revered. You have the

# Our purpose is not to make older people be like 30-year-olds but to realize this period of their lives can be one of the most significant and rewarding of times.

wise old man and the wise old woman. But here, it's a sad fact that people don't have much respect for the elderly. We want to get them out of the way. We don't even want to look at them. A tremendous problem exists, and yet nobody is dealing with it in any meaningful way. That's why I'm here. My hope is that this SAGE program will have an impact on the country."

The idea for the SAGE program was born several years ago when Luce received a visit from her mother, who was suffering from a common problem of the aging: insomnia. "Together we tried some of the things we now do in SAGE, including biofeedback relaxation techniques, and they were very successful," the program's founder recalls. "From this experience it seemed to me I was getting a message. Like a lot of people, I had always avoided thoughts of old age. My idea was I was going to die at 30. Then I made it to 31. I'm not going to live beyond 40, I thought. Somehow it never occurred to me that I was going to actually live and face the problems I was seeing around me on the street. I talked this over with friends, and I found out that they too were beginning to wonder what life was going to be like at 60 and 70."

Convinced that she was into an area of pressing need, Luce—a three-time winner of the American Psychological Association's writer's award—gave up writing and put all her savings and book royalties into the purchase of the Berkeley house that would serve as SAGE headquarters.

"First I undertook to read all the literature I could find on the subject of the aging in America. But I soon gave this up. It was all so negative. Caring for old people seemed to mean 'water, feed and make comfortable.' None of it looked like fun. There was so little of a positive nature being done."

Now, despite the difficulties of keeping SAGE together and running, a rich vein of new ideas about old-age problems flows forth. For example, Luce challenges the modern-day practice of sedating old people to make them sleep longer. "We have so many misconceptions about age in this country. Take sleep and the phenomenon of old people

waking up so early in the morning. This is a universal occurrence. In other countries, such as India, old people get up at 4 or 5 a.m. and go to the ashram for meditation. The early morning is an ideal time to reach the inner self. But in the United States we consider waking early as 'insomnia,' and we prescribe dangerous and detrimental drugs to keep our old people asleep."

Another common notion Luce challenges is the widespread belief that old people should accept illness, stiffness and aching joints as part of the aging process and respond by limiting activities and energy output. "What's needed is more energy output, not less," she insists. "The body itself is constantly regenerating itself, no matter what your age. If you can change the old habits that brought on the aches and pains in the first place, you can change the body and be rid of the ailments. Our belief is 'Your body is as you use it.' "

Also contrary to common professional practice, Luce all but discounts academic degrees in the process of selecting future SAGE leaders. "Of course, there are certain skills we seek in our leaders," she says, "but far more important are the qualities of caring, sensitivity and the ability to listen with sympathy and patience. Also, we want leaders who can drop the role facade and aren't afraid to be themselves."

Such a teacher is Mac Worden. Everybody has been telling me about him. He is 68, and they say he came to the SAGE program a little over a year ago so heavily sedated by doctors he had lost most of his memory. A forlorn, inward, isolated figure then, they say, he is now a changed man. He has gone back to college to qualify as a therapist for the elderly, and he's become one of SAGE's most effective leaders, working with very, very old people in rest-homes. Later, the most compelling memory I have of Mac is not his own story but his account of little breakthroughs with old and very lonely and frightened people.

"With many of these people," Mac explains, "about all I can do is try to get a response, to stimulate them. We have this special soft ball. To this one woman I said, 'Catch the ball.' She said, 'No,

I can't catch the ball.' I dropped it in her lap. 'What's this? What's this?' she asked. 'Come on, it's a ball. Throw it back to me.' 'I can't,' she said, but a few days later, she did. Now she catches the ball regularly, and she teases me. She acts as if she's going to throw it and then she won't. She laughs and has a great time.

"There is another woman who doesn't participate at all. But she holds my hand like an old friend. And the other day she said, 'You won't forget me, will you?' I said, 'No, I won't forget you.' 'I'm counting on you,' she said."

At the end of the first session, Gay Luce and I are back in the living room. Everyone is gone. She is talking about keeping SAGE alive. "The program started in January of 1974 with just a handful of us. It was free of charge to participants, and it is still free of charge. From the beginning it was a success. The word spread, and before we knew it, we couldn't keep up with either the demand from old people who wanted to join, or from the young and old people who wanted to volunteer their services as group leaders. Today, we run eight groups in Marin County, Berkeley, nearby Albany and Oakland. But we still can't keep up with demand. There are long waiting lists and a flood of inquiries coming in from around the country. Because no one is paid anything, we are in the difficult position of working virtually without funds and being unable to adequately handle the response. The future is very uncertain."

It is saddening to hear about SAGE teetering along financially from month to month on volunteer services. It forms a disquieting counterpoint in the mind to all the testimony from Herb, Frances, Eleanor and Mac. SAGE has its techniques, you realize; but, beyond this, there is something refreshingly nontechnical and nonauthoritarian about the program. Here, there are no charts, graphs or statistics kept; no striving or competitive goal setting. Neither is there any bearded Dr. Finkleheimer, giving the definitive word in a Viennese accent. Instead, you have a group of decent people coming together, open and caring, willing to reach out. What SAGE really is is love.

# 47

# Inside the Nursing Home by Claire Townsend

### The Journals

*June 26.* FORGET IT! I AM NEVER GOING BACK!

*June 27.* That was written last night, just after I returned from my first night at the *** home. What is really bad is that instead of coming up with a crusader wish to help the nursing home problem, I came out last night vowing to commit suicide before I get old. (Claire Townsend)

*June 27.* The head nurse or supervisor, a licensed practical nurse, told us that she was glad we had come because usually she had only three people to work her intensive care floor of about fifty-four patients. (Elizabeth Baldwin)

*June 27.* In one home we went to, an aide with no experience was left alone on her second night to prepare twenty bedridden patients for bed. One woman expressed a desire to get out of bed and go to the toilet. The aide, having never actually gotten a patient out of bed, just watched it done once, got the woman into the bathroom, supporting most of the woman's weight, and onto the toilet seat. When the patient was done, the aide walked her back to bed, but as the bed was a high hospital type, the aide was not strong enough to lift the woman in and ended up rolling her onto it with much pain and consternation to both. (Janet Keyes)

*June 27.* I followed one nurse around today and asked her to explain what she was doing—like the tests for sugar and acid in the urine. When the former came out negative, I asked her if that was good and she said, "No . . . yes . . . no . . . wait a minute . . . yes, it's good to be negative, but not too negative."

The nurse I was assigned to, Grace, was so kind to some patients and so mean to others that it was cruel when the two extremes happened in a single room with two patients. While the two of us were putting the favored patient to bed (doing a lot of extra fussing and smiling and taking a long time) the other patient kept saying, "Girlie, please put me to bed." But I did not know how to go about it, so I just stood there feeling helpless and horrible. Then Grace finally ambled over to the second patient, jerked her out of the chair, slammed her against the bed, and roughly undressed her. The patient kept crying and saying that she was about to slip and fall, but Grace just told her to shut up. Finally, I assisted the woman up onto the bed. Then Grace threw the covers over her, covering her face, so I had to uncover her and tuck her in. (Claire Townsend)

*July 4.* The Colonel tried to tip me twenty-five cents for taking him to the bathroom. (Patricia Pittis)

*June 27.* When it came time to give the medicine, the R.N. said she was too busy, and would we please administer it. Later, Grace told me what we had just done was illegal, that only an R.N. can administer medicine. (Claire Townsend)

*July 1.* The aide called all the old people "the little people who do crazy things" and said you can never trust them, because they never take their medicine or do what they are supposed to do.

Schedule for the day shift, 7:00 A.M. to 3:00 P.M. Fourteen people to take care of—seven per aide. All on different floors and all to be waked at different hours. I would go into their rooms with Mrs. B.'s master key, wake them up, wash them down with a brief sponge bath, take them to the bathroom, partially dress them (shoes and dressing gown), and open their breakfast for them if it had already arrived.

Breakfast generally consisted of some form of eggs with cold toast and jam, coffee, milk or orange juice. (Patricia Pittis)

*June 28.* On the lunch tray there were two dry fish

sticks, some mashed potatoes, and puréed peas (everyone gets the puréed food whether or not they are on a special diet), and some cornbread. As one tray was being carried down the hall to a patient, a nurse reached over, picked up a piece of cornbread from the tray, and ate it. (Claire Townsend)

*July 3.* All they ever do is watch TV, eat, and sleep. Some do not even care what they watch—they are not listening anyway. They just sit in their chairs and stare blankly at the noise coming out of the TV. Although the *** home schedules trips regularly (recently went to see the Hershey chocolate factory in Pennsylvania), bingo twice a week, movies on Fridays, birthday parties once a month, religious services on Thursdays and Sundays, all of this does not seem to fill up the time, and few seem to participate. (Patricia Pittis)

*June 28.* A no-legged man died at 9:00 A.M. the morning of my second day; they did not get his body removed until 11:00 that night. The R.N. said she had called the doctor to come over to pronounce him dead (that was what they were waiting for all the time), but he never came. Finally the friendly neighborhood mortician picked up the body and drove it to the hospital where a doctor could be found. (Claire Townsend)

*July 13.* Mrs. M. is totally incontinent. Came in to put her to bed and found her already in her nightgown. She had not been dressed all day. Her nightgown was soaked. Her urine had run down her legs, through her stockings, and into her shoes, which were now soaked also. No one had done anything for her or checked her since she had been gotten up around 8:30 A.M. She should have gone downstairs long ago, but she hated to disturb the nurses—she knows they are so busy. All she does is sit in her urine-soaked clothing all day, watching television, but not really concentrating. (Patricia Pittis)

*June 28.* It got so it seemed that all we did for eight hours was clean up crap and empty urine bags. (Claire Townsend)

*June 27.* The air conditioning got the rooms much too cold and could not be turned off. Most of the patients were shivering and I was shivering too. When we came on the morning round there were not enough blankets for everybody. (Elizabeth Baldwin)

*July 1.* Some rooms smelled atrocious because of little or no ventilation. Some patients had air conditioning; others could not open their windows. Still others said they would be cold if we opened their windows for them. (Patricia Pittis)

*June 27.* The fingernails and toenails of the patients were long and disgustingly dirty. (Elizabeth Baldwin)

*July 2.* There does not seem to be any rehabilitation program. One man, totally bedridden, never even wore any clothes. He sat up to eat, then went right back to bed. Mr. T. is ambulatory with a cane and walker, but we took him down to the taxi in a wheelchair because "it was faster and more convenient," according to Mrs.

B. Mrs. B. said there was a whirlpool in the basement, but did not say how often it was used, or by whom. (Patricia Pittis)

*July 6.* The physical therapist is supposed to come in every Tuesday but sometimes he never comes. (Patricia Pittis)

*June 27.* Mrs. W. was a big black woman in her fifties or sixties who kept saying she was burning "down there." It turned out that her skin had been split open as a result of aides' carelessness in turning her over. This had happened before and she had been hospitalized as a result. This time all they put on it was a towel.

Another lady had a catheter tube without a urinal bag attached to it. (Elizabeth Baldwin)

*July 2.* There are no regular fire drills and Mrs. B. said that patients have no idea what they are supposed to do in case of fire. When some kids came in and pulled the alarm for fun, all the ambulatory patients stood in the halls and wondered what was going on, and where the fire was. It would be a mad house if a fire were to occur. None of the aides or most of the staff have any idea of the best way to evacuate the building; as far as I can see, there is no organized plan. The nearest available exits are not posted anywhere. (Patricia Pittis)

*June 27.* One thing that surprised me was that patients were allowed to smoke in bed at night, a serious fire hazard. (Elizabeth Baldwin)

*June 27.* The nurses were all smoking, so I asked in which rooms was smoking permissible. "Nowhere. But we sneak cigarettes in here and in the lounge all the time. It don't make no difference." Half the time I see the R.N. smoking as she walks down the hall. (Claire Townsend)

*July 2.* Personal records of health are kept. Drugs administered to patients are recorded on same sheet with date. Also each shift writes down what happened during their shift. If anyone fell, died, got sick, sent to the hospital, or went home or away. (Patricia Pittis)

*June 27.* One lady, one of the few who could talk sensibly, said that the doctor comes in, just asks her how she feels, and then leaves, charging her ten dollars. (Elizabeth Baldwin)

*July 6.* According to Mrs. B., there are three doctors at the *** home. Two doctors charge ten dollars per patient per visit, even if it takes place in the office, while the third tells them to leave what they can afford on her desk when they go out. The patients leave two to three dollars, which does not even pay for the shots they are given, much less the doctor's visit. Therefore, it is understandable that she has the most patients in the nursing home. The doctor has reserved Tuesdays and Thursdays for visits, from 10:00 A.M. to 2:00 P.M. Mrs. B. says she never gets a chance to see all her patients during those two days, so some go for two weeks or more without being able to see their doctor. (Patricia Pittis)

*July 10.* Mrs. C. fell during the night. She has lacerations all up her right arm. Her left arm has been put in a cast. The blood on her wounds has already dried and crusted around the edges. It must have been a long time before she called the nursing station to ask for help. When we arrived, the room stank; the bathroom floor, sink, and tub, and the bedroom carpet were covered with blood and feces—Mrs. C. and her bed, too. Beth gave her a quick bath and took her blood pressure; I changed her bed. Both of us were nurses' aides and did not know what else to do. Nurse S. was scheduled to come in that morning but she never showed up—did not call to give an explanation or anything. In fact, when we called her, the phone was disconnected. She had not come in all week. . . . We were not authorized to give medication. At 8:30 we called Mrs. R. when the nurse was still not in. She was furious at us for not telling her sooner. . . . Meanwhile, the diabetic patients had to be given their insulin at the exact time. So a private nurse gave it to them while I took care of her patient. Finally, Mrs. B. came in; she was supposed to be on vacation.

I saw the whole list of applications and changes of personnel. Beth plans to leave; Martha plans to leave eventually; I plan to leave before the end of the summer. Nurse S. never comes in anyway, so there will be no one left in the nursing station in a few weeks.

The conditions are too bad to stay long. Already I am feeling less cheerful, I am less patient and rougher with the patients. They get me down. I begin to think and feel like them with all their pains! (Patricia Pittis)

*July 11*. Beth took money out of the Colonel's coat pocket when she thought I could not see her. But I saw her doing it in the mirror. She is very underhanded and suspicious; she looked guiltily back to see if I were there every few seconds, then took the money. I was in the bathroom helping the Colonel go to the bathroom. (Patricia Pittis)

*June 27*. I heard one of the nurses ask another nurse, "Do you have Mrs. B.'s cold cream?" And the other nurse said, "No, E. has Mrs. B.'s cold cream. But I have her hand lotion." (Claire Townsend)

*July 11*. Mrs. B. came in in the morning and found a plastic jar that had contained a thousand aspirins completely empty. She did not know who had taken them but thought maybe the kitchen help and other employees had asked for them until there were none left. She did not make a big fuss about the issue. (Patricia Pittis)

*July 12*. All the old people have to look forward to is meals—it is one of the only events in their entire daily routine. There are three different servings for dinner: 4:15, 5:15, 6:15. Exactly on the dot they all rush to the door and stampede in like little children in school starving for their lunch. They sit on the sofas and chairs in the hallway up to forty-five minutes or an hour waiting for their mealtime to roll around. Others wait up to an hour in the theater in the front seats waiting for the movie at 7:00 P.M. There is nothing else to look forward to, I guess. (Patricia Pittis)

*June 27*. We sat around the nursing station at 12:20 A.M., talking and playing the radio, drinking water and coffee and eating pizza for about half an hour—right across the hall from a patient's room whose door was open. (Elizabeth Baldwin)

*July 11*. Mrs. R. told me that the only way to get the hospital to send out an ambulance to pick up the Colonel for his checkup would be if he were lying on the floor of his room. When Beth and I took him to the bathroom, he happened to lose his footing, so Beth casually let him drop to the floor of the bathroom and then called Mrs. B. The ambulance men were angry because the manager had lied and told the hospital that the Colonel had had a heart attack. The hospital gave him a quick checkup, but the Colonel says they did not ask him a thing. They sent him back right away.

The man in room 165 is so lonely. He wants a nurse in there every minute of the day and does not let you go until he knows exactly when you will be back and who the nurse is on the next shift, if you will not be back until the next day. I asked him how his dinner had been, and he said, "Never very good and always lonely." (Patricia Pittis)

*June 27*. In the *** home, there were almost no activities. On warm days, the patients were wheeled up to the front porch where they were able to watch the cars rush by on a dirty highway, or overlook the adjacent cemetery. A few watched an unfocused television, while others sat around the nurses' station and stared absently at the opening and shutting of the elevator door. There were no newspapers, magazines, or books in evidence and rarely any planned activities. Once a week, a cart was brought around from the local drugstore and the patients were able to pay exorbitant prices to buy a few items to brighten up their day. Immediately after dinner, the patients started asking the nurses if they could go to bed; they had nothing else to do. (Janet Keyes)

# 48

# Old Folks' Commune

At 82, Kathryn Gabel was trying hard to die. Living alone in an Orlando, Fla., motel room, she was no longer interested in eating and had increased her intake of Miltown to 400 milligrams a day. She had no family to turn to and refused to sign herself into a nursing home. Fortunately, a friend led her to a local "senior citizens' commune" where the elderly help each other to cope with the problems of growing old. With a little support and understanding, Kathryn Gabel stopped taking medication and began to eat regularly. She lived four productive years before dying recently of a stroke.

Gabel was helped by Share-A-Home, a unique network of private residences in Florida where old people form a family unit with legal authority over their lives. Unlike residents of a boarding house, the communards can vote new members in and out and have hiring and firing power over the staff. They can plan their own menus and entertainment—and even sneak into the kitchen for a snack. Started in 1969 by Orlando business-man Jim Gillies for the self-sufficient

elderly, the nonprofit organization currently has 112 members in eight residences. For $274 to $400 a month, members get three meals a day, laundry and maid service. A car and driver take them to church or the doctor. "I call it a halfway house for the elderly," says Orlando psychiatrist E. Michael Gutman. "There is a stage in aging when people are no longer totally independent but not debilitated. At Share-A-Home, they can be assured of getting their basic needs as well as a feeling of belonging."

**Love:** "After my husband passed away, I thought I would live by myself but I couldn't," says Bess Landis, 85, from Eaton, Ohio. "Now, I just love it here." Concert pianist Patricia Price, 41, and retiree Henry Mitchell, 63, came to Share-A-Home to escape loneliness. They are about to marry and set up their own housekeeping.

Gillies, 50, who manages the homes for $15,000 a year, has turned down offers to franchise his communal concept. He prefers to keep it a nonprofit operation, which makes it unattractive to

the private entrepreneurs now in the nursing-home field. If the residences were commercial, the state would consider them boarding houses and they would be forced to locate in commercial sections. At the same time, the communes have no medical staff on the premises. Thus members cannot presently qualify for Medicaid or other state welfare programs designed to underwrite nursing care.

Gillies, who is opening more communes in Tampa and Cleveland, Ohio, would like to see other nonprofit corporations—perhaps even the church—start Share-A-Home projects. "Old people are better off living with people of their own age—at the speed of their own generation," he says. "Old people think differently. They can't cope with the attitudes of the young any more." But in Orlando, at least, senior citizens have taken the communal experiment from the young—and made it work.

—MARY ALICE KELLOGG with ANDREW JAFFE
in Orlando, Fla.

# 49

## AGED PARENTS AND DEPENDENT KIDS: THE MIDDLE-AGED DILEMMA

**Sidney Margolius**

(EDITOR'S NOTE: *In the seventh of its reports on "Today's Families and Their Money Problems,"* FAMILY CIRCLE *tells how a unique, comprehensive agency serving the aged helped relieve the dilemma of a Minneapolis family with elderly parents who were no longer able to take care of themselves.*)

GERALD R. BRIMACOMBE

*Joan and Richard Butler (above, with their grandson, Joshua) learned to cope with a problem common to a growing number of modern families: The struggle to provide for themselves, their children—and help their elderly parents. For a while things were bleak—until aid came from the Minneapolis Age and Opportunity Center, which offers diversified services to senior citizens. Thanks to the center's medical, financial and emotional support, Frank Butler, 75, and his wife, Marie, 71, chatting at right with M.A.O. chairwoman Daphne Krause, are back in their own house, enjoying security and independence.*

WHEN their doctor told Marie and Frank Butler that they would have to go to a nursing home, their daughter-in-law Joan spent a frantic day phoning almost every nursing home in Minneapolis. The doctor felt that Marie, 71 and suffering from diabetes, and Frank, 75, chair-ridden with emphysema, no longer could take care of themselves in their own home.

Joan found what she and her husband, Dick, considered to be a suitable nursing home— one run by a local church group.

Marie and Frank stayed less than three months and insisted on going home. After 45 years of their own apartments and then a house, they couldn't stand being limited to one room—one not even as big as

just their living room at home. Moreover, proud people who survived the Depression of the 1930's, when Frank worked 78 hours a week for $22 as a butcher, they rejected the prospect that after they consumed most of their assets they would have to ask for state aid to pay the nursing home. Even that short stay cost Marie and Frank $3,000—a heartbreaking chunk of their life savings.

Marie is a sweet-faced lady with a gentle voice. Even when she tells her troubles she sounds as though she's explaining rather than complaining. "The care at the nursing home was wonderful," she relates. "But they put us in the infirmary. The people there were all senile. It was very expensive; $1,215 a month for the two of us. They tell you to borrow on your insurance and turn over your house. They allow you to keep only $750 in savings. Then you can go on relief. I haven't been on relief my whole life. I don't intend to go now."

If they had remained in the nursing home, state aid was inevitable. Their total income is only $360 a month, mostly Social Security and a pension from the Meat Cutters Union. Their prized house itself, an elderly frame dwelling in a downtown block of two- and four-family houses, might also have to be sold.

For Dick and Joan, their parents' refusal to remain in the nursing home created a guilt-edged dilemma that confronts most middle-aged and even youngish couples sooner or later. Having elderly parents remain in their own home or even in yours is no problem when they're physically capable. But caring for an invalid is another matter. The problem often occurs just when sons and daughters are collecting their own crises, including health difficulties and the needs of growing children.

Despite modern financial helps such as Medicare and state medical aid, the quandary of how to care for older parents is increasing. For one thing, average life expectancy is increasing—no society in history has had to care for such a large elderly population.

Another reason for the spreading concern over care of the elderly is that the proliferation of nursing homes, some launched to soak up increased government funds, has been matched by the increasing number of horror stories about their inadequate care.

When elderly people must enter a nursing home, adding to the inevitable guilt feelings of their relatives is the worry about the quality of care. Only about 20 percent of nursing homes are truly high quality, Senate experts say.

The basic puzzle is, where does an elderly person go? One study found that many who enter nursing homes do so not for unarguable medical reasons but because they simply have no other place to go. Over half of those now in nursing homes really need only some help in their activities.

The dilemma of care for the elderly inevitably has an emotional impact on their grown children. Relations between husband and wife are affected because of the financial help

one spouse may give to an elderly parent, especially when it's without consulting the other. The needs of elderly parents also may cause discord among their sons and daughters by recalling old rivalries and jealousies. A common phenomenon is the resentment of those who help toward those who don't want to help.

Joan and Dick Butler themselves felt some of those concerns when Marie and Frank insisted on leaving the nursing home. Dick is 50—a big, patient man and a skilled machinist employed at the Honeywell factory in Minneapolis most of his work life. But he suffers

from histaminic headaches which have affected his eyes. He had to leave work for seven weeks last fall with his only income from workmen's compensation.

Joan is a tall, lean woman with strong features and a ready smile who dresses in tailored, well-organized separates and runs a tidy, well-organized home. She's able to keep glued together despite the many demands she's had to meet in the course of raising seven children. There has never been any discord between her and Dick over what help they gave his parents, usually more in the way of services—such as doing their laundry—than in cash. In fact, Marie Butler told me she thinks of Joan and her other daughter-in-law, Molly, as her own daughters.

But as is often the case, one son or daughter usually assumes a major role in helping elderly parents. Sometimes it's the one living closest or who left home last. Dick's brother, Bill, two years older, moved to Texas and can no longer help.

Working couples like Joan and Dick rarely have the capacity to aid elderly relatives financially. There was never a time when Dick and Joan didn't have money problems. Today Dick makes around $14,000—before taxes. In earlier years, when his pay was much lower, they had to cope with such expenses as $4,000 for orthodontia for four of their young daughters.

For the past several months, Joan's been working as a supermarket cashier three days a week to bolster the family's finances. Therese, 19, lived at home until she recently married. Mark, 18, is enrolled in an auto-mechanics course that costs $82 a month.

Apart from financial help, with Dick's own health problems, he and Joan now lack even the physical capacity to give his parents the care they need. "We spent sleepless nights worrying," Joan relates. "At least we didn't have to feel we were the ones who pushed them into the nursing home. While they were there we saw to it that someone visited them almost every day. Even when

they wanted to leave . . . if we were upset, it was only because they decided so suddenly. Within a day or two they wanted us to find a housekeeper and bring them home. Grandma was really bothered when she went into the nursing home. Emotionally, they're far better off at home."

At that point a four-alarm crisis would have erupted were it not for the availability of a pioneering agency for elderly people. This is the Minneapolis Age and Opportunity Center, which provides supportive services to help elderly people stay in their own homes rather than go to nursing homes.

The older Butlers' doctor had agreed to their leaving the nursing home only if they got the help of M.A.O., as local people call the Age and Opportunity Center. Marie had really been sick. She had—and still has—diabetic foot ulcers, a heart condition and a medically impressive list of related conditions. She also must care for Frank, who requires constant medication for the chronic bronchitis caused by his years of going in and out of meat-refrigerator rooms.

So when Joan and Dick had restored the older Butlers to their own home and settled them down, it was a great relief for all when M.A.O. took over.

M.A.O.'s services are tailored to the specific needs of its elderly clients. For Marie and Frank, M.A.O. delivers two meals a day—one hot dinner and one cold lunch for the next day. Marie need only prepare breakfast. In fact, it was her ability to prepare at least breakfast that convinced M.A.O. that with its two meals and other services, the Butlers could get along at home.

M.A.O. also sends a homemaker once a week to do the heavier cleaning, such as vacuuming and changing the beds, and a choreman to occasionally spruce up the small yard. Another vital M.A.O. service is transportation to clinics, including its own operated in conjunction with Abbot-Northwestern Hospital.

The transportation has been

*Dick and Joan with four of their seven children—Pam, 21 (the mother of the child shown on the preceding page); Debbie, 22 (soon to be a mother herself); Kathy, 26; and Mark, 18. Dick is a skilled machinist and Joan now works part-time to help boost their finances.*

especially helpful for Frank. One of M.A.O.'s fleet of minibuses and station wagons brings him to the Veterans Administration clinic for periodic treatments. Last fall when he had to go into the hospital for four weeks, M.A.O. brought Marie there almost every day to visit him.

Dick and Joan's children, who range from 26 to 18, three married, supply any transportation that M.A.O. can't, and also do chores when they're in town or have time off from school or work. Marie has two brothers who also help with shopping and transportation.

It's this carefully dovetailed combination of services from M.A.O. and help from relatives that makes such care tolerable for relatives and financially feasible for M.A.O. But what cements the teamwork in this case is that the Butler children and their grandparents care for each other.

For others, M.A.O. also provides personal care if needed, such as help with bathing, financial counseling, information on resources like food stamps, an emergency food shelf and even emergency money, and legal services for wills and estates, Social Security eligibility and other legal problems of the elderly.

M.A.O. even has a handyman whom it sends over to build a wheelchair ramp, if needed, fix a furnace or small appliances, or provide other repairs elderly people often badly need. For Marie and Frank the handyman does any needed painting and puts up the storms and screens—the kind of jobs Dick and Bill used to do for them.

M.A.O. is the creation of an articulate, active, community volunteer, Daphne Krause, now its executive director. As a community worker she perceived the need for a multi-service organization for the elderly. She believes a crisis is developing in their care, for the senior population is increasing by 1,000 a day while the working population that must support the seniors has shrunk because of the low birth rate in the Depression.

The convenient solution of storing the elderly in nursing homes has been accelerated by recent changes in both laws and attitudes. Children are no longer held to be financially responsible for their parents. Frank Butler says 80 percent of the nursing-home residents had their expenses paid for by the State Medicaid program.

But Daphne Krause came to feel that many nursing-home residents could be cared for in their own homes if comprehensive support was available. She felt that both the seniors and the taxpayers, now footing a swelling bill for institutional care, could benefit greatly. She first took her concept to senior-citizen groups. They told her what seniors need and formed the first board of directors. Now it also includes representatives from labor unions, churches, medical groups, family agencies and community organizations such as the

Junior League. Daphne also enlisted the Abbott-Northwestern Hospital in setting up a clinic and won the financial backing of community and government agencies and private donors.

The clinic and full services have been operating just since 1968, but already M.A.O. is getting national attention including from Congress. Senate experts see M.A.O. as a potential model for elderly-care and as an alternative to costly nursing homes.

Today, M.A.O. works on two simple but accurate premises. One is that medical services are not enough: The elderly need a full range of services and need to be able to get them all from one agency. The other concept is to tailor the care to help the elderly maintain various levels of independence.

Thus, M.A.O. even operates an employment service and places elderly people in good health in positions where they can help those in poor health, even as live-in companions.

Some of these activities are on a volunteer basis, such as part-time office work for M.A.O., shopping for other elderly people and so on. For others, such as the senior handyman project, retired men receive pay for repair work, painting, yardwork and similar jobs.

The elderly served by M.A.O. pay modest fees, if they can afford them. Marie and Frank pay only $1 a day for their home-delivered meals. Others may pay up to $1.85—M.A.O.'s cost. Partial payment can even be made in food stamps. There's no charge at all in some circumstances; if, for example, a senior citizen has high medical bills or a Social Security check has been stolen. The program is so carefully planned that the drivers who deliver meals are even coached on how to deal with any medical emergencies they may encounter. Also, there is no set rate for other services. M.A.O. tells clients its costs; for example, that homemaker and handyman services cost M.A.O. about $3.75 an hour. Users contribute whatever they can. (Some oldsters have contributed as little as 25¢.)

The clinic is a key part of the M.A.O. program, especially in a period of rising medical bills, when fixed incomes of older people especially have been eroded by the rise in living costs. In general, the proportion of medical expenses paid by Medicare has shrunk. This means that many older people are deprived of care. Doctors at the clinic found that many patients had not seen a doctor in years and that most needed immediate medical attention.

For that reason, since late '73 the clinic not only has expanded its services but provides them at no charge above the Medicare, Medicaid, or any insurance reimbursement for an individual whose income is $4,500 or less ($5,500 for a couple). There's no "means test." The clinic simply accepts the members' word about finances. The services even include prescriptions filled at hospital

cost, nursing services at home when needed, specialist eye care, emotional counseling and blood-donor service. Some of the expenses of the clinic are absorbed by the Abbott-Northwestern Hospital.

The clinic also provides health check-ups, which brought it temporarily into confrontation with Blue Cross, the Medicare supervisory agency in the Minneapolis area, because Medicare doesn't usually cover "routine check-ups." But the clinic insisted that preventive checkups facilitate early, and thus more effective treatment. This logic won the day but not before the issue became the subject of a U.S. Senate hearing.

## Dollar-a-Day Fee

It's only because Marie and Frank pay just $1 a day toward M.A.O.'s services that they can get along on their $360 a month. They buy no clothes. (The grandchildren provide Marie with housedresses.) Their biggest expense is her medicine. Frank gets his medicines through the V.A. and is still annoyed that the V.A. provided his medicines but the nursing home charged him 75¢ a day "for dishing it out."

Their other major expenses are about $50 a month for utilities, phone and heat; $20–$25 for food other than meals supplied by M.A.O., and $400 a year for property taxes, stabilized for them as senior citizens under local law. As one insight into the spending ways of seniors, they spend nothing at all on entertainment but about $250 a year on birthday and Christmas gifts. Still, the Butlers are in a race with inflation. Frank notes that "every time Social Security goes up, so does Medicare, so the increases don't help much."

If M.A.O. is the wave of the future, it has yet to reach most American towns (except for a similar agency in Athens, Georgia). Many of the individual components of the M.A.O. program probably are available in your area. But if you have the responsibility for the care of elderly relatives, you may have to assemble these fragments yourself, perhaps with the help of a local family service or senior citizens' agency, advises B. C. Fisher of New York's Community Service Society.

One of the most widely available services is "Meals on Wheels," like the M.A.O. program that brings Marie and Frank their meals. This service is partly financed by the Federal Government. In some cities the public school systems operate the "Meals on Wheels" program, putting the school cafeterias to useful double duty.

Many programs have been organized by Senior Citizen and Golden Age Clubs affiliated with the National Council of Senior Citizens, including the Senior Aides program of part-time jobs.

Another widespread service is telephone reassurance, sometimes called "Ring A Day." At prearranged times, volunteers—often seniors themselves—call elderly people living alone. If there is no answer, or in an emergency, the caller knows beforehand which doctor, neighbor and relatives to notify. A specialist in problems of widowhood, Dr. Virginia R. Coevering, has written a booklet, *Guidelines for a Telephone Reassurance Service*, published by the Institute of Gerontology. In the belief that this service can make a vital difference in the lives of isolated and elderly people, the Institute, located at 543 Church St., Ann Arbor, Mich. 48104, offers the booklet free.

Perhaps the most innovative self-help program is the Jamaica, N.Y., Service Program for Older Adults. It brought together community organizations and senior-citizen groups to provide services and activity programs, with the seniors themselves involved in helping elderly residents. A Senior Citizen Ad-

visory Council helped identify what local older people themselves consider to be their primary needs and interests. The Council initiated a senior citizens' crime-prevention program; worked to get free checking accounts for seniors from local banks; helped sponsor health fairs and seminars, and distributed a "health passport"—a wallet card recording essential health data which might be needed in an emergency.

Seniors increasingly are helping others through the nationwide Retired Senior Volunteer Program. R.S.V.P. already operates in 600 communities with help from the Federal ACTION agency.

Homemaker and visiting-nurse services are also available. You can send a stamped self-addressed envelope for a local list of the National Council for Homemaker–Home Health Aide Services, 67 Irving Place, New York, N.Y.

10003.

One type of home care that elderly ill people probably can invoke more often is the home health visits by medical personnel available under Medicare and Medicaid programs. Such care must be approved by the patient's physician as part of a treatment plan. A government survey found this benefit underutilized.

For Marie and Frank Butler, the availability of all these services in one agency has meant a chance to spend more years in their own home with the feeling of independence and dignity they prize. To Joan and Dick, this pioneering agency has brought peace of mind after years of worry over their parents, and more time to deal with their own health problems and their children's needs.

# 50

As mental health ideologies have changed, the system serves a smaller proportion of older persons than in earlier decades. This paper discusses likely future changes in the characteristics of older persons and of mental health professionals and makes recommendations for changes in the system.

# The Mental Health System and the Future Aged[1]

Robert L. Kahn, PhD[2]

Prediction of the future, in considering the mental health needs of the aged, requires an understanding of the past. Accordingly, we will first consider the patterns of mental health care of the aged in the first half of this century and then contrast it with more recent changes. It is our contention that such an analysis discloses a clear-cut pattern of negative age bias, that some of the factors underlying this bias will remain, while others will have altered significantly by the year 2000, and, finally, that it is then possible to make predictions both about what *will* happen and what *should* happen.

The early 1900s were characterized by the great buildup of mental hospitals, particularly those operated by states and counties. In 1904 there were 150,151 persons resident in mental hospitals in the United States, while the total was 633,504 in the peak year of 1955 (Willner, 1974). During this period there was a systematic age bias, with older persons being disproportionately hospitalized.

Fig. 1 shows first admission rates per 100,000 persons of each age group in the state of New York from 1909-1911 to 1949-1951. At every decade there was a consistent age gradient; the older the age, the higher the rate of admission. Although the rates for other age groups remained fairly constant over this 40-year period, remaining between 50 and 150 per 100,000, the aged not only had an initially much higher rate, but the rate continued to rise, more than doubling the 1909-1911 rate by 1949-1951, and

going from around 200 to approximately 435 per 100,000.

After World War II there was a dramatic alteration in our conceptions and patterns of mental health care. With such milestones as the establishment of the National Institute of Mental Health in 1948, the organization of the Joint Commission on Mental Illness and Health in 1955, and the passage of the Community Mental Health Centers Act of 1963, there was a more active and optimistic attitude toward mental illness, characterized by radically reduc-

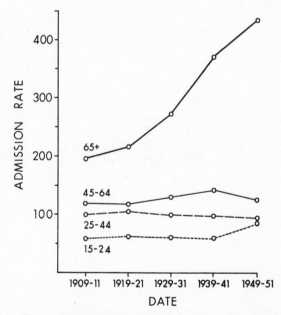

Fig. 1. First admissions to all hospitals for mental disease in New York State, 1910-1950: Rates per 100,000 population in each age group (derived from Malzberg, 1967).

1. With the assistance of Sanford Finkel, MD, Raymond Launier, Jay Magaziner, and Kenneth Sakauye, MD.
2. Associate Professor, Dept. of Psychiatry, and Committee on Human Development, Dept. of Behavioral Sciences, Univ. of Chicago, Chicago 60637.

ing the resident mental hospital population and developing such other services as psychiatric units in general hospitals, outpatient services of all kinds, and the vaunted community mental health centers.

These developments did result in drastically changed patterns of use of psychiatric facilities, but patterns which varied strikingly according to age. In Fig. 2 the percentage of change for each age group is shown in the first admission

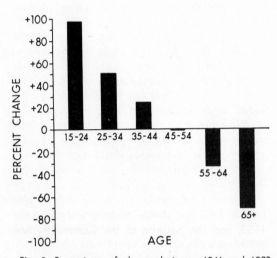

Fig. 2. Percentage of change between 1946 and 1972 for each age group in rate of first admissions per 100,000 population to state and county mental hospitals (USA) (derived from Kramer, 1973a).

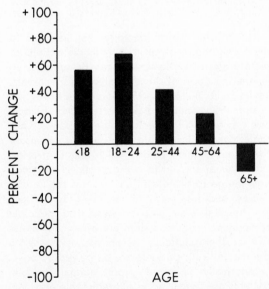

Fig. 3. Percentage of change between 1966 and 1971 for each age group in rate of patient care episodes per 100,000 population for all psychiatric services (USA) (derived from Redick, 1973).

rates to all state and county mental hospitals in the United States between 1946 and 1972. Once more there is an age gradient but now it is diametrically opposite to that shown for the earlier years of this century. In the past 25 years there has been an enormous increase in the first admission rate for the very young, 97%, with the amount of change progressively decreasing with age, being unchanged for the 45-54 year group, and then showing a great *decrease* for the older patients, going down over 71% for those aged 65 and over.

These figures are based on first admissions to mental hospitals, but a similar trend is found when examining patient care episodes in all psychiatric services. Patient care episodes are defined as the number of residents or enrolled patients in all types of psychiatric facilities at the beginning of the year plus the total additions to these facilities during the year. Comparing the years 1966 and 1971, with all the new facilities and services available, there was an increase of 37% in patient care episodes for the total population (Redick, 1973). Again, as shown in Fig. 3, there is an enormous age differential, and a consistent gradient, with younger persons showing the largest increases (as much as 67.5% for those 18-24 years of age), with lesser increases for successively older age groups, and with those aged 65 and over showing an actual *decrease* of almost 22%.

Rather than helping older persons, the great mental health revolution has only led to their dropping out of the psychiatric system. Certainly the new programs have not helped the aged. If we look, for example, at psychiatric units in general hospitals, from 1966 to 1971 there was a 45% reduction in the number of patient care episodes for the aged. In Community Mental Health Centers, in 1971 the aged represented only 7% of inpatient service, and only 3% of their outpatient cases. Of all other outpatient services, the aged were only 2% (Kramer, 1973a).

To the question of what has happened to the aged mental health dropouts, obviously much of the answer can be found in the data on nursing homes. In an analysis by Redick (1974) of changes in the utilization of psychiatric services by the aged mentally ill during the decade 1960-1970, he concludes that there is an "emerging custodialism" in which the aged are now being displaced to nursing homes. Showing an incredible increase from 554,000 residents in 1963 to 1,098,500 10 years later, and with a current bed capacity of over 1,200,000, the nursing homes have replaced the state and county hospitals as the custodial warehouses. This has led to an increase in the total proportions of persons aged 65+ who are institutionalized, with the proportion rising from 4% to 5% from 1960 to 1970.

In 1963 almost two-fifths of the aged who were diagnosed as mentally ill and who were in long-term care institutions were to be found in state and county mental hospitals, while 53% were in nursing homes and personal care homes. These proportions changed drastically in 1969, when 75% of the aged mentally ill were in nursing homes.

It is obvious that the elderly are being neglected by the mental health establishment. The explanation for this unfortunate state of affairs is undoubtedly complex. It is a common stereotype among clinical gerontologists that other mental health professionals avoid the aged because of psychological problems such as ". . . unresolved conflict with parental images and the need to deny our own mortality . . ." (Lawton & Gottesman, 1974). Although there may well be some degree of psychological selectivity in determining which professionals become gerontologists, there is no *a priori* basis for presuming that this group are more mentally healthy than other professionals, or that they have fewer unresolved conflicts over growing old. It could just as well be hypothesized that those who work with the elderly may have *excessive* unresolved parental conflicts, or excessive problems in confronting their own mortality. In any case, such simplistic psychological explanations would damn the aged to continued neglect so long as human beings have parents and so long as human beings die.

Nor can the data be interpreted mechanically in terms of administrative considerations or idiosyncratic financial status of the aged, although these are obviously contributory factors. It is not a situation of the aged against the world. There is a consistent age gradient over the entire life-span which must be accounted for, in which the aged, defined here as those who are 65 and over, are simply the extreme of a continuum.

In contrast to the views just mentioned, the patterns of psychiatric care of the aged can be better explained on the basis of a reciprocal aversiveness between the mental health establishment and older persons, based on the interaction of such factors as mental health ideology,

social class characteristics, and considerations of age appropriateness.

## Ideological Factors

Over the past two centuries in this country, there have been several clear ideological movements and patterns with regard to mental health. Originally the mental hospitals were established as part of a great humanitarian movement to provide treatment for the mentally ill instead of merely depositing them in prisons or poorhouses. In the 19th century the advocates of "moral treatment" endeavored to improve the quality of care in the mental hospitals; but with the increasing flow of lower class immigrants as patients, the hospitals became very custodial in their orientation, relying heavily on the use of restraints (Grob, 1966). In the 20th century the mental hospital continued to deteriorate until our World War II experiences and some new developments in England (e.g., Carse, Panton, & Watt, 1958; Macmillan, 1958) contributed to a reconceptualization of our mental health ideology.

The prevailing practices in hospital treatment were so bad that even politicians could make the obvious criticisms, as evident in President Kennedy's message to Congress on "Mental Illness and Mental Retardation" in 1963:

> . . . (these new programs) have rendered obsolete the traditional methods of treatment which imposed upon the mentally ill a social quarantine, a prolonged or permanent confinement in huge, unhappy mental hospitals where they were out of sight and forgotten.

The mental health ideology that had led to these conditions, often implicit in the actions of society and of professionals, can be summed up in the concept of "custodialism" (Greenblatt, Levinson, & Williams, 1957; Greenblatt, York, & Brown, 1955; Stanton & Schwartz, 1954). Gilbert and Levinson (1956) actually developed a Custodial Mental Illness Ideology Scale to measure the extent of this ideology which they contrasted with "humanism." The components of an ideology can be found in attitudes toward the nature, causes, and treatment of mental illness, including hospital aims and policies. The principal components of custodialism are a basically negative or therapeutically pessimistic approach to the mentally ill; patients are perceived as being categorically different from normal people; patients are perceived as unpredictable and dangerous, requiring care in a highly controlled setting; the setting is concerned mainly with detention and safekeeping; and the institution is conceived as a rigid status hierarchy with lines of communication following the chain of authority, and with the patient occupying the lowest status position in the hierarchy.

Opposition to custodialism took many forms, both inside and outside the institution, with some who challenged the role of the institution itself. Much of the change within the institution was embodied in the concept of the "therapeutic community" which originated in Britain (Jones, 1953; Main, 1946). Taking a more optimistic view of mental illness, the proponents of the therapeutic community believed that much pathology was induced by the institution itself which compelled the patient to learn and act the "sick role." To prevent such a development they advocated democratizing the hospital, flattening the heirarchy, opening up two-way communication channels, and utilizing the skills of the total personnel of the institution, with special emphasis on the expanded role of the patient.

The new philosophy was indeed accompanied by many changes,[3] with meetings of staff and patients on psychiatric wards, by establishing "open" hospitals by unlocking the doors, by increasing personnel, and by accelerating patient turnover. But the application of the ideological shifts were uneven in their effect on different age groups. There seems to be a consistent relationship between custodialism and age. Prior to World War II, with mental illness regarded as a stigma, with custodialism as the dominant philosophy, and with the mental hospital serving primarily to extrude the mentally ill from society, older persons were more frequently hospitalized than younger persons. With the change in orientation after the war, the age gradient was reversed. For the young, the changed ideology represented new possibilities for treatment. For the aged, custodialism continued to prevail but with one difference—earlier the aged were treated custodially in mental hospitals (despite the presence of psychiatrically-trained personnel); now they are treated custodially in nursing homes (without any pretense of psychiatric service).

Part of the great displacement of the mentally ill aged from the state hospitals to nursing homes has resulted from a mechanical adherence to

slogans, such as "alternatives to hospitalization." Based on the principle that state hospitals are unsuitable settings for the elderly, programs have been developed to find alternatives; but this usually means the use of nursing homes, without the realization that nursing homes are even more custodial in their care than the hospitals they are meant to replace (Epstein & Simon, 1968). The confusion of slogan and substance is, of course, common in contemporary mental health trends. The shift from the hospital to the community, for example, may simply represent a changed location but the same old philosophy (Polak & Jones, 1973).

## Custodialism as a Self-Fulfilling Prophecy

In part, the age biases in mental health treatment demonstrated above are a direct consequence of the policy of custodialism. The negative attitudes associated with custodialism resulted in the accumulation of chronic patients, predominantly schizophrenics, who were hospitalized at an early age and then remained institutionalized, commonly for life. Such persons thus constituted an aging resident population for whom custodialism had been a self-fulfilling prophecy, teaching them the "sick role," isolating them from their families and from normal community activities, and making them incapable of living without extensive protective care. Custodialism applied to the young eventually created a cohort of older persons who required it or could be moved out of the mental hospital only by heroic efforts. These patients were galling to the hospital staffs, taking up so much time, space, and money and with such little benefit. On reaching age 65 these patients were routinely shifted to the "geriatric" ward, and their evident need for custodial care was now attributed to their age rather than to their chronic schizophrenia and long-term custodial history. The myth about these patients has been augmented by life-cycle professionals who endeavor to set up programs in mental hospitals for geriatric patients, but who fail to distinguish between those aged who developed mental disorder in their early life, such as schizophrenics, and persons who developed mental disorder in old age (Kahn & Zarit, 1974). Since the management of older patients in mental hospitals did not fit the new treatment philosophy, it was considered preferable to shift them to other institutions, still complacently custodial.

The philosophy of custodialism is so entrenched that benevolent gerontological planners

---

3. Sometimes the effects of the ideological shift are not properly appreciated because of the temporal proximity of the use of chemotherapy. The large-scale use of drugs, which began in the middle 1950s, coincided with the start of the reduction in the resident patient population in mental hospitals. But the changes in ideology and practice antedated the drugs. Macmillan (1958), for example, started opening his hospital in 1945 and completed the changeover in 1952.

talk about the need to provide custodial care as part of any new comprehensive care system. Since there are persons who manifestly fit the custodial operation, it is easy to overlook the fact that the need for custodial care is highly exaggerated and that its very application is self-perpetuating. Studies of aged persons in custodial settings have demonstrated the phenomena of "excess disability" (Kahn, 1971) in which the level of function is poorer than the patient's physiological capability (Brody, Kleban, Lawton, & Silverman, 1971; Kelman, 1962). Excess disability is characteristic of both self-care and cognitive functioning. A person may have all the necessary physiological capacities yet be unable to feed or bathe himself. Cognitively, the old person may show "unorientation" (Kahn, 1971), a state in which the impairment demonstrated in areas where the patient has personal and emotional involvement is greater than the impairment shown in more neutral areas. Thus, he may know the date or the name of the President of the United States, but be unable to state where he is, even after having been in residence for months or years. In a large-scale institutional study it was found that the level of mental status of aged patients was related to certain characteristics of the institutions, being better when the institution was less custodial (Kahn, 1961). It has been demonstrated that breaking down the custodial pattern of a mental hospital ward by mixing young and old patients on the same ward will result in improved cognitive function in the older patient (Kahana & Kahana, 1970).

Although there is much difference of opinion among gerontologists on the use of institutions, assaults are now appearing from new directions, and some of the basic assumptions and practices of custodialism are being challenged. Notable among these are new research findings (Schaie, 1974) which question the generality of cognitive decline with age, findings which, by undercutting one of the stereotypes about "senility," are also undercutting one of the stereotypes about the need for custodial care.

### Effects of Social Class

The relationship between age and custodialism can be explained further on the basis of cohort differences in social class. It is a well-established research finding that mental health treatment varies according to the social status of the patient, with upper-class persons receiving psychological treatment such as psycho-therapy and psychoanalysis, while lower-class patients receive somatic therapy and custodial care (Hollingshead & Redlich, 1958). Since, compared to the young, a higher proportion of the old have been poorly educated, and a higher proportion of old mental patients are working class rather than middle class, differences in treatment reflect these social class differences, thus compounding the age difference.

The effects of social class are complex and do not necessarily reflect discriminating prejudice. The new treatment philosophies, whether represented by the "therapeutic communities" or some form of psychotherapy, emphasize verbal interaction and the patient's recognition of psychological causation of mental disorder. Since these are the very characteristics that distinguish social classes, the aged may be treated custodially not only because they are aged, but because, with their lesser education and other cultural differences, they are less receptive to verbal psychological treatments (Hollingshead & Redlich, 1958; Kahn, Pollack, & Fink, 1957).

Thus there is mutual avoidance; the mental health professionals prefer the young, educated patients, and the aged reject the psychological treatments of psychotherapy and psychoanalysis so highly valued by the professional.

### Age Appropriateness

In addition to the social class factors, there may be an intrinsic life cycle phenomenon of age appropriateness for types of psychiatric treatment. Comparable to attitudes toward other life events, there is apparently a sense that psychiatric treatment is appropriate or optimum at a given time of life. Certainly the professionals, starting with Freud himself, have encouraged the notion that psychological treatment is best undertaken early in life. Among the present-day young it may be almost a status symbol to be in treatment, but for the present-day old it is a disgrace.

### A LOOK AT THE FUTURE

From this analysis insights can be derived regarding critical theoretical issues regarding mental illness and treatment in the aged and how these will be affected by changing social factors by the year 2000.

### Effects of Changes in the Aged

Perhaps the major changes in the relationship of custodialism and the aged in the year 2000 will come about because of predictable changes in the aged themselves. We know that they will have characteristics of higher social status: much better education—the median education will be high school graduation, far fewer numbers of foreign-born, and more social and political awareness. These people will have much less tolerance for custodialism in all its aspects, including the use of custodial institutions such as nursing homes.

The aged are also likely to be much better off because of better economic resources through improved pensions and social security, better comprehensive medical care, and better preparation for, and participation in, retirement. Because of all these changes the aged may actually manifest fewer extreme cases of disordered behavior for which custodial care might be considered.

## Effects of Changes in the Professionals

The mental health professionals can also be expected to change significantly. Responding partly to the improved social status of the aged, no longer contaminated in their thinking by large numbers of chronically institutionalized schizophrenics who will have died off, and with a greater awareness of the etiology and modifiability of acute organic brain syndromes, the professional will also eschew custodialism and will become increasingly concerned with prevention in all its aspects. Although primary prevention through such measures as good nutrition will be major efforts, secondary and tertiary prevention will also receive greater attention than today. These will stress mitigating or terminating a disorder once it is manifest by using such methods as early detection and crisis intervention, and reducing the disabilities consequent upon disorder by using such techniques as the therapeutic community and rehabilitation. At the very least, there will be a recognition that the negative consequences of mental dysfunction can be minimized by exposing old persons to more demanding and stimulating environments, in contrast to the isolation and dependency effects of the custodial institution. There will be less infantilization and greater opportunities for the old person to maintain control of his own situation.

## Needed New Developments

New developments within the mental health system must also be undertaken directly. For one thing, the very fact of increasing numbers of the aged require new approaches.[4]

Concepts for new programs that should be developed, as well as the operational examples, already exist, although decisive evaluative studies remain to be done. Allowing for many variations depending on the resources of specific settings, the following are suggested as guiding principles:

(1) Mental health and illness are not categorically different, and the same individual will have both healthy and pathological components of personality. As much as possible we should respond to the healthy aspects rather than reinforce the "sick role."

(2) Psychopathology is not fixed or inevitable within the organism, even with altered central nervous system dysfunction. Different environments produce different consequences on function, contributing to enhancement or to deterioration.

(3) "Senility" is a psycho-social-biological phenomenon. Although we may have limited means for changing the biological component, the psychological and social factors are modifiable.

(4) If an old person is under protective care, his functional level should correspond to his physiological capacity.

(5) Intervention can be harmful as well as helpful. Although resources for intervention should be available when needed, it is best to follow a policy of *minimal intervention*; that is, intervention that is least disruptive of usual functioning in the usual setting. Thus, it would be more sensible to provide care in the home or day-care center than in the hospital; in the storefront rather than in the clinic; in the neighborhood rather than downtown; for brief rather than for long periods; with neighborhood personnel rather than with explicit medical or social agency professionals.

Minimal intervention as a positive concept must be differentiated from neglect. It must also be differentiated from "maximal-minimal" intervention, in which the person is removed from his community, then placed in an institution that provides no psychological or social compensatory measures.

4. From a conventional viewpoint, the problem would be almost insoluble if we reckoned the fantastic costs or professional needs as described by Kramer (1973b). For example, reckoning on a 20% psychiatric need in the total population in the year 1980, and providing a total of 10 hours of care per year per patient per discipline, he indicates that over 300,000 professionals will be required in each of the disciplines of psychiatry, psychology, and nursing, with an additional 609,000 social workers needed to provide minimal service.

(6) Effective care is quite different from the *number* of services. The structural dynamics may be far more important than the component parts. In particular, *continuity of care is essential, in which* personnel, agencies, and institutions are integrated. The same personnel should be able to deal with the person in a variety of settings, whether in or out of the institution. Institutions will not be as effective if they are encapsulated units, even with high staff/patient ratios, as if they are part of a coordinated comprehensive system.

(7) Both the needs of the old person and his family must be considered. More good may be done for both by providing supportive help to the family, for example, than by dealing directly with the patient's psychosis. One of the most useful techniques is to provide "holiday relief," in which the old person may be hospitalized for a week or two to enable the family to take a vacation. This limited support may often be sufficient to prevent permanent institutionalization of the old person.

There may also be a legitimate conflict of interests. It may relieve emotional pressures on a family to place an old person in an institution permanently, but the effects of the move may be deleterious to the old person. In those cases, ethical as well as clinical judgment is required.

(8) Expectations may be decisive in achieving mental health goals. In using an institution, for example, setting a time limit at the point of entry may help the old person, his family, and the institution to act in ways more likely to lead to his return home.

(9) *Decentralization* and *"de-medicalization"* of services are desirable. Outreach workers, nonprofessionals preferably coming from the same background, same neighborhood, and same general age group as the prospective clients, would be the first line of contact, serving at least in a confidante role, providing the liaison to professionals. The latter would serve as indirect consultants to nonprofessionals, providing brief *direct* service only to a small number of persons, but providing *indirect* consultation to "firing line professionals such as police, clergymen, general physicians, and to others such as bank tellers, bus drivers, and storekeepers." Most persons could be helped without ever becoming an administratively official "patient" or "client."

(10) Instead of being the passive recipient of services which the professional decides are good for him, the old person's sense of control should be maintained. The very act of being helped can have the paradoxical effect of increasing the impairment because of the infantilization and sense of loss of control that results.

(11) Those principles can be carried further by realizing that *"potential service"* may be as useful as any form of *actual* help. The basis of this concept is to guarantee that service will be available when needed. If a community were assured of the validity of the commitment of service it would be increasingly possible to cope with many problems, either autonomously or with minimum help, that might otherwise have involved more extensive use of resources. Thus, guaranteeing that brief hospitalization will always be available when needed should not only reduce the amount of long hospitalization, but the amount of brief hospitalization as well.

(12) The most effective mental health programs for the aged have been achieved in the context of the public health technique of a geographically-defined catchment area (e.g., Macmillan, 1958; Perlin & Kahn, 1967). By explicitly defining the responsibility and commitment for a given target population and physical locale, there has been the greatest opportunity for facilitating such necessary components as comprehensiveness and continuity of care, guaranteed service, and maximum use of community resources. In practice the application of the catchment area concept has resulted in providing for the mental health needs of the entire population. (Without such a definition, programs follow the conventional criteria for selecting patients, resulting in the characteristic biases toward the aged, so that their needs are overlooked or evaded by "dumping" old people into an external institution or resource.)

These concepts and changed practices have considerable promise in meeting the mental health needs of the aged by the year 2000. They will have an impact on both the established mental health system and the innovative community services. The new approaches may have the multiple virtues of not only being more effective than many conventional practices but also far more economical and efficient in the use of our resources.

**References**

Brody, E. M., Kleban, M. M., Lawton, M. P., & Silverman, H. A. Excess disabilities of mental impaired aged: Impact of individualized treatment. **Gerontologist,** 1971, 11, 124-132.

Carse, J., Panton, N. E., & Watt, A. A district mental health service: the Worthing experiment. **Lancet,** 1958, 1, 39-42.

Epstein, L. J., & Simon, A. Alternatives to state hospitalization for the geriatric mentally ill. **American Journal of Psychiatry,** 1968, **124,** 955-961.

Gilbert, D. C., & Levinson, D. J. Ideology, personality and institutional policy in the mental hospital. **Journal of Abnormal & Social Psychology,** 1956, **53,** 263-271.

Greenblatt, M., Levinson, D. J., & Williams, R. **The patient and the mental hospital.** Free Press, Glencoe, IL, 1957.

Greenblatt, M., York, R., & Brown, E. L. **From custodial to therapeutic care in mental hospitals.** Russell Sage Foundation, New York, 1955.

Grob, G. N. **The state and the mentally ill.** Univ. of North Carolina Press, Chapel Hill, 1966.

Hollingshead, A. B., & Redlich, F. C. **Social class and mental illness.** John Wiley, New York, 1958.

Jones, M. **The therapeutic community.** Basic Books, New York, 1953.

Kahana, E., & Kahana, B. Therapeutic potential of age integration: Effects of age integrated hospital environments on elderly psychiatric patients. **Archives of General Psychiatry,** 1970, **23,** 20-29.

Kahn, R. L. Psychological aspects of aging. In I. Rossman (Ed.), **Clinical geriatrics.** J. B. Lippincott, Philadelphia, 1971.

Kahn, R. L., Pollack, M., & Fink, M. Social factors in the selection of therapy in a voluntary mental hospital. **Journal of Hillside Hospital,** 1957, **6,** 216-228.

Kahn, R. L., Pollack, M., & Goldfarb, A. I. Factors related to individual differences in mental status of institutionalized aged. In P. Hoch & J. Zubin (Eds.), **Psychopathology of aging.** Grune & Stratton, New York, 1961.

Kahn, R. L., & Zarit, S. H. Evaluation of mental health programs for the aged. In P. O. Davidson, F. W. Clark, & L. A. Hamerlynck (Eds.), **Evaluation of behavioral programs.** Research Press, Champaign, IL, 1974.

Kellman, H. R. An experiment in the rehabilitation of nursing home patients. **Public Health Reports.** PHS, DHEW, 1962, **77,** 356-366.

Kramer, M. Historical tables in changes in patterns of the use of psychiatric facilities 1946-1971. Biometry Branch, NIMH, Rockville, MD, 1973. (a)

Kramer, M. Implications of expected changes in composition of the U. S. population for the delivery of mental health services during the period 1971-1985. Paper presented at the Southeastern Divisional Meeting of the American Psychiatric Assn., Williamsburg, VA, Oct., 1973. (b)

Lawton, M. P., & Gottesman, L. E. Psychological services to the elderly. **American Psychologist,** 1974, **29,** 689-693.

Macmillan, D. Hospital-community relationships. In **An approach to the prevention of disability from chronic psychoses: The open mental hospital within the community.** Milbank Memorial Fund, New York, 1958.

Main, T. The hospital as a therapeutic institution. **Bulletin of the Menninger Clinic,** 1946, **10,** 66-70.

Malzberg, B. **Mental disease in New York State 1910-1960: A study of incidence.** Research Foundation for Mental Hygiene, Albany, 1967.

Perlin, S., & Kahn, R. L. The development of a community mental health center model. In **Psychiatric Research Report 22,** American Psychiatric Assn., Washington, 1967.

Polak, P., & Jones, M. The psychiatric nonhospital: A model for change. **Community Mental Health Journal,** 1973, **9,** 123-132.

Redick, R. W. Patient care episodes in psychiatric services, United States 1971. **Statistical Note 92.** Biometry Branch, NIMH, Rockville, MD, 1973.

Redick, R. W. Patterns in use of nursing homes by the aged mentally ill. **Statistical Note 107.** Biometry Branch, Rockville, MD, 1974.

Schaie, K. W. Translations in gerontology—from lab to life: Intellectual functioning. **American Psychologist,** 1974, **29,** 802-807.

Stanton, A., & Schwartz, M. **The mental hospital.** Basic Books, New York, 1954.

Willner, S. G. Patients resident in mental hospitals by type of hospitals, United States, 1904-1970. Biometry Branch, NIMH, Rockville, MD, 1974.

# VIII. Death and Dying

Death, which occupied a central position in philosophy and religion since the beginnings of humanity, became a taboo subject in this century. Unable to master death with the same rational, scientific methods that have led to increasing control of our environments and of many disease processes, we have tried to push it out of our consciousness, to deny its mystery and power. At a personal level, the dying are more and more likely to be moved from their homes and into hospitals or nursing homes, thus removing death from the fabric of everyday life.

In recent years, a small group of persons: medical and mental health professionals, clergy, philosophers, and the dying themselves, have vividly described how this situation of denial and avoidance affects both the dying and those who will continue to live (Powers). By excluding death from everyday life, it has become even more fearful. Often we have tried to protect the dying by keeping them in ignorance about their true condition. The patient, aware of what is happening to him or her, shares in the pretense that death does not exist (Glaser and Strauss). But this silence and avoidance is often more painful than awareness of the truth. We also try to shield children from death; but from a very early age children are concerned with the problems of separation and death, and often manifest their feelings in play or fantasies (Kastenbaum).

In some instances, life can be prolonged through the use of medical support systems or other interventions. In the Quinlan case (Clark, et al.), the issues surrounding the use of these life-support systems are dramatically confronted: when can such devices be removed, what role does the individual or his or her family have in making this decision, and what constitutes death from religious, medical, and legal perspectives?

For the survivors, there is the painful task of picking up one's life (as the articles on widowhood in Part V indicate). An immediate concern of theirs is what kind of funeral arrangements to make. As most persons do not formulate these plans before death, and the dying person may not indicate what kind of funeral he or she desires, the bereaved may have no idea of what to do and are sometimes subjected to pressures to provide an expensive funeral (Mitford).

Our ability to provide comfort to the dying person, and to make one's last days meaningful depends on being able to listen openly to what they have to say. Two first-hand accounts of dying persons are included in this section. In the first, Elisabeth Kubler-Ross, one of the pioneers in the movement to enlarge our communication with and understanding of the dying, interviews a 17-year-old girl who is terminally ill. In the second, Ernest Becker, philosopher and author of a landmark book, *Denial of Death,* reflects on his personal experience of dying (Keen).

261

Finally, the student is invited to compare his or her own responses to the questionnaire "You and Death" with the results of the survey of *Psychology Today* readers, and to examine generally what feelings and concepts people hold about death.

# 51

Thomas Powers

# LEARNING TO DIE

The final lesson that few doctors know how to teach

ON NOVEMBER 8, 1970, BARBARA B., a woman in her middle sixties, was admitted to New York Hospital with an unexplained intestinal blockage. Because it was a Sunday and her own doctor was unavailable, the doctor of a friend took over. He had never met Mrs. B. and knew nothing of her medical history. When he asked what was wrong she described her symptoms during the preceding few days but volunteered nothing else. Dr. C. began making arrangements for an exploratory operation in the next day or two if the situation did not correct itself.

A friend had accompanied Mrs. B. to the hospital. Later that day her daughter and son-in-law came up to see her. Mrs. B. was in considerable pain so there was not much conversation. When they did talk, it was about matters of little consequence. Not knowing exactly what Mrs. B.'s condition was they all hoped that an operation would not be necessary, but they did not speculate as to what might have caused the blockage. Each of the four had a pretty good idea of the cause: none of them mentioned it that first day.

On Monday Dr. C. contacted Mrs. B.'s regular doctor and was told she had had a cancerous breast removed in the summer of 1968, that malignant skin nodules had reappeared in the summer of 1970, and that laboratory tests showed spreading cancer. It was obvious to Dr. C. that Mrs. B.'s cancer had reached her abdomen and that she did not have long to live. When he spoke to Mrs. B.'s family, however, he was somewhat more tentative. He said he was not sure (which was true; he was not *absolutely certain*) what was causing the blockage, that the blockage might disappear, that he advised waiting for a few days to see how things developed. He admitted, in response to direct questions, that Mrs. B. was suffering from a serious case of cancer and that serious in her case probably meant fatal. He muted only the probable (but not yet *certain*) fact that Mrs. B. had already begun to die.

During the following few days Mrs. B. was in continual discomfort but nevertheless remained the same person her family had always known: witty, unsentimental, interested in gossip, a passionate reader, a stern critic of everything about President Nixon except the good looks of his daughters, in all things a woman determined to be strong. When friends or family came to visit she talked about politics, life on Tenth Street, what she was reading, and so on. Everyone asked how she was feeling. She always answered, "Oh, all right," with a look of disgust. Once or twice she said she hoped she would not need an operation. A kind of unspoken agreement was in effect: cancer was not to be mentioned. The reasons for the agreement varied. Mrs. B. felt it was weak to discuss bodily ills, and wanted to spare her daughter. Her daughter wanted to spare her mother. Mrs. B. and her family all knew her cancer had reappeared, but discussion of the possible operation was based on the unstated assumption that the cancer and the intestinal blockage were two entirely separate conditions. In other words, everyone knew the end was coming, but resisted the notion that it was coming *now*.

When the blockage persisted into the middle of the next week, however, it became increasingly difficult to ignore the seriousness of Mrs. B.'s condition. Mrs. B. had nothing but contempt for people who complained and was inclined to think that any mention of her own condition was a kind of complaining. In spite of this, she began to refer to it elliptically.

One evening, as her son-in-law was just leaving, she abruptly mentioned a Kingsley Amis novel she had once read in which a character visits a hospitalized friend who is dying with cancer (Mrs. B. winced at the word) of the stomach. In the novel, the dying friend makes little pretense of interest in the conversation; he is simply trying to hold on until his next pain shot.

"I'm beginning to feel that way myself," Mrs. B. said with a bitter smile, apologizing for her failure to keep up her end of the conversation and ashamed of herself for bringing it up. "When something really hurts, all you live for is that pain shot."

A couple of days later Mrs. B.'s son-in-law arrived just as Mrs. B.'s roommate was coming out of anesthesia following an operation to determine if she had breast cancer. The son-in-law asked what the verdict had been. "She had two tumors but neither

*Thomas Powers graduated from Yale in 1964 and subsequently worked as a journalist in Rome, London, and New York. His first book,* Diana: The Making of a Terrorist, *has just been published by Houghton Mifflin.*

was malignant," Mrs. B. said. "Some people have all the luck."

Mrs. B. refrained from talking about her feelings directly on all but one or two occasions. Once she told her daughter, "I've got so little to look forward to," but then regained her composure. "Sometimes I can't help feeling blue," she explained. There were other slips, but generally she refused to talk about what she was going through, or to let anyone else talk about it. Neither she nor anyone else had yet admitted fully what was now the one great fact in her life: she was dying.

DYING IS NOT A SUBJECT to which doctors have traditionally paid much attention. Their first purpose is to preserve life, and once life can no longer be decently extended they tend to lose interest. Until fairly recently, the medical profession reacted to death as if the subject were adequately covered by the children's old skip-rope song:

> *Doctor, doctor, will I die?*
> *Yes, my child, and so will I.*

Since death was inevitable, discussion was restricted to secondary matters, centering on three main questions. The first was how to determine when the patient was really dead. Before the twentieth century, people were occasionally buried while still alive, and wills sometimes included a stipulation that the deceased remain above ground until his body actually began to smell. The second question, still much discussed, was whether or not to tell the patient he was dying. The third question, of more interest to doctors of divinity than of medicine, concerned the individual after the process of dying was complete: specifically, did the soul survive, and if so, in what form? All three questions are still open to dispute, and the first has attracted considerable scientific attention since the advent of organ transplants. Laws that require embalming before burial preclude the possibility of being buried alive, but there is still plenty of contention about identifying the precise moment at which a patient becomes sufficiently dead to justify the removal of vital organs.

The question of dying itself has been ignored. In 1912 a Boston doctor, Roswell Park, suggested that nothing was known about the subject and coined a word for its study—thanatology. No one remembered the word or undertook the study. With the exception of books on death as a religious event, almost nothing was published on the subject. The few books that were often had a cultist flavor, like

*Death: Its Causes and Phenomena,* also published in 1912, which included a chapter on "Photographing and Weighing the Soul." Medical scientists acted as if Woodrow Wilson had adequately described death and dying in his last words before slipping into unconsciousness: "I am a broken machine. I am ready to go." Scientists were interested in the machine during, not after, its breakdown. They described dying exclusively in terms of the specific diseases or conditions which accompanied it, almost as if dying would not occur if there were no disease.

Since the second world war the subject has begun to receive some attention. In 1956, the American Psychological Association held a major symposium on death at its annual convention. In 1965, Dr. Elisabeth Kübler-Ross began a prolonged study of dying patients at the University of Chicago's Billings Hospital. Other organizations, institutes, and centers, usually with a highly specialized focus, have been established in Cleveland, Boston, Durham, North Carolina, and elsewhere. In 1967, a number of doctors in New York created the Foundation of Thanatology (the coincidental use of Dr. Park's word was not discovered until later) to encourage the study of death and dying from a broad perspective. They chose the word thanatology to make it easier to raise funds, figuring that philanthropists, like others, would find the word death so disturbing they would prefer to have nothing to do with it. La Rochefoucauld, the seventeenth-century French writer, said, "One can no more look steadily at death than at the sun." The Foundation of Thanatology has found that the attention span of those they approach for funds is generally just long enough to say no. Independent researchers have experienced similar difficulties and disappointments, including outright hostility on the part of doctors, nurses, and hospital administrators. Nevertheless, some important work has been done, and dying as a biological and psychological event is beginning to be understood.

T HE BIOLOGICAL ASPECTS OF DEATH have received the most attention. In most, but not all, cases an autopsy will reveal exactly how an individual died, by which doctors now usually mean what caused his brain to cease functioning. Since respirators and other machines can keep the heart beating and other organs functioning virtually indefinitely, doctors have begun to accept "brain death" as adequate confirmation that the patient is actually "dead." The brain is considered to be dead when an electroencephalogram (EEG) is flat, which means that it detects no electromagnetic activity within the brain. It is a useful definition, compromised to some degree by the fact that patients have, if only rarely, recovered completely following two or even three days with an absolutely flat EEG. Brain death is generally (but not always) caused by a lack of oxygen, which is generally (but not always) caused by failure of the heart or lungs. The number of exact ways in which a human can die are, however, vast. Medical scientists are successful in describing how the body breaks down, not quite so successful in explaining why it breaks down; they admit that in a significant number of cases death occurs for no apparent medical reason whatever.

Dying as a psychological event, as an experience, is even more elusive. The principal obstacle to its study has been the fear of death on the part of patients, relatives, doctors, nurses, and the dispensers of funds for research. Since no one can say convincingly what death is, it is not easy to say why people fear it. In general, the fear of death has been broken down into the specific fears of pain, loneliness, abandonment, mutilation, and, somewhat more difficult to define, fear of the loss of self. This is not just another way of saying fear of death, but a kind of disassociation of the self as a conscious entity (the sense of *me*-ness one feels) from the self as a particular individual, with his particular history in the everyday world. That individual is one's closest associate and one fears his loss.

The fear of death also has a primitive, non-rational dimension, like fear of the dark and fear of the unknown. Conscious effort can bring such fear under control but cannot suppress it entirely. One doctor in New York uses complaints about the food in hospitals as a rule of thumb for gauging the fear of death: the more passionate and unreasonable the complaint, he has found, the greater the fear of dying. Everyone apparently experiences the fear of death in some degree, but reacts to it in his own way. People tend to die as they have lived, as suggested in the saying, "Death is terrible to Cicero, desirable to Cato, and indifferent to Socrates."

The experience of death is obviously related to its immediate cause. Heart disease and stroke are the conditions most likely to grant the widespread wish for death to occur in sleep. Heart patients who have been saved by modern techniques report they felt only a sudden pain and the beginning of mingled alarm and surprise. In earlier times, those sensations would have been death (as they presumably still are for those not saved). Patients who have suffered severe heart attacks often regain consciousness in some hospital's intensive-care unit with the words, "I'm dying, I'm dying," suggesting that awareness of death can be almost, but not quite, instantaneous. Nurses then find themselves in the awkward position of having to explain that the patient is not dying, without making clear the fact he still might at any moment. Diseases which do not attack vital centers directly and massively, and especially the forms of breakdown associated with old age, allow considerable warning before death actually arrives.

When an individual begins to die, much of what he suffers is the result of the fear of death on his own part and on the part of those around him. He reminds people that they, too, are going to die, which they naturally are not eager to consider. As a result, the first problem faced by the dying individual is to discover the truth about his condition.

In some rare instances doctors make a practice of telling patients the truth immediately, but in most cases the patient has to find out by himself. In their book, *Awareness of Dying,* Barney G. Glaser and Anselm L. Strauss describe a struggle for the truth which is sometimes Byzantine in its complexity, with patients trying to pick up clues while doctors, nurses, and relatives join in a conspiracy to conceal the patient's actual condition. The reason for withholding the truth, doctors say, is that the patient would find it too upsetting, that he needs hope in order to keep on fighting for life, that one can never be absolutely certain of a diagnosis, that patients really do not want to know.

A number of studies have shown, however, that 80 per cent (more or less, depending on the study) of doctors oppose telling dying patients the truth, while 80 per cent of their patients want to be told. Doctors apparently shy from the subject because death represents a defeat and because, like everybody else, they find death upsetting to talk about. The psychological stratagems of medical students confronting death for the first time are notorious. The atmosphere of autopsy rooms is one of macabre humor, a degree or two short of hysteria. Doctors generally end by suppressing awareness of death so thoroughly some researchers speculate that that is why they are drawn to medicine in the first place.

Even while doctors and nurses do everything in their power to withhold the truth, resorting with a smile to outright lies, they customarily believe that the majority of their patients know the truth anyway. Relatives of the dying have the same mixture of feelings, trying to suppress the truth and yet assuming that eventually the patient will realize what is happening. Husbands and wives, each knowing the truth, often tell a third party that *they* know, but not to let the *other* know because he (or she) "couldn't stand it." The pretense naturally grows harder to sustain as the dying patient approaches a final decline. Nevertheless, the pretense is often maintained by sheer will until the end, even when all parties know the truth, and know the others know it too.

In rare instances patients refuse to recognize the truth, ignoring the most obvious clues (such as the visit of a relative who lives thousands of miles away) and insisting up until the end that they will be better in no time. For such patients almost any explanation will suffice. One woman dying of cancer, for example, believed (or pretended to believe) that she was only the victim of a slightly new strain of flu. Dr. Kübler-Ross describes a woman Christian Scientist who insisted until the end that faith in God was sufficient physic for an open cancer which was clearly killing her. As the woman declined she put on ever more garish makeup, until finally she was painting her white and withered cheeks a deep red, suppressing the distinctive smell of cancer with

perfume and using false eyelashes and deep green eye shadow to insist she was still alive and even attractive. In most cases, however, patients eventually sense they are not getting better and either ask their doctors directly (by no means always getting an honest answer) or set verbal traps for nurses, relatives, and other patients, checking their responses for every discrepancy. One woman fatally ill with a rare disease discovered her condition when she casually ran across an article in *Newsweek* which described every symptom in exact detail. Nurses believe that "way deep down" patients sense when they are dying, and there is some evidence this is true. Patients who know they are dying will often tell a nurse, "I'm going to die tonight," and then do so. Occasionally, however, patients feel they are going to die when, in fact, they are going to live. Persuading such a patient he's going to recover can be a frustrating experience, particularly when he has watched doctors and nurses deliberately deceive other patients who really were dying.

When patients finally do realize they are dying, a pattern of behavior often follows which was first described in detail by Dr. Kübler-Ross. Based on interviews with hundreds of dying patients over the past five years, she divides the reaction to knowledge of impending death into five distinctive stages.

The first stage is one of denial, even when a patient has suspected the worst and fought to determine the truth. All his life he has casually accepted the fact that "we all have to go." He is stunned to realize that now *he* has to go. After the discovery, patients often retreat into a self-imposed isolation, remaining silent with friends or relatives or even refusing to see them, while they get used to the fact that no mistake has been made, that they are *now* in the process of dying. Dr. Kübler-Ross believes that the dying never completely lose hope that a cure for their disease will be discovered at the last minute or that an outright miracle will occur ("the Scripture says that nothing is impossible with God"). This hope remains a deep-seated thing, and for practical purposes, such as writing wills and settling their affairs, the dying generally accept the fact they are dying once they have been told, directly or indirectly, that it is truly so.

The second stage is one of anger, especially when the dying individual is young. The anger can be released in any direction: at the doctors for doing nothing, at relatives because they are going to live, at other patients for not being quite so ill, at nurses for being young and healthy, at God for being unjust. In 1603, when Queen Elizabeth was told by her physician, Sir Robert Cecil, that she was seriously ill and must go to bed, she flared back, *"Must!* Is must a word to be addressed to princes? Little man, little man! Thy father, were he alive, durst not have used that word." Her mood quickly shifted to gloomy self-pity. "Thou art so presumptuous," she said, "because thou knowest that I shall die."

Eventually the anger subsides and the dying patient enters a curious stage in which he tries to bar-

"In general, the fear of death has been broken down into the specific fears of pain, loneliness, abandonment, mutilation, and fear of the loss of self."

gain for his life. He begins to talk about all the things he has failed to do but will undertake if he recovers. He laments the fact he spent so much time earning a living and so little with his family, promising to alter his priorities if he gets home again. The most explicit bargains, generally proposed to God, are usually kept a secret. They are often legally precise, offering regular church attendance and sincere belief in return for a few more years. The bargains tend to be selfless, for the dying person knows he is about to lose himself altogether. Bargains can be offered for almost anything, for the chance to attend a son's wedding or to see another spring, but they all have one element in common: they are *never* kept. If the dying person actually does live until spring he immediately proposes another bargain.

Religious individuals often insist they submit themselves happily to God's pleasure ("Thy will be done") but are prepared to propose a reasonable compromise. St. Anselm, the Archbishop of Canterbury, dying in 1109, told fellow clerics gathered about his deathbed, "I shall gladly obey His call. Yet I should also feel grateful if He would grant me a little longer time with you, and if I could be permitted to solve a question—the origin of the soul." God did not accept the offer, and St. Anselm shortly died, but if He had, Dr. Kübler-Ross suggests that St. Anselm would quickly have proposed another bargain.

The fourth stage is one of altogether reasonable depression, part of the process doctors refer to as "anticipatory grief." In effect, the dying patient is grieving for himself before the fact of death, since he is about to lose everything he loves. It is this grieving which is probably most feared by doctors and relatives. It is painful to witness a death, and doubly painful when the dying person reacts in a fearful or hysterical manner. This is exceedingly rare, and yet doctors and relatives, perhaps unsure what their own reactions would be, fear the possibility so greatly that they put off discussion of death as long as possible and sometimes, as mentioned above, deny the truth until the end. In every other circumstance of life, no matter how bleak, some consolation can be genuinely offered; with those who know they are dying, there is nothing to say. Dr. Kübler-Ross has found, however, that the grieving patient will often come out of his depression and face the prospect of death more calmly for having been through it.

The final stage, not always reached, is one of acceptance.

WHEN MRS. B. WOKE UP ONE AFTERNOON following a nap, she saw her daughter standing by her bed with tears streaming down her cheeks. "Now, we're not going to have any tears," Mrs. B. said.

Nevertheless, she, too, had recognized the seriousness of her condition. During the first week she was in the hospital she made a point of telling her daily visitors they really didn't have to come so often. Now she admitted to looking forward to every visit. "It's nice to wake up and find somebody there," she confessed. Her last roommate had remained only a day before moving into a single room, so Mrs. B. was entirely alone between visits. The roommate, a woman in her forties who had also had a cancerous breast removed, had been shifted by her husband when he learned of Mrs. B.'s medical history. He said he wanted to protect the feelings of his wife, but she was acutely embarrassed by the move and came to see Mrs. B. every day. When the woman left the hospital she stopped by to say goodbye and suggested that she and Mrs. B. meet in New York for lunch someday. "Or," she said, "we have a place near you in the country. Maybe we can get together next spring." Mrs. B. said that would be fine and then added, "Good luck."

By the second week it was obvious Mrs. B.'s intestinal blockage was not going to clear by itself. Her doctors told her family the cancer had reached her liver and had probably affected her entire abdominal area. The sole remaining question was how long it would take Mrs. B. to die and whether or not she would be able to go home again in the time remaining. The only way she could leave the hospital, the doctors said, would be to undergo an operation in order to remove whatever was obstructing her intestine. They warned that she was in a weakened condition and might die during the operation, or that cancer might have affected so much of her intestine nothing could be done. The alternatives were also presented to Mrs. B., although in less detail and more tentatively. Both she and her family decided it would be better to go ahead.

Mrs. B.'s eldest daughter, living in California, already had made plans to come East for Thanksgiving, knowing it would probably be her last chance to see her mother. When she was told about the operation she asked over the phone, "Shall I wait until next week or should I come now?"

"I think you'd better come now," her brother-in-law said. She arranged for someone to take care of her three children and made a plane reservation for the day after the operation. Mrs. B.'s two brothers were also called, but they decided to wait until after the operation before coming to New York. "If I came now it would scare her to death," said the brother who lived in Washington.

The operation was scheduled for the morning of Thursday, November 19. Her family remained by the phone throughout the day. At 6 P.M. the surgeon finally called and said Mrs. B.'s intestine was blocked by cancer every two or three inches. There was nothing he could do. He was asked how long Mrs. B. might live. "Perhaps a week," he said.

Later that evening Mrs. B.'s family visited her briefly after she came up from the recovery room. She was pale and drawn and barely able to speak. The operation had obviously been an ordeal. "Never again," she whispered. "Never again."

The next day Mrs. B.'s eldest daughter flew to New York and went to see her mother, already beginning to regain her strength after the operation. Before the family went to see her on Saturday they tried to decide what to say if she should ask about her condition. The hard thing was finding out what Mrs. B. already had been told by her doctors. Until they reached Dr. C., they decided, they would tell Mrs. B. everyone was worried but didn't yet know the full results of the operation. They feared she would press them, and they knew that if she asked directly whether or not the cancer had been cut out, the only possible answers would be the truth or an outright lie. They did not want to lie, knowing how much Mrs. B. would hate being lied to, but they dreaded equally talking about the true situation. They could not have explained why.

As things turned out they need not have worried. Mrs. B. had cross-examined her doctors on a number of occasions since Thursday night, when she had found the strength to say, "It was my cancer, wasn't it?" Dr. C. later explained that Mrs. B. kept after him until she had the truth. His practice was to answer all questions truthfully, leaving it up to the patient to decide which questions to ask. Some patients asked nothing. Others stopped as soon as Dr. C. indicated their condition was serious. Mrs. B. had been unusual, he said, in questioning him precisely about her condition.

On Sunday Mrs. B. began to weaken again. When her son-in-law arrived about 11 A.M., she shooed the nurse out of the room. "I want to be alone with my son-in-law," she said. As soon as the door was closed she said, "I'm dying. There's no use kidding ourselves."

She told her son-in-law where all her papers were and what was in her will, asking him to make sure his mother got the red leather box which Mrs. B. had bought for her in Czechoslovakia the previous summer, and then had liked so much she kept it. "I've been feeling guilty about that," she said.

She also asked her son-in-law to get her lawyer on the phone so she could give him "a pep talk." When she reached him she said, "Now listen, you take care of the kids and try and keep the government from getting it all." She gave her best to his wife and said goodbye.

Finally Mrs. B. asked her son-in-law to make sure her eyes went to the eye bank and that her body was given to "science." (Mrs. B.'s surgeon told her son-in-law he wanted to do an autopsy, but that cancer had destroyed her body's usefulness as far as "science" was concerned. Mrs. B.'s second choice had been cremation without any service, and that wish was carried out.)

After Mrs. B. had straightened out her affairs to her own satisfaction, she relaxed and began to chat and even joke about her situation. A few minutes later she suddenly weakened and seemed to doze off. After awhile she started awake, staring intently at the ceiling. "Is there anything up there, right over my bed?" she asked her son-in-law. He said

there was not. A look of resigned disgust came over Mrs. B.'s face. "I'm afraid I'm going to have hallucinations," she said.

During the following days her decline was obvious to herself and her family. She spent more time dozing, was coherent for shorter periods which came farther apart. During one such moment she told her daughter, "I hadn't believed it would happen so fast."

IN MOST AMERICAN HOSPITALS the experience of death is clouded by drugs. When drugs are necessary to relieve pain there is no alternative, but heavy sedatives, tranquilizers, and pain-killing drugs are also used for purposes of "patient management." In the final stages of dying the greatest fear of patients is abandonment, with good reason. When possible, hospitals will try to send patients home to die. Doctors often cut back their visits, overworked nurses save most of their attention for "those who can be helped," and even the families of the dying frequently begin to detach themselves. The belief that life must go on can be carried to brutal limits, with relatives and even husbands or wives acting as if the dying individual were already dead. When dying patients pester the nursing staff for attention, they are often simply trying to alleviate their loneliness; if the pestering becomes irksome there is a tendency to respond with drugs.

The abandonment which dying patients fear can be as much emotional as literal. Nurses say they do not become hardened to death and often dream about the death of their patients. As a result they attempt to distance themselves from the dying by thinking of them as no longer quite there, referring to the care of unconscious patients, for example, as "watering the vegetables." The terrible moment which demands that life-sustaining equipment be turned off is emotionally masked by the phrase, "pulling the plug."

The impulse to abandon the dying can become overwhelming. It is policy in most hospitals to move dying patients into single rooms as death approaches. Doctors, nurses, and even relatives tend to find good reasons to stay out of the dying patient's room. The pretense is that no one wants to "disturb" the dying person while he is "resting," but nurses say they have seen too many clusters of relatives outside hospital rooms at the moment of death to consider it a coincidence.

As death approaches, the world of the dying gradually shrinks. They talk less of their disease and more about their exact symptoms, how they feel, what they plan to do tomorrow, or this afternoon, or in the next hour. Hope generally remains until the final moments, but its focus tends to shift. The Rev. Robert Reeves, Jr., the chaplain of Columbia-Presbyterian Hospital in New York, tells of one middle-aged man who hoped to get back to his business up until five weeks before his death. During the first week after that he talked about getting

"Heart disease and stroke are the conditions most likely to grant the wide-spread wish for death to occur in sleep."

home for Thanksgiving. During the second week he hoped to be able to get out of bed again. In the third week he hoped to regain the ability to swallow food. At the beginning of his final week of life he hoped for a good night's sleep. A day later he hoped his pain medicine would work. The day before he died he hoped he would die in his sleep. He was denied every hope except the last, and yet each had eased his way toward death.

When the layman speaks of death he is referring to *somatic* death, or the death of the entire organism. The traditional signs of somatic death are *rigor mortis* (the stiffening of certain muscles), *algor mortis* (the cooling of the body) and *liver mortis* (the purplish-red discoloration of the skin caused by the settling of the blood). Somatic death includes the death of all bodily tissues, but an individual is commonly said to be "dead" long before all his tissues have died. The death of the "person," then, is only one stage in what an increasing number of doctors tend to think of as a distinct physiological process.

One doctor likens the process of death to menopause, which has long been known to include profound biological changes in women going far beyond the simple cessation of ovulation. The fact of putrefaction can also be cited as evidence that dying is a coherent biological event, and not simply the exact condition which precipitates death (heart failure, say, or kidney shutdown). When the body dies, organisms escape the gastrointestinal tract and begin the process of general decomposition by which the body is returned to Biblical ashes and dust. Built into the body, in other words, is the biological mechanism of its own dissolution, a fact which hardly can be dismissed as a coincidence. In arguing for an expanded notion of death, doctors also mention the characteristic return of the dying to infancy. Gradually they sleep longer each day, until they wake for only minutes at a time. Emotionally, the dying become increasingly dependent. Waking in the night they may cry if they discover they are alone, or sink back to sleep if someone is there.

Given a choice, the vast majority of people would prefer to die in their sleep. The next best, they say, would be a "peaceful" death, a consummation largely under the control of doctors. "Dear gentlemen," said the eighteenth-century English doctor, Sir Samuel Garth, to physicians whispering together at the foot of his bed, "let me die a natural death." The ability of doctors to extend the process of dying, if not life, is incomparably greater now. Medical "heroics" can keep the heart beating, the lungs breathing, the kidneys functioning, the brain flickering long after death would normally have arrived. The deterioration of the body from disease, and especially from cancer, proceeds further than it would without medical intervention. The result is that patients often lose consciousness long before they die because doctors, or relatives, refuse to give up when the body does. One nurse with years of ex-

perience in an intensive-care unit says she finds it increasingly difficult to tell when a patient has died, since machines sustain his vital signs.

Once the process of dying has begun, death can arrive at any time. Some patients die quickly; some linger for months with conditions that ought to have been quickly fatal. Doctors are still exceedingly cautious about predicting when someone will die, since they are so often surprised. Thomas Lupton, a sixteenth-century English writer, made the following attempt to list sure signs of imminent death:

> *If the forehead of the sick wax red, and his brows fall down, and his nose wax sharp and cold, and his left eye becomes little, and the corner of his eye runs, if he turn to the wall, if his ears be cold, or if he may suffer no brightness, and if his womb fall, if he pulls straws or the clothes of his bed, or if he pick often his nostrils with his fingers, and if he wake much, these are almost certain tokens of death.*

Signs which modern nurses look for are dilated nostrils, sagging of the tongue to one side of the mouth, and a tendency for the thumbs to tuck in toward the palms of the dying patient's hands. Just as dying people frequently sense the imminence of their own death and predict it accurately, nurses develop a sense which tells them (but not always correctly) when a patient is going to die.

In the early stages of dying, the patient remains essentially himself, afflicted only by the knowledge of impending death and the effect of that knowledge on himself and those around him. In the final stages, consciousness in the dying sometimes undergoes qualitative changes. This experience is the least well understood of all, since the nearer a patient approaches to death, the less he can describe what he feels. The crisis for the dying patient characteristically arrives when he stops "fighting" to live. Doctors cannot say just how patients "fight," but they are unanimous in saying that patients do so, and that "fighting" can make all the difference in situations which can go either way. A man fighting to stay alive apparently duplicates the experience of a man fighting to stay awake, i.e., alternating flashes of lucidity and delirium. Patients often signal the approach of death by simply saying, "I can't fight any longer." The period that follows is unlike any other experienced in life.

Until the twentieth century, this final period was often called "the dying hour," although it can last considerably longer than an hour. Physicians described it as being a peaceful period in which the dying person, accepting the lost struggle and the inevitable end, is relaxed and ready to depart. The patient may gradually distance himself from life, actually turning away close friends and relatives, literally turning to the wall (as suggested by Lupton) as he prepares himself to die. Accepting the fact of their own death, the dying frequently turn their attention to those who will live, who are sometimes aggrieved by the readiness of the dying to leave them behind. At the end it is often the dying who comfort the living. Even so self-centered a figure as Louis XIV said to those around his deathbed, "Why weep ye? Did you think I should live forever?" After a pause he reflected with equanimity, "I thought dying had been harder."

Dying patients who remain fully conscious, or nearly so, say they are tired, feel a growing calm, are ready to go, are perhaps even happy. When Stephen Crane died of tuberculosis in England in 1900, only twenty-nine years old, he tried to describe the sensation to a friend: "Robert—when you come to the hedge—that we must all go over. It isn't so bad. You feel sleepy—and you don't care. Just a little dreamy anxiety—which world you're really in—that's all."

Dr. Austin Kutscher, one of the creators of the Foundation of Thanatology, has been studying death and related questions since the death of his wife in 1966. He emphasizes that in some ways the living tyrannize over the dying, studying the experience of the latter for the sake of those who remain. An example is the effort of medical scientists to narrow the definition of death in order to allow the organs of the dying to be used for transplants. The decision to accept brain death as death itself may be valid, Kutscher says, but it can hardly be argued that the definition was framed for the benefit of the dying. As a result of this natural bias on the part of the living, the study of death and dying has tended to ignore the nature of the event, and of its experience.

"Isn't there something rather magical about life that defies measurement by a piece of apparatus?" Dr. Kutscher says. "We are begging the issue by trying to define death when we can't even define life."

The scientific study of dying is relatively recent, but there exists a vast literature, amounting to case studies, of the approach of death. The final moments of great men have always been minutely recorded, these accounts ranging from those in the *Lives of the Saints*, which tend to a dull predictability, to the moment-by-moment narratives of death as experienced by generals, poets, and kings. Again and again the last words of the dying concede their readiness to depart; an unfeigned peace seems to ease the final flickering out. History and modern research agree that, for unknown reasons, the dying do not find it hard to die.

The very last moments are, of course, the least accessible. Some doctors have found evidence that the experience of patients still conscious has an element of the mystical. The doctors are quick to say that they are not talking about God and religion and parapsychological cultism; also they admit that such experiences might be the result of anoxia, or oxygen starvation in the brain. Nevertheless, they say, there is reason to believe the dying can experience a sense of surrender which borders on ecstasy. In a secular age, as practitioners of a science which tends toward mechanism, doctors reluctantly speak of "soul" or "spirit." But, in the safety of anonymity, they return again and again to the puzzle of what it is that dies when the body ceases to function. One doctor, attempting to describe the mystery he had sensed in dying patients, quoted the dying words attributed to the ancient philosopher Plotinus: "I am making my last effort to return that which is divine in me to that which is divine in the universe."

D URING HER FINAL FIVE DAYS OF LIFE, Mrs. B. was rarely conscious. The hospital left the second bed in her room empty. Her doctors and family decided not to attempt extreme efforts which could only prolong her dying, but Mrs. B. continued to receive intravenous feeding and was regularly turned by the nurses as a precaution against pneumonia.

On two occasions Mrs. B. started violently awake and insisted, "Something is terribly wrong." She did not know her daughters and believed her doctors were conspiring against her. She was given heavy sedation, and her daughters felt that, in effect, she had already died. Nevertheless, on a few last occasions she regained consciousness and knew her family, if only briefly. Two days before she died, as her surgeon was examining her, she suddenly asked, "Why don't I die?"

"Because you're tough," the surgeon said.

"I don't want to be tough that way," Mrs. B. said.

Because one test of a patient's grip on life is the ability to respond, the doctors and nurses would call her name loudly from time to time to ask if she wanted anything. "Mrs. B.?" one of the nurses nearly shouted one night. "Mrs. B.?"

"I'm gone," said Mrs. B. in a faint whisper.

"No, you're still with us," the nurse said.

Mrs. B. grew steadily weaker. Her kidneys began to fail. She began to breathe rapidly and heavily, then stopped altogether, and after a moment began again. A nurse called this "Cheyne-Stokes breathing" and said it was probably a sign that the end was approaching. Some of the nurses thought Mrs. B. was completely unconscious; others felt she had only lost the ability to respond. Not knowing who was right, her family spoke as if she could hear and understand everything said in the room.

When Mrs. B.'s youngest daughter arrived about 11 A.M. the morning of Thanksgiving Day, November 26, she found her mother breathing slowly and regularly. Her body was completely relaxed over onto one side. It was a bright sunlit day. Mrs. B.'s daughter sat down by the large bank of windows overlooking Manhattan to the south and tried to read, but found herself thinking of her mother. After a while she looked up and saw that her mother had stopped breathing. So long expected, death had arrived unnoticed. For eighteen days Mrs. B.'s daughter had restrained her tears. Now, finally, when her mother was no longer there to comfort or be comforted, she began to cry.

# 52

# The Ritual Drama of Mutual Pretense

## by Barney G. Glaser and Anselm L. Strauss

When patient and staff both know that the patient is dying but pretend otherwise—when both agree to act as if he were going to live—then a context of mutual pretense exists. Either party can initiate his share of the context; it ends when one side cannot, or will not, sustain the pretense any longer.

The mutual-pretense awareness context is perhaps less visible, even to its participants, than the closed, open, and suspicion contexts, because the interaction involved tends to be more subtle. On some hospital services, however, it is the predominant context. One nurse who worked on an intensive care unit remarked about an unusual patient who had announced he was going to die: "I haven't had to cope with this very often. I may know they are going to die, and the patient knows it, but (usually) he's just not going to let you know that he knows."

Once we visited a small Catholic hospital where medical and nursing care for the many dying patients was efficiently organized. The staff members were supported in their difficult work by a powerful philosophy—that they were doing everything possible for the patient's comfort—but generally did not talk with patients about death. This setting brought about frequent mutual pretense. This awareness context is also predominant in such settings as county hospitals, where elderly patients of low socioeconomic status are sent to die; patient and staff are well aware of imminent death but each tends to go silently about his own business.[1] Yet, as we shall see, sometimes the mutual pretense context is neither silent nor unnegotiated.

1. Robert Kastenbaum has reported that Cushing Hospital, "a Public Medical Institution for the care and custody of the elderly" in Framingham, Massachusetts, "patient and staff members frequently have an implicit mutual understanding with regard to death . . . institutional dynamics tend to operate against making death 'visible' and a subject of open communication. . . . Elderly patients often behave as though they appreciated the unspoken feelings of the staff members and were attempting to make their demise as acceptable and unthreatening as possible." This observation is noted in Robert Kastenbaum, "The Interpersonal Context of Death in a Geriatric Institution, abstract of paper presented at the Seventeenth Annual Scientific Meeting, Gerontological Society (Minneapolis: October 29-31, 1964).

The same kind of ritual pretense is enacted in many situations apart from illness. A charming example occurs when a child announces that he is now a storekeeper, and that his mother should buy something at his store. To carry out his fiction, delicately cooperative action is required. The mother must play seriously, and when the episode has run its natural course, the child will often close it himself with a rounding-off gesture, or it may be concluded by an intruding outside event or by the mother. Quick analysis of this little game of pretense suggests that either player can begin; that the other must then play properly; that realistic (nonfictional) action will destroy the illusion and end the game; that the specific action of the game must develop during interaction; and that eventually the make-believe ends or is ended. Little familial games or dramas of this kind tend to be continual, though each episode may be brief.

For contrast, here is another example that pertains to both children and adults. At the circus, when a clown appears, all but the youngest children know that the clown is not real. But both he and his audience must participate, if only symbolically, in the pretense that he is a clown. The onlookers need do no more than appreciate the clown's act, but if they remove themselves too far, by examining the clown's technique too closely, let us say, then the illusion will be shattered. The clown must also do his best to sustain the illusion by clever acting, by not playing too far "out of character." Ordinarily nobody addresses him as if he were other than the character he is pretending to be. That is, everybody takes him seriously, at face value. And unless particular members return to see the circus again, the clown's performance occurs only once, beginning and ending according to a prearranged schedule.

Our two simple examples of pretense suggest some important features of the particular awareness context to which we shall devote this chapter. The make-believe in which patient and hospital staff engage resembles the child's game much more than the clown's act. It has no institutionalized beginning and ending comparable to the entry and departure of the clown; either the patient or the staff must signal the beginning of their joint pretense. Both parties must act properly if the pretense is to be maintained, because, as in the child's game, the illusion created is fragile, and easily shattered by incongruous "realistic" acts. But if either party slips slightly, the other may pretend to ignore the slip.[2] Each episode between the patient and a staff member tends to be brief, but the mutual pretense is done with terrible seriousness, for the stakes are very high.[3]

### Initiating the Pretense

This particular awareness context cannot exist, of course, unless both the patient and staff are aware that he is dying. Therefore all the structural conditions which contribute to the existence of open awareness (and which are absent in closed and suspicion awareness) contribute also to the existence of mutual pretense. In addition, at least one interactant must indicate a desire to pretend that the patient is not dying and the other must agree to the pretense, acting accordingly.

A prime structural condition in the existence and maintenance of mutual pretense is that unless the patient initiates conversation about his impending death, no staff member is required to talk about it with him. As typical Americans, they are unlikely to initiate such a conversation; and as professionals they have no rules commanding them to talk about death with the patient, unless he desires it. In turn, he may wish to initiate such conversation, but surely neither hospital rules nor common convention urges it upon him. Consequently, unless either the aware patient or the staff members breaks the silence by words or gestures, a mutual pretense rather than an open awareness context will exist; as, for example, when the physician does not care to talk about death, and the patient does not press the issue though he clearly does recognize his terminality.

The patient, of course, is more likely than the staff members to refer openly to his death, thereby inviting them, explicitly or implicitly, to respond in kind. If they seem unwilling, he may decide they do not wish to confront openly the fact of his death, and then he may, out of tact or genuine empathy for their embarrassment or distress, keep his silence. He may misinterpret their responses, of course, but for reasons suggested in previous chapters, he probably has correctly read their reluctance to refer openly to his impending death.

2. I. Bensman and I. Garver, "Crime and Punishment in the Factory," in A. Gouldner and H. Gouldner (eds.), *Modern Society* (New York: Harcourt, Brace and World, 1963), pp. 593–96.

3. A German communist, Alexander Weissberg, accused of spying during the great period of Soviet spy trials, has written a fascinating account of how he and many other persons collaborated with the Soviet government in an elaborate pretense, carried on for the benefit of the outside world. The stakes were high for the accused (their lives) as well as for the Soviet. Weissberg's narrative also illustrated how uninitiated interactants must be coached into their roles and how they must be cued into the existence of the pretense context where they do not recognize it. See Alexander Weissberg. *The Accused* (New York: Simon and Schuster, 1951).

Staff members, in turn, may give him opportunities to speak of his death, if they deem it wise, without their directly or obviously referring to the topic. But if he does not care to act or talk as if he were dying, then they will support his pretense. In doing so, they have, in effect, accepted a complementary assignment of status—they will act with pretense toward his pretense. (If they have misinterpreted his reluctance to act openly, then they have assigned, rather than accepted, a complementary status.)

Two related professional rationales permit them to engage in the pretense. One is that if the patient wishes to pretend, it may well be best for his health, and if and when the pretense finally fails him, all concerned can act more realistically. A secondary rationale is that perhaps they can give him better medical and nursing care if they do not have to face him so openly. In addition, as noted earlier, they can rely on common tact to justify their part in the pretense. Ordinarily, Americans believe that any individual may live—and die—as he chooses, so long as he does not interfere with others' activities, or, in this case, so long as proper care can be given him.

To illustrate the way these silent bargains are initiated and maintained, we quote from an interview with a special nurse. She had been assigned to a patient before he became terminal, and she was more apt than most personnel to encourage his talking openly, because as a graduate student in a nursing class that emphasized psychological care, she had more time to spend with her patient than a regular floor nurse. Here is the exchange between interviewer and nurse:

INTERVIEWER: Did he talk about his cancer or his dying?
NURSE: Well, no, he never talked about it. I never heard him use the word cancer. . . .
INTERVIEWER: Did he indicate that he knew he was dying?
NURSE: Well, I got that impression, yes. . . . It wasn't really openly, but I think the day that his roommate said he should get up and start walking, I felt that he was a little bit antagonistic. He said what his condition was, that he felt very, very ill that moment.
INTERVIEWER: He never talked about leaving the hospital?
NURSE: Never.
INTERVIEWER: Did he talk about his future at all?
NURSE: Not a thing. I never heard a word. . . .
INTERVIEWER: You said yesterday that he was more or less isolated, because the nurses felt that he was hostile. But they have dealt with patients like this many many times. You said they stayed away from him?
NURSE: Well, I think at the very end. You see, this is what I meant by isolation . . . we don't communicate with them. I didn't, except when I did things for him. I think you expect some-

body to respond to, and if they're very ill we don't . . . I talked it over with my instructor, mentioning things that I could probably have done; for instance, this isolation, I should have communicated with him . . .

INTERVIEWER: You think that since you knew he was going to die, and you half suspected that he knew it too, or more than half; do you think that this understanding grew between you in any way?

NURSE: I believe so . . . I think it's kind of hard to say but when I came in the room, even when he was very ill, he'd rather look at me and try to give me a smile, and gave me the impression that he accepted . . . I think this is one reason why I feel I should have communicated with him . . . and this is why I feel he was rather isolated. . . .

From the nurse's account, it is difficult to tell whether the patient wished to talk openly about his death, but was rebuffed; or whether he initiated the pretense and the nurse accepted his decision. But it is remarkable how a patient can flash cues to the staff about his own dread knowledge, inviting the staff to talk about his destiny, while the nurses and physicians decide that it is better not to talk too openly with him about his condition lest he "go to pieces." The patient, as remarked earlier, picks up these signals of unwillingness, and the mutual pretense context has been initiated. A specific and obvious instance is this: an elderly patient, who had lived a full and satisfying life, wished to round it off by talking about his impending death. The nurses retreated before this prospect, as did his wife, reproving him, saying he should not think or talk about such morbid matters. A hospital chaplain finally intervened, first by listening to the patient himself, then by inducing the nurses and the wife to do likewise, or at least to acknowledge more openly that the man was dying. He was not successful with all the nurses.

The staff members are more likely to sanction a patient's pretense, than his family's. The implicit rule is that though the patient need not be forced to speak of his dying, or to act as if he were dying, his kin should face facts. Afer all, they will have to live with the facts after his death. Besides, staff members usually find it less difficult to talk about dying with the family. Family members are not inevitably drawn into open discussion, but the likelihood is high, particularly since they themselves are likely to initiate discussion or at least to make gestures of awareness.

Sometimes, however, pretense protects the family member temporarily against too much grief, and the staff members against too immediate a scene. This may occur when a relative has just learned about the impending death and the nurse controls the ensuing scene by initiating temporary pretense. The reverse situation also occurs: a newly arrived nurse discovers the patient's terminality, and the relative smooths over the nurse's distress by temporary pretense.

### The Pretense Interaction

An intern whom we observed during our field work suspected that the patient he was examining had cancer, but he could not discover where it was located. The patient previously had been told that she probably had cancer, and she was now at this teaching hospital for that reason. The intern's examination went on for some time. Yet neither he nor she spoke about what he was searching for, nor in any way suggested that she might be dying. We mention this episode to contrast it with the more extended interactions with which this chapter is concerned. These have an episodic quality—personnel enter and leave the patient's room, or he occasionally emerges and encounters them—but their extended duration means that special effort is required to prevent their breaking down, and that the interactants must work hard to construct and maintain their mutual pretense. By contrast, in a formally staged play, although the actors have to construct and maintain a performance, making it credible to their audience, they are not required to write the script themselves. The situation that involves a terminal patient is much more like a masquerade party, where one masked actor plays carefully *to* another as long as they are together, and the total drama actually emerges from their joint creative effort.

A masquerade, however, has more extensive resources to sustain it than those the hospital situation provides. Masqueraders wear masks, hiding their facial expressions; even if they "break up" with silent laughter (as a staff member may "break down" with sympathy), this fact is concealed. Also, according to the rules ordinarily governing masquerades, each actor chooses his own status, his "character," and this makes his role in the constructed drama somewhat easier to play. He may even have played similar parts before. But terminal patients usually have had no previous experience with their pretended status, and not all personnel have had much experience. In a masquerade, when the drama fails it can be broken off, each actor moving along to another partner; but in the hospital the pretenders (especially the patient) have few comparable opportunities.

Both situations share one feature—the extensive use of props for sustaining the crucial illusion. In the masquerade, the props include not only masks but clothes and other costuming, as well as the setting where the masquerade takes place. In the hospital interaction, props also abound. Patients dress for the part of not-dying patient, including careful attention to grooming, and to hair and makeup by female patients. The terminal patient may also fix up his room so that it looks and feels "just like home," an activity that supports his enactment of normalcy. Nurses may respond to these props with explicit appreciation—"how lovely your hair looks this morning"—or even help to establish them, as by doing the patient's hair. We remember one elaborate pretense ritual involving a husband and wife who had won the nurses' sympathy. The husband simply would not recognize that his already comatose wife was approaching death, so each morning the nurses carefully prepared her for his visit, dressing her for the occasion and making certain that she looked as beautiful as possible.

The staff, of course, has its own props to support its ritual prediction that the patient is going to get well: thermometers, baths, fresh sheets, and meals on time! Each party utilizes these props as he sees fit, thereby helping to create the pretense anew. But when a patient wishes to demonstrate that he is finished with life, he may drive the nurses wild by refusing to cooperate in the daily routines of hospital life—that is, he refuses to allow the nurses to use their props. Conversely, when the personnel wish to indicate how things are with him, they may begin to omit some of those routines.

During the pretense episodes, both sides play according to the rules implicit in the interaction. Although neither the staff nor patient may recognize these rules as such, certain tactics are fashioned around them, and the action is partly constrained by them. One rule is that dangerous topics should generally be avoided. The most obviously dangerous topic is the patient's death; another is events that will happen afterwards. Of course, both parties to the pretense are supposed to follow the avoidance rule.

There is, however, a qualifying rule: Talk about dangerous topics is permissible as long as neither party breaks down. Thus, a patient refers to the distant future, as if it were his to talk about. He talks about his plans for his family, as if he would be there to share their consummation. He and the nurses discuss today's events—such as his treatments—as if they had implications for a real future, when he will have recovered from his illness. And some of his brave or foolhardy activities may signify a brave show of pretense, as when he bathes himself or insists on tottering to the toilet by himself. The staff in turn permits his activity. (Two days before he returned to the hospital to die, one patient insisted that his wife allow him to travel downtown to keep a speaking engagement, and to the last he kept up a lively conversation with a close friend about a book they were planning to write together.)

A third rule, complementing the first two, is that each actor should focus determinedly on appropriately safe topics. It is customary to talk about the daily routines—eating (the food was especially good or bad), and sleeping (whether one slept well or poorly last night). Complaints and their management help pass the time. So do minor personal confidences, and chatter about events on the ward. Talk about physical symptoms is safe enough if confined to the symptoms themselves, with no implied references to death. A terminal patient and a staff member may safely talk, and at length, about his disease so long as they skirt its fatal significance. And there are many genuinely safe topics

having to do with movies and movie stars, politics, fashions—with everything, in short, that signifies that life is going on "as usual."

A fourth interactional rule is that when something happens, or is said, that tends to expose the fiction that both parties are attempting to sustain, then each must pretend that nothing has gone awry. Just as each has carefully avoided calling attention to the true situation, each now must avert his gaze from the unfortunate intrusion. Thus, a nurse may take special pains an announce herself before entering a patient's room so as not to surprise him at his crying. If she finds him crying, she may ignore it or convert it into an innocuous event with a skillful comment or gesture—much like the tactful gentleman who, having stumbled upon a woman in his bathtub, is said to have casually closed the bathroom door, murmuring "Pardon me, *sir*." The mutuality of the pretense is illustrated by the way a patient who cannot control a sudden expression of great pain will verbally discount its significance, while the nurse in turn goes along with his pretense. Or she may brush aside or totally ignore a major error in his portrayal, as when he refers spontaneously to his death. If he is tempted to admit impulsively his terminality, she may, again, ignore his impulsive remarks or obviously misinterpret them. Thus, pretense is piled upon pretense to conceal or minimize interactional slips.

Clearly then, each party to the ritual pretense shares responsibility for maintaining it. The major responsibility may be transferred back and forth, but each party must support the other's temporary dominance in his own action. This is true even when conversation is absolutely minimal, as in some hospitals where patients take no particular pains to signal awareness of their terminality, and the staff makes no special gestures to convey its own awareness. The pretense interaction in this case is greatly simplified, but it is still discernible. Whenever a staff member is so indelicate, or so straightforward, as to act openly as if a terminal patient were dying, or if the patient does so himself, then the pretense vanishes. If neither wishes to destroy the fiction, however, then each must strive to keep the situation "normal."[4]

### The Transition to Open Awareness

A mutual pretense context that is not sustained can only change to an open awareness context. (Either party, however, may again initiate the pretense context and sometimes get cooperation from the other.) The change can be sudden, when either patient or staff distinctly conveys that he has permanently abandoned

4. A close reading of John Gunther's poignant account of his young son's last months shows that the boy maintained a sustained and delicately balanced mutual pretense with his parents, physicians and nurses. John Gunther, *Death Be Not Proud* (New York: Harper and Bros., 1949). Also see Bensman and Gerver, *op. cit.*

the pretense. Or the change to the open context can be gradual: nurses, and relatives, too, are familiar with patients who admit to terminality more openly on some days than they do on other days, when pretense is dominant, until finally pretense vanishes altogether. Sometimes the physician skillfully paces his interaction with a patient, leading the patient finally to refer openly to his terminality and to leave behind the earlier phase of pretense.

Pretense generally collapses when certain conditions make its maintenance increasingly difficult. These conditions have been foreshadowed in our previous discussion. Thus, when the patient cannot keep from expressing his increasing pain, or his suffering grows to the point that he is kept under heavy sedation, then the enactment of pretense becomes more difficult, especially for him.

Again, neither patient nor staff may be able to avoid bringing impending death into the open if radical physical deterioration sets in, the staff because it has a tough job to do, and the patient for other reasons, including fright and panic. Sometimes a patient breaks his pretense for psychological reasons, as when he discovers that he cannot face death alone, or when a chaplain convinces him that it is better to bring things out into the open than to remain silent. (Sometimes, however, a patient may find such a sympathetic listener in the chaplain that he can continue his pretense with other personnel.) Sometimes he breaks the pretense when it no longer makes sense in light of obvious physical deterioration.

Here is a poignant episode during which a patient dying with great pain and obvious bodily deterioration finally abandoned her pretense with a nurse:

> There was a long silence. Then the patient asked, "After I get home from the nursing home will you visit me?" I asked if she wanted me to. "Yes, Mary, you know we could go on long drives together. . . ." She had a faraway look in her eyes as if daydreaming about all the places she would visit and all the things we could do together. This continued for some time. Then I asked, "Do you think you will be able to drive your car again?" She looked at me, "Mary, I know I'm daydreaming; I know I am going to die." Then she cried, and said, "This is terrible, I never thought I would be this way."

In short, when a patient finds it increasingly difficult to hang onto a semblance of his former healthy self and begins to become a person who is visibly dying, both he and the staff are increasingly prone to say so openly, whether by word or gesture. Sometimes, however, a race occurs between a patient's persistent pretense and his becoming comatose or his actual death—a few more days of sentience or life, and either he or the staff would have dropped the pretense.

Yet, a contest may also ensue when only one side wishes to keep up the pretense. When a patient openly displays his awareness but shows it unacceptably, as by apathetically "giving up," the staff or family may try to reinstate the pretense. Usually the patient then insists on open recognition of his own impending death, but sometimes he is persuaded to return to the pretense. For instance, one patient finally wished to talk openly about death, but her husband argued against its probability, although he knew better; so after several attempts to talk openly, the patient obligingly gave up the contest. The reverse situation may also occur: the nurses begin to give the patient every opportunity to die with a maximum of comfort—as by cutting down on normal routines—thus signaling that he should no longer pretend, but the patient insists on putting up a brave show and so the nurses capitulate.

We would complicate our analysis unduly if we did more than suggest that, under such conditions, the pretense ritual sometimes resembles Ptolemy's cumbersomely patched astronomical system, with interactants pretending to pretend to pretend! We shall only add that when nurses attempt to change the pretense context into an open context, they generally do this "on their own" and not because of any calculated ward standards or specific orders from an attending physician. And the tactics they use to get the patient to refer openly to his terminality are less tried and true than the more customary tactics for forcing him to pretend.

## Consequences of Mutual Pretense

For the patient, the pretense context can yield a measure of dignity and considerable privacy, though it may deny him the closer relationships with staff members and family members that sometimes occur when he allows them to participate in his open acceptance of death. And if they initiate and he accepts the pretense, he may have nobody with whom to talk although he might profit greatly from talk. (One terminal patient told a close friend, who told us, that when her family and husband insisted on pretending that she would recover, she suffered from the isolation, feeling as if she were trapped in cotton batting.) For the family—especially more distant kin—the pretense context can minimize embarrassment and other interactional strains; but for closer kin, franker concourse may have many advantages.

Oscillation between contexts of open awareness and mutual pretense can also cause interactional strains. We once observed a man persuading his mother to abandon her apathy—she had permanently closed her eyes, to the staff's great distress—and "try hard to live." She agreed finally to resume the pretense, but later relapsed into apathy. The series of episodes caused some anguish to both family and patient, as well as to the nurses. When the patient initiates the mutual pretense, staff members are likely to feel relieved. Yet the consequent stress of either maintaining the pretense or changing it to open awareness sometimes may be considerable. Again, both the relief and the stress affect nurses more than medical personnel, principally because the latter spend less time with patients.

But whether staff or patient initiates the ritual of pretense, maintaining it creates a characteristic ward mood of cautious serenity. A nurse once told us of a cancer hospital where each patient understood that everyone there had cancer, including himself, but the rules of tact, buttressed by staff silence, were so strong that few patients talked openly about anyone's condition. The consequent atmosphere was probably less serene than when only a few patients are engaged in mutual pretense, but even one such patient can affect the organizational mood, especially if the personnel become "involved" with him.

A persistent context of mutual pretense profoundly affects the more permanent aspects of hospital organization as well. (This often occurs at county and city hospitals.) Imagine what a hospital service would be like if all terminal patients were unacquainted with their terminality, or if all were perfectly open about their awareness—whether they accepted or rebelled against their fate.[5] When closed awareness generally prevails the personnel must guard against disclosure, but they need not organize themselves as a team to handle continued pretense and its soemtimes stressful breakdown. Also, a chief organizational consequence of the mutual pretense context is that it eliminates any possibility that staff members might "work with" patients psychologically, on a self-conscious professional basis. This consequence was strikingly evident at the small Catholic hospital referred to a few pages ago. It is also entirely possible that a ward mood of tension can be set when (as a former patient once told us) a number of elderly dying patients continually communicate to each other their willingness to die, but the staff members persistently insist on the pretense that the patients are going to recover. On the other hand, the prevailing ward mood accompanying mutual pretense tends to be more serene —or at least less obviously tense—than when open suspicion awareness is dominant.

5. For a description of a research hospital where open awareness prevails, with far-reaching effects on hospital social structure, see Renée Fox, *Experiment Perilous* (New York: Free Press of Glencoe, 1959).

# 53

# The Kingdom Where Nobody Dies

by Robert Kastenbaum

*Dr. Robert Kastenbaum is professor and chairman of the psychology department at the University of Massachusetts in Boston.*

Children are playing and shouting in the early morning sunshine near the end of Alban Berg's opera *Wozzeck*. They are chanting one variant of a very familiar rhyme: "Ring-a-ring-a-roses, all fall down! Ring-a-ring-a-roses, all . . . ." The game is interrupted by the excited entry of other children, one of whom shouts to Marie's child, "Hey, your mother is dead!" But Marie's child responds only by continuing to ride his hobbyhorse, "Hop, hop! Hop, hop! Hop, hop!" The other children exchange a few words about what is "out there, on the path by the pool," and race off to see for themselves. The newly orphaned child hesitates for an instant and then rides off in the direction of his playmates. End of opera.

What begins for Marie's child? Without knowing the details of his fate, we can sense the confusion, vulnerability, and terror that mark this child's entry into the realm of grief and calamity. Adult protection has failed. The reality of death has shattered the make-believe of childhood.

Children are exposed to death on occasions much less dramatic than the sudden demise of a parent. A funeral procession passes by. A pet dies. An innocent question is raised at the dinner table: "Was this meat once a real live cow?" In a society such as ours that has labored so diligently to put mortality out of sight and out of mind, most of the questions children ask about death make parents uncomfortable. It is often thought that there is no appropriate answer that would not be alarming or threatening to children. Therefore, the subject of death is mostly evaded entirely or fantasized.

The intrusion of death places typical parents in an awkward position. They are not able to relax and observe—much less *appreciate*—how the child orients himself toward death. Yet much can be learned by indulging this curiosity. By dropping the adult guard that directs us to protect children from morbid thoughts and threatening events and by concentrating instead upon how children themselves react to death, surprising insights begin to emerge. We find from psychological research, clinical experience, folkways, and incidents shared with children in and around home that, despite the lack of explicit references, death is an integral part of growing up.

A child's fascination with death occurs almost any time, almost any place. Mortality is a theme that wends its way into many of the child's activities, whether solitary or social. Consider games for example. Ring-around-the rosy is a popular childhood play theme in both this country and Europe. Our own parents and grandparents delighted in "all fall down," as did their ancestors all the way back to the fifteenth century. The origin of this game, however, was anything but delightful.

Medieval society was almost totally helpless against bubonic plague—Black Death. If adults could not ward off death, what could children do? They could join hands, forming a circle of life. They could chant ritualistically and move along in a reassuring rhythm of unity. Simultaneously acknowledging and mocking the peril that endangered each of them individually, the children predicted and participated in their own sudden demise: "all fall down!" This was a playing-at-death, but it utilized highly realistic materials. Ring-around-the-rosy had one distinct advantage over its model—one could arise to play again. While the game provided the vehicle to conquer or survive death, it was also a way of saying, "I know that I, too, am vulnerable, but I will enjoy the security of other young, living bodies around me." An exercise in make-believe? Perhaps. Nevertheless, this familiar game also deserves respect as an artful response to harsh and overwhelming reality.

Death has been ritualized in many other children's games as well. In the playful romping of tag, what is the hidden agenda or mystery that makes the chaser "It"? Could "It" be the disguise for death? We may be reluctant even to speculate that the touch of death is at the symbolic root of the tag games that have flourished for so many centuries throughout so much of the world. Yet Death (or the Dead Man) certainly is central to at least some of the chase games beloved to children. In the English game "Dead Man Arise" the central player lies prostrate on the ground while other children either mourn over him or seek to bring him back to life. When least expected, up jumps John Brown, the Dead Man, the Water Sprite, Death himself, or whatever name local custom prefers. The children flee or freeze in surprise as the chaser whirls toward them for a tag that will bestow Dead Man status upon the victim.

Although children today continue to participate in rituals that can be traced centuries back, other death-attuned merriments such as "bang, bang, you're dead!" are of more recent origin, and the repertoire is constantly freshened. When everyday group games do not provide a sufficient outlet for death-oriented play, children are likely to express their own special thoughts and feelings individually through inventive play. Suffocating and burying a doll is an instance of fulfilling a death fantasy. Similarly, a game of repeatedly crashing toy cars into each other or a model plane into the ground effectively permits a youngster to test out feelings that are evoked in certain real situations. Should an adult happen to interrupt this brutal type of play, the youngster may offer some reassuring comment, such as "Nobody gets killed bad" or "All the people come home for supper."

How death becomes a vital element in what we call child's play was illustrated by my eight-year-old son at home just a few weeks ago. David, for no ostensible reason, went to the piano and improvised. A short while later he moved to the floor near the piano and began stacking his wooden blocks. These two spontaneous actions did not have any apparent relationship to each other, nor did they bear the mark of death awareness. Yet the only way to appreciate David's behavior is in terms of response to death and loss. The piano playing and block building occurred within a half-hour of the time David and I had discovered our family cat lying dead in the road. Together we acknowledged the death, discussed the probable cause, shared our surprise and dismay, and removed the body for burial in the woods. David then went his own way for a while, which included the actions already mentioned.

When I asked what he was playing on the piano, David answered, "Lovey's life story." He explained how the various types of music he had invented represented memorable incidents in the life of his lost cat (e.g., "This is music for when she scratched my arm"). The wooden blocks turned out to be a monument for Lovey. A close look revealed that the entire building was constructed in an *L* shape, with several other *L*s at salient points.

If there had been no sharing of the initial death experience, I probably would not have guessed that David's play had been inspired by an encounter with mortality. Adults often fail to fathom the implications of children's play because they have not had the opportunity to perceive the stimulus. It is very easy to misinterpret what children are doing, because the nature of their play does not necessarily convey the meaning behind the activity (children go to the piano or their blocks for many other reasons than memorializing). The fact that a particular behavior does not seem to be death-related by no means rules out the possibility that it must be understood at least partially in those terms.

More systematically now, let us explore the child's relationship to death from encounters with both tragedy and games, starting in infancy. Although the young child does not comprehend death as a concept in the strictest sense of the term, death themes certainly engage his mind very early in life, and they are intimately related to the central development of his personality.

There are two different, although related, realizations that children must eventually develop. The first is that other people die, and the second is that they themselves will die. One of the earliest inquiries into the psychology of death touched upon the question of the child's exposure to the death of others. Around the turn of the century G. Stanley Hall, one of the most distinguished of this nation's first generation of psychologists, and one of his students conducted a study on adult recollections of childhood. Several of the questions they asked concerned early encounters with death. Interestingly, many of the earliest memories involved death in one form or another.

When asked specifically about their earliest experiences with death, many of Hall's respondents answered with considerable detail. He later wrote that ". . . the first impression of death often comes from a sensation of coldness in touching the corpse of a relative and the reaction is a nervous start at the contrast with the warmth that the contact of cuddling and hugging was wont to bring. The child's exquisite temperature sense feels a chill where it formerly felt heat. Then comes the immobility of face and body where it used to find prompt movements of response. There is no answering kiss, pat, or smile. . . . often the half-opened eyes are noticed with awe. The silence and tearfulness of friends are also impressive to the infant, who often weeps reflexly or sympathetically."

Taking careful note of mental reactions to the elaborate funeral proceedings of the era, Hall observed that "little children often focus on some minute detail (thanatic fetishism) and ever after remember, for example, the bright pretty handles or the silver nails of the coffin, the plate, the cloth binding, their own or others' articles of apparel, the shroud, flowers, and wreaths on or near the coffin or thrown into the grave, countless stray phrases of the preacher, the fear lest the bottom of the coffin should drop out or the straps with which it is lowered into the ground should slip or break, a stone in the first handful or shovelful of earth thrown upon the coffin, etc. The hearse is almost always prominent in such memories and children often want to ride in one."

Some adult memories of death went back to age two or three. A child that young could not interpret or symbolize death in anything approaching the adult mode. Yet the exposure to death seemed to make a special impression. Possibly what happens is that the memory is preserved in details of the perception. The scene, or some of its elements that are easily overlooked by an adult, remains charged with emotion and vividly etched in the child's mind. When the adult turns the pages back to early childhood, he cannot show us the text, only the pictures. We do not yet know very much about the place of these early death portraits in the process of individual development, nor can we say with certainty what happens when such seldom-reviewed memories are brought to light in the adult years. However, it is likely that many of us have death perceptions engraved at some level of our memory that predate our ability to preserve our experiences in the form of verbal concepts.

Another way to study the impact of death upon a young child is to learn how he responds to the actual loss of somebody close to him. Albert Cain and his colleagues at the University of Michigan have found that a pattern of disturbed behavior often follows a death in the family. The symptoms occasionally become part of the child's personality from that time forward. One of Cain's studies focused upon responses to the death of a brother or sister. Guilt, as might be expected, was one of the more frequent reactions. "In approximately half our cases," reports Cain, "guilt was rawly, directly present. So, too, was trembling, crying and sadness upon mention of the sibling's death, with the guilt still consciously active five years or more after the sibling's death. Such children felt responsible for the death, sporadically insisted that it was all their fault, felt they should have died, too, or should have died instead of the dead sibling. They insisted they should enjoy nothing, and deserved only the worst. Some had suicidal thoughts and impulses, said they deserved to die, wanted to die—this also being motivated by a wish to join the dead sibling. They mulled over and over the nasty things they had thought, felt, or said to the dead sibling, and became all the guiltier. They also tried to recall the good things they had done, the ways they had protected the dead sibling, and so on."

Many other types of problems were noted in the same study. Some young children developed distorted ideas of what is involved in both illness and death, leading them to fear death for themselves at almost any time or to fantasize that the adults had killed their siblings—fantasies often fed by misinterpretations of emergency respiration and other rescue procedures. The surviving children sometimes became very fearful of physicians and hospitals or resented God as the murderer of their siblings. A few children developed major problems in mental functioning; they suddenly appeared "stupid," did not even know their own age, and seemed to lose their sense of time and causation.

The loss of an expected family member who was not yet born also proved unsettling to many of the children observed by Cain. Although miscarriage, as an event, was difficult for the young child to understand, it was clear enough that something important had gone wrong. Evasive answers by anxious parents increased the problem for some children. In the absence of accurate knowledge they created fantasies that the fetus had been abandoned or murdered. One child insisted that his mother had thrown the baby into a garbage can in a fit of anger; another associated the miscarriage with guppies that eat their babies. At times the insistent questioning by the child had the effect of further unsettling his parents, who had not yet worked through their own feelings about the miscarriage.

Not all children become permanently affected by death in their family. Some weather the emotional crisis with the strong and sensitive help of others. The point is simply that death registers in the minds of young children whether or not adults are fully cognizant of the phenomenon. It need not be either a sibling death or a miscarriage. The death of a playmate, the man across the street, a distant relative, a pet, a sports hero, or a national political figure all make an impression somewhere in the child's mind. Real death is not a rare event in the child's world.

There is no precise way of knowing which death will make the greatest impact upon which child. The death of a pet, especially if it is the first death exposure or occurs in a striking manner, sometimes affects a youngster more than the subsequent death of a person. There is nothing automatic about the different responses to death, even in childhood. Nor can the seemingly in-

consequential or remote death be disregarded if we wish to understand the child's thoughts and feelings on mortality.

Whatever the impact of other deaths, however, the loss of a parent has the most signal and longest-lasting influence on children. Bereavement in early childhood has been implicated as the underlying cause of depression and suicide attempts in later life. In one British study, for example, it was found that boys age four or younger who had lost their fathers were especially vulnerable to severe depression in adulthood. Many of the fathers died in combat. Perhaps some of the psychiatric and physical casualties of our involvement in Vietnam eventually will include the suicide committed in 1990 by the son whose father did not return. The death of a young father, however, does not automatically determine his son's fate. There is no way to predict the surviving child's response. In fact, the responses themselves cannot be explained entirely on the basis of parental death alone. What registered in the child's mind when his parent died? By what process did this first response develop into a way of life or into a sort of psychological time bomb set for later detonation? How might the child have been protected or guided? These questions have been raised only sporadically, and the answers are still elusive.

The significance of experiencing another's death during childhood has prompted many psychotherapists to look for such encounters in their adult patients. Psychiatrist David M. Moriarty, for example, has described a depressed woman who had attempted suicide on three occasions and had received electro-shock therapy twice without notable improvement in her behavior. When she was three years old, her mother had died of appendicitis. In the course of treatment she would call her psychiatrist in a panic, feeling that the world was coming in on her. The thought behind this fear was traced to the graveyard scene, when a shovelful of dirt had been thrown on the lowered coffin. Dr. Moriarty concluded that "Mrs. Q. lived most of her life afraid that she would lose other people whom she loved. The most impressive fact was that she talked and thought about the death of her mother as if it had just happened. This tragic event of forty years ago was still uppermost in her mind."

Of all the methods used to piece together the meaning of death during childhood, none can replace the sharing of a direct death experience with a

young child. It is only in such moments of fortunate sharing that we have a clear glimpse into the child's face-to-face encounter with death. There is something indescribably poignant about the way in which the young child attempts to attune himself to threat, limitations, and mortality at a time when he would appear to be innocent of dark concerns. In a journal that I have kept for each of my children, I recorded my son's first encounter with death.

David, at eighteen months, was toddling around the back yard. He pointed at something on the ground. I looked and saw a dead bird, which he immediately labeled "buh . . . buh." But he appeared uncertain and puzzled. Furthermore, he made no effort to touch the bird. This was unusual caution for a child who characteristically tried to touch or pick up everything he could reach. David then crouched over and moved slightly closer to the bird. His face changed expression. From its initial expression of excited discovery and later of puzzlement, now it took on a different aspect: to my astonishment, his face was set in a frozen, ritualized expression resembling nothing so much as the stylized Greek dramatic mask of tragedy. I said only, "Yes, bird . . . dead bird." In typically adult conflict, I thought of adding, "Don't touch," but then decided against this injunction. In any event, David made no effort to touch.

Every morning for the next few days he would begin his morning explorations by toddling over to the dead-bird-place. He no longer assumed the ritual-mask expression but still restrained himself from touching. The bird was allowed to remain there until greatly reduced by decomposition. I reasoned that he might as well have the opportunity of seeing the natural processes at work. This was, to the best of my knowledge, David's first exposure to death. No general change in his behavior was noted, nor had any been expected. The small first chapter had concluded.

But a few weeks later a second dead bird was discovered. David had quite a different reaction this time. He picked up the bird and gestured with it. He was "speaking" with insistence. When he realized that I did not comprehend his wishes, he reached up toward a tree, holding the bird above his head. He repeated the gesture several times. I tried to explain that being placed back on the tree would not help the bird. David continued to insist, accompanying his command now with gestures that could be interpreted as a bird flying. All too predictably, the bird did not fly when I returned it to the tree. He insisted that the effort be repeated several times; then he lost interest altogether.

There was a sequel a few weeks later—by now autumn. David and I were walking in the woods, sharing many small discoveries. After a while, however, his attention became thoroughly engaged by a single fallen leaf. He tried to place it back on the tree himself. Failure. He gave the leaf to me with "instructions" that the leaf be restored to its rightful place. Failure again. When I started to try once more, he shook his head no, looking both sober and convinced. Although leaves were repeatedly seen to fall and dead animals were found every now and then, he made no further efforts to reverse their fortunes.

David's look of puzzlement and his repeated efforts to reverse death suggest that even the very young child recognizes a problem when he sees one. Indeed, the problem of death very well might be the prime challenge that sets into motion the child's curiosity and mental questing. Instead of constituting only an odd corner of the young child's mental life, death and its related problems may, in fact, provide much of the motivation for his intellectual development. Children obviously do not possess the conceptual structures of the adult; nevertheless, they do try to understand. Curiosity about death and "where things go" is part of a child's early motivation for exploring his environment. While many developmentalists have observed how the young child comes to an appreciation of object constancy, few have noted that this mental achievement is not possible unless there is also an appreciation of inconstancy. In other words, the young child must be aware of changes, losses, and disappearances if he is eventually to comprehend what "stays," what "goes," and what "comes and goes." Even very young children encounter losses, ends, and limits. Without an ability to fathom these experiences, they could not form proto-concepts of constancies, beginnings, and possibilities.

The death of animals, relatives, or friends undoubtedly has some relationship to the child's discovery of his own mortality, but there are other observations that are more germane. Adah Maurer, a school psychologist in California, suggests that an infant as young as three months old has the glimmerings of death awareness. For a while the baby alternates between sleeping and waking states, with bio-

logical imperatives having the upper hand. Soon, Maurer says, "the healthy baby is ready to experiment with these contrasting states. In the game of peek-a-boo, he replays in safe circumstances the alternate terror and delight, confirming his sense of self by risking and regaining complete consciousness. A light cloth spread over his face and body will elicit an immediate and forceful reaction. Short, sharp intakes of breath, vigorous thrashing of arms and legs removes the erstwhile shroud to reveal widely staring eyes that scan the scene with frantic alertness until they lock glances with the smiling mother, whereupon he will wriggle and laugh with joy. . . . To the empathetic observer, it is obvious that he enjoyed the temporary dimming of the light, the blotting out of the reassuring face and the suggestion of a lack of air which his own efforts enabled him to restore, his aliveness additionally confirmed by the glad greeting implicit in the eye-to-eye oneness with another human."

Babies a few months older begin to delight in disappearance-and-return games. Overboard goes a toy, somebody fetches it, then overboard again. The questions When is something gone? and When is it gone "forever"? seem very important to the young explorer. He devises many experiments for determining under what conditions something is "all gone." Maurer suggests that we "offer a two-year-old a lighted match and watch his face light up with demonic glee as he blows it out. Notice the willingness with which he helps his mother if the errand is to step on the pedal and bury his banana peel in the covered garbage can. The toilet makes a still better sarcophagus until he must watch in awed dismay while the plumber fishes out the Tinker-toy from the overflowing bowl."

It makes sense to take these activities seriously. They provide early clues as to how children begin to grasp what "all gone" means. Once children are old enough to begin talking in sentences, part of their verbal repertoire usually includes death words. One conversation between a four-year-old girl and her eighty-four-year-old great-grandmother illustrates the preschool-age child's concept of death: "You are old. That means you will die. I am young, so I won't die, you know." This excerpt suggests that the little girl knows what it means to die, even if she has not entirely grasped the relationship between age and death. However, a moment later she adds: "But it's all right, Gran'mother. Just make sure you wear your white dress. Then,

after you die, you can marry Nomo [great-grandfather] again, and have babies."

The words "dead" and "die" are fairly common in children's conversation and often are used with some sense of appropriateness. Yet an extra comment such as "you can marry Nomo again" or a little adult questioning frequently reveals that a child's understanding of death is quite different from an adult's. Psychologist Maria Nagy, studying Hungarian children in the late 1940s, discovered three phases in the child's awareness of personal mortality. Her interpretation of death ideas expressed by three- to ten-year-olds in drawings and words are classic.

*Stage one: present until about age five.* The preschool child usually does not recognize that death is final. Being dead is like being less alive. The youngest children regard death as sleep or departure. Still, there is much curiosity about what happens to a person after he dies. The children "want to know where and how he continues to live. Most of the children connected the facts of absence and funerals. In the cemetery one lives on. Movement . . . is limited by the coffin, but for all that, the dead are still capable of growth. They take nourishment, they breathe. They know what is happening on earth. They feel it if someone thinks of them and they even feel sorry for themselves." Death disturbs the young child because it separates people from each other and because life in the grave seems dull and unpleasant.

*Stage two: between the ages of five and nine.* The distinguishing characteristic of this stage is that the child now tends to personify death. Death is sometimes seen as a separate person —for example, an angel or a frightening clown. For other children death is represented by a dead person. Death usually makes his rounds in the night. The big shift in the child's thinking from stage one is that death now seems to be understood as final: it is not just a reduced form of life. But there is still an important protective feature here: personal death can be avoided. Run faster than the Death Man, lock the door, trick him, and you will not die, unless you have bad luck. As Nagy puts it, "Death is still outside us and is also not general."

*Stage three: ages nine to ten and thereafter.* The oldest children in Nagy's study recognized that death was not only final but also inevitable. It will happen to them, too, no matter how fast they run or how cleverly they hide. "It is like the withering of flowers," a ten-year-old girl explained to the psychologist.

Nagy's stages offer a useful guide to the development of the child's conception of death, but not all observations fit neatly into these three categories. There are instances in which children as young as five realize their own inevitable mortality. A six-year-old boy worked out by himself the certainty of death. In a shocked voice he revealed, "But I had been planning to live forever, you know." A five-year-old reasoned aloud: "One day you [father] will be died. And one day Mommy will be died . . . . And one day even Cynthia [little sister], she will be died, I mean dead, too . . . . [pause] And one day *I* will be dead . . . . [long pause] *Everybody* there is will be dead . . . . [long, long pause] That's sad, isn't it?" This insight is several years ahead of schedule and is even farther ahead of what one would expect from most theories of mental growth.

Apparently, it is possible to grasp the central facts of death at a surprisingly early age. Children probably tend to retreat from this realization when it comes so early and for several years fluctuate between two states of belief: that death is final and inevitable, and that death is partial, reversible, and perhaps avoidable.

My research indicates that the orientation many adolescents have toward death also fluctuates between a sense of invulnerability and a sense of impending, castastrophic wipeout. Some adults reveal a similar tendency to function at two levels of thought: they "know" that death is final and inevitable, of course, but most of their daily attitudes and actions are more consistent with the belief that personal mortality is an unfounded rumor.

Sooner or later most children come to understand that death is final, universal, and inevitable. Parents might prefer that children remain innocent of what is happening in their lives and sheltered from emotional stress, shock, and anguish. But it is our own make-believe, not theirs, if we persist in behaving as though children are not attuned to the prospect of mortality. It is important to remember that in this century millions of children around the world have grown up literally in the midst of death and the threat of death. They have fewer illusions on the subject than do many adults.

"The kingdom where nobody dies," as Edna St. Vincent Millay once described childhood, is the fantasy of grownups. We want our children to be immortal—at least temporarily. We can be more useful to children if we can share with them realities as well as fantasies about death. This means some uncomfortable moments. Part of each child's adventure into life is his discovery of loss, separation, nonbeing, death. No one can have this adventure for him, nor can death be locked in another room until a child comes of age. At the beginning the child does not know that he is supposed to be scared of death, that he is supposed to develop a fabric of evasions to protect himself, and that his parents are not to be relied upon for support when it really counts. He is ready to share his discoveries with us. Are we?

# 54

# The Death-Dip Hypothesis

Death is admittedly one of the few things left you can still count on. However, observers note that, under certain conditions, people demonstrate an ability to postpone the inevitable, at least for a short period of time. Apparently, if there's something worth living for, the dying find it within themselves to hang on.

Two researchers from State University of New York at Stony Brook believe they've documented this phenomenon occurring before birthdays, elections and one Jewish holiday. Under these circumstances, David P. Phillips and Kenneth A. Feldman reveal evidence to support a "death-dip hypothesis"—that death-rate statistics take a significant nosedive prior to the meaningful event. What's more, when the raison de vivre passes, they found a corresponding increase in departing souls.

**Revealing Records.** In the first instance, the pair examined the birth and death dates of some 1,300 famous people, classifying them by month rather than day. Among the first group of 400, they noted only 16 deaths in the month preceding the birthmonth, while statistical estimates predicted there should be closer to 28. During the birthmonth, and in the three following months, 140 deaths occurred, some 23 more than could be expected by statistical averages. In all five of their samples, the pair reports, "the dip in deaths before the birthmonth and the peak in deaths immediately thereafter are both evident," supporting their hypothesis. This same trend proved even more significant among the very famous, presumably, according to Phillips and Feldman, because their birthdays are grander occasions than those of ordinary or less famous people, often accompanied by public celebrations, "many gifts, much attention and other tokens of respect."

Going back as far as the election of 1904, the researchers compared U.S. death rates in September and October of election years with those in the same months of both preceding and following years. By their calculations, "there is a significant dip in U.S. mortality before U.S. presidential elections" from 1904 to 1968.

**Waiting to Atone.** Similarly, they found a drop in New York City deaths prior to Yom Kippur (the Jewish Day of Atonement on which believers receive forgiveness for the previous year's sins), even though mortality statistics are not classified by religion and Jews account for only 28 percent of New York City's population. This percentage is greater than for any other American city, however, and when New York's pre–Yom Kippur death dip was compared to the country as a whole, the former proved larger nine out of 10 times. Also, the selection of Yom Kippur, which falls on a different day every year, helps separate the effects of the holiday from the effects of the season.

Phillips and Feldman qualify their explanations as tentative; however, they refute such arguments as a seasonal fluctuation in births or deaths, the possibility that deaths may have been misregistered because of the disrupting influences of elections and holidays or the effects of medical intervention. Despite obvious limitations, they believe that their "death-dip interpretation" may come to be valued as a social indicator, measuring changes in the way people react to the ceremonies of their culture.

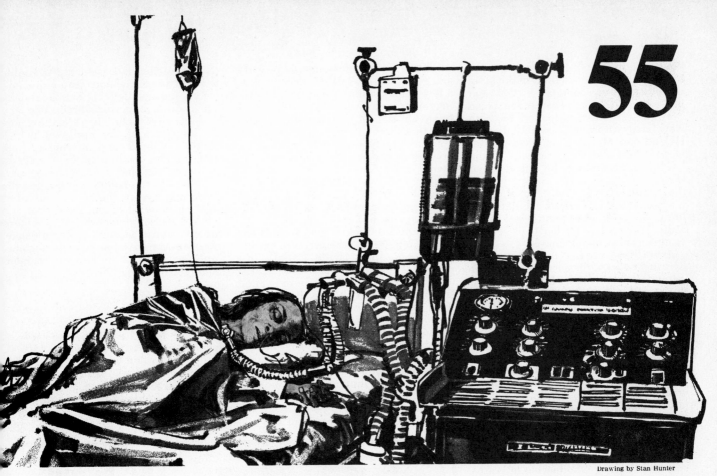

# 55

Drawing by Stan Hunter

**The girl in a coma: Artist's sketch of Karen Quinlan being kept alive on a respirator at St. Clare's Hospital, Denville, N.J.**

# A Right To Die?

She lies curled on her bed in the intensive-care unit at St. Clare's Hospital in Denville, N.J. Once, Karen Ann Quinlan was a vivacious girl with frosted brown hair and a ready smile. Now, she weighs only 70 pounds. Her hair falls on her pillow in dull, matted strands. Her skin, sallow and waxen, is stretched taut over her skull. Her mouth is in a rigid grimace, her eyes are tightly shut. Thin yellow tubes for drainage and intravenous feeding trail from her nose and arm. Beside her bed, a Bennett MA-1 respirator hisses with a steady rhythm, as it has for the past six months, forcing air into her lungs through an incision in her throat. Karen is in a "persistent vegetative state"—but for the respirator, she would almost certainly have died months ago.

How long the respirator will continue to keep Karen alive is problematical. Last week, the girl's fate shifted from the hospital to the judicial arena of the New Jersey Superior Court in Morristown. There, Joseph T. Quinlan has asked to be made guardian of his 21-year-old daughter so that the respirator can be removed and she can be allowed to die "with grace and dignity." Quinlan and his wife, Julia, arrived at this decision because

doctors have offered no hope that Karen can recover. "I didn't want her to die," Joseph Quinlan explained. "I just wanted to put her back in her natural state, and leave her to the Lord. If the Lord wants her to live, she'll live. If He wants her to die, she'll die." The Quinlans were bolstered in their decision by their parish priest, Father Thomas Trapasso, who assured them that under Roman Catholic teaching they had no moral obligation to keep their daughter alive by "extraordinary means" without hope.

The Quinlan case now poses, in a tragically public way, the most delicate of medical and legal issues: whether in addition to the right to live there is, in certain circumstances, a right to die.

Karen Quinlan's plight also raises a number of complex related issues—the question of euthanasia, and the almost theological nuances with which doctors and priests alike seek to differentiate between "active" and "passive" procedures. There is the question of when death really occurs, and what standards shall be used to define it. Finally, there is the fact that all of these issues are so ineluctably bound up with human emotions and human frailty, with the welfare of the living as well as that of the

stricken. Perhaps in the long run the most fundamental question posed by the Quinlan case is whether it or any similar moral dilemma can or should be taken to a court of law for resolution.

This is hardly the first time, though it may be among the most conspicuous, that these questions have been raised. Steps to terminate treatment in hopeless cases have been quietly taken countless times, usually on the mutual agreement of patient, family and physician. But when Quinlan signed a release to permit her doctors to turn off the respirator last July, they refused. Thus the Quinlans' private and personal plight came before the public bar in a case that is probably unique in American jurisprudence. Sometime this week, Judge Robert Muir Jr. is expected to decide whether to grant the Quinlans' request.

To protect her interests during the trial, Karen Quinlan is represented by a court-appointed guardian who made his position in her defense quite clear. "If she were brain-dead," said attorney Daniel Coburn, "I would have said her life was terminated. But that is not the case. This is not a court of love, of compassion, but a court of law. You can't just extinguish life because she is an eyesore." He was supported by both New Jersey Attorney General William F. Hyland and Morris County Prosecutor Donald G. Collester Jr., as well as the lawyers representing the hospital and her physicians. To turn the respirator off, they contend, would be an act of palpable homicide. "Where do we draw the line?" lawyer Ralph Porzio asked Judge Muir. "You are being asked to place your stamp on an act of euthanasia."

Aside from its compelling overtones of personal tragedy, the case is yet another symptom of a changing legal climate in the practice of medicine and new concerns about ethical safeguards insuring respect for human life. The rising number of malpractice suits is causing doctors to revise their thinking about using—or not using—procedures that were once considered routine. Last winter, the profession received a severe shock when Dr. Kenneth Edelin, a Boston obstetrician, was convicted of manslaughter for performing an abortion and not trying to save the life of the infant. "After the Edelin case, doctors are really scared," says Dr. Harold Hirsh, a physician and attorney who teaches at Washington's Georgetown and Catholic universities. "There's a real concern in the profession over criminal liability."

In the Quinlan case, the specter of criminal liability has been extended to the ethical concerns of the doctor's duty to treat a person when, as some say, it is not a matter of prolonging the process of life but of prolonging the process of death. Critics of withdrawing life support in hopeless cases have been quick to cite the calculated euthanasia policy employed by Nazi Germany against cripples, mental incompetents, epileptics, the elderly and others held to be socially undesirable. Few ethical thinkers take a comparison between the Nazi policy and the Quinlan case seriously. "There is a moral difference between killing and allowing to die," says Rev. Richard A. McCormick of Georgetown's Kennedy Center for Bioethics. "When you cease extraordinary effort, it is the disease that kills, not the withdrawal."

McCormick's distinction seems clear, for example, in the case of an elderly patient with widespread cancer. But Karen's illness remains something of a mystery, and though doctors have in recent years (very largely in order to cope with the demand for organ transplants) developed the concept of "brain death" as opposed to "heart death," none of her doctors now claims that Karen Quinlan is in any technical sense already

dead. She lapsed into a coma in the early-morning hours of April 15 after drinking a few gin-and-tonics—and possibly taking some drugs as well (page 60). According to Dr. Robert J. Morse, the neurologist in charge of her case, the coma appeared to have been "metabolic in origin and perhaps drug-induced." One theory is that Karen passed out, and the mixture of drugs and alcohol made her vomit. Inhalation of the vomit could have cut off the supply of oxygen to her brain, causing permanent damage.

Most of the doctors who have examined Karen Quinlan believe she has lost her consciousness of life. "She is in a persistent vegetative state," said neurology professor Dr. Julius Korein in court last week. "I don't believe she can think in any of the senses we talk of. She can't calculate, can't reason ... Let's not confuse mental deficiency and Miss Quinlan. In my opinion she has no awareness, no consciousness. That's a totally different world."

Karen can, for limited periods, breathe on her own, triggering a light on her respirator. Dr. Arshad Javed has made attempts to wean Karen from the ma-

chine, and she has occasionally been able to maintain spontaneous respiration.

Korein concluded that Karen has damage in any of four critical brain areas, and possibly all of them. They are: the reticular formation of the midbrain, which controls arousal and alertness; both halves of the cerebral cortex, the center for reasoning and memory; the basal ganglia, a motor-control center, and the thalamus, a relay center for sensations such as those of touch, pain, heat and cold. Most likely more than one of these are involved to account for Karen's state. Because damage to nerve cells is irreparable, he said that no known treatment could repair Karen's brain.

Judge Muir has little in the way of legal precedents to go by. In general, courts have ruled that an adult who has no dependents can choose to die. In a 1971 case, for example, a Florida judge held that an elderly woman with incurable anemia could refuse any further treatment. In cases involving Jehovah's

## The Family

*"I didn't want her to die. I just wanted to put her back in her natural state, and leave her to the Lord. If the Lord wants her to live in a natural state, she'll live. If he wants her to die, she'll die."*

—Joseph Quinlan

**Vigil for Karen: Mrs. Quinlan, Father Trapasso (right); above, Joseph Quinlan**
Photos by Mark Greenberg

Witnesses, however, the courts have routinely intervened to insure that minors receive transfusions, even though their parents object on religious grounds.

Interestingly, in Tarpon Springs, Fla., last week, reporters uncovered the case of Elaine Esposito, 41, who has been in a coma for 34 years, ever since she suffered a burst appendix at the age of 6. Miss Esposito cannot speak or move, and is still cared for around the clock by her mother. Unlike Karen Quinlan, however, she is not on a respirator and is not being kept alive by artificial means.

Perhaps the closest parallel to the Quinlan case is one decided in New Jersey four years ago involving a 22-year-old Jehovah's Witness named Dolores Heston who required transfusions following an auto accident. Because she was in shock, she could not consent, and her mother tried to prevent treatment on the ground that her daughter would have declined for religious reasons. At the hospital's request, the court ordered treatment, which saved her life. But

there are important differences between the two cases. Dolores was offered a meaningful life after surgery. What Quinlan and his family contend is that there is no such prospect for Karen.

The dilemma doctors face in cases like Karen's is largely due to medical progress and the development of ever more sophisticated means of life support. Thirty years ago, a patient died when his heart stopped, and "extraordinary" treatment consisted of an injection of adrenalin. But with respirators, heart-lung machines, organ

# Who Was Karen Quinlan?

"The last thing we want to do is put Karen Ann Quinlan on trial," says county prosecutor Collester. "It makes no difference whether she was the Virgin Mary or Mary Magdalen," agrees attorney Coburn, who was appointed by the court to defend Karen's interests. But in court, Karen's parents have based their arguments on the belief that she herself would have wanted them to remove the machinery prolonging her life—and that argument has thrust the questions of what Karen was like, what she thought and how she lived, to the very heart of her tragic and curious case.

**Enigma:** In spite of the probing investigations of police, press and physicians, however, Karen Ann Quinlan remains something of an enigma. Adopted at the age of four weeks from a hospital for unwed mothers, she lived until last fall in Julia and Joseph Quinlan's New Jersey home, a two-story frame house with a white Madonna on the lawn. Her activities and ambitions seem to have been the ordinary stuff of middle-class suburbia. She was an average student at local parochial schools, and principals and teachers recall nothing remarkable about her. A bit of a tomboy, she was avidly interested in sports, and at one time even held a job as a gas-station attendant and assistant mechanic.

In August 1974, shortly after she was laid off from her job as a technician at a ceramics factory, Karen moved out of the Quinlan household to live with a friend in an apartment miles away. After that, the accounts of her life-style start to vary tremendously. For one thing, she appears to have lost touch with her old friends from school and to have started running with a wholly new crowd. Her roommate, Robin Croft, scoffs at reports that they lived a drug- and drink-ridden life, saying that they only occasionally "tied one on" and that Karen "might have taken a few pills for a high, but she wasn't into drugs."

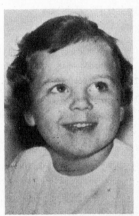

Karen as baby and with Nanette Foit: Who knows what she would choose for herself?

But Thomas R. French, a young Morris County resident who was with Karen during the last few days of her active life, tells a different story. French describes her as "self-destructive, popping whatever pills she could get her hands on" and often drinking to excess.

**Tragedy:** On the night of April 14, Karen accompanied French and several other friends to Falconer's, a roadside tavern in nearby Lake Lackawanna, where they were to celebrate a friend's birthday. According to French, they had prefaced the trip to the tavern with several gin-and-tonics. French says he had seen Karen "popping pills" earlier in the day. He reports that Karen "started to nod out" after only one drink at the bar, so he drove her home. By the time they got there, Karen had passed out entirely. A few minutes later, he realized that she had stopped breathing and began to give her mouth-to-mouth resuscitation. His friends called an ambulance and Karen was carried off, unconscious, to the hospital, never to wake again.

Part of the Quinlans' argument for withdrawing Karen's life supports rests on their claim that Karen had made it quite clear that she was horri-

fied at the idea of being kept alive by mechanical means. Last week in court, Julia Quinlan described three separate occasions when Karen had said she would rather be allowed to die than be kept alive by machines. Lori A. Gaffney, an 18-year-old friend, testified that Karen had told her she "would not want to be kept alive by such extraordinary means—under any circumstances." Miss Gaffney reports that Karen was particularly distressed after the father of a close friend, Nanette Foit, succumbed slowly and painfully to cancer.

"If anyone can make the decision to cut off treatment for an incompetent patient," says Dr. Robert Veatch, a specialist in medical ethics at New York's Institute of Society, Ethics and the Life Sciences, "it must be the person who best knows what she would want for herself." In Karen Ann Quinlan's case, it is not at all clear who knew her best during the last jumbled weeks of her active life. But her parents, who have known her longest and are convinced that the Karen who lived with them was the real one, are convinced beyond doubt that they know what she would choose.

—MERRILL SHEILS with SUSAN AGREST in Morristown, N.J.

transplants and similar measures, patients who would have died can be kept alive, at least technically, for weeks, months and even years. "Technology," says Dr. David Abramson of Washington's Georgetown University Hospital, "has advanced so that no one really has to die, so we have to make a choice."

Harold Hirsh, the physician-lawyer, agrees. "There comes a time when people should die in peace," he declares. Hirsh recalls a woman in a coma as the result of a cerebral hemorrhage, who was sustained for six weeks only by means of a respirator and intravenous feedings. Finally, the woman's doctor went to her family and explained that she could remain this way for years, without a chance of recovery. "You'll start hating to come see her in the hospital," he told the family, "and maybe even start hating her." They agreed, and the doctors unhooked the respirator.

The ethical problems in some cases have been eased by the concept of brain death, spelled out by a Harvard Medical School ad hoc committee in 1968. Under these guidelines, a physician can pronounce a patient dead if he shows the absence of brain waves on an electroencephalogram for 24 hours, together with a lack of spontaneous breathing, fixed and dilated pupils and no response to external stimulation. The Harvard criteria were adopted mainly to enable surgeons to remove organs for transplants while the donor's heart was still beating and the organs remained viable. But they can now also be used by doctors as sure evidence that life supports can be withdrawn with impunity, and eight states (Maryland, Oregon, Michigan, California, Virginia, Kansas, Georgia and New Mexico) have passed laws recognizing the Harvard guidelines as valid to determine brain death.

**B**ut such standards don't apply in cases like Karen's where neurologic signs are present, and the issue isn't whether the patient is dead, but whether there is a prospect of meaningful life. In these instances, the doctor must follow his conscience and the wishes of the family—but at his own risk. "There is no legal safeguard," says Dr. Gordon Avery of Washington, D.C.'s Children's Hospital. "It's like walking on thin ice."

There is no question that "active euthanasia," such as giving a patient a fatal injection in order to end his misery, is homicide. Yet only two doctors have ever come to trial in the U.S. for alleged "mercy killings," and both were acquitted. In 1949, Dr. Hermann Sander of Manchester, N.H., was accused of injecting air into the veins of a cancer patient, and in 1973, Dr. Vincent A. Montemarano, then with New York's Nassau County Medical Center, was charged with giving a cancer patient a lethal dose of potassium chloride. Sympathetic juries

acquitted both on evidence that the patients were already dead before the alleged acts occurred.

But many other physicians regularly flirt with active euthanasia in dealing with dying and suffering patients. In a recent survey of 660 internists, Diana Crane, a University of Pennsylvania sociologist, found that 43 per cent said they would administer increasing doses of narcotics to cancer patients in pain, knowing full well that in addition to easing the pain, the drug could eventually cause fatal respiratory arrest. The law, says Dr. Samuel Klagsbrun of New York's St. Luke's Hospital, "forces doctors to kill secretly, and this happens much more often than we acknowledge." The circumspect way for doctors to help a suffering patient, says Dr. Alvin Goldfarb, a New York psychiatrist and neurologist, is to say, "I have something for your pain. If you take too much, it will be harmful." And then, in effect, the patient decides.

Klagsbrun recalls the case of an elderly woman who was totally crippled and in constant pain from arthritis. She and her son discussed euthanasia with the doctor, and he gave her a prescription for Seconal. But the woman's hands were too badly crippled for her to hold the glass of water, so the son held the glass while she swallowed the pills. "Before she died," Klagsbrun says, "the mother told her son that this was the greatest gift she had ever received from him."

In every case, doctors must make a careful evaluation before taking such steps. Elderly people who express the wish to die, says Goldfarb, are sometimes suffering more from depression than they are from physical illness. "You treat the depression," he says, "and let them make a decision when they're in their right minds."

**D**octors seldom forget a patient whose life they bring to an end. Dr. Joel Posner of Lankenau Hospital, just outside Philadelphia, remembers a desperately ill man on a respirator who was doing a New York Times crossword puzzle the first time the physician saw him. Unable to speak, the man handed

---

## The Doctors

*"She is in a persistent vegetative state ... I don't believe she can think in any of the senses we talk of. She can't calculate, can't reason ... Let's not confuse mental deficiency and Miss Quinlan. In my opinion she has no awareness and no consciousness."*

—Dr. Julius Korein

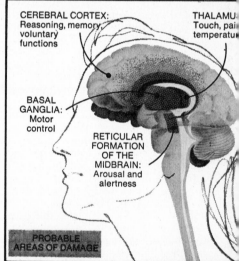

CEREBRAL CORTEX: Reasoning, memory, voluntary functions

THALAMU[S]: Touch, pai[n] temperatu[re]

BASAL GANGLIA: Motor control

RETICULAR FORMATION OF THE MIDBRAIN: Arousal and alertness

PROBABLE AREAS OF DAMAGE

Ib Ohlsson

Morse, Javed with Porzio (center); diagram of Karen's brain
Robert R. McElroy—Newsweek

Posner a note that read: "Please Don't Kill Me." Eventually, the patient became so sick that the respirator tube would slip out of his throat several times a day, causing him to turn blue from near suffocation. Finally, because of the man's suffering, Posner decided that further care on the machine was useless, and that the patient should be allowed to die. Turning off the respirator would be cruel, Posner decided, because it might take the patient twelve hours of choking to die. Morphine to put him to sleep could potentially constitute active euthanasia. So Posner turned off the respirator and administered pure oxygen through the tube. The effect was to suppress the man's respiration and put him to sleep. He died shortly afterward. "It was really no different from morphine," says Posner, "but somehow more legal."

For the vast majority of doctors, however, the use of "passive euthanasia"—failure to apply heroic treatments or, as in Karen's case, the withdrawal of life supports—is widespread. Physicians are less fearful of violating professional ethics or the law in making decisions not to initiate treatment in hopeless cases. "You have a patient with a brain tumor, in coma, and there's just no chance for her," notes a New York neurologist. "If she stops breathing, we don't put her on the respirator." In a case like Karen's, doctors might keep the respirator going, but not order the use of antibiotics if she developed pneumonia or some other infection.

A New York neurologist cites the case of a 30-year-old woman with a brain hemorrhage who never recovered consciousness after surgery. For six months, she was given respiratory care, but remained in a vegetative state. "Finally, we decided with the family that if she developed an infection we wouldn't treat it," he recalls. "And that's what happened: she got pneumonia and died in a week."

So wary are many doctors of actually turning off a life-support system that they work out devious conscience-sparing ploys to accomplish their purposes. Instead of switching off the respirator, for example, they simply don't replace the oxygen tank when it's empty. "They're not likely to get caught not maintaining the oxygen supply," suggests sociologist Crane, "while they might get caught unplugging the machine." But some doctors can be quite casual in facing such problems. Posner remembers with horror the cavalier request he received from one colleague at another hospital. "Do you mind if this patient dies?" the doctor asked of one emergency case. "The respirator's on the fifth floor and the nurse says it's a pain in the ass . . ."

The decision to withhold treatment from a patient unable to express his wishes—a patient like Karen Quinlan—

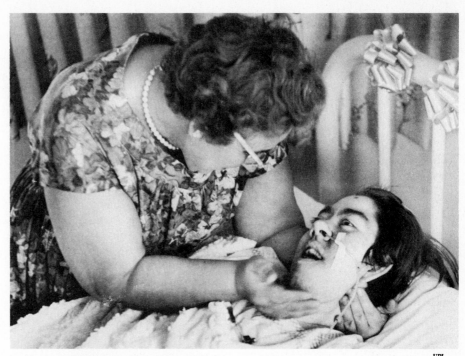

Mrs. Louis Esposito tends daughter Elaine who has been in a coma for 34 years

UPI

is the most difficult of all, and it is particularly controversial in the case of the infant born with severe mental or physical defects. The matter is easiest to decide in babies with anencephaly, the complete absence of the cerebral cortex. "With the best of care they live for only a few months," notes Dr. John Freeman of Johns Hopkins, "so many of us believe it is acceptable to withhold feeding and treatment of infections."

When Julius Korein was asked to testify as to what Karen's mental age would be, he replied: "The best way I can describe this would be to take the situation of the anencephalic monster. If you put a flashlight in back of the head the light comes out of the pupils. They have no brain."

But there is a growing controversy over permitting children with Down's syndrome, popularly known as mongolism, to perish in similar fashion. Many such infants have gastrointestinal or cardiac defects that would be fatal unless surgically repaired. On the parents' request, many pediatricians omit surgery and allow the children to die. But now, there is growing opposition to this practice both within and outside the profession. "The baby," declares Dr. Sheldon Korones of the University of Tennessee Newborn Center, "is not his parents' chattel." In some cases, the matter has been taken to court and judges have ordered the life-saving surgery. No matter how well intended, however, such decisions should not be left to the courts alone, in the view of some doctors. "I'd tell the judge: 'You ordered the surgery to be done'," says Dr. Jordan Weitzman of the University of Southern California, " 'now you find the surgeon'."

Weitzman recalls the case of a baby born with a malformed brain and severe facial deformities, whose unmarried mother left the hospital and abandoned the child. Since the baby couldn't eat except through a tube, the doctors decided, wisely in Weitzman's opinion, to let him die. But on a tip from someone at the hospital, The Los Angeles Times published a heart-rending feature about the baby's plight and doctors were pressured into continuing treatment.

Another child, born with no genitals, intestines or bladder, failed to elicit any such sympathy, Weitzman recalls, even though his condition was treatable. The baby was allowed to die. "Nobody said a word," according to the USC doctor. "I think it's because we live in an era of the Body Beautiful, so the sight of a kid with almost nothing below the waist gave everybody pause."

Legal action to save a retarded child can create bizarre complications for both parent and physician. Dr. Kenneth Kenigsberg, a New York pediatric surgeon, was confronted two years ago by the parents of a mongoloid child with intestinal obstruction. They begged him not to operate: the parents felt that the stress on their marriage of rearing the child would be too great. Through an anonymous phone call, the matter came to the attention of the district attorney, who threatened the father with a jail term if the child wasn't treated. Kenigsberg operated and the child survived. "I thought I had made a humane decision in not operating," the surgeon says. "But now the child is a bouncing, smiling happy mongoloid who lives with a foster mother. I don't know which course was right."

Many doctors are reluctant to use any

means to hasten a patient's death. "Most of us were taught to fight to the very last, and strive as hard as we can to keep people alive," says Dr. Frank M. Weiser, a New York cardiologist. There is also the obvious fact that the physician cannot always be certain that a patient won't recover. Dr. Robert Glaser, president of the Kaiser Family Foundation in Palo Alto, Calif., recalls a 70-year-old man with multiple myeloma, an incurable malignancy of the bone marrow, who seemed to be going progressively downhill. Physicians at a large medical center decided to administer only painkillers and to keep the patient comfortable during his last days. They also transferred him to a hospital nearer his home. But there a new doctor took over and decided to try another course of drug therapy to treat the myeloma. As a result, the patient went into partial remission and has enjoyed another four years of relatively active life. Doctors agree that the patient who is told that he has six months to live but is alive six years later is almost a cliché.

To some doctors, particularly those with profound ethical or religious convictions against any form of euthanasia, the plea of "death with dignity" is specious and misleading. Most people seem to think that if a patient takes a sufficient dose of Demerol, morphine or other painkiller, he probably will die peaceably enough, but often things don't turn out that way. "I have seldom seen anybody die with 'peace and dignity'," says Posner. "They have tubes and pain, and they're scared. It's not like 'Love Story'."

Most physicians oppose attempts to settle cases like those of Karen Quinlan in the courts. If Judge Muir should rule that Karen's treatment must be continued, says Georgetown's Hirsh, "it will have a tremendous impact on the practice of medicine. Doctors are going to fear making any judgments at all, and we're just going to be keeping hopeless cases alive."

The doctors are equally opposed to any attempt to legislate medical procedures. Betty Jane Anderson, director of the American Medical Association's department of health law, puts it this way: "So long as you have advances in medical knowledge, the criteria for death will vary. The definition of death is constantly evolving. If you're locked into a statutory definition of death, you're stuck with it until the law changes. After all, it used to be that death occurred when you held a mirror to a patient's mouth and it did not fog up."

On balance, the medical consensus seems to be that the traditional relationship between the physician, the patient and the family is what must prevail—in the Quinlan issue as well as in most other decisions on medical practice. The decisions involved, according to this view,

are too personal and depend too much on individual circumstances to be left up to the cold impersonality of the law. "There's usually a positive commitment of people within a family to each other's welfare," says Dr. Raymond S. Duff of Yale. "There are covenants that people have toward one another that can be described as sacred. If we look to these bonds, we can probably remove decisions like the Quinlan one from the courts."

Once such a case does go to the courts, however, it is obviously very difficult for any judge to sanction what, from a strictly legal point of view, still amounts to homicide. Observers at the Quinlan trial last week sensed that the case was going badly for the family.

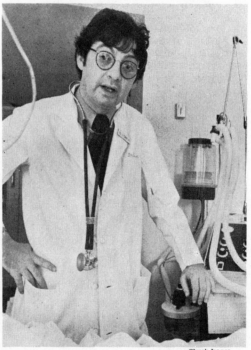

Chuck Isaacs

**Posner: Few die with dignity**

Judge Muir is expected to announce his ruling this week, but whatever the outcome of the case, the appeals process could take months or even years. Meanwhile Karen Quinlan herself will be increasingly prey to pneumonia and infections that regularly afflict intensive-care patients. Some doctors think that she will almost surely die before any ajudication can be reached, and many believe that it would in fact be best for this delicate issue never to be judicially settled. For it is Karen Quinlan's lot, in the final act of her tragically shortened life, to pose one of those fundamental ethical problems that human beings are obliged constantly to confront—and never, perhaps, to resolve.

—MATT CLARK with SUSAN AGREST in Morristown, N.J., MARIANA GOSNELL and DAN SHAPIRO in New York, HENRY McGEE in Washington and bureau reports

# 56

# The Funeral Transaction

## by Jessica Mitford

*A funeral is not an occasion for a display of cheapness.
It is, in fact, an opportunity for the display of a status
symbol which, by bolstering family pride, does much to
assuage grief. A funeral is also an occasion when feelings
of guilt and remorse are satisfied to a large extent by the
purchase of a fine funeral. It seems highly probable that the
most satisfactory funeral service for the average family
is one in which the cost has necessitated some degree of
sacrifice. This permits the survivors to atone for any real
or fancied neglect of the deceased prior to his death. . . .*
— *National Funeral Service Journal,*
*August 1961*

The seller of funeral service has, one gathers, a preconceived, stereotyped view of his customers. To him, the
bereaved person who enters his establishment is a
bundle of guilt feelings, a snob and a status seeker. The
funeral director feels that by steering his customer to
the higher-priced caskets, he is giving him his first dose
of grief therapy. In the words of the *National Funeral
Service Journal:* "The focus of the buyer's interest must
be the casket, vault, clothing, funeral cars, etc.—the
only tangible evidence of how much has been invested
in the funeral—the only real status symbol associated
with a funeral service."

Whether or not one agrees with this rather un-
flattering appraisal of the average person who has
suffered a death in the family, it is nevertheless true that
the funeral transaction is generally influenced by a combination of circumstances which bear upon the buyer
as in no other type of business dealing: the disorientation caused by bereavement, the lack of standards by
which to judge the value of the commodity offered by
the seller, the need to make an on-the-spot decision,
general ignorance of the law as it affects disposal of the
dead, the ready availability of insurance money to
finance the transaction. These factors predetermine to
a large extent the outcome of the transaction.

The funeral seller, like any other merchant, is preoccupied with price, profit, selling techniques. As Mr.
Leon S. Utter, dean of the San Francisco College of
Mortuary Science, writes in *Mortuary Management
Idea Kit:* "Your selling plan should go into operation
as soon as the telephone rings and you are requested to
serve a bereaved family. . . . Never preconceive as to
what any family will purchase. You cannot possibly
measure the intensity of their emotions, undisclosed
insurance or funds that may have been set aside for
funeral expenses."

The selling plan should be subtle rather than high-
pressure, for the obvious "hard sell" is considered inappropriate and self-defeating by modern industry
leaders. Two examples of what *not* to say to a customer
are given in the *Successful Mortuary Operation & Service
Manual:* "I can tell by the fine suit you're wearing, that
you appreciate the finer things, and will want a fine
casket for your Mother," and "Think of the beautiful
memory picture you will have of your dear Father in
this beautiful casket."

At the same time nothing must be left to chance.
The trade considers that the most important element of
funeral salesmanship is the proper arrangement of
caskets in the Selection Room (where the customer is
taken to make his purchase). The sales talk, while
preferably dignified and restrained, must be designed to
take maximum advantage of this arrangement.

The uninitiated, entering a casket selection room
for the first time, may think he is looking at a random
grouping of variously priced merchandise. Actually,
endless thought and care are lavished on the development of new and better selection room arrangements,
for it has been found that the placing of the caskets
materially affects the amount of the sale. There are
available to the trade a number of texts devoted to the
subject, supplemented by frequent symposiums, seminars, study courses, visual aids, scale model selection
rooms complete with miniature caskets that can be
moved around experimentally. All stress the desired
goal: selling consistently in a "bracket that is above
average."

The relationship between casket arrangement and
sales psychology is discussed quite fully by Mr. W. M.
Krieger, managing director of the influential National
Selected Morticians Association, in his book *Successful
Funeral Management.* He analyzes the blunder of placing the caskets in order of price, from cheapest to most
expensive, which he calls the "stairstep method" of
arrangement. As he points out, this plan "makes direct

dollar comparisons very easy." Or, if the caskets are so arranged that the most expensive are the first ones the buyer sees, he may be shocked into buying a very cheap one. A mistake to be avoided is an unbalanced line with too many caskets in a low price range: "The unbalanced line with its heavy concentration of units under $300 made it very easy for the client to buy in this area with complete satisfaction."

In developing his method of display, Mr. Kreiger divides the stock of caskets for convenience into four "quartiles," two above and two below the median price, which in his example is $400. The objective is to sell in the third, or just above median, quartile. To this end the purchaser is first led to a unit in this third quartile—about $125 to $150 *above* the median sale, in the range of $525 to $550. Should the buyer balk at this price, he should next be led to a unit providing "strong contrast, both in price and quality," this time something well below the median, say in the $375 to $395 range. The psychological reasons for this are explained. They are twofold. While the difference in quality is demonstrable, the price is not *so* low as to make the buyer feel belittled. At the same time, if the buyer turns his nose up and indicates that he didn't want to go *that* low, now is the time to show him the "rebound unit"—one priced from $5 to $25 *above* the median, in the $405 to $425 bracket.

Mr. Kreiger calls all this the "Keystone Approach," and supplies a diagram showing units 1, 2, and 3, scattered with apparent artless abandon about the floor. The customer, who has been bounced from third to second quartile and back again on the rebound to the third, might think the "Human Tennis Ball Approach" a more appropriate term.

Should the prospect show no reaction either way on seeing the first unit—or should he ask to see something better—the rebound gambit is, of course, "out." "In" is the Avenue of Approach. It seems that a Canadian Royal Mountie once told Mr. Krieger that people who get lost in the wilds always turn in a great circle to their right. Probably, surmises Mr. Krieger, because 85 percent of us are right-handed? In any event, the Avenue of Approach is a main, wide aisle leading to the right in the selection room. Here are the better-quality third- and fourth-quartile caskets.

For that underprivileged, or stubborn, member of society who insists on purchasing below the median (but who should nevertheless be served "graciously and with just as much courtesy and attention as you would give to the buyer without a limit on what he can spend") there is a narrow aisle leading to the *left*, which Mr. Krieger calls "Resistance Lane." There is unfortunately no discussion of two possible hazards: what if an extremely affluent prospect should prove to be among the 15 percent of *left*-handed persons, and should therefore turn automatically into Resistance Lane? How to extricate him? Conversely, if one of the poor or stubborn, possibly having at some time in his past been lost in Canada, should instinctively turn to the broad, right-hand Avenue of Approach?

The Comprehensive Sales Program offered by Successful Mortuary Operation to its participating members is designed along the same lines as **Mr.** Krieger's plan, only it is even more complicated. Everything is, however, most carefully spelled out, beginning with the injunction to greet the clients with a warm and friendly handshake, and a suggested opening statement, which should be "spoken slowly and with real sincerity: 'I want to assure you that I'm going to do everything I can to be helpful to you!' "

Having made this good beginning, the funeral director is to proceed with the Arrangement Conference, at each stage of which he should "weave in the service story"—in other words, impress upon the family that they will be entitled to all sorts of extras, such as ushers, cars, pallbearers, a lady attendant for hairdressing and cosmetics, and the like—all of which will be included in the price of the casket which it is now their duty to select. These preliminaries are very important for "the Arrangement Conference can *make* or *break* the sale."

The diagram of the selection room in this manual resembles one of those mazes set up for experiments designed to muddle rats. It is here that we are introduced to the Triangle Plan, under which the buyer is led around in a triangle, or rather in a series of triangles. He is started off at position A, a casket costing $587, which he is told is "in the $500 range"—although, as the manual points out, it is actually only $13 short of $600. He is informed that the average family buys in the $500 range—a statement designed to reassure him, explain the authors, because "most of the people believe themselves to be *above* average." Supposing the client does not react either way to the $587 casket. He is now led to position B on the diagram—a better casket priced at $647. However, this price is not to be mentioned. Rather, the words "sixty dollars additional" are to be used. Should the prospect still remain silent, this is the cue to continue *upward* to the most expensive unit.

Conversely, should the client demur at the price of $587, he is to be taken to position C—and told that "he can *save* $100" by choosing this one. Again, the figure of $487 is not to be mentioned. If he now says nothing, he is led to position D. Here he is told that "at sixty dollars additional, we could use this finer type, and all of the services will be just exactly the same." This is the crux of the triangle plan; the recalcitrant buyer has now gone around a triangle to end up unwittingly within forty dollars of the starting point. It will be noted that the prices all end in the number seven, "purposely styled to allow you to quote as: 'sixty dollars additional or save a hundred dollars.' "

The buyer is not likely to have caught the significance of this guided tour. As a customer he finds himself in an unusual situation, trapped in a set of circumstances peculiar to the funeral transaction. His frame of mind will vary, obviously, according to the circumstances which led him to the funeral establishment. He may be dazed and bewildered, his young wife having just been killed in an accident; he may be rather relieved because a crotchety old relative has finally died after a long and painful illness. The great majority of funeral buyers, as they are led through their paces at the mortuary—whether shaken and grief-stricken or merely looking forward with pleasurable anticipation to the reading of the will—are assailed by many a nagging question: What's the *right* thing to do? I am arranging this funeral, but surely this is no time to indulge my own preferences in taste and style; I feel I know what she would have preferred, but what will her family and friends expect? How can I avoid criticism for inadvertently doing the wrong thing? And, above all, it should be a nice, decent funeral—but what *is* a nice, decent funeral?

Which leads us to the second special aspect of the funeral transaction: the buyer's almost total ignorance of what to expect when he enters the undertaker's parlor. What to look for, what to avoid, how much to spend. The funeral industry estimates that the average individual has to arrange for a funeral only once in fifteen years. The cost of the funeral is the third largest expenditure, after a house and a car, in the life of an ordinary American family. Yet even in the case of the old relative, whose death may have been fully expected and even welcomed, it's most unlikely that the buyer will have discussed the funeral with anybody in advance. It just would not seem right to go round saying, "By the way, my uncle is very ill and he's not expected to live; do you happen to know a good, reliable undertaker?"

Because of the nature of funerals, the buyer is in a quite different position from one who is, for example, in the market for a car. Visualize the approach. The man of prudence and common sense who is about to buy a car consults a Consumers' Research bulletin or seeks the advice of his friends; he knows in advance the dangers of rushing into a deal blindly.

In the funeral home, the man of prudence is completely at sea without a recognizable landmark or bearing to guide him. It would be an unusual person who would examine the various offerings and then inquire around about the relative advantages of the Monaco casket by Merit and the Valley Forge by Boyertown. In the matter of cost, a like difference is manifest. The funeral buyer is generally not in the mood to compare prices here, examine and appraise quality there. He is anxious to get the whole thing over with—not only is he anxious for this, but the exigencies of the situation demand it.

The third unusual factor which confronts the buyer is the need to make an on-the-spot decision. Impulse buying, which should, he knows, be avoided in everyday life, is here a built-in necessity. The convenient equivocations of commerce—"I'll look around a little, and let you know," "Maybe, I'll call you in a couple of weeks if I decide to take it," "My partner is going to Detroit next month, he may pick one up for me there"—simply do not apply in this situation. Unlike most purchases, this one cannot be returned in fifteen days and your money refunded in full if not completely satisfied.

Not only is the funeral buyer barred by circumstances from shopping around in a number of establishments; he is also barred by convention and his own feelings from complaining afterwards if he thinks he was overcharged or otherwise shabbily treated. The reputation of the TV repairman, the lawyer, the plumber is public property and their shortcomings are often the subject of dinner party conversation. The reputation of

the undertaker is relatively safe in this respect. A friend, knowing I was writing on the subject, reluctantly told me of her experience in arranging the funeral of a brother-in-law. She went to a long-established, "reputable" undertaker. Seeking to save the widow expense, she chose the cheapest redwood casket in the establishment and was quoted a low price. Later, the salesman called her back to say the brother-in-law was too tall to fit into this casket, she would have to take one that cost $100 more. When my friend objected, the salesman said, "Oh, all right, we'll use the redwood one, but we'll have to cut off his feet." My friend was so shocked and disturbed by the nightmare quality of this conversation that she never mentioned it to anybody for two years.

Popular ignorance about the law as it relates to the disposal of the dead is a factor that sometimes affects the funeral transaction. People are often astonished to learn that in no state is embalming required by law except in certain special circumstances, such as when the body is to be shipped by common carrier.

The funeral men foster these misconceptions, sometimes by coolly misstating the law to the funeral buyer and sometimes by inferentially investing with the authority of law certain trade practices which they find it convenient or profitable to follow. This free and easy attitude to the law is even to be found in those institutes of higher learning, the Colleges of Mortuary Science, where the fledgling undertaker receives his training. For example; it is the law in most states that when a decedent bequeaths his body for use in medical research, his survivors are bound to carry out his directions. Nonetheless an embalming textbook, *Modern Mortuary Science,* disposes of the whole distasteful subject in a few misleading words: "Q: Will the provisions in the will of a decedent that his body be given to a medical college for dissection be upheld over his widow? A: No . . . No-one owns or controls his own body to the extent that he may dispose of the same in a manner which would bring humiliation and grief to the immediate members of his family."

I had been told so often that funeral men tend to invent the law as they go along (for there is a fat financial reward at stake) that I decided to investigate this situation at first hand. Armed with a copy of the California code, I telephoned a leading undertaker in my community with a concocted story: my aged aunt, living in my home, was seriously ill—not expected to live more than a few days. Her daughter was coming here directly; but I felt I ought to have some suggestions, some arrangements to propose in the event that . . . Sympathetic monosyllables from my interlocutor. The family would want something very simple, I went on, just cremation. Of course, we can arrange all that, I was assured. And since we should prefer only cremation, and there will be no service, we should prefer not to buy a coffin. The undertaker's voice at the other end of the phone was now alert, although smooth. He told me, calmly and authoritatively, that it would be "illegal" for him to enter into such an arrangement. "You mean it would be against the law?" I asked. Yes, indeed. "In that case, perhaps we could take the body straight to the crematorium in our station wagon?" A shocked silence, followed by an explosive outburst: "Madam, the average lady has neither the facilities nor the inclination to be hauling dead bodies around!" (Which was actually a good point, I thought.)

I tried two more funeral establishments, and was told substantially the same thing: cremation of an un-coffined body is prohibited under California law. This was said, in all three cases, with such a ring of conviction that I began to doubt the evidence before my eyes in the state code. I reread the sections on cremation, on health requirements; finally I read the whole thing from cover to cover. Finding nothing, I checked with an officer of the Board of Health, who told me there is no law in California requiring that a coffin be used when a body is cremated. He added that indigents are cremated by some county welfare agencies without benefit of coffin.

It is, however, true that most privately owned crematoria have their own privately established rule that they will not cremate without a coffin. After all, why not? Many are in the casket-selling business themselves, and those that are not depend for their livelihood on the good will of funeral directors who are.

Cemetery salesmen are also prone to confuse fact with fiction to their own advantage in discussing the law. Cemeteries derive a substantial income from the sale of "vaults." The vault, a cement enclosure for the casket, is not only a money-maker; it facilitates upkeep of the cemetery by preventing the eventual subsidence of the grave as the casket disintegrates. In response to my inquiry, a cemetery salesman (identified on his card as a "memorial counselor") called at my house to sell me what he was pleased to call a "pre-need memorial estate," in other words, a grave for future occupancy. After he had quoted the prices of the various graves, the salesman explained that a minimum of $120 must be added for a vault, which, he said, is "required by law."

"Why is it required by law?"

"To prevent the ground from caving in."

"But suppose I should be buried in one of those Eternal caskets made of solid bronze?"

"Those things are not as solid as they look. You'd be surprised how soon they fall apart."

"Are you *sure* it is required by law?"

"I've been in this business fifteen years; I should know."

"Then would you be willing to sign this?" (I had been writing on a sheet of paper, "California State Law requires a vault for ground burial.")

The memorial counselor gathered up his colored photographs of memorial estates and walked out of the house.

The fifth unusual factor present in the funeral transaction is the availability to the buyer of relatively large sums of cash. The family accustomed to buying every major item on time—car, television set, furniture —and to spending to the limit of the weekly paycheck, suddenly finds itself in possession of insurance funds and death benefit payments, often from a number of sources. It is unnecessary for the undertaker to resort to crude means to ascertain the extent of insurance coverage. A few simple and perfectly natural questions put to the family while he is completing the vital statistics forms will serve to elicit all he needs to know. For example, "Occupation of the deceased?" Shall we bill the insurance company directly?"

The undertaker knows, better than a schoolboy knows the standings of the major league baseball teams, the death benefit payments of every trade union in the community, the social security and workmen's compensation scale of death benefits, the veterans' and servicemen's death benefits: social security payment, up to $255; if the deceased was a veteran, $250 more and free burial in a national cemetery; burial allowance of $400 and up for military personnel and U. S. Civil Service employees; $700 for retired railroad workers; additional funeral allowance of $300 to $800 under various state workmen's compensation laws if the death was occupationally connected, and so on and on.

The undertaker has all the information he needs to proceed with the sale. The widow, for the first time in possession of a large amount of ready cash, is likely to welcome his suggestions. He is, after all, the expert, the one who knows how these things should be arranged, who will steer her through the unfamiliar routines and ceremonies ahead, who will see that all goes as it should.

At the lowest end of the scale is the old-age pensioner, most of whose savings have long since been spent. He is among the poorest of the poor. Nevertheless, most state and county welfare agencies permit him to have up to $1,000 in cash; in some states he may own a modest home as well, without jeopardizing his pension. The funeral director knows that under the law of virtually every state the funeral bill is entitled to preference in payment as the first charge against the estate. (Efforts in some states to pass legislation limiting the amount of the priority for burial costs to, say, $500 have been frustrated by the funeral lobby.) There is every likelihood that the poor old chap will be sent out in high style unless his widow is a very, very cool customer indeed.

The situation that generally obtains in the funeral transaction was summed up by former Surrogate's Court Judge Fowler of New York in passing upon the reasonableness of a bill which had come before him: "One of the practical difficulties in such proceedings is that contracts for funerals are ordinarily made by persons differently situated. On the one side is generally a person greatly agitated or overwhelmed by vain regrets or deep sorrow, and on the other side persons whose business it is to minister to the dead for profit. One side is, therefore, often unbusinesslike, vague and forgetful, while the other is ordinarily alert, knowing and careful."

There are people, however, who know their own minds perfectly well and who approach the purchase of a funeral much as they would any other transaction. They are, by the nature of things, very much in the minority. Most frequently they are not in the immediate family of the deceased but are friends or representatives of the family. Their experiences are interesting because to some extent they throw into relief the irrational quality of the funeral transaction.

Mr. Rufus Rhoades, a retired manufacturer of San Rafael, California, was charged with arranging for the cremation of a ninety-two-year-old friend who died in a rest home in 1961. He telephoned the crematorium, and was quoted the price of $75 for cremation plus $15 for shipping the ashes to Santa Monica, where his friend's family had cemetery space. He suggested hiring an ambulance to pick up the body, but this idea was quickly vetoed by the crematorium. He was told that he would have to deal through an undertaker, that the body could not be touched by anyone but a licensed funeral director, that a "container" would have to be provided. This he was unaware of; and no wonder, for these are "regulations" of the crematorium, not requirements of California law.

Mr. Rhoades looked in the San Rafael telephone directory, and found five funeral establishments listed. He picked one at random, called, and was told that under no circumstances could price be discussed over the telephone as it was "too private a matter"; that he should come down to the funeral home. There he found that the cheapest price, including "a low priced casket and the complete services" was $480. Mr. Rhoades protested that he did not *wish* the complete services, that there was to be no embalming, that he did not want to see the coffin. He merely wanted the body removed from the rest home and taken to the crematorium, some five miles away. Balking at the $480, Mr. Rhoades returned home and telephoned the other four funeral establishments. The lowest quotation he could obtain was $250.

Not unnaturally, Mr. Rhoades feels he paid a fee of $50 a mile to have his friend's body moved from the rest home to the crematorium. The undertaker no doubt felt, for his part, that he had furnished a service well below his "break even" point, or, in his own terminology, "below the cost at which we are fully compensated."

There was the case of a young widow whose husband died of cancer in 1950 after a long illness in Oakland, California. His death was fully expected by both of them, and they had discussed the matter of his funeral. The day he died, the widow left town to stay with her mother, leaving the funeral arrangements in the hands of their attorney, who was also a close friend. There was to be no religious service, just cremation and disposal of the ashes. Cremation, the attorney learned, would cost $60. The body had already been moved from the hospital to a nearby funeral establishment, so the attorney telephoned the undertaker to instruct him to deliver it to the crematorium. To his astonishment, he was told the minimum price for this would be $350—"including our complete services." There ensued a long conversation full of cross-purposes; for what "service' could now possibly be rendered to the dead man, to his widow who was thousands of miles away, or indeed to anybody? The funeral director insisted that this was the lowest price at which he would be fully compensated. Compensated for what? demanded the attorney. For the complete services . . . and so it went, until the attorney blew up and threatened to complain to the hospital that they had recommended an unscrupulous funeral establishment. At that point, the undertaker reduced his price to $150.

The point of view of the funeral director must here be explored. I talked with Mr. Robert MacNeur, owner of the largest funeral establishment in the Oakland area, with a volume of 1,000 funerals a year. Their cheapest offering is the standard service with redwood casket, at $485. "My firm has never knowingly subjected a person to financial hardship," Mr. MacNeur declared. "We will render a complete funeral service for nothing if the circumstances warrant it. The service is just the same at no charge as it is for a $1,000 funeral."

Mr. MacNeur produced a copy of the "Grant Miller Cooperative Plan," in which this philosophy is spelled out, and is here quoted in full: "Grant Miller Mortuaries have served the families of this community for over sixty years. It has always been their policy to provide funeral service regardless of financial circumstances. If a family finds the First Standard Arrangement including the finer type Redwood Casket at $485 to be beyond their present means or wishes, Grant Miller Mortuaries stand ready to reduce costs in accordance with the following cooperative plan chart, rather than use one or a series of cheap or inferior caskets."

The price chart which accompanies this shows the buyer that if he cannot afford to pay $485 for the cheapest casket in the house, he can have it, with the complete service, for $422.50. If he cannot afford that, he can pay $360, or $297.50, or $235, or $117.50, and so on down the line to "$0" for "persons in Distress Circumstances." It is the undertaker, of course, who decides who is eligible for these dispensations.

The retired manufacturer and the young widow happened to be extremely well off financially. They were not entitled to, neither did they solicit, any sort of charitable contribution from the funeral establishments or any reduction of the charges because of "distress circumstances." But as business people they were astonished that the undertakers should expect them to pay several hundred dollars for merchandise and services they wanted no part of, as a kind of assessment or contribution to the operation of the funeral establishment. The undertakers, it should be added, were equally incredulous, and possibly hurt, that these people should question their method of doing business.

The guiding rule in funeral pricing appears to be "from each according to his means," regardless of the actual wishes of the family. A funeral director in San Francisco says, "If a person drives a Cadillac, why should he have a Pontiac funeral?" The Cadillac symbol figures prominently in the funeral men's thinking. There is a funeral director in Los Angeles who says: his rock-bottom minimum price is $200. But he reserves to himself the right to determine who is eligible for this minimum-priced service. "I won't sell it to some guy who drives up in a Cadillac." This kind of reasoning is peculiar to the funeral industry. A person can drive up to an expensive restaurant in a Cadillac and can order, rather than the $10 dinner, a 25-cent cup of tea and he will be served. It is unlikely that the proprietor will point to his elegant furnishings and staff, and will demand that the Cadillac owner should order something more commensurate with his ability to pay so as to help defray the overhead of the restaurant.

There is, however, one major difference between the restaurant transaction and the funeral transaction. It is clear that while the Cadillac owner may return to the restaurant tomorrow with a party of six and order $10 dinners all around, this will not be true of his dealings with the undertaker. In the funeral business it's strictly one to a customer. Very likely many a funeral director has echoed with heartfelt sincerity the patriotic sentiments of Nathan Hale: "My only regret is that I have but one life to give for my country." The television industry touts the advantages of a TV set in every room; auto salesmen urge the convenience of several cars for every family; cigarette manufacturers urge "a carton for the home and one for the office"; but if the undertaker fails to move in and strike while the iron is hot, the opportunity is literally lost and and gone forever. (The only exception to this is noted by the Clark Metal Grave Vault people, who in their advertisements advance the startling thought: "DISINTERMENTS —RARE BUT REWARDING. It needn't be a problem. *It can lead to repeat business. . . .*")

The funeral industry faces a unique economic situation in that its market is fixed, or inelastic; and as the death rate steadily declines, the problems become sharper.

# 57

# Interview With A 17-Year-Old Girl

## by Elisabeth Kubler-Ross

*The following is an interview of a seventeen-year-old girl with aplastic anemia, who asked to be seen in the presence of the students. An interview with her mother took place immediately afterwards, followed by a discussion among the medical students, attending physician, and nursing staff of her ward.*

DOCTOR: I think I'll make it a little easy on you, okay, and let us know please if you get too tired or are in pain. Do you want to tell the group how long you have been ill and when it all started?

PATIENT: Well, it just came on me.

DOCTOR: And how did it come on?

PATIENT: Well, we were at a church rally in X, a small town from where we live, and I had gone to all the meetings. We had gone over to the school to have dinner and I got my plate and sat down. I got real cold, got the chills and started shaking and got a real sharp pain in my left side. So they took me to the minister's home and put me to bed. The pain kept getting worse and I just kept getting colder and colder. So this minister called his family doctor and he came over and said that I had an appendicitis attack. They took me to the hospital and it seemed like the pain kind of went away; it just kind of disappeared by itself. They took a lot of tests and found that it wasn't my appendix so they sent me home with the rest of the people. Everything was okay for a couple of weeks and I went back to school.

STUDENT: What did you think you had?

PATIENT: Well, I did not know. I went to school for a couple of weeks and then I got real sick one day and fell down the stairs and felt real weak and was blacking out. They called my home doctor and he came and told me that I was anemic. He put me in the hospital and gave me three pints of blood. Then I started getting these pains in here. They were bad and they thought maybe it was my spleen. They were going to take it out. They took a whole bunch of X-rays and everything. I kept having a lot of trouble and they didn't know what to do. Dr. Y. was consulted and I came up here for a checkup and they put me in the hospital for ten days. They ran a whole bunch of tests and that's when they found out that I was aplastic.

STUDENT: When was this?

PATIENT: That was about the middle of May.

DOCTOR: What did this mean to you?

PATIENT: Well, I wanted to be sure it was too, because I was missing so much school. The pain hurt quite a bit and then, you know, just to find out what it was. So I stayed in the hospital for ten days and they ran all kinds of tests and then they told me what I had. They said it was not terrible. They didn't have any idea what had caused it.

DOCTOR: They told you that it was not terrible?

PATIENT: Well, they told my parents. My parents asked me if I wanted to know everything, and I told them yes, I wanted to know everything. So they told me.

STUDENT: How did you take that?

PATIENT: Well, at first I didn't know and then I kind of figured that it was God's purpose that I got sick because it had happened all at once and I had never been sick before. And I figured that it was God's purpose that I got sick and that I was in his care and he would take care of me so I didn't have to worry. And I've just gone on like that ever since and I think that's what kept me alive, knowing that.

STUDENT: Ever get depressed about it?

PATIENT: No.

STUDENT: Do you think others might?

PATIENT: Oh, someone might get real, real sick. I feel that, you know, there's no reassuring thing, but I think everybody who gets sick feels that way once in a while.

STUDENT: Do you wish at times that it was not your parents that had told you about the condition—you wish maybe the doctors had told you about it, had come to you?

PATIENT: No, I like my parents to tell me better. Oh, I guess it was all right that they had told me, but I would have kind of enjoyed that so much . . . if the doctor had shared it with me.*

---

* Here she expresses her ambivalence about being told by her parents instead of the doctor.

STUDENT: The people that have been working around you, the doctors, and nurses, do you think they have been avoiding the issue?

PATIENT: They never tell me anything, you know, just mostly my parents. They have to tell me.

STUDENT: Do you think you've changed your feelings about the outcome of this disease since the first time you heard about it?

PATIENT: No, I still feel the same.

STUDENT: Have you thought about it long?

PATIENT: Uh huh.

STUDENT: And this hasn't changed your feelings?

PATIENT: No, I went through the trouble, they can't find veins on me now. They give me so many other things like that with all these other problems, but we just have to keep our faith now.

STUDENT: Do you think you've got more faith during this time.

PATIENT: Uh huh. I really do.

STUDENT: Do you think this would be one way that you've changed? Your faith is the most important thing then that will pull you through?

PATIENT: Well, I don't know. They say that I might not pull through, but if he wants me to be well, I've got to get well.

STUDENT: Has your personality changed, have you noticed any changes each day?

PATIENT: Yes, because I get along with more people. I usually do, though. I go around and visit a few of the patients and help them. I get along with the other roommates, so I get someone else to talk to. You know, when you feel depressed it helps to talk to someone else.

DOCTOR: Do you get depressed often? Two of you were in this room before, now you are all alone?

PATIENT: I think it was because I was worn out. I haven't been outdoors for a week now.

DOCTOR: Are you getting tired now? Tell me when you get too tired, then we will finish this session.

PATIENT: No, not at all.

STUDENT: Have you noticed any change in your family or friends, in their attitude toward you?

PATIENT: I've been a lot closer to my family. We get along well, my brother and I were always close when we were small. You know he's eighteen and I'm seventeen, just fourteen months apart. And my sister and I were always real close. So now they and my parents are a lot closer. You know, I can talk to them more and they, oh, I don't know, it's just a feeling of more closeness.

STUDENT: It's deepened, enriched your relationship with your parents?

PATIENT: Uh huh, and with other kids, too.

STUDENT: Is this a sense of support for you during this illness?

PATIENT: Yes, I don't think I could go through it now without my family and all the friends.

STUDENT: They want to help you in every way possible. How about you, do you help them, too, in some way?"

PATIENT: Well, I try to . . . whenever they come I try to make them feel at home and make them go home feeling better and things like that.

STUDENT: Do you feel very depressed when you're alone?

PATIENT: Yes, I kind of panic because I like people and I like to be around people and being with someone . . . I don't know, when I'm alone all the problems come up. Sometimes you do feel more depressed when there's nobody there to talk to.

STUDENT: Is there anything in particular that you feel when you're alone, anything that sort of scares you about being alone?

PATIENT: No, I just get to feeling that there's nobody there and nobody to talk to.

DOCTOR: Before you were sick, what kind of girl were you? Were you very outgoing or did you like to be alone?

PATIENT: Well, I was pretty outgoing. I liked to do sporty things, go places, go to games and to a lot of meetings.

DOCTOR: Have you ever been alone for any length of time before you were sick?

PATIENT: No.

STUDENT: If you had to do it over again, would you rather your parents had waited before telling you?

PATIENT: No, I'm glad I knew right from the start. I mean I'd rather know right at the beginning and know that I have to die and they can face me.

STUDENT: What is it that you do have to face, what's your vision of what death is like?

PATIENT: Well, I think it's wonderful because you go to your home, your other one, near to God, and I'm not afraid to die.

DOCTOR: Do you have a visual picture of this "other home," realizing, you know, all of us have some fantasies about it though we never talk about it. Do you mind talking about it

PATIENT: Well, I just kind of think it's like a reunion where everybody is there and it is real nice and where there's someone else there—special, you know. Kind of makes the whole thing different.

DOCTOR: Is there anything else you can say about it, how it feels?

PATIENT: Oh, you would say you have a wonderful feeling, no more needs and just being there and never again alone.

DOCTOR: Everything just right?

PATIENT: Just right, uh huh.

DOCTOR: No need for food to stay strong?

PATIENT: No, I don't think so. You'll have a strength within you.

DOCTOR: You don't need all these earthly things?

PATIENT: No.

DOCTOR: I see. Well, how did you get this strength, all this courage to face it right from the beginning? You know many people have a religion, but very few at the time will just face it like you. Have you always been that way?

PATIENT: Uh huh.

DOCTOR: You never had any real deep hostile—

PATIENT: No.

DOCTOR: Or got angry at people who weren't sick.

PATIENT: No, I think I got along with my parents because they were missionaries for two years in S.

DOCTOR: I see.

PATIENT: And they've both been wonderful workers of the church. They just brought us all up in a Christian home and that has helped a great deal.

DOCTOR: Do you think we, as physicians, should speak to people who face a fatal illness about their future? Can you tell us what you would teach us if your mission was to teach us what we should do for other people?

PATIENT: Well, a doctor will just come in and look you over and tell you "How are you today" or something like that, a real phoney. It just kind of makes you resent being sick because they never speak to you. Or they come in like they are a different kind of people. Most of the ones I know do that. Well, they come down and talk with me for a little while and ask me how I feel and visit with me. They say things about my hair and that I'm looking better. They just talk to you and then they'll ask you how you feel and some get into explaining things as much as then can. It's kind of hard for them because I'm underage and they aren't supposed to tell me anything, because they are supposed to tell my parents. I think that's so important to talk to a patient because if there's a cold feeling between the doctors you kind of dread to have them come in if he's going to be cold and businesslike. When he comes in and is warm and human that means a great deal.

DOCTOR: Did you have a feeling of discomfort or unpleasantness about coming here and talking about it to us?

PATIENT: No, I don't mind talking about it.

STUDENT: How have the nurses handled this problem?

PATIENT: Most of them have been real wonderful and talk a great deal and I know most of them pretty well.

DOCTOR: You have the feeling that the nurses are able to handle it better than the physicians in a way?

PATIENT: Well, yes, because they are there more and they do more than the doctors.

DOCTOR: Uh huh, they just may be less uncomfortable.

PATIENT: I'm sure of that.

STUDENT: May I ask, has anybody in your family ever died since you grew up?

PATIENT: Yes, my dad's brother, my uncle died. I went to his funeral.

STUDENT: How did you feel?

PATIENT: Well, I don't know. He looked kind of funny, he looked different. But, you know that's the first person that I'd ever seen dead.

DOCTOR: How old were you?

PATIENT: I'd say about twelve or thirteen.

DOCTOR: You said, "he looked funny" and you smiled.

PATIENT: Well, he did look different, you know, his hands didn't have any color and they did look so still. And then my grandmother died but I wasn't there. My grandfather died on my mother's side, but I wasn't there either, I just went on, you know. Oh, then my aunt died and I couldn't go to the funeral because it was not too long ago and I was sick and we didn't go.

DOCTOR: It comes in different forms and ways, doesn't it?

PATIENT: Yes, he was my favorite uncle. You don't really have to cry when somebody dies because you know they're going to heaven and it's kind of a happy feeling for them, to know that they're going to be in paradise.

DOCTOR: Did any of them talk about it to you at all?

PATIENT: A real, close friend of mine just died, over a month ago and his wife and I went to his funeral. That meant a lot to me because he had been so wonderful and had done so much for me when I got sick. He left you feeling so comfortable and everything.

DOCTOR: So what you say is to be a little more understanding and take a little time and talk with the patients.

# 58

## The Heroics of Everyday Life: A Theorist of Death Confronts His Own End

# "Joy and hope and trust are things one achieves after one has been through forlornness."

## A conversation with Ernest Becker by Sam Keen

**Ernest Becker:** You are catching me *in extremis*. This is a test of everything I've written about death. And I've got a chance to show how one dies. The attitude one takes. Whether one does it in a dignified, manly way; what kinds of thoughts one surrounds it with; how one accepts his death.

**Sam Keen:** This conversation can be what you want it to be. But I would like to relate your life to your work. And I would like to talk about the work you haven't been able to finish.

**Becker:** That's easy enough. As far as my work is concerned, I think its major thrust is in the direction of creating a merger of science and the religious perspective. I want to show that if you get an accurate scientific picture of the human condition, it coincides exactly with the religious understanding of human nature. This is something Paul Tillich was working on but didn't achieve because he was working from the direction of theology. The problem is to work from the direction of science. If I have anything that I can rub my hands together in glee about in the quiet hours and say, "Tee hee, this is what I've pulled off," I think I have delivered the science of man over to a merger with theology.

**Keen:** How have you done this?

**Becker:** By showing that psychology destroys our illusions of autonomy and hence raises the question of the true power source for human life. Freud, Wilhelm Reich, and particularly Otto Rank, demonstrate how we build character and culture in order to shield ourselves from the devastating awareness of our underlying helplessness and the terror of our inevitable death. Each of us constructs a personality, a style of life or, as Reich said, a character armor in a vain effort to deny the fundamental fact of our animality. We don't want to admit that we stand alone. So we identify with a more powerful person, a cause, a flag, or the size of our bank account. And this picture of the human condition coincides with what theology has traditionally said: man is a creature whose nature is to try to deny his creatureliness.

**Keen:** And when the half-gods go, the gods arrive? When we abandon our pseudocontrol we discover that we are lived by powers over which we have no control? Schleiermacher, the 19th-century theologian, said the human condition was characterized by absolute dependency, or contingency.

**Becker:** Exactly. I also see my work as an extension of the Frankfurt school of sociology, and especially of the work of Max Horkheimer. Horkheimer says man is a willful creature who is abandoned on the planet; he calls for mankind to form itself into communities of the abandoned. That is a beautiful idea and one that I wanted to develop in order to show the implications of the scientific view of creatureliness.

**Keen:** What are the implications?

**Becker:** This gets us into the whole problem of evil. One of the things I won't be able to finish, unfortunately, is a book on the nature of evil. I wrote a book called *The Structure of Evil*, but I didn't talk much about evil there. When I got sick, I was working on a book in which I try to show that all humanly caused evil is based on man's attempt to deny his creatureliness, to overcome his insignificance. All the missiles, all the bombs, all human edifices, are attempts to defy eternity by proclaiming that one is not a creature, that one is something special.

Searching out a scapegoat comes from

the same need to be special. As Arthur Miller said, ''everybody needs his Jew.'' We each need a Jew or a nigger, someone to kick to give us a feeling of specialness. We want an enemy to degrade, someone we can humiliate to raise us above the status of creatures. And I think this is an immense datum, the idea of the dynamic of evil as due fundamentally to the denial of creatureliness. Obviously, the idea is that if you accept creatureliness you no longer have to protest that you are something special.

**Keen:** But in your writing you stress the need to believe that we are special. You say that we must all be heroes in order to be human.

**Becker:** That is true. But the important question is how we are to be heroes. Man is an animal that has to do something about his ephemerality. He wants to overcome and be able to say, ''You see, I've made a contribution to life. I've advanced life, I've beaten death, I've made the world pure.'' But this creates an illusion. Otto Rank put it very beautifully when he said that the dynamic of evil is the attempt to make the world other than it is, to make it what it cannot be, a place free from acci-

> **"Society has to contrive some way to allow its citizens to feel heroic. This is one of the great challenges of the 20th century."**

dent, a place free from impurity, a place free from death.

The popularity of cults like Nazism stems from the need for a heroic role. People never thrive as well as when they feel they are bringing purity and goodness into the world and overcoming limitation and accident.

**Keen.** Do you think any of the present political crisis is due to our lack of heroic ideals? Whatever the reality of the Kennedy Administration, it did produce a sense of Camelot and a new heroic image. Nixon has given us lackluster and short-haired plumbers.

**Becker:** Well, America is very much looking for heroes, isn't it? I think one of the tragedies of this country is that it hasn't been able to express heroics. The last heroic war was World War II. There we were fighting evil and death. But Vietnam was clearly not a fight against evil. It is a terrible problem and I don't pretend to solve it. How does one live a heroic life?

Society has to contrive some way to allow its citizens to feel heroic. This is one of the great challenges of the 20th century. Sometimes there is a glimpse of constructive heroics—the CCC in the mid-'30s,

the camaraderies in a just war, the civil-rights campaigns. Those people felt that they were bringing a certain amount of purity and justice into the world. But how do you get people to feel that society is set up on a heroic order without grinding up some other society, or finding scapegoats the way the Nazis did?

**Keen:** In the terms of your understanding of society, it seems to be a Catch-22 problem. If the mass of people are encapsulated in character armor that prevents them from facing the horror of existence and therefore seeing the necessity for a heroic life, then the mass heroic models must be, by definition, unconscious. Isn't the idea of heroism an elite idea? In *The Hero With a Thousand Faces* Joseph Campbell says the hero's journey is not taken by every man.

**Becker:** I am using the idea of heroism in a broader sense. To be a hero means to leave behind something that heightens life and testifies to the worthwhileness of existence. Making a beautiful cabinet can be heroic. Or for the average man, I think being a provider is heroic enough. In stories and plays they make fun of the old folks when they said, ''Well, I've always provided for you. I've always fed you.'' But those are the heroics of the average man. It is not something that one should disparage. I suppose (I haven't thought about it) that the American heroism is that one has always made a good living, been a good breadwinner and stayed off welfare roles.

**Keen:** The hero as self-sufficient man.

**Becker:** Yes. But I don't think one can be a hero in any really elevating sense without some transcendental referent, like being a hero for God, or for the creative powers of the universe. The most exalted type of heroism involves feeling that one has lived to some purpose that transcends one. This is why religion gives the individual the validation that nothing else gives him.

**Keen:** I remember Hannah Arendt's lovely statement that the Greek polis was formed by the warriors who came back from the Trojan wars. They needed a place to tell their stories, because it was only in the story that they achieved immortality. Democracy was created to make the world safe for telling stories.

**Becker:** In primitive cultures the tribe was a heroic unit because its members and the ancestral spirits were an audience. The tribe secured and multiplied life and addressed itself to the dead ancestors and said, ''You see how good we're doing. We are observing the shrines and we are giving you food.'' Among some Plains Indians, each person had a guardian spirit, a per-

sonal divine referent that helped him to be a hero on earth. I think this accounts for a good deal of the nobility and dignity in some of those Indian faces we see in photographs. They had a sense that they were contributing to cosmic life.

**Keen:** It may be much harder for modern man to be a hero. In tribal cultures, heroism had to do with repeating archetypical patterns, following in the footsteps of the original heroes. The hero was not supposed to do anything new. We have thrown away the past and disowned traditional models. So the terror of the modern hero is that he has to do something new, something that has never been done before. We are justified only by novelty. I

> **"Here we are all eggs, placental eggs. We all hatched on this planet and our main life's task becomes to deny that we're eggs."**

think this is why modern man (and with women's liberation, modern woman) is anxious and continually dissatisfied. We are always trying to establish our uniqueness.

**Becker:** Yeah, that's very true. Tillich concluded that for modern man to be heroic, he has to take nonbeing into himself in the form of absurdity and negate it.

**Keen:** In Buddhism and Eastern philosophy there is an even greater fascination with embracing the Void. The hero is the one who can overcome the desire to exist and embrace nonbeing.

**Becker:** I have a feeling there is a certain cleverness in Buddhism. Since you can't have what you want in the world you renounce it altogether; since you can't beat death, you embrace it. They keep talking about getting off the wheel of karma but with tongue in cheek, hoping they will get on again. Buddhism never appealed to me because it lacks an explanation of why we're here. Western man is interested in whys, and causes.

Here we are all eggs, placental eggs. We all hatched on this planet and our main life's task becomes to deny that we're eggs. We want to protest that we're here for some higher reason and we've been trying to find out what this reason is. There's no answer but the reason must be there. And it seems to me Buddhism never tries to answer these questions: Why are we here? Why do eggs hatch on this planet in the form of embryos? This seems to me our major question, the one that torments us all.

**Keen:** You will need to tell me when you are becoming tired because I can come and go as your energy permits.

**A sketch of Ernest Becker**

# A Day of Loving Combat

For a brief time the spotlight focused on Ernest Becker and then, for some fickle reason, it dimmed and he receded into undeserved obscurity. From 1965 to 1967 Becker was *the* professor at Berkeley. During a time of political high jinx and revolutionary sentiments he was an academic superstar to a generation of students who listened only to men whose ideas were infused with passion. As a visiting lecturer in sociology and anthropology he played to overflow audiences. With conscious drama (he once lectured from the set for King Lear) he unveiled the pathology that lies hidden beneath normality. And then with a flip of the footlights, he changed the scene to show how human a thing madness can be.

Beneath the mask of personality, underneath the facade of character, lurks the fear of death and the vast terror of the world. It is little wonder that we cling to quirks and defense mechanisms. We rather bear those perversions we have than fall into the abyss of absurdity. With bold strokes Becker limned the human condition to show how heroic we must be if we would live with truth.

Becker's thinking did not follow the political style of the '60s. He did not talk revolution. But the students loved his spacious and fiery mind and his willingness to think across departmental lines. Departmental chairmen were not so delighted. To some his popularity seemed adequate evidence that he was superficial. When no department could find funds to renew Becker's contract, 2,000 students petitioned the administration demanding that he be retained. After the administration carefully explained that they were powerless to act in departmental matters, the Berkeley student government took the matter into its hands and voted $13,000 of student-body funds to retain Becker as a visiting scholar.

Instead of accepting the students' offer, Becker traveled across the Bay to teach at San Francisco State. But the political turmoil of that school's mini-apocalypse, when Hayakawa became a household word in California, made it difficult for him to continue the careful scholarship that had always provided the foundation for his intellectual theater. In 1969

Becker, then 44, moved to Simon Fraser University in Vancouver, where he is professor in the department of political science, sociology and anthropology.

His development as a generalist came about gradually. After World War II Becker lived in Europe for several years and served on the staff of the U.S. Embassy in Paris. But foreign service did not satisfy his desire to make a contribution to life. The question that obsessed him—"Why do people act the way they do?"—led him back to Syracuse University for a Ph.D. in cultural and social anthropology (1960). There he became interested in the parallels between Zen and psychoanalysis and began to develop an existential approach to psychological questions. Rather than focusing on symptoms or elaborate intrapsychic explanations for phenomena such as fetishism or paranoia, he kept asking the fundamental question: why do we voluntarily repress ourselves and adopt crippling defense mechanisms? Becker's wide-angle vision led to an outpouring of books and articles that deal with our need to apply scientific psychological knowledge to the critical problems of personal freedom and social morality. His central concern has remained the overlap between the scientific theory of man and the theological image

of him. The titles of his books reflect his persistent global focus:

*Zen: A Rational Critique* (Norton, 1961)
*The Birth and Death of Meaning* (Free Press, Second Edition, 1971)
*The Revolution in Psychiatry* (Free Press, 1967)
*Beyond Alienation* (Braziller, 1967)
*The Structure of Evil* (Braziller, 1968)
*Angel in Armor* (Braziller, 1969)
*The Lost Science of Man* (Braziller, 1971)
*The Denial of Death* (Free Press, 1973)

A year ago *Angel in Armor* created a wave of enthusiasm among PT editors and we put Becker's name on the list for a future conversation. Then in early December his new book, *The Denial of Death*, arrived and the wave swelled. On December 6th, I called his home in Vancouver to see if he would be willing to tape a conversation. His wife Marie informed me that he had just been taken to the hospital and was in the terminal stage of cancer. The next day she called to say that Ernest would very much like to do the conversation if I could get there while he still had strength and clarity. So I went to Vancouver with speed and trembling, knowing that the only thing more presumptuous than intruding into the private world of the dying would be to refuse the invitation.

Our conversation started slowly. I asked leading questions and Becker answered. At times my mind raised objections but I did not have the heart to push critical points. The hours wove us together and our talk became crisper. It was clear that Becker neither wanted nor offered intellectual quarter. The nearness of the unthinkable was not to be an excuse for thinking poorly or softening argument. As our dialogue entered what Karl Jaspers called the stage of "loving combat," the color returned to Becker's face and for two hours death was absent from the room. When it came time for me to go, we shared a paper cup of medicinal sherry the nurse had left on the night stand for Ernest. And I left, having learned something about courage that I will not forget.

—Sam Keen

**Becker:** Well, I don't know what course my illness is going to take, so I would just as soon get the conversation finished. This fatigue is not going to hurt me terribly.

I would like to talk about some of the misgivings I have about my earlier work. One of the big defects with my early work is that I tried to accommodate ideas to the opportunities of the '60s, to be relevant.

**"There is nothing honest for the intellectual to do today in the world mess except to elaborate his picture of what it means to be a man."**

Recently I have tried to present an empirical picture of man irrespective of what we need or want. Today I hold, with the Frankfurt school, that the only honest *praxis* is theory. There is nothing honest for the intellectual to do today in the world mess except to elaborate his picture of what it means to be a man. Man is the animal that holds up a mirror to himself. If he does this in an entirely honest way, it is a great achievement. To just run, to be driven without elaborating an image, without showing oneself what one is, this makes a creature very uninteresting.

**Keen:** Perhaps. But Hegel made just the opposite point: it is in blindness rather than self-knowledge that man serves the purposes of the Absolute Spirit. The cunning of the Spirit is that it uses the partial passions of man to serve the ends of the cosmos. And somehow our self-ignorance is necessary to the whole drama.

**Becker:** I think Hegel may be right after all. We are here to use ourselves up; to burn ourselves out. But it is still the job of the thinker not to be blindly driven and to try to hold up a mirror for man. It doesn't follow that everyone should be in the business of trying to figure things out. In his study of primitive man, Paul Radin makes the distinction between the thinker and the man of action. The Shaman is a thinker and everybody knows he is an oddball, and not a model for other members of the tribe. But the thinker of today imagines that it is the task of everybody to gain insight and be self-realized.

**Keen:** So the task of going beyond character is a very limited human vocation and the ordinary man must live a heroic life within the limits of his character armor?

**Becker:** Yes. Very few people can live without repression, without limitations. Knowing how difficult self-awareness is, and what a hazardous and anxious thing it is to get rid of character armor, I would not recommend it for all people. Fritz Perls said "to die and be reborn is not easy." That is the understatement of the year. I can't imagine what many of the everyday people I know would do without their character armor. For most people mental health is a controlled obsession, the channeling of one's energies in a limited and definite direction. Those people who are self-realized still live in a very obsessed way, don't they? They have to write another book, do another job, grow, improve. They are really not very attractive creatures. They are different from the average man only in knowing that they are obsessed. I mean, here is the proof of that: I am lying in a hospital bed dying and I am putting everything I have got into this interview, as though it were really important, right? And I consider myself to be a self-realized person in the sense of having seen through my Oedipus complex and broken my character armor. But if I am going to live as a creature, I have to focus my energies in a driven way.

**Keen:** Is it accidental that you became fascinated with the question of death and wrote *The Denial of Death* and then became ill? Was the fascination a kind of premonition?

**Becker:** No. That book was finished a full year before I became sick. I came upon the idea of the denial of death strictly from the logical imperatives of all my other work. I discovered that this was the idea that tied up the whole thing. It was primarily my discovery of the work of Otto Rank that showed me that the fear of life and the fear of death are the mainsprings of human activity.

Hi Nurse, am I still alive?

**Nurse:** You're still alive.

**Becker:** This girl takes such excellent care of me. Such excellent care. It's amazing.

**Nurse:** Anything you need?

**Becker:** I would like some ice to suck on.

**Nurse:** OK.

**Keen:** Sometime I want to push you on some critical points. Is your energy high enough now, or should I wait until this afternoon?

**Becker:** My energy is good. My mother [the intravenous glucose] is working well.

**Keen:** OK. Here goes. It seems to me you do an excellent job in reviving the lost realism of the tragic vision of life, but I find a certain distortion in your perspective. Rudolph Otto said that if we look at the holy—life in the raw—it can be characterized by three ideas. It is a mystery; it is terrifying or awesome; it is fascinating and desirable. You seem to overstress the terror of life and undervalue the appeal. Life, like sexuality, is both dreadful and desirable.

**Becker:** Well, all right. I think that is very well put, and I have no argument with it except to say that when one is doing a work, one is always in some way trying to counter prevailing trends. My work has a certain iconoclastic bias. If I stress the terror, it is only because I am talking to the cheerful robots. I think the world is full of too many cheerful robots who talk only about joy and the good things. I have considered it my task to talk about the terror. There is evil in the world. After the reports that came out of Nuremburg about the things that were done in the death camps, it is no longer possible to have a naturally optimistic view of the world. One of the reasons we are on the planet is to be slaughtered. And tragedy strikes so suddenly. We must recognize this even as we shield ourselves against the knowledge. All of our character armor is to shield us from the knowledge of the suddenness with which terror can strike. People are really fragile and insecure. This is the truth. There is a beautiful line from

**"I am lying in a hospital bed dying and I am putting everything I have got into this interview, as though it were really important, right?"**

*The Pawnbroker* where the main character says "I couldn't do anything. I couldn't do anything." We do anything to keep ourselves from the knowledge that there is nothing we can do. We manufacture huge edifices of control. In Russia, for instance, they don't report disasters like plane crashes. In paradise, these things are supposed to have been eliminated.

**Keen:** It is like the *Christian Science Monitor*—it monitors out catastrophes.

**Becker:** Well, this is the control aspect of character armor which is so vital to the human being. I don't know what people would do if they had to live with the knowledge of the suddenness of catastrophe. You just can't worry that any car on the street might strike your child on the way to school. But it might. It is natural for man to be a crazy animal; he must live a crazy life because of his knowledge of death.

**Keen:** Another critical probe. You say: Man lives on two levels: he is an animal and a symbol-maker, hence he lives in one world of fact and another of illusion; and our character armor builds the illusory edifices that keep us from the threatening knowledge of the raw facts of life. But it seems to me you fall into the old positivist distinction between fact and interpretation or data and meaning. I doubt that we have anything like a raw world of facts to which we then add a layer of symbolic interpretations. Tillich always insisted: "Never say *only* a symbol." Symbolic knowledge is the highest form of knowledge we have. How can you justify the position that the *factual* world elicits only primal terror and certainty of the finality of death? The fact is we do not know. As Kierkegaard might have said, "Where do you, Ernest Becker, a historical individual, stand in order to give so certain a separation of fact and illusion?"

**Becker:** Yes, I see. That is a very good point. I don't really know how to answer that. What you are saying is that the symbolic transcendence of death may be just as true as the fact of death.

**Keen:** Right, but let me elaborate a little. Our modes of thinking about the world are basically dual. We can call them right- and left-brain dominance, or Dionysian and Apollonian, or primary- and secondary-process thinking. If we take our clues from the rationalistic, or Apollonian mode of thinking, time is linear and we are all individual atoms that end in death. But in the unconscious there are no straight lines, no time and no death.

**Becker:** I see what you mean. I would have to agree that the transcendence of death, symbolically or from the point of view of the whole universe, may be very real. But as a philosopher I am trying to talk to the consciousness of modern man, who by and large doesn't live in a Dionysian universe and doesn't experience much transcendence of time. I am speaking to the man who doesn't have a canopy of symbols to surround himself with and who is, therefore, quite afraid.

**Keen:** But our experience of being captives within time and victims of time may be more a sociological than a philosophical datum. It may reflect a judgment we should make about our society rather than about the universe. In most pretechnological cultures, death was not as much of a problem as it is today. In some cultures, death was seen as analogous to the transition from winter to spring and the resurrection of the earth.

**Becker:** That's right. Certain peoples believed that death was the final ritual

> "I am speaking to the man who doesn't have a canopy of symbols to surround himself with and who is, therefore, quite afraid."

promotion, the final rite of passage where the person became individuated to the highest degree. But we don't hold those beliefs any more.

**Keen:** But we have to ask ourselves why we don't. Are they intellectually invalid or have we only lost the knack of thinking with anything except the left hemispheres of our brains? One thing that is emerging from the new studies of ESP, psychokinesis and psychic healing is that the orthodox models of mind and reality that have been considered beyond question since the 19th century are no longer adequate. If mind is not an isolated brain-mechanism within a machine-body, if there is something like a field or a pool of consciousness (the metaphors are makeshift) a hypothesis like reincarnation or the survival of consciousness becomes more interesting.

**Becker:** I have to admit that I am of the Apollonian bias and I can't fathom the mind of those who are into ESP and that sort of thing. I want to keep an open mind, but based on the way I see the world and feel about it, people don't communicate. People are really separate minds and separate bodies. Children and parents don't understand each other. It takes 20 years of marriage to finally communicate with one's spouse. Everyone lives in his own little compartmentalized world to an extent that is terrifying. Sam, let's put it this way, I have grown increasingly suspicious of all idealisms and all hopefulnesses. For me, it is works like Samuel Beckett's *Endgame* that give a true picture of the human condition—the terrible, hopeless, isolation of people. To me it seems like grabbing at straws to talk about left brain and right brain.

**Keen:** Your personal philosophy of life seems to be a Stoic form of heroism.

**Becker:** Yes, though I would add the qualification that I believe in God.

**Keen:** And to come to that point of trust you must break all illusions?

**Becker:** Right. The fundamental scientific, critical task is the utter elimination of all consolations that are not empirically based. We need a stark picture of the human condition without false consolations.

**Keen:** I prefer a more pluralistic approach. On certain days, I operate dominantly as a thinking being; on other days I am dominantly a compassionate being. And on some few lucky days I live largely in sensations. From which type of experience should I draw my clues to interpret the world? On my hard days I am a Stoic and I know that the courageous thing to do is look straight at the wintery smile on

the face of truth. But on those soft days when I am permeable to everything around me, anything seems possible and I know that the courageous way is the one with greater trust and greater openness to what is strange.

**Becker:** I think that is good and true but it represents a level of achievement. Joy and hope and trust are things one achieves after one has been through the forlornness. They represent the upper reaches of personality development and they must be cultivated. But for people to talk of joy and happiness and to be dancing around completely under the control of their Oedipus complexes, without any self-knowledge, completely reflexive, driven creatures, doesn't seem honest to me. I always watch Billy Graham because there is something spooky about this kind of reflexive joy that I can't understand. The thing has all the characteristics of straight conditioning phenomena. It is a Skinner box. And at that level I don't like to talk about faith and joy. But in the way you express it, I would want to begin talking about a higher human achievement where intellect is left behind and emotional and other types of experience start coming into play. I suppose that in my writing I have been doing an intellectual house-cleaning to make room for the higher virtues.

**Keen:** In the moment when your mind flips into the space where you can say, "I am a Stoic but I believe in God," what does the world look like? How do you see yourself?

**Becker:** Well, I suppose the most immediate thing I feel is relieved of the burden of responsibility for my own life, putting it back where it belongs, giving it back to whoever or whatever hatched me. I feel a great sense of relief and trust that eggs are not hatched in vain. Beyond accident and contingency and terror and death there is a meaning that redeems, redeems not necessarily in personal immortality or anything like that but a redemption that makes it good somehow. And that is enough. . . .

**Keen:** I realize that this morning I held you at arm's length. My attitude was a perfect illustration of your thesis about the denial of death. I wanted to exile you in a category from which I was excluded—namely, the dying. That is human enough but very silly because it prevents me asking you some questions I would like to ask. As a philosopher you have thought as hard about death as anybody I know. And now, as it were, you are doing your empirical research.

**Becker:** It only hurts when I laugh.

**Keen:** And somehow, I would like to ask you what you can add now that you are closer to experience.

**Becker:** I see what you mean, yes. Gee, I don't know. I can't say anything that anyone else hasn't already said about dying or death. Avery Weisman and Elisabeth Kübler-Ross have been working with patients who were dying. What makes dying easier is to be able to transcend the world into some kind of religious dimension. I would say that the most important thing is to know that beyond the absurd-

**"Based on the way I see the world and feel about it, people don't communicate. People are really separate minds and separate bodies."**

ity of one's life, beyond the human viewpoint, beyond what is happening to us, there is the fact of the tremendous creative energies of the cosmos that are using us for some purposes we don't know. To be used for divine purposes, however we may be misused, this is the thing that consoles. I think of Calvin when he says, "Lord, thou bruises me, but since it is You, it is all right." I think one does, or should try to, just hand over one's life, the meaning of it, the value of it, the end of it. This has been the most important to me. I think it is very hard for secular men to die.

**Keen:** Has this transcendent dimension become more tangible to you since you became ill or were you always connected through some religious tradition?

**Becker:** I came out of a Jewish tradition but I was an atheist for many years. I think the birth of my first child, more than anything else, was the miracle that woke me up to the idea of God, seeing something pop in from the void and seeing how magnificent it was, unexpected, and how much beyond our powers and our ken. But I don't feel more reli-

**"For the child, the process of growing up involves a masking over of fears and anxieties by the creation of character armor."**

gious because I am dying. I would want to insist that my wakening to the divine had to do with the loss of character armor. For the child, the process of growing up involves a masking over of fears and anxieties by the creation of character armor. Since the child feels powerless and very vulnerable, he has to reinforce his power by plugging into another source of power.

I look at it in electrical-circuit terms. Father, mother, or the cultural ideology becomes his unconscious power source. We all live by delegated powers. We are utterly dependent on other people. In personality breakdown, what is revealed to the person is that he is not his own person.

**Keen:** We are all possessed. Perhaps when we reach 40 we begin to have the chance to expel our interiorized parents and make autonomous decisions.

**Becker:** Maybe. It is a fascinating phenomenon because the fundamental deception of social reality is that there are persons, independent, decision-making centers walking around. But the human animal has no strength and this inability to stand on one's own feet is one of the most tragic aspects of life. When you finally break through your character armor and discover your vulnerability, it becomes impossible to live without massive anxiety unless you find a new power source. And this is where the idea of God comes in.

**Keen:** But that is only one side of the story. When the personality defenses are surrendered, there is more anxiety but there is also automatically more energy, more eros, available to deal with the world since less of it is being invested in a holding action. So there is an overflow, a net increase in joy.

**Becker:** Yes, definitely. There is an increase in creative energies.

**Keen:** I would like to go on a different tack. In the days before Job, illness was thought to be the result of a divine judgment. If you were sick, it was proof that you were in a state of sin. With the introduction of the naturalistic theory of disease, suffering was severed from guilt. Now, with the advent of psychosomatic medicine, we have brought Job's comforters back to the bedside and we talk about parallels between styles of life and styles of illness. And the cruelest question that is always present, even if unasked, in the presence of illness is: "Why are you sick?," or worse yet, "Why have you done this thing to yourself?" I wonder what thoughts you have about the relation of styles of life and types of disease.

**Becker:** I think one of the great tragic paradoxes is that we are finding out so much about illness and psychosomatic disease and that we can't do anything about it. I go back to what I said this morning: we are driven creatures. Suppose we find out that a certain style of life leads to heart attacks or cancer. I think the approach still has to be the microscopic one, that is the physiochemical one, because practically, people cannot change their

characters. It is like the knowledge we have about how parents can induce schizophrenia in children. We know about double-binds and things like that, but we still can't envision societies taking children away from their mothers. There is no way to program society so that people aren't helplessly dependent upon other people. And this leads to depression when betrayal or abandonment occurs. So the approach must be a remedial, biochemical one, where you give people shots so they don't feel bad or at least tone down the symptomatology.

**Keen:** It seems to me that in some way your thought is excessively masculine—which is forgivable since you are a man. But when you talk about the effort of man to be self-sufficient, I wonder if the condition you portray is not more the masculine condition than the human condition, and if it is not exaggerated by the kind of rational, competitive, masculine culture in which we live. If you were a woman how would your philosophical perspective differ?

**Becker:** That's some question. I don't know. Certainly heroism, the search for scapegoats, the avoidance of death and the vain attempt to make the planet into something which it is not are as much feminine as masculine traits.

**Keen:** But traditionally women satisfied their immortality drive more by creating children than by fabricating artifacts. Men must create *ex nihilo* while women have the option of biological reproduction. I think because men's creativity inevitably involves the ephemeral world of symbols, there is greater insatiability among males than females. We make a building or write a book and then we have to do it all over again to keep proving to ourselves that we are creative.

**Becker:** A book is such a shallow phenomenon compared to a child, isn't it? And it is such transient heroics compared to a baby.

I don't know about my work. I think there is an awful lot of femininity in it in terms of the kinds of things I had to feel in order to write. When it comes to the drive toward heroism, I think men are more competitive than women. The whole drama of history is the story of men seeking to affirm their specialness. One war after another has been caused by the efforts of man to make the world into something it can't be. And look at the energy we put into symbolic pursuits. You just can't imagine a feminine Bobby Fischer with that fantastic, energetic devotion to a symbolic game—chess.

**Keen:** If you were assigned to the job of

creating a symbolic portrait of Ernest Becker to accompany this conversation, what would it look like?

**Becker:** If I had to do a symbolic portrait? Maybe what is significant is that I hesitate every time you ask me a personal question. My personality is very much in the background in my work. The only dis-

**"A book is such a shallow phenomenon compared to a child, isn't it? And it is such transient heroics compared to a baby."**

tinctive thing I think I have really achieved as a person is a self-analysis of an unusually deep kind.

**Keen:** You were never in analysis?

**Becker:** No, and that is a long story I had hoped at some later date to be able to write up because I think it is very important.

**Keen:** Then why don't you tell me about your self-analysis?

**Becker:** Let me say a word about this other thing first. If I were forced to paint a portrait of myself the things that come to mind are Rembrandt's successive self-portraits, in which we see him aging and see the effects of his life on his face. First, there would be the young man and every successive portrait would show the face marked by the teachings of life, by the disillusionments. It would show maturity as disillusionment into wisdom. But my first choice would be to let my ideas be presented without an accompanying portrait of me. I am very much against the cult of personality. I can't stand actors' faces, or gurus' faces. I object to pushing the image of oneself as the answer to things, as the one who is going to figure things out. I have never forgotten what Socrates said. He claimed that he was obviously a better teacher than the Stoics because of his ugliness. He argued that the Stoics won people over by their handsomeness, so if a person was won over by his doctrine it had to be the doctrine itself. One ought to be won over by the force of intellectual ideas, not by the personality of the thinker. And again there is something false about a face because it implies that there is an independent person behind it, which is very rarely the case.

**Keen:** The self-analysis?

**Becker:** I think that was a big event in my life lasting over a period of years. In my mid-30s, I suddenly started to experience great anxiety, and I wanted to find out why. So I took a pad and pencil to bed and when I would wake up in the middle

of the night with a really striking dream I would write it down, and write out what feeling I had at certain points in the dream. Gradually my dream messages, my unconscious, told me what was bothering me—I was living by delegated powers. My

**"Gradually my dream messages, my unconscious, told me what was bothering me—I was living by delegated powers. My power sources were not my own."**

power sources were not my own and they were, in effect, defunct. I think if you are talking about analysis what you are revealing to the person is his lack of independence, his conditioning, his fears and what his power source is. To find my way out of the dilemma my self-analysis revealed, I started exploring other dimensions of reality, theological dimensions and so on.

**Keen:** How has the theological perspective changed the way you view man?

**Becker:** Well, for instance, I was once a great admirer of Erich Fromm but lately I believe he is too facile and too optimistic about the possibilities of freedom and the possibilities of what human life can achieve. I feel there may be an entirely different drama going on in this planet than the one we think we see. For many years I felt, like Fromm and almost everybody else, that the planet was the stage for the future apotheosis of man. I now feel that something may be happening that is utterly unrelated to our wishes, that may have nothing to do with our apotheosis or our increasing happiness. I strongly suspect that it may not be possible for mankind to achieve very much on this planet. So that throws us back to the idea of mankind as abandoned on the planet and of God as absent. And the only meaningful kind of dialogue is when man asks an absent God, "Why are we here?" I suppose, to use Tillich's terms, I am changing from the horizontal to the vertical dimension: I think a person must address himself to God rather than to the future of mankind. It would be funny, wouldn't it, if Jerusalem did win out over Athens?

**Keen:** The most passionate statement I heard Tillich make in the years I studied with him was that the genuinely prophetic thinkers in the modern age were those who spend a lifetime combating the Grand Inquisitor. It seems that the visions of apotheoses, of ideal states and of utopias in which there is to be no repression inevitably lead to the five-year plans and the bloodiest political purges.

**Becker:** The beautiful thing about America is, that whatever is wrong with us, we have not gone the road of sacrificing people to a utopian ideal.

**Keen:** The Greeks knew what they were doing when they said hope was the last of the plagues in Pandora's box. It seems that disillusionment must come before trust.

**Becker:** And the sense of joy is something achieved after much tribulation where, in the Franciscan sense, all activity stops to listen to a bird. But that is an achievement and not something that one gets in a couple of group sessions or by a few Primal screams. At the very highest point of faith there is joy because one understands that it is God's world, and since everything is in His hands what right have we to be sad—the sin of sadness? But it is very hard to live that.

I think it is the task of the science of man to show us our real condition on this planet. So long as we lie to ourselves and live in false hopes, we can't get anywhere. I don't know where we are going to get, but I think truth is a value, an ultimate value and false hope is a great snare. I always like Nikos Kazantzakis' phrase "hope is the rotten-thighed whore." I think the truth is something we can get to, the truth of our condition, and if we get to it, it will have some meaning. It is this passion for truth that has kept me going.

**Keen:** Are there other things you would like to talk about?

**Becker:** We seem to be all talked out, don't we? In an uncanny way we have covered everything. You have put some questions to me that really stumped me and made me think beyond what I would normally do. I am really surprised that I was able to respond to you as well as I have, because I have been very tired. But the mind works quite a bit better than the body in that sense; it has its own alertness.

I am sorry to have put you through this trial. It is a little bit like the anthropologist with the dying American Indian, you know, trying to get the last names down on the tape recorder before the Indian expires and there isn't time. You never had an interview like this before, did you?

**Keen:** No. But once I opened the possibility and you wanted to do it, it had to be done. And it has been an event in my life.

**Becker:** I am sorry I probably won't get

**"There is joy because one understands that it is God's world, and since everything is in His hands what right have we to be sad?"**

to see it. It's funny, I have been working for 15 years with an obsessiveness to develop these ideas, dropping one book after another into the void and carrying on with some kind of confidence that the stuff was good. And just now, these last years, people are starting to take an interest in my work.

Sitting here talking to you like this makes me very wistful that I won't be around to see these things. It is the creature who wants more experience, another 10 years, another five, another four, another three. I think, gee, all these things going on and I won't be a part of it. I am not saying I won't see them, that there aren't other dimensions in existence but at least I will be out of this game and it makes me feel very wistful.

**Keen:** I hope I will feel that way too. I think the only thing worse would be not to feel wistful. So many people are finished before they die, they desire nothing more: they are empty.

**Becker:** That's a good point.

**Keen:** I know that what I fear more than anything is not having the green edge there until the end.

**Becker:** Well, if you are really a live person, I don't see how that is possible. You are bound to be more and more interested in experience. There is always more to discover.

**Keen:** I guess I should go.

**Becker:** What time is it?

**Keen:** A quarter after six . . .

# 59

## A RESEARCH QUESTIONNAIRE

It was published originally in *psychology today magazine*.

We have reprinted the reply form in two places in *Readings in Aging and Death: Contemporary Perspectives:* immediately following the questionnaire and at the back of the book. The reply forms have been perforated to allow you to remove them from the book. Thus, the survey can be used in a variety of ways:

1. you can use it *by yourself*, and record the changes in your own attitudes about death and dying that take place during the term that you use this book;

2. the survey can be used as a *class project*, either once during the course, or at both the beginning and end of the course—thus you can compare your own attitudes with those of your classmates, and you can record changes that are undergone by the entire class during the term;

3. finally, you can contrast either your own or your class's attitudes with those of the readers of *psychology today*. (The results of that survey are printed in the August 1971 issue of *psychology today*.)

Through the use of this survey you can participate in an interesting and important social research project, and, at the same time, gain some valuable insights that can enrich your own life.

Please answer the questions by circling the appropriate letters on the reply form. It is important that you be as candid and thoughtful as possible; the value of the findings will depend upon your honesty. If some of the questions do not apply to you, simply leave them blank.

# Reply Form

# You & Death

**1** A  B  C  D  E  F  G  H
**2** A  B  C  D
**3** A  B  C  D  E
**4** A  B  C  D  E  F  G  H
**5** A  B  C  D  E  F  G  H  I
_____
**6** A  B  C  D  E  F  G  H
_____
**7** A  B  C  D  E
**8** A  B  C  D  E
**9** A  B  C
**10** A  B  C  D  E
**11** A  B  C  D  E
**12** A  B  C  D
**13** A  B  C  D
**14** A  B  C  D  E  F
**15** A  B  C  D  E  F  G
_____
**16** A  B  C  D  E  F  G  H
_____
**17** A  B  C  D  E  F  G  H  I
**18** A  B  C  D  E
**19** A  B  C  D  E
**20** A  B  C  D  E
**21** A  B  C  D  E  F  G  H
**22** A  B  C  D
_____
**23** A  B  C  D
**24** A  B  C  D  E  F  G
_____
**25** A  B  C  D  E  F
**26** A  B  C  D
**27** A  B  C  D  E
**28** A  B  C  D
**29** A  B  C  D  E  F  G  H  I
_____
**30** A  B  C
**31** A  B
**32** A  B  C
**33** A  B  C  D  E  F  G  H
**34** A  B  C  D
**35** A  B  C  D  E  F
**36** A  B  C  D  E  F  G  H  I

**37** A  B  C  D
**38** A  B  C  D
**39** A  B  C  D  E  F
_____
**40** A  B  C  D  E
**41** A  B  C  D  E  F  G  H  I
_____
**42** A  B  C  D  E  F  G  H
_____
**43** A  B
**44** A  B  C  D
**45** A  B  C  D
**46** A  B  C
**47** A  B  C  D  E  F  G  H
_____
**48** A  B  C  D  E
**49** A  B  C  D
**50** A  B  C  D
**51** A  B  C  D
**52** A  B  C  D
**53** A  B  C
**54** A  B  C  D  E
**55** A  B  C  D  E
**56** A  B  C  D  E
**57** A  B  C  D  E  F  G  H  I
_____
**58** A  B
**59** A  B  C  D  E  F  G  H  I
**60** A  B  C  D  E  F  G
**61** A  B  C  D
**62** A  B  C  D  E  F  G  H
**63** A  B  C  D
**64** A  B  C  D  E
**65** A  B  C  D
**66** A  B  C  D  E
**67** A  B  C  D  E  F  G
**68** A  B  C  D  E  F
**69** A  B  C  D  E  F  G
**70** A  B  C  D  E  F
**71** A  B  C
**72** A  B  C  D  E  F  G  H  I
**73** A  B  C  D  E  F  G  H
**74** _____
**75** A  B  C  D  E
_____

# We need your advice

Because this book will be revised every two years, we would like to know what you think of it. Please fill in the brief questionnaire on the reverse of this card and mail it to us.

## Business Reply Mail

No postage stamp necessary if mailed in the United States

First Class
Permit No. 247
New York, N.Y.

Postage will be paid by

**Dale Tharp**
**Editor**
**Harper & Row Publishers Inc.**
**College Dept.**
**10 East 53rd St.**
**New York, NY 10022**

Aging and Death

# SOCIAL PROBLEMS: CONTEMPORARY PERSPECTIVES

I am a _____ student _____ instructor

Term used _____ 19_____

Name_____School_____

Address_____

_____

City_____ State_____ Zip_____

# How do you rate this book?

**1.** Please list (by number) the articles you liked best.

_____   _____   _____   _____   _____

Why? _____

_____

**2.** Please list (by number) the articles you liked least.

_____   _____   _____   _____   _____

Why? _____

_____

3. Please evaluate the following:

|  | Excell. | Good | Fair | Poor | Comments |
|---|---|---|---|---|---|
| Organization of the book | ____ | ____ | ____ | ____ | _____ |
| Section introductions | ____ | ____ | ____ | ____ | _____ |
| **Overall Evaluation** | ____ | ____ | ____ | ____ | _____ |

**4.** Do you have any suggestions for improving the next edition?

_____

_____

_____

**5.** Can you suggest any new articles to include in the next edition?

_____

_____

_____

_____

_____

_____

_____

_____

**Thank you very much**

NOTE: You must fill in the name of the person (or department) to whom the form should be sent.

# Business Reply Mail

No postage stamp necessary if mailed in the United States

First Class
Permit No. 247
New York, N.Y.

Postage will be paid by

**Harper & Row Publishers Inc.**

**Attention:** _____

**10 East 53rd St.**

**New York, NY 10022**

# ATTENTION

Now you may order individual copies of the books in the CONTEMPORARY PERSPECTIVES READER SERIES directly from the publisher.

The following titles are now available:

Readings in ABNORMAL PSYCHOLOGY, Edited by Lawrence R. Allman and Dennis T. Jaffe (Note: fill in SBN here)

Readings in ADOLESCENT PSYCHOLOGY, Edited by Thomas J. Cottle (SBN)

Readings in ADULT PSYCHOLOGY, Edited by Lawrence A. Allman and Dennis T. Jaffe (SBN)

Readings in AGING AND DEATH, Edited by Steven H. Zarit (SBN)

Readings in ECOLOGY, ENERGY AND HUMAN SOCIETY, Edited by William R. Burch, Jr. (SBN)

Readings in EDUCATIONAL PSYCHOLOGY, Edited by Robert A. Dentler and Bernard J. Shapiro (SBN)

Readings in HUMAN DEVELOPMENT, Edited by David Elkind and Donna C. Hetzel (SBN)

Readings in HUMAN SEXUALITY, Edited by Chad Gordon and Gayle Johnson (SBN)

Readings in SOCIAL PROBLEMS, Edited by Peter M. Wickman (SBN)

Readings in SOCIAL PSYCHOLOGY, Edited by Dennis Krebs (SBN)

Readings in SOCIOLOGY, Edited by Ian Robertson (SBN)

$5.95        Paperback

Order your copies of any of the above titles by filling in the coupon below.

------------------------------------------------------------------------------------------------

Please send me:

_____ copies of _____ (SBN)

_____ copies of _____ (SBN)

_____ copies of _____ (SBN)

_____ copies of _____ (SBN)

at $5.95 each. My check or money order in the amount of $_____ is enclosed. (Harper & Row will pay the postage and handling.)

_____
Name

_____
Address

_____
City

_____
State                           Zip

77 78 79 80 9 8 7 6 5 4 3 2 1